Rajasthan, Delhi & Agra

Delhi
p30

Agra & the Taj Mahal
p78

Rajasthan
p106

Lindsay Brown, Abigail Blasi

Contents

PLAN YOUR TRIP

Welcome to Rajasthan,
Delhi & Agra 4

Rajasthan, Delhi &
Agra Map 6

Rajasthan, Delhi &
Agra's Top 12 8

Need to Know 14

If You Like 16

Month by Month 19

Itineraries 22

Travel with Children 25

Regions at a Glance 27

ON THE ROAD

DELHI 30
History 31
Sights 31
Activities 53
Tours 53
Courses 54
Sleeping 54
Eating 59
Drinking & Nightlife 65
Entertainment 67
Shopping 67
Greater Delhi 75
Gurgaon (Gurugram) 76

AGRA &
THE TAJ MAHAL 78
History 79
Sights 79
Activities 87
Tours 87
Sleeping 88
Eating 91
Drinking
& Nightlife 93
Shopping 93
Around Agra 97
Fatehpur Sikri 97

PUSHKAR P138

HOLI FESTIVAL P19

Rajasthan, Delhi & Agra

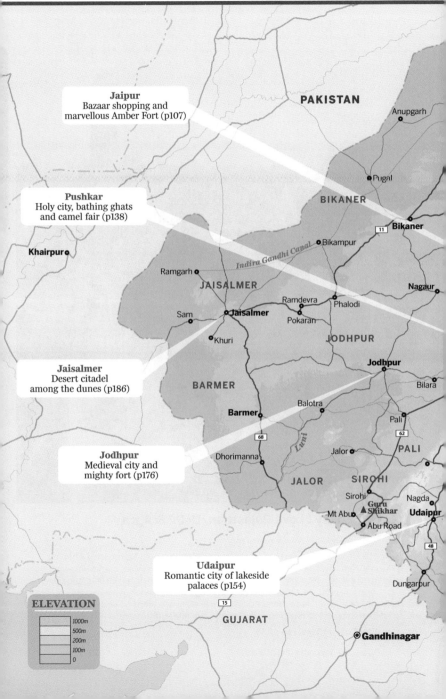

Jaipur
Bazaar shopping and
marvellous Amber Fort (p107)

Pushkar
Holy city, bathing ghats
and camel fair (p138)

Jaisalmer
Desert citadel
among the dunes (p186)

Jodhpur
Medieval city and
mighty fort (p176)

Udaipur
Romantic city of lakeside
palaces (p154)

PAKISTAN

Anupgarh

Pugal

BIKANER

Bikaner

11

Khairpur

Bikampur

Indira Gandhi Canal

Ramgarh

JAISALMER

Nagaur

Ramdevra

Phalodi

Sam

Jaisalmer

Pokaran

JODHPUR

Khuri

Jodhpur

BARMER

Bilara

Balotra

Barmer

Pali

68

Luni

62

Dhorimanna

Jalor

PALI

JALOR

SIROHI

Sirohi

Nagda

Guru
Shikhar

Mt Abu

Udaipur

Abu Road

48

Dungarpur

ELEVATION

1000m
500m
200m
100m
0

15

GUJARAT

Gandhinagar

Welcome to Rajasthan, Delhi & Agra

Rajasthan is the jewel in India's crown. From fairy-tale palaces and epic forts to colourful festivals and wildlife encounters, this is India at its vibrant best.

The Golden Triangle

The famous Golden Triangle is a traveller's survey of Indian icons with Rajasthan's capital, Jaipur, at one of the apexes. It kicks off at the daunting megametropolis of Delhi, with its majestic Mughal heritage, and then angles to Agra, where one of the world's most famous tombs, the Taj Mahal, defines the city. The triangle is completed at Jaipur – a city painted pink with some of the most colourful bazaars in India. Moreover, Jaipur is the gateway to Rajasthan, and once you've slept in a palace, entered a medieval fort or swayed on a camel, you'll want to experience more.

Magnificent Monuments

In Rajasthan, it's the forts and palaces that grab your attention. Massive forts emerge from mountain tops, their battle-scarred ramparts still defying long-dead enemies. Spiked doors that once held war elephants at bay open onto the twisting approaches to the palaces within. Austere and practical gives way to fantasy and opulence once safely inside. Carved marble and stone, fountains and coloured glass decorate the halls of business and rooms of pleasure. All across Rajasthan, there are forgotten forts and lovingly restored palaces, including Jaisalmer's fairy-tale desert outpost, Amber's honey-hued fort-palace and Jodhpur's imposing Mehrangarh, to name just a few.

Land of Kings

Rajasthan is literally the Land of the Kings. It is home to the chivalrous Rajputs, and its battle-scarred heritage has bestowed legacies of pride and tradition. The upper echelons of this medieval society built magnificent palaces and forts, many of which are now glorious hotels and museums. In addition, stunning handicrafts and fine arts were developed and nurtured through patronage by the maharajas. Village life remains steeped in tradition but, just like the rest of India, the pace of change is accelerating. Turbaned men still barter for decorated camels – they just relay the successful deal home via a smartphone.

Celebration of Colour

The colours of Rajasthan are impossible to ignore and the effect of emerald green, canary yellow and fire-engine red turbans and saris is simply dazzling. Little wonder so many fashion designers find their inspiration and raw materials in this state. The lucky visitor might even see a flash of orange while tiger-spotting in Ranthambhore National Park. Easier to collect on a camera are the bright hues of Rajasthan's many festivals: from garishly decorated mounts at the camel and elephant festivals in Pushkar and Jaipur, respectively, to the rainbow explosions of Diwali and Holi, celebrated across the region.

Why I Love Rajasthan, Delhi & Agra

By Lindsay Brown, Writer

My first trip to Rajasthan was part of a quick Golden Triangle tour to 'warm down' after my first trek in the Himalayas. Any apprehensions about heat and dust were quickly dispelled by the desert's cool winter days. I was captivated by camel carts and distinguished, turbaned cameleers bringing produce into Jaipur's pink city. Here was a seemingly timeless world that I had only ever imagined. These glimpses are more fleeting now in the cities, but the sight of an oxen-driven water-lifting device in rural Rajasthan reignites the magic.

For more about our writers, see p288

Above: Chittorgarh Fort (p151)

Contents

RAJASTHAN 106

Eastern Rajasthan 107
Jaipur 107
Around Jaipur 127
Bharatpur & Keoladeo
National Park 128
Alwar 131
Sariska Tiger Reserve
& National Park 133
Ajmer 135
Pushkar 138
Ranthambhore
National Park 143

**Udaipur &
Southern Rajasthan ... 145**
Bundi 145
Kota 150
Chittorgarh (Chittor) 151
Udaipur 154
Around Udaipur 165
Mt Abu 167
**Northern Rajasthan
(Shekhawati) 171**
Nawalgarh 171
Jhunjhunu 173
Fatehpur 174
Mandawa 174
**Jaisalmer, Jodhpur &
Western Rajasthan 176**
Jodhpur 176
Around Jodhpur 185
Jaisalmer 186
Around Jaisalmer 195
Bikaner 196
Around Bikaner 202

UNDERSTAND

**Rajasthan, Delhi &
Agra Today 204**

History 206

**Rajasthani
Way of Life 219**

Sacred India 223

Rajasthani Food 227

**Arts, Crafts &
Architecture 232**

**Wildlife &
Landscapes 236**

SURVIVAL GUIDE

Scams 242

**Women &
Solo Travellers 244**

Directory A–Z 246

Transport 257

Health 266

Language 273

Index 281

Map Legend 287

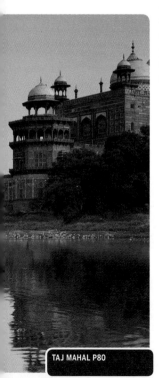

TAJ MAHAL P80

SPECIAL FEATURES

Red Fort in 3D 36
Taj Mahal in 3D 82
Fatehpur Sikri in 3D ... 98
Rajasthani Colour 102

Shekhawati
Magical mural-adorned *havelis* (p171)

Delhi
Mega city boasting monuments aplenty (p30)

Taj Mahal, Agra
Marble monument to love (p80)

Ranthambhore National Park
Tigers in the jungle (p143)

Bundi
Fairy-tale palace and exquisite step-wells (p145)

Chittorgarh
Immense mountain-top fort (p151)

0   200 km
0   100 miles

Ganganagar

Sirsa

Suratgarh

HARYANA

INDIA

Hisar

CHURU

Rajgarh

Delhi

Sardarshahr

Rewari

Ratangarh

Shekhawati

Baggar

Jhunjhunu

Fatehpur

Nawalgarh

Tal Chhapar
Wildlife
Sanctuary

Sikar

Patan

Bansur

Mathura

Sariska
Tiger
Reserve

Alwar

Didwana

SIKAR

Shahpura

JAIPUR

ALWAR

Bharatpur

Fatehpur
Sikri

Agra

UTTAR
PRADESH

Sambhar
Salt Lake

Jaipur

Amber

Keoladeo
National Park

NAGAUR

Sambhar

Bassi

Dausa

Dholpur

Pushkar

Kishangarh

DHOLPUR

Saraswati

Ajmer

TONK

Karauli

AJMER

Tonk

Ranthambhore
National Park

Beawar

Sawai
Madhopur

Chambal

BHILWARA

Deoli

BUNDI

Bhilwara

Bundi

Kota

BARAN

Shivpuri

Chittorgarh
(Chittor)

Bijolia

Rana
Pratap
Sagar

KOTA

Baran

Darrah
Wildlife
Sanctuary

Nimach

Jhalawar

Aklera

MADHYA
PRADESH

UDAIPUR

Gandhi
Sagar

JHALAWAR

Jaisamand Lake &
Wildlife Sanctuary

Rajgarh

BANSWARA

Banswara

Galiakot

Bhopal

Ratlam

Rajasthan, Delhi & Agra's
Top 12

Taj Mahal, Agra

1 Exquisite tomb that's as much a monument to love as it is to death, the Taj Mahal (p80) is arguably the world's most beautiful building, and has been enshrined in the writings of Tagore and Kipling. Built by Emperor Shah Jahan in adoration of his third wife, Mumtaz Mahal, this milky-white marble mausoleum is inlaid with calligraphy, precious and semiprecious stones and intricate floral designs representing eternal paradise, and is the pinnacle of Mughal architecture as well as romance.

Amber Fort, Jaipur

2 Before the capital was moved to Jaipur, the fort palace of Amber (p127) was the capital of the Kachwaha. The honey-coloured citadel rises from a sloping ridge surrounded by higher ridges capped with battlements and watchtowers. From the beautiful geometric gardens and Maota Lake, you can roam up to the main square, Jaleb Chowk. From here, wander freely through the palace grounds, halls of audience, the magnificent three-storey Ganesh Pol, the once-taboo *zenana* (women's quarters) and the still-glittering Jai Mandir.

TURTIX / SHUTTERSTOCK ©

SAIKO2P / SHUTTERSTOCK ©

Delhi

3 India's capital (p30) bears the remnants of former empires, from Mughal tombs to the British-era mansions. Marvel at the splendour of Old Delhi – with the Jama Masjid, Red Fort and *havelis* (ornately decorated residences), the ancient forts of Tughlaqabad and Purana Qila, and the wonders of Qutb Minar and Mehrauli Archaeological Park. Add to this the city's many fine eateries, with offerings from street food to modern Indian, amazing museums and shopping, and it's easy to see why Delhi mesmerises many. Top: Jama Masjid (p40)

Jodhpur

4 The ancient capital of the kingdom of the Marwar, Jodhpur (p176) has Rajasthan's most spectacular fort and, from its ramparts, one of India's iconic views. Mehrangarh seems to emerge organically from its rocky pedestal to protect the Blue City. From this perch the old city of Jodhpur, a maze of blue houses, is like an ocean surrounding an island fortress. Beyond the teeming city, jeep safaris explore the home of the desert-dwelling Bishnoi, a people who have been protecting the natural environment for aeons. Bottom: Mehrangarh (p177)

SAMJQP / SHUTTERSTOCK ©

ALEXANDER MAZURKEVICH / SHUTTERSTOCK ©

Jaisalmer Fort

5 The 12th-century Jaisalmer Fort (p186) defiantly rises from the flat desert lands, a vision from childhood memories of tales such as 'Ali Baba and the Forty Thieves'. The reality is no less romantic. Castellated stone bastions and elephant-size doors protect a warren of narrow bazaars and Jain and Hindu temples, all bustling with life – almost a quarter of the city's population lives inside the fort. Overseeing the bazaars is the former maharaja's seven-storey palace, now a fascinating museum.

Pushkar Camel Fair

6 Some come for the camels, some come to bathe away their sins, some come just for the fun. Pushkar's extraordinary camel fair (p140) is Rajasthan's signature event, combining Hindu spiritualism, camel commerce and cultural celebration. The camels, cattle and Mawari steeds arrive early so that the dealing can be done before the frivolity of the fair takes over and before the full-moon ceremony of Kartik Purnima, when pilgrims bathe and set candles afloat in a holy lake.

Ranthambhore National Park

7 There are only a handful of places left where you can see the magnificent tiger in the wild. Ranthambhore National Park (p143) is one such place and your chances of spotting a tiger are good. This former hunting reserve is a majestic setting for a tiger safari. There are lush ravines, crocodile-infested lakes and a crumbling fort straight out of *The Jungle Book*. Spotted deer graze in the dappled light of an open wood, their eyes, nostrils and ears twitching for the sight, smell or sound of a striped predator.

DMITRY ZIMIN / SHUTTERSTOCK ©

MOROZ NATALIYA / SHUTTERSTOCK ©

KADGPHOTO / SHUTTERSTOCK ©

Udaipur

8 Following the fall of Chittorgarh, Maharana Udai Singh II moved the Mewar capital to Udaipur (p154) in 1568. The city is dominated by the sprawling City Palace, which hugs the eastern shoreline of Udaipur's centrepiece, Lake Pichola. The enormous complex houses a museum, a couple of swish heritage hotels and the erstwhile royals. The mirror-surfaced lake, in turn, hosts one of Rajasthan's most renowned palaces, the wedding-cake Lake Palace, now also an exclusive five-star hotel and occasional movie set.
Above left: City Palace (p155)

Chittorgarh

9 The enormous fortress of Chittorgarh (p151) epitomises the romanticism of Rajput legend, with tales of chivalry, heroism and tragedy all entwined within its architecture. As Rajasthan's greatest fort, it was the capital of the Sisodia rulers of Mewar and attracted numerous invaders, particularly Delhi's sultans and emperors – though its spectacular defences were not as effective as expected. Virtually a ruin now, Chittorgarh crowns the top of a rocky rise, its ramparts protecting empty palaces, temples and extraordinary towers. Top right: Chittorgarh Fort (p151)

Superb Shekhawati

10 In the arid plains of northern Rajasthan, the area known as Shekhawati (p171) boasts a treasure of *havelis*. The walls of these grand homes, built by wealthy traders, can't speak, but they certainly tell a damn good story with their colourful and often whimsical murals. Shekhawati's dusty towns, including Nawalgarh, Fatehpur and Mandawa, offer a lot more than the celebrated *havelis*, however. Travellers who take time out to be immersed in village life will discover a rich and deeply conservative culture.
Bottom right: Le Prince Haveli (p174), Fatehpur

Camel Safari, Thar Desert

11 For an unbeatable cultural experience, hop aboard a ship of the desert for an extended safari (p192) or simple overnight jaunt into the windswept dunes of Rajasthan's Thar Desert. From a camel's back, you can see herds of gazelles and meet desert-dwelling villagers. At the end of the day you can make chapatis over an open fire, witness a cultural performance and fall blissfully asleep under a Persian carpet of glittering stars. You can organise a camel safari in Jaisalmer, as well as Bikaner and Osian.

Bundi

12 Bundi (p145) is a delight. A town where tourism is low key yet the experiences it offers are quintessentially Rajasthan. The picturesque Bundi Palace tumbles down a rock-strewn slope beneath the ramparts of the even more ancient fort of Taragarh. Inside the once-luxurious palace are fading memories – gold and turquoise murals evoking a glorious past. Below the palace, a bazaar bustles with colour around *baoris*, or step-wells, magnificently carved portals to once-precious water reserves. Bottom: Bundi Palace (p147)

Need to Know

For more information, see Survival Guide (p241)

Currency
Indian rupee (₹)

Language
Hindi, Rajasthani (five regional dialects), English

Visas
Apart from citizens of Nepal, Bhutan and the Maldives, everyone needs to apply for a visa before arriving in India.

Money
Most urban centres have ATMS accepting Visa, MasterCard, Cirrus, Maestro and Plus cards. Carry cash as backup. MasterCard and Visa are the most widely accepted credit cards.

Mobile Phones
Roaming connections are excellent in urban areas, poor in the countryside. Local prepaid SIMs are widely available; the paperwork is fairly straightforward but you'll have to wait 24 hours for activation.

Time
India Standard Time (GMT/UTC plus 5½ hours)

When to Go

Warm to hot summers, mild winters
Tropical climate, wet & dry seasons
Dry climate
Desert, dry climate

Delhi
GO Oct–Mar

Agra
GO Oct–Mar

Jaipur •
GO Oct–Mar

Jodhpur •
GO Oct–Mar

High Season
(Dec–Feb)

➡ Pleasant daytime temperatures, but can get cold at night.

➡ Peak tourists, peak prices – prebook all flights and accommodation.

➡ Domestic flights often get delayed owing to fog.

Shoulder Seasons
(Sep–Nov, Feb & Mar)

➡ Warm nights suit many visitors fleeing colder climes.

➡ Ranthambhore National Park opens in October and the migratory birds arrive at Keoladeo Ghana National Park.

Low Season
(Apr–Aug)

➡ By April it's warming up and June is very hot awaiting the monsoon, which brings the rain in July and August.

➡ Ranthambhore National Park closes at the end of June.

Useful Websites

Incredible India (www.incredibleindia.org) Official India tourism site.

IndiaMike (www.indiamike.com) Popular travellers forum.

Lonely Planet (www.lonelyplanet.com/india) Destination information, the popular Thorn Tree Travel Forum and more.

Rajasthan Tourism Development Corporation (www.rtdc.in) Rajasthan government tourism site.

Festivals of India (www.festivalsofindia.in) All about Indian festivals.

Important Numbers

To dial numbers from outside India, dial your international access code, India's country code then the number (minus the '0' used for dialling domestically).

Country code	91
International access code (in India)	00
Emergency (Ambulance/ Fire/Police)	112

Exchange Rates

Australia	A$1	₹48
Bangladesh	Tk100	₹79
Canada	C$1	₹48
Euro zone	€1	₹72
Japan	¥100	₹58
New Zealand	NZ$1	₹46
UK	£1	₹82
US	US$1	₹64

For current exchange rates, see www.xe.com.

Daily Costs

**Budget:
Less than ₹2500**

➡ Dorm bed: ₹200–300

➡ Double room in budget hotel: ₹600–1500

➡ Thali or pizza: ₹150–350

➡ Bus or train ticket: ₹30–150

**Midrange:
₹2500–10,000**

➡ Double room in a hotel: ₹1500–5000

➡ Lunch or dinner in a local restaurant: ₹300–1000

➡ Admission to forts and museums: ₹500

➡ Taxi for a short sightseeing jaunt: ₹500–2000

**Top End:
More than ₹10,000**

➡ Double room in a hotel: ₹5000+

➡ Lunch or dinner in a hotel: ₹1000–3000

➡ Cocktails and wine: ₹1500–3000

➡ Hire car and driver: ₹800–1200

Opening Hours

Official business hours are 9.30am to 5.30pm Monday to Friday, with many offices closing for a lunch hour around 1pm. Many sights are open from dawn to dusk.

Banks 10am–2pm or 4pm Monday to Friday, to noon or 1pm Saturday

Post Offices 10am–4pm Monday to Friday, to noon Saturday

Restaurants 8am–10pm or lunch: noon–2.30pm or 3pm; dinner: 7–10pm or 11pm

Shops 9am–9pm, some closed Sunday

Arriving in New Delhi & Jaipur

Indira Gandhi International Airport (Delhi; p71) This is the closest international airport. There is a prepaid-taxi booth where you can book a taxi for a fixed price (including luggage), thus avoiding commission scams. Many hotels will arrange airport pick-ups with advance notice – these are often complimentary with top-end hotels but for a fee at others. Because of the late-night arrival of many international flights, a hotel-room booking and airport pick-up is advised.

Jaipur International Airport (p124) Jaipur's airport receives flights from the Middle East, Thailand and Singapore, and other destinations are planned. The airport has a prepaid taxi booth and many Jaipur hotels can organise airport pick-ups.

Getting Around

Transport in India is reasonably priced, quick and efficient (if not always comfortable).

Train Extensive coverage of the country, inexpensive and heavily used; advance booking is recommended.

Car Hiring a car with a driver doesn't cost a fortune, and is recommended over driving yourself.

Bus Cheaper and slower than trains, but a useful and practical alternative. Overnight sleeper buses are best avoided.

For much more on **getting around**, see p258

If You Like...

Mighty Forts

The feudal past of Rajasthan has left a sturdy architectural legacy of defensive fortresses. These massive buildings evoke the past and are quite rightly the focus of tourists and would-be time travellers.

Delhi The home of Shah Jahan's Red Fort where the Peacock Throne once resided. (p34)

Agra Akbar initiated construction of the massive fort that became a prison for his grandson, Shah Jahan. (p84)

Chittorgarh A massive citadel capping a mountain plateau – its battle-scarred bastions embrace palaces, temples and towers. (p151)

Jodhpur A blue city spread beneath the ramparts of the hulk of Mehrangarh, Rajasthan's most commanding fort. (p177)

Jaisalmer A golden sandstone castle that drifts in the desert and is still inhabited. (p186)

Bikaner Junagarh is another hulk of over-engineering encompassing a delicately carved peaceful interior. (p196)

Sleeping in a Palace

The phenomenal wealth of the feudal kings and princes was as exclusive as it was vast. At that time, only by luck of birth or special invitation could one have experienced the splendid interiors. But now the erstwhile royals rely on tourism and the palaces have become luxury hotels where you can sleep like a maharaja.

Jaipur Regional nobles built palaces around this city, so you'll find an embarrassment of palatial digs. (p117)

Udaipur Ticks all the boxes for the most romantic setting with the picture-perfect Taj Lake Palace. (p161)

Jodhpur Boasts one of the last palaces to be built before the royals lost their gravy trains – the Umaid Bhawan Palace. (p180)

Bikaner Set in beautiful gardens, the magnificent Laxmi Niwas Palace is a luxurious retreat. (p200)

Wildlife

If you are interested in India's wildlife – particularly its tigers and bird life – then Rajasthan should be high on your list of Indian states to visit. The national parks of Rajasthan started out as hunting reserves for the maharajas. In later years, with modern weapons, this turned into wholesale slaughter and led to a conservation ethos and the establishment of national parks.

Ranthambhore National Park Amazing scenery and one of the best places to spot a wild tiger in India. (p143)

Keoladeo National Park An internationally recognised wetland attracting scores of seasonal migrants – a birdwatcher's paradise. (p129)

Sariska Tiger Reserve Tigers were reintroduced here after the reserve controversially lost its own population to poaching. (p133)

Kumbhalgarh Wildlife Sanctuary No tigers but a leopard hotspot and great birdwatching. (p165)

Top: Kingfisher, Keoladeo National Park (p129)
Bottom: Agra Fort (p84)

Fabulous Festivals

Rich in religion and tradition, Rajasthan has scores of vibrant festivals. Most festivals follow either the Indian lunar calendar (a complex system determined by astrologers) or the Islamic calendar (which falls about 11 days earlier each year; 12 days earlier in leap years) and therefore change annually relative to the Gregorian calendar.

Diwali Celebrated on the 15th day of Kartika (October/November), featuring crazy amounts of fireworks. (p21)

Holi People celebrate the beginning of spring (February/March) by throwing coloured water and *gulal* (powder) at one another. (p19)

Pushkar Camel Fair Rajasthan's biggest event – part agricultural show, part cultural festival and part Hindu pilgrimage. (p140)

Dussehra Mela Kota fills with the smell of fireworks as enormous firecracker-stuffed effigies are burnt to mark the victory of Rama over the demon Ravana. (p114)

Deserts & Camels

Rajasthan's great Thar Desert is criss-crossed by ancient trade routes and dotted with traditional villages where life continues in a fashion very similar to more romantic times. Slow loping camels remain an important method of transport even in this frantic era and they remain integral to traditional desert culture.

Jaisalmer Evocative overnight camel safaris – sweeping sand dunes, traditional dances and a charpoy under the stars. (p192)

Holi Festival (p19)

Jodhpur The centre for exploring the desert homelands of the Bishnoi, a people who hold all animals sacred. (p176)

Bikaner Travel in a traditional camel cart through the arid scrubland while visiting villages and sleeping on dunes. (p197)

Osian For a most authentic experience, staying in village huts or under the stars and eating simple fare. (p185)

Bazaar Shopping

Rajasthan really is one of the easiest places to spend money, with its bustling and vibrant bazaars, colourful arts and crafts, gorgeous fabrics, miniature paintings, blue pottery, magic carpets and much more. The cardinal rule is to bargain, and bargain hard.

Delhi The capital has it all, from modern shopping malls to sidewalk spice sellers and timeless bazaars. (p67)

Jodhpur Antiques (new and old), homewares, bric-a-brac and pungent spices – it's all here. (p183)

Jaipur Arts and crafts, as well as amazing jewellery, abound in the bazaars of the Old City. (p123)

Pushkar Explore cluttered Sadar Bazaar, chock-a-block full with embroidered textiles and hippie paraphernalia. (p143)

Udaipur Among the bounty of art and crafts, the ancient art of miniature painting stands tall here. (p163)

Month by Month

TOP EVENTS

Pushkar Camel Fair, October/November

Diwali, October or November

Jaipur Literature Festival, January

Jaisalmer Desert Festival, January/February

Jaipur Elephant Festival, February/March

January

Midwinter cool lingers throughout the north and it's downright cold in the desert night air. Pleasant daytime weather and several festivals make it a popular time to travel, so book ahead.

✪ Kite Festival

Sankranti, the Hindu festival marking the sun's passage across the Tropic of Capricorn, is celebrated in many ways throughout India. In Jaipur, it's the mass kite-flying that steals the show.

☆ Jaipur Literature Festival

The Jaipur Literature Festival has grown into the world's biggest free literature festival, attracting local and international authors and poets. Readings, debates, music and even the odd controversy keep it energised.

✪ Jaisalmer Desert Festival

Three-day celebration of desert culture, with many events in the Sam Sand dunes. Camel races, turban-tying contests, traditional puppetry and the famous Mr Desert competition are part of the fun. It may fall in February. (p195)

✪ Vasant Panchami

Hindus dress in yellow and place books, musical instruments and other educational objects in front of idols of Saraswati, the goddess of learning, to receive her blessing. The holiday may fall in February.

February

The weather remains comfortable in Rajasthan, with very little rain and plenty of festivals. The days are getting marginally warmer but it's still ideal travelling weather.

✪ Shivaratri

This day of Hindu fasting recalls the *tandava* (cosmic victory dance) of Lord Shiva. Temple processions are followed by the chanting of mantras and anointing of linga (phallic images symbolising Shiva). Shivaratri can also fall in March.

✪ Jaipur Elephant Festival

Taking place on the day before Holi (and so both can fall in March), the Jaipur Elephant Festival celebrates the pachyderm's place in Indian culture. There are elephant dress parades and competitions such as polo and tug-of-war, but animal welfare groups have criticised the treatment of elephants taking part in these events.

✪ Holi

One of North India's most exuberant festivals; Hindus celebrate the beginning of spring, in either February or March, by throwing coloured water and *gulal* (powder) at anyone within range. On the night before Holi, bonfires symbolise the demise of the demoness Holika.

March

The last month of the main travel season, March sees the last of the cool days of winter as daytime temperatures creep above 30°C.

🏃 Wildlife-Watching

As the weather warms up and water sources dry out, animals tend to congregate at the few remaining sources of water. This can improve your chances of spotting tigers and leopards.

✨ Rama's Birthday

During Ramanavami, which lasts anywhere from one to nine days, Hindus celebrate the birth of Rama with processions, music, fasting and feasting, readings and enactments of scenes from the Ramayana and ceremonial weddings of Rama and Sita idols.

May

The region heats up with daytime temperatures over 40°C. Life slows down as the humidity builds up in anticipation of the monsoon.

✨ Summer Festival

Rajasthan's very own hill station, the delightful Mt Abu, celebrates summer with a three-day carnival.

There are boat races on Nakki Lake, fireworks and traditional music and dances.

🍴 Mango Madness

Mangoes are indigenous to India, which might be why they're so ridiculously good here. The season starts in March, but in May the fruit is sweet, juicy and everywhere. A hundred varieties grow here, but the Alphonso is known as 'king'.

✨ Ramadan (Ramazan)

Thirty days of dawn-to-dusk fasting mark the ninth month of the Islamic calendar. Muslims traditionally turn their attention to God, with a focus on prayer and purification. Ramadan begins around 16 May 2018 and 6 May 2019.

June

Life retreats indoors during the hot days when temperatures still soar over 40°C. Monsoon storms increase in energy, bringing much-needed respite, though the nights remain hot and humid.

✨ Eid al-Fitr

Muslims celebrate the end of Ramadan with three days of festivities, starting 30 days after the start of the fast.

July

Now it's really raining, with many a dusty road becoming an impassable quagmire. But you may be tempted by the reduced accommodation rates and smaller crowds.

✨ Brothers & Sisters

On Raksha Bandhan (Narial Purnima), girls fix amulets known as *rakhis* to the wrists of brothers and close male friends to protect them in the coming year. Brothers reciprocate with gifts and promises to take care of their sisters.

August

It's monsoon season and the relief is palpable. In a good season there's copious, but not constant, rainfall and temperatures are noticeably lower but still steamy.

✨ Independence Day

This public holiday on 15 August marks the anniversary of India's independence from Britain in 1947. Celebrations are a countrywide expression of patriotism, with flag-hoisting ceremonies (the biggest one is in Delhi), parades and patriotic cultural programs.

✨ Teej

The festival of Teej celebrates the arrival of the monsoon and the marriage of Parvati to Shiva. Three-day celebrations across Rajasthan, particularly Jaipur, culminate in a street procession of the Teej idol. (p114)

September

The rain begins to ease, though temperatures are still high. By the end of September, Rajasthan and Delhi are all but finished with the monsoon.

✨ Ganesh Chaturthi

Hindus celebrate Ganesh Chaturthi, the birth of the elephant-headed god, with verve, particularly in Ranthambhore Fort. Thousands gather at the abandoned fort and clay idols of Ganesh are paraded. Ganesh Chaturthi may also be in August.

✨ Navratri

This Hindu 'Festival of Nine Nights' leading up to Dussehra celebrates the goddess Durga in all her incarnations. Special dances are performed and the goddesses Lakshmi and Saraswati are also celebrated. Navratri may fall in October.

October

Occasional heavy showers aside, this is when North India starts to get its travel mojo on. October brings festivals, national park openings and more comfortable temperatures, with post-monsoon lushness.

✨ Dussehra

Colourful Dussehra celebrates the victory of the Hindu god Rama over the demon-king Ravana and the triumph of good over evil. Dussehra is big in Kota, where effigies of Ravana are ritually burned. This festival may fall in September.

✨ Gandhi's Birthday

The national holiday of Gandhi Jayanti is a solemn celebration of Mohandas Gandhi's birth, on 2 October, with prayer meetings at his cremation site at Raj Ghat in Delhi. Schools and businesses close for the day. (p41)

✨ Diwali

In the lunar month of Kartika, in October or November, Hindus celebrate Diwali for five days, giving gifts, lighting fireworks and burning lamps to lead Lord Rama home. This is India's main holiday time and it is hard to get transport or hotel rooms.

November

The climate is blissful, with warm days and cooler nights. The peak season is getting into full swing. Lower temperatures mean higher prices and more tourist buses.

✨ Pushkar Camel Fair

Rajasthan's premier cultural event takes place in the Hindu lunar month of Kartika (October or November). As well as camel trading, there is horse and cattle trading and an amazing fairground atmosphere. It culminates with ritual bathing in Pushkar's holy lake. (p140)

✨ The Prophet Mohammed's Birthday

The Islamic festival of Eid-Milad-un-Nabi celebrates the birth of the Prophet Mohammed with prayers and processions. It falls in the third month of the Islamic calendar: around 30 November 2017, 21 November 2018 and 10 November 2019.

December

December is peak tourist season for a reason: the daytime weather is glorious, the humidity is low and the nights are cool. The mood is festive and it seems everyone is getting married.

◉ Weddings!

Marriage season peaks in December and you may see a *baraat* (bridegroom's procession), replete with white horse and brass band, on your travels. Across Rajasthan, loud music and spectacular parties are the way they roll, with brides in *mehndi* (ornate henna designs) and pure gold.

🏂 Birdwatching

Many of India's winter migrants complete their travels and set up nesting colonies. Keoladeo National Park is an internationally renowned wetland and birdwatching mecca. (p129)

🏂 Camel Treks in Rajasthan

The cool winter (November to February) is the time to mount a camel and ride through the Rajasthan sands. See the Thar Desert from a whole new perspective: observe gazelles, make dinner over an open fire and camp out in the dunes.

Itineraries

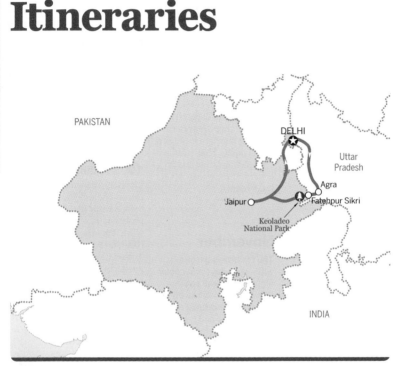

PAKISTAN

DELHI

Uttar
Pradesh

Agra

Jaipur

Fatehpur Sikri

Keoladeo
National Park

INDIA

The Golden Triangle

One route is so well loved it even has a name: the Golden Triangle. This classic Delhi–Agra–Jaipur trip can be squeezed into a single week and gives a tantalising taste of the splendours of Rajasthan.

Spend a day or two in **Delhi** finding your feet and seeing the big-draw sights, such as the magnificent Mughal Red Fort and Jama Masjid, India's largest mosque. Then catch a convenient train to **Agra** to spend a day being awed by the Taj Mahal and the mighty Agra Fort. Only an hour away is **Fatehpur Sikri**, a beautiful Mughal city dating from the apogee of Mughal power. It can be visited on the way to Bharatpur, in Rajasthan, where you can enjoy a rural respite at **Keoladeo National Park**, one of the world's foremost bird reserves. Having relaxed at this beautiful and rewarding place, you can then take a train to **Jaipur**. Spend a couple of days in and around Rajasthan's hectic, dusky-pink capital, seeing the City Palace and Amber Fort and stocking up on blue pottery, dazzling jewellery and Rajasthani puppets before heading back to Delhi.

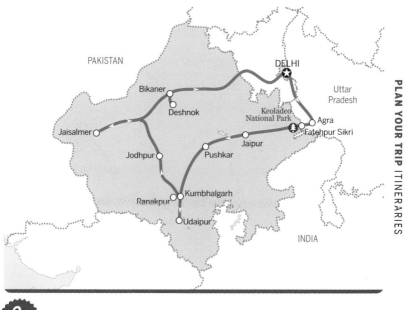

 **Royal Rajasthan**

With a fortnight to spare, you can forget triangles and go all out for a multifaceted loop taking in Rajasthan's most spectacular cities, all erstwhile capitals of former princely states, boasting fairy-tale palaces and stern fortresses.

You will most likely start from the nation's capital of **Delhi** to see the Mughal monuments, such as the massive Red Fort. No trip to India is complete without a visit to the Taj Mahal at **Agra**. Spend two days here viewing the Taj during the day, at night and from the maze-like Agra Fort. Spend a day exploring the ghost city of **Fatehpur Sikri**, before heading to the birdwatching mecca that is **Keoladeo National Park**. Next stop is the pink city of **Jaipur** where you will want to spend two or three days exploring the palaces of Jaipur and Amber.

From Jaipur, take a short trip to the sacred lake of **Pushkar**, where you can release your inner hippie or attend the camel fair. Move on to the romantic lake-town of **Udaipur**, visiting the fine City Palace and the impressive Jagdish Temple as well as doing some shopping and relaxing on rooftops while peering at the lake and its famous palace. From Udaipur head towards the extraordinary, bustling, blue city of Jodhpur. Take time to stop at the milk-white Jain temple complex of **Ranakpur** and the isolated, dramatic fortifications of **Kumbhalgarh** – as they are fairly close together, you can visit them en route to Jodhpur within a day. In **Jodhpur**, visit the spectacular Mehrangarh, a fort that towers protectively over the city like a storybook fortress.

Next take an overnight train to the Golden City, **Jaisalmer**, a giant sandcastle in the desert, with its beautiful Jain temples and exquisite merchants' *havelis* (traditional, ornately decorated mansions). Take a short camel safari through the bewitching landscape of sweeping dunes and sleep under the stars. If you have the time on your way back to Delhi, break your journey with a stop in the desert city of **Bikaner**, home of the impregnable Junagarh Fort and nearest city to the famous rat temple at **Deshnok**.

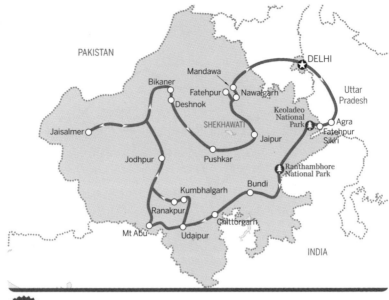

1 MONTH A Month-Long Sojourn

A month will allow you to explore Delhi, Agra and Rajasthan to their fullest extent, with plenty of time to linger along the way whenever a particular destination takes your fancy.

After arriving in **Delhi** and exploring the city sights, take the train to **Agra** to gaze at the picture-perfect Taj Mahal, explore Agra Fort and have a day-trip out to the abandoned Mughal city of **Fatehpur Sikri**. To experience Rajasthan's wild side, first head to the World Heritage–listed birdwatching paradise of **Keoladeo National Park**, where the sheer numbers of nesting birdlife will astound you. This can be followed by a tiger safari at **Ranthambhore National Park**, one of your best bets in all India for spotting a tiger.

Take a Kota-bound train southwest for a stop at the charming small town of **Bundi** to explore the crumbling palace. From here it is a short train ride to **Chittorgarh**, where one of Rajasthan's most impressive fortresses occupies a mountain plateau. Next stop is **Udaipur**, where you can relax after your travels with a few easy days of sightseeing, elegant dining and souvenir shopping.

From Udaipur it's worth side-tripping to **Mt Abu** to see the magnificent Delwara Temples before going north to Jodhpur. Alternatively, head north to Jodhpur, stopping on the way to see the magnificent fort at **Kumbhalgarh** and the Jain temples of **Ranakpur**. From **Jodhpur** it's an easy train or bus ride to **Jaisalmer**, the desert town with a romantic, picturesque fort rising from the golden sands. Here you can spend a few days exploring *havelis* and palaces, before taking an overnight camel trek into the desert. After Jaisalmer, head to **Bikaner**.

Travel south from Bikaner, stopping at the fascinating rat temple at **Deshnok** before coming to rest at the sacred pilgrimage town of **Pushkar**. At Pushkar you may be in time for the famous camel festival; otherwise, just put your feet up for a few days and soak in the serenity.

From Pushkar, it's a short hop to **Jaipur**, with its fabulous citadel at Amber and great shopping. Head north to **Shekhawati** for a few days, inspecting *havelis* at **Mandawa**, **Nawalgarh** and **Fatehpur**, before returning to Delhi.

Plan Your Trip
Travel with Children

Fascinating, frustrating, thrilling and fulfilling – India is as much of an adventure for children as it is for parents. Though the sensory overload may be, at times, overwhelming for younger kids, the colours, scents, sights and sounds of India more than compensate by setting young imaginations ablaze.

Rajasthan for Kids

Being a family-oriented society, Rajasthan is a very child-friendly destination. That doesn't necessarily translate into a travelling-with-children-friendly destination, however. Smaller children, in particular, will be constantly coddled, offered treats and smiles and warm welcomes. And while all this is fabulous for outgoing children, it may prove tiring, or even disconcerting or frightening, for those of a more retiring disposition. Remember, though, that the attention your children will inevitably receive is almost always good natured; kids are the centre of life in many Indian households and your own will be treated – usually for better rather than worse – just the same.

Eating

Feeding your brood is fairly easy in the well-touristed parts of Rajasthan and you'll find Western and Chinese dishes with a bit of searching. Look out for multi-cuisine restaurants, should your little one be saying 'not curry again'.

Adventurous eaters will delight in experimenting with a vast range of tastes and textures: paneer (unfermented cheese) dishes, simple dhal (a curried lentil dish), creamy korma, buttered naan (bread baked

Best Regions for Kids

Keoladeo National Park

Here, the kids can let go of your hand and jump on a bike. Let them ride along the car-free road and tick off as many feathered species as they can.

Jodhpur

Let imaginations run wild at mighty Mehrangarh; older kids can let fly on the exhilarating Flying Fox.

Ranthambhore National Park

What kid won't be thrilled to see a wild tiger? And there's a mesmerising jungle fortress straight out of Kipling's *Jungle Book* to explore.

Amber

Climbing up to Amber Fort and learning about the splendid, if tyrannical, lives of the ruling classes is sure to inspire.

Sam Sand Dunes

Riding a gentle and dignified camel across the shifting sand dunes is a delight for young and old.

in a tandoor oven), pilau (rice) and *momos* (steamed or fried dumplings) are all firm favourites. Few children, no matter how culinarily unadventurous, can resist the finger-food fun of a vast South Indian dosa (rice pancake).

Sleeping

Rajasthan offers such an array of accommodation – from budget boxes to former palaces of the maharajas – that you're bound to be able to find something that will appeal to the whole family. Hotels will almost always come up with an extra bed or two for a nominal charge. Most places won't mind fitting one, or maybe two, children into a regular-sized double room along with their parents. Any more is pushing your luck – look for two rooms that have an adjoining door.

On the Road

Travel in Rajasthan can be arduous for the whole family. Plan fun, easy days to follow longer car, bus or train rides, and pack plenty of diversions. An iPod, iPad or laptop with a stock of movies downloaded make invaluable travel companions, as do books, light toys and games. The golden rule is to expect your best-laid plans to take a hit every now and then.

Travelling on the road with kids anywhere in India requires constant vigilance. Be especially cautious of road traffic – pedestrians are at the bottom of the feeding chain and road rules are routinely ignored.

Health

Health care of a decent standard, even in the most traveller-frequented parts of Rajasthan, is not as easily available as you might be used to. The recommended way to track down a doctor at short notice is through your hotel. In general, the most common concerns for on-the-road parents include heat rash, skin complaints such as impetigo, insect bites or stings and diarrhoea. If your child takes special medication, bring along an adequate stock in case it's not easily found locally.

Children's Highlights
Fortress Splendours

Jaipur (p127) Live out legends in the majestic citadel of Amber.

Jaisalmer (p186) Recreate the *Arabian Nights* in Jaisalmer's desert fortress.

Jodhpur (p177) Amaze their imaginations with the story-book fort and palace.

Wildlife Wonders

Ranthambhore National Park (p143) Tigers, jungles, jeep safaris and an abandoned mountain-top fort.

Keoladeo National Park (p129) The chance to go cycling on car-free roads to spot wildlife.

Sariska Tiger Reserve & National Park (p133) Numerous deer, monkeys and other wildlife, and just maybe a tiger.

Planning
Before You Go

Visit your doctor to discuss vaccinations, health advisories and other health-related issues involving your children well in advance of travel. For helpful hints, see Lonely Planet's *Travel with Children*, and the 'Kids To Go' section of Lonely Planet's Thorn Tree forum (lonelyplanet.com/thorntree).

What to Pack

If you're travelling with a baby or toddler, there are items worth packing in quantity: nappies, nappy rash cream, extra bottles, wet wipes, infant formula and jars or dehydrated packets of favourite foods. You can get these items in many parts of Rajasthan, too, but brands may be unfamiliar. Another good idea is a fold-up cot; a pusher or pram, though, is superfluous, since there are few places with pavements wide enough to use one. For older children, make sure you bring sturdy footwear, a hat, child-friendly insect repellent and sun lotion.

Regions at a Glance

Rajasthan is India in microcosm. Its history rises out of the landscape, from the monumental architecture of the forts and palaces of the Rajput maharajas to the great swaths of desert dunes. But this is not simply an empty desert. Instead, it is a timeless, surprisingly well-populated, arid region. Cleverly cultivated and with monsoonal blessings and ancient groundwater, this desert supports the villages of Rajasthan and is even abundant with wildlife. In an already colourful country, Rajasthan might be the most dazzling of India's regions – there are festivals galore, tigers to spot, desert vistas to explore by camel and enough fine arts and crafts to make you wish you had a bigger luggage allowance.

Delhi

Food
Shopping
Ruins

From Street Food to Modern Indian

Delhi proffers a stunning calvacade of flavour; sample modern Indian fusion cuisine or munch on fresh-from-the-fire *Dilli-ka-chaat* (Delhi's delectable street food).

Bazaars & Boutiques

Shopping in Delhi is a wonderland of bazaars, boutiques and emporiums. Take your pick from intricately wrought handicrafts, modern Indian design, the bookshops of your dreams, and music shops piled high with Indian classical instruments.

Mughal Sights

The ruins of seven imperial cities are scattered throughout Delhi, but its Mughal ruins are among the finest: wander in and out of centuries of history at the Red Fort, Humayun's Tomb, Hauz Khas, Qutb Minar, Mehrauli, Purana Qila, and more.

p30

Agra &
the Taj Mahal

Architecture
Tombs
Forts

Mughal Splendours

Agra has India's finest
Mughal remains, not just
the Taj Mahal, but many
other beautiful tombs and
the magnificence of Shah
Jahan's former fortress.

World's Finest
Mausoleums

The Taj Mahal, built for
Shah Jahan's lamented
wife, is the pinnacle of
Mughal architectural
achievement, and don't
miss Akbar's mausoleum, a
decorative masterpiece.

Mighty Defences

Agra Fort is a red-sandstone
complex surrounded by
2.5km of walls and containing beautiful palaces and
mosques.

p78

Rajasthan

Forts & Palaces
Animal Encounters
Festivals

Rajput Grandeur

The splendid palaces and
mighty forts of Rajasthan
demonstrate the wealth
and power of the Rajputs
who once dominated the
region. The region is replete
with magnificent architecture, from Jaipur's graceful
Hawa Mahal, to the fairy-
tale fort of Jaisalmer.

One Safari

Rajasthan is a great place
to get closer to nature:
whether it's tracking tigers
in Ranthambhore National
Park, spotting colourful
birds in Keoladeo National
Park or exploring the desert
on a camel safari out of
Jaisalmer or Bikaner.

Holidays &
Celebrations

Heading the list is the celebrated camel fair in the
Hindu pilgrimage town
of Pushkar. Other show-
stoppers include Jaipur's
famous literature and elephant festivals and Jaisalmer's Desert Festival. As with
the rest of India, Diwali
and Holi are celebrated
with lots of exuberance.

p106

On the Road

Delhi
p30

Agra & the
Taj Mahal
p78

Rajasthan
p106

Delhi

☎ 011 / POP 25.7 MILLION / ELEV 293M

Includes ➜

History 31
Sights 31
Activities 53
Tours 53
Courses 54
Sleeping 54
Eating 59
Drinking & Nightlife . . .65
Entertainment 67
Shopping 67
Greater Delhi 75
Gurgaon (Gurugram) . .76

Best Places to Eat

➡ Bukhara (p63)

➡ Indian Accent (p64)

➡ Masala Library (p62)

➡ Cafe Lota (p63)

➡ Andhra Pradesh Bhawan Canteen (p62)

Best Places to Sleep

➡ Lodhi (p58)

➡ Manor (p59)

➡ Madpackers Hostel (p58)

➡ Stops @ The President (p54)

Why Go?

Delhi is a city where time travel is feasible. Step aboard your time machine (the sleek and efficient metro) and you can go from Old Delhi, where labourers haul sacks of spices and jewellers weigh gold on dusty scales, to modern New Delhi, with its colonial-era parliament buildings and penchant for high tea. Then on to the future: Gurgaon, a satellite city of skyscraping offices and glitzy malls.

This pulsating metropolis has a bigger population than Australia, and is one of the world's most polluted cities. But woven into its rich fabric are moments of pure beauty: an elderly man threading temple marigolds; Sufi devotional songs; a boy flying a kite from a rooftop.

So don't be put off. Delhi is a city that has been repeatedly ravaged and reborn, with vestiges of lost empires in almost every neighbourhood. There's so much to experience here, it's like a country in itself.

When to Go
Delhi

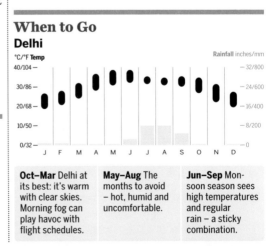

Oct–Mar Delhi at its best: it's warm with clear skies. Morning fog can play havoc with flight schedules.

May–Aug The months to avoid – hot, humid and uncomfortable.

Jun–Sep Monsoon season sees high temperatures and regular rain – a sticky combination.

History

Delhi is said by Hindus to be the site of ancient Indraprastha, home of the Pandavas in the Mahabharata. Excavations near the Purana Qila have revealed evidence of human habitation dating back 3000 years. The name Delhi is linked to the Maurya king Dhilu, who ruled the region in the 1st century BC, but for most of its existence, the city has been known by the multiple different names given to it by its conquerors.

The first city for which clear archaeological evidence remains was Lal Kot, or Qila Rai Pithora, founded by the Hindu king Prithviraj Chauhan in the 12th century. The city fell to Afghan invaders in 1191, and for the next 600 years, Delhi was ruled by a succession of Muslim sultans and emperors. The first, Qutub-ud-din Aibak, razed the Hindu city and used its stones to construct Mehrauli and the towering Qutb Minar.

Qutub-ud-din Aibak's 'Mamluk' (Slave) dynasty was quickly replaced by the Khilji dynasty, following a coup. The Khiljis constructed a new capital at Siri, northeast of Mehrauli, supplied with water from the royal tank at Hauz Khas. Following another coup, the Tughlaq sultans seized the reins, creating a new fortified capital at Tughlaqabad, and two more cities – Jahanpurah and Firozabad – for good measure.

The Tughlaq dynasty fell after Tamerlane stormed through town in 1398, opening the door for the Sayyid and Lodi dynasties, the last of the Delhi sultanates, whose tombs are scattered around the Lodi Gardens. The scene was set for the arrival of the Mughals. Babur, the first Mughal emperor, seized Delhi in 1526, and a new capital rose at Shergarh (the present-day Purana Qila), presided over by his son, Humayun.

Frantic city building continued throughout the Mughal period. Shah Jahan gained the Peacock Throne in 1627 and raised a new city, Shahjahanabad, centred on the Red Fort. The Mughal city fell in 1739, to the Persian Nadir Shah, and the dynasty went into steep decline. The last Mughal emperor, Badahur Shah Zafar, was exiled to Burma (Myanmar) by the British for his role in the 1857 First War of Independence; there were some new rulers in town.

When the British shifted their capital to Delhi from increasingly rebellious Calcutta in 1911, it was time for another bout of construction. The architect Edwin Lutyens drew up plans for a new city of wide boulevards and stately administrative buildings to accommodate the colonial government – New Delhi was born.

In 1947 Partition – the division of India and Pakistan – saw Delhi ripped apart as many inhabitants fled to the north and migrants flooded inwards, a trauma from which some say the city has never recovered. The modern metropolis certainly faces other challenges too – traffic, population, crime and the deepening chasm between rich and poor. However, the city on the Yamuna River continues to flourish, with its new satellite cities spreading Delhi further and further outwards.

◉ Sights

Most sights in Delhi are easily accessible by metro, though to reach some you'll have to take a rickshaw or taxi from the stop, even though it bears the same or similar name

---

DELHI'S TOP FESTIVALS

To confirm exact dates contact India Tourism Delhi (p71).

Republic Day (⊘ 26 Jan) A spectacular military parade in Rajpath.

Beating of the Retreat (⊘ 29 Jan) More military pageantry in Rajpath.

St.Art (⊘ Dec-Mar) Street art festival.

Independence Day (⊘ 15 Aug) India celebrates its Independence from Britain.

Dussehra (Durga Puja; ⊘ Sep/Oct) Hindu celebration of good over evil with parades of colourful effigies.

Qutb Festival (⊘ Oct/Nov) Sufi singing and classical music and dance at the Qutb Minar complex.

Diwali (Festival of Light; ⊘ Oct/Nov) Fireworks across the city for the Festival of Light.

Delhi International Arts Festival (DIAF; www.diaf.in; ⊘ Nov/Dec) Exhibitions, performing arts, film, literature and culinary events.

Delhi Highlights

1 Red Fort (p34)
Exploring this Mughal masterpiece, imagining its former traumas and splendours.

2 Humayun's Tomb (p43) Enjoying the architectural virtuosity and mirror-image gardens of Delhi's most spectacular resting place.

3 Jama Masjid (p40) Experiencing the serenity of the 'Friday Mosque', with its wide open courtyard.

4 Qutb Minar Complex (p75) Visiting Delhi's first Islamic city at sunrise.

5 Hazrat Nizam-ud-din Dargah (p43) Drinking in the mystical, magical atmosphere and hearing qawwali

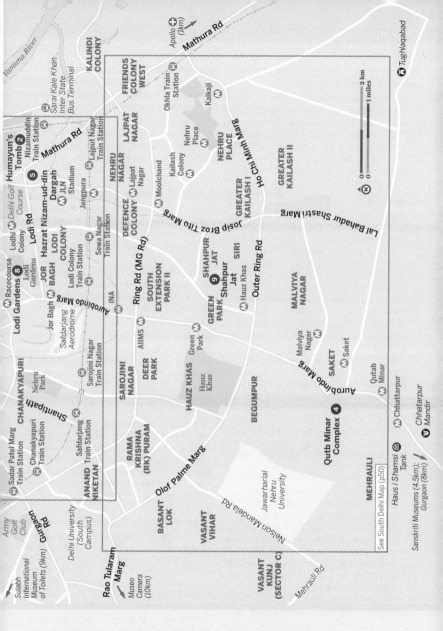

6 Cycling (p53)
Taking a rollicking, eye-opening bike ride through Old Delhi at dawn.

7 Street food (p60) Sampling some of Old Delhi's flavour-packed street food, such as Gali Paratha Wali's stuffed breads with attitude.

8 Lodi Gardens (p44) Roaming around Delhi's favourite tree-shaded, tomb-dotted park.

9 Shahpur Jat (p70) Browsing contemporary Indian fashion designs at this independently minded village.

(Islamic devotional singing) at this hallowed Sufi shrine.

to the sight, eg Qutb Minar and Tughlaqabad. Note that many places are closed on Monday.

⊙ Old Delhi

'Old Delhi' is roughly equivalent to the the Mughal city of Shahjahanabad. The main drag is Chandni Chowk, stretching from Red Fort to Fatehpur Masjid, which is a cacophonous tumult of noise, colour and traffic. Narrow lanes spiderweb off the street, lined by brilliantly colourful bazaars. The easiest way to get around is by cycle rickshaw or on foot.

★ Red Fort   FORT

(Map p38; Indian/foreigner ₹30/500, with museum ticket ₹35/500, video ₹25, audio guide in Hindi/English or Korean ₹69/115; ⊙ dawn-dusk Tue-Sun, museums 10am-5pm; Ⓜ Chandni Chowk) Founded by Emperor Shah Jahan and just a few decades older than the Palace of Versailles in France, this fort took 10 years to construct (1638–48). It had the decapitated bodies of prisoners built into the foundations for luck, and is surrounded by an 18m-high wall. It once overlooked the Yamuna River, which has now shrunk to some distance away. A tree-lined waterway, known as *nahr-i-bihisht* (river of paradise), ran out of the fort and along Chandni Chowk, fed by the Yamuna.

Shah Jahan never took up full residence here, after his disloyal son, Aurangzeb, imprisoned him in Agra Fort.

The last Mughal emperor of Delhi, Bahadur Shah Zafar, was flushed from the Red Fort in 1857 and exiled to Burma (Myanmar) for his role in the First War of Independence. The British destroyed buildings and gardens inside the fortress walls and replaced them with ugly barrack blocks for the colonial army.

The fort is the setting for an evening **sound and light show** (Map p38; www.theashokgroup.com; Tue-Fri ₹60, Sat & Sun ₹80; ⊙ in Hindi/English 7/8.30pm Feb-Apr, Sep & Oct, 7.30/9pm May-Aug, 6/7.30pm Nov-Jan), narrated by Amitabh Bachchan.

The audio guide tour, by acclaimed company Narrowcasters, is worthwhile as it brings the site to life.

➡ Lahore Gate

(Map p38) The main gate is hidden by a defensive bastion built in front by Shah Jahan's son Aurangzeb. During the struggle for independence, nationalists promised to raise the Indian flag over the gate, an ambition that became a reality on 15 August 1947. The Prime Minister makes a speech here every Independence Day.

➡ Chatta Chowk

(Covered Bazaar) This imperial bazaar used to cater to royal women and glitter with silk and jewels for sale. Today's wares are rather more mundane souvenirs.

➡ Naubat Khana

(Drum House) At the eastern end of Chatta Chowk, the arched 'Drum House' once accommodated royal musicians and served as parking for royal horses and elephants.

➡ Indian War Memorial Museum

(⊙ 10am-5pm Tue-Sun) Upstairs at Naubat Khana is the Indian War Memorial Museum, which contains ferocious-looking and fascinating historical weaponry.

➡ Museum on India's Struggle for Freedom

(⊙ 10am-5pm Tue-Sun) Housed in ugly British-built barracks, the Museum on India's Struggle for Freedom tells the story of the struggle against the British that led to Independence.

➡ Salimgarh

(Map p38; ⊙ 10am-5pm Tue-Sun) This fort was established by Salim Shah Suri in 1546, so predates its grander neighbour. Salimgarh was later used as a prison, first by Aurangzeb and later by the British; you can visit the ruined mosque and a small museum.

➡ Diwan-i-Am

This arcade of sandstone columns was the hall of public audience, where the emperor greeted guests and dignitaries from a throne on the raised marble platform, which is backed by fine pietra-dura (inlaid stone) work that features Orpheus, incongruously, and is thought to be Florentine.

➡ Diwan-i-Khas

The Hall of Private Audience was used for bowing and scraping to the emperor. Above the corner arches to the north and south is inscribed in Urdu, 'If there is paradise on the earth – it is this, it is this, it is this'. Nadir Shah looted the legendary jewel-studded Peacock Throne from here in 1739. Bahadar Shah Zafar became the last Mughal emperor here in May 1857, but was tried (here, again) by the British seven months later following the Mutiny, and exiled.

South of the Diwan-i-Khas is the dainty **Khas Mahal** (Special Palace), containing the emperor's private apartments, shielded from prying eyes by lace-like carved marble screens. An artificial stream, the *nahr-i-*

bihisht (river of paradise), once flowed through the apartments to the adjacent Rang Mahal (Palace of Colour), home to the emperor's chief wife. The exterior of the palace was once lavishly painted; inside is an elegant lotus-shaped fountain.

➤ Mumtaz Mahal

South of the Rang Mahal is this pavilion, thought to have been built for Arjumand Banu Begum (also known as Mumtaz Mahal) – the Taj Mahal is her mausoleum. Today it houses the Museum of Archaeology (⊙10am-5pm Tue-Sun), with imperial objects from those of Akbar to the rose-water sprinklers and calligraphy of the last emperor, Badapur Shah.

➤ Royal Baths

Closed to the public, the royal *hammams* once contained a sauna and hot baths for the royal family.

➤ Moti Masjid

(Pearl Mosque) This small white mosque was built by Aurangzeb as his private place of worship. The outer walls align with the fort walls, while the inner walls are askew to align with Mecca. It is closed to visitors.

➤ Shahi Burj

The Shahi Burj is a three-storey octagonal tower that was Shah Jahan's favoured workplace. From here he planned the running of his empire. In front of the tower is what remains of an elegant formal garden, centred on the Zafar Mahal, a sandstone pavilion surrounded by a deep, empty water tank.

Chandni Chowk   AREA

(Map p38; Ⓜ Chandni Chowk) Old Delhi's main drag is lined by Jain, Hindu and Sikh temples, plus a church, with the Fatehpuri Masjid at one end. Tree-lined and elegant in Mughal times, the thoroughfare is now mind-bendingly chaotic, with tiny little ancient bazaars tentacling off it. In the Mughal era, Chandni Chowk centred on a pool that reflected the moon, hence the name, 'moonlight place'. The main street is almost impossible to cross, full as it is of cars, hawkers, motorcycles, rickshaws and porters.

Digambara Jain Temple   JAIN TEMPLE

(Map p38; Chandni Chowk; ⊙6am-noon & 6-9pm; Ⓜ Chandni Chowk) Opposite the Red Fort is the red sandstone Digambara Jain Temple, built in 1658. It houses a fascinating bird hospital (Map p38; donations appreciated; ⊙10am-5pm) established in 1956 to further the Jain principle of preserving all life,

treating 30,000 birds a year. Squirrels and vegetarian birds are admitted; predators are treated as outpatients. Remove shoes and leather items before entering the temple.

Sunehri Masjid   MOSQUE

(Golden Mosque; Map p38; ⊙dawn-dusk; Ⓜ Chandni Chowk) Built in 1721, this mosque has gilded domes, hence its name. In 1739, the Persian invader Nadir Shah stood on the roof and watched his soldiers massacre thousands of Delhi's inhabitants.

Sisganj Gurdwara   SIKH TEMPLE

(Map p38; Chandni Chowk) The icing-sugar-white 18th-century Sisganj Gurdwara marks the martyrdom site of the ninth Sikh guru, Tegh Bahadur, executed by Aurangzeb in 1675 for resisting conversion to Islam. A banyan tree marks the spot where he was killed.

Fatehpuri Masjid   MOSQUE

(Map p38; Chandni Chowk; ⊙5am-9.30pm; Ⓜ Chandni Chowk) Built by Fatehpuri Begum, one of Shah Jahan's wives, this 17th-century mosque is a haven of tranquillity after the frantic streets outside. The central pool was taken from a noble house, hence the elaborate shape. After the 1857 uprising the mosque was sold to a Hindu nobleman by the British for ₹19,000 and returned to

DELHI SIGHTS

THE PIGEONS OF OLD DELHI

Pigeon rearing *(kabootar bazi)* is a popular hobby in Old Delhi, among those who can afford it – it costs from ₹5000 per bird. Some pigeons are trained to fight, some are fast, some are noted for their endurance. The practice first gained popularity during Mughal rule, when the birds were used for communication, and when Shahjahanabad was first built there were rival pigeon clubs all over the city. It's said that Nadir Shah's Delhi massacre was sparked after a row over the sale of a pigeon between one of his soldiers and a local fancier. Today there are still so many keepers that flying has to follow a timetable so that flocks don't clash. There are strict hierarchies among the owners; it takes more than 20 years to become a Khalifa (master pigeon keeper). The most spectacular event, of pigeon racing *(haqaana)*, takes place on Republic Day.

Red Fort

HIGHLIGHTS

The main entrance to the Red Fort is through ❶ **Lahore Gate** – the bastion in front of it was built by Aurangzeb for increased security. You can still see bullet marks on the gate, dating from 1857, the First War of Independence, when the Indian army rose up against the British.

Walk through the Chatta Chowk (Covered Bazaar), which once sold silks and jewellery to the nobility; beyond it lies ❷ **Naubat Khana**, a russet-red building, which houses Hathi Pol (Elephant Gate), so called because visitors used to dismount from their elephants or horses here as a sign of respect. From here it's straight on to the ❸ **Diwan-i-Am**, the Hall of Public Audiences. Behind this are the private palaces, the ❹ **Khas Mahal** and the ❺ **Diwan-i-Khas**. Entry to this Hall of Private Audiences, the fort's most expensive building, was only permitted to the officials of state. The artificial stream the Nahr-i-Behisht ('stream of paradise') used to run a cooling channel of water through all these buildings. Nearby is the ❻ **Moti Masjid (Pearl Mosque)** and south is the ❼ **Mumtaz Mahal**, housing the Museum of Archaeology, or you can head north, where the Red Fort gardens are dotted by palatial pavilions and old British barracks. Here you'll find the ❽ **baoli**, a spookily deserted water tank. Another five minutes' walk – across a road, then a railway bridge – brings you to the island fortress of ❾ **Salimgarh**.

TOP TIPS

➡ To avoid crowds, get here early or late in the day; avoid weekends and public holidays.

➡ An atmospheric way to see the Red Fort is by night; you can visit after dark if you attend the nightly Sound & Light Show.

Salimgarh
Salimgarh is the 16th-century fort built by Salim Shah Sur. It was constructed on an island of the Yamuna River and only recently opened to the public. It is still partly used by the Indian army.

Museum on India's Struggle for Freedom

Chatta Chowk

Lahore Gate
Lahore Gate is particularly significant, as it was here that Jawaharlal Nehru raised the first tricolour flag of independent India in 1947.

Naubat Khana
The Naubat Khana (Drum House) is carved in floral designs and once featured musicians playing in the upper gallery. It housed Hathi Pol (Elephant Gate), where visitors dismounted from their horse or elephant.

Baoli
The Red Fort step well is seldom visited and is a hauntingly deserted place, even more so when you consider its chambers were used as cells by the British from August 1942.

Moti Masjid
The Moti Masjid (Pearl Mosque) was built by Aurangzeb in 1662 for his personal use. The domes were originally covered in copper, but the copper was removed and sold by the British.

Diwan-i-Khas
This was the most expensive building in the fort, consisting of white marble decorated with inlay work of cornelian and other stones. The screens overlooking what was once the river (now the ring road) were filled with coloured glass.

Baidon Pavilion

Zafar Mahal

Hammam

6

Rang Mahal

5

4

Mumtaz Mahal

7

3

2

PIT STOP
To refuel, head to Gali Paratha Wali, a foodstall-lined lane off Chandni Chowk noted for its many varieties of freshly made paratha (traditional flat bread).

Delhi Gate

←NORTH

Diwan-i-Am
These red sandstone columns were once covered in shell plaster, as polished and smooth as ivory, and in hot weather heavy red curtains were hung around the columns to block out the sun. It's believed the panels behind the marble throne were created by Florentine jeweller Austin de Bordeaux.

Khas Mahal
Most spectacular in the Emperor's private apartments is a beautiful marble screen at the northern end of the rooms; the 'Scales of Justice' are carved above it, suspended over a crescent, surrounded by stars and clouds.

Old Delhi

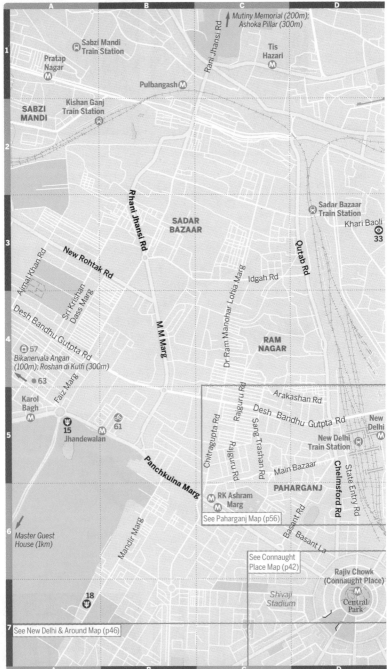

Mutiny Memorial (200m); Ashoka Pillar (300m)

Sabzi Mandi Train Station

Pratap Nagar

SABZI MANDI

Kishan Ganj Train Station

Pulbangash

Rani Jhansi Rd

Tis Hazari

Sadar Bazaar Train Station

Khari Baoli
33

SADAR BAZAAR

Rhani Jhansi Rd

Qutab Rd

New Rohtak Rd

Ajmal Khan Rd

Sri Krishan Dass Marg

Idgah Rd

Dr Ram Manohar Lohia Marg

RAM NAGAR

Desh Bandhu Gutpta Rd

M M Marg

Bikanervala Angan (100m); Roshan di Kulfi (300m)
57
63

Karol Bagh

Faiz Marg

15
Jhandewalan

61

Arakashan Rd

Chitragupta Rd

Rajguru Rd

Desh Bandhu Gutpta Rd

Sang Trashan Rd

Rajguru Rd

New Delhi

New Delhi Train Station

Panchkuina Marg

Main Bazaar

PAHARGANJ

Chelmsford Rd

State Entry Rd

RK Ashram Marg

See Paharganj Map (p56)

Master Guest House (1km)

Mandir Marg

Basant Rd

Basant La

See Connaught Place Map (p42)

Rajiv Chowk (Connaught Place)

Central Park

18

Shivaji Stadium

See New Delhi & Around Map (p46)

DELHI

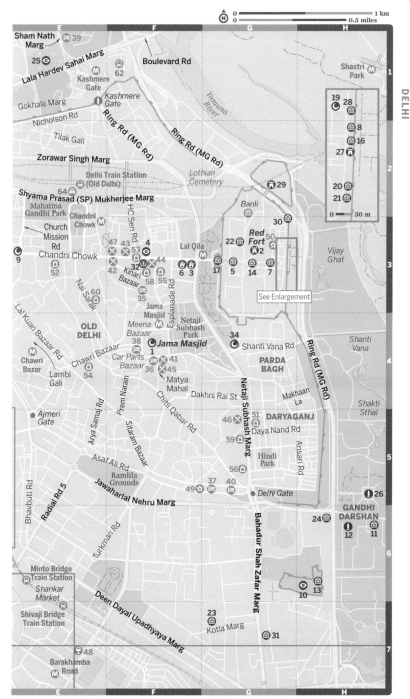

DELHI

0 ___ 1 km
0 ___ 0.5 miles

Sham Nath Marg
25
Lala Hardev Sahai Marg
Kashmere Gate
62
Boulevard Rd
Gokhale Marg
Kashmere Gate
Nicholson Rd
Ring Rd (MG Rd)
Tilak Gali
Ring Rd (MG Rd)
Zorawar Singh Marg
Delhi Train Station (Old Delhi)
Lothian Cemetery
29
64
Shyama Prasad (SP) Mukherjee Marg
Mahatma Gandhi Park
Chandni Chowk
Church Mission Rd
Chandni Chowk
47 43 4
53
32 44
9
52
42 Kinari Bazaar
58 55
60
Nai Sarak
35
Lal Qila
Lal Kuan Bazaar Rd
Jama Masjid
Meena Bazaar
Chawri Bazaar
Lambi Gali
OLD DELHI
38
Jama Masjid
1
Car Parts Bazaar
Matya Mahal
36 41
45
Netaji Subhash Park
34
Shanti Vana Rd
Chawri Bazar
54
Esplanade Rd
Dakhni Rai St
Chitli Qabar Rd
Prem Narain
Arya Samaj Rd
Sitaram Bazaar
Ajmeri Gate
Asaf Ali Rd
Ramlila Grounds
Jawaharlal Nehru Marg
49 37 40
Delhi Gate
46
59
DARYAGANJ
51
Daya Nand Rd
Ansari Rd
Hindi Park
56
Makhaan La
PARDA BAGH
Netaji Subhash Marg
Bahadur Shah Zafar Marg
Bhavbuti Rd
Radial Rd 5
Turkman Rd
Deen Dayal Upadhyaya Marg
Minto Bridge Train Station
Shankar Market
Shivaji Bridge Train Station
48
Barakhamba Road
23
Kotla Marg
31
Shastri Park
19 28
8
16
27
20
21
0 ___ 50 m
30
22 Red Fort 2 50
17 5 14 7
See Enlargement
Vijay Ghat
Shanti Vana
Shakti Sthal
24
12 11
GANDHI DARSHAN
26
10 13
Baoli
Yamuna River
Ring Rd (MG Rd)

Old Delhi

◎ Top Sights
1 Jama Masjid...................................F4
2 Red Fort..G3

◎ Sights
3 Bird Hospital.................................F3
4 Chandni Chowk............................F3
5 Chatta Chowk...............................G3
6 Digambara Jain Temple................F3
7 Diwan-i-Am...................................G3
8 Diwan-i-Khas...............................H2
9 Fatehpuri Masjid...........................E3
10 Feroz Shah Kotla...........................H6
11 Gandhi Darshan............................H6
12 Gandhi Memorial..........................H6
13 Hawa Mahal..................................H6
14 Indian War Memorial Museum.............G3
15 Jhandewalan Hanuman Temple.........A5
16 Khas Mahal...................................H2
17 Lahore Gate..................................G3
18 Lakshmi Narayan Temple.....................A7
19 Moti Masjid...................................H1
20 Mumtaz Mahal..............................H2
21 Museum of Archaeology................H2
22 Museum on India's Struggle for
    Freedom....................................G3
23 National Bal Bhavan......................G7
24 National Gandhi Museum..................H6
   Naubat Khana........................(see 14)
25 Nicholson Cemetery......................E1
26 Raj Ghat.......................................H5
27 Rang Mahal...................................H2
28 Royal Baths..................................H1
29 Salimgarh.....................................G2
30 Shahi Burj....................................G3
31 Shankar's International Dolls
    Museum.....................................G7
32 Sisganj Gurdwara.........................F3
33 Spice Market................................D3
34 Sunehri Masjid..............................G4

◎ Sleeping
35 Haveli Dharampura.......................F3
36 Hotel Bombay Orient.....................F4
37 Hotel Broadway............................G5
38 Hotel New City Palace...................F4
39 Maidens Hotel..............................E1

40 Stops @ The President...................G5

⊗ Eating
41 Al-Jawahar...................................F4
   Chor Bizarre.........................(see 37)
42 Gali Paratha Wali.........................F3
43 Haldiram's...................................F3
44 Jalebiwala....................................F3
45 Karim's..F4
   Lakhori..................................(see 35)
46 Moti Mahal...................................G5
47 Natraj Dahi Balle Wala..................F3

◎ Drinking & Nightlife
48 24/7...E7

◎ Entertainment
49 Delite Cinema...............................F5
50 Sound & Light Show.......................G3

◎ Shopping
51 Aap Ki Pasand (San Cha)..............G5
52 Ballimaran....................................E3
53 Chandni Chowk............................F3
54 Chawri Bazaar..............................E4
55 Dariba Kalan.................................F3
56 Daryaganj Kitab Bazaar.................G5
57 Karol Bagh Market........................A4
58 Kinari Bazaar................................F3
59 Musical Instrument Shops..............G5
60 Nai Sarak.....................................E3

❶ Transport
   Delhi Transport Corporation.......(see 62)
   Haryana Roadways.................(see 62)
61 Jhandewalan Cycle Market............B5
62 Kashmere Gate Inter State Bus
    Terminal....................................F1
63 Lalli Motorbike Exports..................A4
64 Prepaid Autorickshaws.................E2
   Punjab Roadways...................(see 62)
   Rajasthan Roadways................(see 62)
   Rajasthan State Road
    Transport Corporation.............(see 62)
   Uttar Pradesh Roadways...........(see 62)
   Uttar Pradesh State Road
    Transport Corporation.............(see 62)

Muslim worship in exchange for four villages 20 years later.

★ **Jama Masjid** MOSQUE
(Friday Mosque; Map p38; camera & video each ₹300, tower ₹100; ⊙ non-Muslims 8am-1hr before sunset, minaret 9am-5.30pm; Ⓜ Chawri Bazaar) A beautiful pocket of calm at the heart of Old Delhi's mayhem, India's largest mosque is built on a 10m elevation, towering above the surrounding hubbub. It can hold a mind-blowing 25,000 people. The marble and red-sandstone 'Friday Mosque' was Shah Jahan's final architectural triumph, built between 1644 and 1658. The four watchtowers were used for security. There are two minarets standing 40m high, one of which can be climbed for amazing views. All of the three gates allow access to the mosque.

The eastern gate was originally for imperial use only. Buy a ticket at the entrance to climb 121 steps up the narrow southern minaret (notices say that unaccompanied women are not permitted). From the top of the minaret, you can see how architect Edwin Lutyens incorporated the mosque into his design of New Delhi – the Jama Masjid, Connaught Place and Sansad Bhavan (Parliament House) are in a direct line.

Visitors should remove their shoes at the top of the stairs. There's no charge to enter the mosque, but you'll have to pay the camera charge whether you want to use your camera or not.

Raj Ghat   MONUMENT

(Map p38; ⊙10am-8pm; M Jama Masjid) FREE On the banks of the Yamuna River, this peaceful park contains a simple black-marble platform marking the spot where Mahatma Gandhi was cremated following his assassination in 1948. This memorial (Map p38) is a thought-provoking spot, inscribed with what are said to have been Gandhi's final words, *Hai Ram* (Oh, God). Every Friday (the day he died) commemorative prayers are held here at 5pm, as well as on 2 October and 30 January, his birth and death anniversaries.

Across Kisan Ghat Rd is the Gandhi Darshan (Map p38; ⊙10am-5pm Mon-Sat; M Indraprastha) FREE, a pavilion displaying photos relating to the Mahatma. Nearby memorials commemorate where Jawaharlal Nehru, Indira Gandhi and Rajiv Gandhi were cremated.

National Gandhi Museum   MUSEUM

(Map p38; ☑ 011-23310168; http://gandhimuseum.org; Raj Ghat; ⊙ 9.30am-5.30pm Tue-Sun; M Jama Masjid) FREE An interesting museum preserving some of Gandhi's personal belongings, including his spectacles and even two of his teeth. Movingly and somewhat macabrely, also here are the dhoti, shawl and watch he was wearing when he was assassinated, and one of the bullets that killed him.

Feroz Shah Kotla   HISTORIC SITE

(Map p38; Bahadur Shah Zafar Marg; Indian/foreigner ₹15/200, video ₹25; ⊙dawn-dusk; M ITO) Firozabad, the fifth city of Delhi, was built by Feroz Shah Tughlaq in 1354, the first city here to be built on the river. Only the fortress remains, with crumbling walls protecting the Jama Masjid (Friday mosque), a *baoli* (step-well), and the pyramid-like Hawa Mahal (Map p38), topped by a 13m-high sandstone Ashoka Pillar inscribed with 3rd-century-BC Buddhist edicts. There's an otherworldly atmosphere to the ruins.

On Thursday afternoon, crowds gather at the mosque to light candles and incense and leave bowls of milk to appease Delhi's djinns (invisible spirits), who are said to

occupy the underground chambers beneath the mosque. Shoes should be removed when entering the mosque and Hawa Mahal.

Shankar's International Dolls Museum   MUSEUM

(Map p38; ☑ 011-3316970; www.childrensbooktrust.com; Nehru House, 4 Bahadur Shah Zafar Marg; adult/child ₹17/6; ⊙10am-6pm Tue-Sun; M ITO) Set up by K Shankar Pillai, a political cartoonist, who started collecting dolls in 1950, this museum has an impressive if quirky collection of 6500 costumed dolls from 85 countries.

National Bal Bhavan   MUSEUM

(Map p38; www.nationalbalbhavan.nic.in; Kotla Marg; adult/child ₹20/free; ⊙ 9am-5.30pm Tue-Sat; M Mandi House) Delhi's children's museum is a charming hodgepodge, with a polychrome-painted toy train ride, parrots, guinea pigs, rabbits and a small aquarium.

Nicholson Cemetery   CEMETERY

(Map p38; Lala Hardev Sahai Marg; ⊙ 8am-6pm Apr-Sep, 9am-5pm Oct-Mar; M Kashmere Gate) Close to Kashmere Gate, this fascinating, forgotten cemetery is the last resting place for hundreds of Delhi's colonial-era residents, many of whom perished in childhood. The most famous (ex)-resident is the eponymous Brigadier General John Nicholson, who died from injuries sustained during the 1857 First War of Independence. He had a formidable reputation, and was so admired by some of his troops that he inspired a religious cult, but he was also contemptuous of the 'natives' and sadistically violent towards his adversaries.

Take the metro to see the British-erected Mutiny Memorial (Rani Jhansi Rd; M Pulbangash) and Ashoka Pillar (Rani Jhansi Rd; M Kashmere Gate), transported here by Feroz Shah.

Coronation Durbar Site   MONUMENT

(Shanti Swaroop Tyagi Marg; M Model Town) This historical oddity is worth seeking out if you like exploring forgotten corners. Around 10km north of Old Delhi, a lone obelisk marks the site where King George V was declared emperor of India in 1911, and where the great durbars (fairs) were held to honour India's British overlords in 1877 and 1903. A few marble busts of British officials and a mammoth statue of George V decorate the neighbouring park. Take an autorickshaw from the metro.

Lakshmi Narayan Temple   HINDU TEMPLE

(Birla Mandir; Map p38; Mandir Marg; ⊙4.30am-1.30pm & 2.30-9pm; M Ramakrishna Ashram Marg) This Orissan-style temple was erected by

Connaught Place

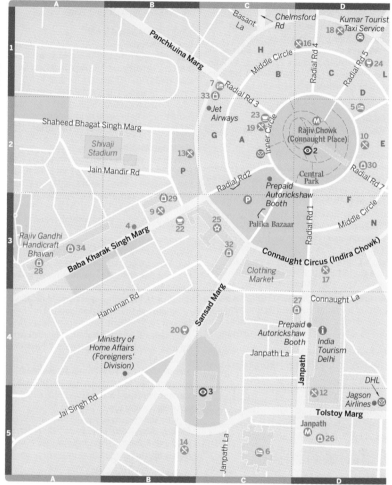

the wealthy industrialist BD Birla in 1939; the main shrine honours Lakshmi, goddess of wealth. Gandhi inaugurated the complex as a temple for all castes; a sign on the gate says 'Everyone is Welcome'.

Jhandewalan
Hanuman Temple HINDU TEMPLE
(Map p38; Link Rd, Jhandewalan; ☉dawn-dusk; M Jhandewalan) This temple is not to be missed (it's actually hard to miss) if you're in Karol Bagh. Take a short detour to see the 34m-high Hanuman statue that soars above the train tracks. Getting up close, there are passageways through the mouths of

demons to a series of atmospheric, deity-filled chambers.

◉ Connaught Place Area

Connaught Place AREA
(Map p42; M Rajiv Chowk) This confusing circular shopping district was named after George V's uncle, the Duke of Connaught, and fashioned after the Palladian colonnades of Bath. Greying, whitewashed, colonnaded streets radiate out from the central circle of Rajiv Chowk, with blocks G to N in the outer circle and A to F in the inner circle. Today they mainly harbour brash, largely

Agrasen ki Baoli MONUMENT
(Map p42; Hailey Lane; ⊙dawn-dusk; Ⓜ Janpath)
This atmospheric 14th-century step-well
was once set in the countryside, till the city
grew up around it; 103 steps descend to the
bottom, flanked by arched niches. It's a remarkable thing to discover among the office
towers southeast of Connaught Place. It's
garnered more attention since it was used as
a shelter by Aamir Khan in the 2015 movie
PK.

⊙ New Delhi & Around

★**Humayun's Tomb** HISTORIC BUILDING
(Map p46; Mathura Rd; Indian/foreigner/under 15
₹30/500/free, video ₹25; ⊙dawn-dusk; Ⓜ JLN
Stadium) Humayun's tomb is sublimely well
proportioned, seeming to float above its
symmetrical gardens. It's thought to have
inspired the Taj Mahal, which it predates
by 60 years. Constructed for the Mughal
emperor in the mid-16th century by Haji
Begum, Humayun's Persian-born wife, the
tomb marries Persian and Mughal elements,
with restrained decoration enhancing the
architecture. The arched facade is inlaid
with bands of white marble and red sandstone, and the building follows strict rules of
Islamic geometry, with an emphasis on the
number eight.

The tomb has had six years of restoration,
and a new visitor centre is due to open at
the site. The surrounding gardens contain
the tombs of the emperor's favourite barber
– an entrusted position given the proximity
of the razor to the imperial throat – and Haji
Begum. This was where the last Mughal emperor, Bahadur Shah Zafar, took refuge before being captured and exiled by the British
in 1857.

To the right as you enter the complex, Isa
Khan's tomb (Map p46; ⊙dawn-dusk) is a fine
example of Lodi-era architecture, constructed in the 16th century. Further south is the
monumental Khan-i-Khanan's tomb (p49),
plundered in Mughal times to build Safdarjang's tomb.

★**Hazrat Nizam-ud-din Dargah** SHRINE
(Map p46; off Lodi Rd; ⊙24hr; Ⓜ JLN Stadium)
Visiting the marble shrine of Muslim Sufi
saint Nizam-ud-din Auliya is Delhi's most
mystical, magical experience. The dargah is
hidden away in a tangle of bazaars selling
rose petals, attars (perfumes) and offerings,
and on Thursday evenings from sunset you
can hear Sufis singing *qawwali* (Islamic

interchangeable but popular bars, and international chainstores, plus a few good hotels
and restaurants. Touts are rampant.

Jantar Mantar HISTORIC SITE
(Map p42; Sansad Marg; Indian/foreigner ₹25/200,
video ₹25; ⊙dawn-dusk; Ⓜ Patel Chowk) This is
one of five observatories built by Maharaja
Jai Singh II, ruler of Jaipur. Constructed in
1725, Jantar Mantar (derived from the Sanskrit word for 'instrument', but which has
also become the Hindi word for 'abracadab-
ra') is a collection of curving geometric buildings that are carefully calibrated to monitor
the movement of the stars and planets.

Connaught Place

⊙ Sights
1 Agrasen ki Baoli F5
2 Connaught Place................................... D2
3 Jantar Mantar....................................... C5

⊕ Activities, Courses & Tours
4 Delhi Tourism & Transport
   Development Corporation
   Booth.. B3

⊟ Sleeping
5 Hotel Palace Heights............................ D2
6 Imperial C5
7 Radisson Blu Marina............................. C1

⊗ Eating
8 Caara Cafe E4
9 Coffee Home B3
10 Farzi Cafe.. D2
11 Haldiram's... E1
12 Hotel Saravana Bhavan D5
13 Hotel Saravana Bhavan B2
14 Kerala House B5
15 Naturals.. E1
16 Nizam's Kathi Kabab D1
17 Rajdhani.. D3
18 Sagar Ratna D1

19 Wenger's.. C2
   Zaffràn ....(see 5)

⊙ Drinking & Nightlife
   1911 ....(see 6)
20 Aqua.. B4
   Atrium, Imperial...........................(see 6)
21 Cha Bar... E3
22 Indian Coffee House............................ B3
23 Keventer's Milkshakes......................... C2
24 Unplugged... D1

⊗ Entertainment
25 Regal Cinema...................................... C3

⊟ Shopping
26 Central Cottage Industries
   Emporium.. D5
27 Janpath & Tibetan Markets D4
28 Kamala.. A3
29 Khadi Gramodyog Bhawan.................. B3
30 M Ram & Sons D2
31 Oxford Bookstore................................ E3
32 People Tree... C3
33 Rikhi Ram C1
34 State Emporiums A3

devotional singing), amid crowds of devotees. The ascetic Nizam-ud-din died in 1325 at the ripe old age of 92. His doctrine of tolerance made him popular not only with Muslims, but with Hindus, Sikhs and Buddhists as well.

Later kings and nobles wanted to be buried close to Nizam-ud-din, hence the number of nearby Mughal tombs. Other tombs in the compound include the graves of Jahanara (daughter of Shah Jahan) and the renowned Urdu poet Amir Khusru. Scattered around the surrounding alleyways are more tombs and a huge *baoli* (step-well). Entry is free, but visitors may be asked to make a donation.

A tour with the Hope Project (p53), which ends at the shrine, is recommended for some background.

Lodi Gardens PARK
(Map p46; Lodi Rd; ⊙ 6am-8pm Oct-Mar, 5am-8pm Apr-Sep; Ⓜ Khan Market or Jor Bagh) Delhi's loveliest escape was originally named after the wife of the British Resident, Lady Willingdon, who had two villages cleared in 1936 in order to landscape a park to remind her of home. Today named after their Lodi-era tombs, the gardens, favoured getaway for Delhi's elite and courting couples, contain

the 15th-century **Bara Gumbad** (Map p46) tomb and mosque, the strikingly different tombs of **Mohammed Shah** (Map p46) and **Sikander Lodi** (Map p46; Ⓜ JLN Stadium), and the Athpula (eight-piered) bridge across the lake, which dates from Emperor Akbar's reign.

Rajpath AREA
(Map p46; Ⓜ Central Secretariat) Rajpath (Kingsway) is a vast parade linking India Gate to the offices of the Indian government. Built on an imperial scale between 1914 and 1931, this complex was designed by Edwin Lutyens and Herbert Baker, and underlined the ascendance of the British rulers. Yet just 16 years later, the Brits were out on their ear and Indian politicians were pacing the corridors of power.

At the western end of Rajpath, the official residence of the president of India, Rashtrapati Bhavan (p45), now partially open to the public via guided tour, is flanked by the mirror-image dome-crowned **North Secretariat** (Map p46) and **South Secretariat** (Map p46), housing government ministries. The Indian parliament meets nearby at the **Sansad Bhavan** (Parliament House; Map p46; Sansard Marg), a circular, colonnaded edifice at the end of Sansad Marg.

At Rajpath's eastern end is mighty India Gate (Map p46; ⊙ 24hr). This 42m-high stone memorial arch, designed by Lutyens, pays tribute to around 90,000 Indian army soldiers who died in WWI, the Northwest Frontier operations and the 1919 Anglo-Afghan War.

Rashtrapati Bhavan HISTORIC BUILDING

(President's House; Map p46; ☑ 011-23015321; www.presidentofindia.nic.in/visit-to-rashtrapati-bhavan.htm; ₹50, online reservation required; ⊙ 9am-4pm Fri-Sun; Ⓜ Central Secretariat) Formerly home to the British Viceroy, the President's House has 340 rooms, with 2.5km of corridors, and it's fascinating to take a peek inside. Your guided visit takes in the domed Durbar Hall, the intimate presidential library and the gilded Ashoka Hall.

Rashtrapati Bhavan Museum MUSEUM

(Map p46; ☑ 011-23792177; www.presidentofindia.nic.in; gate 30, Mother Theresa Crescent Rd; tour ₹50; ⊙ 9am-4pm Fri-Sun; Ⓜ Patel Chowk) Occupying the presidential stables and garages, this swish museum has state-of-the-art displays including a virtual-reality walk with Gandhi and 3D images of presidential speeches, plus vehicles, such as a Mercedes given to Rajiv Gandhi by the King of Jordan. Book ahead online.

Mughal Gardens GARDENS

(Map p46; ⊙ usually 9.30am-4pm Tue-Sun mid-Feb–mid-Mar; Ⓜ Central Secretariat) FREE The extravagance of these glorious gardens is such that Mountbatten, India's last viceroy, was said to have employed 418 gardeners. There are fountains, cypress, bougainvillea, climbing roses, symmetrical lawns and wandering peacocks. If you're in town when the gardens are in flower (the same months they're open), they're not to be missed.

National Museum MUSEUM

(Map p46; ☑ 011-23019272; www.nationalmuseumindia.gov.in; Janpath; Indian/foreigner ₹20/650, camera Indian/foreigner ₹20/300; ⊙ 10am-5pm Tue-Sun, free guided tour 10.30am & 2.30pm Tue-Fri, 10.30am, 11.30am & 2.30pm Sat & Sun; Ⓜ Central Secretariat) This glorious if dusty museum is full of treasures. Mind-bogglingly ancient, sophisticated figurines from the Harappan civilisation, almost 5000 years old, include the remarkable Dancing Girl, and there are also some fine ceramics from the even older Nal civilisation. Other items include Buddha relics, exquisite jewellery, miniature paint-ings, medieval woodcarvings, textiles and musical instruments.

Allow at least two hours. Bring identification to obtain an audio guide (included in the foreigner ticket price; ₹150 extra for Indian tourists). There's also a cafe.

National Gallery of Modern Art GALLERY

(Map p46; ☑ 011-23386111; www.ngmaindia.gov.in; Jaipur House, Dr Zakir Hussain Marg; Indian/foreigner ₹20/500; ⊙ 10am-5pm Tue-Sun; Ⓜ Khan Market) Housed in the Maharaja of Jaipur's domed former palace (built in 1936), Delhi's flagship art gallery displays collections tracing the development of Indian art from the mid-19th century to the present day, from 'Company Paintings' created by Indian artists to please their British rulers to the artworks of Nobel Prize–winner Rabindranath Tagore. Photography is prohibited.

Gandhi Smriti MUSEUM

(Map p46; ☑ 011-23012843; 5 Tees Jan Marg; ⊙ 10am-5pm Tue-Sun, closed every 2nd Sat of month; Ⓜ Racecourse) FREE This poignant memorial to Mahatma Gandhi is in Birla House, where he was shot dead on the grounds by a Hindu zealot on 30 January 1948, after campaigning against intercommunal violence.

The house itself is where Gandhi spent his last 144 days. The exhibits include rooms preserved just as Gandhi left them, a detailed account of his life and last 24 hours, and vivid miniature dioramas depicting scenes from his life.

Indira Gandhi Memorial Museum MUSEUM

(Map p46; ☑ 011-23010094; 1 Safdarjang Rd; ⊙ 9.30am-4.45pm Tue-Sun; Ⓜ Racecourse) FREE In the residence of controversial former prime minister Indira Gandhi is this interesting museum devoted to her life and family, India's Kennedys. It displays her personal effects, including the blood-stained sari she was wearing when she was assassinated in 1984. Many rooms are preserved as they were, providing a window into the family's life. An exhibit at the rear charts the life of Indira's son, Rajiv, who met a similarly violent end and was assassinated in 1991.

Nehru Memorial Museum MUSEUM

(Map p46; ☑ 011-23016734; www.nehrumemorial.nic.in; Teen Murti Rd; ⊙ 9am-5.30pm Tue-Sun; Ⓜ Udyog Bhawan) FREE Built for the British commander-in-chief and previously called 'Flagstaff House', the stately Teen Murti Bhavan was later the official residence of

New Delhi & Around

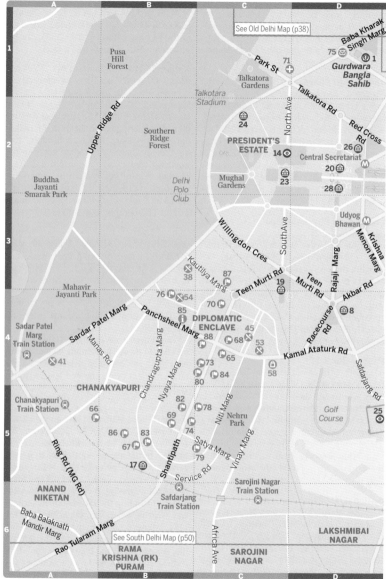

Jawaharlal Nehru (India's first prime minister). It's now a museum devoted to Nehru's life and work; the bedroom, study and drawing room are preserved as if he'd just popped out.

On the grounds is a 14th-century hunting lodge, built by Feroz Shah, and a more recent **planetarium** (Map p46; ☎ 011-23014504; www.nehruplanetarium.org; 45min show adult/child ₹60/40; ⏰ shows English 11.30am & 3pm, Hindi 1.30pm & 4pm), which has shows about the stars in Hindi and English.

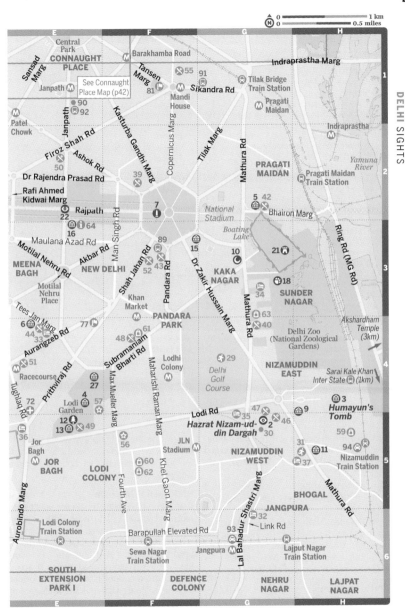

Purana Qila   FORT
(Old Fort; Map p46; ☎ 011-24353178; Mathura Rd; Indian/foreigner ₹5/200, video ₹25, sound & light show adult/child ₹100/50; ⏱ dawn-dusk; Ⓜ Pragati Maidan) The unimaginatively named 'Old Fort' is where Mughal Emperor Humayun met his end in 1556, tumbling down the steps of the **Sher Mandal**, which he used as a library. The fort had been built by Afghan ruler Sher Shah (1538–45), during his brief ascendancy over Humayun. It's well worth a visit, with its peaceful garden studded

New Delhi & Around

◎ Top Sights
1 Gurdwara Bangla Sahib D1
2 Hazrat Nizam-ud-din Dargah G5
3 Humayun's Tomb H4

◎ Sights
4 Bara Gumbad E4
5 Crafts Museum G2
6 Gandhi Smriti E4
7 India Gate F2
8 Indira Gandhi Memorial Museum D4
9 Isa Khan's Tomb H4
10 Khairul Manazil G3
11 Khan-i-Khanan's Tomb H5
12 Lodi Gardens E5
13 Mohammed Shah's Tomb E5
14 Mughal Gardens C2
15 National Gallery of Modern Art F3
16 National Museum E3
17 National Rail Museum B5
18 National Zoological Gardens G3
19 Nehru Memorial Museum C3
   Nehru Planetarium .... (see 19)
20 North Secretariat D2
21 Purana Qila G3
22 Rajpath E2
23 Rashtrapati Bhavan C2
24 Rashtrapati Bhavan Museum C2
25 Safdarjang's Tomb D5
26 Sansad Bhavan D2
27 Sikander Lodi's Tomb E4
28 South Secretariat D2

◎ Activities, Courses & Tours
   Aura .... (see 61)

29 Delhi Golf Club G4
30 Hope Project G5
   Lodhi Spa .... (see 35)
31 Torch H5

◎ Sleeping
32 Bloom Rooms @ Link Rd G6
33 Claridges E4
34 Devna G3
35 Lodhi G5
36 Lutyens Bungalow E5
37 Zaza Stay H5

◎ Eating
38 Alkauser B3
   Altitude Cafe .... (see 62)
39 Andhra Pradesh Bhawan Canteen F2
40 Basil & Thyme G4
41 Bukhara A4
42 Cafe Lota G2
   Chicken Inn .... (see 52)
43 Chor Bizarre F3
44 Dhaba E4
   Diva Spiced .... (see 62)
45 Gujarat Bhawan C4
   Gulati .... (see 52)
   Havemore .... (see 52)
46 Karim's G5
47 Kebab Stands G4
48 La Bodega F4
49 Lodi Garden Restaurant E5
50 Masala Library E2
51 Nagaland House E4
52 Pandara Market F3
   Perch .... (see 48)

with well-preserved ancient red-stone monuments, including the intricately patterned **Qila-i-Kuhran Mosque** (Mosque of Sher Shah).

A popular boating lake has been created from Purana Qila's former moat, with pedalos for hire.

Across busy Mathura Road are more relics from the city of Shergarh, including the beautiful **Khairul Manazil mosque** (Map p46), still used by local Muslims and favoured haunt of flocks of pigeons.

Crafts Museum   MUSEUM
(Map p46; ☑ 011-23371641; Bhairon Marg; ☻ 10am-5pm Tue-Sun; Ⓜ Pragati Maidan) FREE Much of this lovely museum is outside, including tree-shaded carvings and buildings. Displays celebrate the traditional crafts of India, with some beautiful textiles on display indoors, such as embroidery from Kashmir and cross-stitch from Punjab. Highlights include an exquisite reconstructed Gujarati

haveli (traditional house). Artisans sell their products in the rear courtyard. The museum includes the excellent Cafe Lota (p63) and a very good shop.

National Rail Museum   MUSEUM
(Map p46; ☑ 011-26881816; Service Rd, Chanakyapuri; adult/child ₹20/10, video ₹100; ☻ 10am-5pm Tue-Sun; Ⓜ Safdarjung) A contender for one of Delhi's best (and best-value) museums, the National Rail Museum has steam locos and carriages spread across 11 acres. Among the venerable bogies are the former Viceregal Dining Car, and the Maharaja of Mysore's rolling saloon. The new indoor gallery includes some hands-on exhibits, a miniature railway, and three simulators (weekends only). A toy train (adult/child ₹20/10) chuffs around the grounds.

National Zoological Gardens   ZOO
(Map p46; ☑ 011-24359825; www.nzpnewdelhi.gov.in; Mathura Rd; adult/child Indian ₹40/20, foreigner

Pindi..(see 52)
53 Sagar Ratna...C4
54 Sana-di-ge B4
    Sodabottleopenerwala..................(see 61)
55 Triveni Terrace Cafe...............................F1

◉ **Drinking & Nightlife**
    Café Turtle ....(see 59)
    Café Turtle ....(see 61)

◉ **Entertainment**
56 Habitat World F5
57 India International Centre.....................E4

◉ **Shopping**
58 Aap Ki Pasand (San Cha) C4
    Anand Stationers..........................(see 61)
    Anokhi ....(see 58)
    Anokhi ....(see 61)
59 Anokhi H5
    Bahrisons ....(see 61)
    Fabindia...(see 61)
60 Fabindia...F5
    Full Circle Bookstore....................(see 61)
    Kama ....(see 61)
61 Khan Market...F4
62 Meharchand Market..............................F5
    Mehra Bros ....(see 61)
    OCM Suitings...................................(see 61)
63 Sunder Nagar Market............................G3
    The Shop ....(see 60)

ℹ **Information**
64 Archaeological Survey of India E3
65 Australian High Commission C4

66 Bangladeshi High Commission A5
67 Bhutanese Embassy B5
68 British High Commission C4
69 Canadian High Commission B5
70 Chinese Embassy...................................C4
71 Dr Ram Manohar Lohia Hospital..........C1
72 East West Medical Centre.....................E4
73 French Embassy......................................C4
74 German Embassy....................................B5
75 India Post...D1
76 Irish Embassy...B4
77 Israeli Embassy......................................E4
78 Japanese Embassy C5
79 Malaysian High Commission C5
80 Myanmar Embassy C4
81 Nepali Embassy......................................F1
82 Netherlands Embassy B5
83 New Zealand High Commission B5
84 Pakistani Embassy..................................C4
85 Sikkim House..B4
86 Singaporean High Commission............B5
87 Sri Lankan High Commission C3
88 US Embassy...C4

ℹ **Transport**
89 Bikaner House F3
90 Chanderlok House...................................E1
91 Himachal Bhawan G1
92 Himachal Pradesh Tourism
    Development Corporation E1
93 Metropole Tourist Service.....................G6
94 Prepaid Autorickshaws H5
    Rajasthan Tourism........................(see 89)

₹200/100, camera/video ₹50/200, battery-operated vehicle adult/child ₹67/34; ⊙9am-4.30pm Sat-Thu, to 4pm Oct-Mar; Ⓜ Pragati Maidan) Founded in 1952, this is a vast green space in the city, covering 86 hectares. Kept in reasonable conditions are lions, tigers, elephants, hippos, rhinos, spectacular birds and monkeys. You can hire battery-operated vehicles to get around.

Safdarjang's Tomb   TOMB
(Map p46; Aurobindo Marg; Indian/foreigner ₹15/200, video ₹25; ⊙dawn-dusk; Ⓜ Jor Bagh) Built by the Nawab of Avadh for his father, Safdarjang, this grandiose, highly decorative mid-18th-century tomb is an example of late Mughal architecture. There were insufficient funds for all-over marble, so materials to cover the dome were taken from the nearby mausoleum of Khan-i-Khanan, and it was finished in red sandstone.

Khan-i-Khanan's Tomb   HISTORIC BUILDING
(Map p46; Indian/foreigner ₹15/200; ⊙dawn-dusk; Ⓜ Jangpura) This is the monumental tomb of a poet and minister in Akbar's court. Khan-i-Khanan had it built for his wife in 1598, and was buried here himself in 1627. It was later plundered to build nearby Safdarjang's tomb, and more of its decoration was stripped in the 19th century.

★**Gurdwara Bangla Sahib**   SIKH TEMPLE
(Map p46; Ashoka Rd; ⊙4am-9pm; Ⓜ Patel Chowk) This magnificent, huge, white-marble gurdwara, topped by glinting golden onion domes, was constructed at the site where the eighth Sikh guru, Harkrishan Dev, stayed before his 1664 death. Despite his tender years, the six-year-old guru tended to victims of Delhi's cholera and smallpox epidemic, and the waters of the large tank are said to have healing powers. It's full of colour and life, yet tranquil, and live devotional songs waft over the compound.

South Delhi

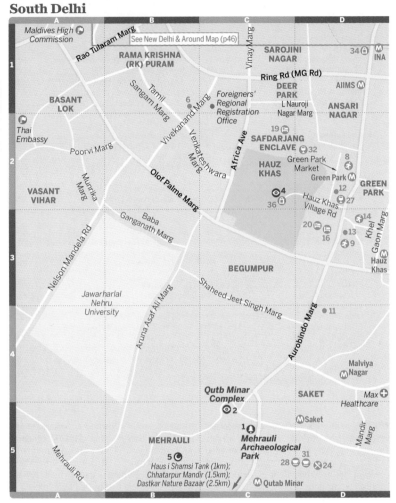

South Delhi

Hauz Khas AREA

(Map p50; ⊙dawn-dusk; Ⓜ Green Park) Built by Sultan Ala-ud-din Khilji in the 13th century, Hauz Khas means 'noble tank', and its reservoir once covered 28 hectares. It collected enough water during the monsoon to last Siri Fort throughout the dry season. Today it's much smaller, but still a beautiful place to be, thronged by birds and surrounded by parkland. Alongside it are the ruins of Feroz Shah's 14th-century madrasa (religious school) and **tomb** (Map p50), which he had built before his death in 1388.

To reach the lake shore, cut through the adjacent **Deer Park** (daylight hours), which has more ruined tombs and a well-stocked deer enclosure. There are numerous Lodi-era tombs scattered along the access road to Hauz Khas Village, and in nearby Green Park.

Bahai House of Worship TEMPLE

(Lotus Temple; Map p50; ☑ 011-26444029; www.bahaihouseofworship.in; Kalkaji; ⊙ 9am-7pm Tue-Sun Apr-Sep, to 5.30pm Oct-Mar; Ⓜ Kalkaji Mandir)

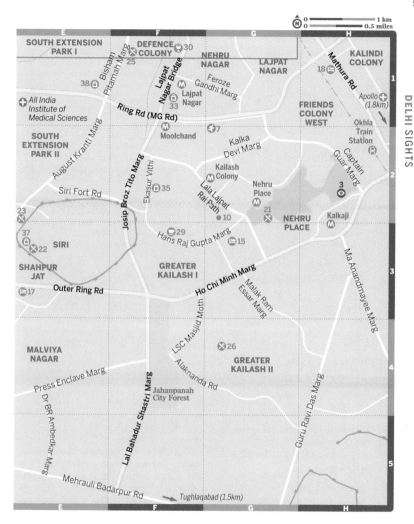

Designed for tranquil worship, Delhi's beautiful Lotus Temple offers a rare pocket of calm in the hectic city. This architectural masterpiece was designed by Iranian-Canadian architect Fariburz Sahba in 1986. It is shaped like a lotus flower, with 27 delicate-looking white-marble petals. The temple was created to bring faiths together; visitors are invited to pray or meditate silently according to their own beliefs. The attached visitor centre tells the story of the Bahai faith. Photography is prohibited inside the temple.

Chhatarpur Mandir   HINDU TEMPLE
(Shri Adya Katyayani Shakti Peeth Mandir; ☑011-26802360; www.chhattarpurmandir.org; Main Chhatarpur Rd; ◷4am-midnight; ⓜChhatarpur) India's second-largest temple (after Akshardham), this impressive sandstone and marble complex dates from 1974, and is dedicated to the goddess Katyayani (one of the nine forms of Parvati). There are dozens of shrines with towering South Indian *gopurams* (temple towers), and an enormous statue of Hanuman stands guard over the compound. Weekdays tend to be fairly sedate, but it gets crowded at weekends

South Delhi

◎ **Top Sights**
1 Mehrauli Archaeological Park C5
2 Qutb Minar Complex C5

◎ **Sights**
3 Bahai House of Worship H2
Feroz Shah's Tomb .... (see 4)
4 Hauz Khas C2
5 Hijron ka Khanqah B5
Iron Pillar .... (see 2)
Qutb Minar .... (see 2)
Quwwat-ul-Islam Masjid .... (see 2)

◎ **Activities, Courses & Tours**
6 Central Hindi Directorate B1
7 Concern India Foundation G2
8 Kerala Ayurveda D2
9 Saffron Palate D3
10 Sivananda Yoga G2
11 Sri Aurobindo Ashram D4
12 Studio Abhyas D2
13 Tushita Meditation Centre D3
14 Yoga Studio D3

◎ **Sleeping**
15 Bed & Chai G3
16 Jugaad Hostel D3
17 Madpackers Hostel E3
18 Manor H1
19 Scarlette C2
20 Treetops D3

◎ **Eating**
Coast .... (see 36)

21 Epicuria G2
22 Greenr E3
Indian Accent .... (see 18)
23 Potbelly E2
24 Rose Cafe D5
Sagar Ratna .... (see 25)
25 Swagath F1
26 Swagath G4

◎ **Drinking & Nightlife**
Anandini Tea Room .... (see 37)
27 Bandstand D2
28 Blue Tokai C5
29 Café Turtle F3
30 Ek Bar F1
Hauz Khas Social .... (see 36)
31 Jugmug Thela D5
Kunzum Travel Cafe .... (see 36)
32 Piano Man Jazz Club D2
Summer House .... (see 27)

◎ **Shopping**
Anokhi .... (see 35)
Claymen .... (see 36)
33 Delhi Musical Stores F1
34 Dilli Haat D1
35 Greater Kailash I: M-Block &
N-Block Markets F2
36 Hauz Khas Village C2
37 NeedleDust E3
Nimai .... (see 22)
38 Timeless E1

and during the Navratri celebrations in September/October.

Other Areas

★ **Akshardham Temple** HINDU TEMPLE
(☎ 011-43442344; www.akshardham.com; National Hwy 24, Noida turning; temple admission free, exhibitions ₹170, water show ₹80; ☉ temple 9.30am-6.30pm Tue-Sun, exhibitions 9.30am-5pm, water show after sunset; Ⓜ Akshardham) In the eastern suburbs, the Gujarati Hindu Swaminarayan Group's Akshardham Temple was built in 2005, and is breathtakingly lavish. Artisans used ancient techniques to carve the pale red sandstone into elaborate reliefs, including 20,000 deities, saints and mythical creatures. The centrepiece is a 3m-high gold statue of Bhagwan Shri Swaminarayan.

The complex includes a boat ride through 10,000 years of Indian history, animatronics telling stories from the life of Swaminarayan, and musical fountains.

Sulabh International Museum of Toilets MUSEUM
(☎ 011-25031518; www.sulabhtoiletmuseum.org; Sulabh Complex, Mahavir Enclave, Palam Dabri Rd; ☉ 10am-5pm Apr-Sep, 10.30am-5pm Oct-Mar; Ⓜ Janakpuri West) ✆ FREE More than half of India's 1.2 billion people still don't have a toilet in their homes, but since 1970 the Sulabh NGO has worked to address India's sanitation issues, constructing new public toilets and developing 'scavenger-free' pour-flush toilets – it's long been illegal for people to work as manual scavengers in order to empty untreated waste, but this caste-defined task is still prevalent in many areas. The organisation also educates, and their small, quirky museum traces the history of the water closet from 2500 BC to modern times. Take a rickshaw from the metro stop.

Sanskriti Museums MUSEUM
(www.sanskritifoundation.org; Anandagram, Mehrauli Gurgaon Rd; ☉ 10am-5pm Tue-Fri; Ⓜ Arjangarh) FREE On the way to Gurgaon, this

little-known, well-kept place contains museums devoted to 'everyday art' and Indian terracotta and textiles. Much of the museum is outside and covers 7 acres. Objects such as kitchenware and hookahs are works of art, and there are expressive terracotta sculptures and intricate textiles from Gujarat, Rajasthan, Kashmir and Bengal.

🏊 Activities

Delhi Golf Club   GOLF
(Map p46; ☑ 011-24307100; www.delhigolfclub.org; Dr Zakir Hussain Marg; 18 holes weekdays/weekends Indian ₹6000/8000, foreigner US$100/150; ☺ dawn-dusk; ⓂKhan Market) Carved out of the undergrowth in 1931, this golf club now covers 220 acres and is a spectacular place to tee off, with beautiful, well-tended fairways, peacocks and Mughal tombs. Weekends are busy.

Kerala Ayurveda   AYURVEDA
(Map p50; ☑ 011-41754888; www.ayurvedancr. com; E-2 Green Park Extn; 1hr synchronised massage with steam ₹1500, sirodhara ₹3000; ☺ 8am-8pm; ⓂGreen Park) Treatments from *sarvang ksheerdhara* (massage with buttermilk) to *sirodhara* (warm oil poured on the forehead).

Aura   SPA
(Map p46; ☑ 8800621206; www.aurathaispa. com; Middle Lane, Khan Market; 1hr dry/oil massage ₹1400/2800; ☺ 10am-9pm; ⓂKhan Market) Glitzy spa offering Thai-inspired massages and treatments. There are also branches at Karol Bagh, GK1, GK2 and Green Park.

👉 Tours

★**Reality Tours & Travel**   TOURS
(☑ 9818227975; http://realitytoursandtravel.com; 2hr tour ₹850; ☺ 10am-6pm) Long-established in Mumbai, the highly professional Reality Tours are now offering tours of Delhi, including the excellent Sanjay Colony tour – a visit to a slum area of Delhi (no photographs permitted out of respect for locals' privacy). The tour guides are knowledgable and friendly, and 80% of profits go to supporting development projects in the colony.

★**DelhiByCycle**   CYCLING
(☑ 9811723720; www.delhibycycle.com; per person ₹1850; ☺ 6.30-10am) Founded by a Dutch journalist, these cycle tours are the original and the best, and a thrilling way to explore Delhi. Tours focus on specific neighbourhoods – Old Delhi, New Delhi, Nizamuddin,

and the banks of the Yamuna – and start early to miss the worst of the traffic. The price includes chai and a Mughal breakfast. Child seats are available.

★**Salaam Baalak Trust**   WALKING
(SBT; Map p56; ☑ 011-23584164; www.salaam baalaktrust.com; Gali Chandiwali, Paharganj; suggested donation ₹200; ⓂRamakrishna Ashram Marg) 🖊 Founded on the proceeds of Mira Nair's 1988 film about the life of street children, *Salaam Bombay!*, this charitable organisation offers two-hour 'street walks' guided by former street children, who will show you firsthand what life is like for Delhi's homeless youngsters. The fees help the Trust assist street children.

Intach   WALKING
(☑ 011-41035557; www.intachdelhichapter.org; tour ₹200) Intach runs walking tours with expert guides, exploring different areas, such as Chandni Chowk, Nizamuddin, Hauz Khas and Mehrauli. Custom walks can also be arranged.

Delhi Heritage Walks   WALKING
(www.delhiheritagewalks.com; 3hr walk ₹500) Fascinating walks led by knowledgable guides around Mehrauli, Old Delhi, Tughlaqabad and more.

Delhi Metro Walks   WALKING
(www.delhimetrowalks.com; half- to full-day group walks per person ₹300-600) Delhi-wallah Surekha Nurain shares her extensive knowledge about architecture, history and culture on recommended group or private tours, visiting both mainstream sights and off-the-beaten-track locations. She has several specially themed walks for families.

Street Connections   WALKING
(www.walk.streetconnections.co.uk; 3hr walk ₹500; ☺ 9am-noon Mon-Sat) 🖊 This fascinating walk through Old Delhi is guided by former street children who have been helped by the Salaam Baalak Trust (p53). It explores the hidden corners of Old Delhi, starting at Jama Masjid and concluding at one of the SBT shelters.

Hope Project   WALKING
(Map p46; ☑ 011-24357081; www.hopeprojectindia. org; 127 Hazrat Nizamuddin; 1½hr walk suggested donation ₹300; ⓂJLN Stadium) 🖊 The Hope Project guides interesting walks around the Muslim basti (slum) of Nizamuddin. Take the walk in the afternoon to end at the *qawwali* (Islamic devotional singing) at the

Hazrat Nizam-ud-din Dargah, or at the more intimate session at the shrine of Hazrat In-ayat Khan on Friday. Wear modest clothing.

Peteindia
WALKING

(www.peteindia.org; 2hr tour ₹750) An NGO of-fering guided walks around the central area that's home to Delhi's magicians, puppet-eers and circus performers, also known as the tinsel slum (the 'Kathputli Colony'). It's not the best organised tour but nonetheless a unique opportunity to see some of the performers, subject of the 2015 documenta-ry *Tomorrow We Disappear*, and discover more about their communities.

Ho Ho Bus Service
TOURS

(Hop-on, Hop-off; ☑ 1280; http://hohodelhi. com; Indian/foreigner ₹350/700, two-day ticket ₹600/1200; ⊘ departures 8.30am-2.40pm Tue-Sun) The Delhi Tourism & Transport Develop-ment Corporation runs the air-conditioned Ho Ho Dilli Dekho bus service, which cir-cuits the major sights every 45 minutes or so from 8.30am to 6.30pm, with the last stop at Jantar Mantar at 6.45pm (last departure at 2.40pm). Buy tickets from the **booth** (Map p42) near the DTTDC office.

🍴 Courses

Sivananda Yoga
HEALTH & WELLBEING

(Map p50; www.sivananda.org.in; A41 Kailash Colo-ny; suggested donation per class ₹400; Ⓜ Kailash Colony) This excellent ashram offers courses and workshops for both beginners and the advanced, plus drop-in classes ranging from one to two hours. On Sunday there is a free introductory drop-in class.

Yoga Studio
YOGA

(Seema Sondhi; Map p50; www.theyogastudio. info; 43 D-Block Hauz Khas; 4/8/12 classes ₹2200/3200/3700, drop in ₹800; Ⓜ Hauz Khas) Seema Sondni's 75-minute classes practise various forms of Ashtanga Vinyasa. From beginners to advanced practioners: contact in advance so you can attend an appropriate class.

Studio Abhyas
MEDITATION, YOGA

(Map p50; ☑ 011-26962757; www.abhyastrust.org; F-27 Green Park; Ⓜ Green Park) Yoga and medi-tation classes and Vedic chanting, for prac-titioners at any level; also offer children's classes.

Sri Aurobindo Ashram
MEDITATION, YOGA

(Map p50; ☑ 011-26567863; www.sriaurobindoash ram.net; Aurobindo Marg; Ⓜ Hauz Khas) Ashram

offering free yoga and meditation classes for serious practitioners.

Tushita Meditation Centre
MEDITATION

(Map p50; ☑ 011-26513400; www.tushitadelhi.com; 9 Padmini Enclave; by donation; ⊘ 6.30-7.30pm Mon & Thu; Ⓜ Hauz Khas) Guided Tibetan/Bud-dhist meditation sessions.

Saffron Palate
COOKING

(Map p50; ☑ 9971389993; www.saffronpalate.com; R21 Hauz Khas Enclave; cooking class without/with market visit ₹6000/8000; ⊘ varies; Ⓜ Hauz Khas) Recommended 2½-hour Indian cookery classes, where you eat the food afterwards, are run by Neha Gupta in her family home. You can also arrange a 4½-hour course in-cluding a market visit.

Central Hindi Directorate
LANGUAGE

(Map p50; ☑ 011-26178454; http://hindinidesha laya.nic.in/english; West Block VII, RK Puram, Vivekanand Marg; 60hr basic course ₹6000) Runs certificate and diploma courses in Hindi; ba-sic courses last 60 hours, with three classes a week.

🛏 Sleeping

Delhi hotels range from wallet-friendly dives to lavish five-stars; wherever you are on the scale, it's wise to book ahead, and reconfirm 24 hours before arrival. Most places offer airport pick-up, arranged in advance.

Hotel rooms above ₹1500 per night at-tract a 8.4% service tax, a 15% luxury tax and nominal Krishi Kalyan Cess (a national agriculture initiative) and Swaccha Bharat Abhiyan Cess (a national sanitation and infrastructure initiative) charges of 0.05% each.

🏛 Old Delhi

★ Stops @ The President
HOSTEL $

(Map p38; ☑ 011-41056226; www.gostops. com; 4/23B Asaf Ali Rd; dm ₹500-800, d ₹3000; ❋ @ ⊚; Ⓜ New Delhi) This is one of the best of Delhi's new breed of hostels, in a great location on the edge of Old Delhi, with a brightly tiled kitchen, lounge areas, three friendly dogs, and comfortable, clean dorms and rooms.

Hotel New City Palace
HOTEL $

(Map p38; ☑ 011-23279548; www.hotelnewcity palace.in; 726 Jama Masjid; r ₹700; ❋; Ⓜ Chawri Bazaar) A palace it's not, but this mazelike hotel has an amazing location overlooking the Jama Masjid. Rooms aren't big, and have small, hard beds with greying sheets, but some have windows and views. The bathrooms (squat toilets) could do with a good scrub, but staff are friendly.

Hotel Bombay Orient
HOTEL $$

(Map p38; ☑011-43101717; Matya Mahal; s/d from ₹970/1430, with AC ₹1370/1830; ☒; Ⓜ Jama Masjid) Opposite famous restaurant Karim's in Old Delhi, this is a friendly place to stay and you'll be in the thick of it. Rooms are clean and tidy, but ask to see a few before you commit. Bookings are recommended.

Hotel Broadway
HOTEL $$

(Map p38; ☑011-43663600; www.hotelbroadwaydelhi.com; 4/15 Asaf Ali Rd; s/d incl breakfast from ₹3250/4805; ☒@☎; Ⓜ New Delhi) The Broadway was Delhi's first high-rise when it opened in 1956. Today it's comfortable, quirky, and in a great Old Delhi location. It's worth staying here for the restaurant Chor Bizarre (p60) and Thugs bar. Some rooms have old-fashioned wood panelling, while others have been quirkily kitted out by French designer Catherine Lévy. Ask for one with views over Old Delhi.

★ Haveli Dharampura
HERITAGE HOTEL $$$

(Map p38; ☑011-23263000; www.havelidharampu|ra.com; 2293 Gali Guliyan; d from ₹13,640; ☒☎; Ⓜ Jama Masjid) This is a beautiful restored *haveli*, full of Mughal atmosphere and centred around a courtyard. Rooms have grandiose polished-wood beds, but it's worth paying for a larger room, as the smallest are a little cramped. The excellent restaurant, Lakhori (p60), serves historic Mughal recipes, and there's *kathak* dancing Friday to Sunday evenings.

Maidens Hotel
HOTEL $$$

(Map p38; ☑011-23975464; www.maidenshotel.com; 7 Sham Nath Marg; r from ₹19,840; ☒@☎☒; Ⓜ Civil Lines) Oberoi-owned Maidens is a grand heritage hotel dating from 1903 – a creamy neoclassical confection fronted by pea-green lawns. Lutyens stayed here while supervising the building of New Delhi, and the high-ceilinged rooms have a colonial-era charm but contemporary comforts. There are two restaurants, a pool and a bar.

🛏 Paharganj & Around

Love it or hate it, this hectic traveller hub is no oasis of serenity. But it is packed with hotels, trinket shops, and restaurants of every

cuisine, and is convenient for New Delhi Railway Station/Airport metro.

If your hotel is on the the Main Bazaar or Arakashan Rd, taxi drivers can make it all the way to the door, though they may be reluctant as it's so congested. If you're having issues, ask to be dropped at Chhe Tooti Chowk and complete your journey on foot.

You can walk to the Main Bazaar in minutes from Ramakrishna Ashram Marg metro. The New Delhi metro is more convenient for Arakashan Rd, which is around 10 minutes' walk from the stop, over a bridge.

★ Backpacker Panda
HOSTEL $

(Map p56; http://backpackerpanda.com; dm 8-bed ₹400, 6-bed ₹450; ☎; Ⓜ Ramakrishna Ashram Marg) A great alternative to Paharganj's less-than-fancy cheap hotels, Panda offers bright, clean dorms (one is female only) with attached bathrooms, charge points, lockers, windows, clean linen and comfortable mattresses. It's close to the metro. Win-win!

★ Hotel Amax Inn
HOTEL $

(Map p56; ☑011-23543813; www.hotelamax.com; 8145/6 Arakashan Rd; s/d/tr from ₹850/950/1350; ☒@☎; Ⓜ New Delhi) In a lane off chaotic Arakashan Rd, the Amax is a long-running traveller favourite, with clean, occasionally stuffy, good-value budget rooms. Staff are friendly, and clued up about traveller needs, and there's a small greenery-fringed terrace. The triple (Room 403) opening onto the rooftop has the added advantage of a window and a nicely stencilled wall.

Zostel
HOSTEL $

(Map p56; ☑011-39589005; www.zostel.com/zostel/Delhi; 5 Arakashan Rd; 6-8-bed dm ₹549, d ₹1499; ☎; Ⓜ New Delhi) Part of the Zostel chain, this place is shabbier than some of Delhi's other backpacker hostels. However, it's got the obligatory cheerful murals, the dorms are a pretty good deal, and it's a friendly place to meet other backpackers.

Paharganj

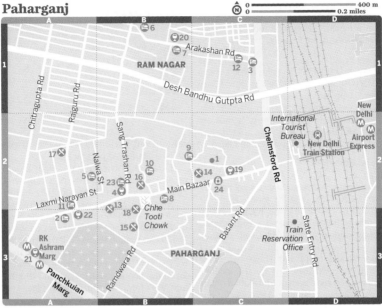

Paharganj

⊕ Activities, Courses & Tours
1 Salaam Baalak Trust C2

⊜ Sleeping
2 Backpacker Panda................................ A3
3 Bloom Rooms @ New Delhi.................. C1
4 Cottage Ganga Inn............................... B2
5 Diya... A2
6 Hotel Amax Inn..................................... B1
7 Hotel Godwin Deluxe............................ B1
8 Hotel Hari Piorko.................................. B2
9 Hotel Namaskar.................................... B2
10 Hotel Rak International........................ B2
11 Metropolis Tourist Home...................... A2
12 Zostel... C1

⊗ Eating
13 Brown Bread Bakery B2

Cafe Fresh ....(see 11)
14 Everest Bakery......................................C2
Malhotra ....(see 11)
15 Narula Bakery.. B3
16 Shimtur... B2
17 Sita Ram Dewan Chand........................ A2
18 Tadka..B3

⊖ Drinking & Nightlife
19 Gem..C2
20 Karen Cafe.. B1
21 Metro Bar..A3
22 My Bar...A3
23 Sam's Bar..B2

⊖ Shopping
24 Main Bazaar C2

Hotel Namaskar　　　　　　　HOTEL $

(Map p56; ☑ 011-23583456; www.namaskarhotel.
com; 917 Chandiwalan, Main Bazaar; r ₹400-650,
with AC ₹700; ❄ 🛜) Up a narrow alley opposite the Dayal Boot House, this long-running traveller cheapo is run by two amiable
brothers and offers a friendly welcome. It
may be humid and noisy, but the rooms get
a fresh coat of powder-pink paint annually,
which gives it a fresher feel than many of
its peers.

Cottage Ganga Inn　　　　　　HOTEL $

(Map p56; ☑ 011-23561516; www.cottageganga
inn.com; 1532 Bazar Sangtrashan; s/d from
₹1000/1300; ❄ @ 🛜; Ⓜ Ramakrishna Ashram
Marg) Quieter than most Paharganj choices,
this place is tucked in a courtyard off the
Main Bazaar, next to a nursery school. It's
clean, calm, comfortable and good value.
Rooms at the front have windows and cost
more.

Hotel Rak International　　HOTEL $
(Map p56;　☎ 011-23562478;　www.hotelrakinter national.com; 820 Main Bazaar, Chowk Bawli; s/d ₹650/750, with AC ₹850/950; ✳; Ⓜ Ramakrishna Ashram Marg) Hotel Rak International is off the Main Bazaar (so it's quieter) and overlooks a little square and temple. The modest rooms at this popular place are a good choice in this price range, with marble floors and bathrooms, plus, unusually, twin rooms and...windows! The pricier rooms overlook the square.

★**Bloom Rooms @ New Delhi**　　HOTEL $$
(Map p56;　☎ 011-40174017;　http://bloomrooms. com; 8591 Arakashan Rd; s/d incl breakfast from ₹2200/2900; ✳@⎙; Ⓜ New Delhi) Bloom Rooms' white-and-yellow, pared-down designer aesthetic is unlike anything else in the 'hood. Plus there are soft pillows, comfortable beds, good wi-fi and free mineral water. Its Re restaurant is a bit gloomy but the food is tasty.

Diya　　B&B $$
(Map p56;　☎ 9811682348;　http://stay.street connections.co.uk;　Tilak St;　s/d incl breakfast ₹2000/2750; ⎙; Ⓜ Ramakrishna Ashram Marg) The kind of place you'd really like kept secret, this is like a South Delhi guesthouse, but on a Paharganj backstreet, and has three lovely, well-cared-for rooms, one with a balcony. There's also a shared kitchen. It's run by Street Connections, and the staff and management are former street kids from the Salaam Baalak Trust. Reservations are essential. Great for solo women.

Hotel Hari Piorko　　HOTEL $$
(Map p56; Main Bazaar; r ₹1450-1850; ✳⎙; Ⓜ Ramakrishna Ashram Marg) It's worth paying just that bit extra to have a fish tank in your room – this is the only hotel in Delhi, to our knowledge, with this option. Even without the fish tanks, this is a good choice – the pricier rooms are also more spacious. There's the Fire & Ice restaurant too, with a balcony overlooking the Main Bazaar.

Hotel Godwin Deluxe　　HOTEL $$
(Map p56; ☎ 011-23613797; www.godwinhotels.com; 8501 Arakashan Rd; s/d incl breakfast ₹3000/3250; ✳@⎙; Ⓜ New Delhi) Run by the same owners as the Grand Godwin next door, Godwin Deluxe offers similar good service, and comfortable, spacious, clean rooms.

Metropolis Tourist Home　　HOTEL $$
(Map p56;　☎ 011-23561794;　www.metropolis touristhome.com;　1634-5 Main Bazaar;　r from

₹2000; ✳@⎙; Ⓜ Ramakrishna Ashram Marg) A long-standing favourite in the backpacking district, this hotel has comfortable, renovated rooms decorated in a hundred shades of brown. The slightly pricey rooftop restaurant feels almost European, with its greenery, low lights and foreign clientele.

Connaught Place & Around

★**Imperial**　　HOTEL $$$
(Map p42;　☎ 011-23341234;　www.theimperialindia. com; Janpath; r from ₹24,300; ✳@⎙✉; Ⓜ Janpath) Classicism meets art deco at the Imperial, which dates from 1931 and was designed by FB Blomfield, an associate of Lutyens. Rooms have high ceilings, flowing curtains, French linen and marble baths. There's the temple-like Thai restaurant Spice Route; the 1911 bar (p65) is highly recommended; and the Atrium cafe (p65) serves the perfect high tea.

The hallways and atriums are lined with the hotel's venerable 18th- and 19th-century art collection.

Hotel Palace Heights　　HOTEL $$$
(Map p42;　☎ 011-43582610;　www.hotelpalace heights.com;　26-28 D-Block;　s/d ₹8100/8650; ✳@⎙; Ⓜ Rajiv Chowk) This small-scale boutique hotel offers some of busy Connaught Place's nicest rooms, with gleaming white linen, and caramel and amber tones. There's an excellent restaurant, Zäffrän (Map p42; ☎ 011-43582610; Hotel Palace Heights, 26-28 D-Block; mains ₹350-650; ⊙ noon-3.30pm & 6.30-11.30pm; Ⓜ Rajiv Chowk).

Radisson Blu Marina　　HOTEL $$$
(Map p42;　☎ 011-46909090;　www.radisson.com/ hotels/indnedl;　59 G-Block;　s/d ₹10,000/11,000; ✳@⎙;　Ⓜ Rajiv Chowk) Connaught Place's swishest choice, the Radisson feels pleasingly luxurious, with sleek, stylish, all-modcon rooms, the Great Kebab Factory, and a cool bar, the Connaught, where you can sip drinks under hanging red lamps.

West Delhi

Master Guest House　　GUESTHOUSE $$
(☎ 011-28741089;　www.master-guesthouse.com; R-500 New Rajendra Nagar; s/d incl breakfast from ₹2071/3270; ✳@⎙; Ⓜ Rajendra Place) In a quiet suburban area, this smart and polished home is a tight ship run by the knowledgable Ushi and Avnish, and has three tastefully furnished rooms with spotless bathrooms. There's a leafy rooftop terrace.

Shanti Home HOTEL $$$
(☑ 011-41573366; www.shantihome.com; A-1/300 Janakpuri; s/d incl breakfast from ₹5500/6500; ❄@⛫; Ⓜ Uttam Nagar East) In west Delhi, this small boutique place is close to the metro and offers beautifully decorated rooms that get gradually swisher the more you spend. There are spacious lounge areas, an excellent, lantern-lit rooftop restaurant, a gym, cooking classes and spa service.

🛏 New Delhi

Bloom Rooms @ Link Rd HOTEL $$
(Map p46; ☑ 011-41261400; bloomrooms.com; 7 Link Rd; s/d incl breakfast from ₹2900/3700; ❄@⛫; Ⓜ Jangpura) A few minutes' walk from the metro, this is a quiet and convenient spot for Khan Market, Humayun's Tomb and Lodi Gardens. Bloom Rooms' designer white-and-yellow aesthetic is pleasingly Scandi-esque. Pillows are soft, wi-fi is fast, and there's a branch of Amici, a respected local Italian restaurant.

★**Lodhi** HOTEL $$$
(Map p46; ☑ 011-43633333; www.thelodhi.com; Lodi Rd; r from ₹21,800; ❄⛫☒; Ⓜ JLN Stadium) The Lodhi is one of Delhi's finest luxury hotels, with huge, lovely rooms and suites. Each room has a balcony with private plunge pool, and those on the upper floors have great views, some over to Humayun's Tomb. Attention to detail is superb. There's also a top-notch spa (Map p46; ☑ 011-43633333; www.thelodhi.com; Lodhi Hotel, Lodi Rd; 1hr massage from ₹3800; Ⓜ JLN Stadium).

Claridges HOTEL $$$
(Map p46; ☑ 011-39555000; www.claridges.com; 12 Aurangzeb Rd; d from ₹13,050; ❄@⛫☒; Ⓜ Racecourse) Fronted by manicured green lawns, elegant Claridges was built in 1952. Colonial-era-styled rooms have all comforts, and there are some excellent dining options, including romantic Mediterranean Sevilla, with its curtained pavilions, and imagine-you're-on-the-highway **Dhaba** (Map p46; ☑ 011-39555000; The Claridges, 12 Aurangzeb Rd; dishes ₹700-2000; ⊙12.30-2.30pm & 7-11.30pm; Ⓜ Racecourse), with traditional Punjabi food.

Zaza Stay GUESTHOUSE $$$
(Map p46; ☑ 011-47373450; www.zaza.co.in; G54, Nizamuddin West; s/d incl breakfast from ₹4000/5000) Owned by a couple who have their own homewares brand, this guesthouse has beautifully decorated rooms with leafy outlooks in Nizamuddin; a quiet and restful area, but still close to the Dargah and Humayun's Tomb.

Lutyens Bungalow GUESTHOUSE $$$
(Map p46; ☑ 011-24611341; www.lutyensbungalow.co.in; 39 Prithviraj Rd; s/d incl breakfast from ₹6500/8000; ❄@⛫☒; Ⓜ Racecourse) A rambling bungalow with a colonial feel, surrounded by verandahs and hanging lamps, this family-run guesthouse has a wonderful garden, with lawns, flowers and fluttering parakeets. Rooms are pleasant, with wooden furnishings and an old-fashioned vibe, and it's a particularly good place to stay with kids because of the unusual amount of rambling space.

🛏 South Delhi

★**Madpackers Hostel** HOSTEL $
(Map p50; S39-A 3rd fl, Panchsheel Park Sth; 6-14-bed dm ₹650-850; ❄⛫; Ⓜ Hauz Khas) A friendly, relaxed hostel with a bright and airy sitting room that's one of the best places in town to hang out and meet like-minded travellers. It has mixed dorms (with one female-only) and graffitied walls, and it's in a leafy area of south Delhi.

Jugaad Hostel HOSTEL $
(Map p50; Mohamed Pur; dm ₹600-800, r ₹2400) In a nicely untouristed if out-of-the-way area, this is a great hostel close to a huge Friday market. There are dorms including a women-only dorm, private rooms, swing chairs on the rooftop and a friendly, helpful welcome.

Bed & Chai HOSTEL $$
(Map p50; www.bedandchai.com; R55 Hans Raj Gupta Marg; dm ₹850, d without/with bathroom from ₹2500/3100) For a quiet stay, this French-owned guesthouse has simple rooms, decorated with flashes of colour and some quirky, original design touches. There's a dorm, a roof terrace and, of course, excellent chai.

Treetops GUESTHOUSE $$
(Map p50; ☑ 9899555704; baig.murad@gmail.com; R-8B Hauz Khas Enclave; s/d from ₹2500/3500; ❄⛫; Ⓜ Hauz Khas) Motor-journalist-novelist-philosopher Murad and his hobby-chef wife Tannie have a gracious home. To stay here feels rather like visiting some upper-crust relatives from another era. There are two large rooms opening onto a leafy rooftop terrace; the smaller room downstairs is cheaper but can feel less private. Evening meals are available.

MAJNU-KA-TILLA

Majnu-ka-Tilla is an enclave that has served as a base for Tibetan refugees since around 1960. It's a popular alternative traveller hub for those who prefer something more relaxed than Paharganj, with a laid-back, little Lhasa vibe. It's named after a local hermit boatman who was nicknamed 'crazy' *(majnu)* and who met Guru Nanak, the founder of Sikhism, here on a small hill *(tilla)*; the nearby 18th-century Majnu-ka-Tilla Gurdwara was built to commemorate the Guru's soujourn here.

Majnu-ka-Tilla's streets are too narrow for traffic, and it's close to the Yamuna River. There's a monastery here, and plenty of maroon-robed Buddhist monks and Tibetans. There are also rather a lot of beggars, but the streets have a small-town, safe-feeling vibe.

Cheapie **Ga-Kyegu House** (☎011-23815196; gakyeguhouse@hotmail.com; H-158, Block 7, Tibetan Colony; r ₹700, without bathroom ₹550; 🖥; Ⓜ Vidhan Sabha) has some bargain rooms with Yamuna River views. Friendly **Wongdhen House** (☎011-23816689; 15-A New Tibetan Colony; r ₹800-1000, without bathroom ₹500; ❈🖥; Ⓜ Vidhan Sabha) has simple, shabby rooms and a good restaurant; next-door **Lhasa House** (☎011-23939888; lhasahouse@rediffmail.com; 16 New Aruna Nagar; r ₹500-1000; Ⓜ Vidhan Sabha) is better value. **Ama** (H40, New Aruna Nagar; ⊙7am-9.30pm; 🖥; Ⓜ Vidhan Sabha) and **Kham Cafe** (New Aruna Nagar; ⊙7am-7.30pm; Ⓜ Vidhan Sabha) are splendid places to chill over coffee, and below Ama is good-value **Akama** (⊙9am-7.30pm; Ⓜ Vidhan Sabha), selling Tibetan artefacts. Two good eating options are **Tee Dee** (32 New Aruna Nagar; dishes ₹60-210; ⊙8.30am-10.30pm; Ⓜ Vidhan Sabha) and long-running and popular **Dolma House** (Block 10, New Tibetan Colony; dishes ₹70-180; ⊙7am-10pm). For a refreshing change, try Korean **Kori's** (Tsampa Café; Tsampa House, 18-19 New Camp; dishes ₹80-290; ⊙7.30am-10pm; 🖥).

To reach here, take the metro to Vidhan Sabha, from where shared auto-/cycle-rickshaws (₹40/20) will take you to the enclave on KB Hedgewar Marg. Ask for the 'wrong side'.

★**Manor**   HOTEL $$$
(Map p50; ☎011-26925151; www.themanordelhi.com; 77 Friends Colony (West); d incl breakfast from ₹11,000; ❈@🖥) With only 16 rooms, this boutique hotel oozes privacy and elegance. Set amid manicured lawns off Mathura Rd, the Manor has large rooms with contemporary furnishings in soothing earth colours and offering the utmost comfort. The restaurant, Indian Accent (p64), is one of Delhi's best.

★**Devna**   GUESTHOUSE $$$
(Map p46; ☎011-41507176; www.tensundernagar.com; 10 Sunder Nagar; s/d ₹5450/5800; ❈@🖥) Devna has lots of charm, with antique wooden furniture, photographs of maharajas, and works of art. The upstairs rooms open onto small terraces, with views over the pretty courtyard garden, and it's close to the expansive grounds of Delhi's zoo.

Scarlette   GUESTHOUSE $$$
(Map p50; ☎011-41023764; www.scarlettenewdelhi.com; B2/139 Safdarjung Enclave; d from ₹7000; ❈🖥) In serene, leafy Safdarjung Enclave, close to Hauz Khas Village and the Deer Park, Scarlette is a *maison d'hôtes* (guest-house) with four rooms, plus an apartment, decorated with beautiful artistic flair by the French textile-designer owner. It's a good choice for solo women.

Airport Area & Beyond

Delhi's Aerocity is a convenient area of big hotels, only 4km from the airport – ideal if you're only stopping over for a night. It's served by the Delhi Aerocity metro stop. Take your pick from brands such as Hotel Pullman, Lemon Tree, and the super-luxurious Hilton-run Andaz Delhi; the cheapest option is the Hotel Delhi Aerocity. There are also a few choices in nearby Vasant Kunj.

See www.newdelhiairport.in for details of several sleeping options at the airport..

🍴 Eating

Old Delhi

★**Jalebiwala**   SWEETS $
(Map p38; Dariba Corner, Chandni Chowk; jalebis per 100g ₹50; ⊙8am-10pm; Ⓜ Lal Qila) Century-old Jalebiwala does Delhi's – if not India's – finest *jalebis* (deep-fried, syrupy dough),

so pig out and worry about the calories tomorrow.

★ **Gali Paratha Wali**　　　STREET FOOD **$**
(Map p38; Gali Paratha Wali; parathas ₹15-35; ⊙7am-11pm; Ⓜ Jama Masjid) This lane off Chandni Chowk has been serving up delectable *parathas* (traditional flat bread) fresh off the *tawa* (hotplate) for generations, originally serving pilgrims at the time of the Mughals. Choose from a spectacular array of stuffings, from green chilli and paneer to lemon and banana.

Natraj Dahi Balle Wala　　STREET FOOD **$**
(Map p38; 1396 Chandni Chowk; plates ₹50; ⊙10.30am-11pm; Ⓜ Chandni Chowk) This tiny place with the big red sign and the big crowds is famous for its *dahi bhalle* (fried lentil balls served with yoghurt and garnished with chutney) and deliciously crispy *aloo tikki* (spiced potato patties).

Haldiram's　　　　　　FAST FOOD **$**
(Map p38; 1454/2 Chandni Chowk; mains ₹70-180; ⊙10am-10.30pm; Ⓜ Chandni Chowk) This clean, bright cafeteria-cum-sweet-shop is a popular stop for its top-notch dosas (large South Indian savoury crêpes), and thalis, and it also sells *namkin* (savouries) and *mithai* (sweets) to eat on the hoof. There's a popular branch at **Connaught Place** (Map p42; 6 L-Block, Connaught Place; snacks ₹70-230; ⊙8.30am-10.30pm; Ⓜ Rajiv Chowk).

★ **Karim's**　　　　　　　MUGHLAI **$$**
(Map p38; Gali Kababyan; mains ₹120-400; ⊙9am-12.30am; Ⓜ Jama Masjid) Just off the lane leading south from Jama Masjid, Karim's has been delighting carnivores since 1913. Expect meaty Mughlai treats such as mutton *burrah* (marinated chops), delicious mutton Mughlai, and the breakfast mutton and bread combo *nahari*. There are branches all over town, including at **Nizamuddin West** (Map p46; 168/2 Jha House Basti; dishes ₹120-400;

⊙8am-10pm Tue-Sat; Ⓜ JLN Stadium), but this location is the oldest and best.

Al-Jawahar　　　　　　MUGHLAI **$$**
(Map p38; Matya Mahal; mains ₹60-350; ⊙7am-midnight; Ⓜ Jama Masjid) Although overshadowed by its famous neighbour, Karim's (p60), Al-Jawahar is also fantastic, serving up tasty Mughlai cuisine at formica tables in an orderly dining room, and you can watch breads being freshly made at the front. Kebabs and mutton curries dominate the menu, but it also does good butter chicken and korma.

Lakhori　　　　　　　　INDIAN **$$$**
(Map p38; Haveli Dharampura, 2293 Gali Guliyan; tasting menus veg/non-veg ₹1800/2200, other dishes around ₹400-600; ⊙10am-10.30pm; 🅖; Ⓜ Jama Masjid) A different experience in the old city, this restored *haveli* is a labour of love by politician Vijay Goel, and it's good to see one of Old Delhi's grand *havelis* finally get some TLC. The restaurant is especially atmospheric in the evening, with tables in the courtyard and Mughlai and local recipes on the menu.

Moti Mahal　　　　　　MUGHLAI **$$$**
(Map p38; ☏011-23273661; 3704 Netaji Subhash Marg; mains ₹290-620; ⊙noon-midnight) There's only one true Moti Mahal, and this been open for six generations – it's full of charm, with a stuck-in-time atmosphere; it'd make a perfect film set for Wes Anderson. Delhi-ites rate the place for its superior butter chicken and *dhal makhani*. There's live *qawwali* (Islamic devotional singing) Wednesday to Monday from 8pm to 11.30pm.

Chor Bizarre　　　　　KASHMIRI **$$$**
(Map p38; ☏011-23273821; Hotel Broadway, 4/15 Asaf Ali Rd; mains ₹325-500; ⊙noon-3pm & 7.30-11pm; Ⓜ New Delhi) A dimly lit cavern filled with bric-a-brac, including a vintage car, Chor Bizarre (meaning 'thieves market') offers delicious and authentic Kashmiri cuisine, including *wazwan,* the traditional Kashmiri feast.

🍴 Paharganj & West Delhi

Paharganj is the main backpacker hub, and its restaurants proffer a wide-ranging mishmash of global cuisine ranging from pizza to banana pancakes. There are more cheap eats in the bazaars at Karol Bagh.

FOOD & DRINK TAXES

Drinks taxes ratchet your bill up by 20% (alcoholic) or 12.5% (nonalcoholic), and restaurants also levy 12.5% VAT on food, plus AC places have to charge a 14% service tax on the 'service' element of your bill. Many also add a 10% service charge. So be aware that all up you may have to pay around 30% or more above what's shown on the menu.

★**Sita Ram Dewan Chand**　　　INDIAN $
(Map p56; 2243 Chuna Mandi; half-/full plate
₹30/55;　⊘8am-5pm;　M Ramakrishna Ashram
Marg) A family-run hole-in-the-wall serving
inexpensive portions of just one dish – *chole
bhature* (spicy chickpeas), accompanied by
delicious, freshly made, puffy, fried bread.
It's a traditional breakfast but many people
are partial to some at any time of day.

Narula Bakery　　　BAKERY $
(Map p56; sandwiches ₹15-25;　⊘9am-10pm;
M Ramakrishna Ashram Marg) A tip-top takeaway bakery if you're looking for a bargain
lunch, this place has veg, cheese and corn or
paneer *kulcha* sandwiches.

Everest Bakery　　　NEPALI $
(Map p56; Chandiwalan; dishes ₹50-250; ⊘8am-
11pm; M Ramakrishna Ashram Marg) This chilled
little fan-cooled place off the Paharganj
main drag offers the usual every-sort cuisine, but including *momos* and impressive
salads. There's also a real Italian coffee machine, a rare beast in Paharganj.

Brown Bread Bakery　　　BAKERY $
(Map p56; Ajay Guest House, 5084-A, Main Bazaar;
snacks ₹65-150; ⊘7am-11pm; 🛜; M Ramakrishna
Ashram Marg) A popular traveller hang-out,
with a rustic, wicker-heavy interior, organic
Brown Bread has simple food that hits the
spot, with omelettes, pizzas, lots of different
breads and very good chips.

Bikanervala Angan　　　FAST FOOD $
(82 Arya Samaj Rd, Karol Bagh; mains ₹35-170;
⊘11am-10.30pm; M Karol Bagh) This small but
buzzing Karol Bagh canteen is a useful pit-
stop for South Indian treats, fast food and
snacks. Thalis start at ₹165.

Roshan di Kulfi　　　ICE CREAM $
(Ajmal Khan Rd, Karol Bagh; kulfi around ₹70;
⊘8.30am-9.30pm; M Karol Bagh) A Karol Bagh
institution for its scrumptious special *pista
badam kulfi* (frozen milk dessert with pistachio, almond and cardamom). It's around
500m northwest of Karol Bagh metro.

★**Shimtur**　　　KOREAN $$
(Map p56; 3rd fl, Navrang Guesthouse, Tooti Galli;
meals ₹240-500; ⊘10am-11pm; M Ramakrishna
Ashram Marg) It takes determination to find
this place: take the turning for the Hotel Rak
International, opposite which is the grotty,
unsigned Navrang Guesthouse. Follow the
stairs to its rooftop and you'll find a small,
bamboo-lined, softly lit terrace. The Kore-

an food is fresh and delicious here. Try the
bibimbap (rice bowl with a mix of vegeta-
bles, egg and pickles; ₹240). Beer is available
(₹170).

Cafe Fresh　　　VEGETARIAN $$
(Map p56; Laxmi Narayan St; dishes ₹115-240;
⊘8am-11pm; 🛜; M Ramakrishna Ashram Marg)
This cafe has veg appeal, catering to a mix
of Indians and foreigners; it's an attractive-
ly calm place to retreat (down a few steps)
from the busy street.

Tadka　　　INDIAN $$
(Map p56; 4986 Ramdwara Rd; mains ₹150-190;
⊘8.30am-10.30pm;　M Ramakrishna　Ashram
Marg) Named for everyone's favourite dhal,
Tadka is a reliable vegetarian choice, serving
up perfectly fine paneer dishes and other
veg treats (ordinary/special thali ₹200/280)
under whirring fans.

Malhotra　　　MULTICUISINE $$
(Map p56; 1833 Laxmi Narayan St; mains ₹80-425;
⊘7am-11pm; 🛜) One street back from the
Main Bazaar chaos, Malhotra is a reliable
local choice, popular with locals and foreigners, with a good menu of set breakfasts
and North Indian standards, such as *mattar
paneer* (pea and cottage cheese curry).

✗ Connaught Place

★**Naturals**　　　ICE CREAM $
(Map p42; 8 L-Block, Connaught Place; cup/cone
₹65, double scoop ₹130; ⊘11am-midnight; M Rajiv Chowk) Founder Mr Kamath's dad was a
mango vendor in Bangalore, which apparently inspired his love of fruit. He went on to
start Naturals, with its wonderfully creamy,
fresh flavours, such as watermelon, coconut,
(heavenly) mango and roasted almond.

★**Hotel Saravana Bhavan**　　　SOUTH INDIAN $$
(Map p42; 46 Janpath; dishes ₹95-210, thali ₹210;
⊘8am-11pm; M Janpath) Fabulous dosas, *idlis*
and other South Indian delights. This is the
biggest and the best of Delhi's Saravana Bha-
van branches, and you can see dosas being
made in the back. Also offers great South
Indian coffee.

Kerala House　　　SOUTH INDIAN $
(Map p42; 3 Jantar Mantar Rd; meals ₹50; ⊘8-
10am, 12.30-3pm & 7-9.45pm; M Patel Chowk) The
Kerala staff canteen is open to the public and
tasty meals here are a lip-smacking bargain,
including unlimited rice, fish curry, fish fry,
sambar, a couple of veg dishes and pickle.

Coffee Home
INDIAN $

(Map p42; Baba Kharak Singh Marg; meals ₹50-150; ⊙ 11am-8pm; Ⓜ Shivaji Stadium) With a shaded garden eating area, and a spacious interior under whirring fans, Coffee Home is always busy with office workers lingering over chai and feasting on South Indian snacks such as *masala dosa*. It is handily located next to the government emporiums.

Hotel Saravana Bhavan
SOUTH INDIAN $

(Map p42; 15 P-Block, Connaught Place; mains ₹95-210; ⊙ 8am-11pm; Ⓜ Rajiv Chowk) Delhi's best thali is served up in unassuming surroundings – a simple Tamil canteen on the edge of Connaught Place. There are queues every meal time to sample the splendid array of richly spiced veg curries, dips, breads and condiments that make it onto every thali plate.

Wenger's
BAKERY $

(Map p42; 16 A-Block, Connaught Place; snacks ₹30-100; ⊙ 10.45am-7.45pm; Ⓜ Rajiv Chowk) Legendary Wenger's was opened by a Swiss couple in 1926, and has been baking up a storm ever since. Come for cakes, sandwiches, biscuits and savoury patties.

Nizam's Kathi Kabab
FAST FOOD $

(Map p42; 5 H-Block, Connaught Place; kebabs ₹80-270; ⊙ 11.30am-11pm; Ⓜ Rajiv Chowk) This takeaway eatery creates masterful kebabs, biryani and *kati* rolls (kebabs wrapped in a hot *paratha*). It's always busy with meat-loving hoards, but there are also paneer, mushroom and egg options available so vegies don't have to miss out.

★ Masala Library
MODERN INDIAN $$$

(Map p46; 21A Janpath; tasting menu ₹2600; ⊙ noon-2.45pm & 7pm-1am; Ⓜ Janpath) Restaurateur Zorawar Kalra has brought his Masala Library to Delhi (the first was in Mumbai), with creative cooking that adds a dash of magic to your meal, with molecular cuisine and dishes such as coconut and mango *amuse-bouche* disguised as a bird's nest and levitating chocolate balls. Arrive hungry and try the 19-course tasting menu.

★ Rajdhani
INDIAN $$$

(Map p42; ☑ 011-43501200; 1/90 P-Block, Connaught Place; thalis ₹475; ⊙ noon-3.30pm & 7-11pm; Ⓜ Rajiv Chowk) Thalis fit for a king. Treat yourself with food-of-the-gods vegetarian thalis that encompass a fantastic array of Gujarati and Rajasthani dishes.

Farzi Cafe
MODERN INDIAN $$$

(Map p42; ☑ 9599889700; 38 E-Block, Connaught Place; mains ₹360-560; ⊙ noon-12.30am; Ⓜ Rajiv Chowk) This buzzy CP joint signifies the Delhi foodie penchant for quirkiness, with all sorts of 'molecular gastronomy' and unusual fusion dishes such as butter chicken *bao* (in a bun). It's only ₹85 for Kingfisher beer, and there are *banta* (traditional homemade fizzy pop) cocktails. There's live Sufi, Hindi and pop music on Friday and Saturday nights from 10pm.

Chor Bizarre
KASHMIRI $$

(Map p46; ☑ 011-23071574; Bikaner House, Pandara Rd; mains ₹325-500; ⊙ 12.30-3pm & 7.30-11pm; Ⓜ Khan Market) In the beautifully restored colonial-era Bikaner House, Chor Bizarre ('Thieves' Market') is a new branch of the famous Old Delhi restaurant. The interior is full of quirky old-fashioned charm, and the menu includes authentic, delicious dishes such as Kashmiri *haaq* (spinach with chilli).

✕ New Delhi & Around

New Delhi, with its dazzlingly opulent five-star hotels, malls and upmarket enclaves around Khan Market, Lodi Rd and Mathura Rd, is where to head if you feel like a swanky meal, with a fabulously wide mix of cuisines.

★ Andhra Pradesh Bhawan Canteen
SOUTH INDIAN $

(Map p46; 1 Ashoka Rd; dishes ₹130-160, thalis ₹110; ⊙ 8-10.30am, noon-3pm & 7.30-10pm; Ⓜ Patel Chowk) A hallowed bargain, the canteen at the Andhra Pradesh state house serves cheap and delicious unlimited South Indian thalis to a seemingly unlimited stream of patrons. Come on Sunday for the fabled Hyderabadi biryani (₹200).

★ Triveni Terrace Cafe
CAFE $

(Map p46; 205 Tansen Marg, Mandi House; dishes ₹55-220; ⊙ 10am-7.30pm; Ⓜ Mandi House) Run by the same folks in charge of the Craft Museum's Cafe Lota, this is a focus for Delhi's arty set, with good-value tasty Indian meals and snacks, such as chilli toast, and nice seating on a leafy terrace overlooking a grassy amphitheatre or inside in a fan-cooled room.

Gujarat Bhawan
GUJARATI $

(Map p46; 11 Kautilya Marg, Chanakyapuri; breakfast ₹60, thali ₹110-140; ⊙ 8-10am, 12.30-2.30pm &

7.30-10pm; M Racecourse) The Gujarat Stater-un canteen is nothing fancy, but serves up nourishing, plentiful, cheap-as-chips vege-tarian home-style Gujarati thalis.

Kebab Stands STREET FOOD $

(Map p46; Hazrat Nizam-ud-din Dargah; kebabs from ₹30; ⊙noon-11pm; M JLN Stadium) The al-ley in front of Hazrat Nizam-ud-din Dargah becomes a hive of activity every evening as devotees leave the shrine in search of sus-tenance. Canteen-style kebab houses cook up lip-smacking beef, mutton and chicken offerings at bargain prices, with biryani and roti as filling side orders.

Nagaland House INDIAN $

(Map p46; 29 Dr APJ Abdul Kalam Rd; thalis ₹120 200; ⊙noon-2pm & 7.30-10pm; M Racecourse) The Nagaland canteen is a simple room overlooking a tangle of palm trees and is worth seeking out for punchy pork offer-ings, with dishes such as pork with bamboo shoots and a Naga-style pork thali. Veg and chicken thalis are also available.

★**Cafe Lota** MODERN INDIAN $$

(Map p46; Crafts Museum; dishes ₹215-415; ⊙8am-10pm; M Pragati Maidan) Bamboo slic-es the sunlight into flattering stripes at this outdoor restaurant offering delicious cook-ing with a twist. Sample their take on fish and (sweet potato) chips, or *palak patta chaat* (crispy spinach, potatoes and chick-peas with spiced yoghurt and chutneys), as well as amazing desserts and breakfasts. It's great for kids.

Caara Cafe CAFE $$

(Map p42; ☑1204569000; British Council, 17, Kasturba Gandhi Marg; mains ₹160-350; ⊙8am-8pm Mon-Sat, 8am-6pm Sun) In the British Council is this most serene, light-filled cafe, hung with Brit art from their collection, so you can sip tea and coffee and nibble on healthy-looking cakes, vegetable curry and salads against the backdrop of a few Dami-an Hirsts.

★**Sodabottleopenerwala** PARSI $$

(Map p46; Khan Market; dishes ₹85-900; ⊙noon-11pm; M Khan Market) The name is like a typ-ical trade-based Parsi surname, the place emulates the Iranian cafes of Mumbai, and the food is authentic Persian, including veg-etable berry *pulav*, mixed-berry trifle and *lagan nu custer* (Parsi wedding custard).

★**Alkauser** STREET FOOD $$

(Map p46; www.alkausermughlaifood.com; Kautilya Marg; kebabs from ₹170, biryani from ₹280; ⊙6-10.30pm) The family behind this hole-in-the-wall takeaway earned their stripes cooking kebabs for the Nawabs of Lucknow in the 1890s. The house speciality is the *kakori* kebab, a pâte-smooth combination of lamb and spices, but other treats include biryani and perfectly prepared lamb *burra* (mari-nated chops) and *murg malai tikka* (chick-en marinated with spices and paneer).

Epicuria FOOD HALL $$

(Map p50; Nehru Place; fast-food dishes ₹100-300; M Nehru Place) This is a food court where you can select fast food from a variety of outlets, including Karim's, Khanchacha, Sagar Ratna and more. You buy a card for ₹500 then pay with it at any outlet – if there's change you can get the money back from the cashier. It also houses some more formal restaurants, including Italian Fio and Dhaba by Claridges.

Sagar Ratna SOUTH INDIAN $$

(Map p46; The Ashok, 50B, Diplomatic Enclave; dishes ₹240-350; ⊙8am-11pm) Considered the best of all the Sagar Ratna locations around town, this venerable South Indian restaurant is always buzzing with families, couples and kitty parties, and does a great line in dosas, *idlis, uttapams* (savoury rice pancakes) and thalis. There are other branches in **Connaught Place** (Map p42; 15-K Block, Connaught Place; dishes ₹115-170; ⊙8am-11pm; M Rajiv Chowk) and **Defence Colony** (Map p50; Defence Colony Market; dishes ₹115-170; ⊙8am-11pm; M Lajpat Nagar).

★**Sana-di-ge** MANGALOREAN $$$

(Map p46; ☑011-405077777; 24/48 Commercial Centre, Malcha Marg; mains ₹345-900; ⊙noon-3.45pm & 7-11.30pm) Fresh fish is flown in daily from Mangalore to this buzzing res-taurant in the diplomatic district. There are an intimate three levels, decorated with ge-ometric screens and with a terrace and bar. Food is wonderful and authentic, so head here for *anjal* fry, crab pepper fry, *marvai* (clams) or the signature *elaneer payasam*.

★**Bukhara** INDIAN $$$

(Map p46; ☑011-26112233; ITC Maurya, Sardar Patel Marg; mains ₹800-2600; ⊙12.30-2.45pm & 7-11.45pm) One of Delhi's best restaurants, this hotel eatery with low seating and crazy-paving walls serves wow-factor Northwest Frontier–style cuisine, with silken kebabs

DELHI EATING

and its famous Bukhara dhal. Reservations are essential.

Perch
INTERNATIONAL **$$$**

(Map p46; Khan Market; snacks & dishes ₹110-950, wine by the glass ₹300-650, cocktails ₹450-650; ⊘11.30am-1am; 🛜; Ⓜ Khan Market) The coolification of upscale shopping enclave Khan Market continues apace with Perch, a wine bar–cafe that's all pared-down aesthetic, waiters in pencil-grey shirts, soothing music, international wines and pleasing international snacks such as Welsh rarebit and tiger prawn with soba noodles.

La Bodega
MEXICAN **$$$**

(Map p46; ☑ 011-43105777; 29, 1st fl, Middle Lane, Khan Market; dishes ₹325-925; ⊘noon-midnight; Ⓜ Khan Market) This chic-yet-cool restaurant has big windows over leafy views, and offers interesting Mexican street food in small plates such as duck tacos with refried beans, *pico de gallo* and guacamole, as well as quesadillas or burritos with chicken and interesting salads.

Basil & Thyme
ITALIAN **$$$**

(Map p46; Sundar Nagar Market; mains ₹465-745; ⊘11am-11pm; Ⓜ Khan Market) This elegant icon has shifted locales but still buzzes with expats and locals, who flock to dine on delicate Mediterranean flavours (no alcohol), in a serene, leafy setting.

Lodi Garden Restaurant
MEDITERRANEAN **$$$**

(Map p46; ☑ 011-24652808; Lodi Rd; mains ₹600-1400; ⊘12.30pm-12.30am; Ⓜ Jor Bagh) This garden restaurant is mostly about ambience: there are lanterns dangling from the trees, tables in curtained pavilions and wooden carts. Although not quite as impressive as the surroundings, the menu traverses Europe and the Middle East, and there's a popular Sunday brunch.

Pandara Market
INDIAN **$$$**

(Map p46; Pandara Rd; mains ₹400-800; ⊘noon-1am; Ⓜ Khan Market) This is the enduring go-to place for excellent Mughlai and Punjabi food. Prices, standards and atmosphere are high along the strip. For quality food, try **Gulati** (Map p46; Pandara Market; mains ₹385-685; ⊘noon-midnight; Ⓜ Khan Market), **Havemore** (Map p46; Pandara Market; mains ₹375-725; ⊘noon-2am; Ⓜ Khan Market), **Pindi** (Map p46; Pandara Market; mains ₹330-570; ⊘noon-midnight; Ⓜ Khan Market) or **Chicken Inn** (Map p46; Pandara Market; mains ₹380-700; ⊘noon-midnight; Ⓜ Khan Market).

South Delhi

There are some fantastic independent restaurants tucked into the southern suburbs of Hauz Khas, Shahpur Jat, Saket and Mehrauli.

Potbelly
NORTH INDIAN **$$**

(Map p50; 116C Shahpur Jat Village; mains ₹250-420, thalis ₹250; ⊘12.30-11pm; Ⓜ Hauz Khas) It's a rare treat to find a Bihari restaurant in Delhi, and this artsy, shabby-chic place with fabulous views has authentic thalis and dishes such as *litti* chicken (whole-wheat balls stuffed with *sattu* and served with *khada masala* chicken).

★Indian Accent
INDIAN **$$$**

(Map p50; ☑ 011-26925151; Manor, 77 Friends Colony (West); dishes ₹725-1425, tasting menu non-veg/veg ₹2995/3095) In the boutique hotel Manor (p59), chef Manish Mehrotra creates inspired modern Indian cuisine, where seasonal ingredients are married in surprising and beautifully creative combinations. The tasting menu is astoundingly good, with wow-factor combinations such as tandoori bacon prawns or paper dosa filled with wild mushroom and water chestnuts. Book well ahead.

Rose Cafe
CAFE **$$$**

(Map p50; ☑ 011-29533186; 2 Westend Marg, Saidullajab; dishes ₹299-520; ⊘noon-9pm; Ⓜ Saket) Almost opposite the fake Dilli Haat market, 'Delhi Haat', an unprepossessing building harbours the Rose Cafe, prettily pale blue and pink. It's all cake stands and freshly prepared Mediterranean and comfort food, with heart-warming dishes such as shepherd's pie, pancakes and all-day breakfasts.

Swagath
SOUTH INDIAN **$$$**

(Map p50; M9 M-Block Market; dishes ₹300-1300; ⊘noon-11.45pm; Ⓜ Kailash Colony) Serving supremely scrumptious Indian seafood (especially crab, prawns, lobster and fish), Swagath will take you on a culinary tour through the fishing villages of South India in inauthentically smart surroundings. There are several branches, including at **Defence Colony Market** (Map p50; 14 Defence Colony Market; dishes ₹365-1300; ⊘11.30am-11.30pm; Ⓜ Lajpat Nagar).

Coast
SOUTH INDIAN **$$$**

(Map p50; above Ogaan, Hauz Khas; dishes ₹360-580; ⊘noon-midnight; Ⓜ Green Park) A light, bright restaurant on several levels, with views over the parklands of Hauz Khas, chic Coast serves light South Indian dishes, such as *avial* (vegetable curry) with pumpkin *erisheri* (with black lentils), plus tacos, salads and hit-the-spot mustard-tossed fries.

🍺 Drinking & Nightlife

Delhi's ever-growing cafe scene has given rise to some cafes with artisanal coffee beans, coffee menus and Turkish pastries. The city's bar and live-music choices are also burgeoning, though licences rarely extend later than 12.30am. For the latest places to go at night, check the hip and informative Little Black Book (http://littleblackbookdelhi.com) or Brown Paper Bag (http://bpbweekend.com/delhi). For gigs, check Wild City (thewildcity.com).

Cafes

⭐ **Blue Tokai**   CAFE

(Map p50; Khasra 258, Lane 3 West End Marg, Saidulajab; ⊗9am-8.30pm; Ⓜ Saket) In an unlikely, tiny lane behind the fake Dilli Haat shopping centre ('Delhi Haat'), Blue Tokai produces and grinds its own amazing coffee; you can get serious caffeine hits such as nitrogen-infused cold brew – there's even a tasting menu. Snacks include 'no leaf salad with pumpkin'.

Feeling more like San Francisco than a dusty Mehrauli lane, it's full of hipster Delhi-ites saying things like 'that is so millennial!'

⭐ **Atrium, Imperial**   CAFE

(Map p42; Janpath; ⊗8am-11.30pm; Ⓜ Janpath) Is there anything more genteel than high tea at the Imperial? Sip tea from bone-china cups and pluck dainty sandwiches and cakes from tiered stands, while discussing the latest goings-on in Shimla and Dalhousie. High tea is served in the Atrium from 3pm to 6pm daily (weekday/weekend ₹1200/1500 plus tax).

Indian Coffee House   CAFE

(Map p42; 2nd fl, Mohan Singh Place, Baba Kharak Singh Marg; ⊗9am-9pm; Ⓜ Rajiv Chowk) Indian Coffee House has faded-to-the-point-of-dilapidated charm, with the waiters' plummage-like hats and uniforms giving them a rakish swagger. You can feast on finger chips and sandwiches like it's 1952, and the roof terrace is a tranquil spot to linger.

Jugmug Thela   TEAHOUSE

(Map p50; Khasra 258, Westend Marg, Saidulajab; ⊗10am-8.30pm; Ⓜ Saket) A hidden surprise in a tiny back lane, this is an artisanal tea specialist styled as a streetside tea stall. They have more than 180 herbs and spices to work with, and serve delicious ayurvedic teas and fine blends such as Kinnow and Rose Earl Grey, iced teas and coffees, plus organic coffee and homebaked cookies.

Keventer's Milkshakes   CAFE

(Map p42; 17 A-Block, Connaught Place; ⊗9am-11pm; Ⓜ Rajiv Chowk) Keventer's has a cult following for its legendary creamy milkshakes (₹100), slurped out of milk bottles on the pavement in front of the stand.

Café Turtle   CAFE

(Map p46; Full Circle Bookstore, Khan Market; ⊗9.30am-8.30pm; Ⓜ Khan Market) Allied to the Full Circle Bookstore (p69), this brightly painted boho cafe gets busy with chattering bookish types, and is ideal when you're in the mood for coffee and cake in cosy surroundings, with a leafy outdoor terrace as well. There are branches in GK1's **N-Block Market** (Map p50; N-Block Market, Greater Kailash I; ⊗8.30am-8.30pm; Ⓜ Kailash Colony) and **Nizamuddin East** (Map p46; 8 Nizamuddin East Market, Full Circle Bookstore; ⊗8.30am-8.30pm; Ⓜ Jangpura).

Kunzum Travel Cafe   CAFE

(Map p50; www.kunzum.com; T49 Hauz Khas Village; ⊗11am-7.30pm Tue-Sun; 🛜; Ⓜ Green Park) 🍃 Quirky Kunzum has a pay-what-you-like policy for the self-service French-press coffee and tea, and sells its own brand of travel guides to Delhi. There's free wi-fi and travel books and magazines to browse.

Bars

⭐ **1911**   BAR

(Map p42; Imperial Hotel, Janpath; ⊗11am-12.45am; Ⓜ Janpath) The Imperial, built in the 1930s, resonates with bygone splendour. This bar is a more recent addition, but still riffs on the Raj. Here you can sip the perfect cocktail (around ₹900) amid designer-clad clientele, against a backdrop of faded photos and murals of maharajas.

⭐ **Piano Man Jazz Club**   CLUB

(Map p50; http://thepianoman.in; B 6 Commercial Complex, Safdarjung Enclave; ⊗noon-3pm & 7.30pm-12.30am) The real thing, this popular, atmospheric place with proper-musos is a dim-lit speakeasy with some excellent live jazz performances.

★ Bandstand
BAR

(Map p50; Aurobindo Market; ⊙noon-1am; 🛜; Ⓜ Green Park) This popular place is near Hauz Khas and has a great glass-covered terrace with views over the tombs of Green Park. It's also one of Delhi's live-music venues, with gigs from 9pm on Thursday and Sunday.

★ Ek Bar
BAR

(Map p50; D17, 1st fl, Defence Colony; ⊙noon-3.30pm & 6pm-12.30am; Ⓜ Lajpat Nagar) On the upper floors of a building in the exclusive area of the Defence Colony, this place has stylish, kooky decor in deep, earth-jewel colours, serious mixology (drinks ₹250 to ₹800) showcasing Indian flavours (how about a gin and tonic with turmeric?), modern Indian bar snacks, nightly DJs, and a see-and-be-seen crowd.

★ Unplugged
BAR

(Map p42; ☑ 011-33107701; 23 L-Block, Connaught Place; ⊙noon-midnight; Ⓜ Rajiv Chowk) There's nowhere else like this in Connaught Place. You could forget you were in CP, in fact, with the big garden, wrought-iron chairs and tables, and swing seats, all under the shade of a mother of a banyan tree hung with basket-weave lanterns. In the evenings there are regular live gigs, anything from alt-rock to electro-fusion. A Kingfisher costs ₹100.

Hauz Khas Social
BAR

(Map p50; 9A & 12 Hauz Khas Village; ⊙10.30am-midnight; Ⓜ Green Park) This chilled-out place is a Hauz Khas hub, and has large rooms with plate-glass windows overlooking lush greenery. There are cocktails and snacks, and a busy smokers' terrace. There's also regular live music and DJs.

Summer House
BAR

(Map p50; 1st fl, Aurobindo Place Market; ⊙11am-1am; Ⓜ Green Park) Close to Hauz Khas, this roomy, rustic 1st-floor bar has a spacious terrace and is a popular, lively evening haunt for a mixed crowd of men and women. There's regular live music. A Kingfisher costs ₹175.

24/7
BAR

(Map p38; Lalit Hotel, Maharaja Rajit Singh Marg; ⊙24hr; Ⓜ Barakhamba Rd) The 24-hour lobby bar at the Lalit Hotel is the perfect spot for a welcome-to-Delhi drink after a long flight.

Aqua
BAR

(Map p42; Park Hotel, 15 Sansad Marg; ⊙11am-midnight; 🛜; Ⓜ Janpath) If you feel the need for some five-star style after visiting Jantar Mantar or shopping in Connaught Place, Aqua is an ideal place to flop, forget the world outside, and sip cocktails by the pool.

Karen Cafe
BAR

(Map p56; Arakashan Rd; ⊙9am-11pm; Ⓜ New Delhi) An escape from the fraught street level, this tiny rooftop cafe has a few tables and a good viewpoint for overlooking the street. It's decorated with Bob Marley posters, wicker chairs and hanging lamps, and, while the service is slow and the food basic, it's as chilled as you'll get on this strip.

Sam's Bar
BAR

(Map p56; Main Bazaar; ⊙11am-1am; Ⓜ Ramakrishna Ashram Marg) Sam's Bar is more laid-back than most Paharganj bars, and a good choice for a drink and a chat, with a mixed crowd of men and women, locals and foreigners. There are snacks and a range of local (₹150 Kingfishers) and international beers and spirits.

Gem
BAR

(Map p56; 1050 Main Bazaar, Paharganj; ⊙11am-12.30am; Ⓜ Ramakrishna Ashram Marg) This wood-panelled dive is the kind of place you can forget what time of day it is – a dark, long-standing Paharganj hang-out that's popular with (male) locals and other travellers; bottles of local beer cost from ₹140. The upstairs area has more atmosphere.

My Bar
BAR

(Map p56; Main Bazaar, Paharganj; ⊙11am-12.30pm; Ⓜ Ramakrishna Ashram Marg) A dark and dingy bar, this place is lively, loud and fun, with a cheery, mixed crowd of backpackers and locals, who may even start dancing... There are several other branches, in CP and Hauz Khas. Drinks are ₹70 to ₹300 (beer from ₹85).

Metro Bar
BAR

(Map p56; 19 Panchkuian Rd; ⊙11am-1am; Ⓜ Ramakrishna Ashram Marg) Tucked around the corner from the Ramakrishna Ashram Marg metro station is a row of much-of-a-muchness bars that are favoured by local businessmen, with not particularly talented female singers belting out requests from the clientele. Metro Bar is the pick of the bunch – fun and friendly, with good Indian food.

☆ Entertainment

Music & Cultural Performances

Habitat World   LIVE PERFORMANCE
(Map p46; ☑ 011-43663333; www.habitatworld.
com; India Habitat Centre, Lodi Rd; Ⓜ Jor Bagh)
This is an important Delhi cultural address,
with art exhibitions, performances and concerts, mostly free. They also arrange regular
Delhi walks.

India International Centre   LIVE PERFORMANCE
(Map p46; ☑ 011-24619431; www.iicdelhi.nic.in;
40 Max Mueller Marg; Ⓜ Khan Market) The IIC is
a key location for a sector of Delhi society,
usually elderly intellectuals. Although the
club is for members only, the public is welcome to the regular, quality, free exhibitions,
talks and concerts.

Cinemas

Delite Cinema   CINEMA
(Map p38; ☑ 011-23272903; www.delitecinemas.
com; 4/1 Asaf Ali Rd; Ⓜ New Delhi) Founded in
1954 as the tallest building in Delhi, the
Delite was renovated in 2006 and it's no
ordinary cinema, with a painted dome and
Czech chandeliers. It's a great place to see
a masala picture (full-throttle Bollywood, a
mix of action, comedy, romance and drama),
with famous extra-large samosas available
in the interval.

Regal Cinema   CINEMA
(Map p42; front/back stalls ₹80/100, balcony
₹100/120; Ⓜ Rajiv Chowk) With a regular turn-
around of Bollywood hits, this Connaught
Place cinema, open since 1932, is a popular
place to catch the latest releases. As of 2017
it also includes the Delhi branch of Madame
Tussauds.

🛍 Shopping

Meharchand Market   MARKET
(Map p46; Lodi Colony; Ⓜ Lodhi Colony) Across
the road from the government housing of
the Lodi Colony, this is a long strip of small
boutiques selling homewares and clothes.
Shops include Fabindia (Map p46; ⊘ 11am-
8pm), the Shop (Map p46; ⊘ 10am-8pm Mon-
Sat, 11am-6pm Sun), and stand-out eateries are
the organic Altitude Cafe (Map p46; mains
₹340-580; ⊘ 8am-5pm; 🖉) and Asian-tapas
restaurant Diva Spiced (Map p46; tapas ₹320-
560, mains ₹390-1200; ⊘ 11.30am-11.30pm).

Timeless   BOOKS
(Map p50; ☑ 011-46056198; 46 Housing Society,
Part I, South Extension; ⊘ 10am-7pm Mon-Sat)
Hidden in a back lane (ask around), Timeless has a devoted following for its quality
coffee-table books on topics from Indian textiles to architecture.

Delhi Musical Stores   MUSIC
(Map p50; ☑ 23276909; www.indianmusicalinstru-
ments.com; C99 Lajpat Nagar; ⊘ 11am-8pm Mon-
Sat; Ⓜ Lajpat Nagar) Delhi Musical Stores has
a fine choice of tablas, harmoniums, sitars
and more.

KUSHTI

Wander the districts north of Kashmere Gate in Old Delhi and you may notice a dispro-
portionately high number of muscular men. No, it's not your imagination. This dusty
quarter is the favoured stomping ground for Delhi's traditional mud wrestlers. *Kushti*, or
pehlwani, is a full-contact martial art, fusing elements of yoga and philosophy with combat and intense physical training.

Young men enrol at *akharas* (training centres) in their early teens, and follow a strict
regimen of daily exercise, climbing ropes, lifting weights and hauling logs to build up the
necessary muscle bulk for this intensely physical sport. Even diet and lifestyle is strictly
controlled; sex, tobacco and alcohol are forbidden, and wrestlers live together in rustic
accommodation under the supervision of a coach who doubles as spiritual guide.

Bouts take place on freshly tilled earth, adding an extra element of grit to proceedings. As with other types of wrestling, the aim is to pin your opponent to the ground, but
fights often continue until one wrestler submits or collapses from exhaustion. At regional
championships, wrestlers compete for golden *gadas* (ceremonial clubs), a tribute to the
favoured weapon of Hanuman, patron deity of wrestling.

Most *akharas* welcome spectators at the daily dawn and dusk training sessions, so
long as this doesn't interfere with training. Seek permission first to avoid offending these
muscle-bound gents – the blog http://kushtiwrestling.blogspot.com is a good introduction to the sport and the main *akharas*.

Aap Ki Pasand (San Cha) DRINKS
(Map p38; 15 Netaji Subhash Marg; ⊙10am-7pm Mon-Sat) Specialists in the finest Indian teas, from Darjeeling and Assam to Nilgiri and Kangra. You can try before you buy, and teas come lovingly packaged in drawstring bags. There's another branch at Santushti Shopping Complex (Map p46; ☑011-264530374; www.sanchatea.com; Racecourse Rd; ⊙10am-6.30pm Mon-Sat; Ⓜ Racecourse).

Daryaganj Kitab Bazaar MARKET
(Book Market; Map p38; ⊙8am-6pm Sun) Come Sunday, books spread across the pavements for around 2km from Delhi Gate northwards to the Red Fort, and a shorter distance west along Jawaharlal Nehru Marg. Rummage for everything from Mills & Boon to vintage children's books. It's best to arrive early, as it gets busy.

Anokhi CLOTHING
(Map p46; www.anokhi.com; 32 Khan Market; ⊙10am-8pm; Ⓜ Khan Market) Anokhi specialises in block-print clothes and homewares, showcasing traditional designs with a modern design sensibility. There are branches at the Santushti Shopping Complex (Map p46; ⊙10am-7pm Mon-Sat; Ⓜ Racecourse) and N-Block Market (Map p50; Greater Kailash I; ⊙10am-8pm; Ⓜ Kailash Colony), with a discount store in Nizamuddin East (Map p46; ⊙10am-8pm Mon-Sat).

OCM Suitings CLOTHING
(Map p46; ☑011-24618937; Khan Market; ⊙11am-8pm Mon-Sat; Ⓜ Khan Market) Men's wool suits from ₹9500 (including material) and ankle-length skirts from ₹550 (excluding material). Suits are ready in around seven to 10 days.

Musical Instrument Shops MUSICAL INSTRUMENTS
(Map p38; Netaji Subhash Marg; ⊙approx 10am-8pm Mon-Sat) For competitively priced instruments, inspect the instrument shops along Netaji Subhash Marg in Daryaganj.

Rikhi Ram MUSIC
(Map p42; ☑011-23327685; www.rikhiram.com; 8A G-Block, Connaught Place; ⊙noon-8pm Mon-Sat; Ⓜ Rajiv Chowk) A beautiful old shop selling professional classic and electric sitars, tablas and more.

Old Delhi

Main Bazaar HANDICRAFTS, CLOTHING
(Map p56; Paharganj; ⊙10am-9pm Tue-Sun; Ⓜ Ramakrishna Ashram Marg) The backpacker-oriented bazaar that runs through Paharganj sells almost everything you want, and a whole lot more. It's great for buying presents, clothes, inexpensive jewellery bits and bobs, and luggage to put everything in as you're leaving India, or for hippy-dippy

OLD DELHI'S BAZAARS

Old Delhi's bazaars are a bamboozling, sensual whirlwind, combining incense, spices strong enough to make you sneeze, rickshaw fumes, brilliant colours, and hole-in-the-wall shops packed with goods that shimmer and glitter. This is less retail therapy, more heightened reality. The best time to visit is midmorning or later in the day, when the streets are less busy.

Whole districts here are devoted to individual items. Chandni Chowk (Map p38; ⊙10am-7pm Mon-Sat; Ⓜ Chandni Chowk) is all clothing, electronics and break-as-soon-as-you-buy-them novelties. For silver jewellery, head for Dariba Kalan (Map p38; ⊙approx 10am-8pm; Ⓜ Chawri Bazaar), the alley near the Sisganj Gurdwara. Off this lane, the Kinari Bazaar (Map p38; Kinari Bazaar; ⊙11am-8pm; Ⓜ Jama Masjid), literally 'trimmings market', is famous for zardozi (gold embroidery), temple trim and wedding turbans. Running south from the old Town Hall, Nai Sarak (Map p38; ⊙approx 10am-8pm; Ⓜ Jama Masjid) is lined with stalls selling saris, shawls, chiffon and lehanga, while nearby Ballimaran (Map p38; Ballimaran; ⊙10am-8pm; Ⓜ Chandni Chowk) has sequined slippers and fancy, curly-toed jootis (traditional slip-on shoes). For gorgeous wrapping paper and wedding cards, head to Chawri Bazaar (Map p38; ⊙10am-7pm), leading west from the Jama Masjid.

Beside the Fatehpuri Masjid, on Khari Baoli, is the nose-numbing Spice Market (Gadodia Market; Map p38; Khari Baoli; Ⓜ Chandni Chowk), ablaze with piles of scarlet-red chillis, ginger and turmeric roots, peppercorns, cumin, coriander seeds, cardamom, dried fruit and nuts. There's a constant trail of workers carrying huge sacks on their heads, and the spices in the air are so strong that everyone keeps sneezing.

clothes to wear on your trip. Haggle with purpose.

Karol Bagh Market
MARKET

(Map p38; ⊙approx 10am-7pm Tue-Sun; Ⓜ Karol Bagh) Favoured for clothes and wedding shopping, this market shimmers with all things sparkly, from dressy *lehanga choli* (skirt-and-blouse sets) to princess-style shoes. There are also electronics at Gaffar market (head here if you need a cracked phone screen replaced) and chrome motorcycle parts.

🏠 Connaught Place

★ Central Cottage Industries Emporium
ARTS & CRAFTS

(Map p42; ☑ 011-23326790; Janpath; ⊙10am-7pm; Ⓜ Janpath) This government-run multilevel store is a wonderful treasure trove of fixed-price, India-wide handicrafts. Prices are higher than in the state emporiums, but the selection of woodcarvings, jewellery, pottery, papier mâché, stationery, brassware, textiles (including shawls), toys, rugs, beauty products and miniature paintings makes it a glorious one-stop shop for beautiful crafts. Downstairs there's the Smoothie Factory cafe.

★ Kamala
ARTS & CRAFTS

(Map p42; Baba Kharak Singh Marg; ⊙10am-7pm Mon-Sat; Ⓜ Rajiv Chowk) Crafts, curios, textiles and homewares from the Crafts Council of India, designed with flair and using traditional techniques but offering some contemporary, out-of-the-ordinary designs.

★ People Tree
HANDICRAFTS, CLOTHING

(Map p42; Regal Bldg, Sansad Marg; ⊙11am-7pm; Ⓜ Rajiv Chowk) 🌿 This hole-in-the-wall shop sells fixed-price, fair-trade, ubercool T-shirts with funky Indian designs and urban attitude, as well as bags, jewellery and Indian-god cushions.

★ State Emporiums
HANDICRAFTS, CLOTHING

(Map p42; Baba Kharak Singh Marg; ⊙11am-1.30pm & 2-6.30pm Mon-Sat; Ⓜ Shivaji Stadium) Handily in a row are these regional treasure-filled emporiums. They may have the air of torpor that often afflicts governmental enterprises, but shopping here is like travelling around India – top stops include Kashmir, for papier mâché and carpets; Rajasthan, for miniature paintings and puppets; Uttar Pradesh, for marble inlay work; Karnataka, for sandalwood sculptures; Tamil Nadu, for metal statues; and Odisha, for stone carvings.

Janpath & Tibetan Markets
ARTS & CRAFTS

(Map p42; Janpath; ⊙11.30am-7pm Mon-Sat; Ⓜ Rajiv Chowk) These twin markets sell shimmering mirrorwork embroidery, colourful shawls, Tibetan bric-a-brac, brass Oms and dangly earrings. There are some good finds if you rummage through the junk, and if you haggle you can get some excellent bargains.

Khadi Gramodyog Bhawan
CLOTHING

(Map p42; Baba Kharak Singh Marg; ⊙10.30am-8pm; Ⓜ Rajiv Chowk) 🌿 Known for its excellent *khadi* (homespun cloth), including good-value shawls, plus handmade paper, incense, spices, henna and lovely natural soaps.

M Ram & Sons
CLOTHING

(Map p42; ☑ 011-23416558; 21 E-Block, Connaught Place; ⊙10.30am-8pm; Ⓜ Rajiv Chowk) A popular Delhi tailor, offering suits from ₹8000. Tailoring is possible in 24 hours.

Oxford Bookstore
BOOKS

(Map p42; N81 Connaught Place; ⊙10am-9.30pm Mon-Sat, 11am-9.30pm Sun; Ⓜ Rajiv Chowk) A swish but somewhat soulless bookstore, where you could nevertheless browse for hours. Staff are not as knowledgable as at other Delhi bookshops, although it sells good gifts, such as handmade paper notebooks. The attached Cha Bar (Map p42; Oxford Bookstore, N81 Connaught Place; ⊙10am-9.30pm Mon-Sat, 11am-9.30pm Sun; Ⓜ Rajiv Chowk) is a buzzing meeting spot.

🏠 New Delhi

★ Khan Market
MARKET

(Map p46; ⊙approx 10.30am-8pm Mon-Sat; Ⓜ Khan Market) 🌿 Khan Market is Delhi's most upmarket shopping enclave, the most expensive place to rent a shop in India, and is favoured by the elite and expats. Its boutiques focus on fashion, books and homewares, and it's also a good place to eat and drink.

For handmade paper, check out Anand Stationers (Map p46; ⊙10am-8pm Mon-Sat, noon-6pm Sun), or try Mehra Bros (Map p46; ⊙10am-7pm Mon-Thu & Sat, 10am-8pm Fri, 11am-6pm Sun) for cool papier-mâché ornaments. Literature lovers should head to Full Circle Bookstore (Map p46; www.fullcirclebooks.in; ⊙9.30am-8.30pm) and Bahrisons (Map p46; www.booksatbahri.com; ⊙10.30am-7.30pm Mon-Sat, 11.30am-7.30pm Sun). For Indian clothes and homewares, hit Fabindia (Map p46; ⊙10.30am-9.30pm) and Anokhi (p68), and

DELHI INFORMATION

SHAHPUR JAT

A 1km rickshaw ride northeast from Hauz Khas metro, the urban village of Shahpur Jat is one of the best places in Delhi to buy upmarket independent designer threads. Stores to seek out include Nimai (Map p50; ☑011-64300113; 416 Shahpur Jat Village; ⊙11am-7.30pm; Ⓜ Hauz Khas) for one-of-a-kind costume jewellery and NeedleDust (Map p50; www.needledust.com; 40B, ground fl, Shahpur Jat; ⊙10.30am-7.30pm Mon-Sat, 11am-6.30pm Sun; Ⓜ Hauz Khas) for embroidered leather shoes, and there are some choice independent restaurants, such as artsy Bihari Potbelly (p64), and vegan organic Greenr (Map p50; ☑7042575339; mains ₹250-375; ⊙11am-7.30pm; 🛜; Ⓜ Hauz Khas). For superb fine tea tastings head to Anandini Tea Room (Map p50; 12A, DDA Flats; ⊙11am-7pm; Ⓜ Hauz Khas).

for elegantly packaged ayurvedic remedies, browse Kama (Map p46; ⊙10.30am-8.30pm).

Sunder Nagar Market   ARTS & CRAFTS
(Map p46; Mathura Rd; ⊙approx 10.30am-7.30pm Mon-Sat) Long-time genteel and sleepy Sundar Nagar has turned increasingly chic. It's long specialised in Indian and Nepali handicrafts, replica 'antiques', furniture and fine Indian teas, but much-loved restaurant Basil & Thyme (p64) has moved here, and there's the cool watering hole, No 8.

South Delhi

★ **Dilli Haat**   ARTS & CRAFTS
(Map p50; Aurobindo Marg; foreigner/Indian ₹100/20; ⊙10.30am-10pm; Ⓜ INA) This open-air food-and-crafts market is a cavalcade of colour and sells regional handicrafts from all over India; bargain hard. With lots of food stands, it's also a good place to sample cheap, delicious regional specialities – try food from Nagaland or Tamil Nadu (dishes are around ₹70 to ₹100).

★ **Hauz Khas Village**   HANDICRAFTS, CLOTHING
(Map p50; ⊙11am-7pm Mon-Sat; Ⓜ Green Park) It's not as hip as it was a few years ago, but still well worth a browse. This arty little enclave has narrow lanes crammed with boutiques selling designer Indian clothing,

handicrafts, contemporary ceramics, hand-made furniture and old Bollywood movie posters. Shops to seek out include Claymen (Map p50; ⊙hours vary), Maarti, Ogaan and Bodice.

Dastkar Nature Bazaar   MARKET
(http://dastkar.org; Andheria Modh; ⊙10am-7pm Tue-Sun; Ⓜ Chhatarpur) Not-for-profit NGO Dastkar promotes regional crafts, and its outdoor craft bazaar holds monthly themed events, showcasing cutting-edge regional culture, craft and food.

Greater Kailash I: M-Block & N-Block Markets   MARKET
(Map p50; ⊙approx 10am-8pm Wed-Mon; Ⓜ Kailash Colony) A two-part midrange shopping enclave with swanky boutiques and posh eateries, best known for Fabindia, which has several branches here. Also check out clothes store Anokhi.

ℹ Information

DANGERS & ANNOYANCES
Delhi is relatively safe in terms of petty crime, though pickpocketing can be a problem in crowded areas so keep your valuables safe.

Train Station Hassle
Touts at New Delhi train station endeavour to steer travellers away from the legitimate International Tourist Bureau and into private travel agencies where they earn a commission. Touts often tell people that their tickets are invalid, there's a problem with the trains, or say they're not allowed on the platform. They then 'assist' in booking expensive taxis or 3rd-class tickets passed off as something else. You're particularly vulnerable when arriving tired at night. As a rule of thumb: don't believe anyone who approaches you trying to tell you anything at the train station, even if they're wearing a uniform or have an official-looking pass.

Women Travellers
Delhi has, unfortunately, a deserved reputation as being unsafe for women. Precautions include never walking around in lonely, deserted places, even during daylight hours, keeping an eye on your route so you don't get lost (download a map that you can use offline) and taking special care after dark – ensure you have a safe means of transport home with, for example, a reputable cab company or driver.

Touts
Taxi-wallahs at the airport and around tourist areas frequently act as touts for hotels, claiming that your hotel is full, poor value, dangerous, burnt down or closed, or that there are riots in

Delhi. Any such story is a ruse to steer you to a hotel where they will get a commission. Insist on being taken to where you want to go – making a show of writing down the registration plate number, and phoning the autorickshaw/taxi helpline may help. Men who approach you at Connaught Place run similar scams to direct you to shops and tourist agents, often 'helpfully' informing you that wherever you're headed is closed.

INTERNET ACCESS

Almost all hotels and many cafes offer free wi-fi access these days.

MEDIA

➜ For printed listings see the weekly calendar pamphlet *Delhi Diary* (₹30), which is available at local bookshops. *Motherland* (www.mother landmagazine.com) is a stylish bi-monthly cultural magazine.

➜ To check out what's on, see the ubercool Little Black Book (www.littleblackbookdelhi. com) or Brown Paper Bag (brownpaperbag.in/ delhi). Don't miss the Delhi Walla blog (www. thedelhiwalla.com), a wonderful window into Delhi's daily life.

MEDICAL SERVICES

Pharmacies are found on most shopping streets and in most suburban markets. Hospitals:

All India Institute of Medical Sciences (AIIMS; Map p50; ☑ 011-65900669; www. aiims.edu; Ansari Nagar; Ⓜ AIIMS)

Apollo Hospital (☑ 011-29871090; www. apollohospdelhi.com; Mathura Rd, Sarita Vihar; Ⓜ Sarita Vihar)

Dr Ram Manohar Lohia Hospital (Map p46; ☑ 011-23365525; www.rmlh.nic.in; Baba Kharak Singh Marg; Ⓜ Patel Chowk)

East West Medical Centre (Map p46; ☑ 011-24690429; www.eastwestrescue.com; 37 Prithviraj Rd; Ⓜ Racecourse)

Max Healthcare (Map p50; ☑ 011-26515050; Press Enclave Rd, Saket; Ⓜ Saket)

POST

There are post offices all over Delhi that can handle letters and parcels (most with packing services nearby). Poste restante is available at the New Delhi office of **India Post** (Map p46; ☑ 011-23743602; Gole Dakhana, Baba Kharak Singh Marg; ⊙ 10am-5pm Mon-Sat); ensure mail is addressed to GPO, New Delhi – 110001. There is a convenient India Post branch at **Connaught Place** (Map p42; 6 A-Block, Connaught Place; ⊙ 8am-7.30pm Mon-Sat; Ⓜ Rajiv Chowk).

Courier services may be arranged through **DHL** (Map p42; ☑ 011-23737587; ground fl, Mercantile Bldg, Tolstoy Marg; ⊙ 8am-8pm Mon-Sat; Ⓜ Rajiv Chowk) at Connaught Place.

TOURIST INFORMATION

Archaeological Survey of India (Map p46; ☑ 011-23010822; www.asi.nic.in; Janpath; ⊙ 9.30am-1pm & 2-6pm Mon-Fri; Ⓜ Central Secretariat) Next door to the National Museum, the Archaeological Survey of India stocks publications about India's main archaeological sites.

India Tourism Delhi (Government of India; Map p42; ☑ 011-23320005, 011-23320008; www. incredibleindia.org; 88 Janpath; ⊙ 9am-6pm Mon-Fri, to 2pm Sat; Ⓜ Janpath) This is the only official India Tourism office, apart from the booth at the airport. Ignore touts who (falsely) claim to be associated with this. It's a useful source of advice on Delhi, getting out of Delhi, and visiting surrounding states. Has free Delhi maps and brochures, and publishes a list of recommended agencies and B&Bs. Come here to report tourism-related complaints.

❶ Getting There & Away

AIR

Indira Gandhi International Airport (☑ 01243376000; www.newdelhiairporty.in) is about 14km southwest of the centre. International and domestic flights use gleaming Terminal 3. Terminal 1 is reserved for low-cost carriers. Free shuttle buses (present your boarding pass and onward ticket) run between the two terminals every 20 minutes, but can take much longer. Leave at least three hours between transfers to be safe.

The arrivals hall at Terminal 3 has 24-hour foreign exchange, ATMs, prepaid taxi and car-hire counters, tourist information, a pharmacy, bookshops, cafes and a **Plaza Premium Lounge** (☑ 011-61233922; s/d 3 hr US$37/52, 6 hr 52/66) with short-stay rooms (there's another of these at Terminal 1 arrivals).

You'll need to show your boarding pass to enter the terminal. At check-in be sure to collect tags for all your carry-on bags and ensure these are stamped as you go through security.

Delhi's airport can be prone to thick fog from November to January (often disrupting airline schedules) – it's wise to allow a day between connecting flights during this period.

Air India (☑ 1800 1801407; www.airindia.com)

Jagson Airlines (Map p42; ☑ 011-23721593; www.jagsongroup.in; Vandana Bldg, 11 Tolstoy Marg; ⊙ 10am-6pm Mon-Sat; Ⓜ Janpath)

Jet Airways (Map p42; ☑ 011-39893333; www. jetairways.com; 11/12 G-Block, Connaught Place; ⊙ 9.30am-6pm Mon-Sat; Ⓜ Rajiv Chowk)

SpiceJet (☑ 1800 1803333; www.spicejet.com)

BUS

Most travellers enter and leave Delhi by train, but buses are a useful option to some destinations and if the trains are booked up.

DELHI GETTING THERE & AWAY

Most state-run services leave from the large **Kashmere Gate Inter State Bus Terminal** (ISBT; Map p38; ☑ 011-23860290; Ⓜ Kashmere Gate) in Old Delhi, accessible by metro. Offices at the terminal:

Delhi Transport Corporation (Map p38; ☑ 011-23370210; www.dtc.nic.in)

Haryana Roadways (Map p38; ☑ 011-23868271; www.hartrans.gov.in)

Punjab Roadways (Map p38; ☑ 011-44820000; www.punbusonline.com)

Rajasthan Roadways (Map p38; ☑ 011-23386658, 011-23864470; Counter 36, Kashmere Gate Inter State Bus Terminal)

Rajasthan State Road Transport Corporation (Map p38; ☑ 011-23864470; http://rsrtc.rajasthan.gov.in)

Uttar Pradesh Roadways (Map p38; ☑ 011-23868709)

Uttar Pradesh State Road Transport Corporation (Map p38; ☑ 011-2622363; www.upsrtc.com)

The **Anand Vihar Inter State Bus Terminal** (ISBT) has some services to Nainital and Kumaun in Uttarakhand. Some cheaper buses to destinations in Uttar Pradesh, Madhya Pradesh and Rajasthan leave from the **Sarai Kale Khan Inter State Bus Terminal** (ISBT) on the ring road near Nizamuddin train station.

Arrive at least 30 minutes ahead of your departure time. You can avoid the hassle by paying a little more for private deluxe buses that leave from locations in central Delhi – enquire at travel agencies or your hotel for details. You can also book tickets or check information on **Cleartrip** (www.cleartrip.com), **Make My Trip** (www.makemytrip.com) or **Goibibo** (www.goibibo.com).

There are buses to Agra, but considering the traffic at either end, you're better off taking the train. **Himachal Pradesh Tourism Development Corporation** (HPTDC; Map p46; hptdc.gov.in; Chanderlok Building, 36 Janpath; Ⓜ Janpath) runs buses from **Himachal Bhawan** (Map p46; ☑ 011-23716689; Sikandra Rd; Ⓜ Mandi House) to Manali (₹1300, nine hours) and Shimla (₹900, 10 hours) at 6.30pm. Tickets are sold at Himachal Bhawan and **Chanderlok House** (Map p46; ☑ 011-23325320; 36 Janpath).

Himachal Road Transport Corporation (HRTC; ☑ 011-23868694; www.hrtc.gov.in) also has AC buses starting from Himachal Bhawan, to Shimla (₹935, seven daily) and to Manali (₹1430, 7pm). These stop at the ISBT Kashmiri Gate an hour later.

Rajasthan Tourism (Map p46; ☑ 011-23381884; www.rtdc.com; Bikaner House, Pandara Rd; Ⓜ Khan Market) runs deluxe buses from **Bikaner House** (Map p46; ☑ 011-23383469; Pandara Rd; Ⓜ Khan Market), near India Gate, to the following destinations:

Ajmer Volvo ₹1200, nine hours, three daily

Jaipur non AC/super deluxe/Volvo ₹400/625/900, six hours, every one to two hours

Jodhpur Volvo ₹1625, 11 hours, two daily

Udaipur Volvo ₹1800, 15 hours, one daily

Women receive a discount of 30% on all Rajasthan Tourism bus prices.

TRAIN

There are three main stations in Delhi: (Old) Delhi train station (aka Delhi Junction) in Old Delhi, New Delhi train station near Paharganj, and Nizamuddin train station, south of Sunder Nagar. Make sure you know which station your train is leaving from.

The best option for foreign travellers is to visit the helpful **International Tourist Bureau** (ITB; Map p56; ☑ 011-23405156; 1st fl, New Delhi Train Station; ⊘ 24hr). The entrance to the ITB is before you go onto platform 1 (on the Paharganj side of New Delhi train station), via a staircase just to the right of the entrance to the platform. Do *not* believe anyone who tells you it has shifted, closed or burnt down – this is a scam to divert you elsewhere. Walk with confidence and ignore all 'helpful' or 'official' approaches. The ITB is a large room with about 10 or more computer terminals – don't be fooled by other 'official' offices.

When making reservations here, you can pay in cash (rupees) only. Bring your passport.

When you arrive, take a ticket from the machine that gives you a place in the queue. Then complete a reservation form – ask at the information counter to check availability. You can then wait to complete and pay for your booking at the relevant counter. This is the best place to get last-minute bookings for quota seats to popular destinations, but come prepared to queue.

There's also a public **Train Reservation Office** (Map p56; Chelmsford Rd; ⊘ 8am-8pm Mon-Sat, to 2pm Sun) closer to Connaught Place, but touts here are notorious for targetting travellers.

ⓘ Getting Around

TO/FROM THE AIRPORT

Whatever time your flight arrives, it's a good idea to book a hotel in advance and notify staff of your arrival time – some places may allow you to check in early. Organised city transport runs to/from Terminal 3; a free shuttle bus runs every 20 minutes between Terminal 3 and Terminal 1.

Pre-arranged Pick-ups Hotels offer pre-arranged airport pick-up, but these are usually more expensive than arranging a taxi yourself – however, it may be worth it to ease your arrival. You'll pay extra to cover the airport parking fee (up to ₹220) and ₹100 charge to enter the arrivals hall. To avoid the entry fee, drivers may wait outside Gates 4 to 6.

Metro The Airport Express line (www.delhimetrorail.com) runs every 10 to 15 minutes from 5.15am to 11.40pm, completing the journey from Terminal 3 to New Delhi train station in around 20 minutes (International/domestic terminal–New Delhi, ₹60/50). It's usually empty because it's a separate line from the rest of the metro. You can use a smart card, or buy a token for the other lines at Airport station; check with customer services.

Bus Air-conditioned buses run from outside Terminal 3 to Kashmere Gate ISBT every 10

MAJOR TRAINS FROM DELHI

DESTINATION	TRAIN NO & NAME	FARE (₹)	DURATION (HR)	FREQUENCY	DEPARTURES & TRAIN STATION
Agra	12280 Taj Exp	100/370 (A)	3	1 daily	7am NZM
	12002 Bhopal Shatabdi	515/1010 (B)	2	1 daily	6am NDLS
Amritsar	12029/12013 Swarna/Amritsar Shatabdi	790/1620 (B)	6	1-2 daily	7.20am/4.30pm NDLS
Bengaluru	22692 Bangalore Rajdhani	2960/4095/6775 (C)	34	4 weekly	8.50pm NZM
Chennai	12434 Chennai Rajdhani	2795/3860/6355 (C)	28	2 weekly	3.55pm NZM
	12622 Tamil Nadu Exp	780/2040/2990 (D)	33	1 daily	10.30pm NDLS
Goa (Madgaon)	12432 Trivandrum Rajdhani	3385/4730/7815 (C)	26	3 weekly	10.55am NZM
	12780 Goa Exp	170/540/740 (D)	27	1 daily	3pm NZM
Haridwar	12017 Dehradun Shatabdi	595/1190 (B)	4½	1 daily	6.45am NDLS
Jaipur	12958 ADI Swama Jayanti Rajdani	1210/1660/2755 (C)	4½	1 daily	7.55pm NDLS
	12916 Ashram Exp	235/590/825 (D)	5	1 daily	3.20pm DLI
	12015 Ajmer Shatabdi	355/740 (B)	4½	1 daily	6.05am NDLS
Kalka (for Shimla)	12011 Kalka Shatabdi	640/1295 (B)	4	2 daily	7.40am NDLS
Khajuraho	12448 UP Sampark Kranti Exp	365/955/1350 (D)	10½	1 daily	8.10pm NZM
Lucknow	12004 Lucknow Swran Shatabdi	885/1850 (B)	6½	1 daily	6.10am NDLS
Mumbai	12952 Mumbai Rajdhani	2085/2870/4755 (C)	16	1 daily	4.45pm NDLS
	12954 August Kranti Rajdani	2085/2870/4755 (C)	17½	1 daily	4.50pm NZM
Udaipur	12963 Mewar Exp	415/1095/1555 (D)	12½	1 daily	7pm NZM
Varanasi	12560 Shivganga Exp	415/1100/1565 (D)	12½	1 daily	6.55pm NDLS

Train stations: NDLS – New Delhi; DLI – Old Delhi; NZM – Hazrat Nizamuddin

Fares: (A) 2nd class/chair car; (B) chair car/1st-class AC; (C) 3AC/2AC/1st-class AC; (D) sleeper/3AC/2AC

minutes, via the Red Fort, LNJP Hospital, New Delhi Station Gate 2, Connaught Place, Parliament St and Ashoka Rd.

Taxi In front of the arrivals buildings at Terminal 3 and Terminal 1 are **Delhi Traffic Police Prepaid Taxi counters** (☑ complaints 56767, women's helpline 1091; www.delhitrafficpolice. nic.in) offering fixed-price taxi services. You'll pay about ₹350 to New or Old Delhi, and ₹450 to the southern suburbs in a battered old black-and-yellow taxi. There's a 25% surcharge between 11pm and 5am. Travellers have reported difficulty in persuading drivers to go to their intended hotel. Firmly insist that the driver takes you to your chosen destination and only surrender your voucher when you arrive where you want.

You can also book a prepaid taxi at the **Megacabs counter** (☑ 011-41414141; www.megacabs. com) at both the international and domestic terminals. It costs ₹600 to ₹700 to the centre, but you get a cleaner car with air-con.

AUTORICKSHAW & TAXI

Local taxis (recognisable by their black and yellow livery) and autorickshaws have meters but these are effectively ornamental as most drivers refuse to use them. Delhi Traffic Police run a network of prepaid autorickshaw booths, where you can pay a fixed fare, including 24-hour stands at the New Delhi, **Old Delhi** (Map p38; ⊙24hr) and **Nizamuddin** (Map p46) train stations; elsewhere, you'll need to negotiate a fare before you set off.

Other booths are **outside the India Tourism Delhi office** (Map p42; 88 Janpath; ⊙11am-8.30pm) and at **Central Park** (Map p42), Connaught Place.

Fares are invariably elevated, especially for foreigners, so haggle hard, and if the fare sounds too outrageous, find another cab. For an autorickshaw ride from Connaught Place, fares should be around ₹30 to Paharganj, ₹60 to the Red Fort, ₹70 to Humayun's Tomb and ₹100 to Hauz Khas. However, it will be a struggle to get these prices. Visit www.taxiautofare.com for suggested fares for these and other journeys. To report overcharging, harassment, or other problems take the licence number and call the Auto Complaint Line on 011-42400400/25844444.

Taxis typically charge twice the autorickshaw fare. Note that fares vary as fuel prices go up and down. From 11pm to 5am there's a 25% surcharge for autorickshaws and taxis.

Kumar Tourist Taxi Service (Map p42; ☑ 011-23415930; www.kumarindiatours.com; 14/1 K-Block, Connaught Place; ⊙9am-9pm) is a reliable company; a day of Delhi sightseeing costs from ₹2000 (an eight-hour and 80km limit applies).

Metropole Tourist Service (Map p46; ☑ 011-24310313; www.metrovista.co.in; 224 Defence Colony Flyover Market; ⊙7am-7pm) is another reliable and long-running taxi service, and good value, charging ₹1500 for up to 80km for one day's car and driver hire, plus ₹100/15 per hour/kilometre thereafter.

Shared electric rickshaws are also a possibility, which means cheaper fares, but only if you're going in the same direction as other passengers.

Radiocabs

You'll need a local mobile number to order a radiocab, or ask a shop or hotel to assist you. These air-conditioned cars are clean, efficient, and use reliable meters, usually charging ₹23 at flagfall then ₹23 per kilometre. Try **Easycabs** (☑ 011-43434343; www.easycabs.com) or **Quickcabs** (☑ 011-45333333; www.quickcabs.in).

Taxi & Auto Apps

Car-sharing services **Uber** (www.uber.com) and **Ola Autos & Cabs** (www.olacabs.com) have transformed travel around Delhi. If you have a local number and a smartphone, download these apps and you can arrange pick-ups from your exact location (though the car/auto will sometimes stop a little way away), then pay the electronically calculated fee in cash when you complete the journey and thus side-stepping much haggling. Uber was banned in 2014 following an assault by one of its drivers but checks have been improved since.

BUS

With the arrival of the metro, travellers rarely use Delhi's public buses, which can get crowded, but there are several useful routes, including the Airport Express bus (₹75) and Bus GL-23, which connects the Kashmere Gate and Anand Vihar bus stations. AC fares are ₹10 to ₹25.

CYCLE-RICKSHAW

Cycle-rickshaws are useful for navigating Old Delhi and the suburbs, but are banned from many parts of New Delhi, including Connaught Place. Negotiate a fare before you set off – expect to pay around ₹10 per kilometre.

METRO

Delhi's **metro** (☑ 011-23417910; www.delhimetrorail.com) is superb: fast and efficient, with signs and arrival/departure announcements in Hindi and English. Trains run from around 6am to 11pm and the first carriage in the direction of travel is reserved for women only. Trains can get insanely busy at peak commuting times (around 9am to 10am and 5pm to 6pm) – avoid travelling with luggage during rush hour if at all possible (however, the Airport Express is always empty, as it's separate from the other lines).

Tokens (₹8 to ₹50) are sold at metro stations. There are also one-/three-day 'tourist cards' (₹150/300, ₹50 deposit, ₹30 refundable when you return it) for unlimited short-distance travel, and a Smart Card (₹150, ₹50 deposit, ₹30 refundable), which can be recharged for amounts from ₹200 to ₹1000 – these make fares 10% cheaper than paying by token.

Because of security concerns, all bags are X-rayed and passengers must pass through an airport-style scanner.

GREATER DELHI

★Qutb Minar Complex   HISTORIC SITE
(Map p50; ☎011-26643856; Indian/foreigner ₹30/500, video ₹25, Decorative Light Show Indian/foreigner ₹20/250, audio guide ₹100; ⊙dawn-dusk; Ⓜ Qutab Minar) If you only have time to visit just one of Delhi's ancient ruins, make it this. The first monuments here were erected by the sultans of Mehrauli, and subsequent rulers expanded on their work, hiring the finest craftsmen and artisans to set in stone the triumph of Muslim rule. The Qutb Festival (p31) of Indian classical music and dance takes place here every October/November. To reach the complex, take the metro to Qutab Minar station, then take an autorickshaw for the 1km to the ruins.

➡ Qutb Minar

(Map p50) The Qutb Minar that gives the complex its name is an unmissable, soaring Afghan-style victory tower and minaret, erected by sultan Qutb-ud-din in 1193 to proclaim his supremacy over the vanquished Hindu rulers of Qila Rai Pithora. Ringed by intricately carved sandstone bands bearing verses from the Quran, the tower stands nearly 73m high and tapers from a 15m-diameter base to a mere 2.5m at the top.

➡ Quwwat-ul-Islam Masjid

(Might of Islam Mosque; Map p50) At the foot of the Qutb Minar stands the first mosque to be built in India. An inscription over the east gate states that it was built with materials obtained from demolishing '27 idolatrous temples'. As well as intricate carvings that show a clear fusion of Islamic and pre-Islamic styles, the walls of the mosque are studded with sun disks, *shikharas* and other recognisable pieces of Hindu and Jain masonry. This was Delhi's main mosque until 1360.

➡ Iron Pillar

(Map p50) In the courtyard of the Quwwat-ul-Islam Masjid is a 6.7m-high iron pillar that is much more ancient than any of the surrounding monuments. It hasn't rusted over the past 1600 years, due to both the dry atmosphere and its incredible purity. A six-line Sanskrit inscription indicates that it was initially erected outside a Vishnu temple, possibly in Bihar, in memory of Chandragupta II, who ruled from AD 375 to 413. Scientists are at a loss as to how the iron was cast using the technology of the time.

★Mehrauli Archaeological Park   PARK
(Map p50; ⊙dawn-dusk; Ⓜ Qutab Minar) FREE
There are extraordinary riches scattered around Mehrauli, with more than 440 monuments – from the 10th century to the British era – dotting a forest and the village itself. In the forest, most impressive are the time-ravaged tombs of Balban and Quli Khan, his son, and the Jamali Khamali mosque, attached to the tomb of the Sufi poet Jamali. To the west is the 16th-century Rajon ki Baoli, Delhi's finest step-well, with a monumental flight of steps.

At the northern end of Mehrauli village is Adham Khan's Mausoleum, which was once used as a British residence, then later as a police station and post office. Leading northwards from the tomb are the pre-Islamic walls of Lal Kot.

To the south of the village are the remains of the Mughal palace, the Zafar Mahal, once in the heart of the jungle. Next door to it is the Sufi shrine, the Dargah of Qutb Sahib. There is a small burial ground with one empty space that was intended for the last king of Delhi, Bahadur Shah Zafar, who died in exile in Burma (Myanmar) in 1862. South of here is a Lodi-era burial ground for *hijras* (tranvestites and eunuchs), Hijron ka Khanqah (Map p50; Kalka das Marg; ⊙dawn-dusk). The identity of those buried here is unknown, but it's a well-kept, peaceful place, revered by Delhi's *hijra* community. A little further south are Jahaz Mahal ('ship palace', also built by the Mughals) and the Haus i Shamsi tank (off Mehrauli-Gurgaon Rd).

You can reach the forested part of the park by turning right from the metro station onto Anuvrat Marg and walking around 500m. A good way to explore the ruins is by guided walking tour.

★Tughlaqabad   FORT
(Indian/foreigner ₹15/200, video ₹25; ⊙dawn-dusk; Ⓜ Tughlakabad) This magnificent 14th-century ruin, half reclaimed by jungle and gradually being encroached on by villages, was Delhi's third incarnation, built by Ghiyas-ud-din Tughlaq. The sultan poached workers from the Sufi saint Nizam-ud-din,

who issued a curse that shepherds would inhabit the fort. However, it's monkeys rather than shepherds that have taken over. There are fantastic emerald-green views. Interlinking underground rooms were used as storehouses. To reach the fort, take an autorickshaw from the Tughlakabad metro (one way/return ₹80/160).

Gurgaon (Gurugram)

The area of Gurgaon (Gurugram) is said to have been presented to Guru Dronacharaya in gratitude for his teaching by its rulers, the Kaurava and Pandava, hence its recent Mahabharata-inspired name change to Gurugram. Delhi's foremost satellite city was once a collection of villages and farmland, but its fortunes changed when the car company Maruti Suzuki India Limited set up a manufacturing base here in the 1970s. Change accelerated in the 1990s, and Gurgaon is now a booming new town, a concrete-laden development of telecommunications companies, call centres, malls, office blocks and hotels, with India's third-highest income per capita.

⊙ Sights

Sultanpur National Park   NATIONAL PARK
(http://haryanaforest.gov.in/SultanpurNationalPark.aspx; Sultanpur; foreigner/Indian ₹40/5, camera/video ₹25/500; ⊙ 7am-4.30pm) It's incredible to think that Gurgaon is only 15km away from Sultanpur National Park. These wetlands shimmer with local and visiting migratory birds, including kingfishers, flamingoes, geese, teal and storks. It's best to get here in early morning, and you can stay overnight at government-run **Rosy Pelican Tourist Complex** (☑ 0120-4355020; r from ₹2175). The easiest way to get here is by taxi from Gurgaon.

Museo Camera   MUSEUM
(☑ 9810009099; www.indiaphotoarchive.org; T-23/5, DLF Phase III; requested donation per person ₹300; Rapid Metro Phase III) This wonderful museum grew out of the collection of Indian photographer Aditya Arya, with the oldest photographs here dating to the 1880s. Meet the Sinar – the Rolls-Royce of cameras – and the same model of Hasselblad that went to the moon and back. You can also see some incredible early photos, dating to the 1850s.

🛏 Sleeping

Gurgaon is full of five-star and luxury business hotels, catering to the many business travellers who stay here, as well as to holidaymakers who fancy luxurious accommodation that is less expensive than in Delhi's city centre, and close to the area's many luxury shopping malls. There is also a smattering of guesthouses and humbler hotels.

Harry's Bed & Breakfast   B&B $$
(☑ 987169996, 9810158515; www.harrysbedandbreakfast.com; Plot 40, Silver Oaks Avenue, DLF 1; s/d ₹2300/2800; ❄ 🕾; Ⓜ Sikanderpur) The unmistakable aromas of southern spices welcome you into this Tamil-owned B&B in a quiet corner of Gurgaon. Spacious, well-lit rooms have plush interiors and en suite bathrooms, and there's complimentary wi-fi and a sumptuous breakfast. One room comes kitted out with its own tiny garden. With notice, the hosts can rustle up a full Tamil meal.

★Tikli Bottom   HOTEL $$$
(www.tiklibottom.com; Manender Farm, Gairatpur Bas; s/d incl full board ₹12,000/21,000; 🕾 🏊) Around 50km south of central Delhi, this peachy Lutyens-style bungalow surrounded by wooded hills, run by a British couple, seems to come from another era, one of toasted teacakes, lawns and chintz. There are four high-ceilinged guest rooms and spacious lounges, plus a beautiful pool with hill views overlooked by a pagoda.

You can also come here for a day, hang out for lunch (adult/aged 12 to 18/under 12 ₹1750/800/300) and explore the countryside with its rambling chickens and emus. For day visitors wanting to swim, the day charge for a room is ₹4500.

Trident   HOTEL $$$
(www.tridenthotels.com; 443, Udyog Vihar, Phase V, Sector 19; r from ₹15,500; ❄ 🕾 🏊; Ⓜ IFFCO Chowk) A contemporary palace, with Mughal-style domes and reflection pools, this has huge rooms and all facilities, and offers good value compared with city-centre five stars. There are excellent eating options and a separate Sunday brunch for kids as well as adults.

✗ Eating

Gurgaon has many great places to eat, though only in the midrange to top-end price brackets, and as it's all so new, places can feel rather soulless. However, not only are there some great hotel restaurants, but there's also DLF Cyber Hub, which is dedicated entirely to gastronomy.

Fat Lulu's PIZZA $$
(☑0124-4245497; Cross Point DLF City IV, DLF Galleria Rd, Gurgaon; pizzas from ₹425; ⊘11.30am-11pm) A delightful little eatery opposite the popular Galleria Market, Fat Lulu's has thin-crust pizzas loaded with toppings, from classic Italian to those with an Indian twist (chicken tikka masala). It has a quirky and colourful dining room that will appeal to those who like a bit of ambience on the side.

DLF Cyber Hub INTERNATIONAL $$
(www.dlfcyberhub.com; DLF Cyber City, Phase II, NH8; mains from ₹200; ⊘most restaurants 11am-midnight; Rapid Metro DLF Cyber City) This is a food court par excellence, and you'll find any type of cuisine you fancy here. Standouts include **Sodabottleopenerwala**, for Parsi cusine; the cool **Gurgaon Social**, with private rooms; **Farzi Cafe**, for molecular cuisine and cheap beer; the **People & Co** for live comedy; **Yum Yum Cha** for funky decor and pan-Asian food; and **Sion 7** for craft beer brewed on site.

★Amaranta SEAFOOD, INDIAN $$$
(☑0124-2451234; The Oberoi, 443 Udyog Vihar, Phase V; mains ₹1900-2100; ⊘12.30-3pm & 7pm-midnight; MIFFCO Chowk) The Oberoi Gurgaon's restaurant wins plaudits for its creativity. Its seafood is outstanding, flown in daily from the coast, but for the full experience try a seven- or nine-course tasting menu (veg/non-veg ₹4000/5900).

🍷 Drinking

Gurgaon has lots of drinking and nightlife options, particularly at DLF Cyber Hub and along Golf Course Rd, and is popular with middle-class locals for a night out, with plenty of bars and restaurants offering live music. DLF Cyber Hub also includes a popular comedy club, the People & Co. As in Delhi, most places only open until 12.30am.

☆ Entertainment

Kingdom of Dreams THEATRE
(☑0124-4528000; www.kingdomofdreams.in; Auditorium Complex, Sector 29; Culture Gully ₹599 refundable on a purchase, shows from ₹1099 Tue-Fri, ₹1199 Sat & Sun; ⊘12.30pm-midnight Tue-Fri, noon-midnight Sat & Sun, showtimes vary; MIFFCO Chowk) An entertainment extravaganza for lovers of Bollywood cinema, Kingdom of Dreams offers an out-and-out sensory assault. You can take in one of three musicals at the Nautanka Mahal, supported by world-class techno-wizardry, as the cast swing, swoop and sing from the rafters. There's a free shuttle here from the metro every 15 minutes.

🛍 Shopping

Gurgaon offers a certain kind of shopping heaven, whole streets lined by flashy malls, with lots of big-name labels and chainstores, plus a few local independent names to spice up the mix, such as **Atelier Mon** (www.ateliermon.com; 27/4, Deodar Marg, Block A, Sector 26A; ⊘11am-6pm Mon-Sat; MSikanderpur).

ℹ Transport

Rapid Metrorail Gurgaon (http://rapidmetro gurgaon.com/home; fare ₹20) This 5km circular track has trains running every five minutes, and connects Sikanderpur with DLF Cyber City.

DELHI GURGAON (GURUGRAM)

Agra & the Taj Mahal

Includes ➡

History 79
Sights 79
Activities 87
Tours 87
Sleeping 88
Eating 91
Drinking
& Nightlife 93
Shopping 93
Fatehpur Sikri 97

Best Places to Eat

➡ Pinch of Spice (p92)

➡ Mama Chicken (p92)

➡ Esphahan (p92)

➡ Vedic (p92)

Best Places to Sleep

➡ Tourists Rest House (p90)

➡ N Homestay (p89)

➡ Oberoi Amarvilas (p89)

➡ The Retreat (p89)

Why Go?

The magical allure of the Taj Mahal draws tourists to Agra like moths to a wondrous flame. And despite the hype, it's every bit as good as you've heard. But the Taj is not a stand-alone attraction. The legacy of the Mughal empire has left a magnificent fort and a liberal sprinkling of fascinating tombs and mausoleums; and there's also fun to be had in the bustling *chowks* (marketplaces). The downside comes in the form of hordes of rickshaw-wallahs, touts, unofficial guides and souvenir vendors, whose persistence can be infuriating at times.

Agra straddles a large bend along the holy Yamuna River. The fort and the Taj, 2km apart, both overlook the river on different parts of the bend. The main train and bus stations are a few kilometres southwest.

When to Go
Agra

Sep–Oct The best time to visit. Most of the monsoon rains are over and summer temperatures have cooled.

Nov–Feb Daytime temperatures are comfortable but big sights are overcrowded. Evenings are nippy.

Mar Evening chill is gone but raging-hot midsummer temperatures haven't yet materialised.

Agra & the Taj Mahal Highlights

1 Taj Mahal (p80)
Basking in the beauty of one of the most famous buildings in the world – a must-see!

2 Fatehpur Sikri (p97)
Roaming a sprawling palace complex from Mughal times, with an immense and fascinating 450-year-old mosque next door.

3 Agra Fort (p84)
Wandering the many rooms of one of India's most impressive ancient forts.

4 Mehtab Bagh (p84)
Relaxing in gardens with perfect sunset views of the Taj.

5 Itimad-ud-Daulah (p86)
Marveling at the marble-work of an exquisite tomb nicknamed the Baby Taj.

6 Akbar's Mausoleum (p86) Visiting the impressive resting place of the greatest Mughal emperor.

7 Agra Walks (p87)
Strolling deeper into ancient Agra with local guides.

8 Kinari Bazaar (p93)
Boggling your senses in one of India's most mesmerising – and hectic – markets.

History

In 1501 Sultan Sikander Lodi established his capital here, but the city fell into Mughal hands in 1526, when Emperor Babur defeated the last Lodi sultan at Panipat. Agra reached the peak of its magnificence between the mid-16th and mid-17th centuries during the reigns of Akbar, Jehangir and Shah Jahan. During this period the fort, the Taj Mahal and other major mausoleums were built. In 1638 Shah Jahan built a new city in Delhi, and his son Aurangzeb moved the capital there 10 years later.

In 1761 Agra fell to the Jats, a warrior class who looted its monuments, including the Taj Mahal. The Marathas took over in 1770, but were replaced by the British in 1803. Following the First War of Independence of 1857, the British shifted the administration of the province to Allahabad. Deprived of its ad-ministrative role, Agra developed as a centre for heavy industry, quickly becoming famous for its chemicals industry and air pollution, before the Taj and tourism became a major source of income.

Agra

☑ 0562 / POP 1.7 MILLION

⊙ Sights

The entrance fee for Agra's five main sights – the Taj, Agra Fort, Fatehpur Sikri, Akbar's Tomb and Itimad-ud-Daulah – comprises charges from two different bodies: the Archaeological Survey of India (ASI) and the Agra Development Association (ADA). Of the ₹1000 ticket for the Taj Mahal, ₹500 is a special ADA ticket, which gives you small savings on the other four sights if visited in the same day. You'll save ₹50 at Agra Fort and ₹10 each at Fatehpur Sikri, Akbar's Tomb and Itimad-ud-Daulah. You can buy this ₹500 ADA ticket at any of the five sights – just say you intend to visit the Taj later that day.

All the other sights in Agra are either free or have ASI tickets only, which aren't included in the ADA one-day offer.

Admission to all sights is free for children under 15. On Fridays, many sights offer a discount of ₹10 (but note that the Taj is closed on Friday).

★ Taj Mahal   HISTORIC BUILDING

(Map p88; Indian/foreigner ₹40/1000, video ₹25; ☉dawn-dusk Sat-Thu) Poet Rabindranath Tagore described it as 'a teardrop on the cheek of eternity'; Rudyard Kipling as 'the embodiment of all things pure'; while its creator, Emperor Shah Jahan, said it made 'the sun and the moon shed tears from their eyes'. Every year, tourists numbering more than twice the population of Agra pass through its gates to catch a once-in-a-lifetime glimpse of what is widely considered the most beautiful building in the world. Few leave disappointed.

The Taj was built by Shah Jahan as a memorial for his third wife, Mumtaz Mahal, who died giving birth to their 14th child in 1631. The death of Mumtaz left the emperor so heartbroken that his hair is said to have turned grey virtually overnight. Construction of the Taj began the following year; although the main building is thought to have been built in eight years, the whole complex was not completed until 1653. Not long after it was finished, Shah Jahan was overthrown by his son Aurangzeb and imprisoned in Agra Fort, where for the rest of his days he could only gaze out at his creation through a window. Following his death in 1666, Shah Jahan was buried here alongside his beloved Mumtaz.

In total, some 20,000 people from India and Central Asia worked on the building. Specialists were brought in from as far away as Europe to produce the exquisite marble screens and pietra dura (marble inlay work) made with thousands of semiprecious stones.

The Taj was designated a World Heritage Site in 1983 and looks nearly as immaculate today as when it was first constructed – though it underwent a huge restoration project in the early 20th century.

➡ Entry & Information

Note: the Taj is closed every Friday to anyone not attending prayers at the mosque.

The Taj can be accessed through the west, south and east gates. Tour groups tend to enter through the east and west gates. Independent travellers tend to use the south gate, which is nearest to Taj Ganj, the main area for budget accommodation, and generally has shorter queues than the west gate. The east gate has the shortest queues of the lot, but this is because the ticket office is inconveniently located a 1km walk away at Shilpgram, a large, government-run tourist centre. There are separate queues for men and women at all three gates. Once you get your ticket, you can skip ahead of the lines of Indians waiting to get in – one perk of your pricey entry fee.

Cameras and videos are permitted but you can't take photographs inside the mausoleum itself, and the areas in which you can take videos are quite limited. Tripods are banned.

Remember to retrieve your free 500ml bottle of water and shoe covers (included in Taj ticket price). If you keep your ticket you get small entry-fee discounts when visiting Agra Fort, Fatehpur Sikri, Akbar's Tomb or the Itimad-ud-Daulah on the same day. You can also pick up an audio guide (₹120). Bags much bigger than a money pouch are not allowed inside; free bag storage is available at the west gate. Any food or tobacco will be confiscated when you go through security.

From the south gate, entry to the inner compound is through a very impressive 30m red-sandstone gateway on the south side of the forecourt, which is inscribed with verses from the Quran.

ⓘ BEST TIMES TO SEE THE TAJ

The Taj is arguably at its most atmospheric at sunrise. This is certainly the most comfortable time to visit, with far fewer crowds. Sunset is another magical viewing time.

You can also view the Taj for five nights around the full moon. Entry numbers are limited, though, and tickets must be purchased a day in advance from the Archaeological Survey of India office (p94); see its website for details. (Note: this office is known as the Taj Mahal Office by some rickshaw riders.)

TAJ MAHAL MYTHS

The Taj is a Hindu Temple

The well-publicised theory that the Taj was originally a Shiva temple built in the 12th century, and only later converted into Mumtaz Mahal's famous mausoleum, was developed by Purushottam Nagesh Oak in 1989. (Oak also claims that the Kaaba, Stonehenge and Vatican City all have Hindu origins.) He petitioned parliament to open the Taj's sealed basement rooms to prove his theory (request denied) and in 2000 India's Supreme Court dismissed his plea to officially name a Hindu king as the builder of the Taj. But the matter is still alive, with a similar court case filed as recently as 2015, this one naming a form of Shiva as one of the plaintiffs. Archaeologists and the Indian government remain unconvinced.

The Black Taj Mahal

The story goes that Shah Jahan planned to build a negative image of the Taj Mahal in black marble on the opposite side of the river as his own mausoleum, and that work began before he was imprisoned by his son Aurangzeb in Agra Fort. Extensive excavations at Mehtab Bagh have found no trace of any such construction.

Craftsmen Mutilations

Legend has it that on completion of the Taj, Shah Jahan ordered the hands of the project's craftsmen to be chopped off, preventing them from ever building anything as beautiful again. Some even say he went so far as to have their eyes gouged out. Thankfully, no historical evidence supports either story.

Sinking Taj

Some experts believe there is evidence to show that the Taj is slowly tilting towards and sinking into the riverbed due to the changing nature of the soil beside an increasingly dry Yamuna River. The Archaeological Survey of India has dismissed any marginal change in the elevation of the building as statistically insignificant, adding that it has not detected any structural damage at its base in the seven decades since its first scientific study of the Taj was carried out, in 1941.

➡ **Inside the Grounds**

The **ornamental gardens** are set out along classical Mughal *charbagh* (formal Persian garden) lines – a square quartered by watercourses, with an ornamental marble plinth at its centre. When the fountains are not flowing, the Taj is beautifully reflected in the water.

The Taj Mahal itself stands on a raised marble platform at the northern end of the ornamental gardens, with its back to the Yamuna River. Its raised position means that the backdrop is only sky – a masterstroke of design. Purely decorative 40m-high white **minarets** grace each corner of the platform. After more than three centuries they are not quite perpendicular, but they may have been designed to lean slightly outwards so that in the event of an earthquake they would fall away from the precious Taj. The redsandstone **mosque** (Map p88) to the west is an important gathering place for Agra's Muslims. The identical building to the east, the **jawab** (Map p88), was built for symmetry.

The central Taj structure is made of semitranslucent white marble, carved with flowers and inlaid with thousands of semi-precious stones in beautiful patterns. A perfect exercise in symmetry, the four identical faces of the Taj feature impressive vaulted arches embellished with pietra dura scrollwork and quotations from the Quran in a style of calligraphy using inlaid jasper. The whole structure is topped off by four small domes surrounding the famous bulbous central dome.

Directly below the main dome is the **Cenotaph of Mumtaz Mahal**, an elaborate false tomb surrounded by an exquisite perforated marble screen inlaid with dozens of different types of semiprecious stones. Beside it, offsetting the symmetry of the Taj, is the **Cenotaph of Shah Jahan**, who was interred here with little ceremony by his usurping son Aurangzeb in 1666. Light is admitted into the central chamber by finely cut marble screens. The real tombs of Mumtaz Mahal and Shah

Taj Mahal

TIMELINE

1631 Emperor Shah Jahan's beloved third wife, Mumtaz Mahal, dies in Buhanpur while giving birth to their 14th child. Her body is initially interred in Buhanpur itself, where Shah Jahan is fighting a military campaign, but is later moved, in a golden casket, to a small building on the banks of the Yamuna River in Agra.

1632 Construction of a permanent mausoleum for Mumtaz Mahal begins.

1633 Mumtaz Mahal is interred in her final resting place, an underground tomb beneath a marble plinth, on top of which the Taj Mahal will be built.

1640 The white-marble mausoleum is completed.

1653 The rest of the Taj Mahal complex is completed.

1658 Emperor Shah Jahan is overthrown by his son Aurangzeb and imprisoned in Agra Fort.

1666 Shah Jahan dies. His body is transported along the Yamuna River and buried underneath the Taj, alongside the tomb of his wife.

1908 Repeatedly damaged and looted after the fall of the Mughal empire, the Taj receives some long-overdue attention as part of a major restoration project ordered by British viceroy Lord Curzon.

1983 The Taj is awarded Unesco World Heritage Site status.

2002 Having been discoloured by pollution in more recent years, the Taj is spruced up with an ancient recipe known as multani mitti – a blend of soil, cereal, milk and lime once used by Indian women to beautify their skin.

Today More than three million tourists visit the Taj Mahal each year. That's more than twice the current population of Agra.

GO BAREFOOT

Help the environment by entering the mausoleum barefoot instead of using the free disposable shoe covers.

Pishtaqs
These huge arched recesses are set into each side of the Taj. They provide depth to the building while their central, latticed marble screens allow patterned light to illuminate the inside of the mausoleum.

Minaret

Entrance

Plinth

Marble Relief Work
Flowering plants, thought to be representations of paradise, are a common theme among the beautifully decorative panels carved onto the white marble.

LIGHT THE WAY

Bring a small torch into the mausoleum to fully appreciate the translucency of the white marble and semiprecious stones.

Filigree Screen

This stunning screen was carved out of a single piece of marble. It surrounds both cenotaphs, allowing patterned light to fall onto them through its intricately carved *jali* (latticework).

Central Dome

The Taj's famous central dome, topped by a brass finial, represents the vault of heaven, a stark contrast to the material world, which is represented by the square shape of the main structure.

Yamuna River

NORTH →

Pietra Dura

It's believed that 35 different precious and semi-precious stones were used to create the exquisite pietra dura (marble inlay work) found on the inside and outside of the mausoleum walls. Again, floral designs are common.

Calligraphy

The strips of calligraphy surrounding each of the four pishtaqs get larger as they get higher, giving the impression of uniform size when viewed from the ground. There's also calligraphy inside the mausoleum, including on Mumtaz Mahal's cenotaph.

Cenotaphs

The cenotaphs of Mumtaz Mahal and Shah Jahan, decorated with pietra dura inlay work, are actually fake tombs. The real ones are located in an underground vault closed to the public.

TAJ MUSEUM

Within the Taj complex, on the western side of the gardens, is the small but excellent **Taj Museum** (Map p88; ◎9am-5pm Sat-Thu) **FREE**, housing a number of original Mughal miniature paintings, including a pair of 17th-century ivory portraits of Emperor Shah Jahan and his beloved wife Mumtaz Mahal. It also has some very well-preserved gold and silver coins dating from the same period, plus architectural drawings of the Taj and some nifty celadon plates, said to split into pieces or change colour if the food served on them contains poison.

Jahan are in a locked basement room below the main chamber and cannot be viewed.

★**Mehtab Bagh**   PARK
(Map p86; Indian/foreigner ₹15/200, video ₹25; ◎dawn-dusk) This park, originally built by Emperor Babur as the last in a series of 11 parks on the Yamuna's east bank (long before the Taj was conceived), fell into disrepair until it was little more than a huge mound of sand. To protect the Taj from the erosive effects of the sand blown across the river, the park was reconstructed and is now one the best places from which to view the great mausoleum.

The gardens in the Taj are perfectly aligned with the ones here, and the view of the Taj from the fountain directly in front of the entrance gate is a special one.

★**Agra Fort**   FORT
(Map p86; Indian/foreigner ₹40/550, video ₹25; ◎dawn-dusk) With the Taj Mahal overshadowing it, one can easily forget that Agra has one of the finest Mughal forts in India. Walking through courtyard after courtyard of this palatial red-sandstone and marble fortress, your amazement grows as the scale of what was built here begins to sink in.

Its construction along the bank of the Yamuna River was begun by Emperor Akbar in 1565. Further additions were made, particularly by his grandson Shah Jahan, using his favourite building material – white marble. The fort was built primarily as a military structure, but Shah Jahan transformed it into a palace, and later it became his gilded prison for eight years after his son Aurangzeb seized power in 1658.

The ear-shaped fort's colossal double walls rise more than 20m and measure 2.5km in circumference. The Yamuna River originally flowed along the straight eastern edge of the fort, and the emperors had their own bathing ghats here. It contains a maze of buildings, forming a city within a city, including vast underground sections, though many of the structures were destroyed over the years by Nadir Shah, the Marathas, the Jats and finally the British, who used the fort as a garrison. Even today, much of the fort is used by the military and off-limits to the general public.

The **Amar Singh Gate** (Map p86) to the south is the sole entry point to the fort these days and where you buy your entrance ticket. Its dogleg design was meant to confuse attackers who made it past the first line of defence – the crocodile-infested moat.

A path leads straight from here up to the large **Moti Masjid** (Pearl Mosque; Map p86), which is closed to the public. To your right, just before you reach Moti Masjid, is the large, open **Diwan-i-Am** (Hall of Public Audiences; Map p86), which was used by Shah Jahan for domestic government business, and features a throne room where the emperor listened to petitioners. In front of it is the small and rather incongruous **grave of John Colvin**, a lieutenant-governor of the northwest provinces who died of an illness in the fort during the 1857 First War of Independence.

A tiny staircase just to the left of the Diwan-i-Am throne leads up to a large courtyard. To your left is the tiny but exquisite **Nagina Masjid** (Gem Mosque), built in 1635 by Shah Jahan for the ladies of the court. Down below was the **Ladies' Bazaar**, where the court ladies bought their goods.

On the far side of the large courtyard, along the eastern wall of the fort, is **Diwan-i-Khas** (Hall of Private Audiences), which was reserved for important dignitaries or foreign representatives. The hall once housed Shah Jahan's legendary Peacock Throne, which was inset with precious stones – including the famous Koh-i-noor diamond. The throne was taken to Delhi by Aurangzeb, then to Iran in 1739 by Nadir Shah and dismantled after his assassination in 1747. Overlooking the river and the distant Taj Mahal is **Takhti-i-Jehangir**, a huge slab of black rock with an inscription around the edge. The throne that stood here was made for Jehangir when he was Prince Salim.

Off to your right from here (as you face the river) is Shish Mahal (Mirror Palace), with walls inlaid with tiny mirrors. At the time of research it had been closed for some time due to restoration, although you can peek through cracks in the doors at the sparkling mirrors inside.

Further along the eastern edge of the fort you'll find Musamman Burj and Khas Mahal, (Map p86) the wonderful white-marble octagonal tower and palace where Shah Jahan was imprisoned for eight years until his death in 1666, and from where he could gaze out at the Taj Mahal, the tomb of his wife. When he died, Shah Jahan's body was taken from here by boat to the Taj. The now closed Mina Masjid, set back slightly from the eastern edge, was his private mosque.

The large courtyard here is Anguri Bagh, a garden that has been brought back to life in recent years. In the courtyard is an innocuous-looking entrance – now locked – that leads down a flight of stairs into a two-storey labyrinth of underground rooms and passageways where Akbar used to keep his 500-strong harem.

Continuing south, the huge red-sandstone Jehangir's Palace (Map p86) was probably built by Akbar for his son Jehangir. It blends Indian and Central Asian architectural styles, a reminder of the Mughals' Afghani cultural roots. In front of the palace is Hauz-i-Jehangir, a huge bowl carved out of a single block of stone, which was used for bathing. Walking past this brings you back to the main path to Amar Singh Gate.

TOP TAJ VIEWS

Inside the Taj Grounds
You may have to pay ₹1000 for the privilege, but it's only when you're inside the grounds themselves that you can really get up close and personal with the world's most beautiful building. Don't miss inspecting the marble inlay work (pietra dura) inside the *pishtaqs* (large arched recesses) on the four outer walls. And don't forget to bring a small torch with you so that you can shine it on similar pietra dura work inside the dark central chamber of the mausoleum. Note the translucency of both the white marble and the semiprecious stones inlaid into it.

From Mehtab Bagh
Tourists are no longer allowed to wander freely along the riverbank on the opposite side of the Yamuna River, but you can still enjoy a view of the back of the Taj from the 16th-century Mughal park Mehtab Bagh, with the river flowing between you and the mausoleum. A path leading down to the river beside the park offers the same view for free, albeit from a more restricted angle.

Looking up from the South Bank of the River
This is a great place to be for sunset. Take the path that hugs the outside of the Taj's eastern wall and walk all the way down to the small temple beside the river. You should be able to find boat-hands down here willing to row you out onto the water for an even more romantic view. Expect to pay around ₹100 per boat. For safety reasons, it's best not to wander down here on your own for sunset.

From a Rooftop Cafe in Taj Ganj
Perfect for sunrise shots: there are some wonderful photos to be had from the numerous rooftop cafes in Taj Ganj. We think the cafe on Saniya Palace Hotel (p88) is the pick of the bunch, with its plant-filled design and great position, but many of them are good. And all offer the bonus of being able to view the Taj with the added comfort of an early-morning cup of coffee.

From Agra Fort
With a decent zoom lens you can capture some fabulous images of the Taj from Agra Fort, especially if you're willing to get up at the crack of dawn to see the sun rising up from behind it. The best places to snap from are probably Musamman Burj and Khas Mahal, the octagonal tower and palace where Shah Jahan was imprisoned for eight years until his death.

AGRA & THE TAJ MAHAL AGRA

Agra

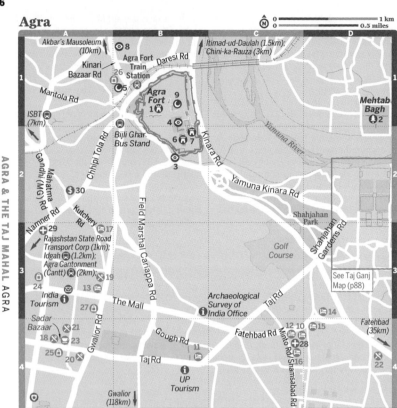

You can walk here from Taj Ganj, or else take a cycle-rickshaw for ₹40.

Akbar's Mausoleum
HISTORIC BUILDING

(Indian/foreigner ₹15/300, video ₹25; ⊙ dawn-dusk) This outstanding sandstone and marble tomb commemorates the greatest of the Mughal emperors. The huge courtyard is entered through a stunning gateway. It has three-storey minarets at each corner and is built of red sandstone strikingly inlaid with white-marble geometric patterns.

The mausoleum is at Sikandra, 10km northwest of Agra Fort. Catch a bus (₹25, 45 minutes) headed to Mathura from Bijli Ghar bus stand (p96); they go past the mausoleum. Or else take a taxi (return trip about ₹800).

Itimad-ud-Daulah
HISTORIC BUILDING

(Indian/foreigner ₹20/210, video ₹25; ⊙ dawn-dusk) Nicknamed the Baby Taj, the exquisite tomb of Mizra Ghiyas Beg should not be missed. This Persian nobleman was Mumtaz Mahal's grandfather and Emperor Jehangir's *wazir* (chief minister). His daughter, Nur Jahan, who married Jehangir, built the tomb between 1622 and 1628, in a style similar to the tomb she built for Jehangir near Lahore in Pakistan.

It doesn't have the same awesome beauty as the Taj, but it's arguably more delicate in appearance thanks to its particularly finely carved *jalis* (marble lattice screens). This was the first Mughal structure built completely from marble, the first to make extensive use of pietra dura and the first tomb to be built on the banks of the Yamuna, which until then had been a sequence of beautiful pleasure gardens.

You can combine a trip here with Chinika-Rauza and Mehtab Bagh, all on the east bank. A cycle-rickshaw covering all four should cost about ₹300 return from the Taj, including waiting time. An autorickshaw should be ₹450.

Agra

◎ **Top Sights**
1 Agra Fort B1
2 Mehtab Bagh D1

◎ **Sights**
3 Amar Singh Gate B2
4 Diwan-i-Am B1
5 Jama Masjid B1
6 Jehangir's Palace B2
7 Khas Mahal B2
8 Kinari Bazaar B1
9 Moti Masjid B1

◎ **Sleeping**
10 Bansi Homestay C4
11 Clarks Shiraz Hotel B4
   Dasaprakash .... (see 28)
12 Hotel Amar C4
13 Hotel Yamuna View A3
14 Howard Plaza D3
15 Mansingh Palace D4
16 N Homestay C4
17 Tourists Rest House A3

◎ **Eating**
18 Brijwasi A4
19 Dasaprakash A3
   Dasaprakash .... (see 28)
20 Lakshmi Vilas A4
21 Mama Chicken A4
22 Pinch of Spice D4
   Vedic .... (see 19)

◎ **Drinking & Nightlife**
23 Café Coffee Day A4
   Costa Coffee .... (see 10)

◎ **Shopping**
24 Khadi Gramodyog A3
25 Modern Book Depot A4
26 Subhash Bazaar B1
27 Subhash Emporium A3

◎ **Information**
28 Amit Jaggi Memorial Hospital C4
   Bagpacker Travel .... (see 17)
29 SR Hospital A3
30 State Bank of India A2

Chini-ka-Rauza　HISTORIC BUILDING

(◎dawn-dusk) **FREE** This Persian-style riverside tomb of Afzal Khan, a poet who served as Shah Jahan's chief minister, was built between 1628 and 1639. Rarely visited, it is hidden away down a shady avenue of trees on the east bank of the Yamuna.

Jama Masjid　MOSQUE

(Map p86; Jama Masjid Rd) This fine mosque, built in the Kinari Bazaar (p93) by Shah Jahan's daughter in 1648, and once connected to Agra Fort, features striking marble patterning on its domes.

🏃 Activities

Hotels allowing nonguests to use their swimming pools include Howard Plaza (p90), per hour ₹500, and Amar (p90), all day ₹575 – with slide.

🎫 Tours

Agra Walks　WALKING

(☑9027711144; www.agrawalks.com; ₹2200) Many folks spend but a day in Agra, taking in the Taj and Agra Fort and sailing off into the sunset. If you're interested in digging a little deeper, this excellent walking/cyclerickshaw combo tour will show you sides of the city most tourists don't see.

The guides are darling and Old Agra highlights include going deeper into Kinari Bazaar and a few off-the-beaten-path temples such as Mankameshwar Mandir and Radha Krishna Mandir. A delectable food tour is also offered (₹2000, includes tastings).

Amin Tours　CULTURAL

(☑9837411144; www.daytourtajmahal.com) If you can't be bothered handling the logistics, look no further than this recommended agency for all-inclusive private Agra day trips from Delhi by car (from ₹9900, depending on number in group) or train (from ₹10,200). Caveat: if they try to take you shopping and you're not interested, politely decline.

UP Tourism　BUS

(☑0562-2421204; www.uptourism.gov.in; incl entry fees Indian/foreigner ₹650/3000) UP Tourism runs coach tours that leave Agra Cantonment train station at 10.30am Saturday to Thursday, after picking up passengers arriving from Delhi on the Taj Express. The tour includes the Taj Mahal, Agra Fort and Fatehpur Sikri, with a 1¼-hour stop in each place.

Tours return to the station so that day trippers can catch the Taj Express back to Delhi at 6.55pm. Contact either of the UP Tourism offices – at the train station (p95) or on Taj Rd (p95) – to book a seat, or just turn up at the train station tourist office at 9.45am to sign up for that day. Tours only depart with five people or more, unless you book via the UP Tourism website – in that

Taj Ganj

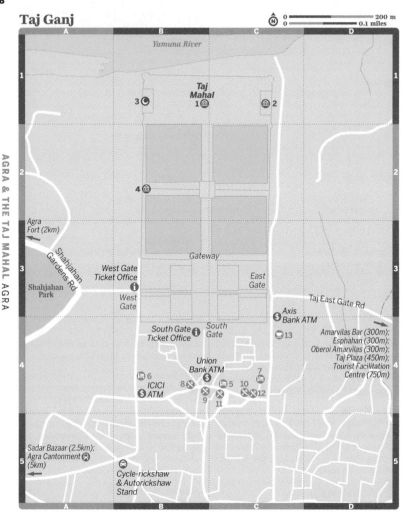

Taj Ganj

N 0 _____ 200 m
0 _____ 0.1 miles

Yamuna River

Taj Mahal 1

3

2

4

Agra Fort (2km)

Shahjahan Gardens Rd

Shahjahan Park

West Gate Ticket Office

West Gate

Gateway

East Gate

Taj East Gate Rd

South Gate Ticket Office

South Gate

Axis Bank ATM

13

Amarvilas Bar (300m); Esphahan (300m); Oberoi Amarvilas (300m); Taj Plaza (450m); Tourist Facilitation Centre (750m)

Union Bank ATM

6

ICICI ATM

8

9

5

11

10

7

12

Sadar Bazaar (2.5km); Agra Cantonment (5km)

Cycle-rickshaw & Autorickshaw Stand

AGRA & THE TAJ MAHAL AGRA

case, we've been told, your tour will go no matter how many sign up. (The website is a bit difficult to navigate: From the home page, click Online Booking Portal > Package Tours at a Glance > Agra Package Tour (under Package Tours, *not* One Day Tour) and take it from there...)

🛏 Sleeping

The main place for budget accommodation is the bustling area of Taj Ganj, immediately south of the Taj, while there's a high concentration of midrange hotels further south, along Fatehabad Rd. Sadar Bazaar, an area boasting good-quality restaurants, offers another option.

Be forewarned: free wi-fi hasn't really caught on in Agra's nicer hotels; expect to pay upwards of ₹500 for 24 hours.

🛏 Taj Ganj Area

Saniya Palace Hotel   HOTEL **$**
(Map p88; ☑ 0562-3270199; www.saniyapalace.in; Chowk Kagziyan, Taj South Gate; r without/with AC from ₹600/1300; ❋@🛜) Set back from the main strip down an undesirable alleyway, this isn't the sleekest Taj Ganj option, but it

Taj Ganj

◉ **Top Sights**
1 Taj Mahal B1

◉ **Sights**
2 Jawab C1
3 Mosque B1
4 Taj Museum B2

🛏 **Sleeping**
5 Hotel Kamal C4
6 Hotel Sidhartha B4
7 Saniya Palace Hotel C4

✗ **Eating**
8 Joney's Place B4
Saniya Palace Hotel .... (see 7)
9 Shankara Vegis B4
10 Shanti Lodge Restaurant C4
11 Taj Cafe C4
12 Yash Cafe C4

◎ **Drinking & Nightlife**
13 Café Coffee Day C4

tries to imbue character with marble floors and Mughal-style framed carpet wall hangings. The rooms are clean and large enough, although the bathrooms in the non-AC rooms are minuscule.

The real coup is the very pleasant, plant-filled (and recently expanded) rooftop, which trumps its rivals for optimum Taj views.

Hotel Kamal HOTEL $

(Map p88; ✆ 0562-2330126; hotelkamal@hot-mail.com; Taj South Gate; r ₹700-1400, with AC ₹2000; ❄✿) The smartest hotel in Taj Ganj proper, Kamal has clean, comfortable rooms with nice touches, such as framed photos of the Taj on the walls and rugs on the tiled floors. Five rooms in the newer annexe are a definite step up, with welcoming woodwork, extra space and stone-walled showers.

There's a cosy, bamboo-enclosed ground-floor restaurant and an underused rooftop restaurant with a somewhat obscured Taj view.

Hotel Sidhartha HOTEL $

(Map p88; ✆ 0562-2230901; www.hotelsidhartha .com; Taj West Gate; r incl breakfast from ₹950, with AC from ₹1200; ❄✿) Of the 21 rooms in this West Gate staple, those on the ground floor are stylish for the price, with marble walls, cable TV and clean bathrooms with hot water (room 111A is the standard to

which all future ground-floor rooms will eventually be renovated). Upper-floor rooms are smaller and not as exciting.

Either way, all rooms surround or over-look a small, leafy courtyard over-run by a shade-providing *tameshwari* plant.

Taj Plaza HOTEL $$

(✆ 0562-2232515; www.hoteltajplazaagra.com; Shilpgram VIP Rd; d ₹1500, with AC ₹2500, Taj-facing ₹3200; ❄@✿) Depending on demand, this well-positioned hotel fluctuates between budget and midrange; when slow, prices can drop 50%. You won't be disappointed if you stay here. It has professional reception and clean rooms with TV – six of which look out at the Taj. There's also a pleasant rooftop with decent Taj and sunset views.

It's a whole lot closer to the Taj than most hotels in the same price range.

★ **Oberoi Amarvilas** HOTEL $$$

(✆ 0562-2231515; www.oberoihotels.com; Taj East Gate Rd; d with/without balcony ₹97,750/80,500; ❄@✿☼) Following Oberoi's iron-clad MO of maharaja-level service, exquisite dining and properties that pack some serious wow, Agra's best hotel by far oozes style and luxury. Elegant interior design is suffused with Mughal themes, a composition carried over into the exterior fountain courtyard and swimming pool, both of which are set in a delightful water garden.

All rooms (and even some bath-tubs) have wonderful Taj views.

The Retreat BOUTIQUE HOTEL $$$

(✆ 8810022200; www.theretreat.co.in; Shilp-gram Rd; s/d incl breakfast from ₹5750/6900; ❄@✿☼) Everything in this sleek, 52-room hotel is done up boutique-style with Indian sensibilities (lots of soothing mauve, mocha and turquoise throughout) and modern fixtures abound. There's a small pool and multicuisine restaurant offering countrywide specialities such as Goan fish curries and Lahori kebabs. Free wi-fi.

🏠 Fatehabad Road Area

★ **N Homestay** HOMESTAY $$

(Map p86; ✆ 9690107860; www.nhomestay.com; 15 Ajanta Colony, Vibhav Nagar; s/d incl breakfast ₹1800/2000; ❄@✿) Matriarch Naghma and her helpful sons are a riot at this wonderful homestay. Their beautiful home, tucked away in a residential neighbourhood 15

SLEEPING PRICE RANGES

Accommodation price ranges for this region:

$ below ₹1500

$$ ₹1500–4000

$$$ above ₹4000

minutes' walk from the Taj's Western Gate, is nothing short of a fabulous place to stay.

The three-storey house features marble floors throughout, and some of the six large and authentically appointed rooms have pleasant balconies (first-come, first-served). Naghma will even cook you dinner (₹400) – and what a cook she is! You'll rarely break through the cultural surface with such ease.

Bansi Homestay   HOMESTAY $$

(Map p86; ☑0562-2333033; www.bansihome stayagra.com; 18 Handicraft Nagar, Fatehabad Rd; s/d incl breakfast ₹3000/3500; ❋ 🛜) 🍴
A retired director of Uttar Pradesh Tourism is your host at this wonderful upscale homestay tucked away in a quiet residential neighbourhood near Fatahabad Rd. The five large rooms boast huge bathrooms with pressurised solar-powered rain-style showers and flank extremely pleasant common areas with bespoke furniture and Krishna paintings. It feels more like a boutique hotel than a homestay.

The immensely pleasurable 2nd-floor garden is a fabulous retreat for watching the world go by, and the food – notably the home-made pickles and *aloo paratha* (potato-stuffed flatbread) – excels, along with the hospitality in general. Bansi is Krishna's flute, a symbol of peace and tranquillity, which is exactly what you'll find here.

Dasaprakash   HOTEL $$

(Map p86; ☑0562-4016123; www.dasaprakash group.com; 18/163A/6 Shamshabad Rd; s/d incl breakfast ₹3100/3450; ❋ 🛜) This friendly and clean retreat offers 28 modern and functional rooms with small desks, flat-screen TVs and nice bathrooms, all of which haven't been around long enough to show signs of deterioration. It all works well as a good-value escape from the diesel and dust, and is located far enough from Fatahabad Rd to offer relative R&R. Free wi-fi.

Walk-ins can easily get discounts of more than 50% if rooms are available.

Howard Plaza   HOTEL $$$

(Map p86; ☑0562-4048600; www.howardplaza agra.com; Fatehabad Rd; s/d incl breakfast from ₹8050/9200; ❋ @ 🛜 ☀) Standard rooms in this very welcoming hotel are decked out in elegant dark-wood furniture and stylish decorative tiling. Deluxe rooms boast soothing aqua colour schemes. You won't find much to fault in either category.

The pool is starting to show its age, but there's a small, well-equipped gym and a very pleasant spa offering a whole range of ayurvedic and massage treatments, including the so-called 'erotic bath'. The breezy, open-air rooftop restaurant doubles as one of the few atmospheric bars in town at night (beer from ₹175, cocktails ₹400), and distant Taj views are on offer from the 4th-floor terrace. Wi-fi is enabled throughout.

Hotel Amar   HOTEL $$$

(Map p86; ☑0562-4027000; www.hotelamar .com; Fatehabad Rd; s/d incl breakfast from ₹4000/4600; ❋ @ 🛜 ☀) Though a little worn, the 66 rooms at the friendly Amar come with wi-fi, big TVs and clean bathrooms. The marble-inlay entrance halls and funky, mirrored-ceiling hallways drive home a palpable sense of place. There's a great pool area, complete with a lush green lawn and a 3.5m-tall water slide. Rooms are usually discounted by at least 15%.

Mansingh Palace   HOTEL $$$

(Map p86; ☑0562-2331771; www.mansingh hotels.com; Fatehabad Rd; r from ₹5200; ❋ @ ☀) The service isn't up to scratch for the quality of this hotel, but if you can put up with the grumpy staff on reception you'll find plush rooms inside a complex crammed with Mughal design themes and exotic furnishings. The garden has an interestingly shaped pool and outdoor barbecue area. There's a gym and the quality **Sheesh Mahal** restaurant has live *ghazal* (Urdu songs) nightly.

🛏 Sadar Bazaar Area

★ Tourists Rest House   HOTEL $

(Map p86; ☑0562-2463961; www.dontworry chickencurry.com; 4/62 Kutchery Rd; s/d from ₹500/600, with AC from ₹950/1100; ❋ @ 🛜) If you aren't set on sleeping under the nose of the Taj, this centrally located travellers' hub offers better value than most Agra spots. It's been under the watchful eye of the same family since 1965 (though you can't tell it's going on 50 years old).

If you can forgo AC, the newly renovated cheapies are great value – and things only get better from there. All rooms come with free wi-fi, TV, hot water and large windows, and are set around a peaceful plant-filled, palm-shaded courtyard (a real highlight) and a North Indian pure veg restaurant. The bend-over-backwards owners speak English and French. They couldn't be more helpful, right down to occasionally carting you off somewhere in their hotel rickshaw. Phone ahead for a free pick-up; otherwise, it's ₹40 in a cycle-rickshaw from the train station. Damn fine masala chai, too.

Clarks Shiraz Hotel   HOTEL $$$
(Map p86; ☑0562-2226121; www.hotelclarks shiraz.com; 54 Taj Rd; r incl breakfast from ₹9200; ❋@☎≋) Agra's original five-star hotel, opened in 1961, has done well to keep up with the hotel Joneses. The standard doubles are nothing special for this price range, but the marble-floored deluxe versions are a pleasant step up and all bathrooms have been re-tiled and are spotless.

There are three very good restaurants, two bars (three in season), a gym, a shaded garden and pool area (one of Agra's best) and ayurvedic massages. Some rooms have distant Taj views.

Hotel Yamuna View   HOTEL $$$
(Map p86; ☑0562-3293777; www.hotelyamuna viewagra.com; 6B The Mall; s/d from ₹7500/8500; ❋@☎≋) This reliably excellent hotel was getting a full makeover when we visited – when completed we expect it to be even more modern and more comfortable than before. Prices listed here are estimates of what they might be when the hotel reopens.

There's a great garden pool, a sleek cocktail bar and a plush Chinese restaurant (with a real Chinese chef – good for a sabbatical from Indian food).

✗ Eating

Dalmoth is Agra's famous version of *namkin* (spicy nibbles). *Peitha* is a square-shaped sweet made from pumpkin and glucose that is flavoured with rosewater, coconut or saffron. You can buy it all over Agra. From October to March look out for *gajak,* a slightly spicy sesame-seed biscuit strip.

Taj Ganj Area

Saniya Palace Hotel   MULTICUISINE $
(Map p88; mains ₹100-200; ☉6am-10pm; ☎) With cute tablecloths, dozens of potted plants and a bamboo pergola for shade, this is the most pleasant rooftop restaurant in Taj Ganj. It also has the best rooftop view of the Taj, bar none. The kitchen is a bit rough and ready, but its mix of Western dishes and Western-friendly Indian dishes usually go down without complaints.

Taj Cafe   MULTICUISINE $
(Map p88; mains ₹50-200; ☉7am-11pm; ☎) Up a flight of steps and overlooking Taj Ganj's busy street scene, this friendly, family-run restaurant is a nice choice if you're not fussed about Taj views. There's a good choice of breakfasts, thalis (₹90 to ₹140) and pizza (₹160 to ₹200), and the lassis here won't disappoint.

Shanti Lodge Restaurant   MULTICUISINE $
(Map p88; mains ₹90-250; ☉6.30am-10pm) The rooftop Taj view here is superb so this is a great place for breakfast or a sunset beer. There's some shade for hot afternoons, although it's not as comfortable as nearby Saniya Palace. The only let-down is the

---

TOP AGRA FESTIVALS

Taj Mahotsav (www.tajmahotsav.org; ☉Feb) This 10-day carnival of culture, cuisine and crafts is Agra's biggest and best party. Held at Shilpgram, the festival features more than 400 artisans from all over India, a pot-pourri of folk and classical music, dances from various regions and enough regional food to induce a curry coma.

Kailash Fair (☉Aug/Sep) Held at the Kailash temple, 12km from Agra, this cultural and religious fair honours Lord Shiva, who legendarily appeared here in the form of a stone lingam. It attracts devotees from all over North India.

Ram Barat (☉Sep) Celebrated before the Hindu festival of Dussehra, Ram Barat is a dramatic recreation of the royal/divine wedding procession of Rama and Sita. Expect three days of colourful lights and pounding Hindu rhythms, highlighted by the 12-hour parade itself, featuring caparisoned elephants, horses, more than 125 mobile floats depicting mythological events and 30 marching bands.

menu which, although not bad, lacks invention. Banana pancakes, anyone?

Shankara Vegis
VEGETARIAN $

(Map p88; Chowk Kaghzi; mains ₹90-150; ⊙ 8am-10.30pm; 🛜) Most restaurants in Taj Ganj ooze a distinctly average air of mediocrity – Shankara Vegis is different. This cosy old-timer, with its red tablecloths and straw-lined walls, stands out not only for its decor, but for great vegetarian thalis (₹120 to ₹160) and, most pleasantly, the genuinely friendly, non-pushy ethos of its hands-on owners.

Joney's Place
MULTICUISINE $

(Map p88; Kutta Park, Taj Ganj; mains ₹70-120; ⊙ 5am-10.30pm) This pocket-sized institution whipped up its first creamy lassi in 1978 and continues to please despite cooking its meals in what must be Agra's smallest kitchen. The cheese and tomato 'jayfelles' (toasted sandwich), the banana lassi (with money-back guarantee) and the *malai* kofta all come recommended, but it's more about crack-of-dawn sustenance than culinary dazzle.

Yash Cafe
MULTICUISINE $$

(Map p88; 3/137 Chowk Kagziyan; mains ₹100-260; ⊙ 7am-10.30pm; 🛜) This chilled-out, 1st-floor cafe has wicker chairs, sports channels on TV, DVDs shown in the evening and a good range of meals, from good-value set breakfasts to thalis (₹90), pizza (₹90 to ₹300) and Indian-style French toast (with coconut – we think they made that up). It also offers a shower and storage space (₹50 for both) to day visitors.

★Esphahan
NORTH INDIAN $$$

(☑2231515; Taj East Gate Rd, Oberoi Amarvilas Hotel; mains ₹1550-3500; ⊙ dinner 6.30pm & 9pm; 🌡) There are only two sittings each evening at Agra's finest restaurant (6.30pm and 9.30pm), so booking a table is essential. The exquisite menu is chock-full of unique delicacies and rarely seen regional heritage dishes.

Anything that comes out of the succulent North Indian tandoor is a showstopper (especially the *bharwan aloo,* a potato kebab stuffed with nuts, spices, mint and coriander). Melt-in-your-mouth dishes such as *aloobukhara maaz* (a Mughlai lamb kebab stuffed with prunes) and *safri gosht* (braised lamb with pickled onions, dried tomatoes and spiced pickle) redefine lamb as most know it. It's all set to a romantic background soundtrack of a live *santoor* (a stringed instrument) player.

🍴 Fatehabad Road Area

Dasaprakash
SOUTH INDIAN $$

(Map p86; www.dasaprakashgroup.com; 18/163A/6 Shamshabad Rd; thalis ₹230-330, mains ₹230-330; ⊙ 7am-11pm) The Vibhav Nagar branch of this perennial South Indian upscale staple ups the ante with a North Indian tandoor. You get the pure veg love of other Dasaprakash branches, plus North Indian options such as veg tandoori kebabs, available from noon (that tandoor needs a few hours to heat up). It's inside the hotel of the same name.

Vedic
NORTH INDIAN $$

(Map p86; www.vedicrestaurant.com; 1 Gwalior Rd; mains ₹150-275; ⊙ 11am-10.45pm; 🌡🖉) Modern decor meets traditional ambience at this North Indian veg hot spot, with paneer (unfermented cheese) dishes featuring highly. The paneer tikka masala and Navaratan korma are particularly good. There's also a range of delicious vegetarian kebabs.

★Pinch of Spice
MODERN INDIAN $$$

(Map p86; www.pinchofspice.in; Fatehabad Rd; mains ₹280-410; ⊙ noon-11.30pm) This modern North Indian superstar is the best spot outside five-star hotels to indulge yourself in rich curries and succulent tandoori kebabs. The *murg boti masala* (chicken tikka swimming in a rich and spicy country gravy) and the paneer *lababdar* (unfermented cheese cubes in a spicy red gravy with sauteed onions) are outstanding. Located opposite the ITC Mughal Hotel.

Portions are huge.

🍴 Sadar Bazaar Area

★Mama Chicken
DHABA $

(Map p86; Stall No 2, Sadar Bazaar; items ₹40-440; ⊙ noon-midnight) This superstar *dhaba* is a must: duelling veg and nonveg glorified street stalls employing 24 cooks during the rush, each of whom is handling outdoor tandoors or other traditional cookware. They whip up outrageously good *kathi* (flatbread wrap) rolls (try chicken tikka or paneer tikka), whole chickens numerous ways, curries and chow meins for a standing-room-only crowd hell-bent on sustenance.

Bright lights, obnoxious signage and funky Indian tunes round out the festive atmosphere – a surefire Agra must.

Lakshmi Vilas
SOUTH INDIAN $

(Map p86; 50A Taj Rd; mains ₹110-130; ⊙ 11am-10.30pm; 🌡🖉) This no-nonsense, plainly

THE SPA MAHAL

If India's most glorious monument looks particularly glowing on your visit, it could come down to a day at the spa. After years of research, Indian and American scientists have identified the culprits behind the ongoing discolouration of the mausoleum, which was originally gleaming white. The dust and air pollution that's a feature of daily life in Agra have tarnished the surface of the Taj over the years, giving it a brownish hue. More recently, a greenish tint has begun to appear, due to the excrement of millions of insects that breed in the polluted Yamuna River and are drawn to the Taj's white-ish walls.

In an effort to restore the marble to some of its earlier glory, a mud-pack cleanse has been developed – based on a traditional recipe used by Indian women to restore their own facial radiance. The next full treatment is scheduled to last from April 2017 to March 2018, using a newly improved formula that experts say won't mar the Taj's surface, as previous applications may have done. Though it should look brilliant when finished, note that if you plan to visit during cleaning time, you'll find this wonder of the world covered by scaffolding! And of course, things may not go according to schedule... So if seeing the Taj is a top priority, check to confirm that the work is complete before you book your flights.

decorated, nonsmoking restaurant is *the* place in Agra to come for affordable South Indian fare. The thali meal (₹145), served from noon to 3.30pm and 7pm to 10.30pm, is good though comes across as relatively expensive.

Brijwasi SWEETS $
(Map p86; Sadar Bazaar; sweets from ₹320 per kg, mains ₹95-170; ☻7am-11pm; ※) Sugar-coma–inducing selection of traditional Indian sweets, nuts and biscuits on the ground floor, with a decent-value Indian restaurant upstairs. It's most famous for its *peda* (milk-based sweets).

Dasaprakash SOUTH INDIAN $$
(Map p86; www.dasaprakashgroup.com; Meher Theater Complex, Gwailor Rd; mains ₹210-325; ☻noon-10.45pm; ※🖈) Fabulously tasty and religiously clean, Dasaprakash whips up consistently great South Indian vegetarian food, including spectacular thalis (₹230 to ₹330), dosas and a few token Continental dishes. The ice-cream desserts (₹100 to ₹220) are another speciality. Comfortable booth seating and wood-lattice screens make for intimate dining.

🍷 Drinking & Nightlife

A night out in Agra tends to revolve around sitting at a rooftop restaurant with a couple of bottles of beer. None of the restaurants in Taj Ganj are licensed, but they can find alcohol for you if you ask nicely, and don't mind if you bring your own drinks, as long as you're discreet.

Amarvilas Bar BAR
(Taj East Gate Rd, Oberoi Amar Vilas Hotel; ☻noon-midnight) For a beer or cocktail in sheer opulence, look no further than the bar at Agra's best hotel. A terrace opens out to views of the Taj. Nonguests can wander onto the terrace, but staff can be funny about it.

Costa Coffee CAFE
(Map p86; www.costacoffee.com; 8 Handicraft Nagar, Fatehabad Rd; ☻8am-11pm; 🕾) Agra's only outlet of this UK coffee chain offers a cool and clean caffeine fix (coffee ₹90 to ₹240) off Fatahabad Rd – and wi-fi.

Café Coffee Day CAFE
(Map p88; www.cafecoffeeday.com; 21/101 Taj East Gate; ☻6am-8pm) This AC-cooled branch of the popular cafe chain is the closest place to the Taj selling proper coffee (₹90 to ₹140). Another branch is located at Sadar Bazaar (Map p86; ☻9am-11pm).

🛍 Shopping

Agra is well known for its marble items inlaid with coloured stones, similar to the pietra dura work on the Taj. Sadar Bazaar, the old town and the area around the Taj are full of emporiums.

Other popular buys include rugs, leather and gemstones, though the latter are imported from Rajasthan and are cheaper in Jaipur.

Be sure to wander narrow streets behind Jama Masjid, where the crazy maze of overcrowded lanes bursting with colourful markets is known collectively as Kinari Bazaar (Map p86; ☻11am-9pm Wed-Mon).

STAYING AHEAD OF THE SCAMS

As well as the usual commission rackets and ever-present gem-import scam, some specific methods to relieve Agra tourists of their hard-earned cash include the following.

Rickshaws

When taking an auto- or cycle-rickshaw to the Taj, make sure you are clear which gate you want to go to when negotiating the price. Otherwise, almost without fail, riders will take you to the roundabout at the south end of Shahjahan Gardens Rd – where expensive tongas (horse-drawn carriage) or camels wait to take tour groups to the west gate – and claim that's where they thought you meant. Only nonpolluting autos can go within a 500m radius of the Taj because of pollution rules, but they can get a lot closer than this.

Fake Marble

Lots of 'marble' souvenirs are actually alabaster, or even just soapstone. So you may be paying marble prices for lower quality stones. The mini Taj Mahals are always alabaster because they are too intricate to carve quickly in marble.

★ Subhash Emporium   ARTS & CRAFTS
(Map p86; ☎9410613616; www.subhashemporium.com; 18/1 Gwalior Rd; ◎9.30am-7pm) Some of the pieces on display at this renowned marble shop are simply stunning. While more expensive than many other shops, you definitely get what you pay for: high-quality stone and master craftsmanship. Some of the work is decorative, but some is functional, such as tabletops, trays, lamp bases, and candle holders that glow from the flame inside.

Subhash Bazaar   MARKET
(Map p86; ◎8am-8pm Apr-Sep, 9am-8pm Oct-Mar) Skirts the northern edge of Agra's Jama Masjid and is particularly good for silks and saris.

Modern Book Depot   BOOKS
(Map p86; Sadar Bazaar; ◎10.30am-9.30pm Wed-Mon) Great selection of novels (plus Lonely Planet guides) at this friendly, 60-year-old establishment.

Khadi Gramodyog   CLOTHING
(Map p86; MG Rd; ◎11am-7pm Wed-Mon) Stocks simple, good-quality men's Indian clothing made from the homespun *khadi* fabric famously recommended by Mahatma Gandhi. There's no English sign – on Mahatma Gandhi (MG) Rd, look for the *khadi* logo of hands clasped around a mud hut.

ℹ Information

Agra is more wired than most, even in restaurants. Taj Ganj is riddled with internet cafes, most charging from ₹40 per hour.

Archaeological Survey of India Office (ASI; Map p86; ☎0562-2227261; www.asiagracircle.in; 22 The Mall; Indian/foreigner ₹540/1000; ◎9.30am-5pm Mon-Fri) The place to buy your full-moon Taj tickets. See its website for more info.

EMERGENCY

Tourist Police (☎0562-2421204; Agra Cantonment Train Station; ◎6.30am-9.30pm) The helpful crew in sky-blue uniforms are based on Fatahabad Rd, but have an office here in the Tourist Facilitation Centre. Officers also hang around the East Gate ticket office and the UP Tourism office on Taj Rd, as well as at major sites.

MEDICAL SERVICES

Amit Jaggi Memorial Hospital (Map p86; ☎0562-2230515, 9690107860; www.ajmh.in; off Minto Rd, Vibhav Nagar) If you're sick, Dr Jaggi, who runs this private clinic, is the man to see. He accepts most health-insurance plans from abroad; otherwise a visit runs ₹1000 (day) or ₹2000 (night). He'll even do house calls.

SR Hospital (Map p86; ☎0562-4025200; Laurie's Complex, Namner Rd) Agra's best private hospital.

MONEY

ATMs are everywhere. There are four close to the Taj, one near each gate (though the East Gate Axis Bank ATM is often on the fritz) and another next to the East Gate ticket office complex. If you need to change money and are worried about being swindled in Taj Ganj, there is a government-sanctioned money changer at the East Gate ticket office complex as well.

POST

India Post (Map p86; www.indiapost.gov.in; The Mall; ◎10am-5pm Mon-Fri, to 4pm Sat)

Agra's historic GPO (General Post Office) dates to 1913 and includes a handy 'facilitation office' for foreigners.

TOURIST INFORMATION

India Tourism (Map p86; ☑ 0562-2226378; www.incredibleindia.org; 191 The Mall; ☺9am-5.30pm Mon-Fri) Very helpful branch; has brochures on local and India-wide attractions.

Tourist Facilitation Centre (Taj East Gate; ☺9.30am-5pm Sat-Thu) This helpful tourist office is part of the East Gate ticket office complex at Shilpgram.

UP Tourism (☑ 0562-2421204; www.up-tourism.com; Agra Cantonment Train Station; ☺6.30am-9.30pm) The friendly train-station branch inside the Tourist Facilitation Centre on Platform 1 offers helpful advice and is where you can book day-long bus tours of Agra. This branch doubles as the Tourist Police. There's another UP Tourism (Map p86; ☑ 0562-2226431; www.uptourism.gov.in; 64 Taj Rd; ☺10am-5pm Mon-Sat) office on Taj Rd.

TRAVEL AGENCIES

Bagpacker Travel (Map p86; ☑ 9997113228; www.bagpackertravels.com; 4/62 Kutchery Rd; ☺9am-9pm) An honest agency for all your travel and transport needs, run by the friendly Anil at Tourists Rest House. English and French spoken.

❶ Getting There & Away

AIR

There are currently no commercial flights departing from Agra's Kheria Airport, but Agra will probably see better air service in the near future, as a long-planned Taj International Airport finally received approval to be built in 2016. Officials say they plan to have it operational

sometime in 2017, but it's too early to tell whether or not they'll meet that goal.

BUS

The opening of the 165km Yamuna Expressway toll highway in 2012 cut drive time from Delhi to Noida, a southeastern suburb, by 30%. Some luxury coaches now use this route and reach central Delhi faster.

Some services from **Idgah Bus Stand** (off National Hwy 2, near Sikandra):

Bharatpur (₹65, 1½ hours, every 30 minutes, 6am to 6.30pm)

Delhi Non-AC (₹180, 4½ hours, every 30 minutes, 5am to 11pm)

Fatehpur Sikri (₹40, one hour, every 30 minutes, 6am to 6.30pm)

Gwalior (₹115, three hours, hourly, 6am to 6.30pm)

Jaipur (₹262, six hours, every 30 minutes, 5am to 11pm)

Jhansi (₹215, six hours, 8.30pm and 10.30pm)

A block east of Idgah, just in front of Hotel Sakura, the **Rajasthan State Road Transport Corporation** (RSRTC; ☑ 0562-2420228; www.rsrtc.rajasthan.gov.in) runs more comfortable coaches to Jaipur throughout the day. Services include non-AC (₹256, 5½ hours, 7.30am, 10am, 1pm and 11.59pm), AC (₹440, five hours, 6.30am and 8.30am) and luxury Volvo (₹530, 4½ hours, 11.30am and 2.30pm).

From **ISBT Bus Stand** (☑ 0562-2603536), luxury Volvo coaches leave for Delhi (₹595, four hours, 7am, 1pm, 3.30pm and 6.30pm) and Lucknow (₹930, 7½ hours, 10am and 10pm); there are also standard non-AC services to Gorakhpur (₹625, 16 hours, 3.30pm and 9.30pm) and Allahabad (₹450, nine hours, 4.30am, 5.30am and 4pm) which continue on to Varanasi (₹600, 13 hours). Several classes of buses to Dehra Dun

AGRA & THE TAJ MAHAL AGRA

DELHI–AGRA TRAINS FOR DAY TRIPPERS

TRIP	TRAIN NO & NAME	FARE (₹)	DURATION (HR)	DEPARTURES
New Delhi–Agra	12002 Shatabdi Exp	550/1010 (A)	2	6am
Agra–New Delhi	12001 Shatabdi Exp	690/1050 (A)	2	9.15pm
Hazrat Nizamuddin–Agra	12280 Taj Exp	100/370 (B)	2¾	7am
Agra–Hazrat Nizamuddin	12279 Taj Exp	100/370 (B)	3	6.55pm
Hazrat Nizamuddin–Agra*	12050 Gatimaan Exp	755/1505 (A)	1¾	8.10am
Agra–Hazrat Nizamuddin*	12049 Gatimaan Exp	755/1505 (A)	1¾	5.50pm

Fares: (A) AC chair/ECC, (B) 2nd-class/AC chair; * departs Saturday to Monday

also depart from here: Volvo (₹1190, 9.30pm); AC (₹700, 4.30pm); non-AC (₹425, 7pm, 8pm, 9pm and 9.30pm). A few evening buses also run to Haridwar (AC/non-AC ₹1050/400, 10 hours), from where you can transfer to a bus for Rishikesh.

Bijli Ghar Bus Stand (Agra Fort Bus Stand; Map p86) serves Mathura (₹65, 90 minutes, every 30 minutes, 6am to 6.30pm), and also Tundla (₹35, one hour, every 30 minutes, 8am to 7pm), from where you can catch the 12382 Poorva Express train to Varanasi at 8.15pm if the trains from Agra are sold out.

Shared autos (₹10) run between Idgah and Bijli Ghar bus stands. To get to ISBT, catch an autorickshaw (₹200 to ₹250, depending on where your trip starts).

TRAIN

Most trains leave from **Agra Cantonment (Cantt) train station**, although some go from Agra Fort station. A few trains, such as Kota PNBE Express, run as slightly different numbers on different days than those listed, but timings remain the same.

Express trains are well set up for day trippers to/from Delhi but trains run to Delhi all day. If you can't reserve a seat, just buy a 'general ticket' for the next train (about ₹90), find a seat in sleeper class then upgrade when the ticket collector comes along (most of the time, he won't even make you pay any more). A new semi-express train between Delhi and Agra, the Gatimaan Express, is now up and running. It travels 160km per hour (India's fastest), a full 30km per hour faster than the Shatabdi Express.

For Orchha, catch one of the many daily trains to Jhansi (sleeper from ₹165, three hours), then take a shared auto to the bus stand (₹10), from where shared autos run all day to Orchha (₹20). An autorickshaw runs ₹200 for the same route.

If you are heading to Jaipur on Thursday, the best option is 12403/12404 ALD JP Express, departing Agra at 7.15am.

ⓘ Getting Around

AUTORICKSHAW

Just outside Agra Cantt station is the **prepaid autorickshaw booth** (⊙24hr), which gives you a good guide for haggling elsewhere. Usually, trips shorter than 3km should not cost more than ₹50. Always agree on the fare before entering the rickshaw.

Sample prices from Agra Cantt station: Fatahabad Rd ₹150; ISBT bus stand ₹200; Sadar Bazaar ₹70; Sikandra ₹400; Taj Mahal (Taj West Gate) ₹100, Taj South Gate ₹130, Shilpgram (Taj East Gate) ₹150; half-day (four-hour) Agra tour ₹400; full-day (eight-hour) Agra tour ₹600. If you just want to shoot to the Taj and back with waiting time, they will charge ₹250. Note: autorickshaws aren't allowed to go to Fatehpur Sikri.

CYCLE-RICKSHAW

Prices from the Taj Mahal's South Gate: Agra Cantt train station ₹80; Agra Fort ₹40; Biili Ghar bus stand ₹50; Fatahabad Rd ₹30; Kinari Bazaar ₹100; Sadar Bazaar ₹50; half-day tour ₹400. Tack on another ₹10 to ₹20 if two people are riding.

TAXI

Outside Agra Cantt the **prepaid taxi booth** (⊙24hr) gives a good idea of what taxis should cost. Non-AC prices: Delhi ₹3500; Fatahabad Rd ₹200; Sadar Bazaar ₹100; Taj Mahal ₹200; half-day (four-hour) tour ₹750; full-day (eight-

MORE HANDY TRAINS FROM AGRA

DESTINATION	TRAIN NO & NAME	FARE (₹)	DURATION (HR)	DEPARTURES
Gorakhpur*	19037/9 Avadh Exp	335/910/1305 (A)	15¾	10pm
Jaipur*	12036 Shatabdi Exp	660/1225 (C)	3½	5.40pm (except Thu)
Khajuraho	12448 UP Sampark Kranti	280/720/1010 (A)	7½	11.10pm
Kolkata (Howrah)	13008 UA Toofan Exp	555/1500 (B)	31	12.15pm
Lucknow	12180 LJN Intercity	145/515 (D)	6	5.50am
Mumbai (CST)	12138/7 Punjab Mail	580/1530/2215 (A)	23	8.35am
Varanasi*	14854/64/66 Marudhar Exp	340/930/1335 (A)	14	8.30pm

Fares: (A) sleeper/3AC/2AC, (B) sleeper/3AC only, (C) AC chair/ECC, (D) 2nd-class/AC chair;
* leaves from Agra Fort station

DANCING BEAR RETIREMENT HOME

For hundreds of years, sloth bear cubs were stolen from their mothers (who were often killed) and forced through painful persuasion to become 'dancing bears', entertaining kings and crowds with their fancy footwork. In 1996, Wildlife SOS (www.wildlifesos.org) – an animal rescue organisation that is often called around Agra to humanely remove pythons and cobras from local homes – began efforts to emancipate all of India's 1200 or so dancing bears. By 2009, nearly all were freed, and more than 200 of them live at the Agra Bear Rescue Facility (☑9756205080; www.wildlifesos.org; Sur Sarovar Bird Sanctuary; 2hr/full day ₹2000/₹4000; ☺9am-4pm), inside Sur Sarovar Bird Sanctuary, 30km outside of Agra on the road to Delhi.

Visitors are welcome to tour the park-like grounds and watch the bears enjoying their new, better lives. Wildlife SOS also runs a refuge for rescued circus elephants (two-hour/full day ₹1500/₹3000), closer to Mathura, which is more hands-on, as you can feed and walk with the elephants. Email or phone in advance to arrange visits.

hour) tour ₹1000. Prices here do not include the ₹10 booking fee and tolls or parking charges (if applicable).

Around Agra

Fatehpur Sikri

☑05613 / POP 30,000

This magnificent fortified ancient city, 40km west of Agra, was the short-lived capital of the Mughal empire between 1572 and 1585, during the reign of Emperor Akbar. Earlier, Akbar had visited the village of Sikri to consult the Sufi saint Shaikh Salim Chishti, who predicted the birth of an heir to the Mughal throne. When the prophecy came true, Akbar built his new capital here, including a stunning mosque, still in use today, and three palaces, one for each of his favourite wives – one a Hindu, one a Muslim and one a Christian (though Hindu villagers in Sikri dispute these claims). The city was an Indo-Islamic masterpiece, but erected in an area that supposedly suffered from water shortages and so was abandoned shortly after Akbar's death.

It's easy to visit this World Heritage Site as a day trip from Agra, but there are a couple of decent places to stay. In addition to the main attractions, the colourful bazaar in the village of Fatehpur, just below the ruins, as well as the small village of Sikri, a few kilometres north, are worth exploring.

The palace buildings lie beside the Jama Masjid mosque. Both sit on top of a ridge that runs between Fatehpur and Sikri. The red-sandstone palace walls are at their most atmospheric and photogenic near sunset.

⊙ Sights

Jama Masjid   MOSQUE

This beautiful, immense mosque was completed in 1571 and contains elements of Persian and Indian design. The main entrance, at the top of a flight of stone steps, is through the spectacular 54m-high Buland Darwaza (Victory Gate), built to commemorate Akbar's military victory in Gujarat. Inside is the stunning white marble tomb of Sufi saint Shaikh Salim Chishti, where women hoping to have children come to tie a thread to the *jalis* (carved lattice screens).

The saint's tomb was completed in 1581 and is entered through an original door made of ebony. Inside it are brightly coloured flower murals, while the sandlewood canopy is decorated with mother-of-pearl shell, and the marble *jalis* are among the finest in India. To the right of the tomb lie the gravestones of family members of Shaikh Salim Chishti and nearby is the entrance to an underground tunnel (barred by a locked gate) that reputedly goes all the way to Agra Fort. Behind the entrance to the tunnel, on the far wall, are three holes, part of the ancient ventilation system; you can still feel the rush of cool air forcing its way through them. Just east of Shaikh Salim Chishti's tomb is the red-sandstone tomb of Islam Khan, the final resting place of Shaikh Salim Chishti's grandson and one-time governor of Bengal.

On the east wall of the courtyard is a smaller entrance to the mosque – the Shahi Darwaza (King's Gate), which leads to the palace complex.

Palaces & Pavilions   PALACE

(Indian/foreigner ₹40/510, video ₹25; ☺dawn-dusk) The main sight at Fatehpur Sikri is the

Fatehpur Sikri

A WALKING TOUR OF FATEHPUR SIKRI

You can enter this fortified ancient city from two entrances, but the northeast entrance at Diwan-i-Am (Hall of Public Audiences) offers the most logical approach to this remarkable Unesco World Heritage site. This large courtyard (now a garden) is where Emperor Akbar presided over the trials of accused criminals. Once through the ticket gate, you are in the northern end of the **❶ Pachisi Courtyard**. The first building you see is **❷ Diwan-i-Khas** (Hall of Private Audiences), the interior of which is dominated by a magnificently carved central stone column. Pitch south and enter **❸ Rumi Sultana**, a small but elegant palace built for Akbar's Turkish Muslim wife. It's hard to miss the **❹ Ornamental Pool** nearby – its southwest corner provides Fatehpur Sikri's most photogenic angle, perfectly framing its most striking building, the five-storey Panch Mahal, one of the gateways to the Imperial Harem Complex, where the **❺ Lower Haramsara** once housed more than 200 female servants. Wander around the Palace of Jodh Bai and take notice of the towering ode to an elephant, the 21m-high **❻ Hiran Minar**, in the distance to the northwest. Leave the palaces and pavilions area via Shahi Darwaza (King's Gate), which spills into India's second-largest mosque courtyard at **❼ Jama Masjid**. Inside this immense and gorgeous mosque is the sacred **❽ Tomb of Shaikh Salim Chishti**. Exit through the spectacular **❾ Buland Darwaza** (Victory Gate), one of the world's most magnificent gateways.

Buland Darwaza
Most tours end with an exit through Jama Masjid's Victory Gate. Walk out and take a look behind you: Behold! The magnificent 15-storey sandstone gate, 54m high, is a menacing monolith to Akbar's reign.

Shahi
Darwaza
(King's Gate)

Tomb of Shaikh Salim Chishti
Each knot in the strings tied to the 56 carved white marble designs of the interior walls of Shaikh Salim Chishti's tomb represents one wish of a maximum three.

Jama Masjid
The elaborate marble inlay work at the Badshahi Gate and throughout the Jama Masjid complex is said to have inspired similar work 82 years later at the Taj Mahal in Agra.

Hiran Minar

This bizarre, seldom-visited tower off the north-west corner of Fatehpur Sikri is decorated with hundreds of stone representations of elephant tusks. It is said to be the place where Minar, Akbar's favourite execution elephant, died.

Pachisi Courtyard

Under your feet just past Rumi Sultana is the Pachisi Courtyard where Akbar is said to have played the game *pachisi* (an ancient version of ludo) using slave girls in colourful dress as pieces.

Diwan-i-Khas

Emperor Akbar modified the central stone column inside Diwan-i-Khas to call attention to a new religion he called Din-i-Ilahi (God is One). The intricately carved column features a fusion of Hindu, Muslim, Christian and Buddhist imagery.

Panch Mahal

Diwan-i-Am (Hall of Public Audiences)

Rumi Sultana

Don't miss the headless creatures carved into Rumi Sultana's palace interiors: a lion, deer, an eagle and a few peacocks were beheaded by jewel thieves who swiped the precious jewels that originally formed their heads.

Ornamental Pool

Tansen, said to be the most gifted Indian vocalist of all time and one of Akbar's treasured nine *Navaratnas* (Gems), would be showered with coins during performances from the central platform of the Ornamental Pool.

Lower Haramsara

Akbar reportedly kept more than 5000 concubines, but the 200 or so female servants housed in the Lower Haramsara were strictly business. Knots were tied to these sandstone rings to support partitions between their individual quarters.

stunning imperial complex of pavilions and palaces spread among a large, abandoned 'city' peppered with Mughal masterpieces: courtyards, intricate carvings, servants quarters, vast gateways and ornamental pools.

A large courtyard dominates the northeast entrance at Diwan-i-Am (Hall of Public Audiences). Now a pristinely manicured garden, this is where Akbar presided over the courts – from the middle seat of the five equal seatings along the western wall, flanked by his advisors. It was built to utilise an echo sound system, so Akbar could hear anything at any time from anywhere in the open space. Justice was dealt with swiftly if legends are to be believed, with public executions said to have been carried out here by elephants trampling convicted criminals to death.

The Diwan-i-Khas (Hall of Private Audiences), found at the northern end of the Pachisi Courtyard, looks nothing special from the outside, but the interior is dominated by a magnificently carved stone central column. This pillar flares to create a flat-topped plinth linked to the four corners of the room by narrow stone bridges. From this plinth Akbar is believed to have debated with scholars and ministers who stood at the ends of the four bridges.

Next to Diwan-i-Khas is the Treasury, which houses secret stone safes in some corners (one has been left with its stone lid open for visitors to see). Sea monsters carved on the ceiling struts were there to protect the fabulous wealth once stored here. The so-called Astrologer's Kiosk in front has roof supports carved in a serpentine Jain style.

Just south of the Astrologer's Kiosk is Pachisi Courtyard, named after the ancient game known in India today as ludo. The large, plus-shaped game board is visible surrounding the block in the middle of the courtyard. In the southeast corner is the most intricately carved structure in the whole complex, the tiny but elegant Rumi Sultana, which was said to be the palace built for Akbar's Turkish Muslim wife. Other theories say it was used by Akbar himself as a palace powder room or for a rest break during court sessions. On one corner of the Ladies Garden just west of Pachisi is the impressive Panch Mahal, a pavilion with five storeys that decrease in size until the top consists of only a tiny kiosk. The lower floor has 84 different columns; in total there are 176 columns.

Continuing anticlockwise will bring you to the Ornamental Pool. Here, singers and musicians would perform on the platform above the water while Akbar watched from the pavilion in his private quarters, known as Daulat Khana (Abode of Fortune). Behind the pavilion is the Khwabgah (Dream House), a sleeping area with a huge stone bunk bed. Nowadays the only ones sleeping here are bats, hanging from the ceiling; the small room in the far corner is full of them.

Heading west from the Ornamental Pool reveals the Palace of Jodh Bai, and the one-time home of Akbar's Hindu wife, said to be his favourite. Set around an enormous courtyard, it blends traditional Indian columns, Islamic cupolas and turquoise-blue Persian roof tiles. Just outside, to the left of Jodh Bai's former kitchen, is the Palace of the Christian Wife. This was used by Akbar's Goan wife Mariam, who gave birth to Jehangir here in 1569. (Some believe Akbar never had a Christian wife and that Mariam was short for Mariam-Ut-Zamani, a title he gave to Jodh Bai meaning 'Beautiful like a Rose', or 'Most Beautiful Woman on Earth'.) Like many of the buildings in the palace complex, it contains elements of different religions, as befitted Akbar's tolerant religious beliefs. The domed ceiling is Islamic in style, while remnants of a wall painting of the Hindu god Shiva can also be found.

Walking past the Palace of the Christian Wife once more will take you west to Birbal Bhavan, ornately carved inside and out, and thought to have been the living quarters of one of Akbar's most senior ministers. The Lower Haramsara, just to the south, housed Akbar's large number of live-in female servants.

Plenty of ruins are scattered behind the whole complex, including the Caravanserai, a vast courtyard surrounded by rooms where visiting merchants stayed. Badly defaced carvings of elephants still guard Hathi Pol (Elephant Gate), while the remains of the small Stonecutters' Mosque and a hammam (bath) are also a short stroll away. Other unnamed ruins can be explored north of what is known as the Mint but is thought to have in fact been stables, including some in the interesting village of Sikri to the north.

Archaeological Museum   MUSEUM
(near Diwan-i-Am; ⊙9am-5pm Sat-Thu) FREE
Inaugurated in 2014 inside Akbar's former

Treasury house, this museum about 100m from Diwan-i-Am showcases pre-Mughal artefacts excavated over many years at Fatehpur Sikri. Small but well presented, highlights include a few remarkably preserved sandstone Jain *tirthankars* (the 24 holy Jain supreme beings) dating between AD 982 and 1034.

Tours

Official Archaeological Society of India guides can be hired from the ticket office for ₹450 (English), but they aren't always the most knowledgeable (some are guides thanks to birthright rather than qualifications). The best guides are available in Agra, and charge ₹750. Our favourite is Pankaj Bhatnagar (☑ 8126995552; ₹750); he prefers to be messaged on WhatsApp.

Sleeping & Eating

Fatehpur Sikri's culinary specialty is *khataie,* the biscuits you can see piled high in the bazaar. For restaurants, head to one of the hotels.

Hotel Goverdhan   HOTEL **$**
(☑ 05613-282643; www.hotelfatehpursikriviews. com; Agra Rd; r ₹750-950, with AC ₹1300; ✽ @ 🛜) There are a variety of rooms at this old-time favourite, all of which surround a very well-kept garden. There's a communal balcony and terrace seating, free wi-fi, new beds in every room, air-coolers in the non-ACs and CCTV. The restaurant does decent work as well (meals ₹70 to ₹180).

Hotel Ajay Palace   GUESTHOUSE **$**
(☑ 9548801213; Agra Rd; r ₹500) This friendly family-run guesthouse isn't pretty but offers a few very simple and cheap double rooms with marble floors and sit-down flush toilets. It's also a very popular lunch stop (mains ₹50 to ₹150). Sit on the rooftop at the large, elongated marble table and enjoy a view of the village streets with the Jama Masjid towering above.

Note that it's not 'Ajay Restaurant By Near Palace' at the bus stand – it's 50m further along the road.

ⓘ Information

DANGERS & ANNOYANCES
Take no notice of anyone who gets on the Fatehpur Sikri–Agra bus before the final stop at Idgah Bus Stand, telling you that you have arrived at the city centre or the Taj Mahal. You haven't. You're still a long autorickshaw ride away, and the man trying to tease you off the bus is – surprise surprise – an autorickshaw driver.

ⓘ Getting There & Around

From the Fatehpur bus stand, buses run to Agra's **Idgah Bus Stand** (p95) every half-hour (₹40) from 5.30am to 6.30pm. If you miss those, walk 1km to Agra Gate and another 350m to Bypass Crossing Stop on the main road and wave down an Agra-bound bus. They pass every 30 minutes or so, day and night.

For Bharatpur (₹25, 40 minutes) or Jaipur (₹190, 4½ hours), wave down a westbound bus from Bypass Crossing Stop.

Regular trains for Agra Fort Station leave Fatehpur Sikri at 4.43am (59811 Haldighati Pass) and 8.16pm (19037/9 Avadh Express), but there are simpler passenger trains at 10.14am and 3.54pm, as well as four other trains that fly through at various times. Just buy a 'general' ticket at the station and pile in (₹20, one to two hours).

GLEN ALLISON / GETTY IMAGES ©

1. Colourful Rajasthani bangles, Pushkar (p138) 2. Detail of elephant parade in mural, Udaipur (p154) 3. Women in Jodhpur (p176), the 'Blue City' 4. Handmade carpets, Jodhpur (p176)

Rajasthani Colour

MAX PADDLER / GETTY IMAGES ©

The most vivid impression on visitors to Rajasthan is that of colour: brilliant, bright tribal dress, glittering gold jewellery and rainbow-coloured bangles adorn the locals and illuminate the bazaars. Inside the palaces, *havelis* (traditional residences) and even humble homes, this trend continues.

The people of Rajasthan have a passion for decoration, having taken advantage of their position on trade routes to acquire artistic skills from many lands. This passion is evident in the manifold variations of Rajasthani turbans and in the attire of the state's women, from their block-printed *odhnis* (headscarves) right down to their brilliantly embroidered jootis (leather shoes). Utilitarian items are transported into the world of art with ceramics such as the famous blue-glazed pottery from Jaipur.

Tie-dyed, block-printed and embroidered textiles and hand-woven carpets are functional yet decorative and colourful. Traditionally, all Rajasthan's textile colours were derived from natural sources such as vegetables, minerals and even insects. Yellow, for instance, came from turmeric and buttermilk; green from banana leaves; orange from saffron and jasmine; blue from the indigo plant; and purple from the kermes insect. Today, however, the majority are synthetically dyed; while they may not possess the subtlety of the traditional tones, they will, at least, stand a better chance in a 40°C machine wash.

BEST PLACES TO SEE...

Block-printed textiles Sanganer

Blue pottery Jaipur

Carpets Jaipur

Embroidery Jaisalmer

Jewellery Jaipur

Miniature Paintings Udaipur

1. **Rajasthani textiles (p233)**
Vibrantly dyed saris drying in the open air.

2. **City Palace, Jaipur (p107)**
Detail of the Peacock Gate at Pitam Niwas Chowk (p111).

3. **Block printing**
A craftsman uses the traditional method of block printing Rajasthani fabrics.

4. **Henna decoration**
Intricate henna designs and bridal jewellery at a wedding in Jaipur.

Rajasthan

Includes ➜
Jaipur 107
Bharatpur & Keoladeo
National Park 128
Pushkar 138
Ranthambhore
National Park 143
Bundi 145
Chittorgarh
(Chittor). 151
Udaipur 154
Mt Abu 167
Jodhpur 176
Jaisalmer 186
Bikaner. 196

Best Forts & Palaces

➜ Jaisalmer (p186)

➜ Jodhpur (p176)

➜ Bundi (p145)

➜ Chittorgarh (p151)

Best Heritage Hotels

➜ Rambagh Palace (p119)

➜ Pal Haveli (p181)

➜ Taj Lake Palace (p161)

➜ Bundi Vilas (p148)

➜ Laxmi Niwas Palace (p200)

Why Go?

It is said there is more history in Rajasthan than in the rest of India put together. Welcome to the Land of the Kings – a realm of maharajas, majestic forts and lavish palaces. India is littered with splendid architecture, but nowhere will you find fortresses quite as magnificent as those in Rajasthan, rising up imperiously from the landscape like fairy-tale mirages or adventure movie sets.

As enchanting as they are, though, there is more to this most royal of regions than its architectural wonders. This is also a land of sand dunes and jungle, of camel trains and wild tigers, of glittering jewels, vivid colours and vibrant culture. There are enough colourful festivals here to fill a calendar, while the shopping and cuisine are nothing short of spectacular. In truth, Rajasthan just about has it all – it is the must-see state of India, brimming with startling, thought-provoking and, ultimately, unforgettable attractions.

When to Go
Jaipur

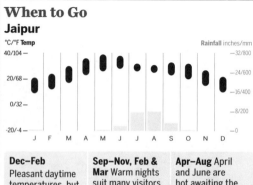

Dec–Feb
Pleasant daytime temperatures, but can get cold at night. Peak tourists, peak prices.

Sep–Nov, Feb & Mar Warm nights suit many visitors fleeing colder climes.

Apr–Aug April and June are hot awaiting the monsoon, which brings the rain in July and August.

History

Rajasthan is the ancestral home of the Rajputs, warrior clans who claim to originate from the sun, moon and fire, and who have controlled this part of India for more than 1000 years. While they forged marriages of convenience and temporary alliances, pride and independence were always paramount, and this lack of unity led to the Rajputs becoming vassals of the Mughal empire.

Mughal rule of Rajasthan was marked by rebellion, uprisings and tragedy, as whole cities committed *jauhar* (ritual mass suicide) rather than submit to the Mughals. Nevertheless, As the Mughal empire declined, the Rajputs clawed back their independence and signed treaties with the British allowing individual Rajput kingdoms to operate as independent princely states under the umbrella of British rule.

At Independence, Rajasthan's many maharajas were allowed to keep their titles and property holdings and were paid an annual stipend commensurate with their status to secure their participation in the union. However, this favourable arrangement lapsed in the 1970s and Rajasthan submitted fully to central control.

EASTERN RAJASTHAN

Jaipur

📞 0141 / POP 3.05 MILLION

Enthralling, historical Jaipur, Rajasthan's capital, is the gateway to India's most flamboyant state.

The city's colourful, chaotic streets ebb and flow with a heady brew of old and new. Careering buses dodge dawdling camels, leisurely cycle-rickshaws frustrate swarms of motorbikes, and everywhere buzzing autorickshaws watch for easy prey. In the midst of this mayhem, the splendours of Jaipur's majestic past are islands of relative calm evoking a different pace and another world.

At the city's heart, the City Palace continues to house the former royal family; the Jantar Mantar, the royal observatory, maintains a heavenly aspect; and the honeycomb Hawa Mahal gazes on the bazaar below. And just out of sight, in the arid hill country surrounding the city, is the fairy-tale grandeur of Amber Fort, Jaipur's star attraction.

History

Jaipur is named after its founder, the great warrior-astronomer Jai Singh II (1688–1743), who came to power at age 11 after the death of his father, Maharaja Bishan Singh. Jai Singh could trace his lineage back to the Rajput clan of Kachhwahas, who consolidated their power in the 12th century. Their capital was at Amber (pronounced 'amer'), about 11km northeast of present-day Jaipur, where they built the impressive Amber Fort.

The kingdom grew wealthier and wealthier, and this, plus the need to accommodate the burgeoning population and a paucity of water at the old capital at Amber, prompted the maharaja in 1727 to commence work on a new city – Jaipur.

Northern India's first planned city, it was a collaborative effort using Singh's vision and the impressive expertise of his chief architect, Vidyadhar Bhattacharya. Jai Singh's grounding in the sciences is reflected in the precise symmetry of the new city.

In 1876 Maharaja Ram Singh had the entire Old City painted pink (traditionally the colour of hospitality) to welcome the Prince of Wales (later King Edward VII). Today all residents of the Old City are compelled by law to preserve the pink facade.

👁 Sights

Old City (Pink City)

The Old City (often referred to as the Pink City) is both a marvel of 18th-century town planning, and a place you could spend days exploring – it's the beating heart of Jaipur.

Avenues divide the Pink City into neat rectangles, each specialising in certain crafts, as ordained in the Shilpa Shastra (ancient Hindu texts). The main bazaars in the Old City include Johari Bazaar, Tripolia Bazaar, Bapu Bazaar and Chandpol Bazaar.

The whole is partially encircled by a crenellated wall punctuated at intervals by grand gateways. The major gates are Chandpol (*pol* means 'gate'), Ajmer Gate and Sanganeri Gate.

⭐ **City Palace** PALACE

(📞0141-4088888; www.royaljaipur.in; Indian/foreigner incl camera ₹130/500, guide from ₹300, audio guide free, Royal Grandeur tour Indian/foreigner ₹2000/2500; ⊙9.30am-5pm) A complex of courtyards, gardens and buildings, the impressive City Palace is right in the centre of the Old City. The outer wall was

Rajasthan Highlights

① Jaisalmer (p186)
Wandering the bustling alleys of the honey-coloured fort, then riding a camel among desert dunes.

② Pushkar (p138)
Making a lakeside pilgrimage to Rajasthan's holiest town.

③ Ranthambhore National Park (p143)
Searching for tigers in the ravines and forests.

④ Mehrangarh (p177) Taking in the views of the Blue City from the imposing ramparts of Jodhpur's mighty fortress.

⑤ Udaipur (p154)
Kicking back in Rajasthan's romantic idyll with palaces and a picturesque lake.

⑥ Pink City (p107)
Wandering the colourful bazaars of Jaipur and the marvellous Amber Fort.

⑦ Bundi (p145)
Resting up in this town with its low-key backpacker vibe, fairy-tale palace and a solemn fort.

⑧ Shekhawati (p175) Admiring the whimsical frescos adorning the crumbling havelis.

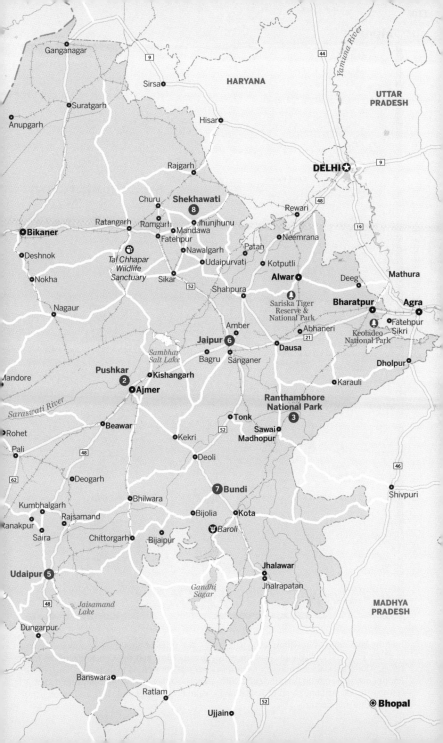

Jaipur

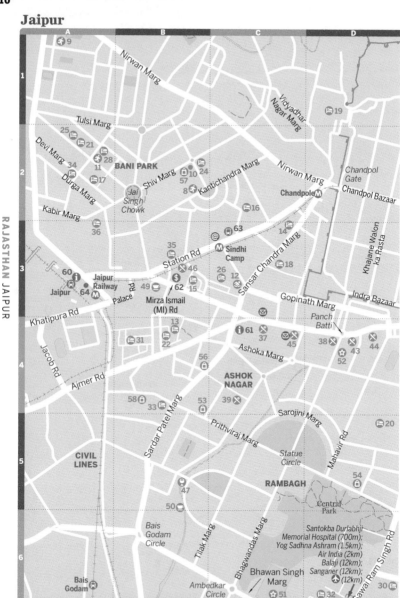

built by Jai Singh II, but within it the palace has been enlarged and adapted over the centuries. There are palace buildings from different eras, some dating from the early 20th century. It is a striking blend of Rajasthani and Mughal architecture.

The price of admission includes entry to Royal Gaitor and the Cenotaphs of the Maharanis, as well as to Jaigarh, a long climb above Amber Fort. This composite ticket is valid for two days and costs Indians an extra

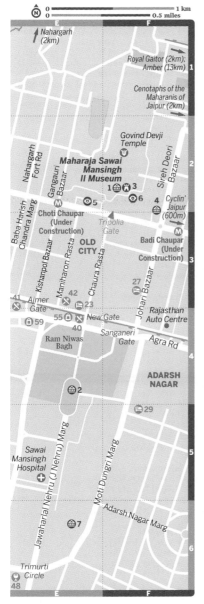

RAJASTHAN JAIPUR

Singh II as a reception centre for visiting dignitaries. Its multiarched and colonnaded construction was cooked up in an Islamic, Rajput and European stylistic stew by the architect Sir Swinton Jacob. It now forms part of the **Maharaja Sawai Mansingh II Museum**, containing a collection of royal costumes and superb shawls, including Kashmiri pashmina. One remarkable exhibit is Sawai Madho Singh I's capacious clothing; it's said he was a cuddly 2m tall, 1.2m wide and 250kg.

➡ The Armoury

The Anand Mahal Sileg Khana – the Maharani's Palace – houses the Armoury, which has one of the best collections of weapons in the country. Many of the ceremonial items are elegantly engraved and inlaid, belying their grisly purpose.

➡ Diwan-i-Khas (Sarvatobhadra)

Set between the Armoury and the Diwan-i-Am art gallery is an open courtyard known in Sanskrit as Sarvatobhadra. At its centre is a pink-and-white, marble-paved gallery that was used as the Diwan-i-Khas (Hall of Private Audience), where the maharajas would consult their ministers. Here you can see two enormous silver vessels, each 1.6m tall and reputedly the largest silver objects in the world.

➡ Diwan-i-Am Art Gallery

Within the lavish Diwan-i-Am (Hall of Public Audience) is this art gallery. Exhibits include a copy of the entire Bhagavad Gita (scripture) handwritten in tiny script, and miniature copies of other holy Hindu scriptures, which were small enough to be easily hidden in the event that zealot Mughal armies tried to destroy the sacred texts.

➡ Pitam Niwas Chowk & Chandra Mahal

Located towards the palace's inner courtyard is Pitam Niwas Chowk. Here four glorious gates represent the seasons – the **Peacock Gate** depicts autumn, the **Lotus Gate** signifies summer, the **Green Gate** represents spring, and finally the **Rose Gate** embodies winter.

Beyond this *chowk* (square) is the private palace, the Chandra Mahal, which is still the residence of the descendants of the royal family and where you can take a 45-minute **Royal Grandeur guided tour** of select areas.

★ Jantar Mantar HISTORIC SITE
(Indian/foreigner ₹50/200, guide ₹200, audio guide ₹100; ⊙9am-4.30pm) Adjacent to the

₹60 on top of City Palace entry (no extra cost for foreigners).

➡ Mubarak Mahal

Entering through Virendra Pol, you'll see the Mubarak Mahal (Welcome Palace), built in the late 19th century for Maharaja Madho

Jaipur

◉ Top Sights
1 Maharaja Sawai Mansingh II
Museum F2

◉ Sights
2 Central Museum E4
3 City Palace...F2
4 Hawa Mahal...F2
5 Iswari Minar Swarga Sal.......................E2
6 Jantar Mantar..F2
7 SRC Museum of Indology.....................E6

◎ Activities, Courses & Tours
8 Charak Ayurveda B2
9 Kerala Ayurveda Kendra.......................A1
10 Kripal Kumbh.. B2
11 Madhavanand Girls College..................A2
12 Mansingh Hotel.....................................C3
RTDC .... (see 60)
Vintage Jeep Tour......................... (see 31)

◎ Sleeping
13 All Seasons Homestay B4
14 Alsisar Haveli...C3
15 Atithi Guest House............................... B3
16 Dera Rawatsar.......................................C2
17 Hotel Anuraag Villa A2
18 Hotel Arya Niwas C3
19 Hotel Bissau Palace...............................D1
20 Hotel Diggi Palace................................ D5
21 Hotel Meghniwas A2
22 Hotel Pearl Palace B4
23 Hotel Sweet Dream E3
24 Jaipur Inn.. B2
25 Jas Vilas A2
26 Karni Niwas..C3
27 LMB Hotel...F3
28 Madhuban... A2
29 Nana-ki-Haveli.......................................F5
30 Narain Niwas Palace Hotel D6
31 Pearl Palace Heritage........................... B4
32 Rambagh Palace.................................... D6
33 Roadhouse Hostel Jaipur B4
34 Shahpura House A2
35 Tony Guest House B3
36 Vinayak Guest House A3

◎ Eating
Anokhi Café ....(see 53)
37 Copper Chimney.....................................C4
38 Dāsaprakash..D4

39 Four Seasons C4
40 Ganesh Restaurant E4
Handi Restaurant .... (see 37)
Hotel Sweet Dream.......................(see 23)
41 Indian Coffee House...............................E3
Jaipur Modern Kitchen .... (see 56)
Jal Mahal.......................................(see 43)
Little Italy.......................................(see 53)
LMB ....(see 27)
42 Mohan E3
43 Natraj D4
44 Niro's... D4
45 Old Takeaway the Kebab Shop C4
Peacock Rooftop Restaurant ...... (see 22)
46 Rawat Kachori.. B3
Surya Mahal ....(see 43)

◎ Drinking & Nightlife
47 100% Rock.. B5
48 Bar Palladio E6
49 Café Coffee Day.................................... B3
50 Curious Life... B5
Lassiwala ....(see 43)
Polo Bar ....(see 32)

◎ Entertainment
51 Polo Ground C6
52 Raj Mandir Cinema............................... D4

◎ Shopping
53 Anokhi.. B4
Crossword .... (see 53)
54 Fabindia... D5
55 Gem-Testing Laboratory.......................E4
Inde Rooh .... (see 22)
56 Jaipur Modern....................................... B4
57 Kripal Kumbh... B2
58 Mojari... B4
59 Rajasthali...E4
Silver Shop .... (see 22)

ⓘ Information
60 RTDC Tourist Office.............................. A3
RTDC Tourist Office.....................(see 63)
61 RTDC Tourist Office Main branch.........C4
62 Thomas Cook... B3

ⓘ Transport
63 Main Bus Station C3
Reservation Office.........................(see 63)
64 Reservation Office................................. A3

City Palace is Jantar Mantar, an observatory begun by Jai Singh II in 1728 that resembles a collection of bizarre giant sculptures. Built for measuring the heavens, the name is derived from the Sanskrit *yanta mantr,* meaning 'instrument of calculation', and in 2010 it was added to India's list of Unesco World Heritage Sites. Paying for a local guide is highly recommended if you wish to learn how each fascinating instrument works.

Jai Singh liked astronomy even more than he liked war and town planning. Before constructing the observatory he sent scholars abroad to study foreign constructs. He built five observatories in total, and this is the largest and best preserved (it was restored in 1901). Others are in Delhi, Varanasi and Ujjain. No traces of the fifth, the Mathura observatory, remain.

A valid Amber Fort/Hawa Mahal composite ticket will also gain you entry.

★**Hawa Mahal**   HISTORIC BUILDING
(Sireh Deori Bazaar; Indian/foreigner incl camera ₹50/200, guide ₹200, audio guide Hindi/English ₹115/170; ⊘9am-5.30pm) Jaipur's most distinctive landmark, the Hawa Mahal is an extraordinary pink-painted delicately honeycombed hive that rises a dizzying five storeys. It was constructed in 1799 by Maharaja Sawai Pratap Singh to enable ladies of the royal household to watch the life and processions of the city. The top offers stunning views over Jantar Mantar and the City Palace in one direction and over Sireh Deori Bazaar in the other.

There's a small museum (open Saturday to Thursday), with miniature paintings and some rich relics, such as ceremonial armour, which help evoke the royal past.

Claustrophobes should be aware that the narrow corridors can sometimes get extremely cramped and crowded inside the Hawa Mahal.

Entrance is from the back of the complex. To get here, return to the intersection on your left as you face the Hawa Mahal, turn right and then take the first right again through an archway. Shopkeepers can show you another way – past their shops!

A valid Amber Fort composite ticket will also gain you entry.

◉ New City

By the mid-19th century it became obvious that the well-planned city was bulging at the seams. During the reign of Maharaja Ram Singh (1835–80) the seams ruptured and the city burst out beyond its walls. Civic facilities, such as a postal system and piped water, were introduced. This period gave rise to a part of town very different from the bazaars of the Old City, with wide boulevards, landscaped grounds and grand European-influenced buildings.

Central Museum   MUSEUM
(Albert Hall; J Nehru Marg; Indian/foreigner ₹40/300, audio guide Hindi/English ₹115/175; ⊘9am-6pm) This museum is housed in the spectacularly florid Albert Hall, south of the Old City. The building was designed by Sir Swinton Jacob, and combines elements of English and North Indian architecture, as

HEAVEN-PIERCING MINARET

Piercing the skyline near the City Palace is this unusual minaret, **Iswari Minar Swarga Sal** (Heaven-Piercing Minaret; Indian/foreigner ₹50/200; ⊘9am-4.30pm) erected in the 1740s by Jai Singh II's son and successor Iswari. The entrance is around the back of the row of shops fronting Chandpol Bazaar – take the alley 50m west of the minaret along the bazaar or go via the Atishpol entrance to the City Palace compound, 150m east of the minaret. You can spiral to the top of the minaret for excellent views.

Iswari ignominiously killed himself by snakebite (in the Chandra Mahal) rather than face the advancing Maratha army – his 21 wives and concubines then did the necessary noble thing and committed *jauhar* (ritual mass suicide by immolation) on his funeral pyre.

A valid Amber Fort/Hawa Mahal composite ticket will also gain you entry.

well as huge friezes celebrating the world's great cultures. It was known as the pride of the new Jaipur when it opened in 1887. The grand old building hosts an eclectic array of tribal dress, dioramas, sculptures, miniature paintings, carpets, musical instruments and even an Egyptian mummy.

SRC Museum of Indology   MUSEUM
(24 Gangwell Park, Prachyavidya Path; Indian/foreigner incl guide ₹40/100; ⊘8am-6pm) This ramshackle, dusty treasure trove is an extraordinary private collection. It contains folk-art objects and other pieces – there's everything from a manuscript written by Aurangzeb and a 200-year-old mirror work swing from Bikaner to a glass bed (for a short queen). The museum is signposted off J Nehru Barg.

◉ City Edge

Surrounding the city are several historic sites including forts, temples, palaces and gardens. Some of these can be visited on the way to Amber Fort.

Nahargarh   FORT
(Tiger Fort; Indian/foreigner ₹50/200; ⊘10am-5pm) Built in 1734 and extended in 1868, this sturdy fort overlooks the city from a sheer ridge to the north. The story goes that the

fort was named after Nahar Singh, a dead prince whose restless spirit was disrupting construction. Whatever was built in the day crumbled in the night. The prince agreed to leave on condition that the fort was named for him. The views are glorious and there's a restaurant that's perfect for a beer.

The best way to visit is to walk or take a cycle-rickshaw (₹50 from MI Rd) to the end of Nahargarh Fort Rd, then climb the steep, winding 2km path to the top. To drive, you have to detour via the Amber area in a circuitous 8km round trip.

A valid Amber Fort/Hawa Mahal composite ticket will also gain you entry.

Royal Gaitor   HISTORIC SITE
(Gatore ki Chhatriyan; Indian/foreigner ₹40/100; ⊘9am-5pm) The royal cenotaphs, just outside the city walls, beneath Nahargarh, are an appropriately restful place to visit and feel remarkably undiscovered. The stone monuments are beautifully and intricately carved. Maharajas Pratap Singh, Madho Singh II and Jai Singh II, among others, are honoured here. Jai Singh II has the most impressive marble cenotaph, with a dome supported by 20 carved pillars.

Jal Mahal   HISTORIC BUILDING
(Water Palace; ⊘closed to the public) Near the cenotaphs of the maharanis of Jaipur, and beautifully situated in the watery expanse of Man Sagar, is this dreamlike palace. It's origins are uncertain, but it was believed to have been extensively restored if not built by Jai Singh II (1734). It's accessed via a causeway at the rear, and is undergoing restoration under the auspices of the Jal Tarang (www.jaltarang.in) project.

Cenotaphs of the
Maharanis of Jaipur   HISTORIC SITE
(Maharani ki Chhatri; Amber Rd; Indian/foreigner ₹40/100; ⊘9am-5pm) Located between Jaipur and Amber, 5km from the centre, the cenotaphs of the maharanis of Jaipur are worth a visit for a stroll.

Galta   HINDU TEMPLE
Squeezed between cliffs in a rocky valley, Galta is a desolate, if evocative, place. The temple houses a number of sacred tanks, into which some daring souls jump from the adjacent cliffs. The water is claimed to be several elephants deep and fed from a spring that falls through the mouth of a sculpted cow.

There are some original frescos in reasonable condition in a chamber at the end of the bottom pool, including those depicting athletic feats, the maharaja playing polo, and the exploits of Krishna and the *gopis* (milkmaids).

It is also known as the Monkey Temple and you will find hundreds of monkeys living here – bold and aggressive macaques and more graceful and tolerable langurs. You can purchase peanuts at the gate to feed to them, but be prepared to be mobbed by teeth-barring primates.

Although only a few kilometres east of the City Palace, Galta is about 10km by road from central Jaipur. An autorickshaw should charge around ₹300 return with waiting time, a taxi will charge at least ₹600.

TOP STATE FESTIVALS

Jaisalmer Desert Festival (⊘Jan/Feb) A chance for moustache twirlers to compete in the Mr Desert contest.

Gangaur (⊘Mar/Apr) A festival honouring Shiva and Parvati's love, celebrated statewide but with fervour in Jaipur.

Mewar Festival (p159) Udaipur's version of Gangaur, with free cultural events and a colourful procession down to the lake.

Teej (⊘Jul/Aug) Jaipur and Bundi honour the arrival of the monsoon and Shiva and Parvati's marriage.

Dussehra Mela (⊘Oct/Nov) Commemorates Rama's victory over Ravana (the demon king of Lanka). It's a spectacular time to visit Kota – the huge fair features 22m-tall firecracker-stuffed effigies.

Marwar Festival (p180) Celebrates Rajasthani heroes through music and dance; one day is held in Jodhpur, the other in Osian.

Pushkar Camel Fair (p140) The most famous festival in the state; it's a massive congregation of camels, horses and cattle, pilgrims and tourists.

On the ridge above Galta is the **Surya Mandir** (Temple of the Sun God), which rises 100m above Jaipur and can be seen from the eastern side of the city. A 2.5km-long walking trail climbs up to the temple from Suraj Pol, or you can walk up from the Galta side. There are hazy views over the humming city.

🏃 Activities

Several hotels will let you use their pool for a daily fee; try those at Narain Niwas Palace Hotel (p119) and **Mansingh Hotel** (Sansar Chandra Marg; nonguests ₹350; ⊘ 7am-8pm).

Kerala Ayurveda Kendra   AYURVEDA
(☑ 0141-4022446; www.keralaayurvedakendra. com; 32 Indra Colony, Bani Park; ⊘ 9am-9pm) Is Jaipur making your nerves jangle? Get help through ayurvedic massage and therapy. Treatments include *sirodhara* (₹1500/2400 for 50/90 minutes), where medicated oil is steadily streamed over your forehead to reduce stress, tone the brain and help with sleep disorders. Massages (male therapist for male clients and female for female clients) cost from ₹500 for 55 minutes.

It offers free transport to/from your hotel.

Charak Ayurveda   AYURVEDA
(☑ 0141-2205628; www.charakayurveda.com; E-7 Kantichandra Marg, Bani Park; ⊘ 9am-2pm & 3-7pm Mon-Sat, 9am-1pm Sun) A full range of ayurvedic treatments are available. Massages start at ₹500.

Yog Sadhna Ashram   YOGA
(☑ 9314011884; www.yogsadhnaindia.org; Bapu Nagar; ⊘ Wed-Mon) Free classes take place among trees off University Rd (near Rajasthan University) and incorporate breathing exercises, yoga asanas (postures) and exercise. Most of the classes are in Hindi, but some English is spoken in the 7.30am to 9.30am class. You can visit for individual classes, or register for longer courses.

Madhavanand Girls College   YOGA
(C19 Behari Marg, Bani Park; ⊘ 6-7am) This college runs free casual yoga classes every day in both Hindi and English. Very convenient if you happen to be lodging in Bani Park – the college is next door to Madhuban hotel.

📖 Courses

Jaipur Cooking Classes   COOKING
(☑ 9928097288; www.jaipurcookingclasses.com; 33 Gyan Vihar, Nirman Nagar, near Ajmer Rd; class veg/nonveg from ₹2000/3700) Popular cooking classes with chef Lokesh Mathur, who boasts more than 25 years' experience working in the restaurant and hotel business. Classes cover both classic dishes and Rajasthani menus and can be veg or nonveg. After a three-hour lesson, you sit down for a lunch or dinner of what you've prepared. Lokesh's kitchen is outside the western outskirts of Jaipur.

Call ahead for exact directions for your autorickshaw driver.

Kripal Kumbh   ART
(☑ 0141-2201127; B18A Shiv Marg, Bani Park) Advance bookings are essential for these free lessons in blue pottery. Lessons aren't possible during the monsoon, from late June to mid-September. There's also a **showroom** (www.kripalkumbh.com; ⊘ 9.30am-6pm Mon-Sat).

Dhamma Thali Vipassana Meditation Centre   HEALTH & WELLBEING
(☑ 0141-2680220; www.thali.dhamma.org; courses by donation) This serene *vipassana* meditation centre is tucked away in the hilly countryside near Galta, a 12km drive east of the city centre. It runs courses in meditation for both beginners and more advanced students throughout the year. Courses are usually for 10 days, during which you must observe noble silence – no communication with others.

🧭 Tours

Cyclin' Jaipur   CYCLING
(☑ 7728060956; www.cyclinjaipur.com; 4hr tour ₹2000; ⊘ tour 6.45am) Get up early to beat the traffic for a tour of the Pink City by bike, exploring the hidden lanes, temples, markets and food stalls of Jaipur. It's a unique and fun way to learn about the workings and culture of the city. Breakfast and refreshments during the tour are included, and helmets are provided on demand.

Tours start at Karnot Mahal, on Ramganj Chaupar in the Old City. Tailor-made walking and food tours are also available.

Vintage Jeep Tour   SIGHTSEEING
(☑ 9829404055, 0141-2373700; www.pearlpalace heritage.com/exclusive-vintage-jeep-tour-jaipur; Lane 2, 54 Gopal Bari; per person ₹2500; ⊘ 9am-5.30pm) A fun way to explore Jaipur's major sights (including Amber and the City Palace) is by jeep – a genuine US Army 1942 Ford Jeep. With a dedicated driver and a guide on board, you are guaranteed to be part of a small tour group (maximum three guests), giving great flexibility. Admission prices and lunch costs are not included.

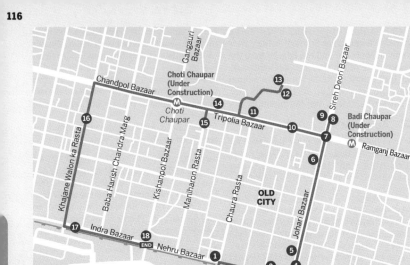

Walking Tour
Pink City

START NEW GATE
END AJMER GATE
LENGTH 4.5KM; THREE TO FIVE HOURS

Entering the old city from **1 New Gate**, turn right into **2 Bapu Bazaar**, inside the city wall. Brightly coloured bolts of fabric, jootis (traditional shoes) and aromatic perfumes make the street a favourite destination for Jaipur's women. At the end of Bapu Bazaar you'll come to **3 Sanganeri Gate**. Turn left into **4 Johari Bazaar**, the jewellery market, where you will find jewellers, goldsmiths and artisans doing highly glazed meenakari (enamelwork), a speciality of Jaipur.

Continuing north you'll pass the famous **5 LMB Hotel**, the **6 Jama Masjid**, with its tall minarets, and the bustling **7 Badi Chaupar**. Be very careful crossing the road here. To the north is **8 Sireh Deori Bazaar**, also known as Hawa Mahal Bazaar. The name is derived from the spectacular **9 Hawa Mahal** (p113), a short distance to the north. Turning left on **10 Tripolia Bazaar**, you will

see a lane leading to the entrance to the Hawa Mahal. A few hundred metres west is the **11 Tripolia Gate**. This is the main entrance to the **12 Jantar Mantar** (p111) and **13 City Palace** (p107), but only the maharaja's family may enter here. The public entrance is via the less ostentatious Atishpol (Stable Gate), a little further along.

After visiting the City Palace complex, head back to Tripolia Bazaar and resume your walk west past **14 Iswari Minar Swarga Sal** (p113), which is well worth the climb for the view. Cross the bazaar at the minaret and head west. The next lane on the left is **15 Maniharon Rasta**, the best place to buy colourful lac (resin) bangles.

Back on Tripolia Bazaar, continue west to cross Choti Chaupar to Chandpol Bazaar until you reach a traffic light. Turn left into **16 Khajane Walon ka Rasta**, where you'll find marble and stoneware carvers at work. Continue south until you reach a broad road just inside the city wall, **17 Indra Bazaar**. Follow the road east towards **18 Ajmer Gate**, which marks the end of the tour.

RTDC
TOURS

(☑ 2200778; tours@rtdc.in; RTDC Tourist Office, Platform 1, Jaipur Train Station; half-/full-day tour ₹400/500; ☺ 8am-6.30pm Mon-Sat) Full-day tours (9am to 6pm) take in all the major sights of Jaipur (including Amber Fort), with a lunch break at Nahargarh. The lunch break can be as late as 3pm, so have a big breakfast. Rushed half-day tours (8am to 1pm, 11.30am to 4.30pm, and 1.30pm to 6.30pm) still squeeze in Amber. The tour price doesn't include admission charges.

Departing at 6.30pm, the Pink City by Night tour (₹700) explores several well-known sights and includes dinner at Nahargarh.

Tours depart from Jaipur train station; the company also picks up and takes bookings from the RTDC Hotel Teej, RTDC Hotel Gangaur and the tourist office at the main bus station.

🛏 Sleeping

Jaipur accommodation pretty much covers all bases, and travellers are spoiled for choice in all budget categories. From May to September, most midrange and top-end hotels offer bargain rates, dropping prices by 25% to 50%.

🛏 Around MI Road

★ Hotel Pearl Palace
HOTEL $

(☑ 0141-2373700, 9414236323; www.hotelpearl palace.com; Hari Kishan Somani Marg, Hathroi Fort; dm ₹400, r with AC ₹1310-1910; ❄ @ 🛜) The dependable Pearl Palace continues to surprise. Ongoing renovations means many excellent rooms simply defy their ordinary tariffs. There's quite a range of rooms to choose from – small, large, some with AC or fan cooling, and all are spotless. Services include money changing, city tours and travel arrangements, and the hotel boasts the excellent Peacock Rooftop Restaurant (p120). Advance booking is recommended.

Karni Niwas
GUESTHOUSE $

(☑ 0141-2365433, 9929777488; www.hotelkarni niwas.com; C5 Motilal Atal Marg; r ₹1000, with AC ₹1500; ❄ @ 🛜) This friendly hotel has clean, cool and comfortable rooms, often with balconies. There's no restaurant, but there are relaxing plant-decked terraces to enjoy room service on. And being so central, restaurants aren't far away. The owner shuns commissions for rickshaw drivers; free pickup from the train or bus station is available.

Roadhouse Hostel Jaipur
HOSTEL $

(☑ 9945522299; www.roadhousehostels.com; D-76 Shiv Heera Path; dm/s/d ₹300/1000/1200; ❄ 🛜) This bright and friendly hostel is in a quiet residential part of town, but it's not too far from all the restaurants on MI Rd. Six- and eight-bed dorms are spotless and air-conditioned and there are a couple of private rooms. There is a free-use kitchen and games room, and management will help with transport tickets.

There's a handy rickshaw stand at the end of the road.

Tony Guest House
GUESTHOUSE $

(☑ 9928871717; www.facebook.com/tonyguesthouse jaipur; 11 Station Road; dm/s/d ₹180/280/340, r with bathroom ₹600; ❄ @ 🛜) This friendly choice on a busy road is well set up for travellers and backpackers on a tight budget, with a rooftop garden, honest travel advice, internet and free-flowing chai. Rooms are extremely basic, some with plywood partition walls, and only one has a private bathroom, although it's with a cold-water shower. The common shower is hot.

★ Atithi Guest House
GUESTHOUSE $$

(☑ 0141-2378679; www.atithijaipur.com; 1 Park House Scheme Rd; s/d ₹1200/1310, with AC ₹1530/1750; ❄ @ 🛜) This nicely presented modern guesthouse, well situated between MI and Station Rds, offers strikingly clean, simple rooms dotted around a quiet courtyard. It's central but peaceful, and the service is friendly and helpful. Meals are available (the thali is particularly recommended) and you can have a drink on the very pleasant rooftop terrace.

Pearl Palace Heritage
HOTEL $$

(☑ 0141-4106599, 9772558855; www.pearlpalace heritage.com; Lane 2, 54 Gopal Bari; r ₹3260-3815; ❄ 🛜) The second hotel for the successful Pearl Palace team is a midrange property boasting some very special characteristics. Stone carvings adorn the halls and each spacious room vibrantly recreates an individual cultural theme, such as a village hut, a sandstone fort, or a mirror-lined palace boudoir. Modern luxuries and facilities have been carefully integrated into the appealing traditional designs.

Dera Rawatsar
HOTEL $$

(☑ 0141-2200770; www.derarawatsar.com; D194 Vijay Path; r incl breakfast ₹4500-5500, ste ₹8000; ❄ @ 🛜 🏊) Situated in a quiet suburban street and yet close to the bus station, this

RAJASTHAN JAIPUR

tranquil hotel is managed by three generations of women of a gracious Bikaner noble family. The hotel has a range of lovely decorated rooms, sunny courtyards, and offers home-style Indian meals. It is an excellent choice for young families and solo female travellers.

All Seasons Homestay
HOMESTAY **$$**

(☏0141-2369443, 9460387055; www.allseasons homestayjaipur.com; 63 Hathroi Fort; s/d from ₹1600/1700, deluxe ₹2000; ✷🛜) Ranjana and her husband Dinesh run this welcoming homestay in their lovely bungalow on a quiet backstreet behind Hathroi Fort. There are 10 pristine guest rooms, two of which have small kitchens for longer stays. There's a pleasant lawn, home-cooked meals and cooking lessons. Advance booking is recommended.

Nana-ki-Haveli
HERITAGE HOTEL **$$**

(☏0141-2615502; www.nanakihaveli.com; Fateh Tiba; r ₹1800-3000; ✷@🛜) Tucked-away off Moti Dungri Marg is this tranquil place with attractive, comfortable rooms decorated with traditional flourishes (discreet wall painting, wooden furniture). It's hosted by a lovely family and is a good choice for solo female travellers. It's fronted by a relaxing lawn and offers home-style cooking and discounted rooms in summer.

Hotel Arya Niwas
HOTEL **$$**

(☏0141-4073456; www.aryaniwas.com; Sansar Chandra Marg; s ₹1635-2725, d ₹2350-3110; ✷@🛜) Just off Sansar Chandra Marg, behind a high-rise tower, this very popular travellers' haunt has a travel desk, bookshop and yoga lessons. For a hotel of 92 rooms it is very well run, though its size means it's not as personal as smaller guesthouses. The spotless rooms vary in layout and size so check out a few.

Outside, there's an extensive terrace facing a soothing expanse of lawn. The self-service vegetarian restaurant doesn't sell beer, but you can bring your own.

Alsisar Haveli
HERITAGE HOTEL **$$$**

(☏0141-2368290; www.alsisar.com; Sansar Chandra Marg; s/d from ₹7605/10,530; ✷@🛜⛶) This genuine heritage hotel housed in a gracious 19th-century mansion is set in beautiful green gardens, and boasts a lovely swimming pool and grand dining room. Its bedrooms don't disappoint either, with elegant Rajput arches and antique furnishings. Though a little impersonal, perhaps because it hosts many tour groups, occasional discounts can be found by booking directly online.

Hotel Diggi Palace
HERITAGE HOTEL **$$$**

(☏0141-2373091; www.hoteldiggipalace.com; off Sawai Ram Singh Rd; s/d incl breakfast from ₹4000/5000; ✷@) About 1km south of Ajmer Gate, this former residence of the *thakur* (nobleman) of Diggi is surrounded by vast shaded lawns. Once a budget hotel, the more expensive rooms are substantially better than the cheaper options. Management prides itself on using organic produce from the hotel's own gardens and farms in the restaurant.

🛏 Bani Park

The Bani Park area is relatively peaceful, away from the main roads, about 2km west of the Old City (northwest of MI Rd).

Vinayak Guest House
HOTEL **$**

(☏0141-2205260; vinayakguesthouse@yahoo.co.in; 4 Kabir Marg, Bani Park; r ₹500-1100; ✷🛜) This welcoming guesthouse is actually in a small, quiet street behind busy Kabir Marg, very convenient to the train station. There is a variety of different rooms and tariffs; those with air-con also have great renovated bathrooms and are your best option. The vegetarian restaurant on the rooftop gets good reports.

★Madhuban
HOTEL **$$**

(☏0141-2200033; www.madhuban.net; D237 Behari Marg; s/d/ste from ₹2290/2615/3865; ✷@🛜⛱) Madhuban has bright, antique-furnished, spotlessly clean rooms, plus a private enclosed garden for alfresco meals. The vibrantly frescoed restaurant serves Rajasthani specialities in addition to Continental and North Indian dishes, and sits beside the courtyard plunge pool. The relatively peaceful locale of Bani Park makes this place a comfortable stay. Bus and train station pickup available.

Hotel Anuraag Villa
HOTEL **$$**

(☏0141-2201679; www.anuraagvilla.com; D249 Devi Marg; s/d ₹1080/1310, with AC from ₹1800/1970; ✷@🛜) This quiet and comfortable option has no-fuss, spacious rooms and an extensive lawn where you can find some quiet respite from the hassles of sightseeing. It has a highly commended vegetarian restaurant with its kitchen on view, and efficient, helpful staff.

Jaipur Inn   HOTEL **$$**
(☎ 9829013660, 0141-2201121; www.jaipurinn.
com; B17 Shiv Marg, Bani Park; r from ₹1500-2000;
❄ @ 🛜) Once a budget travellers' favourite,
this is now a midrange hotel offering an as-
sortment of eclectic and individual rooms.
Inspect a few before settling in. Plus points
include the helpful manager and several
common areas where travellers can make
a coffee, use the wi-fi, or grab a meal. Yoga
and Bollywood dance lessons can be had on
the rooftop.

Hotel Meghniwas   GUESTHOUSE **$$$**
(☎ 0141-4060100; www.meghniwas.com; C9 Sawai
Jai Singh Hwy; r/ste ₹5760/8220; ❄ @ 🛜 ≋) In
a building erected by Brigadier Singh in
1950 and run by his gracious descendants,
this very welcoming hotel has comfortable
and spotless rooms, with traditional carved-
wood furniture and leafy outlooks. The
standard rooms are spacious, and although
it's on a major road it is set well back behind
a leafy garden. There's a first-rate restaurant
and an inviting pool.

Jas Vilas   GUESTHOUSE **$$$**
(☎ 0141-2204638; www.jasvilas.com; C9 Sawai Jai
Singh Hwy; s/d incl breakfast from ₹6250/6960;
❄ @ 🛜 ≋) This small but impressive hotel
was built in 1950 and is still run by the same
charming family. It offers spacious rooms,
most of which face the large sparkling pool
set in a romantic courtyard. Three garden-
facing rooms are wheelchair accessible. In
addition to the relaxing courtyard and gar-
den, there is a cosy dining room and helpful
management.

Shahpura House   HERITAGE HOTEL **$$$**
(☎ 0141-2203069; www.shahpura.com; D257 Devi
Marg; s/d/ste from ₹7140/8330/9520; ❄ @ 🛜 ≋)
Elaborately built and decorated in traditional style, this heritage hotel offers immaculate rooms, some with balconies, featuring murals, coloured-glass lamps, flat-screen TVs,
and even ceilings covered in small mirrors
(in the suites). This rambling palace boasts a
durbar hall (royal reception hall) with a huge
chandelier, and a cosy cocktail bar.

There's also an inviting swimming pool
and an elegant rooftop terrace restaurant
that stages cultural shows.

🏠 Old City

Hotel Sweet Dream   HOTEL **$**
(☎ 0141-2314409;   www.hotelsweetdreamjaipur.
in; Nehru Bazaar; s/d ₹900/1150, with AC from

₹1600/1850; ❄ 🛜) Probably the best option
right inside the Old City, and one of Jaipur's
better budget hotels. Several of the rooms
have been renovated and enlarged (reducing the overall room count). There are increasing amenities the higher up the price
scale (and rickety elevator) you go. There's
a bar plus an excellent rooftop terrace
restaurant.

Hotel Bissau Palace   HERITAGE HOTEL **$$**
(☎ 0141-2304391; www.bissaupalace.com; out-
side Chandpol; r ₹3270-6540; ❄ @ 🛜 ≋) This
is a worthy choice if you want to stay in a
palace on a budget. It's actually just outside
the city walls, less than 10 minutes' walk
from Chandpol (a gateway to the Old City).
There's a swimming pool, a handsome wood-
panelled library and three restaurants. The
hotel has oodles of heritage atmosphere,
with antique furnishings and mementos.

🏠 Rambagh Environs

Rambagh Palace   HERITAGE HOTEL **$$$**
(☎ 0141-2385700; www.tajhotels.com; Bhawani
Singh Marg; r from ₹43,560; ❄ @ 🛜 ≋) This
splendid palace was once the Jaipur pad
of Maharaja Man Singh II and his glam-
orous wife Gayatri Devi. Veiled in hectares
of manicured gardens, the hotel – run by
the luxury Taj Group brand – has fantastic
views across the immaculate lawns. More
expensive rooms are naturally the most
sumptuous.

Nonguests can join in the magnificence
by dining in the lavish restaurants or drinking tea on the gracious verandah. At least
treat yourself to a drink at the spiffing Polo
Bar (p122).

**Narain Niwas
Palace Hotel**   HERITAGE HOTEL **$$$**
(☎ 0141-2561291; www.hotelnarainniwas.com; Narain
Singh Rd;   s/d incl breakfast from ₹8425/
10,530, deluxe d ₹13,455; ❄ @ 🛜 ≋) In Kano-
ta Bagh, just south of the city, this genuine
heritage hotel has ramshackle splendour.
There's a lavish dining room with liveried
staff, an old-fashioned verandah on which to
drink tea, and antiques galore. The standard
rooms are in a garden wing and aren't as
spacious as the high-ceilinged deluxe rooms,
which vary in atmosphere and amenities.

Out back you'll find a large secluded pool
(nonguests ₹300 for two hours between 8am
and 4pm), a heavenly spa, and sprawling
gardens complete with peacocks.

✕ Eating

✕ Around MI Rd

Indian Coffee House
CAFE **$**

(MI Rd; coffee ₹20-40, snacks ₹35-60; ☺6am-9pm) Set back from the street, down an easily missed alley, this traditional coffee house (a venerable co-op–owned institution) offers a pleasant cup of filtered coffee in very relaxed surroundings. Aficionados of Indian Coffee Houses will not be disappointed by the fan-cooled, pale-green ambience. Inexpensive *pakoras* (deep-fried battered vegetables) and dosas grace the menu.

Jal Mahal
ICE CREAM **$**

(MI Rd; cups & cones ₹30-120; ☺10am-11pm) This great little ice-cream parlour has been going since 1952. There are around 50 flavours to choose from, but if it's hot outside, it's hard to beat mango. There are also plenty of other ice-cream concoctions, including sundaes and banana splits, many with fanciful names.

Old Takeaway the Kebab Shop
KEBAB **$**

(151 MI Rd; kebabs ₹90-180; ☺6-11pm) One of several similarly named roadside kebab shops on this stretch of MI Road, this one (next to the mosque) is the original (so we're told) and the best (we agree). It knocks up outstanding tandoori kebabs, including paneer *sheesh,* mutton *sheesh* and tandoori chicken. Like the sign says: a house of delicious nonveg corner.

Rawat Kachori
SWEETS **$**

(Station Rd; kachori ₹30, lassi ₹50, sweets per kg ₹350-850; ☺6am-10pm) Head to this popular takeaway with an attached restaurant for delicious Indian sweets and famous kachori (potato masala in a fried pastry case), a scrumptious savoury snack. A salty or sweet lassi or a delicious milk crown (fluffy dough with cream) should fill you up for the afternoon.

★ Peacock Rooftop Restaurant
MULTICUISINE **$$**

(☏0141-2373700; Hotel Pearl Palace, Hari Kishan Somani Marg; mains ₹175-340; ☺7am-11pm) This multilevel rooftop restaurant at the Hotel Pearl Palace gets rave reviews for its excellent yet inexpensive cuisine (Indian, Chinese and Continental) and fun ambience. The attentive service, whimsical furnishings and romantic view towards Hathroi Fort make it a first-rate restaurant. In addition to the dinner menu, there are healthy breakfasts and great-value burgers, pizzas and thalis for lunch.

It's wise to make a booking for dinner.

Four Seasons
MULTICUISINE **$$**

(☏0141-2375450; D43A Subhash Marg; mains ₹125-295; ☺11am-3.30pm & 6.30-11pm; ❄☑) Four Seasons is one of Jaipur's best vegetarian restaurants. It's a popular place with dining on two levels and a glass wall to the busy kitchens. There's a great range of dishes on offer, including tasty Rajasthani specialities, South Indian dosas, Chinese fare, and a selection of thalis and pizzas. No alcohol.

Anokhi Café
INTERNATIONAL **$$**

(☏0141-4007245; 2nd fl, KK Square, C-11 Prithviraj Marg; mains ₹250-350; ☺10am-7.30pm; ☏☑) This relaxing cafe with a fashionable organic vibe is the perfect place to come if you're craving a crunchy, well-dressed salad, a quiche or a thickly filled sandwich – or just a respite from the hustle with a latte or an iced tea. The delicious organic loaves of bread are made to order and can be purchased separately.

Handi Restaurant
NORTH INDIAN **$$**

(MI Rd; mains ₹220-440; ☺noon-3.30pm & 6-11pm) Handi has been satisfying customers since 1967, with scrumptious tandoori and barbecue dishes and rich Mughlai curries. In the evenings it sets up a smoky kebab stall at the entrance to the restaurant. Good vegetarian items are also available. No beer.

It's opposite the main post office, tucked at the back of the Maya Mansions.

Surya Mahal
SOUTH INDIAN **$$**

(☏0141-2362811; MI Rd; mains ₹130-310, thalis ₹240-350; ☺8am-11pm; ❄☑) This popular option near Panch Batti specialises in South Indian vegetarian food; try the delicious *masala dosa* and the tasty *dhal makhani* (black lentils and red kidney beans). There are also Chinese and Italian dishes, and good ice creams, sundaes and cool drinks.

Natraj
INDIAN **$$**

(☏0141-2375804; MI Rd; mains ₹150-250, thalis ₹250-520; ☺9am-11pm; ❄☑) Not far from Panch Batti is this classy vegetarian place, which has an extensive menu featuring North Indian, Continental and Chinese cuisine. Diners are blown away by the potato-encased 'vegetable bomb' curry. There's a good selection of thalis and South Indian food – the *paper masala dosa* is delicious – as well as a great array of Indian sweets.

Dāsaprakash SOUTH INDIAN $$
(☑ 0141-2371313; 5 Kamal Mansions, MI Rd; mains ₹115-240, thalis ₹310-345; ⊙ 9am-10.30pm; 🕸 ✎)
Part of a renowned chain established in 1921, Dāsaprakash specialises in vegetarian South Indian cuisine, including thalis and several versions of dosa and *idli* (spongy, round, fermented rice cake). Afterwards you can choose from a wonderful selection of cold drinks and over-the-top ice-cream sundaes.

★**Niro's** INDIAN $$$
(☑ 0141-2374493; MI Rd; mains ₹250-500; ⊙ 10am-11pm; 🕸) Established in 1949, Niro's is a long-standing favourite on MI Rd that, like a good wine, only improves with age. Escape the chaos of the street by ducking into its cool, clean, mirror-ceilinged sanctum to savour veg and nonveg Indian cuisine with professional service. Classic Chinese and Continental food are available, but the Indian menu is definitely the pick.

Even locals rave about the butter chicken and rogan josh. Beer and wine are served.

Copper Chimney INDIAN $$$
(☑ 0141-2372275; Maya Mansions, MI Rd; mains ₹300-475, thali veg/nonveg ₹490/575; ⊙ noon-3.30pm & 6.30-11pm; 🕸) Copper Chimney is casual, verging on elegant, and is definitely welcoming, with the requisite waiter army and a fridge of cold beer. It offers excellent veg and nonveg Indian cuisine (with generous servings), including aromatic Rajasthani specials. Continental and Chinese food is also on offer, as is a small selection of Indian wine, but the curry-and-beer combos are hard to beat.

Little Italy ITALIAN $$$
(☑ 0141-4022444; 3rd fl, KK Square, Prithviraj Marg; mains ₹300-500; ⊙ noon-10pm; 🕸) The best Italian restaurant in Jaipur, Little Italy is part of a small national chain that offers excellent vegetarian pasta, risotto, and wood-fired pizzas in cool, contemporary surroundings. The menu is extensive and includes some Mexican items, plus first-rate Italian desserts. It's licensed and there's an attached sister concern, Little India, with an Indian and Chinese menu.

Jaipur Modern Kitchen MEDITERRANEAN $$$
(☑ 0141-4113000; www.jaipurmodern.com; 51 Sardar Patel Marg, C-Scheme; mains ₹300-550; ⊙ 11am-11pm; 🕸 ✎) 🍴 In addition to the homewares and fashion, Jaipur Modern boasts this super Mediterranean cafe showcasing organic ingredients and supporting

local sustainable agriculture. The tasty pizzas, pasta, *momos* and wraps are all made in-house. There's even a special emphasis on locally grown quinoa; the Q menu features soups, appetisers, mains and desserts, all containing the versatile seed.

🍴 **Old City**

Ganesh Restaurant NORTH INDIAN $
(Nehru Bazaar; mains ₹100-160; ⊙ 9am-11.30pm; ✎) This pocket-sized outdoor restaurant is in a fantastic location on the top of the Old City wall near New Gate. The chef is in a pit on one side of the wall, so you can check out your pure vegetarian food being cooked. If you're looking for a local eatery with fresh tasty food such as paneer butter masala, you'll love it.

There's an easy-to-miss signpost, but no doubt a stallholder will show you the narrow stairway.

Mohan INDIAN $
(144-5 Nehru Bazaar; mains ₹25-150, thali ₹80; ⊙ 9am-10.30pm; ✎) Tiny Mohan is easy to miss: it's a few steps down from the footpath on the corner of the street. It's basic, cheap and a bit grubby, but the thalis, curries (half-plate and full plate) and snacks are freshly cooked and very popular.

LMB INDIAN $$
(☑ 0141-2560845; Johari Bazaar; mains ₹210-320; ⊙ 8am-11pm; 🕸 ✎) Laxmi Misthan Bhandar, LMB to you and me, is a vegetarian restaurant in the Old City that's been going strong since 1954. A welcoming air-conditioned refuge from frenzied Johari Bazaar, LMB is also an institution with its singular decor, attentive waiters and extensive sweet counter. Now it is no longer purely *sattvik* (pure vegetarian), you can now order meals with onion and garlic.

Popular with both local and international tourists, try the Rajasthan thali (₹540) followed by the signature *kulfa* (₹100, a fusion of *kulfi* and *falooda* with dry fruits and saffron).

Hotel Sweet Dream MULTICUISINE $$
(☑ 0141-2314409; www.hotelsweetdreamjaipur.in; Nehru Bazaar; mains ₹130-285; 🕸) This hotel in the Old City has a splendid restaurant on the roof with views down to bustling Nehru Bazaar. It's a great place to break the shopping spree and grab a light lunch or a refreshing *makhania* lassi (₹140) made with fresh fruits and curd. The menu includes pizza and Chinese, but the Indian is best.

RAJASTHAN JAIPUR

🍸 Drinking & Nightlife

⭐ Lassiwala
CAFE

(MI Rd; lassi small/large ₹25/50; ⊘7.30am until sold out) This famous, much-imitated institution is a simple place that whips up fabulous, creamy lassis in clay cups. Get here early to avoid disappointment! Will the real Lassiwala please stand up? It's the one that says 'Shop 312' and 'Since 1944', directly next to the alleyway. Imitators spread to the right as you face it.

⭐ Curious Life
CAFE

(📞0141-2229877; www.facebook.com/curiouslife coffeeroasters; P25 Yudhisthira Marg, C-Scheme; coffees from ₹75; ⊘9am-10pm; 🛜) The latest coffee trends brew away in this showcase of Indian hipster-hood. Single-origin, espresso, French press, AeroPress, V60 pour over – you name it, and you'll find it brewing here among the predominantly 20-something crowd. There are also cold brews, smoothies, shakes and muffins, all underscored by a curiously retro soundtrack.

⭐ Bar Palladio
BAR

(📞0141-2565556; www.bar-palladio.com; Narain Niwas Palace Hotel, Narain Singh Rd; cocktails ₹500-700; ⊘6-11pm) This cool bar-restaurant boasts an extensive drinks list and an Italian food menu (mains ₹350 to ₹400). The vivid blue theme of the romantic Orientalist interior flows through to candlelit outdoor seating, making this a very relaxing place to sip a drink, snack on bruschetta and enjoy a conversation. Il Teatro is an occasional live-music event at the bar – see the website for dates.

100% Rock
BAR

(Hotel Shikha, Yudhishthir Marg, C-Scheme; pint of beer/cocktails from ₹190/300; ⊘11am-12.30am; 🛜) Attached to, but separate from Hotel Shikha, this is the closest thing there is to a beer garden in Jaipur, with plenty of outdoor seating as well as air-conditioned side rooms and a clubby main room with a small dance floor. Two-for-one beer offers are common, making this popular with local youngsters.

Polo Bar
BAR

(Rambagh Palace Hotel, Bhawan Singh Marg; ⊘noon-midnight) This spiffing watering hole adorned with polo memorabilia boasts arched, scalloped windows framing the neatly clipped lawns. A bottle of beer costs from ₹400 according to the label, a glass of wine starts at ₹550, and cocktails cost from

₹600. Delicious snacks are also available throughout the day.

Café Coffee Day
CAFE

(Country Inn & Suites, MI Rd; coffees ₹80-150; ⊘10am-10pm) The franchise that successfully delivers espresso to coffee addicts, as well as the occasional creamy concoction and muffin, has several branches in Jaipur. In addition to this one, sniff out the brews at Paris Point on Sawai Jai Singh Hwy (aka Collectorate Rd), at the central museum, and near the exit point at Amber Fort.

☆ Entertainment

Jaipur isn't a big late-night party town, though many of its hotels put on some sort of evening music, dance or puppet show. English-language films are occasionally screened at some cinemas – check the cinemas and local press for details.

Raj Mandir Cinema
CINEMA

(📞0141-2379372; www.therajmandir.com; Baghwandas Marg; tickets ₹120-400; ⊘reservations 10am-6pm, screenings 12.30pm, 3pm, 6.30pm & 10pm) Just off MI Rd, Raj Mandir is *the* place to go to see a Hindi film in India. This opulent cinema looks like a huge pink cream cake, with a meringue auditorium and a foyer somewhere between a temple and Disneyland. Bookings can be made one hour to seven days in advance at windows 9 and 10.

Advance booking is your best chance of securing a seat, but forget it in the early days of a new release. Alternatively, sharpen your elbows and join the queue when the current booking office opens 45 minutes before curtain up. Avoid the cheapest tickets, which seat you very close to the screen.

Chokhi Dhani
LIVE PERFORMANCE

(📞0141-5165000; www.chokhidhani.com; Tonk Rd; adult/child incl Rajasthani thali from ₹600/350; ⊘6-11pm) Chokhi Dhani, meaning 'special village', is a mock Rajasthani village 20km south of Jaipur, and is a fun place to take kids. There are open-air restaurants, where you can enjoy a tasty Rajasthani thali, plus a bevy of traditional entertainment – dancers, acrobats, snack stalls – and adventure-park-like activities for kids to swing on, slide down and hide in.

There are more expensive tickets depending on which dining experience you opt for. A return taxi from Jaipur, including waiting time, will cost about ₹800.

Polo Ground SPECTATOR SPORT
(☑ ticket info 0141-2385380; Ambedkar Circle, Bhawan Singh Marg) Maharaja Man Singh II indulged his passion for polo by building an enormous polo ground next to Rambagh Palace, which is still a polo-match hub today. A ticket to a match also gets you into the lounge, which is adorned with historic photos and memorabilia. The polo season extends over winter. Contact the Rajasthan Polo Club for info about tickets.

🛍 Shopping

Jaipur is a shopper's paradise. Commercial buyers come here from all over the world to stock up on the amazing range of jewellery, gems, textiles and crafts that come from all over Rajasthan. You'll have to bargain hard, particularly around major tourist sights.

Many shops can send your parcels home for you – often cheaper than if you do it yourself.

The city is still loosely divided into traditional artisans' quarters. Bapu Bazaar is lined with saris and fabrics, and is a good place to buy trinkets. Johari Bazaar and Sireh Deori Bazaar are where many jewellery shops are concentrated, selling gold, silver and highly glazed enamelwork known as meenakari, a Jaipur speciality. You may also find better deals for fabrics with the cotton merchants of Johari Bazaar.

Kishanpol Bazaar is famous for textiles, particularly *bandhani* (tie-dye). Nehru Bazaar also sells fabric, as well as jootis (traditional shoes), trinkets and perfume. The best place for bangles is Maniharon Rasta.

Plenty of factories and showrooms are strung along the length of the road to Amber, between Zorawar Singh Gate and the Park Regis Hotel, to catch the tourist traffic. Here you'll find huge emporiums selling block prints, blue pottery, carpets and antiques. Note that these shops are used to busloads of tourists swinging in to blow their cash, so you'll need to wear your bargaining hat.

Rickshaw-wallahs, hotels and travel agents will be getting a hefty cut from any shop they steer you towards. Many unwary visitors get talked into buying things for resale at inflated prices, especially gems. Beware of these get-rich-quick scams.

Jaipur Modern FASHION & ACCESSORIES
(☑ 0141-4112000; www.jaipurmodern.com; 51 Sardar Patel Marg, C-Scheme; ⊙ 11am-11pm) This contemporary showroom offers local arts

---

SHOPPING FOR GEMS

Jaipur is famous for precious and semi-precious stones. There are many shops offering bargain prices, but you do need to know your gems. The main gem-dealing area is around the Muslim area of Pahar Ganj, in the southeast of the Old City. Here you can see stones being cut and polished in workshops tucked off narrow backstreets.

One of the oldest scams in India is the gem scam, where tourists are fooled into thinking they can buy gems to sell at a profit elsewhere. To receive an authenticity certificate, you can deposit your gems at the gem-testing laboratory (☑ 0141-2568221; www.gtljaipur. info; Rajasthan Chamber Bhawan, MI Rd; ⊙ 10am-4pm Mon-Sat) between 10am and 4pm, then return the following day between 4pm and 5pm to pick up the certificate. The service costs ₹1050 per stone, or ₹1650 for same-day service, if deposited before 1pm.

---

and crafts, clothing, homewares, stationary and fashion accessories. The staff are relaxed (no hard sell here) and if you are not in the mood to shop, there's a great cafe serving Lavazza coffee and Mediterranean snacks.

Inde Rooh CLOTHING
(☑ 9829404055, 9929442022; www.inderooh. com; Hotel Pearl Palace, Hari Kishan Somani Marg; ⊙ 10.30am-10.30pm) This tiny outlet in the Hotel Pearl Palace highlights the talents of Jaipur's traditional block printers blended with contemporary design. Handmade and stitched, the quality and value of the women's and menswear compares well with Jaipur's more famous fashion houses. Homewares are also available.

Rajasthali ARTS & CRAFTS
(MI Rd; ⊙ 11am-7.30pm Mon-Sat) This state-government-run emporium, opposite Ajmer Gate, is packed with quality Rajasthani artefacts and crafts, including enamelwork, embroidery, pottery, woodwork, jewellery, puppets, block-printed sheets, miniatures, brassware, mirrorwork and more. Scout out prices here before launching into the bazaar; items can be cheaper at the markets, but the quality is often higher at the state emporium for not much more money.

Anokhi
CLOTHING, TEXTILES

(www.anokhi.com; 2nd fl, KK Square, C-11 Prithviraj Marg; ⊙9.30am-8pm Mon-Sat, 11am-7pm Sun) Anokhi is a classy, upmarket boutique selling stunning high-quality textiles such as block-printed fabrics, tablecloths, bed covers, cosmetic bags and scarves, as well as a range of well-designed, beautifully made clothing that combines Indian and Western influences. There's a wonderful little cafe on the premises and an excellent bookshop in the same building.

Fabindia
CLOTHING

(☑0141-4015279; www.fabindia.com; B 4 E- Prithviraj Road; ⊙11am-9pm) A great place to co-ordinate colours with reams of rich fabrics, plus furniture and home accessories. You can also find organically certified garments, beauty products and condiments. Located opposite Central Park, gate number 4.

Silver Shop
JEWELLERY

(Hotel Pearl Palace, Hari Kishan Somani Marg; ⊙6-10pm) A trusted jewellery shop backed by the hotel management that hosts the store. A money-back guarantee is offered on all items. Find it under the peacock canopy in the hotel's Peacock Rooftop Restaurant.

Crossword
BOOKS

(1st fl, KK Square, Prithvirag Marg; ⊙11am-9pm) Crossword is an excellent bookshop with all sorts of fiction and nonfiction, including the latest best sellers, pictorial books and books on Indian history. Music CDs and DVDs are also available. There is a cafe and restaurant in the same building.

Mojari
CLOTHING

(☑0141-2377037; D-67 Shiv Heera Marg; ⊙10am-6.30pm) Named after the traditional decorated shoes of Rajasthan, Mojari is a UN-supported project that helps rural leatherworkers, traditionally among the poorest members of society. A wide variety of footwear (₹300 to ₹1000) is available, including embroidered, appliquéd and open-toed shoes, mules and sandals. There's a particularly good choice for women, plus a small selection of handmade leather bags and purses.

ⓘ Information

INTERNET ACCESS

Internet cafes are thin on the ground, but almost all hotels and guesthouses provide wi-fi and/or internet access.

Mewar Cyber Café (Station Rd; per hr ₹30; ⊙7am-11pm) Near the main bus station.

MEDICAL SERVICES

Most hotels can arrange a doctor on-site.

Santokba Durlabhji Memorial Hospital (SDMH; ☑0141-2566251; www.sdmh.in; Bhawan Singh Marg) Private hospital, with 24-hour emergency department, helpful staff and clear bilingual signage. Consultancy fee ₹400.

Sawai Mansingh Hospital (SMS Hospital; ☑0141-2518222, 0141-2518597; Sawai Ram Singh Rd) State-run, but part of Soni Hospitals group (www.sonihospitals.com). Before 3pm, outpatients go to the CT & MRI Centre; after 3pm, go to the adjacent Emergency Department.

MONEY

There are plenty of places to change money, including numerous hotels, and masses of ATMs, most of which accept foreign cards.

Thomas Cook (☑0141-2360940; Jaipur Towers, MI Rd; ⊙9.30am-6pm) Changes cash and travellers cheques.

POST

DHL Express (☑0141-2361159; www.dhl.co.in; G8, Geeta Enclave, Vinobha Marg; ⊙10am-8pm) Look for the sub-branch on MI Rd then walk down the lane beside it to find DHL Express. For parcels, the first kilogram is expensive, but each 500g thereafter is cheap. All packaging is included in the price. Credit cards and cash accepted.

Main Post Office (☑0141-2368740; MI Rd; ⊙8am-7.45pm Mon-Fri, 10am-5.45pm Sat) A cost-effective and efficient institution, though the back-and-forth can infuriate. Parcel-packing-wallahs in the foyer must first pack, stitch and wax seal your parcel for a small fee before sending.

TOURIST INFORMATION

Jaipur Vision and *Jaipur City Guide* are two useful, inexpensive booklets available at bookshops and some hotel lobbies (where they are free). They feature up-to-date listings, maps, local adverts and features.

RTDC Tourist Office (☑0141-5155137; www.rajasthantourism.gov.in; former RTDC Tourist Hotel, MI Rd; ⊙9.30am-6pm Mon-Fri) has maps and brochures on Jaipur and Rajasthan. Additional branches at the **airport** (☑0141-2722647; ⊙9am-5pm Mon-Fri), **Amber Fort** (☑0141-2530264; ⊙9.30am-5pm Mon-Fri), **Jaipur train station** (☑0141-2200778; platform 1; ⊙24hr) and the **main bus station** (☑0141-5064102; platform 3; ⊙10am-5pm Mon-Fri).

ⓘ Getting There & Away

AIR

Jaipur International Airport (☑0141-2550623; www.jaipurairport.com) is located 12km southeast of the city.

It's possible to arrange flights to Jaipur from Europe, the US and other places, via Delhi. A few direct flights run to Bangkok and Singapore and the Gulf.

Air India (☑ 0141-2743500, airport 0141-2721333; www.airindia.com; Nehru Place, Tonk Rd) Daily flights to Delhi and Mumbai.

IndiGo (☑ 9212783838; www.goindigo.in; Terminal 2, Jaipur International Airport) Flights to Ahmedabad, Bengaluru (Bangalore), Chennai (Madras), Delhi, Hyderabad, Kolkata (Calcutta), Mumbai and Pune.

Jet Airways (☑ 0141-2725025, 1800 225522; www.jetairways.com; ☺ 5.30am-9pm) Flights to Delhi and Mumbai.

SpiceJet (☑ 9871803333; www.spicejet.com; Terminal 2, Jaipur International Airport; ☺ 6am-7pm) Daily flights to Delhi.

Scoot (☑ 8000016354; www.scoot.com) Three weekly flights to Singapore.

Thai Smile (☑ Thailand +662-1188888; www.thaismileair.com) Three weekly flights to Bangkok.

BUS

Rajasthan State Road Transport Corporation (RSRTC, aka Rajasthan Roadways) buses all leave from the **main bus station** (Station Rd; left luggage per bag per 24hr ₹10), picking up passengers at Narain Singh Circle (where you can also buy tickets). There's a left-luggage office at the main bus station, as well as a prepaid autorickshaw stand.

Ordinary buses are known as 'express' buses, but there are also 'deluxe' buses (coaches, really, but still called buses), which vary a lot but are generally much more expensive and comfortable (usually with air-con but not always) than ordinary express buses. Deluxe buses leave from Platform 3, tucked away in the right-hand corner of the bus station. Unlike ordinary express buses, seats can be booked in advance from the **reservation office** (☑ 0141-5116032; Main Bus Station).

With the exception of those going to Delhi (half-hourly), deluxe buses are much less frequent than ordinary buses.

CAR & MOTORCYCLE

Most hotels and the RTDC tourist office can arrange a car and driver. Depending on the vehicle, costs are ₹9 to ₹12 per kilometre, with a minimum rental rate equivalent to 250km per day. Also expect to pay a ₹200 overnight charge, and note that you will have to pay for the driver to return to Jaipur even if you are not returning.

Rajasthan Auto Centre (p261) You can hire, buy or fix a Royal Enfield Bullet (and lesser motorbikes) at Rajasthan Auto Centre, the cleanest little motorcycle workshop in India. To hire a 350cc Bullet costs ₹600 per day (including helmet) within Jaipur.

TRAIN

The **reservation office** (☑ enquiries 131, reservations 135; ☺ 8am-2pm & 3-8pm) is to your left as you enter Jaipur train station. It's open for advance reservations only (more than five hours before departure). Join the queue for 'Freedom Fighters and Foreign Tourists' (counter 769).

For same-day travel, buy your ticket at the northern end of the train station at Platform

MAIN BUSES FROM JAIPUR

DESTINATION	FARE (₹)	DURATION (HR)	FREQUENCY
Agra	261-289, AC 470-573	5½	11 daily
Ajmer	150, AC 316	2½	at least hourly
Bharatpur	195, AC 410	4½	at least hourly
Bikaner	334, AC 596	5½-7	hourly
Bundi	216	5	5 daily
Chittorgarh	339, AC 585	7	6 daily
Delhi	273, AC 800	5½	at least hourly
Jaisalmer	593	14	2 daily
Jhunjhunu	181, AC 321	3½-5	half-hourly
Jodhpur	340, AC 741	5½-7	every 2 hours
Kota	252	5	hourly
Mt Abu (Abu Road)	486, AC 866	10½-13	6 daily
Nawalgarh	145, AC 258	2½-4	hourly
Pushkar	161	3	daily
Udaipur	420, AC 914	10	6 daily

1, window 10 (closed 6am to 6.30am, 2pm to 2.30pm and 10pm to 10.30pm).

Station facilities on Platform 1 include an RTDC tourist office, Tourism Assistance Force (police), a cloakroom for left luggage (₹16 per bag per 24 hours), retiring rooms, restaurants and air-con waiting rooms for those with 1st-class and 2AC train tickets.

There's a prepaid autorickshaw stand and local taxis at the road entrance to the train station.

Services include the following:

Agra sleeper ₹185, 3½ to 4½ hours, nine daily

Ahmedabad sleeper ₹350, nine to 13 hours, seven daily (12.30am, 2.20am, 4.25am, 8.40am, 11.45am, 2.20pm and 8.35pm)

Ajmer (for Pushkar) sleeper ₹90, two hours, 21 daily

Bikaner sleeper ₹275, 6½ to 7½ hours, three daily (12.45am, 4.15pm, 9.45pm)

Delhi sleeper ₹245, 4½ to six hours, at least nine daily (1am, 2.50am, 4.40am, 5am, 6am, 2.35pm, 4.25pm, 5.50pm and 11.15pm), more on selected days

Jaisalmer sleeper ₹350, 12 hours, three daily (11.10am, 4.15pm and 11.45pm)

Jodhpur sleeper ₹250, 4½ to six hours, 10 daily (12.45am, 2.45am, 6am, 9.25am, 11.10am, 11.25am, 12.20pm, 5pm, 10.40pm and 11.45pm)

Ranthambhore NP (Sawai Madhopur) sleeper ₹180, two to three hours, at least nine daily (12.30am, 5.40am, 6.40am, 11.05am, 2pm, 4.50pm, 5.35pm, 7.35pm and 8.45pm), more on selected days

Udaipur sleeper ₹270, seven to eight hours, three daily (6.15am, 2pm and 11pm)

ⓘ Getting Around

TO/FROM THE AIRPORT

There are no bus services from the airport. An autorickshaw/taxi costs at least ₹350/450. There's a prepaid taxi booth inside the terminal.

AUTORICKSHAW

Autorickshaw drivers at the bus and train stations might just be the pushiest in Rajasthan. Use the fixed-rate prepaid autorickshaw stands instead. Keep hold of your docket to give to the driver at the end of the journey. In other cases be prepared to bargain hard – expect to pay at least ₹80 from either station to the Old City.

CYCLE-RICKSHAW

You can do your bit for the environment by flagging down a lean-limbed cycle-rickshaw rider. Though it can be uncomfortable watching someone pedalling hard to transport you, this *is* how they make a living. A short trip costs about ₹50.

PUBLIC TRANSPORT

Jaipur Metro (☑ 0141-2385790; www.jaipur metrorail.info) operates about 10km of track, known as the Pink Line, and nine stations. The

MAJOR TRAINS FROM JAIPUR

DESTINATION	TRAIN	DEPARTURE TIME	ARRIVAL TIME	FARE (₹)
Agra (Cantonment)	19666 Udaipur-Kurj Exp	6.15am	11am	185/510 (A)
Agra (Fort)	12035 Jaipur-AF Shatabdi	7.05am	10.35am	505/1050 (D)
Ahmedabad	12958 Adi Sj Rajdhani	12.30am	9.40am	1130/1580 (B)
Ajmer (for Pushkar)	12195 Ajmer-AF Intercity	9.40am	11.50am	100/325 (C)
Bikaner	12307 Howrah-Jodhpur Exp	12.45am	8.15am	275/705 (A)
Delhi (New Delhi)	12016 Ajmer Shatabdi	5.50pm	10.40pm	570/1205 (D)
Delhi (S Rohilla)	12985 Dee Double Decker	6am	10.30am	505/1205 (D)
Jaisalmer	14659 Delhi-JSM Exp	11.45pm	11.40am	350/935 (A)
Jodhpur	22478 Jaipur-Jodhpur SF Exp	6am	10.30am	515/625 (E)
Sawai Madhopur	12466 Intercity Exp	11.05am	1.15pm	180/325/560 (F)
Udaipur	19665 Jaipur–Udaipur Exp	11pm	6.45am	270/715 (A)

Fares: (A) sleeper/3AC, (B) 3AC/2AC, (C) 2nd-class seat/AC chair, (D) AC chair/1AC, (E) AC chair/3AC, (F) sleeper/AC chair/3AC

track starts southwest of the Pink City in Mansarovar, travels through Civil Lines, and currently terminates at Chandpole. At the time of writing, the continuation of this track through the Pink City from Chandpole to Badi Chaupar was under construction. Fares are between ₹5 and ₹15.

TAXI

There are unmetered taxis available, which will require negotiating a fare.

Metro Cabs (☐ 0414-4244444; www.metro-cabs.in; flagfall incl 2km ₹50, then per km ₹10-12, plus per min ₹1, night surcharge 10pm-6am 25%; ☉ 24hr) Taxis can be hired for sightseeing for four-/eight-hour blocks for ₹700/1350.

Around Jaipur

Amber

The magnificent, formidable, honey-hued fort of Amber (pronounced 'amer'), an ethereal example of Rajput architecture, rises from a rocky mountainside about 11km northeast of Jaipur, and is the city's must-see sight.

Amber was the former capital of Jaipur state. It was built by the Kachhwaha Rajputs, who hailed from Gwalior, in present day Madhya Pradesh, where they reigned for over 800 years. The construction of the fort, which was begun in 1592 by Maharaja Man Singh, the Rajput commander of Akbar's army, was financed with war booty. It was later extended and completed by the Jai Singhs before they moved to Jaipur on the plains below.

The town of Amber, below the fort, is also worth visiting, especially the Anokhi Museum of Hand Printing. From the museum you can walk around the ancient town to the restored Panna Meena Baori and Jagat Siromani Temple (known locally as the Meera Temple).

◉ Sights

★ Amber Fort   FORT
(Indian/foreigner ₹100/500, night entry ₹100, guide ₹200, audio guide ₹200-250; ☉ 8am-6pm, last entry 5.30pm, night entry 7-9pm) This magnificent fort comprises an extensive palace complex, built from yellow and pink sandstone, and white marble, and is divided into four sections, each with its own courtyard. It is possible to visit the fortress on elephant-back, but animal welfare groups have criticised the keeping of elephants at Amber because of reports of abuse, and because carrying passengers can cause lasting injuries to the animals.

WORTH A TRIP

ABHANERI

Abhaneri is home to one of Rajasthan's most spectacular step-wells. With around 11 visible levels (depending on groundwater level) of zigzagging steps, the 10th-century Chand Baori (☉ dawn-dusk) FREE is an incredible geometric wonder. Flanking the well is a small crumbling palace, where royals used to picnic and bathe in private rooms (water was brought up by ox-power).

Abhaneri is about 95km from Jaipur and about 10km from National Hwy 21, the main Agra–Jaipur highway. From Jaipur catch a bus to Sikandra (₹70, 1½ hours), from where you can hop in a crowded share taxi (₹10) for the 5km trip to Gular. From Gular catch a share taxi or minibus to Abhaneri (another 5km and ₹10). If you have your own transport, Abhaneri and its step-well is a worthwhile stop between Jaipur and Agra/Bharatpur.

As an alternative, you can trudge up to the fort from the road in about 10 minutes, or take a 4WD to the top and back for ₹400 (good for up to five passengers), including a one-hour wait time. For night entry, admission for foreigners drops to the Indian price.

However you arrive, you will enter Amber Fort through the Suraj Pol (Sun Gate), which leads to the Jaleb Chowk (Main Courtyard), where returning armies would display their war booty to the populace – women could view this area from the veiled windows of the palace. The ticket office is directly across the courtyard from the Suraj Pol. If you arrive by car you will enter through the Chand Pol (Moon Gate) on the opposite side of Jaleb Chowk. Hiring a guide or grabbing an audio guide is highly recommended, as there are very few signs and many blind alleys.

From Jaleb Chowk, an imposing stairway leads up to the main palace, but first it's worth taking the steps just to the right, which lead to the small Siladevi Temple, with its gorgeous silver doors featuring repoussé (raised relief) work.

Heading back to the main stairway will take you up to the second courtyard and the Diwan-i-Am (Hall of Public Audience), which has a double row of columns, each topped by a capital in the shape of an elephant, and latticed galleries above.

The maharaja's apartments are located around the third courtyard – you enter through the fabulous Ganesh Pol, decorated with beautiful frescoed arches. The Jai Mandir (Hall of Victory) is noted for its inlaid panels and multimirrored ceiling. Carved marble relief panels around the hall are fascinatingly delicate and quirky, depicting cartoon-like insects and sinuous flowers. Opposite the Jai Mandir is the Sukh Niwas (Hall of Pleasure), with an ivory-inlaid sandalwood door and a channel that once carried cooling water right through the room. From the Jai Mandir you can enjoy fine views from the palace ramparts over picturesque Maota Lake below.

The zenana (secluded women's quarters) surrounds the fourth courtyard. The rooms were designed so that the maharaja could embark on his nocturnal visits to his wives' and concubines' respective chambers without the others knowing, as the chambers are independent but open onto a common corridor.

The Amber Sound & Light Show (☎0141-2530844; Kesar Kiyari complex; Indian/foreigner ₹100/200; ☉English 7.30pm, Hindi 8.30pm) takes place below the fort in the complex near Maota Lake.

Jaigarh   FORT

(Indian/foreigner ₹50/100, car ₹50, Hindi/English guide ₹200/300; ☉9am-5pm) A scrubby green hill rises above Amber and is topped by the imposing Jaigarh, built in 1726 by Jai Singh. The stern fort, punctuated by whimsical-hatted lookout towers, was never captured and has survived intact through the centuries. It's an uphill walk (about 1km) from Amber and offers great views from the Diwa Burj watchtower. The fort has reservoirs, residential areas, a puppet theatre and the world's largest wheeled cannon, Jaya Vana.

During the Mughal empire, Jaipur produced many weapons for the Mughal and Rajput rulers. The cannon, a most spectacular example, was made in the fort foundry, which was constructed in Mughal times. The huge weapon dates from 1720, has a barrel around 6m long, is made from a mix of eight different metals and weighs 50 tonnes. To fire it requires 100kg of gunpowder, and it has a range of 30km. It's debatable how many times this great device was used.

A sophisticated network of drainage channels feed three large tanks that used to provide water for all the soldiers, residents and livestock living in the fort. The largest tank has a capacity for 22.8 million litres

of water. The fort served as the treasury of the Kachhwahas, and for a long time people were convinced that at least part of the royal treasure was still secreted in this large water tank. The Indian government even searched it to check, but found nothing.

Within the fort is an armoury and museum, with the essential deadly weapons collection and some royal knick-knacks, including interesting photographs, maps of Jaigarh, spittoons, and circular 18th-century playing cards. The structure also contains various open halls, including the Shubhat Niwas (Meeting Hall of Warriors), which has some weather-beaten sedan chairs and drums lying about.

Admission is free with a valid ticket from the Jaipur City Palace that is less than two days old.

Anokhi Museum of Hand Printing   MUSEUM

(☎0141-2530226; Anokhi Haveli, Kheri Gate; adult/child ₹80/25; ☉10.30am-4.30pm Tue-Sat, 11am-4.30pm Sun, closed May–mid-Jul) This interesting museum in a restored *haveli* documents the art of hand-block printing, from old traditions to contemporary design. You can watch masters carve unbelievably intricate wooden printing blocks and even have a go at printing your own scarf or T-shirt. There's a cafe and gift shop, too.

🛏 Sleeping

★Mosaics Guesthouse   GUESTHOUSE $$
(☎0141-2530031, 8875430000; www.mosaics guesthouse.com; Siyaram Ki Doongri; s/d incl breakfast ₹3300/3800; ❄@🛜) Get away from it all at this gorgeous arty place (the French owner is a mosaic artist and will show off his workshop) with four lovely rooms and a rooftop terrace with beautiful fort views. Set-price Franco-Indian meals cost ₹800/1000 for veg/nonveg. It's about 1km past the fort near Kunda Village – head for Siyaram Ki Doongri, where you'll find signs.

Bharatpur & Keoladeo National Park

☎05644252,350 / POP 252,350

Bharatpur is famous for its wonderful Unesco-listed Keoladeo National Park, a wetland and significant bird sanctuary. Apart from the park, Bharatpur also has a few historic vestiges, though it wouldn't be worth making the journey for these alone. The town is dusty, noisy and not particularly

Bharatpur

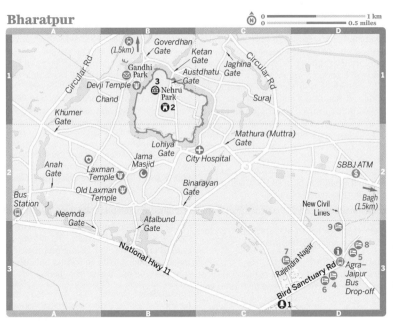

visitor-friendly. Bharatpur hosts the boisterous and colourful **Brij Festival** just prior to Holi celebrations.

◉ Sights

Lohagarh   FORT

FREE The still-inhabited, 18th-century Lohagarh, or Iron Fort, was so named because of its sturdy defences. Despite being somewhat forlorn and derelict, it is still impressive, and sits at the centre of town, surrounded by a moat. There's a northern entrance, at **Austdhatu (Eight-Metal) Gate** – apparently the spikes on the gate are made of eight different metals – and a southern entrance, at **Lohiya Gate**.

Maharaja Suraj Mahl, constructor of the fort and founder of Bharatpur, built two towers, the **Jawahar Burj** and the **Fateh Burj**, within the ramparts to commemorate his victories over the Mughals and the British. The fort also contains three much decayed palaces within its precincts.

One of the palaces, centred on a tranquil courtyard, houses a **museum** (Indian/foreigner ₹20/100, photography prohibited inside museum; ⊘ 9.45am-5.15pm Tue-Sun). Upstairs is a ragtag display of royal artefacts, including weaponry. More impressive is the Jain sculpture gallery, which includes some beautiful 7th- to

Bharatpur

◉ **Top Sights**
1 Keoladeo National Park C3

◉ **Sights**
2 Lohagarh...B1
3 Museum B1

🛏 **Sleeping**
4 Birder's Inn D3
5 Falcon Guest House D3
6 Hotel Sunbird D3
7 Kiran Guest House...............................C3
8 New Spoonbill Guesthouse D3
9 Royal Guest House D3

Flexible category 3
State Bank of India ATM..............(see 5)

10th-century pieces. The most spectacular feature of the museum, however, is the palace's original *hammam* (bathhouse), which retains some fine carvings and frescos.

◉ Keoladeo National Park

This tremendous bird sanctuary and **national park** (Indian/foreigner ₹75/500, video ₹600/900, guide per hr ₹150, bike/mountain-bike/ binoculars rental per day ₹25/40/100; ⊘ 6am-6pm Apr-Sep, 6.30am-5pm Oct-Mar) has long been recognised as one of the world's most important bird breeding and feeding grounds. In a good monsoon season over one-third of the park can be submerged, hosting more than 360 species within its 29 sq km. The marshland patchwork is a wintering area for aquatic birds, including visitors from Afghanistan, Turkmenistan, China and Siberia. The park is also home to deer, nilgai (antelope) and boar, which can be readily spotted.

Keoladeo originated as a royal hunting reserve in the 1850s. It continued to supply the tables of the maharajas with fresh game until as late as 1965. In 1982 Keoladeo was declared a national park and it was listed as a World Heritage Site in 1985.

By far the best time to visit this park is October to February, when you should see many migratory birds. At other times it can be dry and relatively bird-free.

Visiting the Park

Park admission entitles you to one entrance per day. One narrow road (no motorised vehicles are permitted past checkpoint 2) runs through the park, but a number of tracks and pathways fan out from it and thread their way between the shallow wetlands. Generally speaking, the further away from the main gate you go, the more interesting the scenery, and the more varied the wildlife becomes.

Only the government-authorised cycle-rickshaws (recognisable by the yellow license plate) are allowed beyond checkpoint 2, and they can only travel along the park's larger tracks. You don't pay an admission fee for the drivers, but they charge ₹100 per hour; some are very knowledgeable.

An excellent way to see the park is by hiring a bicycle at the park entrance. Having a bike is a wonderfully quiet way to travel, and allows you to avoid bottlenecks and take in the serenity on your own. However, we recommend that lone female travellers who wish to cycle do so with a guide (who will cycle alongside you), as we've had more than one report of lone women being harassed by young men inside the park in recent years.

You get a small map with your entrance ticket, though the park isn't big, so it's difficult to get lost.

🛏 Sleeping

There are plenty of sleeping options, suiting all budgets, near the park on Bird Sanctuary Rd, so don't feel pressured by touts at Bharatpur's train or bus stations.

New Spoonbill Guesthouse   HOTEL $
(☏ 05644-223571, 7597412553; www.hotelspoon bill.com; Gori Shankur Colony; s/d ₹700/800, with AC ₹1100/1200; 🅰@🛜) Owned and run by the same family as the original Spoonbill Hotel down the road, this place has simple but smart rooms, each with a small terrace. The larger rooms are great, with lots of windows. The dining room looks onto the garden and delicious home-cooked meals are available.

Royal Guest House   HOTEL $
(☏ 9414315457; www.royalguesthousebharatpur. com; B-15 New Civil Lines, near Saras Circle; r ₹300-900; 🅰@🛜) Rooms at the Royal are all very clean and fresh, and the rooftop restaurant is cosy, making the whole place feel more like a homestay than a guesthouse. Guests can use a kitchen for self-catering, and have free access to the internet. The ultrakeen management, who live on the premises, do money changing and run a sister operation, Royal Farmhouse, 3.5km from here.

Falcon Guest House   GUESTHOUSE $
(☏ 05644-223815; falconguesthouse@hotmail. com; Gori Shankur Colony; s/d from ₹600/800, r with AC ₹1200-1500; 🅰@) The Falcon may well be the pick of a bunch of hotels all in a row and all owned by the same extended family. It's a well-kept, snug place to stay, run by the affable Mrs Rajni Singh. There is a range of comfortable, good-sized rooms at different prices, including a family room. The best rooms have balconies.

Kiran Guest House   GUESTHOUSE $
(☏ 05644-223845; www.kiranguesthouse.com; 364 Rajendra Nagar; r ₹400-800, with AC ₹1100; 🅰) Managed by eager-to-please brothers, this guesthouse delivers great value, with seven simple, clean and spacious rooms and a pleasant rooftop where you can eat tasty home cooking. It's on a quiet road not far from Keoladeo park. Nature guiding and free pick-up from the Bharatpur train and bus stations are offered.

⭐ Hotel Sunbird   HOTEL $$
(☏ 05644-225701; www.hotelsunbird.com; Bird Sanctuary Rd; s/d from ₹2100/2550, ste ₹2950; 🅰🛜) This popular, well-run place close to the Keoladeo park entrance may look modest from the road, but out back boasts a lovely garden (with bar) and spacious rooms with balconies. Rooms are clean and comfortable and the restaurant dishes up a good range of tasty veg and nonveg dishes. Packed lunches and guided tours for the park are available.

MAJOR TRAINS FROM BHARATPUR

DESTINATION	TRAIN	DEPARTURE	ARRIVAL	FARE (₹)
Agra (Cantonment)	19666 Udz-Kurj Exp	9.46am	10.55am	150/510 (A)
Delhi (Hazrat Nizamuddin)	12059 Kota-Jan Shatabdi	9.25am	12.30pm	135/415 (B)
Jaipur	19665 Kurj-Udaipr Exp	6.55pm	10.50pm	150/510 (A)
Sawai Madhopur	12904 Golden Temple Mail	10.30am	12.55pm	180/560 (A)

Fares: (A) sleeper/3AC, (B) 2nd-class/AC chair

★ Birder's Inn   HOTEL $$
(☑ 05644-227346; www.birdersinn.com; Bird Sanctuary Rd; r incl breakfast from ₹3500; ❄ @ 🛰 🏊) The Birder's Inn is a popular, long-standing base for exploring the national park. There is a multicuisine restaurant and a small pool to cool off in. The rooms are airy, spacious and nicely decorated, and are set far back from the road in well-tended gardens. Guides from the hotel are available for Keoladeo.

ℹ Information

Main Post Office (⊘ 10am-1pm & 2-5pm Mon-Sat) Near Gandhi Park.
Tourist Office (☑ 05644-222542; Saras Circle; ⊘ 9am-5pm) On the crossroads about 700m from the national park entrance; has a free map of Bharatpur and Keoladeo National Park.

ℹ Getting There & Away

BUS

Buses running between Agra and Jaipur will drop you by the tourist office or outside the Keoladeo park entrance if you ask.

Services from Bharatpur **bus station** include the following:
Agra non-AC/AC ₹68/171, 1½ hours, half-hourly around the clock
Alwar ₹136, four hours, hourly until 8pm
Deeg ₹39, one hour, hourly until 8pm
Delhi ₹192, five hours, half-hourly from 6am to 7pm, then hourly until 11pm
Fatehpur Sikri ₹28, 45 minutes, half-hourly around the clock
Jaipur ₹195, 4½ hours, half-hourly, 24 hours

TRAIN

The **train station** is about 4km from Keoladeo and the main hotel area; a rickshaw should cost around ₹70.

Agra 2nd-class seat/sleeper/3AC ₹60/150/510, 1½ to two hours, nine daily between 4.45am and 8.10pm
Delhi 2nd-class seat/sleeper/3AC ₹95/180/510, three to four hours, 12 trains

daily, plus three other services on selected days
Jaipur 2nd-class seat/sleeper/3AC ₹110/150/510, three to four hours, nine daily between 2am and 10pm
Ranthambhore NP (Sawai Madhopur) 2nd-class seat/sleeper/3AC ₹135/180/560, two to three hours, 10 daily between 1am and 9.40pm. These trains all continue to Kota (four hours) from where you can catch buses to Bundi.

ℹ Getting Around

A cycle- or autorickshaw from the bus station to the main hotel area should cost around ₹40 (add an extra ₹30 from the train station).

Alwar

☑ 0144 / POP 341,430

Alwar is perhaps the oldest of the Rajasthani kingdoms, forming part of the Matsya territories of Viratnagar in 1500 BC. It became known again in the 18th century under Pratap Singh, who pushed back the rulers of Jaipur to the south and the Jats of Bharatpur to the east, and who successfully resisted the Marathas. It was one of the first Rajput states to ally itself with the fledgling British empire, although British interference in Alwar's internal affairs meant this partnership was not always amicable.

Alwar is the nearest town to Sariska Tiger Reserve and National Park and boasts a good museum, but it sees few tourists.

◎ Sights

City Palace   HISTORIC BUILDING
(Vinay Vilas Mahal) Under the gaze of Bala Quila fort sprawls the colourful and convoluted City Palace complex, with massive gates and a tank reflecting a symmetrical series of ghats and pavilions. Today most of the complex is occupied by government offices, overflowing with piles of dusty papers and soiled by pigeons and splatters of *paan* (a mixture of betel nut and leaves for chewing).

RAJASTHAN ALWAR

SURAJ MAHL'S PALACE, DEEG

At the centre of Deeg – a small, rarely visited, dusty tumult of a town about 35km north of Bharatpur – stands the incongruously glorious **Suraj Mahl's Palace** (Indian/foreigner ₹15/200; ⊙ 9.30am-5.30pm Sat-Thu), edged by stately formal gardens. It's one of India's most beautiful and carefully proportioned palace complexes. Pick up a map and brochure at the entrance; photography is not permitted in some of the bhavans (buildings).

Built in a mixture of Rajput and Mughal architectural styles, the 18th-century **Gopal Bhavan** is fronted by imposing arches to take full advantage of the early-morning light. Downstairs is a lower storey that becomes submerged during the monsoon as the water level of the adjacent tank, **Gopal Sagar**, rises. It was used by the maharajas until the early 1950s, and contains many original furnishings, including faded sofas, huge punkas (cloth fans) that are over 200 years old, chaise longues, a stuffed tiger, elephant-foot stands, and fine porcelain from China and France.

In an upstairs room at the rear of the palace is an Indian-style marble dining table – a stretched oval-shaped affair raised just 20cm off the ground. Guests sat around the edge, and the centre was the serving area. In the maharaja's bedroom is an enormous 3.6m by 2.4m wooden bed with silver legs.

Two large tanks lie alongside the palace, the aforementioned Gopal Sagar to the east and **Rup Sagar** to the west. The well-maintained gardens and flowerbeds, watered by the tanks, continue the extravagant theme with over 2000 fountains. Many of these fountains are in working order and coloured waters pour forth during the monsoon festival in August.

The **Keshav Bhavan** (Summer or Monsoon Pavilion) is a single-storey edifice with five arches along each side. Tiny jets spray water from the archways and metal balls rumble around in a water channel imitating monsoon thunder. Deeg's massive walls (which are up to 28m high) and 12 vast bastions, some with their cannons still in place, are also worth exploring. You can walk up to the top of the walls from the palace.

Other bhavans (in various states of renovation) include the marble **Suraj Bhavan**, reputedly taken from Delhi and reassembled here, the **Kishan Bhavan** and, along the northern side of the palace grounds, the **Nand Bhavan**.

Deeg is an easy day trip (and there's nowhere good to stay) from Bharatpur or Alwar by car. All the roads to Deeg are rough and the buses crowded. Frequent buses run to and from Alwar (₹60, 2½ hours) and Bharatpur (₹28, one hour).

Hidden within the City Palace is the excellent **Alwar Museum** (Indian/foreigner ₹50/100; ⊙ 9.45am-5.15pm Tue-Sun).

The museum's eclectic exhibits evoke the extravagance of the lifestyle of the maharajas: stunning weapons, stuffed Scottish pheasants, royal ivory slippers, erotic miniatures, royal vestments, a solid silver table, and stone sculptures, such as an 11th-century sculpture of Vishnu.

Somewhat difficult to find in the Kafkaesque tangle of government offices, the museum is on the top floor of the palace, up a ramp from the main courtyard. There should be plenty of people around to point you in the right direction and from there you can follow the signs.

Cenotaph of Maharaja Bakhtawar Singh   HISTORIC BUILDING

This double-storey edifice, resting on a platform of sandstone, was built in 1815 by Maharaja Vinay Singh, in memory of his father. To gain access to the cenotaph, take the steps to the far left when facing the palace. The cenotaph is also known as the Chhatri of Moosi Rani, after one of the mistresses of Bakhtawar Singh who performed *sati* (self-immolation) on his funeral pyre – after this act she was promoted to wifely status.

Bala Quila   FORT

This imposing fort stands 300m above Alwar, its fortifications hugging the steep hills that line the eastern edge of the city. Predating the time of Pratap Singh, it's one of the few forts in Rajasthan built before the rise of the Mughals, who used it as a base for attacking Ranthambhore. Mughal emperors Babur and Akbar have stayed overnight here, and Prince Salim (later Emperor Jehangir) was exiled in Salim Mahal for three years.

Now in ruins, the fort houses a radio transmitter station and parts can only be visited with permission from the superintendent of police. However, this is easy to get: just ask at the superintendent's office in the City Palace complex. You can walk the very steep couple of kilometres up to the fort entrance or take a 7km rickshaw ride.

🛏 Sleeping & Eating

⭐ Aravali Clarks Inn   HOTEL $$
(📲 0144-2332316; www.clarksinn.in; Nehru Rd; s/d incl breakfast from ₹2500/3000, ste ₹6000; 🌸@🛜🏊) One of the town's best choices, this conveniently located hotel has recently come under the patronage of Clarks Inn and is undergoing refurbishment. Rooms are large and well furnished and boast big bathrooms. The multicuisine Bridge restaurant is one of the best in town, and there's a bar. The pool is summer only.

Turn left out of the train station and it's about 300m down the road.

Hotel Hill View   HOTEL $$
(📲 0144-2700989; www.hillviewalwar.com; 19 Moti Dungri Rd; r from ₹2100; 🌸🛜) Rooms at this centrally located hotel vary so much that you may prefer a cheaper 'deluxe' to a pricier 'super deluxe'; inspect a few before deciding. The same management runs three Inderlok restaurants in town, including one here, so the food is good. The attached bar may or may not be an advantage depending on the clientele.

It is found south of the city centre on the road that encircles Moti Dungri.

RTDC Hotel Meenal   HOTEL $$
(📲 0144-2347352; meenal@rtdc.in; Topsingh Circle; s/d ₹900/1100, with AC ₹1100/1300; 🌸) A respectable option with tidy yet bland rooms typical of the chain. It's located about 1km south of town on the way to Sariska, so it's quiet and leafy, though a long way from the action.

Prem Pavitra Bhojnalaya   INDIAN $
(📲 9314055521; near Hope Circle; mains ₹75-100; ⊙10.30am-4pm & 6.30-10pm; 🍴) Alwar's renowned restaurant has been going since 1957. In the heart of the old town, it serves fresh, tasty pure-veg food – try the delicious *aloo parathas* (bread stuffed with spicy potato) and *palak paneer* (unfermented cheese cubes in spinach puree). The servings are big; half-serves are available. Finish off with the famous *kheer* (creamy rice pudding).

You have to pay 10% extra to eat in the air-conditioned section – but it is worth it. Turn right out of the bus station, take the first left (towards Hope Circle) and it's on your left after 100m.

ℹ️ Information

State Bank of Bikaner & Jaipur (Company Bagh Rd; ⊙9.30am-4pm Mon-Fri, to 12.30pm Sat) Changes major currencies and travellers cheques and has an ATM. Near the bus stand.

Tourist Office (📲 0144-2347348; Nehru Rd; ⊙10am-5pm Mon-Sat) Helpful centre (if actually open when it should be) offering a map of Alwar and information on Sariska. Near the train station.

ℹ️ Getting There & Around

A cycle-rickshaw between the bus and train stations costs ₹80. Look out for the shared taxis (₹10) that ply fixed routes around town. They come in the form of white minivans and have the word 'Vahini' printed on their side doors. One handy route goes past Aravali Clarks Inn, the tourist office and the train station before continuing on to the bus station and terminating a short walk from the City Palace complex.

A return taxi to Sariska Tiger Reserve will cost you around ₹1500.

BUS
The Alwar **bus station** is on Old Bus Stand Rd, near Manu Marg. Services:

Bharatpur ₹128, four hours, hourly from 5am to 8.30pm

Deeg ₹87, 2½ hours, hourly from 5am to 8.30pm

Delhi ₹176, four hours, every 20 minutes from 5am to 9pm

Jaipur ₹160, four hours, half-hourly from 6am to 10.30pm

Sariska ₹35, one hour, half-hourly from 6am to 10.30pm

TRAIN
The **train station** is fairly central, on Naru Marg. Around a dozen daily trains leave for Delhi (sleeper/3AC ₹180/560, three to four hours) throughout the day.

It's also three to four hours to Jaipur (sleeper/3AC ₹180/510) from here. Sixteen trains depart daily and prices are almost identical to those for Delhi.

Sariska Tiger Reserve & National Park

📲 0144

Enclosed within the dramatic, shadowy folds of the Aravalli Hills, the Sariska Tiger Reserve & National Park (📲 0144-2841333; www.rajasthanwildlife.in; Indian/foreigner ₹105/570, vehicle ₹250; ☺ morning safari 7-10.30am, evening safari 2-5.30pm Nov-Feb, timings vary by 30min Mar-Jun & Oct, no safaris Jul-Sep, tickets on sale an hour before entry time) is a tangle of remnant semideciduous jungle and craggy canyons sheltering streams and lush greenery. It covers 866 sq km (including a core area of 498 sq km), and is home to peacocks, monkeys, majestic sambars, nilgai, chital, wild boars and jackals.

Unfortunately, despite its name, you're unlikely to spot a tiger in Sariska. It is, however, still a fascinating sanctuary. The best time to spot wildlife is November to March, and you'll see most wildlife in the evening. The park is closed to safaris from 1 July to 30 September. Your chances of spotting wildlife at this time is minimal, in any case, and the park is only open for temple pilgrimage.

◎ Sights

Besides wildlife, Sariska has some fantastic sights within the reserve or around its peripheries, which are well worth seeking out. If you take a longer tour, you can ask to visit one or more of these. Some are also accessible by public bus.

Kankwari Fort
FORT

Deep inside the sanctuary, this imposing small jungle fort, 22km from Sariska, offers amazing views over the plains of the national park, dotted with red mud-brick villages. A four- to five-hour 4WD safari (one to five passengers plus mandatory guide) to Kankwari Fort from the Forest Reception Office near the reserve entrance costs ₹2600, plus guide fee (₹300).

This fort is the inaccessible place that Aurangzeb chose to imprison his brother, Dara Shikoh, Shah Jahan's chosen heir to the Mughal throne, for several years before he was beheaded.

Bhangarh
HISTORIC SITE

Around 55km from Sariska, beyond the inner park sanctuary and out in open countryside, is this deserted, well-preserved and notoriously haunted city. Founded in 1631 by Madho Singh, it had 10,000 dwellings, but was suddenly deserted about 300 years ago for reasons that remain mysterious. Bhangarh can be reached by a bus (₹39) that runs twice daily through the sanctuary to nearby Golaka village. Check what time the bus returns, otherwise you risk getting stranded.

☞ Tours

Private cars, including taxis, are limited to sealed roads heading to the temple and are allowed only on Tuesday and Saturday. The best way to visit the park is by gypsy (open-topped, six-passenger 4WD), which can explore off the main tracks. Gypsy safaris start

SARISKA'S TIGER TALE

Sariska Tiger Reserve took centre stage in one of India's most publicised wildlife dramas. In 2005 an Indian journalist broke the news that the tiger population here had been eliminated, a report that was later confirmed officially after an emergency census was carried out.

An inquiry into the crisis recommended fundamental management changes before tigers be reintroduced to the reserve. Extra funding was proposed to cover relocation of villages within the park as well as increasing the protection force. But action on the recommendations has been slow and incomplete despite extensive media coverage and a high level of concern in India.

Nevertheless, a pair of tigers from Ranthambhore National Park were moved by helicopter to Sariska in 2008. By 2010, five tigers had been transferred. However, in November 2010 the male of the original pair was found dead, having been poisoned by local villagers, who are not supportive of the reintroduction. The underlying problem: the inevitable battle between India's poorest and ever-expanding village populace with the rare and phenomenally valuable wildlife on their doorstep. Plans to relocate and reimburse villagers inside the park have largely failed to come to fruition, and illegal marble mining and clashes between cattle farmers and park staff have remained a problem.

In early 2012 the first cubs were sighted. At the time of writing, Sariska's tiger population was thought to be 14.

Only time will tell if this reintroduction is successful – inbreeding in the small population is an understandably high concern. Despite much vaunted successes for Project Tiger (www.projecttiger.nic.in) at a national level, Sariska remains a sad indictment of tiger conservation in India, from the top government officials down to the underpaid forest guards.

at the park entrance, and vehicle plus driver hire is ₹2100 for a three-hour safari; the vehicles can take up to five people (including guide). The bigger 20-seat canters cost ₹5000 for the vehicle and driver, but offer a much diminished experience. Guides are mandatory (₹300 for three hours).

Bookings can be made at the **Forest Reception Office** (☑0144-2841333; www.rajasthanwildlife.in; Jaipur Rd; ⊘ticket sales 6.55-7.30am & 1-3pm Nov-Jan, timings vary by 30min Mar-Jun & Oct), where buses will drop you.

🛏 Sleeping

RTDC Hotel Tiger Den   HOTEL $$
(☑0144-2841342; tigerden@rtdc.in; s/d incl breakfast ₹1860/2645, with AC ₹2505/3290, ste ₹4780; ❄) Hotel Tiger Den isn't fancy – a cement block fronted by a lawn and backed by a rambling garden. It's best feature is that it is very close to the reserve entrance. On the plus side the management is friendly, there is a bar, and the rooms have balconies with a pleasant outlook. Bring a mosquito net or repellent.

Hotel Sariska Palace   HERITAGE HOTEL $$$
(☑7073474870; www.thesariskapalace.in; r incl breakfast ₹8400, ste from ₹13,500; ❄🛜🏊) Near the reserve entrance is this imposing former hunting lodge of the maharajas of Alwar. There's a driveway leading from opposite the Forest Reception Office. Rooms have soaring ceilings and soft mattresses, and those in the annexe by the swimming pool have good views. The Fusion Restaurant here serves expensive Indian and Continental dishes, as well as hosting a buffet (lunch/dinner ₹750/900).

Sariska Tiger Heaven   HOTEL $$$
(☑9251016312; www.sariskatigerheaven.com; r incl all meals from ₹7500; ❄🛜🏊) This isolated place about 3km west of the bus stop at Thanagazi village has free pick-up on offer. Rooms are set in stone-and-tile cottages and have big beds and windowed alcoves. It's a tranquil, if overpriced, place to stay. Staff can arrange 4WDs and guides to the reserve.

❶ Getting There & Away

Sariska is 35km from Alwar, a convenient town from which to approach the reserve. There are frequent (and crowded) buses from Alwar (₹35, one to 1½ hours, at least hourly) and on to Jaipur (₹129, four hours). Buses stop in front of the Forest Reception Office.

Ajmer

☑0145 / POP 542.330

Ajmer is a bustling, chaotic city, 130km southwest of Jaipur and just 13km from the Hindu pilgrimage town of Pushkar. It surrounds the expansive lake of Ana Sagar, and is itself ringed by rugged Aravalli Hills. Ajmer is Rajasthan's most important site in terms of Islamic history and heritage. It contains one of India's most important Muslim pilgrimage centres, the shrine of Khwaja Muin-ud-din Chishti, who founded the Chishtiya order, the prime Sufi order in India. As well as some superb examples of early Muslim architecture, Ajmer is also a significant centre for the Jain religion, possessing an amazing golden Jain temple. However, with Ajmer's combination of high-voltage crowds and traffic, especially during Ramadan and the anniversary of the saint's death, most travellers choose to use Ajmer as a stepping stone to laid-back Pushkar.

◉ Sights

Dargah of Khwaja Muin-ud-din Chishti   ISLAMIC SHRINE
(www.dargahajmer.com; ⊘4am-9pm summer, 5am-9pm winter) This is the tomb of Sufi saint Khwaja Muin-ud-din Chishti, who came to Ajmer from Persia in 1192 and died here in 1236. The tomb gained its significance during the time of the Mughals – many emperors added to the buildings here. Construction of the shrine was completed by Humayun, and the gate was added by the Nizam of Hyderabad. Mughal emperor Akbar used to make the pilgrimage to the dargah from Agra every year.

You have to cover your head in certain parts of the shrine, so remember to take a scarf or cap – there are plenty for sale at the colourful bazaar leading to the dargah, along with floral offerings and delicious toffees.

The main entrance is through **Nizam Gate** (1915). Inside, the green and white mosque, **Akbari Masjid**, was constructed in 1571 and is now an Arabic and Persian school for religious education. The next gate is called the **Shahjahani Gate**, as it was erected by Shah Jahan, although it is also known as 'Nakkarkhana', because of the two large *nakkharas* (drums) fixed above it.

A third gate, **Buland Darwaza** (16th century), leads into the dargah courtyard.

Ajmer

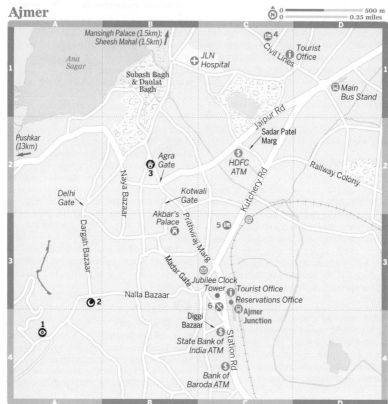

Ajmer

◉ Sights
1 Adhai-din-ka-Jhonpra A4
2 Dargah of Khwaja Muin-ud-din
   Chishti A3
3 Nasiyan (Red) Temple B2

◉ Sleeping
4 Badnor House C1
5 Haveli Heritage Inn C3

◉ Eating
6 Madina Hotel C3

Flanking the entrance of the courtyard are the *degs* (large iron cauldrons), one donated by Akbar in 1567, the other by Jehangir in 1631, for offerings for the poor.

Inside this courtyard, the saint's domed tomb is surrounded by a silver platform. Pilgrims believe that the saint's spirit will intercede on their behalf in matters of illness, business or personal problems, so the notes and holy string attached to the railings around are thanks or requests.

Pilgrims and Sufis come from all over the world on the anniversary of the saint's death, the Urs, in the seventh month of the Islamic lunar calendar. Crowds can be suffocating.

Bags must be left in the cloakroom (₹10 each, with camera ₹20) outside the main entrance.

Nasiyan (Red) Temple   JAIN TEMPLE
(Prithviraj Marg; ₹10; ⊙8.30am-5.30pm) This marvellous Jain temple, built in 1865, is also known as the Golden Temple, due to its amazing golden diorama in the double-storey temple hall. The intricate diorama depicts the Jain concept of the ancient world, with 13 continents and oceans, the golden city of Ayodhya, flying peacock and elephant gondolas, and gilded elephants with many tusks. The hall is also decorated with gold, silver and precious stones. It's unlike any

other temple in Rajasthan and is well worth a visit.

Adhai-din-ka-Jhonpra HISTORIC SITE

(Two-and-a-Half-Day Building; ⊙dawn-dusk) Beyond the Dargah of Khwaja Muin-ud-din Chishti, on the town outskirts, are the extraordinary ruins of the Adhai-din-ka-Jhonpra mosque. According to legend, construction in 1153 took only 2½ days. Others say it was named after a festival lasting 2½ days. It was originally built as a Sanskrit college, but in 1198 Mohammed of Ghori seized Ajmer and converted the building into a mosque by adding a seven-arched wall covered with Islamic calligraphy in front of the pillared hall.

🛏 Sleeping & Eating

Haveli Heritage Inn HOTEL $$

(☑ 0145-2621607; www.haveliheritageinn.com; Kutchery Rd; r ₹1340-3000; ❄ @) Set in a 140-year-old *haveli,* this welcoming city-centre oasis is arguably Ajmer's best midrange choice. The high-ceilinged rooms are spacious (some are almost suites), simply decorated, air-cooled and set well back from the busy road. There's a pleasant, grassy courtyard and the hotel is infused with a family atmosphere, complete with home-cooked meals.

Badnor House GUESTHOUSE $$

(☑ 0145-2627579; www.badnorhouse.com; Savitri Girl's College Rd, Civil Lines; s/d incl breakfast ₹2600/3000; ❄ 🛜) This guesthouse provides an excellent opportunity to stay with a delightful family and receive down-to-earth hospitality. There are three heritage-style doubles and an older-style, spacious and comfortable self-contained suite with private courtyard. The host is also an occasional travel photographer.

Mansingh Palace HOTEL $$$

(☑ 0145-2425956; www.mansinghhotels.com; Circular Rd; r from ₹4200, ste ₹7000; ❄ @ 🛜 ☰) This modern place, on the shores of Ana Sagar about 3km from the centre, is rather out of the way, but has attractive and comfortable rooms, some with views and balconies. The hotel has a shady garden, a bar and a good restaurant, the Sheesh Mahal.

Madina Hotel NORTH INDIAN $

(Station Rd; mains ₹30-100; ⊙9am-11pm) Handy if you're waiting for a train (it's opposite the station), this simple, open-to-the-street eatery cooks up cheap veg and nonveg fare, with specialities such as chicken Mughlai and *rumali roti* (huge paper-thin chapati).

Sheesh Mahal MULTICUISINE $$

(Circular Rd; mains ₹150-375; ⊙noon-3pm & 7-10.30pm) This upmarket restaurant, located in Ajmer's top hotel, the Mansingh Palace (p137), offers excellent Indian, Continental and Chinese dishes, as well as a buffet when the tour groups pass through. The service is slick, the air-con is on the chilly side, and the food is very good; it also boasts a bar.

ℹ Information

JLN Hospital (☑ 0145-2625500; Daulat Bagh; ⊙24hr)

Main Post Office (Prithviraj Marg; ⊙10am-1pm & 1.30-6pm Mon-Sat) Less than 500m from the train station.

Satguru's Internet (60-61 Kutchery Rd; per hr ₹30; ⊙9am-10pm)

Tourist Office Ajmer Junction Train Station (⊙9am-5pm); RTDC Hotel Khadim (☑ 0145-2627426; ⊙9am-5pm Mon-Fri)

ℹ Getting There & Away

For those pushing on to Pushkar, haggle hard for a private taxi – ₹350 is a good rate.

BUS

Government-run buses leave from the **main bus stand** in Ajmer, from where buses to Pushkar (₹14, 30 minutes) also leave throughout the day. In addition to these buses, there are less-frequent 'deluxe' coach services running to major destinations such as Delhi and Jaipur. There is a 24-hour cloakroom at the bus stand (₹10 per bag per day).

DESTINATION	FARE (₹)	DURATION (HR)
Agra	392	10
Ahmedabad	543	13
Bharatpur	330	7
Bikaner	267	7
Bundi	184	5
Chittorgarh	195, AC 348	5
Delhi	404, AC 1096	8½
Jaipur	148, AC 314	2½
Jaisalmer	458	11
Jodhpur	205, AC 445	6
Udaipur	285, AC 542	9

TRAIN

Ajmer is a busy train junction. To book tickets, go to booth 5 at the train station's **reservations office** (⊙8am-8pm Mon-Sat, to 2pm Sun). Services include the following:

MAJOR TRAINS FROM AJMER

DESTINATION	TRAIN	DEPARTURE	ARRIVAL	FARE (₹)
Agra (Agra Fort Station)	12988 Ajmer-SDAH Exp	12.50pm	6.50pm	275/695 (A)
Delhi (New Delhi)	12016 Ajmer Shatabdi	2.05pm	10pm	720/1530 (B)
Jaipur	12991 Udaipur-Jaipur Exp	11.30am	1.30pm	100/325/440 (C)
Jodhpur	15014 Ranighat Exp	1.40pm	5.35pm	185/510 (A)
Udaipur	09721 Jaipur-Udaipur SF SPL	8.25am	1.15pm	140/245/490/560 (D)

Fares: (A) sleeper/3AC, (B) AC chair/1AC, (C) 2nd-class seat/AC chair/1AC, (D) 2nd-class seat/sleeper/AC chair/3AC

Agra (Agra Fort Station) sleeper/AC Chair ₹275/570, 6½ hours, three daily (2.10am, 12.50pm and 3pm)

Chittorgarh sleeper/3AC ₹180/560, three hours, at least six daily (1.25am, 2.15am, 1pm, 4.10pm, 8.30pm and 9.05pm)

Delhi (mostly to Old Delhi or New Delhi stations) 2nd-class seat/sleeper ₹165/300, eight hours, 11 daily around the clock

Jaipur 2nd-class seat/sleeper/AC chair ₹100/150/325, two hours, at least 24 throughout the day

Jodhpur sleeper/3AC ₹185/510, four to five hours, two direct daily (1.40pm and 2.25pm)

Mt Abu (Abu Road) sleeper ₹245, five hours, 12 daily

Mumbai sleeper ₹495, around 19 hours, three daily (6.35am, 9.20am and 12.40pm)

Udaipur sleeper ₹245, five hours, four daily (1.25am, 2.15am, 8.25am and 4.10pm)

Pushkar

☎ 0145 / POP 21,630

Pushkar has a magnetism all of its own – it's quite unlike anywhere else in Rajasthan. It's a prominent Hindu pilgrimage town and devout Hindus should visit at least once in their lifetime. The town curls around a holy lake, said to have appeared when Brahma dropped a lotus flower. It also has one of the world's few Brahma temples. With 52 bathing ghats and 400 milky-blue temples, the town often hums with *puja* (prayers), generating an episodic soundtrack of chanting, drums and gongs, and devotional songs.

The result is a muddle of religious and tourist scenes. The main street is one long bazaar, selling anything to tickle a traveller's fancy, from hippy-chic tie-dye to didgeridoos. Despite the commercialism and

banana pancakes, the town remains enchantingly small and authentically mystic.

Pushkar is only 11km from Ajmer, separated from it by rugged Nag Pahar (Snake Mountain).

◉ Sights

Fifty-two bathing ghats surround the lake, where pilgrims bathe in the sacred waters. If you wish to join them, do so with respect. Remember, this is a holy place: remove your shoes and don't smoke, kid around or take photographs.

Some ghats have particular importance: Vishnu appeared at **Varah Ghat** in the form of a boar, Brahma bathed at **Brahma Ghat**, and Gandhi's ashes were sprinkled at **Gandhi Ghat**, formerly Gau Ghat.

Pushkar boasts hundreds of temples, though few are particularly ancient, as they were mostly desecrated by Aurangzeb and subsequently rebuilt.

Old Rangji Temple　　　　HINDU TEMPLE
Old Rangji Temple is close to the bazaar and is often alive with worshippers.

Savitri Mata Temple　　　　HINDU TEMPLE
(Saraswati Temple; ropeway return trip ₹92; ☉ ropeway 9.30am-7.30pm) The ropeway makes the ascent to the hilltop Saraswati Temple a breeze. The temple overlooks the lake and the views are fantastic at any time of day. Alternatively, you could take the one-hour trek up before dawn to beat the heat and capture the best light.

Brahma Temple　　　　HINDU TEMPLE
Pushkar's most famous temple is the Brahma Temple, said to be one of the few such temples in the world as a result of a curse by Brahma's consort, Saraswati. The temple is

Pushkar

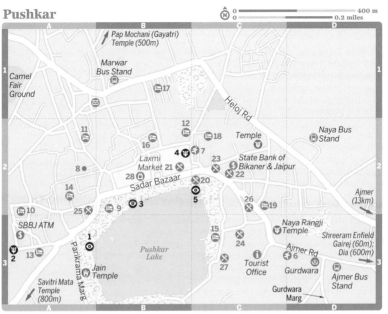

Pap Mochani (Gayatri) Temple (500m)

Marwar Bus Stand

Camel Fair Ground

Heloj Rd

Naya Bus Stand

Temple

Laxmi Market 21

State Bank of Bikaner & Jaipur

Sadar Bazaar

Ajmer (13km)

SBBJ ATM

Pushkar Lake

Naya Rangji Temple

Shreeram Enfield Gairej (60m); Dia (600m)

Ajmer Rd

Tourist Office

Gurdwara

Ajmer Bus Stand

Jain Temple

Savitri Mata Temple (800m)

Gurdwara Marg

Pushkar

Sights
1 Brahma Ghat A3
2 Brahma Temple A3
3 Gandhi Ghat B2
4 Old Rangji Temple B2
5 Varah Ghat C2

Activities, Courses & Tours
Cooking Bahar .... (see 8)
6 Government Homeopathic Hospital D3
7 Roshi Hiralal Verma C2
8 Saraswati Music School A2

Sleeping
9 Bharatpur Palace B2
10 Hotel Akash A2
11 Hotel Everest A2
12 Hotel Kanhaia Haveli B2
13 Hotel Navaratan Palace A3
14 Hotel Paramount Palace A2

15 Hotel Pushkar Palace C3
16 Hotel Tulsi Palace B2
17 Hotel White House B1
18 Inn Seventh Heaven C2
19 Shyam Krishna Guesthouse C2

Eating
20 Falafel Wrap Stalls C2
21 Honey & Spice B2
22 Naryan Café C2
23 Om Baba Restaurant C2
24 Om Shiva Garden Restaurant C3
25 Out of the Blue A2
26 Shri Vankatesh C2
Sixth Sense .... (see 18)
27 Sunset Café C3

Shopping
28 Sadar Bazaar B2

marked by a red spire, and over the entrance gateway is the *hans* (goose symbol) of Brahma. Inside, the floor and walls are engraved with dedications to the dead.

Pap Mochani (Gayatri) Temple   HINDU TEMPLE

The sunrise views over town from Pap Mochani (Gayatri) Temple, reached by a track

behind the Marwar bus stand, are well worth the 30-minute climb.

Activities

Government Homeopathic Hospital   AYURVEDA

(Ajmer Rd; 1hr full-body massage ₹500; ⊙9am-1pm & 4-6pm) For a noncommercial massage-treatment experience, try the ayurvedic

PUSHKAR CAMEL FAIR

Come the month of Kartika, the eighth lunar month of the Hindu calendar and one of the holiest, Thar camel drivers spruce up their ships of the desert and start the long walk to Pushkar in time for Kartik Purnima (Full Moon). Each year around 200,000 people converge on the **Pushkar Camel Fair** (⊙ Oct/Nov), bringing with them some 50,000 camels, horses and cattle.

The place becomes an extraordinary swirl of colour, sound and movement, thronged with musicians, mystics, tourists, traders, animals, devotees and camera crews.

Trading begins a week before the official fair (a good time to arrive to see the serious business), but by the time the RTDC mela (fair) starts, business takes a back seat and the bizarre sidelines (snake charmers, children balancing on poles etc) jostle onto centre stage. Even the cultural program seems peculiar, with contests for the best moustache, and most beautifully decorated camel. Visitors are encouraged to take part: pick up a program from the RTDC office and see if you fancy taking part in the costumed wedding parade, or join a Visitors versus Locals sports contest such as traditional Rajasthani wrestling.

It's hard to believe, but this seething mass is all just a sideshow. Kartik Purnima is when Hindu pilgrims come to bathe in Pushkar's sacred waters. The religious event builds in tandem with the camel fair in a wild, magical crescendo of incense, chanting and processions to dousing day, the last night of the fair, when thousands of devotees wash away their sins and set candles afloat on the holy lake.

Although fantastical, mystical and a one-off, it must be said that it's also crowded, touristy, noisy (light sleepers should bring earplugs) and occasionally tacky. Those affected by dust and/or animal hair should bring appropriate medication. However, it's a grand epic, and not to be missed if you're anywhere within camel-spitting distance.

The fair usually takes place in November, but dates change according to the lunar calendar.

department at the small and basic Government Homeopathic Hospital.

Roshi Hiralal Verma   REIKI, YOGA
(✆ 9829895906; Ambika Guest House, Laxmi Market) Offers reiki, yoga and shiatsu; costs depend on the duration and nature of your session.

⚲ Courses

Saraswati Music School   MUSIC
(✆ Birju 9828297784, Hemant 9829333548; saraswati_music@hotmail.com; Mainon ka Chowk) Teaches tabla (drums), flute, harmonium, singing, and *kathak* (classical dance) and Bollywood dance. For music, contact Birju, who's been playing for around 20 years, and charges from ₹350 for two hours. He often conducts evening performances (7pm to 8pm), and also sells instruments. For dance, contact Hemant.

Cooking Bahar   COOKING
(✆ 0145-2773124; www.cookingbahar.com; Mainon ka Chowk; 2-3hr class ₹1100) Part of the Saraswati Music School family, Deepa conducts cooking classes that cover three vegetarian courses.

🛌 Sleeping

Owing to Pushkar's star status among backpackers, there are far more budget options than midrange, though many budget properties have a selection of midrange-priced rooms. At the time of the camel fair, prices multiply up to three-fold or more, and it's essential to book several weeks ahead.

★ Hotel Everest   HOTEL $
(✆ 9414666958, 0145-2773417; www.pushkarhotel everest.com; off Sadar Bazaar; r ₹300-850, with AC ₹1000-1150; ❄ @ 🛜) This welcoming budget hotel is nestled in the quiet laneways north of Sadar Bazaar. It's run by a friendly father-and-son team who can't do too much for their appreciative guests. The rooms are variable in size, colourful and spotless, and the beds are comfortable. The rooftop is a pleasant retreat for meals or just relaxing with a book.

Hotel Tulsi Palace   HOTEL $
(✆ 8947074663; www.hoteltulsipalacepushkar. com; VIP Rd, Holika Chowk; r ₹500-700, with AC ₹1000-1500; 🛜) Tulsi Palace is a great budget choice with a variety of bright and

airy rooms around a central courtyard. The attached Little Prince Cafe on the 1st-floor verandah serves Continental breakfasts and Indian lunch and dinner, and boasts prime street-life views. The friendly staff will help with your transport needs.

Hotel White House GUESTHOUSE $
(☎0145-2772147; www.pushkarwhitehouse.com; off Heloj Rd; r ₹350-950, with AC ₹1000-1500; ❄@📶) This place is indeed white, with spotless rooms. Some are decidedly on the small side, but the nicest are generous and have balconies to boot. There is good traveller fare and green views from the plant-filled rooftop restaurant. It's efficiently run by a woman and her two sons. Yoga is offered, as is a welcome brew of mango tea for every guest.

Hotel Akash HOTEL $
(☎0145-2772498; filterboy21@yahoo.com; Badi Basti; d ₹600, s/d without bathroom ₹300/500; 📶) A simple budget place with keen young management and a large tree sprouting up from the courtyard to shade the rooftop terrace. Rooms are basic fan-cooled affairs that open out to a balcony restaurant good for spying on the street below.

Bharatpur Palace HOTEL $
(☎0145-2772320; bharatpurpalace_pushkar@yahoo.co.in; Sadar Bazaar; r ₹400-1000, without bathroom ₹250-600; ❄) This rambling building occupies one of the best spots in Pushkar, on the upper levels adjacent to Gandhi Ghat. It features aesthetic blue-washed simplicity: bare-bones rooms with unsurpassed views of the holy lake. The rooftop terrace (with restaurant) has sublime vistas, but respect for bathing pilgrims is paramount for intended guests.

Room 1 is the most romantic place to wake up: it's surrounded on three sides by the lake. Rooms 9, 12, 13 and 16 are also good.

Shyam Krishna Guesthouse GUESTHOUSE $
(☎0145-2772461; skguesthouse@yahoo.com; Sadar Bazaar; s/d ₹400/700, without bathroom ₹300/500; 📶) Housed in a lovely old blue-washed building with lawns and gardens, this guesthouse has ashram austerity and genuinely friendly management. Some of the cheaper rooms are cell-like, though all share the simple, authentic ambience. The outdoor kitchen and garden seating are a good setting for a relaxing meal of hearty vegetarian fare, but watch out for passing troops of monkeys.

Hotel Paramount Palace HOTEL $
(☎0145-2772428; www.pushkarparamount.com; r ₹200-1000; 📶) Perched on the highest point in Pushkar overlooking an old temple, this welcoming hotel has excellent views of the town and lake (and lots of stairs). The rooms vary widely; the best (106, 108, 109) have lovely balconies, stained-glass windows and are good value, but the smaller rooms can be dingy. There's a dizzyingly magical rooftop terrace.

Hotel Navaratan Palace HOTEL $
(☎0145-2772145; www.navratanpalace.com; s/d incl breakfast ₹800/900, with AC ₹1000/1200; ❄📶🏊) Located close to the Brahma Temple, this hotel has a lovely enclosed garden with a fabulous pool (₹100 for nonguests), children's playground and pet tortoises. The rooms, crammed with carved wooden furniture, are clean and comfortable but small.

★**Inn Seventh Heaven** HERITAGE HOTEL $$
(☎0145-5105455; www.inn-seventh-heaven.com; Choti Basti; r ₹1350-3300; ❄@📶) Enter this lovingly converted *haveli* through heavy wooden doors into an incense-perfumed courtyard, with a marble fountain in the centre and surrounded by tumbling vines. There are just a dozen individually decorated rooms situated on three levels, all with traditionally crafted furniture and comfortable beds. Rooms vary in size, from the downstairs budget rooms to the spacious Asana suite.

On the roof you'll find the excellent Sixth Sense restaurant (p142), as well as sofas and swing chairs for relaxing with a book. Early booking (two-night minimum, no credit cards) is recommended.

Hotel Kanhaia Haveli HOTEL $$
(☎0145-2772146; www.pushkarhotelkanhaia.com; Choti Basti; r ₹400-600, with AC ₹1500-1800; ❄📶) Boasting a vast range of rooms, from budget digs to suites, you are sure to find a room and price that suits. Rooms get bigger and lighter, with more windows, the more you spend. Some rooms have balconies, while all have cable TV. There is a multicuisine restaurant with views on the rooftop.

Dia B&B $$
(☎0145-5105455; www.diahomestay.com; Panch Kund Marg; r incl breakfast ₹3550-4950; ❄@📶) This beautifully designed B&B by the folks at Inn Seventh Heaven has five very private doubles a short walk from town. The rooms are straight out of a design magazine and will have you swooning (and extending your

booking). You can dine here at the cosy rooftop restaurant or head to the Sixth Sense restaurant at Inn Seventh Heaven.

Hotel Pushkar Palace   HERITAGE HOTEL $$$

(📞0145-2772001; www.hotelpushkarpalace.com; s/d/ste incl breakfast ₹7715/8310/17,805; ❋@) Once belonging to the maharaja of Kishangarh, the top-end Hotel Pushkar Palace boasts a romantic lakeside setting. The rooms have carved wooden furniture and beds, and all rooms above the ground floor, and all the suites, look directly out onto the lake: no hotel in Pushkar has better views. A pleasant outdoor dining area overlooks the lake.

Ananta Spa & Resort   RESORT $$$

(📞0145-3054000; www.anantahotels.com; Leela Sevri, Ajmer Rd; r incl breakfast from ₹6000; ❋@⟁☀) The arrival of Ananta, an (almost) five-star resort sprawling on 3.5 hectares in the rugged ranges 4km from Pushkar, heralds a new era in pilgrimages. Lucky pilgrims zip from reception to the Balinese-style cottages on golf buggies. Rooms are spacious and fully appointed, but most guests will gravitate to the luscious pool, spa, games room, restaurant, lounge or bar.

🍴 Eating

Pushkar has plenty of atmospheric eateries with lake views, and menus reflecting backpacker preferences. Strict vegetarianism, forbidding even eggs, is the order of the day.

Naryan Café   CAFE $

(Mahadev Chowk, Sadar Bazaar; breakfast from ₹100; ⊙7.30am-10pm) Busy any time of day, this is particularly popular as a breakfast stop: watch the world go by with a fresh coffee (from ₹40) or juice (from ₹80) and an enormous bowl of homemade muesli, topped with a mountain of fruit.

Shri Vankatesh   INDIAN $

(Choti Basti; mains ₹60-100; ⊙9am-10pm) Head to this no-nonsense local favourite and tuck into some dhal, paneer or kofta, before mopping up the sauce with some freshly baked chapatis and washing it all down with some good old-fashioned chai. The thalis (₹70 to ₹150) are excellent value, too. Watch your food being cooked or head upstairs to people-watch the street below.

Falafel Wrap Stalls   MIDDLE EASTERN $

(Sadar Bazaar; wraps ₹70-130; ⊙7.30am-10.30pm) Perfect for quelling a sudden attack of the munchies, and a big hit with Israeli travellers,

these adjacent roadside joints knock up a choice selection of filling falafel-and-hummus wraps. Eat them while sitting on stools on the road or devour them on the hoof.

Out of the Blue   MULTICUISINE $$

(Sadar Bazaar; mains ₹170-280; ⊙8am-11pm; ⟁) Distinctly a deeper shade of blue in this sky-blue town, Out of the Blue is a reliable restaurant. The menu ranges from noodles and *momos* (Tibetan dumplings) to pizza, pasta, falafel and pancakes. A nice touch is the street-level espresso coffee bar (coffees ₹60 to ₹80) and German bakery.

Sixth Sense   MULTICUISINE $$

(Inn Seventh Heaven, Choti Basti; mains ₹100-200; ⊙8.30am-4pm & 6-10pm; ⟁) This chilled rooftop restaurant is a great place to head to even if you didn't score a room in the popular hotel. The pizza and the Indian seasonal vegetables and rice are all serviceable, as is the filter coffee and fresh juice. Its ambience is immediately relaxing and the pulley apparatus that delivers food from the ground-floor kitchen is very cunning.

Save room for the desserts, such as the excellent homemade tarts.

Om Shiva Garden
Restaurant   MULTICUISINE $$

(📞0145-2772305; www.omshivagardenrestaurant.com; mains ₹140-250; ⊙8am-11pm; ⟁) This traveller stalwart near Naya Rangji Temple continues to satisfy, with wood-fired pizzas and espresso coffee featuring on its predominately Italian and North Indian menu. It's hard to pass on the pizzas, but there are also some Mexican and Chinese dishes and 'German bakery' items to try.

Honey & Spice   MULTICUISINE $$

(Laxmi Market, off Sadar Bazaar; mains ₹90-250; ⊙8am-5.30pm; ✍) 🌿 Run by a friendly family, this tiny wholefood breakfast and lunch place has delicious South Indian coffee and homemade cakes. Even better are the salads and hearty vegetable combo stews served with brown rice – delicious, wholesome and a welcome change from frequently oil-rich Indian food.

Sunset Café   MULTICUISINE $$

(mains ₹80-250; ⊙7.30am-midnight; ⟁) Right on the eastern ghats, this cafe has sublime lake views. It offers the usual traveller menu, including curries, pizza and pasta, plus there's a German bakery serving reasonable cakes. The lakeside setting is perfect at sunset and gathers a crowd.

BUSES FROM PUSHKAR (NAYA BUS STAND)

DESTINATION	FARE (₹)	DURATION (HR)	FREQUENCY
Bikaner	225	6	hourly
Bundi	200	6	daily (11am)
Jaipur	160	4	7 daily (7.15am, 7.45am, 8am, 8.30am, 9.30am, 2pm & 4pm)
Jodhpur	185	5	3 daily (8am, 10.30am & 12.30pm)

Om Baba Restaurant   MULTICUISINE **$$**
(☑ 0145-2772858; off Sadar Bazaar; mains ₹130-220; ⊙ 8.30am-11pm) Om Baba Rooftop Restaurant serves all the traveller favourites so common in the neighbourhood (pizza, pasta, falafel, hummus), but it's the views from the rooftop that sets this place apart.

🛍 Shopping

Sadar Bazaar   MARKET
Pushkar's Sadar Bazaar is lined with enchanting little shops and is a good place for picking up gifts. Many of the vibrant Rajasthani textiles originate from Barmer, south of Jaisalmer. There's plenty of silver and beaded jewellery catering both to local and foreign tastes, including some heavy tribal pieces. As Pushkar is touristy, you'll have to haggle.

The range of Indian-music CDs makes this market an excellent place to sample local tunes.

ⓘ Information

Foreign-card-friendly ATMs and unofficial money changers are dotted around Sadar Bazaar.
Post Office (off Heloj Rd; ⊙ 9.30am-5pm Mon-Fri) Near the Marwar bus stand.
State Bank of Bikaner & Jaipur (SBBJ; Sadar Bazaar; ⊙ 10am-4pm Mon-Fri, to 12.30pm Sat) Changes travellers cheques and cash. The SBBJ ATM accepts international cards.
Tourist Office (☑ 0145-2772040; Hotel Sarovar; ⊙ 10am-5pm) Free maps and camel fair programs.

DANGERS & ANNOYANCES

Beware of anyone giving you flowers to offer a *puja* (prayer): before you know it you'll be whisked to the ghats in a well-oiled hustle and asked for a personal donation of up to ₹1000. Other priests do genuinely live off the donations of others and this is a tradition that goes back centuries – but walk away if you feel bullied and always agree on a price before taking a red ribbon (a 'Pushkar passport') or flowers.

During the camel fair, Pushkar is besieged by pickpockets working the crowded bazaars. You can avoid the razor gang by not using thin-walled day packs and by carrying your pack in front of you. At any time of year, watch out for rampaging motorbikes ridden by inconsiderate youths in the bazaar.

ⓘ Getting There & Away

Pushkar's tiny train station is so badly connected it's not worth bothering with. Use Ajmer junction train station instead.

A private taxi to Ajmer costs around ₹300 (note that it's almost always more expensive in the opposite direction). When entering Pushkar by car there is a toll of ₹20 per person.

BUS

Frequent buses to/from Ajmer (₹14, 30 minutes) depart from the **Naya Bus Stand**, and also from the **Ajmer Bus Stand** on the road heading eastwards out of town. Most other buses leave from the Naya Bus Stand, though some may still use the old **Marwar Bus Stand** (but not RSRTC buses).

Local travel agencies sell tickets for private buses – you should shop around. These buses often leave from Ajmer (p137), but the agencies should provide you with free connecting transport. Check whether your bus is direct, as many services from Pushkar aren't. And note, even if they are direct buses they may well stop for some time in Ajmer, meaning it's often quicker to go to Ajmer first and then catch another bus from there.

ⓘ Getting Around

There are no autorickshaws in central Pushkar, but it's a breeze to get around on foot. If you want to explore the surrounding countryside, you could try hiring a motorbike (₹400 per day) from one of the many places around town. For something more substantial, try **Shreeram Enfield Gairej** (Ajmer Rd; Enfield Bullet hire per day ₹700, deposit ₹50,000), which hires Enfield Bullets and sells them.

Ranthambhore National Park
☑ 07462
This famous **national park** (www.rajasthan wildlife.in; ⊙ Oct-Jun) is the best place to spot wild tigers in Rajasthan. Comprising 1334

sq km of wild jungle scrub hemmed in by rocky ridges, at its centre is the 10th-century Ranthambhore Fort. Scattered around the fort are ancient temples and mosques, hunting pavilions, crocodile-filled lakes and vine-covered *chhatris* (burial tombs). The park was a maharajas' hunting ground until 1970, a curious 15 years after it had become a sanctuary.

Seeing a tiger (around 52 to 55 in 2016) is partly a matter of luck; leave time for two or three safaris to improve your chances. But remember there's plenty of other wildlife to see, including more than 300 species of birds.

It's 10km from Sawai Madhopur (the gateway town for Ranthambhore) to the first gate of the park, and another 3km to the main gate and Ranthambhore Fort.

◎ Sights

Ranthambhore Fort FORT
(⊙6am-6pm) FREE From a distance, the magical 10th-century Ranthambhore Fort is almost indiscernible on its hilltop perch – as you get closer, it seems almost as if it is growing out of the rock. It covers an area of 4.5 sq km, and affords peerless views from the disintegrating walls of the Badal Mahal (Palace of the Clouds), on its northern side. The ramparts stretch for more than 7km, and seven enormous gateways are still intact.

To visit the on the cheap, join the locals who go there to visit the temple dedicated to Ganesh. Shared 4WDs (₹40 per person) go from the train station to the park entrance – say 'national park' and they'll know what you want. From there, other shared 4WDs (₹20 per person) shuttle to and from the fort, which is inside the park. Alternatively hire your own gypsy (and driver) for about ₹1000 for three hours through your hotel.

✦ Activities

Safaris take place in the early morning and late afternoon, starting between 6am and 7am or between 2pm and 3.30pm, depending on the time of year. Each safari lasts for around three hours. The mornings can be exceptionally chilly in the open vehicles, so bring warm clothes.

The best option is to travel by gypsy (six-person, open-topped 4WD; Indian/foreigner ₹730/1470). You still have a chance of seeing a tiger from a canter (20-seat, open-topped truck; ₹510/1250), but other passengers can be very rowdy.

Be aware that the rules for booking safaris (and prices) are prone to change. You can book online through the park's official website (www.rajasthanwildlife.in), or go in person to the safari booking office, which is inconveniently located 1.5km from Hammir Circle, in the opposite direction to the park. And to be sure of bagging a seat in a vehicle, start queuing at least an hour (if not two) before the safaris are due to begin – meaning a very early start for morning safaris! Booking with hotels is much simpler, but be aware that they add commission to the rates.

🛏 Sleeping

Hotel Aditya Resort HOTEL $
(🕿9414728468; www.hoteladityaresort.com; Ranthambhore Rd; r ₹400-700, with AC ₹900; ❄@🖦) This friendly place is one of the better of the few ultracheapies along Ranthambhore Rd. There are just six simple, unadorned rooms (get one with an outside window; only a couple have air-conditioning), and a basic rooftop restaurant. The staff will help with safari bookings, but be sure to ask how much they are charging for the service.

★Hotel Ranthambhore Regency HOTEL $$
(🕿07462-221176; www.ranthambhor.com; Ranthambhore Rd; s/d incl all meals from ₹6500/7500; ❄@🖦🏊) A very professional place that caters to tour groups but can still provide great service to independent travellers. It has immaculate, well-appointed rooms (think marble floors, flat-screen TVs etc), which would rate as suites in most hotels. The central garden with an inviting pool is a virtual oasis, and there's a pampering spa next to the restaurant.

Tiger Safari Resort HOTEL $$
(🕿07462-221137; www.tigersafariresort.com; Ranthambhore Rd; r incl breakfast ₹1800-2200; ❄@🖦🏊) A reasonable midrange option, with spacious doubles and 'cottages' (larger rooms with bigger bathrooms) facing a garden and small pool. The management is adept at organising safaris, wake-up calls and early breakfasts before the morning safari. As per the other hotels, a commission is added for this service, so ask for a breakdown of the costs.

Ankur Resort HOTEL $$
(🕿07462-220792; www.ankurresorts.com; Ranthambhore Rd; s/d incl all meals ₹3500/4000, cottages ₹4000/5000; ❄@🖦🏊) Ankur Resort is good at organising safaris, wake-up calls and

early breakfasts for tiger spotters. Standard rooms are fairly unadorned, but clean and comfortable with TVs. The cottages boast better beds, a fridge and settee, and overlook the surrounding gardens and pool.

★ **Khem Villas**   BOUTIQUE HOTEL $$$
(☑ 07462-252099; www.khemvillas.com; Khem Villas Rd; s/d incl all meals ₹12,000/14,000, tents ₹19,000/23,000, cottages ₹21,000/25,000; ✳@శ) Set in 9 hectares of organic farmland and reforested land, this splendid ecolodge was created by the Singh Rathore family, the driving force behind the conservation of tigers at Ranthambhore. The accommodation ranges from colonial-style bungalow rooms to luxury tents and sumptuous stone cottages. Privacy is guaranteed – you can even bathe under the stars.

In addition to jungle safaris, Khem Villas runs a river safari (₹5000 for two people) on the Chambal river where you can see gharial and mugger crocodiles plus numerous bird species.

ℹ Information

There's an ATM just by Hammir Circle, as well as others by the train station.

Ranthambore Adventure Tours
(☑ 9414214460; ranthambhoretours@rediff.mail.com; Ranthambhore Rd) Safari agency that gets good reviews.

Tourist Office (☑ 07462-220808; Train Station; ◷ 9.30am-6pm Mon-Fri) Has maps of Sawai Madhopur, and can offer suggestions on safaris.

Safari Booking Office (www.rajasthanwildlife.com; ◷ 5.30am-3.30pm) Seats in gypsies and canters can be reserved on the website, though a single gypsy (with a premium price) and five canters are also kept for direct booking at the Forest Office. Located 500m from the train station.

ℹ Getting There & Away

There are very few direct buses to anywhere of interest, so it's always preferable to take the train.

TRAIN

Sawai Madhopur junction station is near Hammir Circle, which leads to Ranthambhore Rd.

Agra (Agra Fort Station) sleeper ₹210, six hours, three daily (11.10am, 4.10pm, 11.15pm)

Delhi 2nd-class/sleeper/3AC ₹190/260/660, 5½ to eight hours, 13 daily

Jaipur 2nd-class seat/sleeper/3AC ₹100/180/560, two hours, 11 to 13 daily

Keoladeo NP (Bharatpur) 2nd-class/sleeper/3AC ₹95/180/560, 2½ hours, 12 to 13 daily

Kota (from where you can catch buses to Bundi) 2nd-class/sleeper/3AC ₹90/180/560, one to two hours, hourly

ℹ Getting Around

Bicycle hire (around ₹40 per day) is available in the main bazaar. Autorickshaws are available at the train station; it's ₹50 to ₹100 for an autorickshaw from the train station to Ranthambhore Rd, depending on where you get off. Many hotels will pick you up from the train station for free if you call ahead.

If you want to walk, turn left out of the train station and follow the road up to the overpass (200m). Turn left and cross the bridge over the railway line to reach a roundabout (200m), known as Hammir Circle. Turn right here to reach the safari booking office (1.5km) or left to find accommodation.

UDAIPUR & SOUTHERN RAJASTHAN

Bundi

☑ 0747 / POP 103,290

A captivating town with narrow lanes of Brahmin-blue houses, lakes, hills, bazaars, and a temple at every turn, Bundi is dominated by a fantastical palace of faded parchment cupolas and loggias rising from the hillside above the town. Though an increasingly popular traveller hang-out, Bundi attracts nothing like the tourist crowds of places such as Jaipur or Udaipur. Few places in Rajasthan retain so much of the magical atmosphere of centuries past.

Bundi came into its own in the 12th century when a group of Chauhan nobles from Ajmer were pushed south by Mohammed of Ghori. They wrested the Bundi area from the Mina and Bhil tribes and made Bundi the capital of their kingdom, known as Hadoti. Bundi was generally loyal to the Mughals from the late 16th century on, but it maintained its independent status until incorporated into the state of Rajasthan after 1947.

◉ Sights

Bundi has around 60 beautiful *baoris* (stepwells), some right in the town centre. The majesty of many of them is unfortunately diminished by their lack of water today – a result of declining groundwater levels – and

Bundi

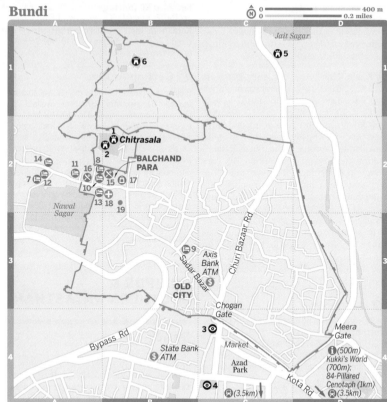

Bundi

◎ Top Sights
1 Chitrasala...B2

◎ Sights
2 Bundi Palace...B2
3 Nagar Sagar Kund...................................C4
4 Raniji-ki-Baori..C4
5 Sukh Mahal...C1
6 Taragarh...B1

🛌 Sleeping
7 Annpurna Haveli......................................A2
8 Bundi Vilas..A2
9 Dev Niwas...B3
10 Haveli Braj Bhushanjee..........................A2
11 Haveli Katkoun.......................................A2

12 Hotel Bundi Haveli..................................A2
13 Kasera Heritage View.............................A2
14 Shivam Tourist Guest House...................A2

🍴 Eating
Bundi Vilas.......................................(see 8)
15 Morgan's Place.......................................B2
16 Rainbow Cafe...A2

🛍 Shopping
17 Yug Art...B2

ℹ Information
18 Ayurvedic Hospital.................................B2
19 Roshan Tour & Travel.............................B2

by the rubbish that collects in them which no one bothers to clean up. The most impressive, **Raniji-ki-Baori** (Queen's Step-Well; Indian/foreigner ₹50/200; ⊙9.30am-5pm), is 46m deep and decorated with sinuous carvings, including the avatars of Lord Vishnu. The **Nagar Sagar Kund** is a pair of matching step-wells just outside the old city's Chogan Gate.

Three sights around town, the Rani-ji-ki-Baori, **84-Pillared Cenotaph** (Indian/foreigner ₹50/200; ⊙9.30am-5pm) and Sukh Mahal, can be visited using a composite ticket (Indian/foreigner ₹75/350) – a great saving if you plan to visit two or more of these sights.

Bundi Palace   PALACE
(Garh Palace; Indian palace/fort/camera ₹80/100/50, foreigner palace, fort & camera ₹500; ⊙8am-6pm) This extraordinary, partly decaying edifice – described by Rudyard Kipling as 'the work of goblins rather than of men' – almost seems to grow out of the rock of the hillside it stands on. Though large sections are still closed up and left to the bats, the rooms that are open hold a series of fabulous, fading turquoise-and-gold murals that are the palace's chief treasure. The palace is best explored with a local guide (₹700 half-day), who will be charged ₹100 to enter.

The palace was constructed during the reign of Rao Raja Ratan Singh (r 1607–31) and added to by his successors. Part of it remained occupied by the Bundi royals until 1948.

If you are going up to Taragarh as well as the palace, get tickets for both at the palace entrance. Once inside the palace's **Hathi Pol** (Elephant Gate), climb the stairs to the Ratan Daulat or **Diwan-e-Aam** (Hall of Public Audience), with a white marble coronation throne. You then pass into the **Chhatra Mahal**, added by Rao Raja Chhatra Shabji in 1644, with some fine but rather weathered murals. Stairs lead up to the **Phool Mahal** (1607), the murals of which include an immense royal procession, and then the **Badal Mahal** (Cloud Palace; also 1607), with Bundi's very best murals, including a wonderful Chinese-inspired ceiling, divided into petal shapes and decorated with peacocks and Krishnas.

★ Chitrasala   PALACE
(Umaid Mahal; ⊙8am-6pm) Within the Bundi Palace complex is the Chitrasala, a small 18th-century palace built by Rao Ummed Singh. To find it, exit through the palace's Hathi Pol (Elephant Gate) and walk round the corner uphill. Above the palace's garden courtyard are several rooms covered in beautiful paintings. There are some great Krishna images, including a detail of him sitting up a tree playing the flute after stealing the clothes of the *gopis* (milkmaids).

The back room to the right is the **Sheesh Mahal**, badly damaged but still featuring some beautiful inlaid glass, while back in the front room there's an image of 18th-century Bundi itself.

Taragarh   FORT
(Star Fort; ₹100, camera/video ₹50/100; ⊙8am-5pm) This ramshackle, partly overgrown 14th-century fort, on the hilltop above Bundi Palace, is a wonderful place to ramble around – but take a stick to battle the overgrown vegetation, help the knees on the steep climb and provide confidence when surrounded by testosterone-charged macaques. To reach it, just continue on the path up behind the Chitrasala.

Jait Sagar   LAKE
Round the far side of the Taragarh hill, about 2km north from the centre of town, this picturesque, 1.5km-long lake is flanked by hills and strewn with pretty lotus flowers during the monsoon and winter months. At its near end, the **Sukh Mahal** (Indian/foreigner ₹50/200; ⊙9.30am-5pm) is a small summer palace surrounded by terraced gardens where Rudyard Kipling once stayed and wrote part of *Kim*.

☞ Tours

Keshav Bhati   TOURS
(☎9414394241; bharat_bhati@yahoo.com) Keshav Bhati is a retired Indian Air Force officer with a passion for Bundi. He is also an official tour guide with an encyclopaedic knowledge of the region and is highly recommended. Tour prices are negotiable.

Kukki's World   TOURS
(☎9828404527; www.kukkisworld.com; 43 New Colony; half-/full-day tour for 2 people US$56/78) OP 'Kukki' Sharma is a passionate amateur archaeologist who has discovered around 70 prehistoric rock-painting sites around Bundi. His trips get you out into the villages and countryside, which he knows like the back of his hand. You can visit his collection of finds and select sites from his laptop at his house (about 300m south of the tourist office) beforehand.

🛏 Sleeping

Shivam Tourist Guest House   GUESTHOUSE $
(☎9460300272, 0747-2447892; Balchand Para; s/d ₹450/500, r with AC ₹800-1000) This guesthouse is run by an energetic young couple who are keen to help travellers get the most from their stay in Bundi. Rooms are simple but comfortable and spotless; the better

rooms are upstairs. There is an all-veg rooftop restaurant, cooking and henna-design classes are offered, plus they can help with booking transport.

Annpurna Haveli
GUESTHOUSE $

(☎ 0747-2447055, 9602805455; www.annpurna havelibundi.com; Balchand Para; r ₹800, r with breakfast & AC ₹1200; ❀ 🛜) Annpurna is a very peaceful family-run guesthouse of just six rooms opposite Nawal Sagar. The simple and clean rooms are a great budget choice, and the best rooms have lake views. Home-cooked meals are enjoyed either in the dining room or on the roof in fine weather.

★ Haveli Braj Bhushanjee
HERITAGE HOTEL $$

(☎ 0747-2442322, 9783355866; www.kiplingsbundi. com; Balchand Para; r ₹1500-6000; ❀ 🛜) This rambling 200-year-old *haveli* is run by the very helpful and knowledgeable Braj Bhushanjee family, descendants of the former prime ministers of Bundi. It's Bundi's first guesthouse and an enchanting place with original stone interiors, a private garden, splendid rooftop views, beautiful, well-preserved murals, and all sorts of other historic and valuable artefacts.

The terrific range of accommodation includes some lovely, modernised rooms that are still in traditional style. It's a fascinating living museum where you can really get a feel for Bundi's heritage. The *haveli* is opposite the Ayurvedic Hospital, though the main entrance is around the corner.

★ Hotel Bundi Haveli
HOTEL $$

(☎ 9929291552, 0747-2447861; www.hotelbundi haveli.com; Balchand Para; r ₹1300-4750; ❀ 🛜) The exquisitely renovated Bundi Haveli leads the pack in terms of contemporary style and sophistication. Spacious rooms, white walls, stone floors, colour highlights and framed artefacts are coupled with modern plumbing and electricity. Yes, it's very comfortable and relaxed and there's a lovely rooftop dining area boasting palace views and an extensive, mainly Indian menu (mains ₹100 to ₹280).

Dev Niwas
HERITAGE HOTEL $$

(☎ 0747-2442928, 8233345394; www.jagatcollection. com; Maaji Sahib-ki-Haveli; r ₹870-1300, with AC ₹3050, ste ₹4350; ❀ 🛜) 🍃 Dev Niwas is a fine *haveli,* just off the busy Sadar Bazaar. Inside is a peaceful oasis with courtyards and open-sided pavilions. Rooms are all very different, yet they are all comfortably furnished and fitted with modern bathrooms.

The open-sided restaurant has cushion seating and there are great views of the fort.

Bundi Vilas
HERITAGE HOTEL $$

(☎ 0747-2444614, 9214803556; www.bundivilas. com; r incl breakfast ₹4000-5000; ❀ @ 🛜) This 300-year-old *haveli* up a side alley has been tastefully renovated with golden Jaisalmer sandstone, earth-toned walls and deft interior design. The five deluxe and two suite rooms exude period character yet boast excellent bathrooms. Set in the lee of the palace walls, this guesthouse has commanding views of the town below and palace above from the rooftop terrace restaurant.

Kasera Heritage View
GUESTHOUSE $$

(☎ 9983790314, 0747-2444679; www.kaseraheritage view.com; s/d from ₹800/1000, r with breakfast & AC from ₹2000; ❀ @ 🛜) A revamped *haveli,* Kasera has an incongruously modern lobby, but offers a range of slightly more authentic rooms. The welcome is friendly, it's all cheerfully decorated, the rooftop restaurant has great views, and discounts of 20% to 30% are offered in summer. The owners' sister *haveli,* Kasera Paradise, just below the palace, has the same contact details and rates.

Haveli Katkoun
GUESTHOUSE $$

(☎ 0747-2444311, 9414539146; www.katkounhaveli bundi.com; s/d ₹700/1200, r incl breakfast & AC ₹2400; ❀ 🛜) Just outside the town's western gate, Katkoun is a completely revamped *haveli* with friendly family management who live downstairs. It boasts large, spotless rooms offering superb views on both sides, to either the lake or palace, and has a good rooftop restaurant (mains ₹65 to ₹200), known for its Indian nonveg dishes.

✖ Eating

★ Bundi Vilas
INDIAN $$

(☎ 0747-2444614; www.bundivilas.com; Balchand Para; mains ₹210-250, set dinners ₹700; ⊙ 7.30-10am, 1-3pm & 7-10pm; 🛜 🍴) The most romantic restaurant in Bundi welcomes visitors from other hotels. Dine in the sheltered yet open-sided terrace, or on the rooftop with uninterrupted views of the fort. It's wise to book for dinner as spots are limited for the candlelit experience beneath the floodlit palace. The set dinner offers several courses of exquisite food and wine is available.

Bundi Vilas has its own farm on the outskirts of Bundi that supplies much of its fresh fruit and vegetables. Do try the home-made jams if you get the chance.

Morgan's Place
MULTICUISINE $$

(Kasera Paradise Hotel; mains ₹130-240; ⊗9am-10pm; 🛜) Morgan's Place is a relaxed (possibly overly relaxed) rooftop restaurant with good espresso (coffees ₹60 to ₹100). If you're in the mood for caffeine, don't mind climbing lots of stairs, and aren't in a hurry, then it delivers. It also serves fresh juice, respectable pizza and pasta, and falafel.

Rainbow Cafe
MULTICUISINE $$

(🖉9887210334; mains ₹120-260, thalis ₹250-500; ⊗7am-11pm; 🛜) Bohemian ambience with chill-out tunes, floor-cushion seating, good snacks and special lassis. You need to be patient, but food eventually emerges from the tiny kitchen. Located on the rooftop of the town's western gate and caged off from marauding macaques with a bamboo trellis.

🛍 Shopping

Yug Art
ART

(www.yugartbundi.com; near Surang Gate; portrait postcard ₹800-1600, comics from ₹3000; ⊗10am-7.30pm) Many art shops will offer you Rajasthani miniatures, but Yug Art offers to put you into one. Provide a photo and you can be pictured on elephant-back or in any number of classical scenes. Alternatively, Yug will record your India trip in a unique travel comic – you help with the script and he'll provide the artwork.

ℹ Information

Head to Sadar Bazar to find ATMs.

Ayurvedic Hospital (🖉0747-2443708; Balchand Para; ⊗9am-1pm & 4-6pm Mon-Sat, 9-11am Sun) This charitable hospital prescribes natural plant-based remedies. There are medicines for all sorts of ailments, from upset tummies to arthritis, and many of them are free.

Roshan Tour & Travel (internet per hr ₹40; ⊗8am-10pm) Travel agency that books train tickets, exchanges currency and has an internet cafe. Located 300m south of the palace.

Tourist Office (🖉0747-2443697; Kota Rd; ⊗9.30am-6pm Mon-Fri) Offers bus and train schedules, free maps and helpful advice.

ℹ Getting There & Away

BUS

For Ranthambhore, it's quicker to catch the train or a bus to Kota, then hop on a train to Sawai Madhopur.

Direct services from **Bundi bus stand**:

Ajmer ₹186, four hours, hourly

Jaipur ₹216, five hours, hourly

Jodhpur ₹376, eight hours, five per day

Kota ₹39, 40 minutes, every 15 minutes

Pushkar ₹200, 4½ hours, two daily

Sawai Madhoper ₹120, five hours, three daily

TRAIN

Bundi station is 4km south of the old city. There are no daily trains to Jaipur, Ajmer or Jodhpur. It's better to take a bus, or to catch a train from Kota or Chittorgarh.

Agra (Agra Fort Station) sleeper ₹160, 12½ hours, daily (5.35pm)

Chittorgarh sleeper ₹180, 2½ to 3½ hours, three to five daily (2.08am, 2.24am, 7.05am, 9.16am and 11pm)

Delhi (Hazrat Nizamuddin) sleeper ₹325, eight to 12 hours, two daily (5.48pm and 10.35pm)

THE MINI-MASTERPIECES OF KOTA & BUNDI

Some of Rajasthan's finest miniature and mural painting was produced around Bundi and Kota, the ruling Hada Rajputs being keen artistic patrons. The style combined the dominant features of folk painting – intense colour and bold forms – with the Mughals' concern with naturalism.

The Bundi and Kota schools were initially similar, but developed markedly different styles, though both usually have a background of thick foliage, cloudy skies and scenes lit by the setting sun. When architecture appears it is depicted in loving detail. The willowy women sport round faces, large petal-shaped eyes and small noses – forerunners of Bollywood pin-ups.

The Bundi school is notable for its blue hues, with a palette of turquoise and azure unlike anything seen elsewhere. Bundi Palace (p147) in particular hosts some wonderful examples.

In Kota you'll notice a penchant for hunting scenes with fauna and dense foliage – vivid, detailed portrayals of hunting expeditions in Kota's once thickly wooded surrounds. Kota's City Palace (p150) has some of the best-preserved wall paintings in the state.

Sawai Madhopur sleeper ₹180, 2½ to five hours, three daily (5.35pm, 5.48pm and 10.35pm; the last train is the fastest)

Udaipur sleeper ₹220, five hours, daily (12963 Mewar Express; 2.08am)

ⓘ Getting Around

An autorickshaw from town to the train station costs ₹70 by day and ₹100 to ₹120 at night.

Kota

☏ 0744 / POP 1 MILLION

An easy day trip from Bundi, Kota is a gritty industrial and commercial city on the Chambal, Rajasthan's only permanent river. You can take boat trips on the river here, for bird- and crocodile-watching, or explore the city's old palace.

◎ Sights

City Palace   PALACE, MUSEUM
(Kotah Garh; www.kotahfort.com; Indian/foreigner ₹100/300; ☉10am-4.30pm) The City Palace, and the fort that surrounds it, make up one of the largest such complexes in Rajasthan. This was the royal residence and centre of power, housing the Kota princedom's treasury, courts, arsenal, armed forces and state offices. The palace, entered through a gateway topped by rampant elephants, contains the offbeat **Rao Madho Singh Museum**, where you'll find everything for a respectable Raj existence, from silver furniture to weaponry, as well as perhaps India's most depressingly moth-eaten stuffed trophy animals.

The oldest part of the palace dates from 1624. Downstairs is a durbar (royal audience) hall with beautiful mirrorwork, while the elegant, small-scale apartments upstairs contain exquisite, beautifully preserved paintings, particularly the hunting scenes for which Kota is renowned.

To get here, it's around ₹40 in an autorickshaw from the bus stand, and at least ₹70 from the train station.

🏃 Activities

Boat Trips   BOATING
(per person 5min/1hr ₹60/1300, max 6 people; ☉10.30am-dusk) A lovely hiatus from the city is a Chambal River boat trip. The river upstream of Kota is part of the **Darrah National Park** and once you escape the city it's beautiful, with lush vegetation and craggy cliffs on either side. Boats start from **Chambal Gardens** (Indian/foreigner ₹2/5),

1.5km south of the fort on the river's east bank.

Trips provide the opportunity to spot a host of birds, as well as gharials (thin-snouted, fish-eating crocodiles) and muggers (keep-your-limbs-inside-the-boat crocodiles).

🛌 Sleeping

Palkiya Haveli   HERITAGE HOTEL **$$**
(☏0744-2387497; www.palkiyahaveli.com; Mokha Para; s/d ₹2725/3315; ❀ ❀) This exquisite *haveli* has been in the same family for 200 years. Set in a deliciously peaceful corner of the old city, about 800m east of the City Palace, it's a lovely, relaxing place to stay, with welcoming hosts, a high-walled garden and a courtyard with a graceful neem tree.

There are impressive murals and appealing heritage rooms, and the food is top-notch.

ⓘ Information

Tourist Office (☏0744-2327695; RTDC Hotel Chambal; ☉9.30am-6pm Mon-Sat) Has free maps of Kota and helpful staff. Turn left out of the bus stand, right at the second roundabout and it's on your right.

ⓘ Getting There & Away

BUS

Services from the main bus stand (on Bundi Rd, east of the bridge over the Chambal River) include the following:

Ajmer (for Pushkar) ₹230, four to five hours, at least 10 daily

Bundi ₹35, 40 minutes, every 15 minutes throughout the day

Chittorgarh ₹184, four hours, half-hourly from 6am

Jaipur ₹240, five hours, hourly from 5am

Udaipur ₹350 to ₹400, six to seven hours, at least 10 daily

TRAIN

Kota is on the main Mumbai–Delhi train route via Sawai Madhopur, so there are plenty of trains to choose from, though departure times aren't always convenient.

Agra (Fort) sleeper ₹225, five to nine hours, three to four daily (7.30am, 9.50am, 2.40pm and 9pm)

Chittorgarh sleeper ₹150, three to four hours, three to four daily (1.10am, 1.25am, 6.05am and 8.45am)

Delhi (New Delhi or Hazrat Nizamuddin) sleeper ₹315, five to eight hours, almost hourly

MAJOR TRAINS FROM KOTA

DESTINATION	TRAIN	DEPARTURE	ARRIVAL	FARE (₹)
Agra	19037/19039 Avadh Exp	2.40pm	9.50pm	225/600/850 (A)
Chittorgarh	29020 Dehradun Exp	8.45am	11.35am	150/715/1180 (C)
Delhi (Hazrat Nizamuddin)	12903 Golden Temple Mail	11.05am	6.45pm	315/805/1115/1855 (E)
Jaipur	12955 Mumbai–Jaipur Exp	8.55am	12.40pm	225/580/780/1275 (E)
Mumbai	12904 Golden Temple Mail	2.25pm	5.20am	490/1275/1805/3035 (E)
Sawai Madhopur	12059 Shatabdi	5.55am	7.03am	125/370 (D)
Udaipur	12963 Mewar Exp	1.25am	7.15am	245/580/780/1275 (E)

Fares: (A) sleeper/3AC/2AC, (B) sleeper, (C) sleeper/2AC/1AC, (D) 2nd class/AC chair, (E) sleeper/3AC/2AC/1AC

Jaipur sleeper ₹225, four hours, six daily (2.55am, 7.40am, 8.55am, 12.35pm, 5.35pm and 11.50pm), plus other trains on selected days

Mumbai sleeper ₹490, 14 hours, five daily fast trains (7.45am, 2.25pm, 5.30pm, 9.05pm and 11.45pm)

Sawai Madhopur 2nd-class seat/sleeper ₹125/180, one to two hours, more than 24 daily

Udaipur sleeper ₹245, six hours, one or two daily (1.10am and 1.25am)

❶ Getting Around

Minibuses and shared autorickshaws link the train station and main bus stand (₹10 per person). A private autorickshaw costs around ₹50.

Chittorgarh (Chittor)

◪ 01472 / POP 116,410

Chittorgarh (the fort, *garh*, at Chittor) is the largest fort complex in India, and a fascinating place to explore. It rises from the plains like a huge rock island, nearly 6km long and surrounded on all sides by 150m-plus cliffs.

Its history epitomises Rajput romanticism, chivalry and tragedy, and it holds a special place in the hearts of many Rajputs. Three times (in 1303, 1535 and 1568) Chittorgarh was under attack from a more powerful enemy; each time, its people chose death before dishonour, performing *jauhar*. The men donned saffron martyrs' robes and rode out from the fort to certain death, while the women and children immolated themselves on huge funeral pyres. After the last of the three sackings, Rana Udai Singh II fled to Udaipur, where he established a new capital for Mewar. In 1616, Jehangir returned Chittor to the Rajputs. There was no attempt at resettlement, though it was restored in 1905.

⊙ Sights

★ **Chittorgarh**   FORT
(Indian/foreigner ₹15/200, Sound & Light Show (in Hindi) ₹100; ⊘ dawn-dusk, Sound & Light Show dusk) A zigzag ascent of more than 1km starts at **Padal Pol** and leads through six gateways to the main gate on the western side, the **Ram Pol** (the former back entrance). Inside Ram Pol is a still-occupied village (turn right here for the ticket office). The rest of the plateau is deserted except for the wonderful palaces, towers and temples that survive from the fort's heyday, along with a few recent temples. A loop road runs around the plateau.

A typical vehicular exploration of the fort takes two to three hours. Licensed guides charging around ₹400 for up to four hours are available for either walking or autorickshaw tours, usually at the ticket office.

➡ **Meera & Kumbha Shyam Temples**

Both of these temples southeast of the **Rana Kumbha Palace** were built by Rana Kumbha in the ornate Indo-Aryan style, with classic, tall *sikharas* (spires). The **Meera Temple**, the smaller of the two, is now associated with the mystic-poetess Meerabai, a 16th-century Mewar royal who was poisoned by her brother-in-law but survived due to the blessings of Krishna. The **Kumbha Shyam Temple** (Temple of Varah) is dedicated to Vishnu and its carved panels illustrate 15th-century Mewar life.

RAJASTHAN CHITTORGARH (CHITTOR)

Chittorgarh (Chittor)

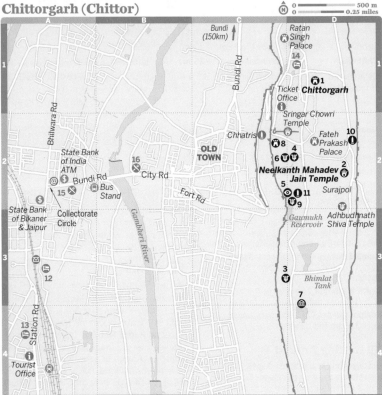

Chittorgarh (Chittor)

◎ **Top Sights**
1 Chittorgarh...D1
2 Neelkanth Mahadev Jain Temple.........D2

◎ **Sights**
3 Kalika Mata Temple...............................C3
4 Kumbha Shyam Temple......................D2
5 Mahasati..D2
6 Meera Temple.......................................C2
7 Padmini's Palace..................................D3
8 Rana Kumbha Palace..........................C2
9 Samidheshwar Temple.......................D2

10 Tower of Fame..D2
11 Tower of Victory.....................................D2

🛏 **Sleeping**
12 Hotel Pratap Palace.............................A3
13 Hotel Shree Ji.......................................A4
14 Padmini Haveli.......................................D1

🍴 **Eating**
15 Chokhi Dhani Garden Family
      Restaurant...A2
16 Saffire Garden Restaurant...................B2

➡ **Tower of Victory**

The glorious **Tower of Victory** (Jaya Stambha), symbol of Chittorgarh, was erected by Rana Kumbha in the 1440s, probably to commemorate a victory over Mahmud Khilji of Malwa. Dedicated to Vishnu, it rises 37m in nine exquisitely carved storeys, and you can climb the 157 narrow stairs (the interior is also carved) to the 8th floor, from where there's a good view of the area.

Below the tower, to the southwest, is the **Mahasati** area, where there are many *sati* (self-immolation) stones – this was the royal cremation ground and was also where 13,000 women committed *jauhar* in 1535. The **Samidheshwar Temple**, built in the

6th century and restored in 1427, is nearby. Notable among its intricate carving is a Trimurti (three-faced) figure of Shiva.

➡ **Gaumukh Reservoir**

Walk down beyond the Samidheshwar Temple and at the edge of the cliff is a deep tank, the Gaumukh Reservoir, where you can feed the fish. The reservoir takes its name from a spring that feeds the tank from a *gaumukh* (cow's mouth) carved into the cliffside.

➡ **Padmini's Palace**

Continuing south, you reach the **Kalika Mata Temple**, an 8th-century sun temple damaged during the first sacking of Chittorgarh and then converted to a temple for the goddess Kali in the 14th century. **Padmini's Palace** stands about 250m further south, beside a small lake with a central pavilion. The bronze gates to this pavilion were carried off by Akbar and can now be seen in Agra Fort.

➡ **Surajpol & Tower of Fame**

Surajpol, on the fort's east side, was the main gate and offers fantastic views across the cultivated plains. Opposite is the **Neelkanth Mahadev Jain Temple**. A little further north, the 24m-high **Tower of Fame** (Kirtti Stambha), dating from 1301, is smaller than the Tower of Victory. Built by a Jain merchant, the tower is dedicated to Adinath, the first Jain *tirthankar* (one of the 24 revered Jain teachers) and is decorated with naked figures of various other *tirthankars,* indicating that it is a monument of the Digambara (sky-clad) order. A narrow stairway leads up the seven storeys to the top. Next door is a 14th-century Jain temple.

🛏 Sleeping & Eating

⭐ **Padmini Haveli**   HERITAGE HOTEL **$$**
(📱 9414734497, 9414110090; www.thepadmini haveli.com; Annapoorna Temple Rd, Shah Chowk, Village, Chittorgarh Fort; r/ste incl breakfast ₹4000/5000; ❋ @ 🛜) This fabulous guesthouse with charming, enthusiastic and well-informed hosts is the only accommodation within the fort. Stylish rooms boast granite bathrooms and traditional decoration, and open onto the communal courtyard of the *haveli*. The hosts are official Chittorgarh guides and they live on-site, providing Italian coffee and homemade meals and jams.

There are only six rooms, three standard and three suites, so booking is advised. This white-washed *haveli* with a large black door can be hard to find in the labyrinthine laneways of the village, so call first.

Hotel Shree Ji   HOTEL **$$**
(📱 9413670931, 01472-249131; hotelshreeji@gmail. com; Station Rd; s/d from ₹1800/2000; ❋ 🛜) A cheerful and efficient business hotel, just 300m from the train station, and a world away from the lacklustre hotels near the bus station. Rooms are bright and spotless and come with complimentary morning tea, newspaper and bottle of water. The restaurant serves an inexpensive thali in the evening.

Hotel Pratap Palace   HOTEL **$$**
(📱 01472-240099; www.hotelpratappalacechittaur garh.com; off Maharana Pratap Setu Marg; r ₹1500, with AC ₹1800-4500; ❋ @ 🛜) This hotel has a wide range of rooms, though its business as a lunch stop for bus groups takes precedence over its accommodation enterprise. Even the more expensive rooms suffer from poor maintenance, and cleanliness standards could be higher. There's a large multicuisine restaurant that produces buffets for tour groups. Try and order à la carte if you can.

The owners also run village tours, horse rides and the upmarket Hotel Castle Bijaipur out of town.

Hotel Castle Bijaipur   HERITAGE HOTEL **$$$**
(📱 01472-240099; www.castlebijaipur.co.in; r from ₹8700; ❋ 🛜 ⊗) This fantastically set 16th-century palace is an ideal rural retreat 41km by road east of Chittorgarh. It's a great place to settle down with a good book, compose a fairy-tale fantasy or just laze around. Rooms are romantic and luxurious, and there's a pleasant garden courtyard and an airy restaurant serving Rajasthani food. It's popular with tour groups.

Reservations should be made through the website or through Chittorgarh's Hotel Pratap Palace. The owners can arrange transfer from Chittor as well as horse and 4WD safaris, birdwatching, cooking classes, massage and yoga.

Chokhi Dhani Garden Family Restaurant   INDIAN **$**
(📱 9413716593; Bundi Rd; mains ₹80-150, thalis ₹110-290; ⊙ 9am-10.30pm; ❋ 🍴) This fancooled roadside *dhaba* (snack bar) with extra seating in the back does a good-value selection of vegetarian dishes, including filling thalis and a variety of North and South Indian dishes.

MAJOR TRAINS FROM CHITTORGARH

DESTINATION	TRAIN	DEPARTURE	ARRIVAL	FARE (₹)
Ajmer (for Pushkar)	12991 Udaipur-Jaipur Exp	8.20am	11.25am	120/410/550 (A)
Bundi	29019 MDS-Kota Exp	3.35pm	5.45pm	160/735/1200 (B)
Delhi (Hazrat Nizamuddin)	12964 Mewar Exp	8.50pm	6.35am	370/975/1380/2325 (C)
Jaipur	12991 Udaipur-Jaipur Exp	8.20am	1.30pm	160/545/750 (A)
Sawai Madhopur	29019 MDS-Kota Exp	3.35pm	9.25pm	210/735/1200 (B)
Udaipur	19329 Udaipur City Exp	4.50pm	7.15pm	160/530/735/1200 (C)

Fares: (A) 2nd-class seat/AC chair/1st-class seat, (B) sleeper/2AC/1AC, (C) sleeper/3AC/2AC/1AC

Saffire Garden Restaurant MULTICUISINE $ (City Rd; mains ₹100-170; ☺8am-10pm; ❄) Sit at tables on the small, tree-shaded lawn or inside the air-conditioned room at the back, and tuck into a variety of standard, but tasty enough, Indian and Chinese dishes.

ⓘ Information

ATMs can be found near Collectorate Circle.
State Bank of Bikaner & Jaipur (SBBJ; Bhilwara Rd; ☺9.30am-4pm Mon-Fri, to noon Sat) ATM and money changing.
Mahavir Cyber Cafe (Collectorate Circle; per hour ₹40; ☺8am-10pm)
Tourist Office (☏01472-241089; Station Rd; ☺10am-1.30pm & 2-5pm Mon-Sat) Friendly and helpful, with a town map and brochure.

ⓘ Getting There & Away

BUS

There are no direct buses to Bundi; take the train instead. Services from the Chittorgarh **bus stand** include the following:
Ajmer (for Pushkar) ₹197, AC ₹350, four hours, hourly until mid-afternoon
Jaipur ₹339, AC ₹667, seven hours, around every 1½ hours
Kota ₹184, four hours, half-hourly
Udaipur ₹120, with AC ₹255, 2½ hours, half-hourly

TRAIN

Ajmer (for Pushkar) sleeper ₹150, three hours, five to seven daily (12.35am, 2.50am, 8.20am, 10.10am, 7.30pm, 7.45pm and 11.30pm)
Bundi sleeper ₹150, two to 3½ hours, three daily (1.50pm, 3.35pm and 8.50pm)
Delhi (Delhi Sarai Rohilla or Hazrat Nizamuddin) sleeper ₹380, 10 hours, two daily fast trains (7.30pm and 8.50pm)
Jaipur sleeper ₹220, 5½ hours, four daily (12.35am, 2.45am, 8.20am and 8.35am)

Sawai Madhopur sleeper ₹210, four to nine hours, three daily (1.50pm, 3.35pm and 8.50pm; the latest is the quickest)
Udaipur sleeper ₹150, two hours, six daily (4.25am, 5.05am, 5.33am, 6.35am, 4.50pm and 7.25pm)

ⓘ Getting Around

A full tour of the fort by autorickshaw should cost around ₹400 return. You can arrange this yourself in town.

Udaipur

☏0294 / POP 451,735

Beside shimmering Lake Pichola, with the ochre and purple ridges of the wooded Aravalli Hills stretching away in every direction, Udaipur has a romance of setting unmatched in Rajasthan and arguably in all India. Fantastical palaces, temples, *havelis* and countless narrow, crooked, timeless streets add the human counterpoint to the city's natural charms. For the visitor there's the tranquillity of boat rides on the lake, the bustle and colour of ancient bazaars, a lively arts scene, the quaint old-world feel of its better hotels, endless tempting shops and some lovely countryside to explore on wheels, feet or horseback.

Udaipur's tag of 'the most romantic spot on the continent of India' was first applied in 1829 by Colonel James Tod, the East India Company's first political agent in the region. Today the romance is wearing slightly thin as ever-taller hotels compete for the best view and traffic clogs ancient thoroughfares.

Udaipur was founded in 1568 by Maharana Udai Singh II following the final sacking of Chittorgarh by the Mughal emperor Akbar. This new capital of Mewar had a much less vulnerable location than Chittorgarh. Mewar still had to contend with repeated invasions by the Mughals and, later, the Marathas, until British intervention in the early 19th century. This resulted in a treaty that protected Udaipur from invaders while allowing Mewar's rulers to remain effectively all-powerful in internal affairs. The ex-royal family remains influential and in recent decades has been the driving force behind the rise of Udaipur as a tourist destination.

◉ Sights

★ City Palace
PALACE

(www.eternalmewar.in; adult/child ₹30/15; ☺9am-11pm) Surmounted by balconies, towers and cupolas towering over the lake, the imposing City Palace is Rajasthan's largest palace, with a facade 244m long and 30.4m high. Construction was begun in 1599 by Maharana Udai Singh II, the city's founder, and it later became a conglomeration of structures (including 11 separate smaller palaces) built and extended by various maharanas, though it still manages to retain a surprising uniformity of design.

You can enter the complex through Badi Pol (Great Gate) at the northern end, or the Sheetla Mata Gate to the south. Tickets for the City Palace Museum are sold at both entrances. Note: you must pay the ₹30 City Palace entrance ticket in order to pass south through Chandra Chowk Gate, en route to the Crystal Gallery or Rameshwar Ghat for the Lake Pichola boat rides, even if you have a City Palace Museum ticket.

Inside Badi Pol, eight arches on the left commemorate the eight times maharanas were weighed here and their weight in gold or silver distributed to the lucky locals. You then pass through the three-arched Tripolia Gate into a large courtyard, Manek Chowk. Spot the large tiger-catching cage, which worked rather like an oversized mousetrap, and the smaller one for leopards.

★ City Palace Museum
MUSEUM

(adult/child ₹250/100, camera or video ₹250, guide ₹250, audio guide ₹200; ☺9.30am-5.30pm, last entry 4.30pm) The main part of the City Palace is open as the City Palace Museum, with rooms extravagantly decorated with mirrors, tiles and paintings, and housing a large and varied collection of artefacts. It's entered from Ganesh Chowk, which you reach from Manek Chowk.

The City Palace Museum begins with the Rai Angan (Royal Courtyard), the very spot where Udai Singh met the sage who told

him to build a city here. Rooms along one side contain historical paintings, including several of the Battle of Haldighati (1576), in which Mewar forces under Maharana Pratap, one of the great Rajput heroes, gallantly fought the army of Mughal emperor Akbar to a stalemate.

As you move through the palace, highlights include the Baadi Mahal (1699), where a pretty central garden gives fine views over the city. Kishan (Krishna) Vilas has a remarkable collection of miniatures from the time of Maharana Bhim Singh (r 1778–1828). The story goes that Bhim Singh's daughter Krishna Kumari drank a fatal cup of poison here to solve the dilemma of rival princely suitors from Jaipur and Jodhpur who were both threatening to invade Mewar if she didn't marry them. The Surya Choupad boasts a huge, ornamental sun – the symbol of the sun-descended Mewar dynasty – and opens into Mor Chowk (Peacock Courtyard) with its lovely mosaics of peacocks, the favourite Rajasthani bird.

The southern end of the museum comprises the Zenana Mahal, the royal ladies' quarters built in the 17th century. It now contains a long picture gallery with lots of royal hunting scenes (note the comic strip–style of the action in each painting). The Zenana Mahal's central courtyard, Laxmi Chowk, contains a beautiful white pavilion and a stable of howdahs, palanquins and other people-carriers.

Crystal Gallery
GALLERY

(City Palace Complex; adult/child incl audio guide & drink ₹550/350, photography prohibited; ☺9am-7pm) The Crystal Gallery houses rare crystal that Maharana Sajjan Singh (r 1874–84) ordered from F&C Osler & Co in England in 1877. The maharana died before it arrived, and all the items stayed forgotten and packed up in boxes for 110 years. The extraordinary, extravagant collection includes crystal chairs, sofas, tables and even beds. The rather hefty admission fee also includes entry to the grand Durbar Hall. Tickets are available at the City Palace gates or the Crystal Gallery entrance.

Government Museum
MUSEUM

(Indian/foreigner ₹20/100; ☺10am-5pm Tue-Sun) Entered from Ganesh Chowk, this museum has a splendid collection of jewel-like miniature paintings of the Mewar school and a turban that belonged to Shah Jahan, creator of the Taj Mahal. Stranger exhibits include

RAJASTHAN UDAIPUR

Udaipur

Savage Garden (100m); Sajjan Garh (7km)

Old Clock Tower

Bara Bazar

Main Post Office (1.3km); GBH American Hospital (2km)

Daiji Footbridge

Gadiya Devra

Gangaur Ghat Rd

HANUMAN GHAT

Heera Cycle Store

Axis Bank ATM

Bajrang Marg

Jagdish Chowk

Jagdish Temple Rd

Jadion-Ki-oi

Bhattiyani Chotta

State Bank of India ATM

City Palace Rd

Navghat Rd

Subhash Rd

Jagniwas Island

Lake Pichola

Bhattiyani Chotta

Vintage & Classic Car Collection (500m); Tourist Office (1.2km); Main (1.5km); (2km); Ahar (3km); (27km)

Thomas Cook

Rameshwar Ghat

Sajjan Niwas Gardens

Lake Palace Rd

0 200 m
0 0.1 miles

a stuffed monkey holding a lamp. There are also regal maharana portraits in profile, documenting Mewar's rulers along with the changing fashions of the moustache.

★ Lake Pichola LAKE

Limpid and large, Lake Pichola reflects the grey-blue mountains on its mirror-like surface. It was enlarged by Maharana Udai Singh II, following his foundation of the city, by flooding Picholi village, which gave the lake its name. The lake is now 4km long and 3km wide, but remains shallow and dries up completely during severe droughts. The City Palace complex, including the gardens at its southern end, extends nearly 1km along the lake's eastern shore.

Boat trips (adult/child 10am-2pm ₹400/200, 3-5pm ₹700/400; ⊙10am-5pm) leave roughly hourly from Rameshwar Ghat, within the City Palace complex (note, you have to pay ₹30 to enter). The trips make a stop at Jagmandir Island, where you can stay for as long as you like before taking any boat back. Take your own drinks and snacks, though, as those sold on the island are extortionately expensive. You can also take 25-minute boat rides from **Lal Ghat** (₹250 per person) throughout the day without the need to enter the City Palace complex: it's worth checking in advance what time the popular sunset departure casts off.

Jagmandir Island ISLAND

The palace on Jagmandir Island, about 800m south of Jagniwas, was built by Maharana Karan Singh II in 1620, added to by his successor Maharana Jagat Singh, and then changed very little until the last few years when it was partly converted into another (smaller) hotel. When lit up at night it has more romantic sparkle to it than the Lake Palace. As well as the seven hotel rooms, the island has a restaurant, bar and spa, which are open to visitors.

Udaipur

◎ Sights
1	Badi Pol	B2
2	Bagore-ki-Haveli	B2
3	City Palace	B3
4	City Palace Museum	B3
5	Crystal Gallery	B3
6	Durbar Hall	B4
7	Government Museum	B3
8	Jagdish Temple	B2
9	Lal Ghat	B2
10	Sheetla Mata Gate	C4
11	Tripolia Gate	B3

◉ Activities, Courses & Tours
	Art of Bicycle Trips	(see 14)
	Ashoka Arts	(see 21)
12	Ayurvedic Body Care	B2
13	Lake Pichola Boat Trips	B4
	Millets of Mewar	(see 36)
14	Prakash Yoga	B1
15	Prem Musical Instruments	B1
16	Shashi Cooking Classes	B1
	Sushma's Cooking Classes	(see 22)

◉ Sleeping
17	Amet Haveli	A2
18	Dream Heaven	A1
19	Fateh Prakash Palace Hotel	B4
20	Hotel Baba Palace	C1
21	Hotel Gangaur Palace	B1
22	Hotel Krishna Niwas	B2
23	Jagat Niwas Palace Hotel	B2
24	Jaiwana Haveli	B2
25	Lal Ghat Guest House	B2
26	Nukkad Guest House	B1
	Poonam Haveli	(see 22)
27	Pratap Bhawan	B2
28	Rangniwas Palace Hotel	D4
29	Shiv Niwas Palace Hotel	B4
30	Taj Lake Palace	A4
31	Udai Garh	B2
32	Udai Kothi	A2

◎ Eating
33	Ambrai	A2
34	Cafe Edelweiss	B1
	Charcoal	(see 27)
	Jagat Niwas Palace Hotel	(see 23)
35	Little Prince	A1
	Mayur Rooftop Cafe	(see 20)
36	Millets of Mewar	A1
37	Queen Cafe	A1

◎ Drinking & Nightlife
	Jaiwana Bistro Lounge	(see 24)
38	Jheel's Ginger Coffee Bar	B1
39	Paps Juices	B1
40	Sunset Terrace	B4

◎ Entertainment
41	Dharohar	B2
42	Mewar Sound & Light Show	C3

◎ Shopping
43	Sadhna	C1

RAJASTHAN UDAIPUR

With its entrance flanked by a row of enormous stone elephants, the island has an ornate 17th-century tower, the **Gol Mahal**, carved from bluestone and containing a small exhibit on Jagmandir's history, plus a garden and lovely views across the lake.

Boat trips (p156) leave roughly hourly from Rameshwar Ghat, within the City Palace complex (note, you have to pay ₹30 to enter). The trips make a stop at Jagmandir Island, where you can stay for as long as you like before taking any boat back. Take your own drinks and snacks, though, as those sold on the island are extortionately expensive.

Jagdish Temple   HINDU TEMPLE
(⊙5.30am-2pm & 4-10pm) Reached by a steep, elephant-flanked flight of steps, 150m north of the City Palace's Badi Pol, this busy Indo-Aryan temple was built by Maharana Jagat Singh in 1651. The wonderfully carved main structure enshrines a black stone image of Vishnu as Jagannath, Lord of the Universe. There's also a brass image of the Garuda (Vishnu's man-bird vehicle) in a shrine facing the main structure.

Bagore-ki-Haveli   MUSEUM
(Indian/foreigner ₹40/80, camera ₹50; ⊙9.30am-5.30pm) This gracious 18th-century *haveli,* set on the water's edge in the Gangaur Ghat area, was built by a Mewar prime minister and has since been carefully restored. There are 138 rooms set around courtyards, some arranged to evoke the period during which the house was inhabited, while others house cultural displays, including – intriguingly enough – the world's biggest turban.

The *haveli* also houses a gallery featuring a fascinating collection of period photos of Udaipur and a surreal collection of world-famous monuments carved out of polystyrene.

Sajjan Garh   PALACE
(Monsoon Palace) Perched up high on top of a distant hill like a fairy-tale castle, this melancholy, neglected late-19th-century palace was

constructed by Maharana Sajjan Singh. Originally an astronomical centre, it became a monsoon palace and hunting lodge. Now government owned, it's in a sadly dilapidated state, but visitors stream up here for the marvellous views, particularly at sunset. It's 5km west of the old city as the crow flies, about 9km by the winding road.

At the foot of the hill you enter the 5-sq-km **Sajjan Garh Wildlife Sanctuary** (Indian/foreigner ₹50/300, car ₹200). A good way to visit is with the daily sunset excursion in a minivan driven by an enterprising taxi driver who picks up tourists at the entrance to Bagore-ki-Haveli at Gangaur Ghat every day at 5pm. The round trip costs ₹300 per person, including waiting time (but not the sanctuary fees). His minivan has 'Monsoon Palace–Sajjangarh Fort' written across the front of it. Alternatively, autorickshaws charge ₹400 including waiting time for a round trip to the sanctuary gate, which they are not allowed to pass. Taxis ferry people the final 4km up to the palace for ₹150 per person.

Vintage & Classic Car Collection   MUSEUM
(Garden Hotel, Lake Palace Rd; adult/child ₹250/150, lunch or dinner ₹230; ⊙9am-9pm) The maharanas' car collection makes a fascinating diversion, for what it tells about their elite lifestyle and for the vintage vehicles themselves. Housed within the former state garage are 22 splendid vehicles, including a seven-seat 1938 Cadillac complete with purdah system, the beautiful 1934 Rolls-Royce Phantom used in the Bond film *Octopussy*, and the Cadillac convertible that whisked Queen Elizabeth II to the airport in 1961. The museum is a 10-minute walk east along Lake Palace Rd.

🏃 Activities

Krishna Ranch   HORSE RIDING
(☑9828059505; www.krishnaranch.com; full day incl lunch ₹1200) Situated in beautiful countryside near Badi village, 7km northwest of Udaipur, and run by the owners of Kumbha Palace guesthouse. Experienced owner-guide Dinesh Jain leads most trips himself, riding local Marwari horses through the surrounding hills. There are also attractive cottages (p161) at the ranch.

Prakash Yoga   YOGA
(☑0294-2524872; inside Chandpol; class by donation; ⊙classes 8am & 7pm) A friendly hatha yoga centre with hour-long classes. The

teacher has more than 20 years' experience. It's tucked inside Chandpol, near the footbridge, but well signed.

Ayurvedic Body Care   AYURVEDA, MASSAGE
(☑0294-2413816; www.ayurvedicbodycare.com; 38 Lal Ghat; ⊙9.30am-8.30pm) A small and popular old-city operation offering ayurvedic massage at reasonable prices, including a 20-minute head or back massage (₹350) and a 50-minute full-body massage (₹850). It also sells ayurvedic products such as oils, moisturisers, shampoos and soaps.

🍲 Courses

Shashi Cooking Classes   COOKING
(☑9929303511; www.shashicookingclasses.blogspot.com; Sunrise Restaurant, 18 Gangaur Ghat Rd; 4hr class ₹1500; ⊙classes 10.30am & 5.30pm) Readers rave about Shashi's high-spirited classes, teaching many fundamental Indian dishes. Classes go for 3½ to four hours and include a free recipe booklet.

Sushma's Cooking Classes   COOKING
(☑7665852163; www.cookingclassesinudaipur.com; Hotel Krishna Niwas, 35 Lal Ghat; 2hr class ₹1000) A highly recommended cooking class run by the enthusiastic Sushma. Classes offer up anything from traditional Rajasthani dishes and learning how to make spice mixes, through bread-making to the all-important method of making the perfect cup of chai.

Prem Musical Instruments   MUSIC
(☑9414343583; 28 Gadiya Devra; per hr ₹700; ⊙10.30am-6pm) Rajesh Prajapati (Bablu) is a successful local musician who gives sitar, tabla and flute lessons. He also sells and repairs those instruments and can arrange performances.

Ashoka Arts   ART
(Hotel Gangaur Palace, Ashoka Haveli, Gangaur Ghat Rd; per hr ₹200) Learn the basics of classic miniature painting from a local master.

🧭 Tours

Art of Bicycle Trips   CYCLING
(☑8769822745; www.artofbicycletrips.com; 27 Gadiya Devra, inside Chandpol; half-day tour ₹1950) This well-run outfit offers a great way to get out of the city. The Lakecity Loop is a 30km half-day tour that quickly leaves Udaipur behind to have you wheeling through villages, farmland and along the shores of Fateh Sagar and Badi Lakes. Other options include a vehicle-supported trip further afield to

Kumbhalgarh and Ranakpur. Bikes are well maintained and all come with helmets.

Millets of Mewar WALKING
(☑8890419048; www.milletsofmewar.com; Hanuman Ghat; per person ₹1000, min 2 people) Health-food specialists Millets of Mewar (p162) organises 2½-hour city tours on which you can meet local artisans who live and work in Udaipur. Tours should be booked a day in advance; they leave from the restaurant at 10am.

★☆ Festivals & Events

Holi RELIGIOUS
(☉Feb/Mar) If you're in Udaipur in February/March, you can experience the festival of Holi, Udaipur-style, when the town comes alive in a riot of colour.

Mewar Festival RELIGIOUS
(☉Mar/Apr) Holi is followed in March/April by the procession-heavy Mewar Festival – Udaipur's own version of the springtime Gangaur festival.

🛏 Sleeping

Many budget and midrange lodgings cluster close to the lake, especially on its eastern side in Lal Ghat. This area is a tangle of streets and lanes close to the City Palace. It's Udaipur's tourist epicentre and boasts numerous eateries and shops. Directly across the water from Lal Ghat, Hanuman Ghat has a slightly more local vibe and often better views, though you're certainly not out of the touristic zone.

🛏 Lal Ghat

Lal Ghat Guest House GUESTHOUSE $
(☑0294-2525301; lalghat@hotmail.com; 33 Lal Ghat; dm ₹200, r ₹1000, without bathroom ₹750, with AC ₹2000; ❄@🅦) This mellow guesthouse by the lake was one of the first to open in Udaipur, and it's still a sound choice, with an amazing variety of older and newer rooms. Accommodation ranges from a spruce, non-smoking dorm (with curtained-off beds and lockers under the mattresses) to the best room, which sports a stone wall, a big bed, a big mirror and air-con.

Most rooms have lake views and those in the older part of the building generally have more character. There's a small kitchen for self-caterers.

Nukkad Guest House GUESTHOUSE $
(☑0294-2411403; nukkad_raju@yahoo.com; 56 Ganesh Ghati; s/d without bathroom ₹100/200,

r ₹300-500; @🅦) Nukkad has clean and simple fan-cooled good-value rooms, plus a sociable, breezy, upstairs restaurant with very good Indian and international dishes. You can join afternoon cooking classes and morning yoga sessions (by donation) without stepping outside the door – just don't stay out past curfew or get caught washing your clothes in your bathroom.

★ Jagat Niwas Palace Hotel HERITAGE HOTEL $$
(☑0294-2420133, 0294-2422860; www.jagat niwaspalace.com; 23-25 Lal Ghat; r ₹2000-3185, with lake view ₹4860-8100; ❄@🅦) This leading midrange hotel set in two converted lakeside *havelis* takes the location cake, and staff are efficient and always courteous. The lake-view rooms are charming, with carved wooden furniture, cushioned window seats and pretty prints. Rooms without a lake view are almost as comfortable and attractive, and considerably cheaper.

The building is full of character, with lots of pleasant sitting areas, terraces and courtyards, and it makes the most of its position with a picture-perfect rooftop restaurant

Jaiwana Haveli HOTEL $$
(☑0294-2411103, 9829005859; www.jaiwana haveli.com; 14 Lal Ghat; r from ₹3265; ❄@🅦) Professionally run by two helpful, efficient brothers, this smart midrange option has spotless, unfussy rooms with good beds, TVs and attractive block-printed fabrics. Book a corner room for views. The rooftop restaurant has great lake views and Indian food (mains ₹140 to ₹300), plus there's a mod cafe (p162) on the ground floor.

ANIMAL AID UNLIMITED

The spacious refuge of **Animal Aid Unlimited** (☑9352511435, 9602055895; www.animalaidunlimited.com; Badi Village) treats around 200 street animals a day (mainly dogs, donkeys and cows) and answers more than 3000 emergency rescue calls a year. The refuge welcomes volunteers and visitors: you can visit between 9am and 4pm without needing to call first, though avoid lunchtime (1pm to 2pm). The refuge is in Badi village, 7km northwest of Udaipur.

A round trip by autorickshaw, including waiting time, costs around ₹350 to ₹400. Call Animal Aid Unlimited if you see an injured or ill street animal in Udaipur.

RAJASTHAN UDAIPUR

Hotel Baba Palace
HOTEL $$

(☎ 0294-2427126; www.hotelbabapalace.com; Jagdish Chowk; r/deluxe r incl breakfast ₹2250/2750; ❄ 🛜) This slick hotel has sparkling, fresh rooms with decent beds behind solid doors and there's a lift. It's eye to eye with Jagdish Temple, so many of the rooms have interesting views; all have air-conditioning and TVs, some have delightfully canopied beds. On top there's the popular Mayur Rooftop Cafe (p162). Free train station or airport pick-ups available.

Hotel Krishna Niwas
HOTEL $$

(☎ 0294-2420163, 9414167341; www.hotelkrishna niwas.com; 35 Lal Ghat; d ₹1500-2000; ❄ @ 🛜) Run by an artist family, Krishna Niwas has smart, clean, all air-con rooms; those with views are smaller, and some come with balconies. There are splendid vistas from the rooftop, and a decent restaurant. You can also try your own cooking after taking one of the popular cooking lessons (p158) here.

Pratap Bhawan
HOTEL $$

(☎ 0294-2560566; www.pratapbhawanudaipur. com; 12 Lal Ghat; r ₹1450-2250; ❄ 🛜) A curving marble staircase leads up from the wide lobby to large rooms with good, big bathrooms and, in many cases, cushioned window seats. A deservedly popular place, even if recent price hikes have spun the place slighlty out of the budget category. The rooftop Charcoal restaurant is nice for sitting out at night.

Poonam Haveli
HOTEL $$

(☎ 0294-2410303; www.hotelpoonamhaveli.com; 39 Lal Ghat; r incl breakfast ₹3215; ❄ @ 🛜) A fairly modern place decked out in traditional style, friendly Poonam has 16 spacious, spotlessly clean rooms with marble floors, big beds, TVs and spare but tasteful decor, plus pleasant sitting areas. None of the rooms enjoy lake views, but the rooftop restaurant does, and also boasts wood-fired pizzas among the usual Indian and traveller fare.

Hotel Gangaur Palace
HERITAGE HOTEL $

(☎ 0294-2422303; www.ashokahaveli.com; Ashoka Haveli, 339 Gangaur Ghat Rd; s ₹400-2000, d ₹500-2500; ❄ @ 🛜) This elaborate, faded *haveli* is set around a stone-pillared courtyard, with a wide assortment of rooms on several floors. It's gradually moving upmarket and rooms range from windowless with flaking paint to bright and recently decorated with lake views. Many have wall paintings and window seats.

The hotel also boasts an in-house palm reader, art shop, art school (p158), and a rooftop restaurant.

Udai Garh
HOTEL $$

(☎ 9660055500, 0294-2421239; www.udaigarhu daipur.in; 21 Lal Ghat; r incl breakfast ₹2600-3400; ❄ 🛜 ⛱) Set just back from the lakeshore, Udai Garh is an oasis of peace, with a central courtyard and spacious rooms. Unfortunately the rooms don't quite capture a lake view, but the wonderful rooftop, with a neat swimming pool and delightful restaurant, certainly does.

Hanuman Ghat

Dream Heaven
GUESTHOUSE $

(☎ 0294-2431038; www.dreamheaven.co.in; Hanuman Ghat; r ₹400-1200; ❄ @ 🛜) This higgledy-piggledy building boasts clean rooms with wall hangings and paintings. Bathrooms are smallish, though some rooms have a decent balcony and/or views. The food at the rooftop restaurant (dishes ₹100 to ₹150), which overlooks the lake, is fresh and tasty; it's the perfect place to chill out on a pile of cushions and the only place to pick up wi-fi.

Amet Haveli
HERITAGE HOTEL $$$

(☎ 0294-2431085; www.amethaveliudaipur.com; Hanuman Ghat; s/d from ₹4165/4760; ❄ @ 🛜 ⛱) A 350-year-old heritage building on the lakeshore, with delightful rooms featuring cushioned window seats, coloured glass and little shutters. They're set around a pretty courtyard and pond. Splurge on one with a balcony or giant bath tub. One of Udaipur's most romantic restaurants, Ambrai (p162), is part of the hotel.

Udai Kothi
HOTEL $$$

(☎ 0294-2432810; www.udaikothi.com; Hanuman Ghat; r ₹6500-10,000; ❄ @ 🛜 ⛱) A bit like a five-storey wedding cake, Udai Kothi is a glittery, modern building (there's an elevator) with lots of traditional embellishments – cupolas, interesting art and fabrics, and window seats in some rooms, marble bathrooms and carved-wood doors in others – and thoughtful touches such as bowls of floating flowers throughout. Rooms are pretty, individually designed and well equipped.

The apex is the rooftop terrace, where you can dine well at the restaurant and swim in Udaipur's best rooftop pool (nonguests ₹500).

City Palace

Shiv Niwas Palace Hotel   HERITAGE HOTEL **$$$**
(☑0294-2528016; www.hrhhotels.com; City Palace Complex; r ₹18,000-103,000; ❂@🛜🏊) This hotel, in the former palace guest quarters, has opulent common areas such as its pool courtyard, bar and lawn garden. Some of the suites are truly palatial, filled with fountains and silver, but the standard rooms are poorer value. Go for a suite, or just for a drink, meal or massage. Rates drop dramatically from April to September.

Fateh Prakash
Palace Hotel   HERITAGE HOTEL **$$$**
(☑0294-2528016; www.hrhhotels.com; City Palace Complex; r/premier ste ₹23,000/45,000; ❂@🛜🏊) Built in the early 20th century for royal functions, the Fateh Prakash has luxurious rooms and gorgeous suites, all comprehensively equipped and almost all looking straight out onto Lake Pichola. Views aside, the general ambience is a little less regal than at Shiv Niwas Palace Hotel – although the Sunset Terrace bar (p162) is a great place for an evening drink.

Taj Lake Palace   HERITAGE HOTEL **$$$**
(☑0294-2428800; www.tajhotels.com; r from ₹38,250; ❂@🛜🏊) The icon of Udaipur, this romantic white-marble palace seemingly floating on the lake is extraordinary, with open-air courtyards, lotus ponds and a small, mango-tree-shaded pool. Rooms are hung with breezy silks and filled with carved furniture. Some of the cheapest overlook the lily pond rather than the lake; the mural-decked suites will make you truly feel like a maharaja.

Other Areas

★**Krishna Ranch**   COTTAGE **$$**
(☑9828059505, 9828059506; www.krishnaranch.com; s/d incl meals from ₹2000/2500; 🛜) 🐾 This delightful countryside retreat has five cottages set around the grounds of a small farm. Each comes with attached bathroom (with solar-heated shower), tasteful decor and farm views. All meals are included and are prepared using organic produce grown on the farm. The ranch is 7km from town, near Badi village, but there's free pick-up from Udaipur.

It's an ideal base for the hikes and horse treks (p158) that the management – a

Dutch-Indian couple – organises from here, though you don't have to sign up for the treks to stay here.

Rangniwas Palace Hotel   HERITAGE HOTEL **$$**
(☑0294-2523890; www.rangniwaspalace.com; Lake Palace Rd; s ₹1090-1420, d ₹1310-1635, ste ₹3050-4360; ❂🛜🏊) This 19th-century palace boasts plenty of heritage character and a peaceful central garden with a small pool shaded by mature palms. The quaint rooms in the older section are the most appealing, while the suites – full of carved wooden furniture and boasting terraces with swing seats or balcony window seats overlooking the garden – are a delight.

✗ Eating

Udaipur has scores of sun-kissed rooftop restaurants, many with mesmerising lake views. The fare is not always that inspiring or varying, but competition keeps most places striving for improvement.

✗ Lal Ghat

Cafe Edelweiss   CAFE **$**
(73 Gangaur Ghat Rd; coffee from ₹60, sandwiches from ₹140; ⊗8am-8pm; 🛜) The Savage Garden restaurant folks run this itsy cafe with baked goods and coffee. Offerings included sticky cinnamon rolls, blueberry chocolate cake, spinach-and-mushroom quiche or apple strudel, muesli or eggs for breakfast, and various sandwiches.

★**Jagat Niwas Palace Hotel**   INDIAN **$$**
(☑0294-2420133; 23-25 Lal Ghat; mains ₹250-325; ⊗7am-10am, noon-3pm & 6-10pm) A wonderful, classy, rooftop restaurant with superb lake views, delicious Indian cuisine and excellent service. Choose from an extensive selection of mouth-watering curries (tempered for Western tastes) – mutton, chicken, fish, veg – as well as the tandoori classics. There's a tempting cocktail menu, Indian wine and the beer is icy cold. Book ahead for dinner.

Charcoal   MULTICUISINE **$$**
(☑8769160106; www.charcoalpb.com; Pratap Bhawan, 12 Lal Ghat; mains ₹140-480; ⊗8am-11pm; 🛜) As the name implies, barbecue and tandoor specials feature at this innovative rooftop restaurant. There are plenty of vegetarian and juicy meat dishes on offer and the homemade soft corn tacos with a variety of fillings are deservedly popular.

Mayur Rooftop Cafe
MULTICUISINE $$

(Hotel Baba Palace, Jagdish Chowk; mains ₹150-290; ☺7am-10pm; ❀🔊) This delightful rooftop restaurant has a great view of the multihued light show on the Jagdish Temple. You can choose the air-con room or the breezy open section. The usual multicuisine themes fill out the menu, and the quality is top-notch. The thali is great value and vegetarians will love the choice of nine paneer dishes.

Savage Garden
MEDITERRANEAN $$$

(☑8890627181; inside Chandpol; mains ₹280-520; ☺11am-11pm) Tucked away in the backstreets near Chandpol, Savage Garden does a winning line in soups, chicken, and homemade pasta dishes. Try ravioli with lamb ragu, and the sweet-savoury stuffed chicken breast with nuts, cheese and carrot rice. The setting is a whitewashed 250-year-old *haveli* with bowls of flowers, tables in alcoves and a pleasant courtyard. Indian wine is also served.

🍴 Hanuman Ghat

Millets of Mewar
INDIAN $

(www.milletsofmewar.com; Hanuman Ghat; mains ₹110-180; ☺8.30am-10.30pm; 🔊) 🍃 Local millet is used where possible instead of wheat and rice at this environmentally aware, slow-food restaurant. There are vegan options, gluten-free dishes, fresh salads, juices and herbal teas. Also on the menu are multigrain sandwiches and millet pizzas, plus regular curries, Indian snacks, pasta and pancakes.

Little Prince
MULTICUISINE $

(Daiji Footbridge; mains ₹100-160; ☺8.30am-11pm) This lovely open-air eatery looking towards the quaint Daiji Footbridge dishes up delicious veg and nonveg meals. There are plenty of Indian options, along with pizzas, pastas and some original variations on the usual multicuisine theme, including Korean and Israeli dishes. The ambience is super-relaxed and the service friendly.

Queen Cafe
INDIAN $

(14 Bajrang Marg; mains ₹70-80; ☺8am-10pm) This restaurant is like a family's front room, serving up good home-style Indian vegetarian dishes. Try the pumpkin curry with mint and coconut, and the Kashmir *pulao* with fruit, vegies and coconut. Host Meenu also offers cooking classes and walking tours that start with a home-cooked breakfast.

★ Ambrai
NORTH INDIAN $$$

(☑0294-2431085; www.amethaveliudaipur.com; Amet Haveli, Hanuman Ghat; mains ₹315-515; ☺12.30-3pm & 7.30-10.30pm) Set at lake-shore level, looking across the water to the floodlit City Palace in one direction and Jagniwas in the other, this is one highly romantic restaurant at night with candlelit, white-linen tables beneath enormous trees. And the service and cuisine do justice to its fabulous position, with terrific tandoor and curries and a bar to complement the dining.

🍷 Drinking & Nightlife

Jaiwana Bistro Lounge
CAFE

(☑9829005859; Jaiwana Haveli, 14 Lal Ghat; coffees from ₹100; ☺7am-10.30pm; 🔊) This modern, cool and clean cafe has espresso coffee and fresh healthy juices to help wash down the tasty bakery items and other main meals.

Paps Juices
JUICE BAR

(inside Chandpol; juices ₹60-180; ☺9am-8pm) This bright-red spot is tiny but very welcoming, and a great place to refuel during the day with a shot of Vitamin C from a wide range of delicious juice mixes. If you want something more substantial, the muesli mix is pretty good, too.

Jheel's Ginger Coffee Bar
CAFE

(Jheel Palace Guest House, 56 Gangaur Ghat Rd; coffees ₹80-110; ☺8am-8pm; 🔊) This small but slick cafe by the water's edge is on the ground floor of Jheel Palace Guest House. Large windows afford good lake views, and the coffee is excellent. It also does a range of cakes and snacks. Note, you can take your coffee up to the open-air rooftop restaurant if you like.

Sunset Terrace
BAR

(Fateh Prakash Palace Hotel; beer/cocktails from ₹400/650; ☺7am-10.30pm) On a terrace overlooking Lake Pichola, this bar is perfect for a sunset gin and tonic. It's also a restaurant (mains ₹400 to ₹950), with live music performed every night.

☆ Entertainment

Dharohar
DANCE

(☑0294-2523858; Bagore-ki-Haveli; Indian/foreigner ₹90/150, camera ₹150; ☺7-8pm) The beautiful Bagore-ki-Haveli (p157) hosts the best (and most convenient) opportunity to see Rajasthani folk dancing, with nightly shows of colourful, energetic Marwari, Bhil and western Rajasthani dances, as well as traditional Rajasthani puppetry.

Mewar Sound & Light Show   LIVE PERFORMANCE
(Manek Chowk, City Palace; adult/child ₹150/100; ⊙7pm Sep-Mar, 7.30pm Apr, 8pm May-Aug) Fifteen centuries of intriguing Mewar history are squeezed into one atmospheric hour of commentary and light switching – in English from September to April, in Hindi other months.

🔒 Shopping

Tourist-oriented shops – selling miniature paintings, wood carvings, silver jewellery, bangles, spices, camel-bone boxes, and a large variety of textiles – line the streets radiating from Jagdish Chowk. Udaipur is known for its local crafts, particularly miniature painting in the Rajput-Mughal style, as well as some interesting contemporary art.

The local market area extends east from the old clock tower at the northern end of Jagdish Temple Rd, and buzzes loudest in the evening. It's fascinating as much for browsing and soaking up local atmosphere as it is for buying. Bara Bazar, immediately east of the old clock tower, sells silver and gold, while its narrow side street, Maldas St, specialises in saris and fabric. A little further east, traditional shoes are sold on Mochiwada.

Foodstuffs and spices are mainly found around the new clock tower at the east end of the bazaar area, and Mandi Market, 200m north of the tower.

Sadhna   CLOTHING
(☑0294-2454655; www.sadhna.org; Jagdish Temple Rd; ⊙10am-7pm) 🖉 This is the crafts outlet for Seva Mandir, a long-established NGO working with rural and tribal people. The small, hard-to-see shop sells attractive fixed-price textiles; profits go to the artisans and towards community development work.

ℹ️ Information

EMERGENCY
Police (☑0294-2414600, emergency 100) There are police posts at Surajpol, Hatipol and Delhi Gate, three of the gates in the old-city wall.

INTERNET ACCESS
You can surf the internet at plenty of places, particularly around Lal Ghat, for ₹40 per hour. Many places double as travel agencies, bookshops, art shops etc.

MEDICAL SERVICES
GBH American Hospital (☑24hr enquiries 0294-2426000, emergency 9352304050; www.gbhamericanhospital.com; Meera Girls College Rd, 101 Kothi Bagh, Bhatt Ji Ki Bari) Modern, reader-recommended private hospital with 24-hour emergency service, about 2km northeast of the old city.

MONEY
There are lots of ATMs, on City Palace Rd near Jagdish Temple, near the bus stand and outside the train station.
Thomas Cook (Lake Palace Rd; ⊙9.30am-6.30pm Mon-Sat) Changes cash and travellers cheques.

POST
DHL (1 Town Hall Rd; ⊙10am-7pm Mon-Sat) Has a free collection service within Udaipur.
DHL Express (☑0294-2525301; Lal Ghat Guesthouse, Lal Ghat) Conveniently situated inside Lal Ghat Guesthouse.
Main post office (Chetak Circle; ⊙10am-1pm & 1.30-6pm Mon-Sat) North of the old city.

RSRTC BUSES FROM UDAIPUR

DESTINATION	FARE (₹)	DURATION (HR)	FREQUENCY
Ahmedabad	236, AC 585	5	hourly from 5.30am
Ajmer (for Pushkar)	296	7	hourly from 5am
Bundi	328	6	daily (7.45am)
Chittorgarh	120	2½	half-hourly from 5.15am
Delhi	672, AC 1685	15	4 daily
Jaipur	424, AC 903	9	hourly
Jodhpur	273, AC 604	6-8	hourly
Kota	291	7	hourly
Mt Abu (Abu Road)	166	4	10 daily from 5.30am

Post office (City Palace Rd; ⊘10am-4pm Mon-Sat) Tiny post office that sends parcels (including packaging them up), and there are virtually no queues. Beside the City Palace's Badi Pol ticket office.

TOURIST INFORMATION

Small tourist offices operate erratically at the train station and airport.

Tourist office (☑0294-2411535; Fateh Memorial Bldg; ⊘10am-5pm Mon-Sat) Not situated in the most convenient position, 1.5km east of the Jagdish Temple (though only about 500m from the bus stand), this place dishes out a limited amount of brochures and information.

ⓘ Getting There & Away

AIR

Udaipur's airport, 25km east of town, is served by flights from Delhi, Mumbai and other hubs. A prepaid taxi from the airport to the Lal Ghat area costs ₹450.

Air India (☑0294-2410999, airport office 0294-2655453; www.airindia.com; 222/16 Mumal Towers, Saheli Rd) Flies daily to Mumbai and Delhi (via Jodhpur).

IndiGo (☑9212783838; www.goindigo.in) Three flights daily to Delhi and two flights daily to Mumbai.

Jet Airways (☑0294-5134000; www.jetairways.com; Maharana Pratap Airport, Dabok) Flies direct to Delhi and Mumbai daily.

Spice Jet (☑9871803333; www.spicejet.com) Flies twice daily to Delhi and daily to Mumbai.

BUS

RSRTC and private buses run from the **main bus stand**, 1.5km east of the City Palace. Turn left at the end of Lake Palace Rd, take the first right then cross the main road at the end, just after passing through the crumbling old Surajpol Gate. It's around ₹40 in an autorickshaw.

If arriving by bus, turn left out of the bus stand, cross the main road, walk through Surajpol Gate then turn left at the end of the road before taking the first right into Lake Palace Rd.

Private bus tickets can also be bought at any one of the many travel agencies lining the road leading from Jagdish Temple to Daiji Footbridge.

TRAIN

The train station is about 2.5km southeast of the City Palace, and 1km directly south of the main bus stand. An autorickshaw between the train station and Jagdish Chowk should cost around ₹50. There's a prepaid autorickshaw stand at the station.

There are no direct trains to Abu Road, Jodhpur or Jaisalmer.

Agra sleeper ₹370, 13 hours, daily (10.20pm)

Ajmer (for Pushkar) seat/sleeper ₹145/215, five hours, four daily (6am, 3.05pm, 5.15pm and 10.20pm), via Chittorgarh (seat/sleeper ₹95/150, two hours)

Bundi sleeper ₹220, 4½ hours, daily (6.15pm)

Delhi sleeper ₹425, 12 hours, two daily (5.15pm and 6.15pm)

Jaipur seat/sleeper ₹180/270, around seven hours, three daily (6am, 3.05pm and 10.20pm)

ⓘ Getting Around

AUTORICKSHAW

These are unmetered, so you should agree on a fare before setting off – the normal fare anywhere in town is around ₹40. You will usually have to go through the rigmarole of haggling, walking away etc to get this fare. Some drivers ask tourists for ₹100 or more. It costs around ₹350 to hire an autorickshaw for a day of local sightseeing.

The commission system is in place, so tenaciously pursue your first choice of accommodation.

MAJOR TRAINS FROM UDAIPUR

DESTINATION	TRAIN	DEPARTURE	ARRIVAL	FARE (₹)
Agra (Cantonment)	19666 Udaipur-Kurj Exp	10.20pm	11am	370/995 (A)
Ajmer (for Pushkar)	Udaipur-Jaipur SF SPL	3.05pm	8pm	140/490 (B)
Bundi	12964 Mewar Exp	6.15pm	10.33pm	220/560 (A)
Chittorgarh	12982 Chetak Exp	5.15pm	7.10pm	180/560 (A)
Delhi (Hazrat Nizamuddin)	12964 Mewar Exp	6.15pm	6.35am	425/1115 (A)
Jaipur	12991 Udaipur-Jaipur Exp	6am	1.30pm	180/625 (B)

Fares: (A) sleeper/3AC, (B) 2nd-class seat/AC chair

KUMBHALGARH WILDLIFE SANCTUARY

Ranakpur is a great base for exploring the hilly, densely forested **Kumbhalgarh Wildlife Sanctuary** (Indian/foreigner ₹50/300, 4WD or car ₹200, camera/video free/₹400; ⊙ safaris 6-9am & 3-4.30pm), which extends over some 600 sq km. It's known for its leopards and wolves, although the chances of spotting antelopes, gazelles, deer and possibly sloth bears are higher, especially from March to June. You will certainly see some of the sanctuary's 200-plus bird species.

Beside the park office, near the Ranakpur Jain temples, is the recommended tour company **Evergreen Safari** (🗘 7568830065; gypsy safari ₹2500). There are also several safari outfits on the road leading up to Kumbhalgarh Fort, including **A-one Tour & Safari** (🗘 8003854293; Pratap Circle; 2/6 people ₹3000/4500; ⊙ safaris 6-9am & 3-4.30pm). Most hotels will use these or similar outfits to organise your safari.

There's a ticket office for the sanctuary right beside where the bus drops you off for the Jain temples, but the nearest of the sanctuary's four entrances is 2km beyond here.

BICYCLE & MOTORCYCLE

A cheap and environmentally friendly way to buzz around is by bicycle (around ₹200 per day), although motorcycle traffic and pollution make it very tiresome if not dangerous. Scooters and motorbikes, meanwhile, are great for exploring the surrounding countryside.

Heera Cycle Store (🗘 9950611973; off Gangaur Ghat Rd; ⊙ 7.30am-8pm) Hires out bicycles/scooters/Bullets for ₹200/500/800 per day (with a deposit of US$200/400/500); you must show your passport and driver's licence.

Around Udaipur

Kumbhalgarh

🗘 02954

About 80km north of Udaipur, Kumbhalgarh is a fantastic, remote fort, fulfilling romantic expectations and vividly summoning up the chivalrous, warlike Rajput era.

The large and rugged Kumbhalgarh Wildlife Sanctuary can also be visited from Kumbhalgarh.

◉ Sights

Kumbhalgarh   FORT
(Indian/foreigner ₹15/200, Light & Sound Show (in Hindi) ₹100/200; ⊙ 9am-6pm, Light & Sound Show 6.30pm) One of the many forts built by Rana Kumbha (r 1433-68), under whom Mewar reached its greatest extents, this isolated fort is perched 1100m above sea level, with endless views melting into blue distance. The journey to the fort, along twisting roads through the Aravalli Hills, is a highlight in itself.

Kumbhalgarh was the most important Mewar fort after Chittorgarh, and the rulers,

sensibly, used to retreat here in times of danger. Not surprisingly, Kumbhalgarh was only taken once in its entire history. Even then, it took the combined armies of Amber, Marwar and Mughal emperor Akbar to breach its strong defences, and they only managed to hang on to it for two days.

The fort's thick walls stretch about 36km; they're wide enough in some places for eight horses to ride abreast and it's possible to walk right round the circuit (allow two days). They enclose around 360 intact and ruined temples, some of which date back to the Mauryan period in the 2nd century BC, as well as palaces, gardens, step-wells and 700 cannon bunkers.

If you're staying here and want to make an early start on your hike around the wall, you can still get into the fort before 9am, although no one will be around to sell you a ticket.

There's a **Light & Sound Show** (in Hindi) at the fort every evening.

🛏 Sleeping

Kumbhal Castle   HOTEL **$$**
(🗘 02954-242171; www.thekumbhalcastle.com; Fort Rd; r from ₹3130; ❋ 🛜 ❄) The modern Kumbhal Castle, 2km from the fort, has plain but pleasant white rooms featuring curly iron beds, bright bedspreads and window seats, shared balconies and good views. The super-deluxe rooms are considerably bigger and worth considering for the few hundred extra rupees. There's an in-house restaurant.

Aodhi   HOTEL **$$$**
(🗘 8003722333, 02954-242341; www.eternal mewar.in; r from ₹8775; ❋ @ 🛜 ❄) Just under

2km from the fort is this luxurious and blissfully tranquil hotel with an inviting pool, rambling gardens and winter campfires. The spacious rooms, in stone buildings, all boast their own palm-thatched terraces, balconies or pavilions, and assorted wildlife and botanical art and photos.

Nonguests can dine in the restaurant, where good standard Indian fare is the pick of the options on offer, or have a drink in the cosy Chowpal Bar. Room rates plummet from April to September.

ⓘ Getting There & Away

From Udaipur's main bus stand, catch a Ranakpur-bound bus as far as Saira (₹78, 2¼ hours, hourly), a tiny crossroads town where you can change for a bus to Kumbhalgarh (₹41, one hour, hourly). That bus, which will be bound for Kelwara, will drop you at the start of the approach road to the fort, leaving you with a pleasant 1.5km walk to the entrance gate.

The last bus back to Saira swings by at 5.30pm (and is always absolutely jam-packed). The last bus from Saira back to Udaipur leaves at around 8pm. To get to Ranakpur from Kumbhalgarh, head first to Saira then change for Ranakpur (₹20, 40 minutes, at least hourly).

A day-long round trip in a private car from Udaipur to Kumbhalgarh and Ranakpur will cost around ₹2000 per car.

Ranakpur

☎ 02934

On the western slopes of the Aravalli Hills, 75km northwest of Udaipur, and 12km west of Kumbhalgarh as the crow flies (but 50km by road, via Saira), the village of Ranakpur hosts one of India's biggest and most important Jain temple complexes.

The village also makes a great base for exploring the impressive Kumbhalgarh Wildlife Sanctuary (p165) or for taking a day trip to visit the fort at Kumbhalgarh (p165).

◉ Sights

Ranakpur JAIN TEMPLE

(Indian/foreigner incl audio guide free/₹200, camera/tablet ₹100/200; ⏰ Jains 6am-7pm, non-Jains noon-5pm) Built in the 15th century in milk-white marble, the main temple of Ranakpur, **Chaumukha Mandir** (Four-Faced Temple), is dedicated to Adinath, the first Jain *tirthankar* (depicted in the many Buddha-like images in the temple). An incredible feat of Jain devotion, the temple is a complicated series of 29 halls, 80 domes and 1444 individually engraved pillars. The interior is completely covered in knotted, lovingly wrought carving, and has a marvellously calming sense of space and harmony.

Shoes, cigarettes, food and all leather articles must be left at the entrance; women who are menstruating are asked not to enter.

Also exquisitely carved and well worth inspecting are two other Jain temples, dedicated to **Neminath** (the 22nd *tirthankar*) and **Parasnath** (the 23rd *tirthankar*), both within the complex, and a nearby **Sun Temple**. About 1km from the main complex is the **Amba Mata Temple**.

🛏 Sleeping

★ **Aranyawas** HOTEL $$

(☎ 02956-293029; www.aranyawas.com; r incl dinner & breakfast ₹5000; ❄@✺) In secluded, tree-shaded grounds off Hwy 32, 12km south of the temple, Aranyawas has 28 attractive rooms in two-storey stone cottages. They aren't fancy, but are spacious, neat and tasteful, with pine furnishings and, in most cases, balconies overlooking a river and jungle-clad hills. There's a large *baori*-inspired pool surrounded by trees and a bonfire for evening drinks in winter.

The restaurant (mains ₹150 to ₹250, buffet lunch/dinner ₹450/500) is a lovely place to stop for a meal even if you're not staying here.

Ranakpur Hill Resort HOTEL $$$

(☎ 02934-286411; www.ranakpurhillresort.com; Ranakpur Rd; s/d from ₹5850/6435; ❄@🛜✺) This is a well-run hotel with a nice pool and gardens, around which are arranged the attractive cottages sporting marble floors, stained glass, floral wall paintings and touches of mirrorwork. There is also a good multicuisine restaurant, and horse-riding packages can be arranged. Check for discounts on the website. It's 3.5km north of the temple complex, along Hwy 32.

ⓘ Getting There & Away

There are direct buses to Ranakpur leaving roughly hourly from the main bus stands in both Udaipur (₹93, three hours) and Jodhpur (₹189, four to five hours). You'll be dropped outside the temple complex unless you state otherwise. Return buses stop running around 7pm. Buses departing for Udaipur can drop you at Saira (₹20, 40 minutes, hourly), about 25km south of Ranakpur, to connect with a bus to Kumbhalgarh (₹41, one hour, hourly).

A day-long round trip in a private car from Udaipur to Ranakpur and Kumbhalgarh costs around ₹2000.

Mt Abu

🖾 02974 / POP 22,950 / ELEV 1200M

Rajasthan's only hill station nestles among green forests on the state's highest mountain at the southwestern end of the Aravalli Hills and close to the Gujarat border. Quite unlike anywhere else in Rajasthan, Mt Abu provides Rajasthanis, Gujaratis and a steady flow of foreign tourists with respite from scorching temperatures and arid terrain elsewhere. It's a particular hit with honeymooners and middle-class families from Gujarat.

Mt Abu town sits towards the southwestern end of the plateau-like mountain, which stretches about 19km from end to end and 6km from east to west. The town is surrounded by the 289-sq-km Mt Abu Wildlife Sanctuary, which extends over most of the mountain.

The mountain is of great spiritual importance for both Hindus and Jains and has over 80 temples and shrines, most notably the exquisite Jain temples at Delwara, built between 400 and 1000 years ago.

Be mindful that if you arrive during Diwali (October or November), or the following two weeks, prices soar and the place is packed. Mt Abu also gets pretty busy from mid-May to mid-June, before the monsoon. In the cooler months, you'll find everyone wrapped up in shawls and hats; pack something woolly to avoid winter chills in poorly heated hotel rooms.

◉ Sights

The white-clad people you'll see around town are members of the **Brahma Kumaris World Spiritual University** (www.bkwsu. com), a worldwide organisation that has its headquarters here in Mt Abu. The university's **Universal Peace Hall** (Om Shanti Bhawan; ⊙8am-6pm), just north of Nakki Lake, has free 30-minute tours that include an introduction to the Brahma Kumaris philosophy (be prepared for a bit of proselytising). The organisation also runs the **World Renewal**

RAJASTHAN MT ABU

DON'T MISS

DELWARA TEMPLES

The **Delwara Temples** (donations welcome; ⊙ Jains 6am-6pm, non-Jains noon-6pm) are Mt Abu's most remarkable attraction and feature some of India's finest temple decoration. They predate the town of Mt Abu by many centuries and were built when this site was just a remote mountain wilderness. It's said that the artisans were paid according to the amount of dust they collected, encouraging them to carve ever more intricately. Whatever their inducement, there are two temples here in which the marble work is dizzyingly intense.

The older of the two is the **Vimal Vasahi**, on which work began in 1031 and was financed by a Gujarati chief minister named Vimal. Dedicated to the first *tirthankar*, Adinath, it took 1500 masons and 1200 labourers 14 years to build, and allegedly cost ₹185.3 million. Outside the entrance is the **House of Elephants**, featuring a procession of stone elephants marching to the temple, some of which were damaged long ago by marauding Mughals. Inside, a forest of beautifully carved pillars surrounds the central shrine, which holds an image of Adinath himself.

The **Luna Vasahi Temple** is dedicated to Neminath, the 22nd *tirthankar*, and was built in 1230 by the brothers Tejpal and Vastupal for a mere ₹125.3 million. Like Vimal, the brothers were both Gujarati government ministers. The marble carving here took 2500 workers 15 years to create, and its most notable feature is its intricacy and delicacy, which is so fine that, in places, the marble becomes almost transparent. The many-layered lotus flower that dangles from the centre of the dome is a particularly astonishing piece of work.

As at other Jain temples, leather articles (including belts and shoes), cameras and phones must be left at the entrance, and menstruating women are asked not to enter.

Delwara is about 3km north of Mt Abu town centre: you can walk there in less than an hour, or hop aboard a shared taxi (₹10 per person) from up the street opposite Chacha Cafe. A taxi all to yourself should be ₹200 round trip, with one hour of waiting time.

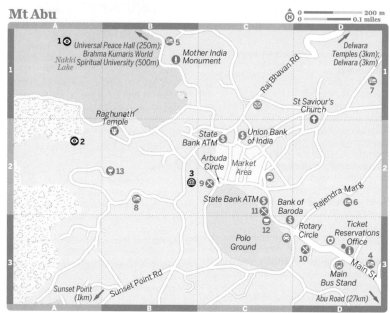

Mt Abu

Mt Abu

◎ Sights
1 Nakki Lake A1
2 Toad Rock A2
3 World Renewal Spiritual Museum B2

✈ Activities, Courses & Tours
Mt Abu Treks .... (see 5)
Shri Ganesh Hotel .... (see 8)

🛏 Sleeping
4 Hotel Hilltone D3
5 Hotel Lake Palace B1
6 Kishangarh House D2

7 Mushkil Aasan D1
8 Shri Ganesh Hotel B2

✖ Eating
9 Arbuda C2
10 Kanak Dining Hall D3
Mulberry Tree Restaurant .... (see 4)
11 Sankalp C2

🍷 Drinking & Nightlife
12 Cafe Coffee Day C3
13 Polo Bar B2

Spiritual Museum (⏱8am-8pm) FREE in the town centre.

Nakki Lake LAKE
Scenic Nakki Lake, the town's focus, is one of Mt Abu's biggest attractions. It's so named because, according to legend, it was scooped out by a god using his *nakh* (nails). Some Hindus thus consider it a holy lake. It's a pleasant 45-minute stroll around the perimeter – the lake is surrounded by hills, parks and strange rock formations. The best known, **Toad Rock**, looks like a toad about to hop into the lake.

Sunset Point VIEWPOINT
Sunset Point is a popular place to watch the brilliant setting sun. Hordes stroll out here every evening to catch the end of the day, the food stalls and all the usual hill-station entertainment. To get there, follow Sunset Point road west of the Polo Ground out of town.

Mt Abu Wildlife Sanctuary WILDLIFE RESERVE
(Indian/foreigner ₹50/300, vehicle ₹200; ⏱8am-5pm) This 289-sq-km sanctuary covers much of the mountain plateau and surrounds the town of Mt Abu. It is home to leopards, deer, foxes and bears. Contact Mt Abu Treks to arrange an overnight stay.

Guru Shikhar　MOUNTAIN

At the northeast end of the Mt Abu plateau, 17km by the winding road from the town, rises 1722m-high Guru Shikhar, Rajasthan's highest point. A road goes almost all the way to the summit and the **Atri Rishi Temple**, complete with a priest and fantastic, huge views. A popular spot, it's a highlight of the RSRTC tour; if you decide to go it alone, a 4WD from Mt Abu will cost ₹600 return.

🖢 Tours

Mt Abu Treks　TREKKING

(📞9414154854; www.mount-abu-treks.blogspot. com; Hotel Lake Palace; 3-4hr trek per person ₹500, full day incl lunch ₹1200) Mahendra 'Charles' Dan arranges tailor-made treks ranging from gentle village visits to longer, wilder expeditions into Mt Abu Wildlife Sanctuary. He's passionate and knowledgeable about the local flora and fauna. Short treks are available as well as an overnight village trek including all meals (₹2000). The sanctuary entrance fee (₹50/300 Indian/foreigner) is not included.

Shri Ganesh Hotel　TREKKING

(📞02974-237292; lalit_ganesh@yahoo.co.in; per person 1hr ₹200, 4hr ₹1000) Organises good short hikes starting at 7am or 4pm.

RSRTC　TOURS

(half-/full-day tours ₹50/110; ⊙half-day tour 1pm, full day 9.30am) The RSRTC runs bus tours of Mt Abu's main sights, leaving from the bus stand where reservations can be made. Both tours visit Achalgarh, Guru Shikhar and the Delwara temples and end at Sunset Point. The full-day tour also includes Adhar Devi, the Brahma Kumaris Peace Hall and Honeymoon Point. Admission and camera fees and the ₹20 guide fee are extra.

🛏 Sleeping

Room rates can double, or treble, during the peak seasons – mid-May to mid-June, Diwali and Christmas/New Year – but generous discounts are often available at other times at midrange and top-end places. If you have to come here during Diwali, you'll need to book way ahead and you won't be able to move for the crowds. Many hotels have an ungenerous 9am checkout time.

Shri Ganesh Hotel　HOTEL $

(📞02974-237292; lalit_ganesh@yahoo.co.in; dm ₹250, s/d ₹500/600, r with bathroom ₹700-1500; @🛜) A fairly central and popular budget spot, Shri Ganesh is well set up for travellers, with an inexpensive cafe and plenty of helpful travel information. Rooms are well used but kept clean. Some have squat toilets and limited hours for hot water. Daily forest walks and cooking lessons are on offer.

Mushkil Aasan　GUESTHOUSE $

(📞9426057837, 02974-235150, 9429409660; mushkilaasan.abu@gmail.com; s/d/q ₹1000/1300/1650; 🛜🛜) A lovely guesthouse nestled in a tranquil vale in the north of town (near Global Hospital), with nine homely decorated rooms and a delightfully planted garden. Home-style Gujarati meals are available, and checkout is a civilised 24 hours. Rooms next to the reception area can be noisy.

Hotel Lake Palace　HOTEL $$

(📞02974-237154; www.savshantihotels.com; r incl breakfast from ₹4165; 🛜🛜) Spacious and friendly, Lake Palace has an excellent location, with small lawns overlooking the lake. Rooms are simple, uncluttered, bright and clean. All have air-conditioning and some have semiprivate lake-view terrace areas. There are rooftop and garden multicuisine restaurants, too.

Kishangarh House　HERITAGE HOTEL $$$

(📞02974-238092; Rajendra Marg; cottages incl breakfast ₹4950, r incl breakfast from ₹6500; 🛜🛜) The former summer residence of the maharaja of Kishangarh is now a plush heritage hotel. The deluxe rooms in the main building are big, with extravagantly high ceilings. The cottage rooms at the back are smaller but cosier. There's a delightful

TREKKING AROUND MT ABU

Getting off the well-worn tourist trail and out into the forests and hills of Mt Abu is a revelation. This is a world of isolated shrines and lakes, weird rock formations, fantastic panoramas, nomadic villagers, orchids, wild fruits, plants used in ayurvedic medicine, sloth bears (which are fairly common), wild boars, langurs, 150 bird species and even the occasional leopard.

A warning from the locals before you set out: it's very unsafe to wander unguided in these hills. Travellers have been mauled by bears and, even more disturbing, have been mugged (and worse) by other people.

sun-filled drawing room and lovely terraced gardens.

Hotel Hilltone
HOTEL $$$

(☑ 02974-238391; www.hotelhilltone.com; Main St; s/d incl breakfast from ₹5355/6545; P✱❄⟲🏊) A modern, well-run hotel in spacious grounds, the punningly named Hilltone takes a leaf out of the more famous hospitality brand with stylishly comfortable and modern rooms that punch above the price tag. The in-house Mulberry Tree Restaurant serves alcohol and nonveg Indian food – a rarity in Mt Abu.

✕ Eating

Kanak Dining Hall
INDIAN $

(Lake Rd; thali Gujarati/Punjabi ₹110/140; ⏱8.30am-3.30pm & 7-11pm) The excellent all-you-can-eat thalis are contenders for Mt Abu's best meals. There's seating indoors in the busy dining hall or outside under a canopy. It's conveniently located near the bus stand for the lunch break during the all-day RSRTC tour.

Arbuda
INDIAN $

(Arbuda Circle; mains ₹100-150; ⏱7am-10.30pm; ☑) This big restaurant is set on a sweeping open terrace filled with chrome chairs. It's very popular for its vegetarian Gujarati, Punjabi and South Indian food, and does fine Continental breakfasts and fresh juices.

Sankalp
SOUTH INDIAN $$

(Hotel Maharaja, Lake Rd; mains ₹90-250; ⏱9am-11pm) A branch of a quality Gujarat-based chain serving up excellent South Indian vegetarian fare. Unusual fillings such as pineapple or spinach, cheese and garlic are available for its renowned dosas and *uttapams* (savoury South Indian rice pancake), which come with multiple sauces and condiments. Order *masala pappad* (wafer with spicy topping) for a tasty starter.

Mulberry Tree Restaurant
MULTICUISINE $$

(Hilltone Hotel, Main St; mains ₹250-350) Mt Abu's Gujarati tourists make veg thalis the order of the day in the town, so if you're craving a bit of nonveg, the smart Mulberry Tree Restaurant at the Hilltone Hotel is the place to go. There are plenty of meaty Indian options on the menu and alcohol is available to wash it down.

🍷 Drinking & Nightlife

Polo Bar
BAR

(☑ 02974-235176; Jaipur House; ⏱11.30am-3.30pm & 7.30-11pm) The terrace at the Jaipur Hotel, formerly the maharaja of Jaipur's summer palace, is a dreamy place for an evening tipple, with divine views over the hills, lake and the town's twinkling lights.

Cafe Coffee Day
CAFE

(Main St; coffee from ₹110; ⏱9am-11pm) A branch of the popular caffeine-supply chain. The tea and cakes aren't bad either.

ℹ Information

There are ATMs on Raj Bhavan Rd, including one outside the tourist office, as well as on Lake Rd.

Bank of Baroda (Main St; ⏱10am-3pm Mon-Fri, to 12.30pm Sat) Changes currency and travellers cheques, and does credit-card advances.

Union Bank of India (Main Market; ⏱10am-3pm Mon-Fri, to 12.30pm Sat) Changes travellers cheques and currency.

Main Post Office (Raj Bhavan Rd; ⏱9am-5pm Mon-Sat)

Tourist Office (⏱9am-5.30pm Mon-Fri) Opposite the main bus stand, this centre distributes free maps of town.

ℹ Getting There & Away

Access to Mt Abu is by a dramatic 28km-long road that winds its way up thickly forested hillsides from the town of Abu Road, where the

MAJOR TRAINS FROM ABU ROAD

DESTINATION	TRAIN	DEPARTURE	ARRIVAL	FARE (₹)
Ahmedabad	19224 Jammu Tawi-Ahmedabad Exp	10.50am	3pm	150/510 (A)
Delhi (New Delhi)	12957 Swarna J Raj Exp	8.50pm	7.30am	1265/1775 (B)
Jaipur	19707 Aravali Exp	10.07am	6.55pm	270/715 (A)
Jodhpur	19223 Ahmedabad-Jammu Tawi Exp	3.30pm	7.55pm	195/510 (A)
Mumbai	19708 Aravali Exp	4.50pm	6.35am	365/985 (A)

Fares: (A) sleeper/3AC, (B) 3AC/2AC

nearest train station is located. Some buses from other cities go all the way up to Mt Abu, others only go as far as Abu Road. Buses (₹30, one hour) run between Abu Road and Mt Abu half-hourly from about 6am to 7pm. A taxi from Abu Road to Mt Abu is ₹350 by day or ₹450 by night. Vehicles are charged when entering Mt Abu (small/large car ₹100/200).

BUS

Services from Mt Abu's **main bus stand**:
Ahmedabad ₹182, seven hours, four daily (6am, 7.30am, 10.15am and 2.45pm)
Jaipur AC ₹924, 11 hours, daily (6.30pm)
Udaipur ₹198, 4½ hours, four daily (8am, 9.15am, 12.45pm and 7pm)

TRAIN

Abu Road station is on the line between Delhi and Mumbai via Ahmedabad. An autorickshaw from Abu Road train station to Abu Road bus stand costs ₹20. Mt Abu has a train **reservations office** (☺8am-2pm Mon-Sat), above the tourist office, with quotas on most of the express trains.

ⓘ Getting Around

To hire a jeep or taxi for sightseeing costs about ₹650/1200 per half-day/day. Many hotels can arrange a vehicle, or you can hire your own vehicle with driver in the town centre.

NORTHERN RAJASTHAN (SHEKHAWATI)

Far less visited than other parts of Rajasthan, the Shekhawati region is renowned for its extraordinary painted *havelis* (ornately decorated residences), highlighted with dazzling, often whimsical, murals. Part of the region's appeal is that these works of art are found in tiny towns connected by single-track roads that run through desolate countryside north of Jaipur. Today it seems curious that such attention and money were lavished on these out-of-the-way houses, but these were once the homelands of wealthy traders and merchants.

From the 14th century onwards, Shekhawati's towns were important trading posts on caravan routes from Gujarati ports to the fertile and booming cities of the Ganges plain. The expansion of the British port cities of Calcutta (now Kolkata) and Bombay (Mumbai) in the 19th century could have been the death knell for Shekhawati, but the merchants moved to these cities, prospered, and sent funds home to construct and decorate their extraordinary abodes.

Nawalgarh

☑ 01594 / POP 63,950

Nawalgarh is a small nontouristy town almost at the very centre of the Shekhawati region, and makes a great base for exploring. It boasts several fine *havelis*, a colourful, mostly pedestrianised bazaar and some excellent accommodation options.

◉ Sights

Dr Ramnath A Podar
Haveli Museum   MUSEUM
(www.podarhavelimuseum.org; Indian/foreigner ₹75/100, camera ₹30; ☺8.30am-6.30pm) Built in 1902 on the eastern side of town, and known locally as 'Podar Haveli', this is one of the region's few buildings to have been thoroughly restored. The paintings of this *haveli* are defined in strong colours, and are the most vivid murals in town, although purists point to the fact that they have been simply repainted rather than restored.

On the ground floor are galleries on Rajasthani culture, including costumes, turbans, musical instruments and models of Rajasthan's forts.

Morarka Haveli Museum   MUSEUM
(₹70; ☺8am-7pm) This museum has well-presented original paintings, preserved for decades behind doorways blocked with cement. The inner courtyard hosts some gorgeous Ramayana scenes; look out for the slightly incongruous image of Jesus on the top storey, beneath the eaves in the courtyard's southeast corner.

Bhagton ki Choti Haveli   HISTORIC BUILDING
(Bhagat Haveli; ₹70) On the external western wall of Bhagton ki Choti Haveli is a locomotive and a steamship. Above them, elephant-bodied *gopis* (milkmaids) dance. Adjacent to this, women dance during the Holi festival. Inside you'll find a host of other murals, including one strange picture (in a room on the western side) of a European man with a cane and pipe, and a small dog on his shoulder.

ⓕ Tours

Ramesh Jangid's Tourist Pension   TOURS
(☑01594-224060; www.touristpension.com; guided hikes 2-3 days per person from ₹2250) Ramesh Jangid organises guided hiking trips, guided camel-cart rides (half-day ₹2000 for two people) to outlying villages, and guided tours by car (full day ₹3500 for up to four

Shekhawati

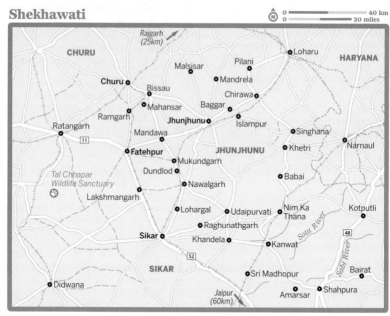

people) to other towns in the region. Lessons in Hindi, tabla, cooking and local crafts such as *bandhani* (tie-dyeing) can also be arranged.

🛏 Sleeping

Ramesh Jangid's
Tourist Pension
GUESTHOUSE **$**

(☑01594-224060; www.touristpension.com; s/d/tr from ₹800/1050/1350; @🖰) 🍃 This guesthouse, run by genial Rajesh, son of Ramesh at Apani Dhani, offers homely, clean accommodation in spacious, cool rooms with big beds. Some rooms have furniture carved by Rajesh's grandfather, and the more expensive rooms also have murals created by visiting artists. Pure veg meals, made with organic ingredients, are available, including a delectable vegetable thali for ₹250.

The family also arranges all sorts of tours (p171) around Shekhawati.

On the western edge of town, near the Maur Hospital, this pension is well known, so if you get lost, just ask a local to point you in the right direction.

DS Bungalow
GUESTHOUSE **$**

(☑9983168916; r ₹400-500) Run by a friendly, down-to-earth couple, this simple place with boxy air-cooled rooms is a little out of town on the way to Roop Niwas Kothi. It's backed by a garden with a pleasant outdoor mud-walled restaurant serving delicious home-cooking. The more energetic can arrange camel tours here.

Shekhawati Guesthouse
GUESTHOUSE **$**

(☑01594-224658; www.shekhawatiguesthouse.com; r incl breakfast ₹600/800, r with AC ₹1000-1500; ✳@🖰) This corner of rural loveliness is more like a homestay run by a very friendly couple. There are six rooms in the main building plus five lovely, mud-walled thatched cottages in the garden. The organic garden supplies most of the hotel's produce needs, which can be enjoyed in the lovely outdoor restaurant.

It's 4km east of the bus stand (₹70 by taxi). Pick-up from the bus or train station can be arranged, as can cooking lessons.

★ Apani Dhani
GUESTHOUSE **$$**

(☑01594-222239; www.apanidhani.com; s/d from ₹1080/1420, r with AC from ₹2500; ✳🖰) 🍃 This award-winning ecotourism venture is a delightfully relaxing place. Rooms with comfortable beds are in cosy mud-hut, thatched-roof bungalows set around a bougainvillea-shaded courtyard. The adjoining organic farm supplies food, and there are solar lights, water heaters and compost toilets. It's on the western side of the Jaipur road. Five per cent of the room tariff goes to community projects.

Tours around the area, via bicycle, car, camel cart or on foot, can be arranged.

Getting There & Away

BUS
The **main bus stand** is little more than a dusty car park accessed through a large yellow double-arched gateway. Services run roughly every hour to Jaipur (₹145 to ₹258, 3½ hours), Jhunjhunu (₹40, one hour) and Mandawa (₹35, 45 minutes).

TRAIN
Nawalgarh is on the route of the biweekly Sikar Dee Express. The train departs Dehli Sarai Rohilla station at 6.50am (on Wednesday and Friday) and arrives at Nawalgarh station at 12.15pm (sleeper/3AC ₹195/510, other classes available). The train continues to Sikar (arrives 1.10pm) on broad gauge, but beyond Sikar to Jaipur work is ongoing to convert the old metre-gauge track. In the opposite direction, the train departs Nawalgarh at 2.45pm (also on Wednesday and Friday) and arrives at Delhi at 9pm (via Jhunjhunu; 2nd class ₹55).

Jhunjhunu

📞 01592 / POP 118,470

Shekhawati's most important commercial centre has a different atmosphere from the smaller towns, with lots of traffic and concrete, and the hustle and bustle that befits the district capital. It does, on the other hand, have some appealing *havelis* and a colourful bazaar.

Sights

Mohanlal Ishwardas
Modi Haveli   HISTORIC BUILDING
(Nehru Bazaar; ₹50) On the northern side of Nehru Bazaar is Mohanlal Ishwardas Modi Haveli (1896). A train runs merrily across the front facade. Above the entrance to the outer courtyard are scenes from the life of Krishna. On a smaller, adjacent arch are British imperial figures, including monarchs and robed judges. Facing them are Indian rulers, including maharajas and nawabs.

Around the archway, between the inner and outer courtyards, there are some glass-covered portrait miniatures, along with some fine mirror-and-glass tilework.

Khetri Mahal   HISTORIC BUILDING
(₹50) A series of small laneways at the western end of Nehru Bazaar (a short rickshaw drive north of the bus station) leads to the imposing Khetri Mahal, a small palace dating from around 1770 and once one of Shekhawati's most sophisticated and beautiful buildings. It's believed to have been built by Bhopal Singh, Sardul Singh's grandson, who founded Khetri. Unfortunately, it now has a desolate, forlorn atmosphere, but the architecture remains a superb open-sided collection of intricate arches and columns.

Modi Havelis   HISTORIC BUILDING
(Nehru Bazaar; ₹50) The Modi Havelis face each other and house some of Jhunjhunu's best murals and woodcarving. The *haveli* on the eastern side has a painting of a woman in a blue sari sitting before a gramophone; a frieze depicts a train, alongside which soldiers race on horses. The spaces between the brackets above show the Krishna legends. The *haveli* on the western side has some comical pictures, featuring some remarkable facial expressions and moustaches.

Sleeping

Hotel Jamuna Resort   HOTEL $$
(📞 9414255035, 01592-232871; www.hotel jamunaresort.in; near Nath Ka Tilla; r ₹1500-3500; ❄@🛰☀) Hotel Jamuna Resort has everything the traveller needs. The rooms in the older wing are either vibrantly painted with murals or decorated with traditional mirrorwork, while the rooms in the newer wing are modern and airy. There's an inviting pool (₹100 for nonguests) set in the garden, plus purpose-built kitchens set up for in-house cooking courses.

The affable owner, Laxmi Kant Jangid has a wealth of knowledge on the villages of Shekhawati and tours can be organised here. Free pick-up from the train or bus stations can be arranged.

Getting There & Away

BUS
There are two bus stands: the **main bus stand** and the **private bus stand**. Both have similar services and prices, but the government-run buses from the main bus stand run much more frequently. Shared autorickshaws run between the two (₹8 per person).

Services from the main bus stand:
Bikaner ₹226, five to six hours, hourly
Delhi ₹230, five to six hours, hourly

RAJASTHAN JHUNJHUNU

Fatehpur ₹45, one hour, half-hourly

Jaipur ₹183, four hours, half-hourly

Mandawa ₹25, one hour, half-hourly

Nawalgarh ₹40, one hour, half-hourly

TRAIN

Jhunjhunu is on the route of the biweekly Sikar Dee Express. The train departs Delhi Sarai Rohilla station at 6.50am (on Wednesday and Friday) and arrives at Jhunjhunu station at 11.30am (sleeper/3AC ₹180/510, other classes available). In the opposite direction, the train departs Jhunjhunu at 3.30pm (also on Wednesday and Friday) and arrives at Delhi at 9pm. The train line to Sikar via Nawalgarh (2nd class ₹55) is broad gauge, but beyond Sikar to Jaipur work is ongoing to convert the old metre-gauge track.

Fatehpur

🌏 01571 / POP 92,600

Established in 1451 as a capital for nawabs (Muslim ruling princes), Fatehpur was their stronghold for centuries before it was taken over by the Shekhawati Rajputs in the 18th century. It's a busy little town, with plenty of *havelis,* many in a sad state of disrepair, but with a few notable exceptions.

⊙ Sights

Apart from the magnificent Le Prince Haveli, other sights include the nearby **Chauhan Well**; **Jagannath Singhania Haveli**; the **Mahavir Prasad Goenka Haveli**, which is often locked but has superb paintings; the **Geori Shankar Haveli**, with mirrored mosaics on the antechamber ceiling; and south of the private bus stand, **Vishnunath Keria Haveli**, and **Harikrishnan Das Saraogi Haveli**, with a colourful facade and iron lacework.

Le Prince Haveli   HISTORIC BUILDING

(🌏 01571-233024; www.cultural-centre.com; incl guided tour ₹200; ⊗ 9am-6pm) This 1802 *haveli* has been stunningly restored by French artist Nadine Le Prince and is one of the most exquisite *havelis* in Shekhawati. Family and visiting artists help to manage the building and conduct the detailed guided tours (30 to 45 minutes). There's a restaurant (bookings required) plus a small gallery. Many of the rooms have been converted into beautifully decorated guest rooms.

The *haveli* is around 2km north of the two main bus stands, down a lane off the main road. Turn right out of the bus stands,

and the turn-off will eventually be on your right, or hop into an autorickshaw.

☞ Tours

Shekhawati Bikers   TOURS

(🌏 01571-233024; per person per day from ₹3600) Le Prince Haveli can get you on a classic Royal Enfield Bullet for a guided tour around the relatively traffic-free roads of Shekhawati.

🛏 Sleeping

★ **Le Prince Haveli**   BOUTIQUE HOTEL $$

(🌏 8094880977, 01571-233024; www.leprincehaveli.com; near Chauhan Well; r from ₹1500, with bathroom from ₹2200, with AC ₹3500-6000; ❄☞🖥) The beautifully restored Le Prince Haveli has opened its artists' residence rooms to travellers. There are 18 highly variable, traditional-style rooms overlooking the central courtyard. The alfresco bar and pool area are great places to unwind, and the restaurant on the terrace serves buffet meals (Indian and French cuisine) and Italian coffee.

There's a 20% discount in summer.

❶ Getting There & Away

At the **private bus stand**, on the Churu–Sikar road, buses leave for the following Shekhawati destinations throughout day, departing as they fill with passengers:

Churu ₹39, one hour

Jhunjhunu ₹45, one hour

Mandawa ₹34, one hour

Ramgarh ₹25, 45 minutes

From the **RSRTC bus stand**, further south down the same road, buses leave for the following:

Bikaner ₹195, 3½ hours, hourly

Delhi ₹288, seven hours, five daily

Jaipur ₹157, 3½ hours, two daily

Mandawa

🌏 01592 / POP 23,350

Of all the towns in the Shekhawati region, Mandawa is the one best set up for tourists, with plenty of places to stay and some decent restaurants. It's a little touristy (a relative term compared to other parts of Rajasthan), but this small 18th-century settlement is still a pleasant base for your *haveli* explorations.

There is only one main drag, with narrow lanes fanning off it. The easy-to-find Hotel Mandawa Haveli is halfway along this street

SHEKHAWATI'S OUTDOOR GALLERIES

In the 18th and 19th centuries, shrewd Marwari merchants lived frugally and far from home while earning money in India's new commercial centres. They sent the bulk of their vast fortunes back to their families in Shekhawati to construct grand *havelis* (traditional, ornately decorated mansions) to show their neighbours how well they were doing and to compensate their families for their long absences. Merchants competed with one another to build ever more grand edifices – homes, temples, step-wells – which were richly decorated, both inside and out, with painted murals.

The artists responsible for these acres of decoration largely belonged to the caste of *kumhars* (potters) and were both the builders and painters of the *havelis*. Known as *chajeras* (masons), many were commissioned from beyond Shekhawati – particularly from Jaipur, where they had been employed decorating the new capital's palaces – and others flooded in from further afield to offer their skills. Soon, there was a cross-pollination of ideas and techniques, with local artists learning from the new arrivals.

The early paintings are strongly influenced by Mughal decoration, with floral arabesques and geometric designs. The Rajput royal courts were the next major influence; scenes from Hindu mythology are prevalent, with Krishna particularly popular.

With the arrival of Europeans, walls were embellished with paintings of the new technological marvels to which the Shekhawati merchants had been exposed in centres such as Calcutta. Pictures of trains, planes, telephones, gramophones and bicycles featured, often painted direct from the artist's imagination. Krishna and Radha are seen in flying motorcars, while the British are invariably depicted as soldiers, with dogs or holding bottles of booze.

These days most of the *havelis* are still owned by descendants of the original families, but not inhabited by their owners, for whom small-town Rajasthan has lost its charm. Many are occupied just by a single *chowkidar* (caretaker), while others may be home to a local family. Though they are pale reflections of the time when they accommodated the large households of the Marwari merchant families, they remain a fascinating testament to the changing times in which they were created. Only a few *havelis* have been restored; many more lie derelict, slowly crumbling away.

For a full rundown on the history, people, towns and buildings of the area, track down a copy of the excellent *The Painted Towns of Shekhawati* by Ilay Cooper, which can be picked up at bookshops in the region or in Jaipur.

and makes a handy point of reference. Most buses drop passengers off on the main street as well as by the bus stand.

☉ Sights

Binsidhar Newatia Haveli   HISTORIC BUILDING
This 1920s *haveli* on the northern side of the Fatehpur–Jhunjhunu road houses the State Bank of Bikaner & Jaipur. There are fantastically entertaining paintings on the external eastern wall, including a European woman in a chauffeur-driven car, the Wright brothers in flight watched by women in saris, a strongman hauling along a car, and a bird-man flying in a winged device.

Murmuria Haveli   HISTORIC BUILDING
The Murmuria Haveli dates back to the 1930s. From the sandy courtyard out front, you can get a good view of the southern external wall of the adjacent double *haveli*: it

features a long frieze depicting a train and a railway crossing. Nehru is depicted on horseback holding the Indian flag. Above the arches on the southern side of the courtyard are two paintings of gondolas on the canals of Venice.

🛏 Sleeping

Hotel Shekhawati   HOTEL **$**
(☎ 01592-223036, 9314698079; www.hotelshekhawati.com;   r ₹400-2800; ✳ @ 🛜) Near Mukundgarh Rd, the only real budget choice in town is run by a retired bank manager and his son (who's also a registered tourist guide). Bright, comically bawdy murals painted by artistic former guests give the rooms a splash of colour. Tasty meals are served on the peaceful rooftop.

Competitively priced camel, horse and 4WD tours can also be arranged.

Hotel Mandawa Haveli
HERITAGE HOTEL **$$**

(✎ 01592-223088, 8890841088; www.hotel mandawahaveli.com; s/ste from ₹1750/5500, d ₹2200-2800; ❋ ☎) Close to Sonathia Gate, on the main road, this hotel is set in a glorious, restored 1890s *haveli* with rooms surrounding a painted courtyard. The cheapest rooms are small, so it's worth splashing out on a suite, filled with arches, window seats and countless small windows.

There's a rooftop restaurant serving delicious food; it's especially romantic at dinner time, when the lights of the town twinkle below. A set dinner costs ₹550.

Hotel Radhika Haveli Mandawa
HERITAGE HOTEL **$$**

(✎ 01592-223045, 9784673645; www.hotelradhika havelimandawa.com; s/d/ste incl breakfast ₹1800/2800/3600; ❋ ☎) This lovely restored *haveli* sits in a quiet part of town with a lawn (and pet rabbit) and boasts comfortable and tasteful rooms that are traditional but without garish murals. There's a good vegetarian restaurant in-house, but it's very close to Monica Rooftop Restaurant should you crave a chicken dish.

Hotel Heritage Mandawa
HERITAGE HOTEL **$$**

(✎ 01592-223742, 9414647922; www.hotelheritage mandawa.com; r ₹1635-6215; ❋ ☎) South of the Subash Chowk is this gracious old *haveli* with traditionally decorated rooms. The eclectic suites have small mezzanine levels either for the bed or the bathroom. Rooms are highly variable, so check a few. Music performances and puppet shows are held in the small garden.

Hotel Castle Mandawa
HERITAGE HOTEL **$$$**

(✎ 01592-223124; www.castlemandawa.com; r incl breakfast from ₹10,230; ❋ @ ☎ ☀) Mandawa's large upmarket hotel in the town's converted fort is a swish and generally comfortable choice. Some rooms are far better appointed than others (the best are the suites in the tower, with four-poster and swing beds), so check a few before you settle in. The gardens and grounds boast restaurants, a coffeeshop and cocktail bar, a pool and an ayurvedic spa.

✖ Eating

Monica Rooftop Restaurant
INDIAN **$$**

(✎ 01592-224178; mains ₹180-400; ☺ 8am-9pm) This delightful rooftop restaurant, in between the fort gate and main bazaar, serves tasty Indian and Chinese meals and cold beer. It's in a converted *haveli*, but only the facade, rather than the restaurant itself, has frescos.

Bungli Restaurant
INDIAN **$$**

(✎ 9929439846; Goenka Chowk; mains ₹140-220, thalis ₹260-360; ☺ 5am-11pm) A popular outdoor travellers' eatery near the Bikaner bus stand, Bungli serves piping-hot tandoori and cold beer from a down-at-heel setting. The food is cooked fresh by a chef who hails from Hotel Castle Mandawa. Early risers can enjoy an Indian breakfast and yoga class (5.30am, 6am, 6.30am) for a total of ₹400.

ⓘ Getting There & Away

The **main bus stand**, sometimes called Bikaner bus stand, has frequent services (roughly half-hourly), including those listed below. Note, there is also a separate **Nawalgarh bus stand**, just off the main drag, with services to Nawalgarh only. Both bus stands are so small they are unrecognisable as bus stands unless a bus is waiting at them. Look for the chai stalls that cluster beside them and you should have the right spot. The main bus stand is at one end of the main street, on your left as the road bears right.

Bikaner ₹223, five hours

Fatehpur ₹34, one hour

Jhunjhunu ₹25, one hour

Nawalgarh ₹35, 45 minutes

JAISALMER, JODHPUR & WESTERN RAJASTHAN

Jodhpur

✎ 0291 / POP 1,033,900

Mighty Mehrangarh, the muscular fort that towers over the Blue City of Jodhpur, is a magnificent spectacle and an architectural masterpiece. Around Mehrangarh's base, the old city, a jumble of Brahmin-blue cubes, stretches out to the 10km-long, 16th-century city wall. The Blue City really is blue! Inside is a tangle of winding, glittering, medieval streets, which never seem to lead where you expect them to, scented by incense, roses and sewers, with shops and bazaars selling everything from trumpets and temple decorations to snuff and saris.

Modern Jodhpur stretches well beyond the city walls, but it's the immediacy and buzz of the old Blue City and the larger-than-life fort that capture travellers' imaginations. This crowded, hectic zone is also Jodhpur's main tourist area. Areas of the old city further west, such as Navchokiya, are just as atmospheric, with far less hustling.

History

Driven from their homeland of Kannauj, east of Agra, by Afghans serving Mohammed of Ghori, the Rathore Rajputs fled west around AD 1200 to the region around Pali, 70km southeast of Jodhpur. They prospered to such a degree that in 1381 they managed to oust the Pratiharas of Mandore, 9km north of present-day Jodhpur. In 1459 the Rathore leader Rao Jodha chose a nearby rocky ridge as the site for a new fortress of staggering proportions, Mehrangarh, around which grew Jodha's city: Jodhpur.

Jodhpur lay on the vital trade route between Delhi and Gujarat. The Rathore kingdom grew on the profits of sandalwood, opium, dates and copper, and controlled a large area, which became cheerily known as Marwar (the Land of Death) due to its harsh topography and climate. It stretched as far west as what's now the India–Pakistan border area, and bordered with Mewar (Udaipur) in the south, Jaisalmer in the northwest, Bikaner in the north, and Jaipur and Ajmer in the east.

◉ Sights & Activities

★ Mehrangarh   FORT

(www.mehrangarh.org) Rising perpendicular and impregnable from a rocky hill that itself stands 120m above Jodhpur's skyline, Mehrangarh is one of the most magnificent forts in India. The battlements are 6m to 36m high, and as the building materials were chiselled from the rock on which the fort stands, the structure merges with its base. Still run by the Jodhpur royal family, Mehrangarh is packed with history and legend. You don't need a ticket to enter the fort itself, only the museum section.

Mehrangarh's main entrance is at the northeast gate, Jai Pol. It's about a 300m walk up from the old city to the entrance, or you can take a winding 5km autorickshaw ride (around ₹120).

Jai Pol was built by Maharaja Man Singh in 1808 following his defeat of invading forces from Jaipur. Past the museum ticket office and a small cafe, the 16th-century Dodh Kangra Pol was an external gate

before Jai Pol was built, and still bears the scars of 1808 cannonball hits. Through here, the main route heads up to the left through the 16th-century Imritia Pol and then Loha Pol, the fort's original entrance, with iron spikes to deter enemy elephants. Just inside the gate are two sets of small hand prints, the *sati* (self-immolation) marks of royal widows who threw themselves on their maharajas' funeral pyres – the last to do so were Maharaja Man Singh's widows in 1843.

Past Loha Pol you'll find a restaurant and Suraj Pol, which gives access to the museum. Once you've visited the museum, continue on from here to the panoramic ramparts, which are lined with impressive antique artillery. The ramparts were fenced off in 2016 after a fatal selfie accident. Hopefully a temporary measure, as the views are spectacular.

Also worth exploring is the right turn from Jai Pol, where a path winds down to the Chokelao Bagh, a restored and gorgeously planted 18th-century Rajput garden (you could lose an afternoon here lolling under shady trees reading a book), and the Fateh Pol (Victory Gate). You can exit here into the old city quarter of Navchokiya.

★ Mehrangarh Museum   MUSEUM

(www.mehrangarh.org; Indian/foreigner incl audio guide ₹100/600, camera/video ₹100/200, Indian/foreign-language guide ₹170/225; ⊗9am-5pm) The fort's museum encompasses the fort's former palace, and is a superb example of Rajput architecture. The network of courtyards and halls features stone-lattice work so finely carved that it often looks more like sandalwood than sandstone. The galleries around Shringar Chowk (Anointment Courtyard) display India's best collection of elephant *howdahs* and Jodhpur's royal palanquin collection. The superb audio guide (available in 11 languages) is included with the museum ticket, but bring ID or a credit card as deposit.

One of the two galleries off Daulat Khana Chowk displays textiles, paintings, manuscripts, headgear and the curved sword of the Mughal emperor Akbar; the other gallery is the armoury. Upstairs is a fabulous gallery of miniature paintings from the sophisticated Marwar school and the beautiful 18th-century Phul Mahal (Flower Palace), with 19th-century wall paintings depicting the 36 moods of classical ragas as well as royal portraits; the artist took 10

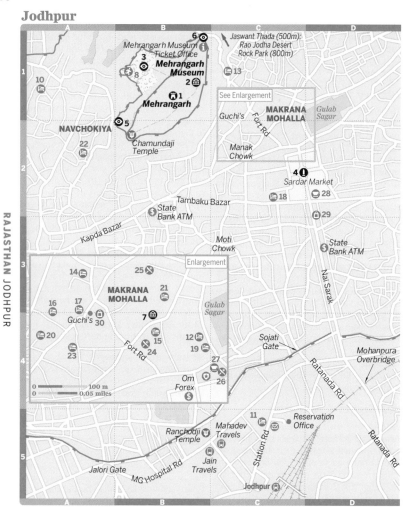

years to create them using a curious concoction of gold leaf, glue and cow's urine.

Takhat Vilas was the bedchamber of Maharaja Takhat Singh (r 1843–73), who had just 30 maharanis and numerous concubines. Its beautiful ceiling is covered with Christmas baubles. You then enter the extensive *zenana,* the lovely latticed windows of which are said to feature over 250 different designs (and through which the women could watch the goings-on in the courtyards). Here you'll find the **Cradle Gallery**, exhibiting the elaborate cradles of infant princes, and the 17th-century **Moti**

Mahal (Pearl Palace), which was the palace's main durbar hall (royal reception hall) for official meetings and receptions, with gorgeously colourful stained glass.

Rao Jodha Desert Rock Park PARK (☑ 9571271000; www.raojodhapark.com; Mehrangarh; ₹100, guide ₹200; ☺ 7am-7pm Apr-Sep, 8am-6pm Oct-Mar) This 72-hectare park – and model of ecotourism – sits in the lee of Mehrangarh. It has been lovingly restored and planted with native species to show the natural diversity of the region. The park is crisscrossed with walking trails that take you up to the city walls, around Devkund Lake,

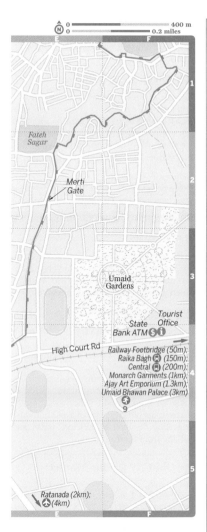

Jodhpur

⊙ **Top Sights**
1	Mehrangarh	B1
2	Mehrangarh Museum	B1

⊙ **Sights**
3	Chokelao Bagh	B1
4	Clock Tower	C2
5	Fateh Pol	B2
6	Jai Pol	B1
7	Tunwarji ka Jhalra	B4

⊕ **Activities, Courses & Tours**
8	Flying Fox	B1
9	Sambhali Trust	F4

⊟ **Sleeping**
10	Cosy Guest House	A1
11	Govind Hotel	C5
12	Haveli Inn Pal	B4
13	Hill View Guest House	C1
14	HosteLavie	A3
15	Hotel Haveli	B4
16	Kesar Heritage Hotel	A3
17	Krishna Prakash Heritage Haveli	A3
18	Nirvana Home	C2
19	Pal Haveli	B4
20	Pushp Paying Guest House	A4
21	Raas	B3
22	Singhvi's Haveli	A2
23	Yogi Guest House	A4

⊗ **Eating**
	Indique	(see 19)
24	Jhankar Choti Haveli	B4
25	Jharokha	B3
	Nirvana	(see 18)
26	Omelette Shops	C4

⊖ **Drinking & Nightlife**
27	Cafe Sheesh Mahal	C4
	Govind Hotel	(see 11)
28	Shri Mishrilal Hotel	D2
	Stepwell Cafe	(see 7)

⊜ **Shopping**
29	MV Spices	D2
30	Sambhali Boutique	A4

RAJASTHAN JODHPUR

spotting local birds, butterflies and reptiles. For an extra insight into the area's native flora and fauna, take along one of the excellent local guides.

Walks here are the perfect restorative if the Indian hustle has left you in need of breathing space. Visit in the early morning or late afternoon for the most pleasant temperatures. The visitors centre is thoughtfully put together, and there's a small cafe, too.

Jaswant Thada   HISTORIC BUILDING
(Indian/foreigner ₹15/50, camera/video ₹25/50, guide ₹50; ⊙9am-5pm) This milky-white marble memorial to Maharaja Jaswant Singh

II, sitting above a small lake 1km northeast of Mehrangarh, is an array of whimsical domes. It's a welcome, peaceful spot after the hubbub of the city, and the views across to the fort and over the city are superb. Built in 1899, the cenotaph has some beautiful *jalis* (carved-marble lattice screens) and is hung with portraits of Rathore rulers going back to the 13th century.

Look out for the memorial to a peacock that flew into a funeral pyre.

Umaid Bhawan Palace   PALACE

(museum Indian/foreigner ₹50/100; ☺museum 9am-5pm) Take an autorickshaw to this hill-top palace, 3km southeast of the old city. The royal incumbent, Gaj Singh II, still lives in part of the building. Built in 1929, the 365-room edifice was designed by the British architect Henry Lanchester for Maharaja Umaid Singh. It took more than 3000 workers 15 years to complete, at a cost of around ₹11 million.

The building is mortarless, and incorporates 100 wagon loads of Makrana marble and Burmese teak in the interior. Apparently its construction began as a royal job-creation program during a time of severe drought. Much of the building has been turned into a suitably grand hotel.

Casual visitors are not welcome at either the royal residence or the hotel, but you can visit the **museum**, housed in one side of the building. It includes photos showing the elegant art-deco design of the palace interior, plus an eccentric collection of elaborate clocks. Don't miss the maharaja's highly polished classic cars, displayed in front of the museum, by the entrance gate.

Tunwarji ka Jhalra   HISTORIC BUILDING

(Step-well; Makrana Mohalla) FREE This geometrically handsome step-well (also known as a *baori* or *wav*) has been rejuvenated after decades as a rubbish dump. It's clean lines and clear, fish-filled water will leave you mesmerised. It's a great place to just sit and watch, but the attached cafe (p183) adds further incentive for a visit.

Clock Tower   MONUMENT

The century-old clock tower is an old city landmark surrounded by the vibrant sounds, sights and smells of Sardar Market, which is marked by triple gateways at its northern and southern ends. The narrow, winding lanes of the old city spread out in all directions from here. Westward, you plunge into the old city's commercial heart, with crowded alleys and bazaars selling vegetables, spices, sweets, silver and handicrafts.

Flying Fox   ADVENTURE SPORTS

(www.flyingfox.asia; adult/child ₹1900/1600; ☺9am-5pm) This circuit of six zip lines flies back and forth over walls, bastions and lakes on the northern side of Mehrangarh. A brief training session is given before you start and safety standards are good: 'awesome' is the verdict of most who dare. Flying Fox has a desk near the main ticket office and its

starting point is in the Chokelao Bagh. Tours last up to 1½ hours, depending on the group size. Book online for a discount on the walk-up price.

✯✯ Festivals & Events

**Rajasthan International
Folk Festival**   MUSIC

(www.jodhpurriff.org; ☺Sep/Oct) The excellent Rajasthan International Folk Festival has five days of music concerts by Indian and international artists held at Mehrangarh.

**Jodhpur Flamenco
& Gypsy Festival**   MUSIC

(www.jfgfestival.com; Mehrangarh; ☺Apr) Mehrangarh, this most spectacular of music venues, hosts April's Jodhpur Flamenco & Gypsy Festival.

Marwar Festival   PERFORMING ARTS

(☺Sep/Oct) In September or October Jodhpur hosts the colourful Marwar Festival, which includes polo and a camel tattoo.

⛏ Sleeping

The old city has something like 100 guesthouses, most of which scramble for your custom as soon as you get within breathing distance of Sardar Market.

If you call ahead, many lodgings can organise a pick-up from the train station or bus stops, even at night. Otherwise, for most places in the old city you can avoid nonsense by getting dropped at the clock tower and walking from there.

Old City (Sadar Market)

HosteLavie   HOSTEL $

(✆0291- 2611001; www.hostelavie.com; Killi Khana, Fort Rd; dm ₹400-450, r ₹1600; ☎) A European-style hostel with clean air-con dorms, where each bed sports a lockable locker and mobile charging point. The dorms are four- and six-bed and each one has its own bathroom. There are also double rooms, making this a good budget option between the fort and the clock tower. It has the obligatory rooftop terrace restaurant.

Rooms are simple and those facing inside are darker but quieter, compared to the airier rooms facing the busy thoroughfare.

Hill View Guest House   GUESTHOUSE $

(✆0291-2441763; hill_view2004@yahoo.com; Makrana Mohalla; dm ₹150, r ₹300-700; ☎) Perched above town and just below the fort walls, this hotel is run by a friendly, enthusiastic Muslim family, who'll make you feel right at home. Rooms are basic, clean and simple, all with bathrooms (but not all with decent windows), and the terrace has a great view over the city. Good, home-cooked veg and nonveg food is on offer.

Village and camel tours can be arranged here.

Kesar Heritage Hotel   GUESTHOUSE $
(☑ 9983216625; www.kesarheritage.com; Makrana Mohalla; r ₹900-1800; ❄ 🛜) A popular budget choice, Kesar plays a good hand with large airy rooms (a few have balconies, air-con and flat-screen TVs) and friendly, helpful management. The sidestreet location puts noisily sputtering rickshaws out of earshot of light sleepers. The rooftop restaurant looks up to Mehrangarh.

Pushp Paying Guest House   GUESTHOUSE $
(☑ 0291-2648494; www.pushpguesthouse.com; Pipli-ki-Gali, Naya Bass, Manak Chowk; r ₹600, with AC ₹900; ❄ @ 🛜) A small family-run guesthouse with five clean, colourful rooms with windows. It's tucked down the narrowest of alleys, but you get an up-close view of Mehrangarh from the rooftop restaurant, where owner Nikhil rustles up great vegetarian fare (dishes ₹30 to ₹90). Nikhil will send a rickshaw to the railway station to pick you up for ₹60 to ₹100.

Yogi Guest House   GUESTHOUSE $
(☑ 0291-2643436; www.yogiguesthouse.com; r ₹800, with AC ₹1500-1900; ❄ 🛜) Yogi's is a venerable travellers' hang-out, with budget and midrange rooms in a 500-year-old blue-washed *haveli* just below the fort walls. It's a friendly place with well-kept, clean rooms. There's also a lovely rooftop restaurant with great views.

★ Krishna Prakash
Heritage Haveli   HERITAGE HOTEL $$
(☑ 0291-2633448; www.kpheritage.com; Nayabas; r incl breakfast ₹1550-3850; ❄ @ ✈) This multilevel heritage hotel right under the fort walls is great value and a peaceful choice. It has decorated carved furniture and colourful murals, and rooms are well proportioned; the deluxe ones are a bit more spruced up, generally bigger, and set on the upper floors, so airier. There's a shaded swimming pool and a relaxing terrace restaurant.

Free bus and train station pick-ups are offered and there are facilities for drivers.

Haveli Inn Pal   HERITAGE HOTEL $$
(☑ 0291-2612519; www.haveliinnpal.com; Gulab Sagar; r incl breakfast ₹3500-4680; ❄ @ 🛜) This smaller sibling of Pal Haveli is accessed through the same grand entrance, but is located around to the right in one wing of the grand *haveli*. It's a simpler heritage experience, with comfortable rooms, and lake or fort views from the more expensive ones. It has its own very good rooftop restaurant, Panorama 360, a mere chapati toss from Indique.

Free pick-ups from Jodhpur transport terminals are offered, and discounts are often available for single occupancy.

Hotel Haveli   HOTEL $$
(Haveli Guesthouse; ☑ 0291-2614615; www.hotel haveli.net; Makrana Mohalla; s/d from ₹1465/1815; ❄ @ 🛜) This 250-year-old building inside the walled city is a popular, efficient and friendly place. Rooms vary greatly and are individually decorated with colour themes and paintings; many have semibalconies and fort views. The rooftop restaurant, Jharokha (p182), has excellent views and nightly entertainment. It's opposite the restored and beautiful Tunwarji ka Jhalra step-well.

Nirvana Home   HOTEL $$
(☑ 0291-5106280; www.nirvana-home.com; 1st fl, Tija Mata ka Mandir, Tambaku Bazaar; s/d from ₹1200/1600, ste ₹3000; ❄ 🛜) It's not often you get to lay your head down in a converted Hindu temple, but Nirvana Home gives you the chance. The hotel is in a busy bazaar, but rooms run off a lovely internal courtyard thick with pot plants. Windows face inside, with views of original 300-year-old temple frescos (fixtures are thankfully newer).

★ Pal Haveli   HERITAGE HOTEL $$$
(☑ 0291-3293328; www.palhaveli.com; Gulab Sagar; r incl breakfast ₹5935-11,115; ❄ @ 🛜) This stunning *haveli,* the best and most attractive in the old city, was built by the Thakur of Pal in 1847. There are 21 charming, spacious rooms, mostly large and elaborately decorated in traditional heritage style, surrounding a central courtyard. The family retain a small museum here. The rooftop restaurant, Indique (p182), is one of the city's finest and boasts unbeatable views.

Raas   BOUTIQUE HOTEL $$$
(☑ 0291-2636455; www.raasjodhpur.com; Tunwarji ka Jhalara; r incl breakfast ₹19,000-41,000; ❄ @ 🛜 ✈) Developed from a 19th-century city mansion, Jodhpur's first contemporary-

RAJASTHAN JODHPUR

style boutique hotel is a splendid retreat of clean, uncluttered style, hidden behind castle-like gates. The red-sandstone-and-terrazzo rooms come with plenty of luxury touches. Most have balconies with great Mehrangarh views – also to be enjoyed from the lovely pool in the garden-courtyard. There are two restaurants and a highly indulgent spa.

🛏 Old City (Navchokiya)

Cosy Guest House
GUESTHOUSE $

(✆9829023390, 0291-2612066; www.cosyguesthouse.com; Chuna Ki Choki, Navchokiya; r ₹400-1550, without bathroom ₹250; @🛜) A friendly place in an enchanting location, this 500-year-old glowing blue house has several levels of higgledy-piggledy rooftops and a mix of rooms, some monastic, others comfortable. Ask the rickshaw driver for Navchokiya Rd, from where the guesthouse is signposted, or call the genial owner, Mr Joshi.

★Singhvi's Haveli
GUESTHOUSE $$

(✆0291-2624293; www.singhvihaveli.com; Ramdevji-ka-Chowk, Navchokiya; r ₹700-2800; ❄@🛜) This 500-odd-year-old, family-run, red-sandstone *haveli* is an understated gem. Run by two friendly brothers, Singhvi's has 13 individual rooms, ranging from simple places to lay your head to the magnificent Maharani Suite, with its 10 windows and fort view. The relaxing vegetarian restaurant is a great place to sample a Rajasthani thali and is decorated with sari curtains and floor cushions.

🛏 Train Station Area

Govind Hotel
HOTEL, HOSTEL $

(✆0291-2622758; www.govindhotel.com; Station Rd; dm ₹250, s/d from ₹800/900, s/d with AC from ₹1400/1600; ❄@🛜) Well set up for travellers, with helpful management, an internet cafe, and a location convenient to the Jodhpur train station. All rooms are clean and tiled, with fairly smart bathrooms. There's a rooftop restaurant and a coffeeshop (Govind Hotel, Station Rd; ⊙10am-10pm) with excellent espresso and cakes.

🍴 Eating

Omelette Shops
STREET FOOD $

(omelettes from ₹25; ⊙10am-10pm) On your right and left as you leave Sadar Market through its northern gate, these two omelette stalls compete for the attentions of passing travellers by knocking up seemingly

endless numbers and varieties of cheap, delicious omelettes. Both do a decent job, and are both run by characters worth spending a few minutes with.

Three tasty, spicy boiled eggs cost ₹15, and a two-egg masala and cheese omelette with four pieces of bread is ₹30.

★Indique
INDIAN $$

(✆0291-3293328; Pal Haveli Hotel; mains ₹250-400; ⊙11am-11pm) This candlelit rooftop restaurant at the Pal Haveli hotel is the perfect place for a romantic dinner, with superb views to the fort, clock tower and Umaid Bhawan. The food covers traditional tandoori, biryanis and North Indian curries, but the Rajasthani *laal maas* (mutton curry) is a delight. Ask the barman to knock you up a gin and tonic before dinner.

Nirvana
INDIAN $$

(✆0291-5106280; 1st fl, Tija Mata ka Mandir, Tambaku Bazar; mains ₹130-200; ⊙9am-10pm) Sharing premises with a Rama temple and a hotel, Nirvana has both an indoor cafe, covered in ancient Ramayana wall paintings, and a rooftop eating area with panoramic views. The Indian vegetarian food is among the most delicious you'll find in Rajasthan. The special thali is enormous and easily enough for two. Continental and Indian breakfasts are served in the cafe.

Jhankar Choti Haveli
MULTICUISINE $$

(✆9828031291; Makrana Mohalla; mains ₹130-360; ⊙8am-10pm; ❄🛜) Stone walls and big cane chairs in a leafy courtyard, along with prettily painted woodwork and whirring fans, set the scene at this semi-open-air travellers' favourite. It serves up good Indian vegetarian dishes, plus pizzas, burgers and baked-cheese dishes. There's also an air-con section and a rooftop for meals with a view.

On the Rocks
NORTH INDIAN $$

(✆0291-5102701; Circuit House Rd; mains ₹130-375; ⊙12.30-3.30pm & 7.30-11pm) This leafy garden restaurant, 2km southeast of the old city, is very popular with locals and tour groups. It has tasty Indian cuisine, including lots of barbecue options and rich and creamy curries, plus a small playground and a cavelike bar (open 11am to 11pm) with a dance floor (for couples only).

Jharokha
INDIAN $$$

(✆0291-2614615; www.hotelhaveli.net; Hotel Haveli, Makrana Mohalla; mains ₹225-355; ⊙8am-11pm) The rooftop terrace of the Hotel Haveli hosts this classy restaurant, with uniformed staff, Indian wine and Spanish *cerveza*. The excellent veg and nonveg dishes include Rajasthani specialities, such as *govind gatta* (cottage cheese and gram-flour dumplings in a yoghurt curry), plus other North Indian curries; try the *aloo Simla mirch* (green bell peppers and potatoes in a spicy gravy).

🍷 Drinking & Nightlife

★**Shri Mishrilal Hotel**   CAFE

(Sardar Market; lassi ₹30; ⊙8.30am-10pm) Just inside the southern gate of Sardar Market, this place is nothing fancy, but whips up the most superb creamy *makhania* lassis. These are the best in town, probably in all of Rajasthan, possibly in all of India.

★**Cafe Sheesh Mahal**   CAFE

(Pal Haveli Hotel; coffee from ₹100; ⊙9.30am-9pm) Coffee drinkers will enjoy the precious beans and the care that is bestowed on them at the deliciously air-conditioned Cafe Sheesh Mahal. And if you're feeling hungry the pancakes here are gaining legendary status.

Stepwell Cafe   CAFE

(☑0291-2636455; Tunwarji ka Jhalra; coffee from ₹120; ⊙noon-10.30pm; 🛜) This delightful modern cafe with espresso coffee, cakes and Italian dishes sits on one side of the wonderfully restored step-well, Tunwarji ka Jhalra. It's a great place to relax and contemplate the time when step-wells such as these kept the city alive. Or you can just watch the kids jump into the water with an impressive booming splash.

🛍️ Shopping

Plenty of Rajasthani handicrafts are available in Jodhpur, with shops selling textiles and other wares clustered around Sardar Market and along Nai Sarak. You'll need to bargain hard. The town is known for antiques.

MV Spices   FOOD

(www.mvspices.com; 107 Nai Sarak; ⊙9am-9pm) The most famous spice shop in Jodhpur (and believe us, there are lots of pretenders!), MV Spices has several small branches around town, including one at Meherangarh, that are run by the seven daughters of the founder of the original stall. It will cost around ₹100 to ₹500 for 100g bags of spices, and the owners will email you recipes so you

JODHPUR'S JODHPURS

A fashion staple for self-respecting horsey people all around the world, jodhpurs are riding breeches – usually of a pale cream colour – that are loose above the knee and tapered from knee to ankle. It's said that Sir Pratap Singh, a legendary Jodhpur statesman, soldier and horseman, originally designed the breeches for the Jodhpur Lancers. When he led the Jodhpur polo team on a tour to England in 1897, the design caught on in London and then spread around the world.

If you fancy taking home an authentic pair of jodhpurs from the city they originated in, head to **Monarch Garments** (☑9352353768; www.monarch-garments. com; A-13 Palace Rd; ⊙10.30am-8.45pm), opposite the approach road leading up to Umaid Bhawan Palace. Here you can buy ready-made jodhpurs or have a pair tailored for you within two days. Prices are polo club–worthy, starting at around ₹9000.

can use your spices correctly when you get home.

Sambhali Boutique   FASHION & ACCESSORIES

(Killi Khana; ⊙10am-7pm) 🧵 This small but interesting shop sells goods made by women who have learned craft skills with the **Sambhali Trust** (☑0291-2512385; www.sambhali-trust.org; c/o Durag Niwas Guest House, 1st Old Public Park, Raika Bagh, Jodhpur), which works to empower disadvantaged women and girls. Items include attractive *salwar* trousers, cute stuffed silk or cloth elephants and horses, bracelets made from pottery beads, silk bags, and block-printed muslin curtains and scarves.

Ajay Art Emporium   ANTIQUES

(Palace Rd; ⊙10am-7pm) Good quality replica Rajasthani antiques and furniture.

ℹ️ Information

There are foreign-card-friendly ATMs dotted around the city, though fewer are in the old city.

Om Forex (Sardar Market; internet per hr ₹30; ⊙9am-10pm) Exchanges currency and also has an internet facility.

Guchi's (Killikhana, Naya Bass, Makrana Mohalla; internet ₹50 per hr; ⊙8am-10pm)

As well as all forms of ticketing and vehicle hire, Guchi's has fast broadband internet and a wealth of knowledge on what to do and where to go, including how to do an excursion to Osian.

Main Post Office (Station Rd; ⊘9am-4pm Mon-Fri, to 3pm Sat, stamp sales only 10am-3pm Sun)

Tourist Office (☑0291-2545083; High Court Rd; ⊘9am-6pm Mon-Fri) Offers a free map and willingly answers questions.

ⓘ Getting There & Away

AIR

The airport is 5km south of the city centre, about ₹400/150 by taxi/autorickshaw.

Jet Airways (☑0291-2515551; www.jetairways.com; Jodhpur Airport) and **Indian Airlines** (☑0291-2510758; www.indian-airlines.nic.in; 2 West Patel Nagar, Circuit House Rd, Ratanader) both fly daily to Delhi and Mumbai.

BUS

Government-run buses leave from the **central bus stand** (Raika Bagh), directly opposite Raika Bagh train station. Walk east along High Court Rd, then turn right under the small tunnel. Services include the following:

Ajmer (for Pushkar) ₹207, AC ₹447, five hours, hourly until 6.30pm

Bikaner ₹243, 5½ hours, frequent from 5am to 6pm

Jaipur ₹336, AC ₹730, seven hours, frequent from 4.45am to midnight

Jaisalmer ₹266, 5½ hours, 10 daily

Mt Abu (Abu Road) ₹271, 7½ hours, nine daily until 9.30pm

Osian ₹62, 1½ hours, half-hourly until 10pm

Rohet ₹47, one hour, every 15 minutes

Udaipur ₹273, AC ₹604, seven hours, 10 daily until 6.30pm

For private buses, you can book through your hotel, although it's cheaper to deal directly with the bus operators on the road in front of Jodhpur train station. **Jain Travels** (☑0291-2643832; www.jaintravels.com; MG Hospital Rd; ⊘7am-11pm) and **Mahadev Travels** (☑0291-2633927; MG Hospital Rd; ⊘7am-10pm) are both reliable. Buses leave from bus stands out of town, but the operator should provide you with free transport (usually a shared autorickshaw) from their ticket office. Example services:

Ajmer (for Pushkar) ₹180, five hours, at least six daily

Bikaner seat/sleeper ₹220/320, five hours, at least five daily

Jaipur seat/sleeper ₹260/380, 7½ hours, five daily

Jaisalmer ₹300, 5½ hours, hourly

Mt Abu (direct) seat/sleeper ₹315/550, 7½ hours, daily

TAXI

You can organise taxis for intercity trips, or longer, through most accommodation places; otherwise, you can deal directly with drivers. There's a taxi stand outside Jodhpur train station. A reasonable price is ₹12 per kilometre (for a non-AC car), with a minimum of 250km per day. The driver will charge at least ₹100 for overnight stops and will charge for his return journey.

TRAIN

The computerised **reservation office** (Station Rd; ⊘8am-8pm Mon-Sat, to 1.45pm Sun) is 300m northeast of Jodhpur train station. Window 786 sells the tourist quota. Services:

Ajmer (for Pushkar) sleeper/3AC ₹185/510, 5½ hours, two daily (6.35am and 7am)

Bikaner sleeper/3AC ₹210/530, 5½ to seven hours, five to eight daily (7.25am, 7.40am, 9.50am, 10.30am, 10.55am, 2.25pm, 4.35pm and 8.10pm)

Delhi sleeper/3AC ₹380/986, 11 to 14 hours, four daily (6.35am, 11.15am, 7.50pm and 9.15pm)

MAJOR TRAINS FROM JODHPUR

DESTINATION	TRAIN	DEPARTURE	ARRIVAL	FARE (₹)
Ajmer (for Pushkar)	54801 Jodhpur-Ajmer Fast Passenger	7am	12.35pm	185/510
Bikaner	14708 Ranakpur Exp	9.50am	3.35pm	210/530
Delhi	12462 Mandor Exp	7.50pm	6.40am	380/986
Jaipur	14854 Marudhar Exp	9.45am	3.30pm	250/625
Jaisalmer	14810 Jodhpur-Jaisalmer Exp	11pm	6am	215/565
Mumbai	14707 Ranakpur Exp	2.45pm	9.40am	485/1270

Fares: sleeper/3AC

Jaipur sleeper/3AC ₹250/625, five to six hours, six to 12 daily from 6.10am to midnight

Jaisalmer sleeper/3AC ₹215/565, five to seven hours, three daily (5.20am, 7.25am, 5.50pm and 11pm)

Mumbai sleeper/3AC ₹485/1270, 16 to 19 hours, two to six daily (5.35am, 2.45pm, 6.20pm, 6.45pm, 7.20pm and 11.55pm); all go via Abu Rd for Mt Abu (4½ hours)

Udaipur There are no direct trains; change at Marwar Junction.

🛈 Getting Around

Despite the absurd claims of some autorickshaw drivers, the fare between the clock tower area and the train stations or central bus stand should be around ₹60 to ₹80. A couple of companies have reliable fixed-price taxis that can be pre-booked.

Around Jodhpur

Southern Villages

A number of traditional villages are strung along and off the Pali road southeast of Jodhpur. Most hotels and guesthouses in Jodhpur offer tours to these villages, often called Bishnoi village safaris. The Bishnoi are a Hindu sect who follow the 500-year-old teachings of Guru Jambheshwar, who emphasised the importance of protecting the environment. Many visitors are surprised by the density – and fearlessness – of wildlife such as blackbuck, nilgai (antelope), chinkara (gazelle) and desert fox around the Bishnoi villages.

The 1730 sacrifice of 363 villagers to protect khejri trees is commemorated in September at **Khejadali village**, where there is a memorial to the victims fronted by a small grove of khejri trees.

At **Guda Bishnoi**, the locals are traditionally engaged in animal husbandry. There's a small lake (full only after a good monsoon) where migratory birds, such as demoiselle cranes, and mammals such as blackbucks and chinkaras, can be seen, particularly at dusk when they come to drink.

The village of **Salawas** is a centre for weaving beautiful *dhurries* (rugs), a craft also practised in many other villages. A cooperative of 42 families here runs the **Roopraj Dhurry Udyog** (☏0291-2896658; roopraj durry@sify.com; ⊙dawn-dusk), through which all profits go to the artisans. A 3ft by 5ft *dhurrie* costs a minimum of ₹3000, a price

For Karachi (Pakistan), the 14889 Thar Express, alias the Jodhpur–Munabao Link Express, leaves Bhagat Ki Kothi station, 4km south of the Jodhpur train station, at 1am on Saturday only. You need to arrive at the station six hours before departure – the same time it takes to reach Munabao (about 7am) on the border. There you undergo lengthy border procedures before continuing to Karachi (assuming you have a Pakistan visa) in a Pakistani train, arriving about 2am on Sunday. Accommodation is sleeper only, with a total sleeper fare of around ₹500 from Jodhpur to Karachi. In the other direction the Pakistani train leaves Karachi at about 11pm on Friday, and Indian train 14890 leaves Munabao at 7pm on Saturday, reaching Jodhpur at 11.50pm. It is currently not possible to book this train online; you will need to go to the station.

based on two weavers working several hours a day for a month at ₹50 per day each. Other families are involved in block-printing.

Bishnoi village tours tend to last four hours in total and cost around ₹800 per person. Those run by Deepak Dhanraj of **Bishnoi Village Safari** (☏9829126398; www.bishnoivillagesafari.com; half-day tour per person ₹800) get good feedback, but many other places do them.

Osian

☏02922 / POP 12,550

The ancient Thar Desert town of Osian, 65km north of Jodhpur, was an important trading centre between the 8th and 12th centuries. Known as Upkeshpur, it was dominated by the Jains, whose wealth left a legacy of exquisitely sculpted, well-preserved temples. The **Mahavira Temple** (Indian/foreigner free/₹10, camera ₹100; ⊙6am-8.30pm) surrounds an image of the 24th *tirthankar* (great Jain teacher), formed from sand and milk. **Sachiya Mata Temple** (⊙6am-7.15pm) is an impressive walled complex where both Hindus and Jains worship.

Osian, along with Jodhpur, co-hosts the Marwar Festival (p180), a colourful display of Rajasthani folk music, dance and costume held every September/October.

Prakash Bhanu Sharma, a personable Brahmin priest, has an echoing **guesthouse** (☑9414440479, 02922-274331; s/d without bathroom ₹400/600) geared towards pilgrims, opposite the Mahavira Temple. **Safari Camp Osian** (☑9928311435; www.safaricamposian. com; d tent incl dinner, breakfast & camel ride from ₹9000) is a fancier tented-camp option.

🚩 Tours

Gemar Singh SAFARI
(☑9460585154; www.hacra.org; per person per day around ₹2050, min 2 people) Gemar Singh arranges popular camel safaris, homestays, camping, desert walks and 4WD trips in the deserts around Osian and its Rajput and Bishnoi villages. Pick-up from Osian bus station, or from Jodhpur, can be arranged.

❶ Getting There & Away

Frequent buses depart from Jodhpur to Osian (₹62, 1½ hours). Buses also run from Phalodi (₹83, two hours). Trains between Jodhpur and Jaisalmer also stop here. A return taxi from Jodhpur costs about ₹1500.

Jaisalmer

☑02992 / POP 65,480
The fort of Jaisalmer is a breathtaking sight: a massive sandcastle rising from the sandy plains like a mirage from a bygone era. No place better evokes exotic camel-train trade routes and desert mystery. Ninety-nine bastions encircle the fort's still-inhabited twisting lanes. Inside are shops swaddled in bright embroideries, a royal palace and numerous businesses looking for your tourist rupee. Despite the commercialism, it's hard not to be enchanted by this desert citadel. Beneath the ramparts, particularly to the north, the narrow streets of the old city conceal magnificent *havelis,* all carved from the same golden-honey sandstone as the fort – hence Jaisalmer's designation as the Golden City.

A city that has come back almost from the dead in the past half-century, Jaisalmer may be remote, but it's certainly not forgotten – indeed it's one of Rajasthan's biggest tourist destinations.

History

Jaisalmer was founded way back in 1156 by a leader of the Bhati Rajput clan named Jaisal. The Bhatis, who trace their lineage back to Krishna, ruled right through to Independence in 1947.

The city's early centuries were tempestuous, partly because its rulers relied on looting for want of other income, but by the 16th century Jaisalmer was prospering from its strategic position on the camel-train routes between India and Central Asia. It eventually established cordial relations with the Mughal empire. In the mid-17th century, Maharawal Sabal Singh expanded the Jaisalmer princedom to its greatest extents by annexing areas that now fall within the administrative districts of Bikaner and Jodhpur.

Under British rule the rise of sea trade (especially through Mumbai) and railways saw Jaisalmer's importance and population decline. Partition in 1947, with the cutting of trade routes to Pakistan, seemingly sealed the city's fate. But the 1965 and 1971 wars between India and Pakistan gave Jaisalmer new strategic importance, and since the 1960s, the Indira Gandhi Canal to the north has brought revitalising water to the desert.

Today, tourism, wind-power generation and the area's many military installations are the pillars of the city's economy.

⊙ Sights

★ Jaisalmer Fort FORT
Jaisalmer's fort is a living urban centre, with about 3000 people residing within its walls. It is honeycombed with narrow winding lanes, lined with houses and temples – along with a large number of handicraft shops, guesthouses and restaurants. You enter the fort from the east, near Gopa Chowk, and pass through four massive gates on the zigzagging route to the upper section. The final gate opens into the square that forms the fort's centre, **Dashera Chowk**.

Founded in 1156 by the Rajput ruler Jaisal and reinforced by subsequent rulers, Jaisalmer Fort was the focus of a number of battles between the Bhatis, the Mughals of Delhi and the Rathores of Jodhpur. In recent years, the fabric of the fort has faced increasing conservation problems due to unrestricted water use caused, in the most part, by high tourist numbers.

★ Fort Palace PALACE
(Indian/foreigner incl compulsory audio guide ₹100/500, camera ₹100; ⊙8am-6pm Apr-Oct, 9am-6pm Nov-Mar) Towering over the fort's main square, and partly built on top of

ℹ ARRIVAL IN JAISALMER

Touts work the buses heading to Jaisalmer from Jodhpur, hoping to steer travellers to guesthouses or hotels in Jaisalmer where they will get a commission. Some may even approach you before the bus leaves Jodhpur; others ride part or all of the way from Jodhpur, or board about an hour before Jaisalmer. On arrival in Jaisalmer, buses can be surrounded by touts baying for your attention. Don't believe anyone who offers to take you anywhere you like for just a few rupees, and do take with a fistful of salt any claims that the hotel you want is full, closed or no good any more. Many hotels will offer pick-ups from the bus or train station.

Also be very wary of offers of rooms for ₹100 or similar absurd rates. Places offering such prices are almost certainly in the camel-safari hard-sell game with the objective of getting you out of the room and on to a camel as fast as possible. If you don't take up their safari offers, the room price may suddenly increase or you might be told there isn't a room available any more.

Touts are less prevalent on the trains, but the same clamour for your custom ensues outside the station once you have arrived.

the Hawa Pol (the fourth fort gate), is the former rulers' elegant seven-storey palace. Highlights of the tour include the mirrored and painted Rang Mahal (the bedroom of the 18th-century ruler Mulraj II), a gallery of finely wrought 15th-century sculptures donated to the rulers by the builders of the fort's temples, and the spectacular 360-degree views from the rooftop.

One room contains an intriguing display of stamps from the former Rajput states. On the eastern wall of the palace is a sculpted pavilion-style balcony. Here drummers raised the alarm when the fort was under siege. You can also see numerous round rocks piled on top of the battlements, ready to be rolled onto advancing enemies. Much of the palace is open to the public – floor upon floor of small rooms provide a fascinating sense of how such buildings were designed for spying on the outside world. The doorways connecting the rooms of the palace are quite low. This isn't a reflection on the stature of the Rajputs, but was a means of forcing people to adopt a humble, stooped position in case the room they were entering contained the maharawal.

The last part of the tour moves from the king's palace (Raja-ka-Mahal) into the queen's palace (Rani-ka-Mahal), which contains an interesting section on Jaisalmer's annual Gangaur processions in spring. The worthwhile 1½-hour audio-guide tour (available in six languages) is included with the entry fee, but you must leave a ₹2000 deposit, or your passport, driver's licence or credit card.

Jain Temples   JAIN TEMPLE
(Indian/foreigner ₹50/200, camera ₹50; ⊙Chandraprabhu, Rikhabdev & Gyan Bhandar 8am-noon, other temples 11am-noon) Within the fort walls is a maze-like, interconnecting treasure trove of seven beautiful yellow sandstone Jain temples, dating from the 15th and 16th centuries. Opening times have a habit of changing, so check with the caretakers. The intricate carving rivals that of the marble Jain temples in Ranakpur and Mt Abu, and has an extraordinary quality because of the soft, warm stone. Shoes and all leather items must be removed before entering the temples.

Chandraprabhu is the first temple you come to, and you'll find the ticket stand here. Dedicated to the eighth *tirthankar,* whose symbol is the moon, it was built in 1509 and features fine sculpture in the *mandapa,* the intensely sculpted pillars of which form a series of *toranas.* To the right of Chandraprabhu is the tranquil **Rikhabdev** temple, with fine sculptures around the walls, protected by glass cabinets, and pillars beautifully sculpted with *apsaras* and gods.

Behind Chandraprabhu is **Parasnath,** which you enter through a beautifully carved *torana* culminating in an image of the Jain *tirthankar* at its apex. A door to the south leads to small **Shitalnath,** dedicated to the 10th *tirthankar,* whose image is composed of eight precious metals. A door in the northern wall leads to the enchanting, dim chamber of **Sambhavanth** – in the front courtyard, Jain priests grind sandalwood in mortars for devotional use. Steps lead down to the **Gyan Bhandar,** a fascinating

Jaisalmer

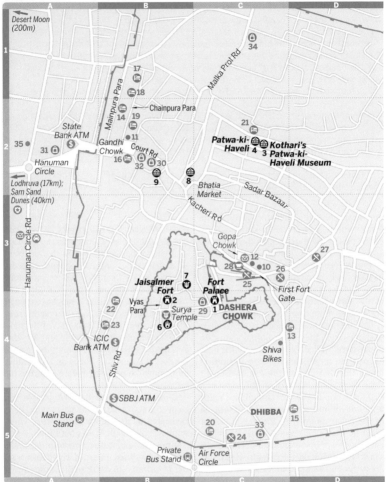

tiny underground library founded in 1500, which houses priceless ancient illustrated manuscripts. The remaining two temples, Shantinath and Kunthunath, were built in 1536 and feature plenty of sensual carving. Note, the restrictive visiting times are for non-Jains. The temples are open all day for worshippers.

Laxminarayan Temple　　　　HINDU TEMPLE
The Hindu Laxminarayan Temple, in the centre of the fort, is simpler than the Jain temples here and has a brightly decorated dome. Devotees offer grain, which is distrib-

uted before the temple. The inner sanctum has a repoussé silver architrave around its entrance, and a heavily garlanded image enshrined within.

★**Patwa-ki-Haveli**　　　　HISTORIC BUILDING
(Government sections Indian/foreigner ₹50/200; ⏱9am-6pm) The biggest fish in the *haveli* pond is Patwa-ki-Haveli, which towers over a narrow lane, its intricate stonework like honey-coloured lace. Divided into five sections, it was built between 1800 and 1860 by five Jain brothers who made their fortunes in brocade and jewellery. It's all very

Jaisalmer

◉ **Top Sights**
1 Fort Palace...............................C4
2 Jaisalmer Fort B4
3 Kothari's Patwa-ki-Haveli
   Museum C2
4 Patwa-ki-Haveli C2

◉ **Sights**
5 Desert Cultural Centre &
   Museum E4
6 Jain Temples B4
7 Laxminarayan Temple B3
8 Nathmal-ki-Haveli..................B2
9 Thar Heritage Museum..........B2

◉ **Activities, Courses & Tours**
10 Sahara Travels.......................C3
11 Thar Desert Tours B2
12 Trotters C3

◉ **Sleeping**
13 1st Gate Home Fusion..........D4
14 Arya Haveli.............................B2
15 Hotel Gorakh Haveli..............D5
16 Hotel Nachana Haveli............B2
17 Hotel Pleasant Haveli............B1
18 Hotel Renuka..........................B1
19 Hotel Swastika.......................B2
20 Hotel Tokyo Palace................C5
21 Killa Bhawan Lodge...............C2
22 Roop Mahal.............................B4
23 Shahi Palace...........................B4

◉ **Eating**
   1st Gate Home Fusion...............(see 13)
24 Desert Boy's Dhani.................C5
25 Jaisal Italy..............................C3
26 Monica Restaurant.................C3
27 Natraj Restaurant..................D3
   Saffron......................................(see 16)

◉ **Drinking & Nightlife**
28 Bhang Shop.............................C3

◉ **Shopping**
29 Bellissima...............................C4
30 Desert Handicrafts Emporium...........B2
31 Gandhi Darshan Emporium.................A2
32 Jaisalmer Handloom..............B2
33 Khadi Gramodyog Bhavan.................C5
34 Zila Khadi Gramodan Parishad...........C1

◉ **Transport**
35 Hanuman Travels....................A2
   Swagat Travels.........................(see 35)

Jethwai Rd

(500m)

Barmer Rd

Buses to
Khuri (150m)
Khuri (48km)

Tourist
Office

Gadi Sagar Rd

Gadi Sagar

RAJASTHAN JAISALMER

impressive from the outside; however, the first of the five sections, the privately owned **Kothari's Patwa-ki-Haveli Museum** (Indian/foreigner ₹100/250; ⊘9am-6pm), richly evokes 19th-century life and is the only one worth paying entry for.

Other sections include two largely empty government-owned 'museums' and two private sections containing shops.

Nathmal-ki-Haveli HISTORIC BUILDING
(donation requested; ⊘8am-7pm) This late-19th-century *haveli,* once used as the prime minister's house, is still partly inhabited. It has an extraordinary exterior, dripping with carvings, and the 1st floor has some beautiful paintings using 1.5kg of gold leaf. The left and right wings were the work

of two brothers, whose competitive spirits apparently produced this virtuoso work – the two sides are similar, but not identical. Sandstone elephants guard the entrance.

Desert Cultural Centre & Museum MUSEUM
(Gadi Sagar Rd; museum ₹50, camera ₹50, combined museum & puppet show ₹100; ⊙ museum 10am-6pm, puppet show 6.30-8.30pm) This interesting little museum tells the history of Rajasthan's princely states and has exhibits on traditional Rajasthani culture. Features include Rajasthani music (with video), textiles, a *kavad* mobile temple, and a *phad* scroll painting depicting the story of the Rajasthani folk hero Pabuji, used by travelling singers as they recite Pabuji's epic exploits. It also hosts nightly half-hour **puppet shows** with English commentary. The ticket includes admission to the Jaisalmer Folklore Museum.

Thar Heritage Museum MUSEUM
(off Court Rd; ₹40, camera ₹20; ⊙ 10am-8pm) This private museum has an intriguing assortment of Jaisalmer artefacts, from turbans, musical instruments, fossils and kitchen equipment to displays on birth, marriage, death and opium customs. It's brought alive by the guided tour you'll get from its founder, local historian and folklorist LN Khatri. Look for the snakes and ladders game that acts as a teaching guide to Hinduism's spiritual journey. If the door is locked you'll find Mr Khatri at his shop, Desert Handicrafts Emporium, nearby on Court Rd.

☞ Tours

The tourist office (p194) runs sunset tours to the Sam Sand Dunes (₹200 per person, minimum four people). Add ₹100 if you'd like a short camel ride, too. Other tours visit Amar Sagar, Lodhruva and Bada Bagh by car.

🛏 Sleeping

While staying in the fort might appear to be Jaisalmer's most atmospheric choice, habitation inside the fort – driven in no small part by tourism – is causing irreparable damage to the monument. As a result, we don't recommend staying inside. Fortunately, there's a wide choice of good places to stay outside the fort. You'll get massive discounts between April and August, when Jaisalmer is hellishly hot.

Unfortunately, some budget hotels are heavily into the high-pressure selling of camel safaris and things can turn sour if you don't take up their propositions; room rates that sound too good to be true almost always are.

Arya Haveli GUESTHOUSE $
(☑ 9782585337; www.aryahaveli.com; Mainpura Para; dm ₹175, with AC ₹275, r incl breakfast ₹450-1500; ✹ 🛜) Helpful staff add to a stay at this spruced-up guesthouse. Rooms are well appointed and looked after; the cheaper ones face an internal courtyard, the best have their own balcony. The top-floor Blues Cafe is a nice place to relax to some good music and tasty food.

Hotel Tokyo Palace HOTEL $
(☑ 02992-255483; www.tokyopalace.net; Dhibba Para; dm ₹150-200, s incl breakfast ₹500-2000, d incl breakfast ₹900-3000; ✹ @ 🛜 ≋) Well run by honest, traveller-friendly management, this hotel has clean midrange rooms, some with lovely window seats, as well as plenty of budget options, including separate basement dorms for men and women (bathrooms are the next level up). A big bonus is the sparkling pool and rooftop restaurant.

Roop Mahal HOTEL $
(☑ 02992-251700; www.hotelroopmahal.com; off Shiv Rd; r ₹600-1500; ✹ 🛜) A solid budget choice with clean spacious rooms, trustworthy management, fort views from the rooftop cafe, and free wi-fi throughout. Cheaper rooms have fan only and windows facing inside; more expensive rooms have air-conditioning and views.

Desert Moon GUESTHOUSE $
(☑ 9414149350, 02992-250116; www.desert moonguesthouse.com; Achalvansi Colony; s ₹600-1200, d ₹900-1800; ✹ @ 🛜) On the northwestern edge of town, 1km from Gandhi Chowk, Desert Moon is in a quiet location beneath the Vyas Chhatri sunset point. The guesthouse is run by a friendly Indian-Kiwi couple who offer free pick-up from the train and bus stations. The 11 rooms are cool, clean and comfortable, with polished stone floors, tasteful decorations and sparkling bathrooms.

Hotel Renuka HOTEL $
(☑ 02992-252757; www.hotelrenuka.net; Chainpura Para; s/d ₹450/550, with AC ₹850/950; ✹ @ 🛜) Spread over three floors, Renuka has squeaky-clean rooms – the best have balconies, bathrooms and air-conditioning. It's

been warmly accommodating guests since 1988, so management knows its stuff. The roof terrace has great fort views and a good restaurant, and the hotel offers free pick-up from the bus and train stations.

Hotel Swastika HOTEL $
(☑ 02992-252483; swastikahotel@yahoo.com; Chainpura Para; dm ₹100, s/d/tr ₹200/300/400, r with AC ₹600; ✹ 🎤) In this well-run place, the only thing you'll be hassled about is to relax. Rooms are plain, quiet, clean and very good for the price; some have little balconies. There are plenty of restaurants nearby.

★ Hotel Nachana Haveli HERITAGE HOTEL $$
(☑ 02992-252110; www.nachanahaveli.com; Goverdhan Chowk; r/ste incl breakfast ₹3950/4950; ✹ @ 🎤) This 280-year-old royal *haveli*, set around three courtyards – one with a tinkling fountain – is a fascinating hotel with a highly regarded restaurant, Saffron. The raw sandstone rooms have arched stone ceilings and the ambience of a medieval castle. They are sumptuously and romantically decorated. The common areas come with all the Rajput trimmings, including swing chairs and bearskin rugs.

Although centrally located, the hotel is set back from the road and the stone walls ensure a peaceful sleep.

Hotel Gorakh Haveli HOTEL $$
(☑ 02992-252978; www.hotelgorakhhaveli.com; Dhibba Para; s/d ₹1000/1500, with AC ₹1500/2500; ✹ 🎤) A pleasantly low-key spot south of the fort, Gorakh Haveli is a modern place built with traditional sandstone and some attractive carving. Rooms are comfy and spacious, staff are amiable, and there's a reasonable all-veg, multicuisine rooftop restaurant (mains ₹30 to ₹150), with fort views, of course. A 30% discount on rooms is offered in summer.

Hotel Pleasant Haveli HOTEL $$
(☑ 02992-253253; www.pleasanthaveli.com; Chainpura Para; r from ₹2450; ✹ 🎤) This welcoming place has lots of lovely carved stone, a beautiful rooftop (with restaurant) and just a handful of spacious and attractive colour-themed rooms, all with modern, well-equipped bathrooms and air-con. Complimentary water bottle and free pick-ups from transport terminals are available.

Shahi Palace HOTEL $$
(☑ 02992-255920; www.shahipalacehotel.com; off Shiv Rd; r ₹350-2000; ✹ @ 🎤) Shahi Palace is a deservedly popular option. It's a modern building in the traditional style with carved sandstone. It has attractive rooms with raw sandstone walls, colourful embroidery, and carved stone or wooden beds. The cheaper rooms are mostly in two annexes along the street, Star Haveli and Oasis Haveli. The rooftop restaurant (mains ₹80 to ₹200) is excellent.

Indian veg and nonveg dishes are available, plus some European fare, cold beer and a superb evening fort view.

★ 1st Gate Home Fusion BOUTIQUE HOTEL $$$
(☑ 02992-254462, 9462554462; www.1stgate.in; First Fort Gate; r incl breakfast from ₹8190; ✹ @ 🎤) Italian-designed and super-slick, this is Jaisalmer's most sophisticated hotel and it is beautiful throughout, with a desert-meets-contemporary-boutique vibe. The location lends it one of the finest fort views in town, especially from its split-level, open-air restaurant-cafe area. Rooms are immaculate with complimentary minibar (soft drinks), fruit basket and bottled water replenished daily.

Killa Bhawan Lodge HOTEL $$$
(☑ 02992-253833; www.killabhawan.com; Patwa-ki-haveli Chowk; r incl breakfast from ₹4165; ✹ 🎤) Near Patwa-ki-Haveli, this small hotel is a delight. There are five big and beautifully decorated rooms, a pleasant rooftop restaurant, KB Cafe, that looks up to the fort, and free tea and coffee all day.

★ Suryagarh HOTEL $$$
(☑ 02992-269269; www.suryagarh.com; Kahala Fata, Sam Rd; r/ste incl breakfast from ₹18,000/23,000; ✹ @ 🎤 ✹) The undisputed king in this category, Suryagarh rises like a fortress beside the Sam road, 14km west of town. It's a brand-new building in traditional Jaisalmer style centred on a huge palace-like courtyard with beautiful carved stonework. Features include a fabulous indoor pool and a multicuisine restaurant, Nosh (mains ₹650 to ₹800; nonguests welcome). Rooms follow the traditional/contemporary theme.

It's a spectacular place, but it doesn't stop there. A great range of activities and excursions are on offer plus nightly entertainment.

🍴 Eating & Drinking

★ 1st Gate Home Fusion ITALIAN, INDIAN $$
(☑ 02992-254462, 9462554462; First Fort Gate; mains ₹220-460; ⏱ 7.30-10.30am, noon-3pm

JAISALMER CAMEL SAFARIS

Trekking around by camel is the most evocative and fun way to sample Thar Desert life. Don't expect dune seas, however – the Thar is mostly arid scrubland sprinkled with villages and wind turbines, with occasional dune areas popping out here and there. You will often come across fields of millet, and children herding flocks of sheep or goats, the neck bells of which tinkle in the desert silence.

Most trips now include 4WD rides to get you to less frequented areas. The camel riding is then done in two two-hour batches, one before lunch, one after. It's hardly camel *trekking*, but it's a lot of fun nevertheless. A cheaper alternative to arranging things in Jaisalmer is to base yourself in the small village of Khuri (p195), 48km southwest, where similar camel rides are available, but where you're already in the desert when you start.

Before You Go

Competition between safari organisers is cut-throat and standards vary. Most hotels and guesthouses are very happy to organise a camel safari for you. While many provide a good service, some may cut corners and take you for the kind of ride you didn't have in mind. A few low-budget hotels in particular exert considerable pressure on guests to take 'their' safari. Others specifically claim 'no safari hassle'.

You can also organise a safari directly with one of the several reputable specialist agencies in Jaisalmer. Since these agencies depend exclusively on safari business it's particularly in their interest to satisfy their clients. It's a good idea to talk to other travellers and ask two or three operators what they're offering.

A one-night safari, leaving Jaisalmer in the afternoon and returning the next morning, with a night on some dunes, is a minimum to get a feel for the experience: you'll probably get 1½ to two hours of riding each day. You can trek for several days or weeks if you wish. The longer you ride, the more understanding you'll gain of the desert's villages, oases, wildlife and people.

The best-known dunes, at Sam (p195), 40km west of Jaisalmer, are always crowded in the evening and are more of a carnival than a back-to-nature experience. The dunes near Khuri are also quite busy at sunset, but quiet the rest of the time. Operators all sell trips now to 'nontouristy' and 'off-the-beaten-track' areas. Ironically, this has made Khuri quieter again, although Sam still hums with day-tripper activity.

With 4WD transfers included, typical rates are between ₹1200 and ₹2500 per person for a one-day, one-night trip (leaving one morning and returning the next). This should include meals, mineral water, blankets and sometimes a thin mattress. Check that there will be one camel for each rider. You can pay for greater levels of comfort (eg tents, better food), but *always* get it all down in writing.

You should get a cheaper rate (₹1000 to ₹1500 per person) if you leave Jaisalmer in the afternoon and return the following morning. A quick sunset ride in the dunes at Sam costs around ₹600 per person, including 4WD transfer. At the other end of the scale, you can arrange for a 20-day trek to Bikaner. Expect to pay between ₹1200 and ₹2000 per person per day for long, multiday trips, depending on the level of support facilities (4WDs, camel carts etc).

& 7-11pm; 🛜✍) Sitting atop the boutique hotel of the same name, this split-level, open-air terrace boasts dramatic fort views and a mouth-watering menu of authentic vegetarian Italian and Indian dishes. Also on offer are excellent wood-fired pizzas and good strong Italian coffee. Snacks and drinks are available outside meal times (7.30am to 11pm).

⭐ **Saffron** MULTICUISINE **$$**
(Hotel Nachana Haveli, Goverdhan Chowk; mains ₹195-415; ⏱7am-11pm) On the spacious roof terrace of Hotel Nachana Haveli, the veg and nonveg food here is excellent. It's a particularly atmospheric place in the evening, with private and communal lounges and more formal seating arrangements. The Indian food is hard to beat, though the Italian isn't too bad either. Alcohol is served.

What to Take

A wide-brimmed hat (or Lawrence of Arabia turban), long trousers, a long-sleeved shirt, insect repellent, toilet paper, a torch (flashlight), sunscreen, a water bottle (with a strap), and some cash (for a tip to the camel men, if nothing else) are recommended. Women should consider wearing a sports bra, as a trotting camel is a bumpy ride. It can get cold at night, so if you have a sleeping bag bring it along, even if you're told that lots of blankets will be supplied. During summer, rain is not unheard of, so come prepared.

Which Safari?

Recommendations shouldn't be a substitute for doing your own research. Whichever agency you go for, insist that all rubbish is carried back to Jaisalmer.

Sahara Travels (02992-252609; www.saharatravelsjaisalmer.com; Gopa Chowk; 6am-8pm) Run by the son of the late LN Bissa (aka Mr Desert), this place is very professional and transparent. Trips are to 'nontouristy' areas only. Prices for an overnight trip (9am to 11am the following day) are ₹1900 per person, all inclusive. A cheaper overnight alternative that avoids the midday sun starts at 2pm and finishes at 11am for ₹1500.

Trotters (9828929974; www.trottersjaisalmer.net; Gopa Chowk; 5.30am-9.00pm) This company is transparently run with a clear price list showing everything on offer, including trips to 'off-the-beaten-track' areas as well as cheaper jaunts to Sam or Khuri. Prices for an overnight trip (6.30am to 11am the following day) are ₹1950 to ₹2450 per person, all inclusive.

Thar Desert Tours (91-9414365333; www.tharcamelsafarijaisalmer.com; Gandhi Chowk; 8.30am-7.30pm) This well-run operator charges ₹1200 per person per day including water and meals, adjusting prices depending on trip times. It limits tours to five people maximum, and we also receive good feedback about them. Customers pay 80% upfront.

In the Desert

Camping out at night, huddling around a tiny fire beneath the stars and listening to the camel drivers' songs, is magical.

There's always a long lunch stop during the hottest part of the day. At resting points the camels are unsaddled and hobbled; they'll often have a roll in the sand before limping away to browse on nearby shrubs, while the camel drivers brew chai or prepare food. The whole crew rests in the shade of thorn trees.

Take care of your possessions, particularly on the return journey. Any complaints you do have should be reported, either to the **Superintendent of Police** (02992-252233), the **tourist office** (p194) or the intermittently staffed **Tourist Assistance Force** (Gadi Sagar Rd) posts inside the First Fort Gate and on the Gadi Sagar access road.

The camel drivers will expect a tip (up to ₹100 per day is welcomed) at the end of the trip; don't neglect to give them one.

Monica Restaurant MULTICUISINE $$
(Amar Sagar Pol; mains ₹100-300, veg/nonveg thali ₹175/375; 8am-3pm & 6-11pm) The airy open-air dining room at Monica just about squeezes in a fort view, but if you end up at a non-view table, console yourself with the excellent veg and nonveg options. Meat from the tandoor is particularly well-flavoured and succulent, the thalis varied, and the salads fresh and tasty.

Jaisal Italy ITALIAN $$
(First Fort Gate; mains ₹180-290; 7.30am-11pm;) Just inside First Fort Gate, Jaisal Italy has a decent vegetarian Italian menu, including bruschetta, antipasti, pasta, pizza, salad and desserts, plus Spanish omelettes. All this is served up in an exotically decorated indoor restaurant (cosy in winter, deliciously air-conditioned in summer) or on a delightful terrace atop the lower fort walls, with cinematic views. Alcohol is served.

RAJASTHAN JAISALMER

Desert Boy's Dhani
INDIAN $$

(Dhibba Para; mains ₹120-250, thali ₹400; ⊙ 11am-4pm & 7-11pm; ❋ 🛜 ✎) A walled-garden restaurant where tables are spread around a large, stone-paved courtyard shaded by a big tree. There's also traditional cushion seating undercover and in an air-con room. Rajasthani music and dance is performed from 8pm to 10pm nightly, and it's a very pleasant place to eat excellent, good-value Rajasthani and other Indian veg dishes.

Natraj Restaurant
MULTICUISINE $$

(Aasani Rd; mains ₹120-180; ⊙ 10am-10pm; 🛜 ✎) This rooftop restaurant has a satisfying view of the upper part of the Salim Singh-ki-Haveli next door. The pure veg food is consistently excellent and the service is great. The delicious South Indian dosas (large savoury crêpes) are fantastic value.

Bhang Shop
CAFE

(Gopa Chowk; lassi from ₹150) Jaisalmer's licensed Bhang Shop is a simple, unpretentious place. The magic ingredient is *bhang*: cannabis buds and leaves mixed into a paste with milk, ghee and spices. As well as lassi, it also does a range of *bhang*-laced cookies and cakes – choose either medium or strong. *Bhang* is legal, but it doesn't agree with everyone, so go easy.

🛍 Shopping

Jaisalmer is famous for its stunning embroidery, bedspreads, mirrorwork wall hangings, oil lamps, stonework and antiques. Watch out when purchasing silver items: the metal is sometimes adulterated with bronze.

There are several good *khadi* (homespun cloth) shops where you can find fixed-price tableclothes, rugs and clothes, with a variety of patterning techniques including tie-dye, block printing and embroidery. Try Zila Khadi Gramodan Parishad (Malka Prol Rd; ⊙ 10am-6pm Mon-Sat), Khadi Gramodyog Bhavan (Dhibba; ⊙ 10am-6pm Mon-Sat) or Gandhi Darshan Emporium (near Hanuman Circle; ⊙ 11am-7pm Fri-Wed).

Bellissima
ARTS & CRAFTS

(Dashera Chowk; ⊙ 8am-9pm) This small shop near the fort's main square sells beautiful patchworks, embroidery, paintings, bags, rugs, cushion covers and all types of Rajasthani art. Proceeds assist underprivileged women from surrounding villages, including those who have divorced or been widowed.

Jaisalmer Handloom
ARTS & CRAFTS

(www.jaisalmerhandloom.com; Court Rd; ⊙ 9am-10pm) This place has a big array of bedspreads, tapestries, clothing (ready-made and custom-made, including silk) and other textiles, made by its own workers and others. If you need an embroidered camel-saddle-cloth (and who doesn't?), try for one here.

Desert Handicrafts Emporium
ARTS & CRAFTS

(Court Rd; ⊙ 9.30am-9.30pm) With some unusual jewellery, paintings, and all sorts of textiles, this is one of the most original of numerous craft shops around town.

ⓘ Information

MONEY
There are ATMs near Hanuman Circle, on Shiv Rd, and outside the train station. Lots of licensed money changers are in and around Gandhi Chowk.

POST
Main post office (Hanuman Circle Rd; ⊙ 10am-5pm Mon-Sat) West of the fort.
Post office (Gopa Chowk; ⊙ 10am-5pm Mon-Fri, to 1pm Sat) Just outside the fort gate; sells stamps and you can send postcards.

TOURIST INFORMATION
Tourist office (🖉 02992-252406; Gadi Sagar Rd; ⊙ 9.30am-6pm) Friendly office with a free town map.

ⓘ Getting There & Away

AIR
Jaisalmer's new airport, 5km south of town, has been lying mothballed for a few years, but there have been signs that regular domestic flights would soon resume. Meanwhile, **Supreme Airlines** (🖉 9820588749; www.supremeairlines.com) was planning to fly a small plane from Delhi to Jaisalmer via Bikaner. Check locally to see if the route is currently operating.

BUS
RSRTC buses leave from the **main bus stand** (Shiv Rd). There are services to Ajmer (₹430, 9½ hours) and Jodhpur (₹266, 5½ hours) throughout the day. Buses to Khuri (₹39, one hour) depart from a **stand** just off Gadi Sagar Rd on Barmer Rd.

A number of private bus companies have ticket offices at Hanuman Circle. **Hanuman Travels** (🖉 9413362367) and **Swagat Travels** (🖉 02992-252557) are typical. The buses them-

MAJOR TRAINS FROM JAISALMER

DESTINATION	TRAIN	DEPARTURE	ARRIVAL	FARE (₹)
Bikaner	12467 Leelan Exp	11.55pm	5.20am	250/625
Delhi	14660 Jaisalmer-Delhi Exp	5pm	10.55am	450/1205
Jaipur	14660 Jaisalmer-Delhi Exp	5pm	4.50am	350/935
Jodhpur	14809 Jaisalmer-Jodhpur Exp	6.45am	1pm	215/565

Fares: sleeper/3AC

selves leave from the **private bus stand** (Air Force Circle). Typical services:

Ajmer (for Pushkar) seat/sleeper ₹300/450, nine hours, two or three daily

Bikaner seat/sleeper ₹200/400, 5½ hours, three to four daily

Jaipur seat/sleeper ₹400/500, 11 hours, two or three daily

Jodhpur seat/sleeper ₹200/400, five hours, half-hourly from 6am to 10pm

Udaipur sleeper ₹350/450, 12 hours, one or two daily

TAXI

One-way taxis should cost about ₹4500 to Jodhpur, ₹5000 to Bikaner or ₹8000 to Udaipur. There's a **taxi stand** on Hanuman Circle Rd.

TRAIN

The **train station** (◷ ticket office 8am-8pm Mon-Sat, to 1.45pm Sun) is on the eastern edge of town, just off the Jodhpur road. There's a reserved ticket booth for foreigners.

Bikaner sleeper/3AC ₹250/625, around six hours, one or two daily (1.10am and 11.55pm)

Delhi sleeper/3AC ₹450/1205, 18 hours, two or three daily (12.45am, 1.10am, 5pm) via Jaipur (12 hours)

Jaipur sleeper/3AC ₹350/935, 12 hours, three daily (12.45am, 5pm, 11.55pm)

Jodhpur sleeper/3AC ₹215/565, five to six hours, three daily (12.45am, 6.45am and 5pm)

ⓘ Getting Around

AUTORICKSHAW

It costs around ₹40 from the train station to Gandhi Chowk.

CAR & MOTORCYCLE

It's possible to hire taxis or 4WDs from the stand on Hanuman Circle Rd. To Khuri, the Sam Sand Dunes or Lodhruva, expect to pay ₹1000 to ₹1200 return including a wait of about an hour or so.

Shiva Bikes (First Fort Gate; motorbike per day ₹500-2000; ◷8am-9pm) A licensed hire place with motorbikes (including Royal Enfield Bullets) and scooters for exploring town and nearby sights. Helmets and area maps are included.

Around Jaisalmer

Sam Sand Dunes

Sam Sand Dunes AREA
(vehicle/camel ₹50/80) The silky Sam Sand Dunes, 41km west of Jaisalmer along a good sealed road (maintained by the Indian army), are one of the most popular excursions from the city. The band of dunes is about 2km long and is undeniably one of the most picturesque in the region. Some camel safaris camp here, but many more people just roll in for sunset, to be chased across the sands by tenacious camel owners offering short rides. Plenty more people stay overnight in one of the several tent resorts near the dunes.

The place acquires something of a carnival atmosphere from late afternoon till the next morning, making it somewhere to avoid if you're after a solitary desert experience.

If you're organising your own camel ride on the spot, expect to pay ₹300 for a one-hour sunset ride, but beware tricks from camel men such as demanding more money en route.

Khuri

📱 03014

The village of Khuri, 48km southwest of Jaisalmer, has quite extensive dune areas attracting their share of sunset visitors, and a lot of mostly smallish 'resorts' offering the same sort of overnight packages as Sam. It also has a number of low-key guesthouses where you can stay in tranquillity in a traditional-style hut with clay-and-dung

RAJASTHAN AROUND JAISALMER

walls and thatched roof, and venture out on interesting camel trips in the relatively remote and empty surrounding area.

Khuri is within the Desert National-al Park, which stretches over 3162 sq km southwest of Jaisalmer to protect part of the Thar ecosystem, including wildlife such as the desert fox, desert cat, chinkara (gazelle), nilgai (antelope), and some unusual bird life including the endangered great Indian bustard.

Be aware that the commission system is entrenched in Khuri's larger accommodation options. If you just want a quick camel ride on the sand dunes, expect to pay around ₹150 per person.

🛏 Sleeping

★ **Badal House** HOMESTAY $

(📞8107339097; r or hut per person incl full board ₹400) Here you can stay in a family compound in the centre of the village with a few spotlessly clean, mud-walled, thatch-roofed huts and equally spotless rooms (one with its own squat toilet), and enjoy good home-cooking. Former camel driver Badal Singh is a charming, gentle man who charges ₹600 for a camel safari with a night on the dunes.

He doesn't pay commission so don't let touts warn you away.

ℹ Getting There & Away

You can catch local buses from Jaisalmer to Khuri (₹30, one hour) from a road just off Gadi Sagar Rd. Walking from Jaisalmer Fort towards the train station, take the second right after the tourist office, then wait by the tree on the left, with the small shrine beside it. Buses pass here at around 10am, 11.30am, 3.30pm and 4pm.

Return buses from Khuri to Jaisalmer leave at roughly 8am, 9am, 10.30am, 11.30am and 2.30pm.

A taxi from Jaisalmer will cost at least ₹1200 to ₹1500. Even if you are staying here you will be paying for the return trip.

Bikaner

📞 0151 / POP 644,400

Bikaner is a vibrant, dust-swirling desert town with a fabulous fort and an energising outpost feel. It's less dominated by tourism than many other Rajasthan cities, though it has plenty of hotels and a busy camel-safari scene, which attracts travellers looking to avoid the Jaisalmer hustle.

History

The city was founded in 1488 by Rao Bika, a son of Rao Jodha, Jodhpur's founder, though the two Rathore ruling houses later had a serious falling out over who had the right to keep the family heirlooms. Bikaner grew quickly as a staging post on the great caravan trade routes from the late 16th century onwards, and flourished under a friendly relationship with the Mughals, but declined as the Mughals did in the 18th century. By the 19th century the area was markedly backward, but managed to turn its fortunes around by hiring out camels to the British during the First Anglo-Afghan War. In 1886 it was the first desert princely state to install electricity.

◉ Sights

★ **Junagarh** FORT

(Indian/foreigner ₹50/300, video ₹150, audio guide ₹50, ID required; ⊙10am-5.30pm, last entry 4.30pm) This most impressive fort was constructed between 1589 and 1593 by Raja Rai Singh, ruler of Bikaner and a general in the army of the Mughal emperor Akbar. You enter through the Karan Prole gate on the east side and pass through three more gates before the ticket office for the palace museum. An audio guide (requiring an identity document as a deposit), is available in English, French, German and Hindi, and is very informative.

The beautifully decorated Karan Mahal was the palace's Diwan-i-Am (Hall of Public Audience), built in the 17th and 18th centuries. Anup Mahal Chowk has lovely carved *jarokhas* (balcony windows) and *jali* screens, and was commissioned in the late 17th century by Maharaja Anup Mahal. Rooms off here include the sumptuous Anup Mahal, a hall of private audience with walls lacquered in red and gold, and the Badal Mahal (Cloud Palace), the walls of which are beautifully painted with blue cloud motifs and red and gold lightning.

The Gaj Mandir, the suite of Maharaja Gaj Singh (r 1745–87) and his two top wives, is a fantastic symphony of gold paint, colourful murals, sandalwood, ivory, mirrors, niches and stained glass. From here you head up to the palace roof to enjoy the views and then down eventually to the superb Ganga Durbar Hall of 1896, with its pink stone walls covered in fascinating relief carvings. You then move into Maharaja Ganga Singh's office and finally into the

BIKANER CAMEL SAFARIS

Bikaner is an excellent alternative to the Jaisalmer camel-safari scene. There are fewer people running safaris here, so the hassle factor is quite low. Camel trips tend to be in the areas east and south of the city and focus on the isolated desert villages of the Jat, Bishnoi, Meghwal and Rajput peoples. Interesting wildlife can be spotted here, such as nilgais (antelope), chinkaras (gazelle), desert foxes, spiny-tailed lizards and plenty of birds including, from September to March, the demoiselle crane.

Three days and two nights is a common camel-safari duration, but half-day, one-day and short overnight trips are all possible. If you're after a serious trip, Jaisalmer is a two-week trek. The best months to head into the desert are October to February. Avoid mid-April to mid-July, when it's searingly hot.

Typical costs are ₹1800 to ₹2500 per person per day including overnight camping, with tents, mattresses, blankets, meals, mineral water, one camel per person, a camel cart to carry gear (and sometimes tired riders), and a guide in addition to the camel men.

Many trips start at Raisar, about 8km east of Bikaner, or Deshnok, 30km south. Travelling to the starting point by bus rather than 4WD is one way of cutting costs.

Vikram Vilas Durbar Hall, where pride of place goes to a WWI De Havilland DH-9 biplane bomber: General Maharaja Sir Ganga Singh commanded the Bikaner Camel Corps during WWI and was the only non-white member of Britain's Imperial War Cabinet during the conflict.

**Prachina Cultural
Centre & Museum**   MUSEUM
(Junagarh; Indian/foreigner ₹30/100; ⊙9am-6pm) Across the fort's main courtyard from the palace entrance, this museum is fascinating and well labelled. It focuses on the Western influence on the Bikaner royals before Independence, including crockery from England and France and menu cards from 1936, as well as some exquisite costumes, jewellery and textiles, and exhibits on contemporary Bikaner crafts.

Old City   AREA
The old city still has a medieval feel despite the motorbikes and autorickshaws. This labyrinth of narrow, winding streets conceals a number of fine *havelis,* and a couple of notable Jain temples just inside the southern wall, 1.5km southwest of Bikaner Junction train station. It makes for an interesting wander – we guarantee you'll get lost at least once. The old city is encircled by a 7km-long, 18th-century wall with five entrance gates, the main entrance being the triple-arched Kothe Gate.

★ **Bhandasar Temple**   JAIN TEMPLE
(⊙5am-1pm & 5.30-11.30pm) Of Bikaner's two Jain temples, Bhandasar is particularly beautiful, with yellow-stone carving and vibrant paintings. The interior of the temple is stunning. The pillars bear floral arabesques and depictions of the lives of the 24 *tirthankars* (great Jain teachers). It's said that 40,000kg of ghee was used instead of water in the mortar, which locals insist seeps through the floor on hot days. The priest may ask for a donation for entry, although a trust pays for the temple upkeep.

☞ Tours

Camel Man   TOURS
(☑9799911117, 9829217331, 0151-2231244; www.camelman.com; Vijay Guest House, Jaipur Rd; half-/full-/multiday trip per person per day from ₹800/1200/1800) The standout Bikaner safari operator in terms of quality, reliability and transparency of what's on offer is Vijay Singh Rathore, aka Camel Man, who operates from Vijay Guest House.

Vino Desert Safari   TOURS
(☑0151-2270445, 9414139245; www.vinodesertsafari.com; Vino Paying Guest House; 1 day, 1 night per person ₹2500, multiday trek per person per day ₹1500-2000) A popular and long-established outfit, Vino Desert Safari is run by Vinod Bhojak, of Vino Paying Guest House.

Vinayak Desert Safari   TOURS
(☑0151-2202634, 9414430948; www.vinayakdesertsafari.com; Vinayak Guest House; half-day 4WD safari per person ₹500, full- or multiday 4WD safari per person ₹900-2000) Vinayak Desert Safari runs 4WD safaris with zoologist Jitu Solanki. This safari focuses on desert animals and

Bikaner

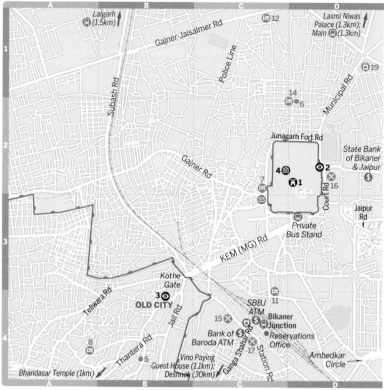

RAJASTHAN BIKANER

birds including the impressive cinereous vulture, with its 3m wingspan, which visits the area in numbers from November to March.

Gouri Guide TOURS
(☎0151-2543306, 9461159796; gouriguide@yahoo. in; Shanti House, New Well, Old City; per person per hr ₹50) Gouri is a knowledgeable and personable guide based in the Old City who can show all the well-known sights and many of the lesser-known sights of Bikaner. He also runs a small guesthouse.

🛏 Sleeping

⭐ **Vijay Guest House** GUESTHOUSE $
(☎0151-2231244, 9829217331; www.camelman. com; Jaipur Rd; r ₹500-1000, with AC ₹1200-1500, ste ₹1800; 🕸🛜) About 4km east of the centre, this is a home away from home, with spacious, light-filled rooms, a warm welcome and good home-cooked meals. Owner

Vijay is a camel expert and a recommended safari operator (p197). Free pick-up and drop-off from rail and bus stations.

As well as camel trips, 4WD outings to sights around Bikaner, and tours to the owner's house in the village of Thelasar, Shekhawati, are offered.

Vino Paying Guest House GUESTHOUSE $
(☎9414139245, 0151-2270445; www.vinodesert safari.com; Ganga Shahar; s ₹250-300, d ₹350-400; @🛜) This guesthouse, in a family home 3km south of the main train station, is a cosy choice and the base of a good camel-safari operator (p197). It has six rooms in the house and six in cool adobe huts around the garden, where there's also a plunge pool. It's excellent value, and the family is helpful and welcoming.

Home-cooked food is served and cooking classes are on offer. It's opposite Gopeshwar Temple; free pick-ups are offered.

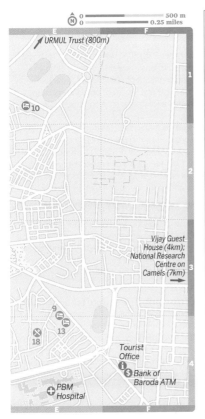

0 — 500 m
0 — 0.25 miles

URMUL Trust (800m)

Vijay Guest House (4km); National Research Centre on Camels (7km)

Tourist Office

Bank of Baroda ATM

PBM Hospital

Bikaner

◉ Top Sights
1 Junagarh D2

◎ Sights
2 Karan Prole..D2
3 Old City..B4
4 Prachina Cultural Centre &
   Museum C2

◔ Activities, Courses & Tours
5 Gouri Guide...B4
6 Vinayak Desert Safari.........................D2

◉ Sleeping
7 Bhairon Vilas C2
8 Bhanwar Niwas A4
9 Chandra Niwas Guest House.............E3
10 Hotel Harasar Haveli E1
11 Hotel Jaswant Bhawan......................C4
12 Hotel Kishan Palace...........................C1
13 Udai Niwas...E4
14 Vinayak Guest House.........................D2

◉ Eating
15 Amberwalla.. C4
   Café Indra .... (see 13)
16 Gallops D2
17 Heeralal's C4
18 Road Runner Cafe...............................E4
   Shakti Dining .... (see 18)

◉ Shopping
19 Bikaner Miniature Arts.......................D1

Vinayak Guest House   GUESTHOUSE $

([☎]0151-2202634, 9414430948; vinayakguesthouse@gmail.com; r ₹400-800, with AC ₹1000; [✳][@][☎]) This place offers six varied and clean rooms in a quiet family house with a little sandy garden (hot water only by bucket in some rooms). On offer are a free pick-up service, good home-cooked food, cooking lessons, bicycles (₹25 per day), and camel safaris and wildlife trips with Vinayak Desert Safari (p197). It's about half a kilometre north of Junagarh.

Chandra Niwas Guest House   HOTEL $

([☎]0151-2200796, 9413659711; chandraniwas@yahoo.in; Rangmanch Rd, Civil Lines; r ₹500, with AC ₹800-1500; [✳][☎]) This small and welcoming guesthouse is in a relatively quiet location, though still handy to Bikaner's sights. The rooms are clean, comfortable and tidy, and there is a lovely terrace restaurant where you can get a veg/nonveg thali for ₹180/250, plus there's a coffeeshop next door.

Hotel Jaswant Bhawan   HOTEL $

([☎]9001554746, 0151-2548848; www.hoteljaswantbhawan.com; Alakh Sagar Rd; r ₹1000-1600; [✳][@][☎]) This is a quiet, welcoming place run by descendants of Bikaner prime ministers. It has a small garden and a comfy, old-fashioned sitting room with historic family photos. The air-conditioned rooms are spacious, plain and airy. Good meals are available (as are cooking lessons). It's a two-minute walk from the main train station, via the station's 'foot over bridge'.

★ Bhairon Vilas   HERITAGE HOTEL $$

([☎]9928312283, 0151-2544751; www.bhaironvilas.com; r from ₹1500-2000; [✳][@][☎][✉]) This hotel on the western side of Junagarh is run by a former Bikaner prime minister's great-grandson. Rooms are mostly large and are eclectically and elaborately decorated with antiques, gold-threaded curtains and old family photographs. There's a bar straight out of the Addams Family, a garden restaurant, a coffeeshop, and a boutique that

THE TEMPLE OF RATS

The extraordinary **Karni Mata Temple** (camera/video ₹30/50; ☉4am-10pm) at Deshnok, 30km south of Bikaner, is one of India's weirder attractions. Its resident mass of holy rodents is not for the squeamish, but most visitors to Bikaner brave the potential for ankle-nipping and put a half-day trip here on their itinerary. Frequent buses leave from Bikaner's main bus stand. A return autorickshaw from Bikaner with a one-hour wait costs ₹400 to ₹450.

Karni Mata lived in the 14th century and performed many miracles during her lifetime. When her youngest son, Lakhan, drowned, she ordered Yama (the god of death) to bring him back to life. Yama said he was unable to do so, but that Karni Mata, as an incarnation of Durga, could restore Lakhan's life. This she did, decreeing that members of her family would no longer die but would be reincarnated as *kabas* (rats). Around 600 families in Deshnok claim to be descendants of Karni Mata and that they will be reincarnated as *kabas*.

The temple isn't, in fact, swarming with rats, but there are a lot of them here, especially in nooks and crannies and in areas where priests and pilgrims leave food for them. And yes, you do have to take your shoes off to enter the temple: it's considered highly auspicious to have a *kaba* run across your feet – you may be graced in this manner whether you want it or not.

You can find food and drinks for yourself at the numerous snack stalls outside.

specialises in beautiful, original wedding saris.

Camel safaris and local guides can be arranged here.

Hotel Harasar Haveli   HOTEL $$
(☎0151-2209891; www.harasar.com; r ₹1800-2800; ❀☎) At this modern hotel with the frontage of an old sandstone *haveli* you'll find unexpectedly grand accommodation. The decor is stylish: that's not fancy blue and gold wallpaper in your room, but exquisitely hand-painted floral patterns. Old dark-wood furniture continues the classy character. Service is great, and the in-house restaurant on the terrace serves alcohol.

Located opposite Karni Singh Stadium, about 1km northeast of Junargarh.

Udai Niwas   HOMESTAY $$
(☎9971795447, 0151-2223447; Rangmanch Rd, Civil Lines; s/d ₹2000/2500; ❀) This friendly and relaxed homestay is set behind its cheerful associated Café Indra. The rooms are large and comfortable, and you can choose to eat the delicious home-cooked meals with the family in the dining room or not. There's even a laundry to do your own washing.

Hotel Kishan Palace   HOTEL $$
(☎9829512610, 0151-2527762; www.hotelkishan palaceheritage.com; 8B Gajner-Jaisalmer Rd; r with fan ₹750, r incl breakfast with AC ₹1500; ❀☎) An old Bikaner house, this hotel was once the home of a colonel of the Bikaner Camel

Corps, and is now run by his grandson. Rooms are unfussy but generously sized, and the place is festooned with old photos and military memorabilia – check out grandfather's MBE and watercolours by the Japanese prisoners of war he once guarded. Get a room at the back away from the main road.

Laxmi Niwas Palace   HERITAGE HOTEL $$$
(☎0151-2202777; www.laxminiwaspalace.com; r ₹10,500-14,500, ste ₹22,000-31,000; ❀@☎☒) Located 2km northeast of the city centre, this pink-sandstone hotel is part of the royal palace, dating from 1902. It has opulent interiors with stone carvings, and is set in large lovely grounds. Rooms are mostly large, elegant and evocative, while the bar and billiards room contain more trophy skins from tigers than are probably still alive in Rajasthan.

Bhanwar Niwas   HERITAGE HOTEL $$$
(☎0151-2529323; www.bhanwarniwas.com; Rampuria St; r ₹6000; ❀@☎) This superb hotel has been developed out of the beautiful Rampuria Haveli – a gem in the old city, 300m southwest of the City Kotwali police station. It has 26 all-different, spacious and delightfully decorated rooms, featuring stencil-painted wallpaper, marble or mosaic floors and antique furnishings. Comfortable common rooms drip with antiques and are arranged around a large courtyard.

🍴 Eating & Drinking

Café Indra   CAFE **$**
(📞 8287895446; Rangmanch Rd, Civil Lines; mains ₹120-170; ⊘ 11.30am-10.30pm; ❄) This bright and clean cafe is a great place to relax with a coffee or a cool drink, and equally good as a place for lunch or dinner, with an array of pizzas, burgers and wraps.

Amberwalla   MULTICUISINE **$**
(📞 0151-2220333; Station Rd; mains ₹60-120, thalis ₹190-200; ⊘ 7am-11pm; ❄ 🍴) This large bright and airy 'diner' caters for everyone with Continental, Chinese, North Indian and South Indian mains, plus sweets, ice cream and a large bakery.

★ Gallops   MULTICUISINE **$$**
(📞 0151-3200833; www.gallopsbikaner.com; Court Rd; mains ₹200-350; ⊘ 10am-10pm; ❄ 📶) This contemporary cafe and restaurant close to the Junagarh entrance is known as 'Glops' to rickshaw-wallahs. There are snacks such as pizzas, wraps and sandwiches, and a good range of Indian and Chinese veg and non-veg dishes. You can sit outside or curl up in an armchair in the air-conditioned interior with a cold beer or an espresso (coffees from ₹100).

Shakti Dining   INDIAN **$$**
(📞 9928900422; Prithvi Niwas, Civil Lines; mains ₹150-260; ⊘ 11am-11pm; ❄ 📶) Central and modern, Shakti's serves good Indian classics in a garden setting or in air-conditoned comfort. Also here is the funky **Road Runner Cafe** (📞 0151-2545033, 9928900422; mains ₹150-260; ⊘ 11am-11pm; ❄ 🍴) for a more casual dining experience.

Heeralal's   MULTICUISINE **$$**
(📞 0151-2205551; Station Rd; mains ₹150-210, thalis ₹165-270; ⊘ 7.30am-10.30pm; ❄ 🍴) This bright and hugely popular 1st-floor restaurant serves up pretty good veg Indian dishes, plus a few Chinese mains and pizzas (but unfortunately no beer), amid large banks of plastic flowers. It's a good place to sit and relax if waiting for a train. The ground-floor fast-food section is less appealing, but it does have a good sweets counter.

🛍 Shopping

Bikaner Miniature Arts   ART
(📞 9829291431; www.bikanerminiturearts.com; Municipal Rd; ⊘ 9am-8pm) The Swami family has been painting miniatures in Bikaner for four generations, and now run this art school and gallery. The quality of work is astounding, and cheaper than you'll find in some of the bigger tourist centres. Art classes can be arranged.

ℹ Information

Main Post Office (⊘ 9am-4pm Mon-Fri, to 2pm Sat) Near Bhairon Vilas hotel.

PBM Hospital (📞 0151-2525312; Hospital Rd) One of Rajasthan's best government hospitals, with 24-hour emergency service.

Tourist Office (📞 0151-2226701; ⊘ 9.30am-6pm Mon-Fri) This friendly office (near Pooran Singh Circle) can answer most tourism-related questions and provide transport schedules and maps.

ℹ Getting There & Away

AIR

Supreme Airlines (p194) flies a small plane (one way from ₹560) Monday to Saturday from Jaipur to Bikaner (departing 7am) and Bikaner to Jaipur (departing 8.45am). These schedules are likely to change.

BUS

There's a **private bus stand** outside the southern wall of Junagarh with similar services (albeit slightly more expensive and less frequent) to the government-run services from the **main bus stand**, which is 2km directly north of the fort (autorickshaw ₹20).

Services from the main bus stand:

Ajmer (for Pushkar) ₹269, six hours, half-hourly until 6pm

MAJOR TRAINS FROM BIKANER JUNCTION

DESTINATION	TRAIN	DEPARTURE	ARRIVAL	FARE (₹)
Delhi (Sarai Rohilla)	22471 Dee Intercity SF Exp	9.30am	5.25pm	305/785
Jaipur	12467 Leelan Exp	6am	12.35pm	275/705
Jaisalmer	12468 Leelan Exp	11.15pm	4.50am	250/625
Jodhpur	14887 KLK-BME Exp	11am	4pm	200/510

Fares: sleeper/3AC

Delhi ₹445, 11 hours, at least four daily

Deshnok ₹35, one hour, half-hourly until 4.30pm

Fatehpur ₹136, 3½ hours, half-hourly until 5.45pm

Jaipur ₹334, with AC ₹596, seven hours, hourly until 5.45pm

Jaisalmer ₹309, 7½ hours, noon daily

Jhunjhunu ₹226, five hours, four daily (7.30am, 8.30am, 12.20pm and 6.30pm)

Jodhpur ₹243, five hours, half-hourly until 6.30pm

Pokaran ₹211, five hours, hourly until 12.45pm

For Jaisalmer, it's sometimes faster to head to Pokaran (which has more departures) and change there.

TRAIN

The main train station is Bikaner Junction, with a computerised **reservations office** (☺ 8am-10pm Mon-Sat, to 2pm Sun) in a separate building just east of the main station building. The foreigner's window is 2931. A couple of other useful services go from Lalgarh station in the north of the city (autorickshaw ₹50).

Delhi (Delhi Sarai Rohilla) sleeper/3AC ₹305/785, eight to 14 hours, three to five daily, 6.30am, 9.30am, 4.45pm, 5.05pm and 11.30pm

Jaipur sleeper/3AC ₹275/705, 6½ hours, five daily, 12.05am, 6am, 6.45pm, 11.05pm and 11.55pm

Jaisalmer sleeper/3AC ₹250/625, 5½ hours, one or two daily, 6.30pm and 11.15pm

Jodhpur sleeper/3AC ₹200/510, five hours, six to seven daily, 12.45am, 6.35am, 9.30am, 11am, 1.40pm, 9.40pm and 10.10pm

No direct trains go to Ajmer for Pushkar.

ℹ Getting Around

An autorickshaw from the train station to Junagarh palace should cost ₹30, but you'll probably be asked for more.

Around Bikaner

National Research Centre on Camels   MUSEUM

(☏ 0151-2230183; www.nrccamel.res.in; Indian/foreigner ₹30/100, camera ₹50, rides ₹50; ☺ 2-6pm) The National Research Centre on Camels is 8km southeast of central Bikaner, beside the Jodhpur–Jaipur Bypass. While here you can visit baby camels, go for a short ride and look around the small museum. There are about 400 camels, of four different breeds. The British Army had a camel corps drawn from Bikaner during WWI. Guides are available for ₹50-plus. The on-site Camel Milk Parlour offers samples to try including *kulfi* and lassi.

The round trip from Bikaner, including a half-hour wait at the camel farm, is around ₹150/₹400 for an autorickshaw/taxi.

Understand Rajasthan, Delhi & Agra

RAJASTHAN, DELHI & AGRA TODAY..........204

Rajasthan leads in sustainable energy and in conserving its cultural and natural heritage, although it grapples with population growth and rapid urbanisation.

HISTORY 206

Few places can boast a more tumultuous history, one peppered with invasions, treachery, heroism and romance, as Rajasthan, Delhi and Agra.

RAJASTHANI WAY OF LIFE...................219

Tradition meets the 21st century, from rural life and indigenous communities to urban sprawl and women's rights.

SACRED INDIA 223

Why can't you become a Hindu? What's the difference between Brahma and a Brahmin? Start here, to unpick Rajasthan's rich religious tapestry.

RAJASTHANI FOOD..........................227

Fancy a curry? Or how about a street-side snack? Taste test Rajasthan's favourite foods.

ARTS, CRAFTS & ARCHITECTURE.............232

Rajasthanis love colour and design, and their artistic skills have been honed for centuries.

WILDLIFE & LANDSCAPES...................236

Internationally renowned wetlands host rare and beautiful birds, and, despite problems, there are still tigers lurking in the jungle.

Rajasthan, Delhi & Agra Today

Rajasthan has old bones and draws great strength from its glorious history and long-held cultural and religious traditions. Conservative forces once kept the state behind when other parts of India rapidly progressed, but lately Rajasthan has been embracing modernisation with gusto. Rajasthan is an early adopter and world leader in renewable energy, yet at the same time Rajasthanis are keen to preserve the best of the past and keep the state prospering as India's premier tourist destination.

Best on Film

Pather Panchali (1955) Haunting masterpiece from Satyajit Ray.

Fire (1996), **Earth** (1998) and **Water** (2005) Classic trilogy of social observation by Deepa Mehta.

Gandhi (1982) The classic biopic.

Lagaan (2001) Raj-era cricketing epic by Ashutosh Gowariker.

The Darjeeling Limited (2007) Train-journey comedy filmed around Jodhpur and Udaipur.

Best in Print

Desert Places (Robyn Davidson; 1996) Travels with Rabari tribespeople through the Thar Desert.

Maharanis (Lucy Moore; 2004) A delightful account of the lives and loves of three generations of Indian princesses.

A Princess Remembers: The Memoirs of the Maharani of Jaipur (Gayatri Devi and Santha Rama Rau; 1976) A life of extraordinary privilege not so much exposed as celebrated, justified and missed.

Rajasthan: An Oral History – Conversations with Komal Kothari (Rustom Bharucha; 2007) The living traditions and folklore of Rajasthan as told by a leading folklorist.

A Thriving Desert

Covering an area of 342,236 sq km, Rajasthan represents roughly 10% of the Indian landmass. Much of it embraces the vast Thar Desert, a surprisingly vibrant and populated desert that is liberally scattered with rural villages, ancient trade-route towns and several rapidly growing cities that were once capitals of princely states.

The desert supports life because of the monsoon rains that percolate through the sands into the water table, to be tapped throughout the year at the ubiquitous wells scattered across the country. In recent years, Rajasthan's life-giving monsoon has become less and less predictable, however, and the scarcity of rain and rapid drop in the water table in many areas have affected people's livelihoods as well as the greater environment.

Chronic droughts have accelerated migration from the parched agricultural lands to the already overburdened cities. Of course, a desert has two things in ample supply – sunshine and space – and so, not surprisingly, Rajasthan leads India in renewable energy generation. In 2015, Rajasthan's solar energy output eclipsed Gujarat, to become the country's number one generator.

The Rajasthan government has committed to achieve 25 gigawatts capacity in solar electricity generation by 2022. And it is well on the way, with many more solar farms being built or planned. The desert also plays host to wind farms and the Jaisalmer wind farm, a pioneering effort that showed great foresight, has grown to become one of the world's biggest such farms.

The State of Tourism

Tourism is probably the most important industry in Rajasthan; it is certainly the most obvious and seems to touch nearly everyone's lives. It brings in valuable foreign revenue and provides much-needed employment. Tourism funds the conservation of Rajasthan's magnificent heritage (including its tigers) and is the life blood of the region's splendid arts and crafts industry. The eminence and durability of the tourism industry have provided many locals from all walks of life with promising career options.

A large number of Rajasthanis now earn a living by working in hotels or souvenir shops, driving taxis or sprucing up their knowledge of history to become tourist guides. Activities such as hot-air ballooning and flying foxes are adding further exhilaration to the more traditional activities of wildlife-watching and camel riding. A more recent development, not unique to Rajasthan, is medical tourism. Udaipur, in particular, seems to have become a centre for dental tourism, with numerous clinics promising clients a princess's smile at a peasant's price.

Trending Now

Living standards in Rajasthan are rising, bringing previously unaffordable luxuries within arm's reach of many of urban Rajasthan's inhabitants. To the outsider, perhaps the most obvious of these luxuries must be the motorcycle and the motor car. Cities such as Jaipur and Jodhpur have rapidly become gridlocked with commuters, the air thick with fumes and beeping horns. Rajasthan's young are on the move – and it's nearly always astride a motorcycle. Infrastructure seems to lag well behind the growing population's needs, even though flyovers, freeways and elevated metros are popping up across the state.

The economy, whether you are talking about Rajasthan or the entire country, has undeniably made giant strides in recent years; however, the challenges for today's politicians – redistribution of wealth and environmental conservation – remain unresolved and at the forefront of cafe conversation. The 2014 election of probusiness prime minister Narendra Modi undoubtedly boosted confidence across the state and the country. When Modi declared war on black money by demonetising the ₹1000 and ₹500 banknotes in 2016, it greatly inconvenienced the populace. And yet, Indians, the vast majority who didn't have stashes of these notes avoiding tax, showed exceptional acceptance and understanding of this brave political move. Here was a politician working for them!

As in much of the world, Rajasthan continues to lose its wildlife, fertile soils and vegetation, yet environmental awareness here is high by global standards and there are admirable ongoing efforts in Rajasthan in developing renewable energy. In a land where the juxtaposition of old and new has become a hackneyed slogan, the visitor must still marvel, and take heart, at the scene of ancient cenotaphs of silk-route nobility standing shoulder to shoulder with state-of-the-art wind turbines, which are helping to address India's burgeoning energy and pollution crises.

POPULATION (RAJASTHAN):
75 MILLION

POPULATION (DELHI):
25.7 MILLION

GDP (PER CAPITA): **US$5195**

NATIONAL GDP GROWTH RATE: **5.75%**

if India were 100 people

30 would be 14 years or younger
65 would be aged between 15 and 64 years
5 would be older than 65 years

belief systems
(% of population)

80.5 Hindu
8.5 Muslim
8.3 Other

1.4 Sikh
1.2 Jain
0.1 Christian

population per sq km

DELHI   RAJASTHAN   INDIA

≈ 200 people

History

A popular Indian saying is that the state of Rajasthan alone has more history than the rest of the country put together. Given that its name literally translates as 'the land of kings', perhaps the idea holds some truth. From war-ravaged forts to elaborate palaces, Rajasthan is a landscape strewn with the legacies of human endeavour, tenacity, skill and ruthlessness.

Back Where It All Began

The desert and scrub areas of Rajasthan have been home to humans for several thousand years. Excavations in Kalibangan, near Ganganagar in northern Rajasthan, have unearthed terracotta pottery and jewellery dating back to around 3000 BC – evidence of the region's earliest known settlements. Some of these urban centres were presumably absorbed into the Harappan segment of the Indus Valley civilisation, where they flourished until the settlement was mysteriously abandoned 3700 years ago. The mass exodus, possibly triggered by flooding or a severe climatic change, rendered the region devoid of human settlement for some time, until indigenous tribes such as the Bhils and the Minas moved in to set up their own squabbling small kingdoms, thereby commencing the long history of argumentative neighbours in the region.

But even as the tribes tore away at each other, another civilisation was sprouting in the fertile plains to the east of Rajasthan, between the rivers Yamuna and Ganga (Ganges), out of the seminomadic Indo-European race known as Aryans or 'noblemen'. It was in this civilisation that Hinduism first evolved as a religious tradition and a way of life, along with a complex patriarchal social structure and the tiered caste system that the greater Indian society adheres to even today. By 1000 BC the province had seen the establishment of at least two prominent kingdoms: the Matsya territory of Viratnagar encompassing Alwar, Bharatpur, Dholpur and Karauli; and Indraprastha, the earliest-known incarnation of Delhi, which was successively built on by several dynasties to come.

Little is known of Rajasthan's development at this time, as the mighty empires that were then strengthening their hold on the subcontinent

> The oldest natural relics in Rajasthan are fossilised remains of a 180-million-year-old forest, located at the Akal Wood Fossil Park in the Thar Desert near Jaisalmer.

TIMELINE

10,000 BC
Stone Age paintings created in the Bhimbetka rock shelters, in what is now Madhya Pradesh; the art continues here for many centuries. Settlements thought to exist across the subcontinent.

2600–1700 BC
The heyday of the Indus Valley civilisation; the settlement spans parts of Rajasthan, Gujarat and the Sindh province in Pakistan.

c 1500 BC
The Indo-Aryan civilisation takes root in the fertile plains of the Indo-Gangetic basin. The settlers speak an early form of Sanskrit, from which several Indian languages later evolve.

largely chose to pass over the state. Alexander the Great, who reached as far as Punjab on his epic campaign to conquer the 'known world', was forced to return when his troops, homesick and weary after the campaign, convinced him to retreat. The Mauryan empire (323–185 BC) had minimal impact too, largely due to its most renowned emperor, Ashoka, taking to nonviolent ways after he converted to Buddhism. In stark contrast to the atrocities he had inflicted on the eastern Indian kingdom of Kalinga, the only evidence Ashoka left of his reign in Rajasthan were Buddhist caves and stupas (Buddhist shrines) near Jhalawar, rock-cut edicts at Bairat, an ancient Buddhist site near Sariska Tiger Reserve, and a 13m-high pillar he inscribed in Delhi.

The 24-spoke wheel, an emblem designed by Ashoka, has been adopted as the central motif on the national flag of India, where it is rendered in blue against a white background.

Marauding Huns & the Advent of Kings

The insulation that Rajasthan enjoyed through its early years came to an abrupt end during the 5th century AD, when armies of fierce Hun warriors rode in from Central Asia to carry out a series of pillaging raids across North India. These raids were to alter the course of the region's history in two major ways. To begin with, they resulted in the disintegration of the Gupta dynasty, which had taken over from the Mauryas as a central power and had reigned over the country from 320 to 550. But, more importantly, they triggered a parallel invasion, as the Rajputs finally came to make Rajasthan their home and, in the absence of an overarching monarchy, grew from strength to strength to usher in the golden age of Rajasthan.

Historical evidence suggests that the Rajputs (their name meaning 'children of kings') fled their homelands in Punjab, Haryana, Gujarat and Uttar Pradesh to settle in Rajasthan, primarily to escape the wrath of the White Huns (and later the Arabs), who had begun to storm in from Pakistan and Afghanistan. Once they had arrived in Rajasthan, the Rajputs trampled over the Bhils and Minas and set up their own small fiefdoms in the face of mounting local chaos. Though they largely belonged to the lower rungs of Hindu society, volatile circumstances demanded that the Rajputs don the role of warriors, if only to fend off further advances by foreign invaders. So in spite of rigid social norms, which didn't allow for any kind of self-promotion, early Rajput clans such as the Gurjara Pratiharas crossed the caste barriers to proclaim themselves Kshatriyas, members of the warrior class, who came second only to the Brahmins (priests) in the caste hierarchy.

To facilitate their smooth transition through social ranks, and to avoid stinging criticism from the Brahmins, these early Rajput clans chose to jettison their worldly ancestry and took to trumpeting a mythological genealogy that supposedly evolved from celestial origins. From the 6th century onward, some of the clans began calling themselves Suryavanshis

The concepts of zero and infinity are widely believed to have been devised by eminent Indian mathematicians, such as Aryabhatta and Varahamihira, during the reign of the Guptas.

1500–1200 BC	c 1000 BC	c 540 BC	563–483 BC
The Rig-Veda, the first and longest of Hinduism's canonical texts, the Vedas, is written; three more books follow. Earliest forms of priestly Brahmanical Hinduism emerge.	Indraprastha, Delhi's first incarnation, comes into being. Archaeological excavations at the site where the Purana Qila now stands continue even today.	The writing of the Mahabharata begins. The longest epic in the world, it takes nearly 250 years to complete and mentions settlements such as Indraprastha, Pushkar and Chittorgarh.	The life of Siddhartha Gautama. The prince attains enlightenment beneath the Bodhi Tree in Bodhgaya (Bihar), thereby transforming into the Buddha (Awakened One).

THE INDOMITABLE SISODIAS

In a region where invasions and political upheavals were historical norms, the Sisodias of Mewar stood out as an exception, using everything from diplomacy to sheer valour to retain an iron grip over their land. Pillage and blood baths notwithstanding, the dynasty administered its kingdom in southern Rajasthan for 1400 years. Lorded over by 76 monarchs throughout the ages, the Sisodias have one of the longest-serving dynasties in the world.

The lineage of the Sisodia kings can be traced back to a prince named Guhil, born to a Rajput queen in the 6th century AD. Orphaned soon after birth and his kingdom ransacked by Huns, at age 11 he forged an alliance with a Bhil chieftain to establish a dynasty called the Guhilots and founded the state of Mewar.

In the 12th century the family split, resulting in a breakaway faction that relocated to the town of Sissoda and rechristened themselves Sisodias. They soon took over Chittorgarh, an ancient garrison that remained under their control until it was sacked by Mughal emperor Akbar in 1568. Though it came as a major military setback, the Sisodias lost no time in retreating into the Aravalli Hills, where they put together a new capital called Udaipur. A serenely beautiful city, Udaipur was never lost to the enemy and remained the capital of Mewar until the kingdom was absorbed into the state of Rajasthan following India's independence.

The Sisodias have been credited with producing some of the most flamboyant kings ever to have reigned in Rajasthan. The family boasts names such as Rana Sanga, who died a valiant death in 1527 while fending off Mughal troops under Babur, and Maharana Pratap (1540–97), who made several daring though unsuccessful attempts to win Chittorgarh back from Akbar during his time in power. Being prolific builders, the Sisodias also gave Mewar some of its finest structures, including the Victory Tower at Chittorgarh, the grand City Palace in Udaipur, the elegant Monsoon Palace atop Sajjangarh Hill and the spectacular Lake Palace, which stands on an island amid the placid waters of Lake Pichola, also in Udaipur.

(Descendants of the Sun), while others chose to be known as Chandravanshis (Descendants of the Moon). A third dynasty, on the other hand, traced their roots to the sacrificial fire that was lit on Mt Abu during the Mauryan era, thereby naming themselves Agnivanshis (Fire-Born).

As the Rajputs slowly consolidated their grip over Rajasthan, they earned a reputation for their chivalry, noble traditions and strict code of conduct. They gave rise to several dynasties, which established some of the most renowned princely states of Rajasthan. The largest of these kingdoms, and the third largest in India after Kashmir and Hyderabad, was Marwar. Founded by the Suryavanshi Rathores who rode in from Uttar Pradesh, it was initially ruled from Mandore, before the seat of

326 BC	323–185 BC	1st century AD	320–550
Alexander the Great invades India. He defeats Porus in Punjab to enter the subcontinent, but a rebellion keeps him from advancing beyond the Beas River in Himachal Pradesh.	India comes under the rule of the Maurya kings. Founded by Chandragupta Maurya, this Pan-Indian empire is ruled from Pataliputra (Patna), and briefly adopts Buddhism.	International trade booms: the region's elaborate overland trade networks connect with ports linked to maritime routes. Trade to Africa, the Gulf, Socotra, Southeast Asia, China and Rome thrives.	The period of the Gupta dynasty, the second of India's great monarchies after the Mauryas. This era is marked by a creative surge in literature and the arts.

power was relocated to the Mehrangarh Fort in nearby Jodhpur. The Sisodias migrated from Gujarat to assemble in the folds of the Aravalli Hills to the south, where they formed the state of Mewar encompassing Chittorgarh and Udaipur. The Kachhwahas, from Gwalior in Madhya Pradesh, settled in Jaipur in eastern Rajasthan, their capital nestled in the twin fort complex of Amber and Jaigarh. Meanwhile, a fourth kingdom, called Jaisalmer, was established in the Thar Desert by the Bhattis. Obscured by the dunes, the Bhattis remained more or less entrenched in their kingdom until Jaisalmer was integrated into the state of Rajasthan after independence.

Over the years, Rajasthan saw the mushrooming of many other smaller dynasties, each of which staked a claim to its own patch of territory in the region and ruled with complete autonomy, often refusing to submit to the whims of the bigger kingdoms. The clans were so content with their tiny fiefdoms that they rarely thought of looking beyond their borders to explore and conquer newer territories.

One dynasty was the exception. The Chauhans settled in Ajmer, from where they gradually extended their rule into Haryana and Uttar Pradesh. Within Rajasthan, the Hada offshoot of the Chauhans crossed over to the Hadoti region and captured the cities of Bundi and Kota, while the Deora branch took over the nearby Sirohi area, making way for successive generations to zero in on the provinces of Ranthambhore, Kishangarh and Shekhawati. The most illustrious of the Chauhan kings, Prithviraj III, even invaded Delhi – then on one of its temporary wanes – and commissioned the building of a settlement called Qila Rai Pithora, the ramparts of which can still be seen near the Qutb Minar in Mehrauli. One of the few Hindu kings to hold fort in Delhi, Prithviraj Chauhan administered his empire from the twin capitals of Qila Rai Pithora and Ajmer, before his reign was put to an end by Islamic warriors, who galloped in by the thousands to change the face of the region forever.

The Sword of Islam

Some 400 years after the Prophet Mohammed introduced Islam into Arabia, northern India saw the arrival of Muslims. With the banner of Islam fluttering high, forces seized the province of Sindh (in Pakistan) and then moved on to occupy the formerly Buddhist city of Ghazni in neighbouring Afghanistan. At the beginning of the 11th century, Turk warriors, led by the fearsome Sultan Mahmud of Ghazni, entered India, razing hundreds of Hindu temples and plundering the region, taking away vast amounts of wealth to fill their coffers back home. The Turks made their raids into India almost an annual affair, ransacking the northern part of the country 17 times in as many years. Jolted out of their internal bickering, the Rajput princes organised some hasty defence, but their army

Upon losing Delhi to the Afghans, Prithviraj Chauhan, the last Hindu king, was captured and taken back to Mohammed of Ghori's court in Ghazni, where he was later blinded and killed.

HISTORY THE SWORD OF ISLAM

Discover the bygone days of Rajasthan's royalty in *A Princess Remembers*, the memoirs of Gayatri Devi, maharani of Jaipur. Cowritten by Santha Rama Rau, it's an enthralling read.

500–600	1024	1192	1206
The emergence of the Rajputs in Rajasthan. Stemming from three principal races supposedly of celestial origin, they form 36 separate clans who claim their own kingdoms across the region.	Mahmud of Ghazni raids India for the last time, ransacking on this occasion the Somnath Temple in Gujarat, where he purportedly smashes the idol with his own hands.	Prithviraj Chauhan loses Delhi to Mohammed of Ghori. The defeat effectively ends Hindu supremacy in the region, exposing Rajasthan and the subcontinent to subsequent Muslim invaders.	Ghori is murdered during a prayer session while returning to Ghazni from a campaign in Lahore. In the absence of an heir, his kingdom is usurped by his generals. The Delhi Sultanate is born.

In 1327 the eccentric Tughlaq emperor Mohammed bin Tughlaq reduced Delhi to a ghost town for two years by moving the entire population to a new capital called Daulatabad, more than 1100km away in the Deccan.

was torn to shreds even before they could retaliate. Rajasthan had been incorporated into the Islamic empire.

Delhi, located further east, was initially spared the wrath of these invaders, as the Sultan largely confined his raids to Rajasthan and parts of Gujarat. Trouble, however, came by the name of Mohammed of Ghori, governor of Ghazni, who invaded India in the late 12th century, defeating Rajput king Prithviraj Chauhan in the Second Battle of Tarain. Ghori left Delhi under the governorship of Qutb-ud-din Aibak, a former Turk slave who had risen to command forces in India. With news of Ghori's death a decade and a half later, Qutb-ud-din claimed the Indian part of Ghori's empire. He declared himself Sultan of the region and founded the Mamluk or Slave dynasty, giving Delhi the first of its many Islamic monarchies.

The enthronement of Qutb-ud-din Aibak began the Sultanate era of Delhi, which lasted for about 350 years. Throughout this period, Delhi was ruled by five different Islamic dynasties, before the first period of Mughal rule in 1526. The Mamluks created the city of Mehrauli, while the Khiljis seated their capital at Siri, and the Tughlaqs constructed the forts of Tughlaqabad and Firoz Shah Kotla. There was one further sultanate, founded by the rebellious governor of Bihar, Sher Shah Suri, who seized control from the Mughal emperor Humayun in 1540 and founded his brief dynasty at Shergarh before Humayun reclaimed his empire in 1555. During this period, the whole of the Gangetic basin came under the Sultanates' control, as did Rajasthan and Gujarat – the princely states there had little option but to bow down to their might.

Despite its many achievements, the Sultanate period was marked by prolonged phases of political turmoil and administrative tension. Having become the jewel of foreign eyes, Delhi was persistently being attacked from the northwest by Mongol, Persian, Turk and Afghan raiders, who all wanted to set up their own outposts in the city. Eventually, two noblemen who were disgraced by Sultan Ibrahim Lodi decided to get even by inviting Babur, prince of Kabul, to invade Delhi, unwittingly paving the way for the most celebrated Islamic dynasty to roll into India.

Enter the Mughals

Rajput armies primarily consisted of cavalries. They were known to breed pedigree horses such as the Marwari and Kathiawari for use by their mounted forces.

Babur, whose Turkic-Mongol lineage included great warriors such as Genghis Khan and Timur the Lame, marched into India through Punjab, defeating Ibrahim Lodi in the First Battle of Panipat (1526) to establish the Mughal dynasty in the country. Once he had seized Delhi, Babur focused his attention on Rajasthan, where many princely states, anticipating his moves, had already banded together to form a united front under the Sisodia king Rana Sanga. Taking advantage of the chaos in Delhi, the Rajputs had meanwhile clawed back into the power race, and states

1303	1321	1336	1398
Ala-ud-din Khilji sacks Chittorgarh with the intention of carrying away the beautiful Sisodia queen Padmini. The queen immolates herself to escape humiliation – the first recorded instance of *sati* in Rajasthan.	The Tughlaqs come to power in Delhi. Mohammed bin Tughlaq expands his empire but becomes known for inelegant schemes, such as creating forgery-prone currency.	Foundation of the mighty Vijayanagar empire, named after its capital city, the ruins of which can be seen today in the vicinity of Hampi (in modern-day Karnataka).	Timur the Lame invades Delhi on the pretext that the Sultans of Delhi are too tolerant with their Hindu subjects. He executes more than 100,000 Hindu captives before the battle for Delhi.

such as Mewar had become formidable enough to pose a considerable threat to the rulers of Delhi. Babur, however, squared everything by defeating the Rajput alliance in a blood-spattered battle where several Rajput chiefs, including Rana Sanga, fell to the enemy's wrath. The defeat, which shook the foundations of the Rajput states, also left the Mughals as the undisputed rulers of northern India.

Mughal supremacy was briefly cut back in the mid-16th century by Sher Shah Suri, who defeated Babur's successor Humayun to give Delhi its sixth and final Sultanate. Humayun reclaimed Delhi 14 years later, and was succeeded upon his accidental death by his 13-year-old son Akbar. Known as the greatest of the Mughal emperors, Akbar ruled for a period of 49 years and, being a master diplomat, used both tact and military force to expand and consolidate the Mughal empire in India. Realising that the Rajputs could not be conquered on the battlefield alone, Akbar arranged a marriage alliance with a princess of the important Kachhwaha clan, which held Amber (and later Jaipur), and even chose Rajput warriors to head his armies. Honoured by these gestures, the Kachhwahas, unlike other Rajputs, aligned themselves with the powerful Mughals, as Akbar indirectly succeeded in winning over one of the biggest Rajput states.

Of course, when diplomacy didn't work, Akbar resorted to war; he conquered Ajmer, and later proceeded to take the mighty forts of Chittorgarh and Ranthambhore. Gradually, all the important Rajput states except Mewar had acknowledged Mughal sovereignty and become vassal states. But even as he was well on his way to becoming the supreme ruler of India, Akbar became more tolerant in many ways. He married a Hindu Rajput princess and encouraged good relations between Hindus and Muslims, giving Rajputs special privileges so that they were embraced within his empire. A monarch with great social insight, he discouraged child marriage, banned *sati* (ritual suicide of a widow on her husband's funeral pyre) and arranged special market days for women. Akbar's reign also saw an unprecedented economic boom in the country, as well as great development in art and architecture.

> Known for his religious tolerance, Akbar propounded a cult called Din-i-Ilahi, which incorporated the best elements of the two principal religions of his empire, Hinduism and Islam.

The Last of the Mughal Greats

Jehangir, Akbar's son, was the next Mughal emperor (r 1605–27) and he ruled alongside his adored Persian wife, Nur Jahan, who wielded considerable power and brought Persian influences to the court. Nur Jahan also commissioned the beautiful Itimad-ud-Daulah, the first Mughal structure to be built in marble, in Agra for her parents. The Rajputs maintained cordial relationships with the Mughals through Jehangir's rule, a notable development being that Udai Singh, king of Udaipur, ended Mewar's reservations about the Muslims by befriending Jehangir.

The Great Mughals

Babur
(r 1526–30)

Humayun
(r 1530–56)

Akbar
(r 1556–1605)

Jehangir
(r 1605–27)

Shah Jahan
(r 1627–58)

Aurangzeb
(r 1658–1707)

1498	1504	1526	1540
Vasco da Gama, a Portuguese voyager, discovers the sea route from Europe to India. He arrives in Kerala and engages in trade with the local kings.	Agra is founded on the banks of the Yamuna River by Sikandar Lodi. Its glory days begin when Akbar makes it his capital and the city is briefly called Akbarabad during his reign.	Babur conquers Delhi and stuns Rajasthan by routing its confederate force, gaining a technological edge on the battlefield due to the early introduction of matchlock muskets in his army.	The Sur dynasty briefly captures Delhi from the Mughals – the loss forces the Mughals to temporarily seek help from the Rajputs.

DELHI'S TWILIGHT YEARS

The death of Aurangzeb marked the beginning of Delhi's twilight years, a period through which the degenerating Mughal empire was laid to waste by the Marathas and the Persians. The Marathas had risen to prominence between 1646 and 1680, led by the heroic Shivaji, under whom their empire was administered by the *peshwas*, or chief ministers, who later went on to become hereditary rulers. At a time when the Mughals were struggling to hold their empire together, the Marathas supplied them with regiments from the south, gaining their own stranglehold on Delhi at the same time. The new army soon went out of control and began to take possession of the land. Contemporary Mughal rulers, who were both ineffective and cowardly, failed to curb the unruly military behaviour. The resulting confusion was capitalised on by the Persian invader Nadir Shah, who sacked Delhi in 1739 and robbed the city of much of its wealth. Seeing which way the wind was blowing, the Marathas abandoned the Mughals and joined the Persians in pillaging the capital. They soon sucked Delhi dry of all its treasures and, when there was nothing left to rob, the Marathas turned their eyes on Rajasthan. Raids and skirmishes with the Rajputs followed; cities were sacked, lives were lost and the Marathas began to win large tracts of Rajput land in the state. The absence of a central Indian authority only contributed to the mayhem, so much so that India had to wait till the early 19th century for another invasion to bring the country under a single umbrella once again.

Good times, however, came to an end soon after Jehangir's period in office, as his descendants' greater emphasis on Islam began to rock the relative peace in the region. Upon Jehangir's death, the prince Khurram took over, assuming the title Shah Jahan, meaning 'monarch of the world'. His reign was the pinnacle of Mughal power. Like his predecessors, Shah Jahan was a patron of the arts and some of the finest examples of Mughal art and architecture were produced during his reign, including the Taj Mahal, an extravagant work of extreme refinement and beauty. Shah Jahan also commenced work on Delhi's seventh incarnation, Shahjahanabad, constructing the Red Fort and the Jama Masjid.

Unfortunately, the emperor harboured high military ambitions and often bled the country's financial resources to meet his whims. His exhaustion of the state treasury didn't go down well with the Rajputs and towards the end of Shah Jahan's rule, the Rajputs and the Mughals had become uneasy bedfellows. Things worsened when Aurangzeb became the last great Mughal emperor in 1658, deposing his father, who died in imprisonment at the Musamman Burj in Agra eight years later. An Islamic hardliner, Aurangzeb quickly made enemies in the region. His zeal saw him devoting all his resources to extending the Mughal empire's boundaries. His government's emphasis on Islam alienated his Hindu subjects.

Best Mughal Monuments

Taj Mahal (Agra)

Fatehpur Sikri (Agra)

Humayun's Tomb (Delhi)

Jama Masjid (Delhi)

Agra Fort (Agra)

Red Fort (Delhi)

1556	1568	1608	1631
Hemu, a Hindu general in Adil Shah Suri's army, seizes Delhi after Humayun's death. He rules for barely a month before losing to Akbar in the Second Battle of Panipat.	Akbar leads his army to Chittorgarh and wrests it from the Sisodias. Udai Singh, then king of Mewar, survives the onslaught and transfers his capital to the new city of Udaipur.	After being granted trading rights by way of a royal charter, the first ships of the British East India Company sail up the Arabian Sea to drop anchor at Surat in Gujarat.	Construction of the Taj Mahal begins after Shah Jahan, devastated by the death of his wife Mumtaz Mahal, vows to build the most beautiful mausoleum in the world in her memory.

Aurangzeb imposed punitive taxes, banned the building of new temples, destroyed many more and forbade music and ceremonies at court. Challenges to his power mounted steadily as people reacted against his dour reign. And when he claimed his rights over Jodhpur in 1678, his relations with the Rajputs turned into full-scale war. Before long, there was insurgency on all sides, which only increased as Aurangzeb died in 1707 to leave the empire in the hands of a line of inefficient successors given to bohemian excesses, who had little or no interest in running the state. The Mughal empire was on a one-way journey towards doom.

The British Drop Anchor

The British invaders came by the sea, following the Portuguese explorer Vasco da Gama, who had first discovered the sea route from Europe to India around Africa in 1498. The British East India Company, a London trading firm that wanted a slice of the Indian spice trade (having seen how well the Portuguese were doing), landed in India in the early 1600s. Granted trading rights by Jehangir, the company set up its first trading outpost in Surat in Gujarat and gradually went about extending its influence across the country, harbouring interests that went beyond mere trade. Extraordinarily enough, this commercial firm ended up nominally ruling India for 250 years.

Sooner or later, all leading European maritime nations came and pitched tent in India. Yet none managed to spread out across the country as efficiently as the British. The early English agents became well assimilated in India, learning Persian and intermarrying with local people, which gave them an edge over other European hopefuls. When the Mughal empire collapsed, they made a calculated political move, filling the power vacuum and taking over the reins of administration through a series of battles and alliances with local rulers. By the early 19th century, India was effectively under British control and the British government in London had begun to take a more direct role in supervising affairs in India, while leaving the East India Company to deal with day-to-day administrative duties.

Outside British territory, the country was in a shambles. Bandits were on the prowl in the rural areas, and towns and cities had fallen into decay. The Marathas' raids in Rajasthan continued and though the British at first ignored the feuding parties, they soon spotted an opportunity for expansion and stepped into the fray. They negotiated treaties with the leaders of the main Rajput states, offering them protection from the Marathas in return for political and military support. The trick worked. Weakened by habitual wrangling and ongoing conflicts, the rulers forfeited their independence in exchange for protection and British residents were installed in the princely states. The British ultimately eliminated

> The Doctrine of Lapse, a policy formulated by Lord Dalhousie, enabled the East India Company to annex any princely state if its ruler was either found incompetent or died without a direct heir.

Best Rajput Monuments

Amber Fort (Jaipur)

Mehrangarh (Jodhpur)

Jaisalmer Fort

Chittorgarh Fort

Kumbhalgarh Fort

Ranthambhore Fort

HISTORY THE BRITISH DROP ANCHOR

1674	1707	1739	1747
Shivaji establishes the Maratha kingdom, spanning western India and parts of the Deccan and north India. He assumes the supercilious title of Chhatrapati (Lord of the Universe).	Death of Aurangzeb, the last of the Mughal greats. His demise triggers the gradual collapse of the Mughal empire as anarchy and rebellion break out across the country.	Nadir Shah plunders Delhi and carries away with him the Peacock Throne, as well as the Koh-i-noor, a magnificent diamond that eventually becomes the property of British royalty.	Afghan ruler Ahmad Shah Durrani sweeps across northern India, capturing Lahore and Kashmir, sacking Delhi and dealing another blow to the rapidly contracting Mughal empire.

the Maratha threat, but, in the process, the Rajputs were effectively reduced to puppets. Delhi's prominence as a national capital dwindled too, as the British chose to rule the country from Calcutta (now Kolkata).

The later British authorities had an elitist notion of their own superiority that was to have a lasting impact on India. The colonisers felt that it was their duty to civilise the nation, unlike the first agents of the East India Company who had seen and recognised the value in India's native culture. During the first half of the 19th century, the British brought about radical social reforms. They introduced education in the English language, which replaced Persian as the language of politics and governance. New roads and canal systems were installed, followed by the foundation of schools and universities modelled on the British system of education. In the later stages, they brought in the postal system, the

THE FIRST WAR OF INDEPENDENCE: THE INDIAN UPRISING

In 1857, half a century after having established firm control of India, the British suffered a serious setback. To this day, the causes of the Uprising (known at the time as the Indian Mutiny and subsequently labelled by nationalist historians as the War of Independence) are the subject of debate. The key factors included the influx of cheap goods, such as textiles, from Britain that destroyed many livelihoods, the dispossession of territories from many rulers and taxes imposed on landowners.

The incident that's popularly held to have sparked the Uprising, however, took place at an army barracks in Meerut in Uttar Pradesh on 10 May 1857. A rumour leaked out that a new type of bullet was greased with what Hindus claimed was cow fat, while Muslims maintained that it came from pigs; pigs are considered unclean to Muslims and cows are sacred to Hindus. Since loading a rifle involved biting the end off the waxed cartridge, these rumours provoked considerable unrest.

In Meerut, the situation was handled with a singular lack of judgement. The commanding officer lined up his soldiers and ordered them to bite off the ends of their issued bullets. Those who refused were immediately marched off to prison. The following morning, the soldiers of the garrison rebelled, shot their officers and marched to Delhi. Of the 74 Indian battalions of the Bengal army, seven (one of them Gurkhas) remained loyal, 20 were disarmed and the other 47 mutinied. The soldiers and peasants rallied around the ageing Mughal emperor in Delhi. They held Delhi for some months and besieged the British Residency in Lucknow for five months before they were finally suppressed. The incident left festering scars on both sides.

Almost immediately the East India Company was wound up and direct control of the country was assumed by the British government, which announced its support for the existing rulers of the princely states, claiming it would not interfere in local matters as long as the states remained loyal to the British.

1756	1757	1857	1858
The rise of the notorious Jat dynasty of Bharatpur in Rajasthan. Under the leadership of Suraj Mahl and his son Jawahar Singh, the Jats join the Marathas and Persians in looting Delhi and Agra.	Breaking out of its business mould, the East India Company registers its first military victory on Indian soil. Siraj-ud-Daulah, nawab of Bengal, is defeated by Robert Clive in the Battle of Plassey.	The short-lived First War of Independence breaks out across India. In the absence of a national leader, the rebels coerce the last Mughal king Bahadur Shah Zafar to proclaim himself emperor of India.	British government assumes control over India – with power officially transferred from the East India Company to the Crown – beginning the period known as the British Raj.

telegraph and the railways, introductions that remain vital to the Indian administrative system today.

But at the same time, British bureaucracy came with controversial policies. Severe taxes were imposed on landowners and, as raw materials from India were used in British industry, cheap British-produced goods began to flood Indian markets and destroy local livelihoods. Mass anger in the country began to rise and found expression in the First War of Independence (Indian Uprising) in 1857. Soldiers and peasants took over Delhi for four months and besieged the British Residency in Lucknow for five months before they were finally suppressed by the East India Company's forces. Rajasthan also saw uprisings among the poor and middle classes, but there was little effect in the royal circles as Rajput kings continued to support the British and were rewarded for their loyalty after the British government assumed direct control of the country the following year.

Plain Tales from the Raj by Charles Allen (ed) is a fascinating series of interviews with people who played a role in British India on both sides of the table.

Independence, Partition & After

Following a lengthy freedom movement, India finally liberated itself from British domination in 1947. The road to Independence was an extraordinary one, influenced by Mohandas Karamchand Gandhi, later known as the Mahatma (Great Soul), who galvanised the peasants and villagers into a nonviolent resistance that was to spearhead the nationalist movement. A lawyer by qualification, he caused chaos by urging people to refuse to pay taxes and boycott British institutions and products. He campaigned for the Dalits (the lower classes of Hindu society, who he called Harijans or the 'Children of God') and the rural poor, capturing the public imagination through his approach, example and rhetoric.

The freedom struggle gained momentum under him, so much so that the British Labour Party, which came to power in 1945, saw Indian independence as inevitable. The process of the handover of power was initiated, but Hindu–Muslim differences took their toll at this crucial moment and the country was divided along religious lines, with the formation of Pakistan to appease the Muslim League, which sought to distance itself from a Hindu-dominated country.

Prior to the change of guard, the British had shifted their capital out of Calcutta (Kolkata) and built the imperial city of New Delhi through the early 1900s, work on which was overseen by architect Edwin Lutyens. Meant to be an expression of British permanence, the city was speckled with grand structures such as the Rashtrapati Bhavan, the Central Vista and hundreds of residential buildings that came to be known as Lutyens Bungalows. After Independence, many of these colonial buildings were used to house the brand-new Indian government, as Delhi was reinstated to its former status as the administrative and political capital of the country.

In an attempt to prevent partition, Mahatma Gandhi unsuccessfully argued that the leader of the Muslim League, Mohammed Ali Jinnah, should lead a united India.

HISTORY INDEPENDENCE, PARTITION & AFTER

1869	1885	1911	1940
The birth of Mohandas Karamchand Gandhi in Porbandar (Gujarat) – the man who would later become popularly known as Mahatma Gandhi and affectionately dubbed 'Father of the Nation'.	The Indian National Congress, India's first home-grown political organisation, is set up. It brings educated Indians together and plays a key role in India's freedom struggle.	Architect Edwin Lutyens begins work on New Delhi, the newest manifestation of Delhi, subsequently considered in architectural circles to be one of the finest garden cities ever built.	The Muslim League adopts its Lahore Resolution, which champions greater Muslim autonomy in India. Subsequent campaigns for a separate Islamic nation are spearheaded by Mohammed Ali Jinnah.

MEANWHILE IN AGRA

As Delhi's light began to shine again, Agra, sadly, slid further from recognition. Being predominantly a satellite capital, where power occasionally spilt over from Delhi, the city had lost most of its political importance after the Mughals had departed. In the modern context, it made little sense to invest it with any kind of government machinery, so much so that it lost out to Lucknow when it came to selecting a state capital for Uttar Pradesh. Nonetheless, Agra continues to be high up on the tourism map of India, as travellers throng the city to visit its many historic sites and monuments.

The long history of insurgency and unrest in India did not end with Independence. In 1962, India had a brief war with China over disputed border territories and went on to engage in three battles with Pakistan over similar issues. Political assassinations didn't recede into history either. Mahatma Gandhi was slain soon after Independence by a Hindu extremist who hated his inclusive philosophy. Indira Gandhi, India's first female prime minister (and daughter of Jawaharlal Nehru, India's prime minister at Independence) was gunned down by her Sikh bodyguards in retaliation for her ordering the storming of the Golden Temple, the holiest of Sikh shrines, in 1984. Her son, Rajiv, who succeeded her to the post of prime minister, was also assassinated, by Tamil terrorists protesting India's stance on Sri Lankan policies.

Rajiv's Italian-born widow, Sonia, was the next of the Gandhis to take up the dynastic mantle of power. She became president of the Congress Party and in 2004 anointed her son Rahul as her chosen successor. However, in Rajasthan, as seen elsewhere across India, the party that fed on the reputation and charisma of the Nehru-Gandhi dynasty since India's formative years was swept away in a 2014 electoral tidal wave that brought the Bharatiya Janata Party (BJP) into power, led by the dynamic figure of Narendra Modi.

Rajasthan is Born

Ever since they swore allegiance to the British, the Rajput kingdoms subjugated themselves to absolute British rule. On the verge of redundancy, they also chose to trade in their real power for pomp and extravagance. Consumption took over from chivalry and, by the early 20th century, many of the kings were spending their time travelling the world with scores of retainers, playing polo and occupying entire floors of expensive Western hotels. Many maintained huge fleets of expensive cars, a fine collection of which can be seen in the automobile museum in Udaipur (p158).

Top History Reads

India: A History, John Keay

The Great Moghuls, Bamber Gascoigne

A History of Rajasthan, Rima Hooja

1947	1948	1948–56	1952
India gains independence on 15 August. Pakistan is formed a day earlier. Thousands of Hindus and Muslims brave communal riots to migrate to their respective nations.	Mahatma Gandhi is assassinated in New Delhi on 30 January by Nathuram Godse. Godse and his coconspirator Narayan Apte are later tried, convicted and executed.	Rajasthan takes shape as the princely states form a beeline to sign the Instrument of Accession and give up their territories, which are incorporated into the newly formed Republic of India.	The first elections are held in Rajasthan and the state gets its first taste of democracy after centuries of monarchical rule. The Congress is the first party to be elected into office.

While it suited the British to indulge them, the maharajas' profligacy was economically and socially detrimental to their subjects, with the exception of a few capable rulers such as Ganga Singh of Bikaner. Remnants of the Raj (the British government in India before 1947) can be spotted all over the region today, from the Mayo College in Ajmer to the colonial villas in Mt Abu, and in the black-and-white photographs, documenting chummy Anglo-Rajput hunting expeditions, which deck the walls of any self-respecting heritage hotel in the state.

After Independence, from a security point of view, it became crucial for the new Indian union to ensure that the princely states of Rajasthan were integrated into the new nation. Most of these states were located near the vulnerable India–Pakistan border and it made sense for the government to push for a merger that would minimise possibilities of rebellion in the region. Thus, when the boundaries of the new nation

MAHARAJAH METAMORPHOSIS

The fate of the royal families of Rajasthan since Independence has been mixed. A handful of the region's maharajas have continued their wasteful ways, squandering their fortunes and reducing themselves to abject poverty. A few zealous ones, who hated to see their positions of power go, have switched to politics and become members of leading political parties in India. Some have skipped politics to climb the rungs of power in other well-known national institutions, such as sports administration bodies or charitable and non-profit organisations in the country. Only a few have chosen to lead civilian lives, earning a name for themselves as fashion designers, cricketers or entertainers.

The majority of kings, however, have refused to let bygones be bygones, and have cashed in on their heritage by opening ticketed museums for tourists and converting their palaces to lavish hotels. With passing time, the luxury hospitality business has begun to find more and more takers from around the world. The boom in this industry can be traced back to 1971, when Indira Gandhi, then India's prime minister, abolished the privileges granted to the Rajasthan princes at the time of accession. Coming as a massive shock to those at the top of the pile, the snipping of the cash cord forced many kings to inadvertently join the long list of heritage hotel owners.

In spite of the abolition, many kings choose to continue using their royal titles for social purposes. While these titles are little more than status symbols now, they still help garner enormous respect from the public. On the other hand, nothing these days quite evokes the essence of Rajput grandeur like a stay in palatial splendour surrounded by vestiges of the regal age, in places such as the Rambagh Palace in Jaipur and the Umaid Bhawan Palace in Jodhpur. Not all the royal palaces of Rajasthan are on the tourist circuit, though. Many of them continue to serve as residences for erstwhile royal families and some of the mansions left out of the tourism pie are crumbling away, ignored and neglected, their decaying interiors home to pigeons and bats.

1971	1984	1998	2001
The Third Indo-Pakistan War spills into Rajasthan, with the Battle of Longewala fought in the Thar Desert. The conflict concludes with the independence of East Pakistan as Bangladesh.	Prime Minister Indira Gandhi is assassinated by her Sikh bodyguards. Her son Rajiv succeeds her as leader but is himself murdered in office in 1991.	India faces international condemnation for carrying out nuclear weapons testing. Pakistan shortly follows suit with its own tests.	A suicide attack on the Indian parliament in New Delhi nearly leads to war with Pakistan, with mass troop mobilisation along the border, including in Rajasthan.

were being chalked out, the ruling Congress Party made a deal with the nominally independent Rajput states to cede power to the republic. To sweeten the deal, the rulers were offered lucrative monetary returns and government stipends, as well as being allowed to retain their titles and property holdings. Having fallen on hard times, the royals could only agree with the government, and their inclination to yield to the Indian dominion gradually brought about the formation of the state of Rajasthan.

To begin with, the state comprised only the southern and southeastern regions of Rajasthan. Mewar was one of the first kingdoms to join the union. Udaipur was initially the state capital, with the maharaja of Udaipur becoming rajpramukh (head of state). The Instrument of Accession was signed in 1949 and Jaipur, Bikaner, Jodhpur and Jaisalmer were then merged, with Jaipur as the state's new capital. Later that year, the United State of Matsya was incorporated into Rajasthan. The state finally burgeoned to its current dimensions in November 1956, with the additions of Ajmer-Merwara, Abu Rd and a tract of Dilwara, originally part of the princely state of Sirohi that had been divided between Gujarat and Rajasthan. Rajasthan is now India's largest state.

2012	2014	2015	2016
The gang-rape and murder of a female medical student in Delhi brings forth protests across the country and internationally as well as new antirape laws.	Narendra Modi becomes prime minister as the centre-right BJP wins parliamentary elections in a landslide.	The anticorruption Aam Aadmi Party (AAP) unexpectedly wins state elections in Delhi, overturning the BJP ascendancy.	Narendra Modi's government demonetises ₹500 and ₹1000 notes in a surprise move to combat 'black money'. Populace takes it surprisingly well. New ₹500 and ₹2000 notes soon circulate.

Rajasthani Way of Life

From the tribal villages of the Thar Desert to the modern hustle of Jaipur, there are few places in India where traditional and modern life jut up against each other as they do in Rajasthan, and in such an exciting and intriguing manner. Camel carts pass hi-tech solar farms, cell phones are ubiquitous and yet conservative social mores underpin everyday life.

Contemporary Life

Indian society as a whole continues to grapple with competition between traditionalism and the effects of globalisation. Cities such as Jaipur may have acquired a liberal sheen on the outside and foreign influences are apparent in the public domain – satellite TV rules the airwaves, mobile phones are nothing short of a necessity and coffee shops are jam-packed on the weekends – but within the walls of a typical home, life often remains conservative at heart, with family affairs dominated by the man of the house. Gender politics are a touchstone issue, from sexual relationships outside marriage to the independence of women.

Rustom Bharucha's *Rajasthan: An Oral History* is a great book for reading your way into the patterns of traditional Rajasthani life.

In the region's backyard, the scene is rather stark. Rural Rajasthan remains one of the poorest areas in the country. Being in close proximity to the Thar Desert, the climate here is harsh and people dwelling in the region's villages are locked in a day-to-day battle for survival, as they have been for ages. Unemployment is rife, which in turn has led to problems such as debt, drug abuse, alcoholism and prostitution. Indigenous tribes have been the worst affected and it isn't uncommon to see members from their communities begging or performing tricks at traffic signals in return for loose change.

Rajasthan also lags behind on the education front, its literacy rate being about 7% behind the national average of 74%. Introduced in 2001, the nationwide 'education-for-all' program aims to impart elementary education to all Indian children. The project focuses on the education of girls, who have historically been deprived of quality schooling; a particular problem in Rajasthan, where the female literacy rate is just 53%, compared to 80.5% for men.

Marriage & Divorce

Indian marriages were always meant to unite families, not individuals. In rural Rajasthan, the case remains much the same today. Unlike in cities, where people now find love through online dating sites, marriages in villages and small towns are still arranged by parents. Those getting married have little say in the proceedings and cross-caste marriages are almost always forbidden. Few move out of their parents' homes after tying the knot; setting up an independent establishment postmarriage is often considered an insult to the elderly.

By and large, marriages in rural areas are initiated by professional matchmakers, who strike a suitable match based on family status, caste

FIRST IMPRESSIONS

It's not the turbaned maharajas or the call-centre graduates or even the stereotypical beggars, for that matter: the first people you run into upon your arrival in Rajasthan are a jostling bunch of overly attentive locals, who ambush travellers the moment they step out of the airport or the railway station and swamp new arrivals in a sea of unsolicited offers. Great hotels, taxi rides at half-price, above-the-rate currency exchange…the list goes on, interspersed with beaming smiles you would usually only expect from long-lost friends. Famed Indian hospitality at work? This is no reception party; the men are touts out on their daily rounds, trying to wheedle a few bucks off unsuspecting travellers. There's no way you can escape them, though a polite but firm 'no, thank you' often stands you in good stead under such circumstances. It's a welcome each and every newcomer is accorded in India.

It's hard not to get put off by the surprise mobbing, but don't let such incidents make you jump to the hasty conclusion that every local is out to hound a few rupees out of you. Walk out of the terminal and into the real India and things suddenly come across as strikingly different. With little stake in your activities, the people you now meet are genuinely warm (even if overtly curious), hospitable and sometimes helpful beyond what you'd call mere courtesy. For example, someone might volunteer to show you around a monument expecting absolutely nothing in return. And while it's advisable to always keep your wits about you, going with the flow often helps you understand the Indian psyche better, as well as making your trip to the region all the more memorable.

and compatible horoscopes. Once a marriage is finalised, the bride's family often arranges for a dowry to be paid to the groom's parents, as an appreciation of their graciously accepting the bride as a member of their family. These dowries are officially illegal, but remain commonplace and can run into hundreds of thousands of rupees, ranging from hard cash to items such as TVs, motorcycles and household furniture.

Despite the exact amount of dowry being finalised at the time of betrothal, there have been sporadic cases reported where the groom's family later insists that the girl's parents cough up more, failing which the bride might be subjected to abuse and domestic violence. Stories of newly married girls dying in kitchen 'accidents' are not uncommon. In most cases, they leave the grooms free to remarry and claim another dowry.

Indian law sets the marriageable age of men and women at 21 and 18 respectively, yet child marriages continue to be practised in rural Rajasthan. It is estimated that one in every two girls in the state's villages are married off before they turn 15. Divorce and remarriage is becoming more common (primarily in bigger cities), but divorce is still not granted by courts as a matter of routine and is not looked upon very favourably by society. Even if a divorce is obtained, it is difficult for a woman to find another husband; as a divorcee, she is considered less chaste than a spinster.

Given the stigma associated with divorce, few people have the courage to walk out on each other, instead preferring to silently endure. Also facing frequent social stigma are widows. While the practice of *sati* (the ritual self-immolation of a wife on her husband's funeral pyre) has passed into history, many expect widows to remain in mourning for the rest of their lives, and face being ostracised from their families and communities.

Matchmaking has embraced the cyber age, with popular sites including www.shaadi.com, www.bharatmatrimony.com and, more progressively, www.second-shaadi.com – for those seeking a partner again.

Women in Rajasthan

According to the most recent census in 2011, India's population is comprised of 586 million women, with an estimated 68% of those working (mostly as labourers) in the agricultural sector. Women are seen primarily as mothers in Indian society and gender equality is a distant aspiration for the majority of Rajasthani women. Being socially disadvantaged, women face many restrictions on their freedoms and, as keepers of a family's honour, they risk accusations of immorality if they mingle freely with strangers. For visitors to India, it can be quite disconcerting to walk through a rural village and see women beating a quick retreat into the privacy of their homes, their faces hidden behind the folds of their saris.

Screened from the outside world, most women in rural Rajasthan live a life that revolves around household tasks and raising children. Where women are permitted to work, this usually involves working in the family fields. Even in professional circles, women are generally paid less than their male counterparts. Besides all this, India's patriarchal society rarely recognises women as inheritors of family property, which almost always goes to male heirs. The birth of a girl child is often seen as unlucky, since it not only means an extra mouth to feed but also a dowry that needs to be given away at the time of marriage. Embryonic sex determination is practised, despite it being illegal, and local media occasionally blows the lid off surgical rackets where surgeons charge huge amounts of money to carry out female-foeticide operations.

Progress has been made, however, in the form of development programs run by the central and state governments, as well as nongovernmental organisations (NGOs) and voluntary outfits that have swung into action. Organisations such as the Barefoot College, URMAL Trust and Seva Mandir all run grass-roots programs in Rajasthan (with volunteering opportunities; see p256) devoted to awareness, education, health issues and female empowerment. Women are entitled to vote and own property; however, they're still notably under-represented in the national parliament, accounting for around 11% of parliamentary members.

In the cities, the scene is much better. Urban women in Jaipur have worked their way to social and professional recognition and feminists are no longer dismissed as fringe extremists. Even so, some of India's first-generation female executives recall a time not very long ago when women encountered resistance when they put in a request for maternity leave, as motherhood had been precluded as an occasion that merited time off from work.

Opium was traditionally served to guests at social functions by several indigenous communities of Rajasthan. Though the sale of opium is now illegal, it continues behind law-enforcers' backs.

Peoples of Rajasthan

Demographically speaking, much of the region's population still lives in its villages, but they are on the move. The cities attract people from all walks of life to create a high-density, multiethnic population. Religious ghettos can be found in places such as Ajmer and Jaipur, where a fair number of Christian families live; the Ganganagar district, home to a large number of Sikhs; and parts of Alwar and Bharatpur, where the populace is chiefly Muslim. Though most Muslims in Rajasthan belong to the Sunni sect, the state also has a small but affluent community of Shiite Muslims, called the Bohras, living in the southeast.

HIJRAS – THE THIRD SEX

India's most visible nonheterosexual group is the *hijras,* a caste of transvestites and eunuchs who dress in women's clothing. Some are gay, some are intersex and some were unfortunate enough to be kidnapped and castrated. Since it has long been traditionally frowned upon to live openly as a gay man in India, *hijras* get around this by becoming, in effect, a third sex of sorts. They work mainly as wandering entertainers at weddings and celebrations of the birth of male children and also as sex workers.

Read more about *hijras* in The Invisibles by Zia Jaffrey, and *Ardhanarishvara the Androgyne* by Alka Pande.

CRICKET

Cricket is a national obsession in India, and Rajasthan is no exception. Nearly everybody claims to understand the game down to its finer points and can comment on it with endless vigour. Shops down shutters and streets take on a deserted look every time India happens to be playing a test match or a crucial one-day game. The arrival of the Twenty20 format and domestic leagues such as the Indian Premier League (IPL) has only taken the game's popularity a notch further.

Keep your finger on the cricketing pulse at www.espncricinfo.com and www.cricbuzz. com. Cricket tragics will be bowled over by *The Illustrated History of Indian Cricket* by Boria Majumdar, and *The States of Indian Cricket* by Ramachandra Guha.

Tribes & Indigenous Communities

Rajasthan has a large indigenous population, comprising communities that are native to the region and have lived there for centuries. Called Adivasis, most of these ethnic groups have been listed as Scheduled Tribes by the government. The majority of the Adivasis are pagan, though some have either taken to Hindu ways or converted to Christianity over time.

Bhils

The largest of Rajasthan's tribes, the Bhils live to the southeast, spilling over into Madhya Pradesh. They speak their own distinct native language and have a natural talent for archery and warfare. Witchcraft, magic and superstition are deeply rooted in their culture. Polygamy is still practised by those who can afford it and love marriages are the norm.

Originally a hunter-gatherer community, the Bhils have survived years of exploitation by higher castes to finally take up small-scale agriculture. Some have left their villages to head for the cities. Literacy is still below average and not too many Bhil families have many assets to speak of, but these trends are slowly being reversed. The Baneshwar Fair is a huge Bhil festival, where you can sample the essence of their culture firsthand.

Minas

The Minas are the second-largest tribal group in Rajasthan and live around Shekhawati and eastern Rajasthan. The name Mina comes from *meen* (fish), and the tribe claims it evolved from the fish incarnation of Vishnu. Minas once ruled supreme in the Amber region, but their miseries began once they were routed by the Rajputs. To make matters worse, they were outlawed during the British Raj, after their guerrilla tactics earned them the 'criminal-tribe' label. Following Independence, the criminal status was lifted and the Minas subsequently took to agriculture.

Festivities, music and dance form a vital part of Mina culture; they excel in performances such as swordplay and acrobatics. Minas view marriage as a noble institution and their weddings are accompanied by enthusiastic celebrations. They are also known to be friendly with other tribes and don't mind sharing space with other communities.

For comprehensive information on India's native and tribal communities, check out the website www.tribal.nic.in, maintained by the Ministry of Tribal Affairs under the Government of India.

Bishnois

The Bishnois are the most progressive of Rajasthan's indigenous communities and even have their presence on the internet (http://bishnoi.org). However, they can't be strictly classified as a tribe. The Bishnois owe their origin to a visionary named Jambho Ji, who in 1485 shunned the Hindu social order to form a casteless faith that took inspiration from nature. Credited as the oldest environmentalist community in India, the Bishnois are animal-lovers and take an interest in preserving forests and wildlife. Felling of trees and hunting within Bishnoi territory are strictly prohibited.

Sacred India

Hindus comprise nearly 90% of Rajasthan's population. Much of the remaining 10% are Muslims, followed by decreasing numbers of Sikhs, Jains, Christians and Buddhists, respectively. In spite of this religious diversity, tolerance levels here are high and incidents of communal violence are rare.

Hinduism & the Caste System

Hinduism is among the world's oldest religious traditions, with its roots going back at least 3000 years. Theoretically, Hinduism is not a religion; it is a way of life, an elaborate convention that has evolved through the centuries, in contrast to many other religions, which can trace their origins to a single founder. Despite being founded on a solid religious base, Hinduism doesn't have a specific theology or even a central religious institution. It also has no provision for conversion; one is always born a Hindu.

Being an extremely diverse religion, Hinduism can't be summed up by a universal definition. Yet, there are a few principal tenets that most Hindu sects tend to go by. Hindus believe that all life originates from a supreme spirit called Brahman, a formless, timeless phenomenon manifested by Brahma, the Hindu lord of creation. Upon being born, all living beings are required to engage in dharma (worldly duties) and samsara (the endless cycle of birth, death and rebirth). It is said that the road to salvation lies through righteous karma (actions which evoke subsequent reactions), which leads to moksha (emancipation), when the soul eventually returns to unite with the supreme spirit.

If that's not complex enough, things are convoluted further by the caste system, which broadly divides Hindus into four distinct classes based on their mythical origins and their occupations. On top of the caste hierarchy are the Brahmins, priests who supposedly originated from Brahma's mouth. Next come the Kshatriyas, the warriors who evolved from the deity's arms – this is the caste that the Rajputs fit into. Vaishyas, tradespeople born from the thighs, are third in the pecking order, below which stand the Shudras. Alternatively called Dalits or Scheduled Castes, the Shudras comprise menial workers such as peasants, janitors or cobblers and are known to stem from Brahma's feet. Caste, by the way, is not changeable.

Hindu Sacred Texts & Epics

Hindu sacred texts fall under two categories: those believed to be the word of God (*shruti*, meaning 'hearing') and those produced by people (*smriti*, meaning 'memory').

Introduced in the subcontinent (supposedly) by the Aryans, the Vedas are regarded as *shruti* knowledge and are considered to be the authoritative basis for Hinduism. The oldest works of Sanskrit literature, the Vedas contain mantras that are recited at prayers and religious ceremonies. The Vedas are divided into four Samhitas (compilations); the Rig-Veda, the oldest of the Samhitas, is believed to have been written

In Hinduism, the syllable 'Om' is believed to be a primordial sound from which the entire universe takes shape. It is also a sacred symbol, represented by an icon shaped like the number three.

more than 3000 years ago. Other Vedic works include the Brahmanas, touching on rituals; the Aranyakas, whose name means the 'wilderness texts', meant for ascetics who have renounced the material world; and the Upanishads, which discuss meditation, philosophy, mysticism and the fate of the soul.

The Puranas comprise a post-Vedic genre that chronicles the history of the universe, royal lineages, philosophy and cosmology. The Sutras,

HINDU GODS & GODDESSES

According to Hindu scriptures, there are around 330 million deities in the Hindu pantheon. All of them are regarded as a manifestation of Brahman (the supreme spirit), which otherwise has three main representations known as the Trimurti – the trio of Brahma, Vishnu and Shiva.

Brahman

The One. The ultimate reality, Brahman is formless, eternal and the source of all existence. Brahman is *nirguna* (without attributes), as opposed to all the other gods and goddesses, which are manifestations of Brahman and therefore *saguna* (with attributes).

Brahma

The only active role that Brahma ever played was during the creation of the universe. Since then he has been immersed in eternal meditation and is therefore regarded as aloof. His vehicle is a swan and he is sometimes shown sitting on a lotus.

Vishnu & Krishna

Being the preserver and sustainer of the universe, Vishnu is associated with 'right action'. He is usually depicted with four arms, each holding a lotus, conch shell, discus and mace, respectively. His consort is Lakshmi, the goddess of wealth, and his vehicle is Garuda, a creature that's half bird, half beast. Vishnu has 10 incarnations, including Rama, Krishna and Buddha. He is also referred to as Narayan.

Krishna, the hugely popular incarnation of Vishnu, was sent to earth to fight for good and combat evil, and his exploits are documented in the Mahabharata. A shrewd politician, his flirtatious alliances with *gopis* (milkmaids) and his love for Radha, his paramour, have inspired countless paintings and songs.

Shiva & Parvati

Although he plays the role of the destroyer, Shiva's creative role is symbolised by his representation as the frequently worshipped lingam (phallus). With snakes draped around his neck, he is sometimes shown holding a trident while riding Nandi the bull. With 1008 names, Shiva takes many forms, including Pashupati, champion of the animals, and Nataraja, performer of the *tandava* (cosmic dance of fury). He is also the lord of yoga.

Shiva's consort is the beautiful goddess Parvati, who in her dark side appears as Kali, the fiercest of the gods who demands sacrifices and wears a garland of skulls. Alternatively, she appears as the fair Durga, the demon slayer, who wields supreme power, holds weapons in her 10 hands and rides a tiger or a lion.

Ganesh

The pot-bellied, elephant-headed Ganesh is held in great affection by Indians. He is the god of good fortune, prosperity and the patron of scribes, being credited with writing sections of the Mahabharata. Ganesh is good at removing obstacles and he's frequently spotted above doorways and entrances of Indian homes.

Hanuman

Hanuman is the hero of the Ramayana and is one of Rajasthan's most popular gods. He is the loyal ally of Lord Rama, and the images of Rama and his wife Sita are emblazoned upon his heart. He is king of the monkeys and thus assures them refuge in temple complexes across the country.

on the other hand, are essentially manuals, and contain useful information on different human activities. Some well-known Sutras are Griha Sutra, dealing with the nuances of domestic life; Nyaya Sutra, detailing the faculty of justice and debate; and Kamasutra, a compendium of love and sexual behaviour. The Shastras are also instructive in nature, but are more technical as they provide information pertaining to specific areas of practice. Vaastu Shastra, for example, is an architect's handbook that elaborates on the art of civic planning, while Artha Shastra focuses heavily on governance, economics and military policies of the state.

The Mahabharata is a 2500-year-old rip-roaring epic that centres on the conflict between two fraternal dynasties, the Pandavas and the Kauravas, overseen by Krishna. Locked in a struggle to inherit the throne of Hastinapura, the Kauravas win the first round of the feud, beating their adversaries in a game of dice and banishing them from the kingdom. The Pandavas return after 13 years and challenge the Kauravas to an epic battle, from which they emerge victorious. Being the longest epic in the world, unabridged versions of the Mahabharata incorporate the Bhagavad Gita, the holy book of the Hindus, which contains the worldly advice given by Krishna to Pandava prince Arjuna before the start of the battle.

Composed around the 2nd or 3rd century BC, the Ramayana tells of Rama, an incarnation of Vishnu, who assumed human form to facilitate the triumph of good over evil. Much like the Mahabharata, the Ramayana revolves around a great war, waged by Rama, his brother Lakshmana and an army of apes led by Hanuman against Ravana, the demon king who had kidnapped Rama's wife Sita and had held her hostage in his kingdom of Lanka (Sri Lanka). After slaying Ravana, Rama returned to his kingdom of Ayodhya, his homecoming forming the basis for the important Hindu festival of Dussehra.

Islam

Islam was founded in Arabia by the Prophet Mohammed in the 7th century AD. The Arabic term 'Islam' means 'surrender' and believers undertake to surrender to the will of Allah (God), which is revealed in the Quran, the holy book of Islam. A devout Muslim is required to pray five times a day, keep day-long fasts through the month of Ramadan and make a pilgrimage to the holy city of Mecca in Saudi Arabia, if possible.

Islam is monotheistic. God is held as unique, unlimited, self-sufficient and the supreme creator of all things. God never speaks to humans directly; his word is instead conveyed through messengers called prophets, who are never themselves divine. The religion has two prominent sects, the minority Shiites (originating from Mohammed's descendants) and the majority Sunnis, who split soon after the death of Mohammed owing to political differences and have since gone on to establish their own interpretations and rituals. The most important pilgrimage site for Muslims in Rajasthan is the extraordinary dargah (burial place) of the Sufi saint Khwaja Muin-ud-din Chishti at Ajmer.

Sikhism

Sikhism was founded on the sermons of 10 Sikh gurus, beginning with Guru Nanak Dev (1469–1539). The core values and ideology of Sikhism are embodied in the Guru Granth Sahib, the holy book of the Sikhs, which is also considered the eternal guru of Sikhism. The Sikhs evolved as an organised community over time and devoted themselves to the creation of a standing militia called the Khalsa, which carried out religious, political and martial duties and protected the Sikhs from foreign threats. The religion, on its part, grew around the central concept of Vaheguru, the universal lord, an eventual union with whom is believed to result in salvation. The Sikhs believe that salvation is achieved through rigorous

Shiva is sometimes characterised as the lord of yoga, a Himalaya-dwelling ascetic with matted hair, an ash-smeared body and a third eye symbolising wisdom.

Sufism is a mystic tradition derived from Islam that originated in medieval times. Being largely secular, it has attracted followers from other religions and is widely practised in North India.

RAJASTHAN FOLK GODS & GODDESSES

Folk deities and deified local heroes abound in Rajasthan. Apart from public gods, families are often known to pay homage to a *kuladevi* (family idol).

Pabuji is one of many local heroes to have attained divine status. Pabuji promised to protect the cows of a woman called Devalde, for which he would receive a mare. He was called upon during his own marriage and, in defending the herd against the villainous Jind Raj Khinchi, was killed, along with all his male relatives. To preserve the family line, Pabuji's sister-in-law cut open her own belly and produced Pabuji's nephew, Nandio, before throwing herself on her husband's funeral pyre.

Professional storytellers called Bhopas pay homage to Pabuji by performing *Pabuji-ka-phad* (reciting poetry alongside *phad,* or a cloth scroll, with paintings that chronicle the life of the hero). You can attend these performances at places such as Chokhi Dhani or Jaisalmer, if they happen at a time when you're around.

Gogaji was an 11th-century warrior and could cure snakebite; today, victims are brought to his shrines by both Hindu and Muslim devotees. Also believed to cure snakebite is Tejaji who, according to tradition, was blessed by a snake, which decreed that anyone honouring Tejaji by tying a thread on to a limb in his name would be cured of snakebite.

Goddesses revered by Rajasthanis include incarnations of Devi (the Mother Goddess), such as the fierce Chamunda Mata, an incarnation of Durga and Karni Mata, worshipped at Deshnok near Bikaner. Women who have committed *sati* (ritual suicide) on their husband's funeral pyres are also frequently worshipped as goddesses, such as Rani Sati, who has an elaborate temple in her honour in Jhunjhunu, Shekhawati.

Barren women pay homage to the god Bhairon, an incarnation of Shiva, at his shrines, which are usually found under khejri trees. In order to be blessed with a child, a woman is required to leave a garment hanging from the branches of the tree. The deified folk hero Ramdev also has an important temple at Ramdevra, near Pokaran in western Rajasthan.

discipline and meditation, which help them overcome the five evils – ego, greed, attachment, anger and lust.

Guru Nanak introduced five symbols, or articles of faith, to bind Sikhs together and display their religious devotion and they are the most obvious public elements of Sikhism that people encounter. These are: *kesh* (uncut hair, covered by a turban for men); *kangha* (a wooden comb, for cleanliness); *kara* (a steel bracelet, for the bonds of faith and community); *kaccha* (breeches, for self-control and chastity); and *kirpan* (a ceremonial sword, to defend against injustice).

Jainism

The Jain religion was founded around 500 BC by Mahavira, the 24th and last of the Jain *tirthankars* (path finders). Jainism originally evolved as a reformist movement against the dominance of priests in Hindu society. It steered clear of complicated rituals, rejected the caste system and believed in reincarnation and eventual moksha by following the example of the *tirthankars*.

Jains are strict vegetarians and revere all forms of life. The religion has two main sects. The Svetambaras (White Clad) wear unstitched white garments; the monks cover their mouths so as not to inhale insects and brush their path before they walk to avoid crushing small creatures. The monks belonging to the Digambaras (Sky Clad), in comparison, go naked. Jainism preaches nonviolence and its followers are markedly successful in banking and business, which they consider nonviolent professions.

Rajasthani Food

Wherever you go in this region of India, you'll never be far away from something tempting and delicious to eat. From the sweet, decadent deep-fry of a street-food stall, to the bliss of a hot cardamom-scented chai (tea) on a cool January morning, food is all around you. Moreover, food is never just food here – it marks celebrations and festivals, honours guests and accompanies births, marriages and deaths.

Making a Meal of It

Rajasthan's cuisine has developed in response to its harsh climate. Fresh fruit and vegetables are rare commodities in desert zones, but these parts of the state overcome the land's shortcomings by serving up an amazing and creative variety of regional dishes, utilising cereals, pulses, spices, milk products and unusual desert fruits in myriad ways. Regal feasts, meanwhile, are the stuff of legend. And modern Rajasthan ranks as one of the best restaurant destinations in the country, with scores of establishments serving up everything from butter chicken to international fusion cuisine.

Bread of Life

A meal is not complete in North India unless it comes with a bountiful supply of roti, little round circles of unleavened bread (also known as chapati), made with fine wholemeal flour and cooked on a *tawa* (hotplate). In Rajasthan you'll also find *sogra,* a thick, heavy chapati made from millet; *makki ki* roti, a fat cornmeal chapati; and *dhokla,* yummy balls of steamed maize flour cooked with coriander, spinach and mint and eaten with chutney. Yet another kind of roti is a pastry-like *purat* roti, made by repeatedly coating the dough in oil, then folding it to produce a light and fluffy bread. *Cheelre,* meanwhile, is a chapati made with gram (chickpea) powder paste, while *bhakri* is a thick roti made from barley, millet or corn, eaten with pounded garlic, red chilli and raw onions by working-class Rajasthanis, and said to prevent sunstroke.

Alongside the world of roti come *puris, parathas* and naans. A *puri* is a delicious North Indian snack of deep-fried wholemeal dough that puffs up like a soft, crispy balloon. Kachori is similar, but here the dough is pepped up with potato, corn or dhal masala. Flaky *paratha* is a soft, circular bread, deliciously substantial and mildly elastic, which makes for a scrumptious early morning snack, and is often jazzed up with a small bowl of pickles and a stuffing of paneer (unfermented cheese), *aloo* (potato) or grated vegetables. Naan bread, made with leavened white flour, is distinguished from roti by being larger, thicker and doughier, cooked on the inner walls of a tandoor (oven) rather than on a *tawa*. Best plain, it is also delicious when laced with garlic and lashings of butter and filled with paneer, *aloo* or coconut and raisins.

Rice

Basmati rice is considered the cream of India's crop, its name stemming from the Hindi phrase for 'queen of fragrance'. Aside from the plain

Spotlighting rice, *Finest Rice Recipes* by Sabina Sehgal Saikia shows just how versatile this humble grain is, with classy creations such as rice-crusted crab cakes.

VEGETARIANS & VEGANS

Vegetarians will have no problem maintaining a varied and exciting diet in India.

Vegetarian food is sometimes divided up in India into 'veg' and 'pure veg', a frequently blurred and confusing distinction. As a general rule of thumb, 'veg' usually means the same as it does in the West: without meat, fowl or seafood, but possibly containing butter (in India's case, ghee), dairy products, eggs or honey. 'Pure veg' often refers to what the West knows as vegan food: dishes containing no dairy products, eggs or honey. Other times, 'pure veg' might also mean no onions, garlic or mushrooms (which some Hare Krishna believe can have a negative effect on one's state of consciousness) or even no root vegetables or tubers (since many Jains, according to the principles of ahimsa, are loath to damage soil organisms).

Though it's extremely easy to be vegetarian in India, finding vegan food – outside 'pure veg' restaurants – can be trickier. Many basic dishes include a small amount of ghee, so ask whether a dish is 'pure veg', even in a vegetarian restaurant.

steamed rice variety, you'll find pilau (aka pilaf), a tasty, buttery rice dish, whose Rajasthani incarnations frequently include cinnamon, cardamom, cloves and a handful or two of almonds and pistachios.

Dhal & Cereals

India has around 60 different varieties of dhal. In Rajasthan, the dhal of choice is *urad,* black lentils boiled in water, then cooked with *garam masala,* red chillies, cumin seeds, salt, oil and fresh coriander.

The state's most popular dhal-based dish is *dhal-bati-choorma,* which mixes dhal with *bati,* buttery hard-baked balls of wholemeal flour, and *choorma,* sweet, fried wholemeal-flour balls mixed with sugar and nuts.

Gram-flour dumplings known as *gatta* are a delicious dish usually cooked in yoghurt or masala and *mangodi* are lentil-flour dumplings served in an onion or potato gravy. A speciality of Jodhpur is *kabuli Jodhpuri,* a dish made with meat, vegetables and yet more fried gram-flour balls. *Govind gatta* offers a sweet alternative: lentil paste with dried fruit and nuts rolled into a sausage shape, then sliced and deep-fried. *Pakora* (fritters), *sev* (savoury nibbles) and other salted snacks generally known as *farsan* are all equally derived from chickpea gram.

Meat Matters

While Rajasthan's Brahmins and traders stuck to a vegetarian diet, the Rajputs have a far more carnivorous history. Goat (known as 'mutton' since the days of the British Raj), lamb and chicken are the mainstays; religious taboos make beef forbidden to Hindus and pork to Muslims.

In the deserts of Jaisalmer, Jodhpur and Bikaner, meats are often cooked without the addition of water, instead using milk, curd, buttermilk and plenty of ghee. Cooked this way, dishes keep for days without refrigeration, a practical advantage in the searing heat of the desert. *Murg ko khaato* (chicken cooked in a curd gravy), *achar murg* (pickled chicken), *kacher maas* (dry lamb cooked in spices), *lal maas* (a rich red dish, usually mutton) and *soor santh ro sohito* (pork with millet dumplings) are all classic desert dishes.

Maas ka sule, a Rajput favourite, is a dry dish that can be made from partridge, wild boar, chicken, mutton or fish. Marinated chunks of meat are cooked on skewers in a tandoor, then glazed with melted butter and a tangy masala spice mix. Mughlai meat dishes, meanwhile, include rich korma and rogan josh, the former mild, the latter cooked with tomatoes and saffron, and both generously spiked with thick, creamy curd.

There's really no such thing in India as a 'curry'. The term is thought to be an anglicisation of the Tamil word *kari* (black or blackened, ie cooked), coined by bewildered Brits for any dish that included tempered spices.

Fruit & Vegetables

Rajasthan's delicious *sabji* (vegetable) dishes have to be admired for their inventiveness under frequently hostile growing conditions. Dishes you might come across include *papad ki sabzi,* a simple pappadam made with vegetables and masala (a mixture of spices), and *aloo mangori,* ground lentil paste sun-dried then added with potato to a curry. Once rolled by hand, the paste is now often forced through a machine in a similar way to making macaroni. A common vegetarian snack is *aloo samosa,* triangular pastry cones stuffed with spicy potato, while another scrumptious local snack is *mirch bada,* a large chilli coated in a thick layer of deep-fried potato and wheatgerm.

There are a few vegetables specific to the deserts of Rajasthan. These include *mogri,* a type of desert bean, which is made into *mogri mangori* (similar to *aloo mangori*), or a sweeter version known as *methi mangori* – *methi* being the leaf of a green desert vegetable. Another use for these *methi* leaves is in *dana methi,* where they are boiled with *dana* (small pea-shaped vegetables) and mixed with sugar, masala and dried fruit.

With developments in infrastructure, more vegetable dishes are now available in Rajasthan than during its barren, warrior-filled past. Heads of cauliflower are usually cooked dry on their own, with potatoes to make *aloo gobi.* Fresh green peas turn up stir-fried with other vegetables in pilaus and biryanis, in samosas along with potato, and in one of North India's signature dishes, *mattar paneer* (peas and fresh, firm white cheese). *Brinjal* (eggplant or aubergine), *bhindi* (okra or ladies' fingers) and *saag* (a generic term for leafy greens) are all popular choices.

The desert bears a handful of fruits, too. The small, round *kair* is a favourite of camels as well as people, to whom it is usually served with mango pickle; *kachri* is frequently made into chutney. If you order something that arrives looking like a plate of dry sticks, these are s*angri* (dried wild desert beans). The seeds and beans are soaked overnight in water, boiled and then fried in oil with masala, dried dates, red chillies, turmeric powder, shredded dried mango, salt, coriander and cumin seeds.

Pickles, Chutneys & Relishes

You're in a pickle without a pickle, or *achar:* no Indian meal is complete without one or two *chatnis* (chutneys) and relishes on the side. A relish can be anything from a roughly chopped onion to a delicately crafted fusion of fruit, nuts and spices. The best known is raita (mildly spiced yoghurt or curd often containing cucumber, tomato or pineapple), which makes a refreshing counter to spicy meals.

Other regional variations include *goonde achar, goonde* being a green fruit that is boiled and mixed with mustard oil and masala. *Kair achar* is a pickle with desert fruit as its base, while *lahsun achar* is an onion pickle. *Lal mirch* is a garlic-stuffed red chilli and *kamrak ka achar* is a pickle made from *kamrak,* a type of desert vegetable with a pungent, sour taste.

To find out more about veganism in India, take a look at www.indianvegan.com. For recipe ideas, pick up a copy of *Spicy Vegan* by Sudha Raina.

Gorge yourself by reading about the extravagant royal recipes of Rajasthan in *Royal Indian Cookery* by Manju Shivraj Singh, the niece of the late Maharaja Bhawani Singh of Jaipur.

TERRIFIC THALIS

Thalis are the traditional cheap and filling meals made up of a combination of curried dishes, served with relishes, pappadams, yoghurt, *puris* and rice. The term 'thali' also covers the characteristic metal tray-plate on which the meal is frequently served. If you're strapped for cash, thalis are a saviour, especially at local hole-in-the-wall restaurants and railway-station dining halls, since they're far heavier on the stomach than the wallet. In southern Rajasthan, many restaurants serve more sophisticated, sweet and lightly spiced Gujarati thalis – one of the best ways to sample a taste of Gujarati cuisine.

For a taste of the desert, try out a few dishes from the recipe collection, *Classic Cooking of Rajasthan,* by Kaira Jiggs and Raminder Malhotra.

The most widely served are made of raw mango, mixed with spices and mustard oil, lime, shredded ginger or tiny whole shallots.

Dairy

Milk and milk products make a staggering contribution to Indian cuisine (hence the sanctity of the cow) and in Rajasthan they're even more important: *dahi* (curd) is served with most meals and is handy for countering heat in terms of both temperature and spiciness of dishes; firm, unmeltable paneer cheese is a godsend for the vegetarian majority and is used in apparently endless permutations; popular lassi (yoghurt-and-iced-water drink) is just one in a host of nourishing sweet or savoury drinks, often with fruit such as banana or mango added; ghee (clarified butter) is the traditional and pure cooking medium; and the best sweets are made with plenty of condensed, sweetened milk or cream.

Sweets & Desserts

Indians have a heady range of tooth-achingly sweet *mithai* (sweets), made from manifold concoctions of sugar, milk, ghee, nuts and yet more sugar. Rajasthani varieties include *badam ki barfi,* a type of fudge made from sugar, powdered milk, almonds and ghee; *chakki,* a *barfi* made from gram flour, sugar and milk. Gram flour, sugar, cardamom, ghee and dried fruits combined make *churma,* while *ladoo* comes in ball form.

Ghewar is a paste based on *urad* (a mung-bean type pulse) that's crushed, deep-fried and dipped in sugar syrup flavoured with cardamom, cinnamon and cloves. It's served hot, topped with a thick layer of unsweetened cream and garnished with rose petals.

Even deities have their favourite dishes. Krishna likes milk products and Ganesh is rarely seen without a bowl of *modak* (sweet rice-flour dumplings).

Kheer is perhaps India's favourite dessert, a delectable, fragrant rice pudding with a light flavour of cardamom, saffron, pistachios, flaked almonds and cashews or dried fruit. *Gulab jamun* are spongy deep-fried balls of milk dough soaked in rose-flavoured syrup. *Kulfi* is addictive once experienced; delicious, substantially firm-textured, made with reduced milk and flavoured with nuts, fruits and berries, and especially tasty in its pale-green pistachio incarnation, *pista kulfi.*

Alongside these more sophisticated offerings are food-stall sweets such as *jalebis* (orange-coloured whirls of fried batter dipped in syrup), which melt in the mouth and hang heavy on the conscience.

Drinks

Tea & Coffee

India runs on chai (tea). It's a unique and addictive brew: more milk than water, stewed for a long time and frequently sugary enough to give you an energy boost. A glass of steaming, sweet chai is the perfect antidote to the heat and stress of Indian travel.

If you just crave a simple cuppa, many cafes and restaurants can serve up 'tray tea' or 'English tea'. Coffee used to be fairly unusual in the region,

PAAN

Meals are often rounded off with *paan,* a fragrant mixture of betel nut (also called areca nut), lime paste, spices and condiments wrapped in an edible, silky *paan* leaf. Peddled by *paan-wallahs, paan* is a digestive and mouth-freshener. The betel nut is mildly narcotic and some aficionados eat *paan* the same way heavy smokers consume cigarettes, which can cause rotten teeth and mouth cancer.

There are two basic types of *paan:* mitha (sweet) and *saadha* (with tobacco). A parcel of *mitha paan* is a splendid way to finish a satisfying meal – pop the whole parcel in your mouth and chew slowly.

BEWARE OF THOSE BHANG LASSIS!

It's rarely printed in menus, but some restaurants in Rajasthan clandestinely whip up bhang lassi, a yoghurt-and-iced-water beverage laced with bhang, a derivative of marijuana. This 'special lassi' can be a potent concoction – some travellers have been stuck in bed for several miserable days after drinking it, others have become delirious and it's not unknown for sufferers to be robbed in such circumstances.

but Delhi and the well-travelled parts of Rajasthan have caught up with the double-mocha-latte ways of the West. At bus and train stations, coffee is still almost indistinguishable from chai: the same combination of water, boiled milk and sugar, but with a dash of instant-coffee powder.

Cooling Off

Aside from the usual gamut of Pepsis and 7Ups, India has a few of its own sugary bottled drinks: the vaguely lemonish Limca and orange Mirinda. *Masala soda* is the quintessential Indian soft drink, but it's an acquired taste. Freshly squeezed orange juice is also widely available, though the most popular street juices are made from sweet lemon and sugar cane, pressed in front of you by a mechanised wheel complete with jingling bells.

Jal jeera is made with lime juice, cumin, mint and rock salt and is sold in large earthenware pots by street vendors as well as in restaurants. *Falooda* is a sweet rose-flavoured Muslim speciality made with milk, cream, nuts and strands of vermicelli.

By far the most popular of all Indian cold drinks, however, is a refreshing sweet or salty lassi (yoghurt drink). Jodhpur is famous for its sweet *makhania* lassis, flavoured with saffron and hearty enough to stand in for a meal. *Chach* is a thin, salted lassi and *kairi chach* is unripe mango juice with water and salt added, widely available in summer and allegedly a good remedy for sunstroke.

Cheers

Most travellers champion Kingfisher beer; other brands here include Royal Challenge, Foster's, Dansberg, London Pilsner and Sandpiper. Served ice-cold, all are equally refreshing. But if you can find draught beer, such as Kingfisher and Golden Peacock, you will certainly notice the better taste over the bottled beer, which has glycerine added as a preservative.

Though the Indian wine industry is still in its infancy, there are strong signs that Indian wines are being accepted into local markets. Two of the best-known Indian wine producers are Sula and Fratelli, which create a whole slew of different varieties of grapes grown in northern Maharashtra. Meanwhile, Grover Vineyards, established in 1988 near Bengaluru (Bangalore), also has a solid reputation, with a smaller range of wines.

At the other end of the scale, *arak* is what the poor drink to get blotto, poignantly called *asha* (hope) in the north of India. The effects of this distilled rice liquor creep up on you quickly and without warning. Only ever drink this from a bottle produced in a government-controlled distillery. *Never* drink it otherwise – hundreds of people die or are blinded every year in India as a result of drinking *arak* produced in illicit stills.

Learn more about Sula Wines and its environmentally friendly sustainable agriculture programs at its website, www.sulawines.com.

Arts, Crafts & Architecture

If the Rajputs knew how to fight a battle, they also knew how to create an artistic legacy. Rajasthan's culture is a celebration of chivalry, hardship and beauty, manifested through its literature, poetry, music, dance, painting and architecture. The state also has a rich tradition of handicrafts, which are prized the world over, both for their intricate craftsmanship and ornamental appeal.

Arts

Dance

Ghungroos are anklets made of metallic bells strung together, worn by Indian classical dancers to accentuate their complex footwork during performances.

Folk dance forms in Rajasthan are generally associated with indigenous tribes and communities of nomadic gypsies. Each region has its own dance specialities. The *ghoomer* (pirouette) is performed by Bhil women at festivals or weddings and its form varies from one village to another. The Bhils are also known for *gair,* a men-only dance, that's performed at springtime festivities. Combine the two and you get *gair-ghoomer,* where women, in a small inner circle, are encompassed by men in a larger circle, who determine the rhythm by beating sticks and striking drums.

Among other popular forms, the *kachhi ghori* dance of eastern Rajasthan resembles a battle performance, where dancers ride cloth or paper horses and spar with swords and shields. To the south, the *neja* is danced by the Minas of Kherwara and Dungarpur just after Holi. A coconut is placed on a large pole, which the men try to dislodge, while the women strike the men with sticks and whips to foil their attempts. A nomadic community called the Kalbelias, traditionally associated with snake charming, performs swirling dances such as the *shankaria,* while the Siddha Jats of Bikaner are renowned for their spectacular fire dance, performed on a bed of hot coals, which supposedly leaves no burns.

Painting & Sculpture

Miniatures

Rajasthan is famed for its miniatures – small-scale paintings that are executed on small surfaces, but cram in a surprising amount of detail by way of delicate brushwork. Originating in the 16th and 17th centuries, they led to the emergence of eminent schools such as Marwar, Mewar, Bundi-Kota, Amber and Kishangarh, among others. Each school had its own stylistic identity; while paintings from the Mewar school depicted court life, festivals, ceremonies, elephant fights and hunts, those from the Marwar school featured vivid colours and heroic, whiskered men accompanied by dainty maidens. Miniatures gained immense value as souvenirs with the coming of the tourism boom.

Get arty with *Indian Art* by Roy Craven, *Contemporary Indian Art: Other Realities* edited by Yashodhara Dalmia and *Indian Miniature Painting* by Dr Daljeet and Professor PC Jain.

Phad

Rajasthan is renowned for a kind of scroll painting called *phad,* which is done on cloth and portrays deities, mythology and legends of Rajput

CINEMA IN INDIA

India has the world's biggest film industry. Films come in all languages, the majority pumped out by the Hindi tinsel town of Bollywood, in Mumbai (Bombay), and Kollywood, its Tamil counterpart, in Chennai (Madras). Most productions, however, are formulaic flicks that seize mass attention with hackneyed motifs – unrequited love, action that verges on caricature, slapstick humour, wet saris and plenty of sexual innuendo. Nonetheless, the past 10 years have seen upscale productions aimed at a burgeoning multiplex audience. Check out the cricket extravaganza *Lagaan,* the patriotic *Rang De Basanti* or Shakespearean adaptations such as *Maqbool* (Macbeth) and *Omkara* (Othello).

India also has a critically acclaimed art-house movement. Pioneered by the likes of Satyajit Ray, Adoor Gopalakrishnan, Ritwik Ghatak and Shyam Benegal, the tradition now boasts directors such as Mira Nair *(Salaam Bombay, Monsoon Wedding, The Namesake)* and Deepa Mehta *(Fire, Earth, Water).*

kings. *Phads* are used by nomadic Bhopas, who travel from village to village singing, dancing and performing and pointing to the scroll to assist the narrative. Bhilwara, near Udaipur, is one of the better-known centres for *phad* scrolls.

Frescoes

Fresco painting, originally developed in Italy, arrived in Rajasthan with the Mughals, and its finest examples can be seen in the exquisitely muralled *havelis* (traditional ornately decorated residences) of Shekhawati. The region's *havelis* form an open-air art gallery, with work in a kaleidoscope of colour and styles.

Crafts

Jewellery, Gems & Enamel Work

Two jewellery-making styles particularly prevalent in Rajasthan are *kundan* and *meenakari* work. *Kundan* involves setting gemstones into silver or gold pieces; one symbolic variation is known as *navratan,* in which nine different gems are set into an item of jewellery, corresponding to the nine planets of Indian astrology. This way, it's an eternally lucky item to have about your person, since you will always be wearing, at any given time, the symbol of the ruling planetary body.

Meenakari, meanwhile, is a gorgeous type of enamelwork, usually applied to a base of silver or gold. Jaipur's pieces of *meenakari* are valued for their vibrant tones, especially the highly prized rich ruby-red; a fantastic selection can be found on sale at the city's Johari Bazaar.

Leatherwork

Leatherworking has a long history in Rajasthan. Leather shoes known as jootis are produced in Jodhpur and Jaipur, often featuring *kashida* (ornate embroidery). Strange to Western eyes and feet, there is no 'right' or 'left': both shoes are identical but after a few wears they begin to conform to the wearer's feet. Jaipur is the best place to buy jootis; try the marvellous UN-supported Mojari (p124).

Textiles

Rajasthan is renowned for the blazing colour of its textiles. Riotously woven, dyed, block- or resist-printed and embroidered, they are on sale almost everywhere you look throughout the state.

During the Mughal period, embroidery workshops *(kaarkhanas)* were established to train artisans so that the royal families were ensured an

Intricate *bandhani* (tie-dye) often carries symbolic meanings when used to make *odhnis* (head-scarves). A yellow background indicates that the wearer has recently given birth, while red circles on that background means she's had a son.

PUPPETRY

Puppetry is one of Rajasthan's most acclaimed, yet endangered, performing arts. Puppeteers first emerged in the 19th century and would travel from village to village like wandering minstrels, relaying stories through narration, music and an animated performance that featured wooden puppets on strings called *kathputlis*. Puppetry is now a dying art; waning patronage and lack of paying audiences has forced many puppeteers to give up the art form and switch to agriculture or menial labour. Those that frequent tourist hotels in the evening usually have a 'day job' and are not paid by the hotel but, rather, hope for donations after the performance and maybe to sell a puppet or two. The colourful puppets have certainly retained their value as souvenirs.

abundant supply of richly embroidered cloth. Finely stitched tapestries, inspired by miniature paintings, were also executed for the royal courts.

Today, Bikaner specialises in embroidery with double stitching, which results in the pattern appearing on both sides of the cloth. In the Shekhawati district, the Jat people embroider motifs of animals and birds on their *odhnis* (headscarves) and *ghaghara* (long cotton skirts), while tiny mirrors are stitched into garments in Jaisalmer. Beautifully embroidered cloth is also produced for livestock and ornately bedecked camels are a common sight, especially at the Pushkar Camel Fair.

Carpets & Weaving

Carpet weaving took off in the 16th century under the patronage of the great Mughal emperor Akbar, who commissioned the establishment of various carpet-weaving factories, including one in Jaipur. In the 19th century, Maharaja Ram Singh II of Jaipur established a carpet factory at the Jaipur jail and soon other jails introduced carpet-making units. Some of the most beautiful *dhurries* (flat-woven rugs) were produced by prisoners and Bikaner jail is still well known for the excellence of its *dhurries*. Recent government training initiatives have seen the revival of this craft and fine-quality carpets are once again being produced across Rajasthan.

Pottery

Of all the arts of Rajasthan, pottery has the longest lineage, with fragments recovered in Kalibangan dating from the Harappan era (around 3000 BC). Before the beginning of the 1st millennium, potters in the environs of present-day Bikaner were already decorating red pottery with black designs.

Today, different regions of Rajasthan produce different types of pottery and most villages in Rajasthan have their own resident potter. The most famous of Rajasthan's pottery is the blue pottery of Jaipur. The blue-glazed work was first evident in tiling on Mughal palaces and cenotaphs and later applied to pottery.

The most famous marble quarries were located in Makrana, west of Jaipur, from where the marble used in the Taj Mahal and the Delwara temples was sourced.

Architecture

The magnificence of Delhi, Agra and Rajasthan's architectural heritage is astounding and the province is home to some of India's best-known buildings. From temples and mosques to mansions and mausoleums, the region has it all. Most spectacular, however, are the fairy-tale forts and palaces built by Rajputs and Mughals, which still bear testimony to the celebrated history of North India.

Temples

Rajasthan's earliest surviving temples date from the Gupta period. Built between the 4th and 6th century, these temples are small and their architecture restrained – the Sheetaleshvara Temple at Jhalrapatan is a notable example. Temple architecture (both Hindu and Jain) developed through the 8th and 9th centuries and began to incorporate stunning sculptural work, which can be seen on temples at Osian and Chittorgarh. Structurally, the temples usually tapered into a single *sikhara* (spire) and had a *mandapa* (pillared pavilion before the inner sanctum). The Delwara complex (p167) at Mt Abu epitomises the architecture of this era. Built in the 11th century, it has marble carvings that reach unsurpassed heights of virtuosity.

Forts & Palaces

The fabulous citadels of Rajasthan were built for a whole slew of reasons, ranging from protection from invading armies to the realisation of extravagant royal whims.

Most of Rajasthan's forts and palaces were built between the 15th and 18th centuries, which coincided with the Mughal reign in Delhi and saw the Rajputs borrowing a few architectural motifs from the Mughals, including the use of pillared arches and the *sheesh mahal* (hall of mirrors). Another ornamentation widely used across Rajasthan was the spired Bengal roof, shaped like an inverted boat. Magnificent examples of Rajput architecture across the state include the Amber Fort (p127), Jaipur's Hawa Mahal (p113) and the City Palace (p155) in Udaipur.

The most famous examples of Mughal architecture lie just beyond Rajasthan's borders in Delhi (p30), with its famous Red Fort and Jama Masjid, and Agra, home to the legendary Taj Mahal (p80).

Towards the end of the British era, a novel architectural style called the Indo-Saracenic school emerged in India, which blended Victorian and Islamic elements into a highly wrought, frilly whole. Some striking buildings were produced in this style, including Albert Hall in Jaipur and Lallgarh Palace in Bikaner.

The Kumbhalgarh Fort, a former Mewar stronghold in the Rajsamand district of Rajasthan, has the second-longest fortification in the world after the Great Wall of China.

Havelis

Rajasthani merchants built ornately decorated residences called *havelis* and commissioned masons and artists to ensure they were constructed and decorated in a manner befitting the owners' importance and prosperity. The Shekhawati district of northern Rajasthan is riddled with such mansions that are covered with extraordinarily vibrant murals. There are other beautiful *havelis* in Jaisalmer, constructed of sandstone, featuring the fine work of renowned local *silavats* (stone carvers).

Step-Wells & Chhatris

Given the importance of water in Rajasthan, it's unsurprising that the architecture of wells and reservoirs rivals other structures in the region. The most impressive regional *baoris* (step-wells) are Raniji-ki-Baori (p146) in Bundi and the extraordinary Chand Baori (p127) near Abhaneri.

Chhatris (cenotaphs) are a statewide architectural curiosity, built to commemorate maharajas, nobles and, as is the case in the Shekhawati district, wealthy merchants. In rare instances, *chhatris* also commemorate women, such as the Chhatri of Moosi Rani at Alwar. Literally translating to 'umbrella', a *chhatri* comprises a central dome, supported by a series of pillars on a raised platform, with a sequence of small pavilions on the corners and sides.

Wildlife & Landscapes

Rajasthan is the India of hot, dry plains. Dominated by desert and scrub, and punctuated by low hills, it's nevertheless home to a rich variety of flora and fauna. Some are easy to spot, such as the monkeys that remain ubiquitous even in the cities, while others require a little more tracking, like the tiger, king of India's cats, which persists in one or two of the region's national parks.

The Lie of the Land

The Thar Desert is the most densely populated desert in the world, with an average of over 60 people per square kilometre.

The rugged Aravalli Range splits Rajasthan like a bony spine, running from the northeast to the southwest. These irregular mountains form a boundary between the Thar Desert to the west and the relatively lusher vegetation to the east. With an average height of 600m, in places the range soars to over 1050m; the highest point, Guru Shikhar (1722m), is near Mt Abu. It's thought to be the oldest mountain range in the world. A second hilly spur, the Vindhya Range, splays around the southernmost regions of Rajasthan.

The state's sole perennial river is the wide, life-giving swell of the Chambal. Rising in Madhya Pradesh from the northern slopes of the Vindhyas, the river enters Rajasthan at Chaurasigarh and forms part of Rajasthan's eastern border with Madhya Pradesh. The south is drained by the Mahi and Sabarmati Rivers; the Luni, which rises about 7km north of Ajmer in the Aravalli, is the only river in western Rajasthan. Seasonal and comparatively shallow, the Luni sometimes billows out to over 2km wide.

The arid region in the west of the state is known as Marusthali or Marwar (the Land of Death), which gives some idea of the terrain. Sprawling from the Aravallis in the east to the Sulaiman Kirthar Range in the west is the Thar Desert, which covers almost three-quarters of the state. It's a dry, inhospitable expanse – the eastern extension of the great Saharo-Tharian Desert – forming 61% of the area covered by desert in India.

Low, rugged hills occasionally punctuate the parched plains. About 60% of the region is also made up of sand dunes, which are formed by the erosion of these low hills and from sand blown from Gujarat's vast desert, the Great Rann of Kutch.

It's hard to believe, but this desolate region was once covered by massive forests and populated by huge animals. In 1996 two amateur palaeontologists working in the Thar Desert discovered animal fossils, some 300 million years old, that included dinosaur fossils. At the Akal Wood Fossil Park, near Jaisalmer, you can visit the incredible remains of fossilised trees that are around 180 million years old. Plant fossils from 45 million years ago show that Rajasthan's metamorphosis into desert is relatively recent – and ongoing.

It's difficult to make out where the desert ends and becomes semiarid. The semiarid zone nestles between the Aravallis and the Thar Desert, extending west from the Aravallis and encompassing the Ghaggar River Plain, parts of Shekhawati and the Luni River Basin.

DESERT – JUST ADD WATER

It sounds too simple and it probably is. Irrigating India's vast arid lands has long been the dream of rulers and politicians. The Indira Gandhi Canal was initiated in 1957 and, though it is still incomplete, it includes an amazing 9709km of canals, with the main canal stretching 649km. Critics suggest that the massive project, connected with Bhakra Dam in Punjab, was concerned with short-term economics and politics to the detriment of the long-term ecology of the region.

The canal has opened up large tracts of the arid region for cash crops, but these tracts are managed by wealthy landowners rather than the rural poor. Environmentalists say that soil has been damaged through over-irrigation, and indigenous plants have suffered, adding to the degeneration of the arid zone. Furthermore, sections of the Indira Gandhi Canal are built on traditional grazing grounds, to which graziers are now denied access. The canal has also been blamed for breeding malaria-carrying mosquitoes.

In 2008, the waters from India's largest westward-flowing river, the Narmada, which were dammed in highly controversial circumstances, trickled into Rajasthan's drought-ravaged regions of Jalore and Barmer. The miraculous appearance of the water brought untold joy to the long-suffering villagers. However, the entire Narmada River project has been heavily criticised both on environmental grounds and for displacing a large number of tribal people in the Narmada Valley.

Delhi lies on the vast flatlands of the Indo-Gangetic Plain, though the northernmost pimples of the Aravallis amount to the Ridge, which lies west of the city centre. The Yamuna River flows southward along the eastern edge of the city. To the south, Agra lies on the banks of the Yamuna, in the neighbouring state of Uttar Pradesh.

Wild Rajasthan

For a place apparently so inhospitable, Rajasthan hosts an incredible array of animals and birds; the stars are the dwindling numbers of tigers now virtually restricted to Ranthambhore National Park and the magnificent migratory bird show of Keoladeo National Park.

Animals

Arid-zone mammals have adapted to the lack of water in various resourceful ways. For example, some top up their fluids with insects that are composed of between 65% and 80% water, and water-bearing plants, while others retain water for longer periods. Faced with the incredible heat, many creatures burrow in the sand or venture out only at night.

Antelopes & Gazelles

Blackbuck antelopes, with their amazing long spiralling horns, are most common around Jodhpur, where they are protected by local Bishnoi tribes. Bishnoi conservation has also helped the chinkaras (Indian gazelles); these delicate, small creatures are extremely fast and agile and are seen in small family herds.

Also notable is the extraordinary nilgai (or blue bull), which is the largest of the antelope family – only the males attain the blue colour. It's a large, muscular animal whose front legs appear longer than its rear legs, giving it a rather ungainly stance.

Big Cats

Tigers were once found along the length of the Aravallis. However, royal hunting parties, poachers and habitat destruction have decimated the population, and the only viable tiger population in Rajasthan can be found in Ranthambhore National Park (p143). Some of

The website of India's premier wildlife magazine, Sanctuary (www.sanctuaryasia.com), highlights the latest conservation issues and has numerous related links.

A Guide to the Wildlife Parks of Rajasthan, by Dr Suraj Ziddi, with photographs by Subhash Bhargava, is a comprehensive guide to Rajasthan's reserves.

Ranthambhore's tigers have been relocated to Sariska Tiger Reserve & National Park (p133) after its population was wiped out by poaching. According to a survey released in January 2015, the parks contained adult populations of approximately 56 and 14 tigers, respectively.

The mainly nocturnal and rarely seen leopard inhabits rocky declivities in the Aravallis and parts of the Jaipur and Jodhpur districts.

Dogs

Jackals are renowned for their unearthly howling. Once common throughout Rajasthan, they would lurk around villages where they scavenged and preyed on livestock. Habitat encroachment and hunting (for their skins) have reduced their numbers, though they are still a very common sight in Keoladeo, Ranthambhore and Sariska parks. The dhole, or Indian wild dog, has also seen its numbers dwindle due to habitat loss, and today sightings are extremely rare.

Wolves used to roam in large numbers in the desert, but farmers hunted them almost to the point of extinction. They have begun to reappear over recent decades, due to concerted conservation efforts. The wildlife sanctuary at Kumbhalgarh (p165) is known for its wolves.

The sandy-coloured desert fox is a subspecies of the red fox and was once prolific in the Thar Desert. As with wolves, the fox population has shrunk due to human endeavours. Keep your eyes open for them scavenging roadkill on the highway near Jaisalmer.

Monkeys

Monkeys seem to be everywhere in Rajasthan. There are two common types: the red-faced and red-rumped rhesus macaque and the shaggy grey, black-faced langur, with prominent eyebrows and long tail. Both

TOP NATIONAL PARKS & WILDLIFE SANCTUARIES

NAME	LOCATION	FEATURES	BEST TIME TO VISIT
Desert National Park	western Rajasthan	great Indian bustards, blackbuck, nilgai, wolves, desert foxes, crested porcupines	Sep–Mar
Keoladeo National Park	eastern Rajasthan	400 bird species, including migratory birds & waterbirds (wetlands)	Oct–Mar, Jul–Aug
Kumbhalgarh Wildlife Sanctuary	southern Rajasthan	wolves in packs of up to 40, chowsinghas (four-horned antelopes), leopards, horse riding	Oct–Jun
Mt Abu Wildlife Sanctuary	southern Rajasthan	forest, sloth bears, wild boar, sambars, leopards	Mar–Jun
Ranthambhore National Park	eastern Rajasthan	tigers, chitals, leopards, nilgai, chinkaras, bird life, ancient fort	Oct–Apr
Sariska Tiger Reserve	eastern Rajasthan	leopards, chitals, chinkaras, bird life, fort, deserted city, temples	Nov–Jun
Tal Chhapar Wildlife Sanctuary	northern Rajasthan	blackbuck, chinkaras, desert foxes, antelopes, harriers, eagles, sparrowhawks	Sep–Mar

GOING, GOING, GONE...

Some of Rajasthan's endangered wildlife is disappearing due to ongoing encroachment on its habitat, but poaching is also a serious problem.

From numbers in excess of 40,000 in the early 20th century, wild tigers in India had crashed as low as 1400 by 2010, although a new survey using camera traps and other techniques estimated that the population had rebounded to 2226 in 2014. Subsequent figures have been extrapolations of this figure and highly contentious. Of this total, Rajasthan's tiger parks – Ranthambhore and Sariska – are thought to hold about 70 adult tigers. Both have been badly hit by poaching in recent decades and Sariska's tigers had to be reintroduced after becoming locally extinct in 2010.

Numbers of the great Indian bustard have also dwindled alarmingly due to hunting and because the bird's eggs are trampled by livestock. However, in Rajasthan, where the bird is the emblem of the state, there is no program for conservation and this has led to calls for a national program similar to Project Tiger to protect this majestic bird.

Three types of vulture have become endangered in recent years. Once common, they joined the endangered ranks after the population in south Asia fell by 95%. The cause was exposure to a veterinary drug, which the vultures absorbed while feeding from livestock carcasses. The reduction in numbers has had knock-on ecological and health effects, as the birds once disposed of many carcasses, thus reducing risks of disease.

types are keen on hanging around human settlements, where they can get easy pickings. Both will steal food from your grasp at temples, but the macaque is probably the more aggressive and the one to be particularly wary of.

Bears

In forested regions you might see a sloth bear – a large creature covered in long black hair with a prominent white V on its chest and a peculiar muzzle with an overhanging upper lip. That lip helps it feed on ants and termites dug out with those dangerous-looking claws on its front paws. Sloth bears feed mostly on vegetation and insects but aren't averse to a bit of carrion. The bears are reasonably common around Mt Abu and elsewhere on the western slopes of the Aravalli Range.

Birds

Keoladeo National Park (p129), a wetland in eastern Rajasthan, is internationally renowned for birdwatching. Resident and winter migrants put on an amazing feathery show. Migratory species include several varieties of storks, spoonbills, herons, cormorants, ibis and egrets. Wintering waterfowl include the common, marbled, falcated and Baikal teal; pintail, gadwall, shoveler, coot, wigeon, bar-headed and greylag geese; common and brahminy pochards; and the beautiful demoiselle crane. Waders include snipe, sandpipers and plovers. Species resident throughout the year include the monogamous sarus crane, moorhens, egrets, herons, storks and cormorants. Birds of prey include many types of eagles (greater spotted, steppe, imperial, Spanish imperial and fishing), vultures (white-backed and scavenger), owls (spotted, dusky horned and mottled wood), marsh harriers, sparrowhawks, kestrels and goshawks.

The remaining forests and jungles that cling to the rugged Aravalli Ranges harbour orioles, hornbills, kingfishers, swallows, parakeets, warblers, mynahs, robins, flycatchers, quails, doves, peacocks, barbets, bee-eaters, woodpeckers and drongos, among others. Birds of prey include numerous species of owls (great horned, dusky, brown fishing and collared scops, and spotted owlets), eagles (spotted and tawny), white-eyed buzzards, black-winged kites and shikras.

If you want to put names to feathers on your travels, pick up a copy of *Birds of Northern India* by Richard Grimmett and Tim Inskipp.

Common birds of the open grasslands include various species of lark. Quails can also be seen, as can several types of shrike, mynahs, drongos and partridges. Migratory birds include the lesser florican, seen during the monsoon, and the Houbara bustard, which winters at the grasslands. Birds of prey include falcons, eagles, hawks, kites, kestrels and harriers.

The Thar Desert also has a prolific variety of bird life. At the small village of Kheechan, about 135km from Jodhpur, you can see vast flocks of demoiselle cranes descending on fields from the end of August to the end of March. Other winter visitors to the desert include Houbara bustards and common cranes. As water is scarce, waterholes attract large flocks of imperial, spotted, pintail and Indian sandgrouse in the early mornings. More desert dwellers include drongos, common and bush quail, blue-tailed and little green bee-eaters and grey partridges. Desert birds of prey include eagles (steppe and tawny), buzzards (honey and long-legged), goshawks, peregrine falcons and kestrels. The most notable of the desert and dry grassland dwellers is the impressive Indian bustard.

Survival Guide

SCAMS 242

WOMEN & SOLO
TRAVELLERS 244

DIRECTORY A–Z . . . 246
Accommodation 246
Customs
Regulations 247
Electricity 248
Embassies &
Consulates 248
Food & Drink 248
GLBTI Travellers 249
Insurance 249
Internet Access 249
Legal Matters 250
Maps 250
Money 250
Opening Hours 251
Photography 251
Post 252
Public Holidays 253
Safe Travel 253
Telephone 253
Time 254
Toilets 254

Tourist
Information 254
Travellers with
Disabilities 254
Visas 255
Volunteering 256

TRANSPORT 257
GETTING THERE &
AWAY 257
Entering the Country 257
Air 257
Land 258
GETTING AROUND 258
Air 258
Bicycle 258
Bus 259
Car 259
Motorcycle 260
Local Transport 262
Train 262

HEALTH 266

LANGUAGE 273
GLOSSARY 278

Scams

India has an unfortunately deserved reputation for scams, both classic and new-fangled. Of course, most can be avoided with some common sense and an appropriate amount of caution. They tend to be more of a problem in the big cities of arrival (such as Delhi or Mumbai), or very touristy spots (such as Rajasthan), though in Goa and Kerala they are relatively rare. Chat with fellow travellers to keep abreast of the latest cons. Look at the India branch of Lonely Planet's Thorn Tree Travel Forum (www.lonelyplanet.com/thorntree), where travellers often post timely warnings about problems they've encountered on the road. Be aware there have been several cases where scammers who can speak the language target Japanese tourists.

Contaminated Food & Drink

➡ The late 1990s saw a scam in North India where travellers died after consuming food laced with dangerous bacteria from restaurants linked to dodgy medical clinics; we've heard no recent reports but the scam could resurface. In unrelated incidents, some clinics have also given more treatment than necessary to procure larger payments from insurance companies.

➡ Most bottled water is legit, but ensure the seal is intact and the bottom of the bottle hasn't been tampered with. While in transit, try and carry packed food if possible. If you eat at bus or train stations, follow the crowd and buy food only from fast-moving places

Credit-Card Con

Be careful when paying for souvenirs with a credit card. While government shops are usually legitimate, private souvenir shops have been known to surreptitiously run off extra copies of the credit-card imprint slip and use them for phoney transactions later. Ask the trader to process the transaction in front of you. Memorising the CVV/CVC2 number and scratching it off the card is also a good idea, to avoid misuse. In some restaurants, waiters will ask you for your PIN with the intention of taking your credit card to the machine – never give your PIN to anyone, and ask to use the machine in person.

Druggings

Occasionally, tourists (especially those travelling solo) have been drugged and robbed or apparently attacked. A spiked drink is the most commonly used method for sending them off to sleep – chocolates, chai from a co-conspiring vendor, 'homemade' Indian food and even bottled water are also known to be used.

Gem Scams

Smooth-talking con artists who promise foolproof 'get rich quick' schemes can be incredibly convincing, so watch

---

KEEPING SAFE

➡ A good travel-insurance policy is essential.

➡ Email copies of your passport identity page, visa and airline tickets to yourself, and keep copies on you.

➡ Keep your money and passport in a concealed money belt or a secure place under your shirt.

➡ Store at least US$100 separately from your main stash.

➡ Don't publicly display large wads of cash when paying for services or checking into hotels.

➡ Consider using your own padlock at cheaper hotels.

➡ If you can't lock your hotel room securely from the inside, stay somewhere else.

out. In this scam, travellers are asked to carry or mail gems home and then sell them to the trader's (nonexistent) overseas representatives at a profit. Without exception, the goods – if they arrive at all – are worth a fraction of what you paid, and the 'representatives' never materialise.

Don't believe hard-luck stories about an inability to obtain an export licence, and don't believe the testimonials they show you from other travellers – they are all fake. Travellers have reported this con happening in Agra, Delhi, and Jaisalmer among other places, but it's particularly prevalent in Jaipur. Carpets, curios and *pashmina* woollens are other favourites for this con.

OTHER TOP SCAMS

➺ Gunk (dirt, paint, poo) suddenly appears on your shoes, only for a shoe cleaner to magically appear and offer to clean it off – for a price.

➺ Some shops are selling overpriced SIM cards and not activating them; it's best to buy your SIM from an official shop and check it works before leaving the area where you bought it (activation can take up to 24 hours).

➺ Shops, restaurants or tour guides 'borrow' the name of their more successful and popular competitor.

➺ Touts claim to be 'government-approved' guides or agents, and sting you for large sums of cash. Enquire at the local tourist office about licensed guides and ask to see identification from guides themselves.

➺ Artificial 'tourist offices' that are actually dodgy travel agencies whose aim is to sell you overpriced tours, tickets and tourist services.

Overpricing

Always agree on prices beforehand while availing services that don't have regulated tariffs. This particularly applies to friendly neighbourhood guides, snack bars at places of touristy interest, and autorickshaws and taxis without meters.

Photography

Use your instincts (better still, ask for permission) while photographing people. If you don't have permission, you may be asked to pay a fee.

Theft

➺ Theft is a risk in India, as anywhere else. Keep luggage locked and chained on buses and trains. Remember that snatchings often occur when a train is pulling out of the station, as it's too late for you to give chase.

➺ Take extra care in dormitories and never leave your valuables unattended.

➺ Remember to lock your door at night; it is not unknown for thieves to take things from hotel rooms while occupants are sleeping.

Touts & Commission Agents

➺ Cabbies and autorickshaw drivers will often try to coerce you to stay at a hotel of their choice, only to collect a commission (included within your room tariff) afterward.

➺ Wherever possible, prearrange hotel bookings (if only for the first night), and request a hotel pick-up. You'll often hear stories about hotels of your choice being 'full' or 'closed' – check things out yourself. Reconfirm and double-check your booking the day before you arrive.

➺ Be very sceptical of phrases like 'my brother's shop' and 'special deal at my friend's place'. Many fraudsters operate in collusion with souvenir stalls.

➺ Avoid friendly people and 'officials' in train and bus stations who offer unsolicited help, then guide you to a commission-paying travel agent. Look confident, and if anyone asks if this is your first trip to India, say you've been here several times. Telling touts that you have already prepaid your transfer/tour/onward journey may help dissuade them.

Transport Scams

➺ Upon arriving at train stations and airports, if you haven't prearranged a pick-up, call an Uber or go to the radio cab, prepaid taxi and airport shuttle bus counters. Never choose a loitering cabbie who offers you a cheap ride into town, especially at night.

➺ While booking multiday sightseeing tours, research your own itinerary, and be extremely wary of anyone in Delhi offering houseboat tours to Kashmir – we've received many complaints over the years about dodgy deals.

➺ When buying a bus, train or plane ticket anywhere other than the registered office of the transport company, make sure you're getting the ticket class you paid for. Use official online booking facilities where possible.

➺ Train station touts (even in uniform or with 'official' badges) may tell you that your intended train is cancelled/flooded/broken down or that your ticket is invalid or that you must pay to have your e-ticket validated on the platform. Do not respond to any approaches at train stations.

Women & Solo Travellers

Women Travellers

Reports of sexual assaults against women and girls are on the increase in India, despite tougher punishments being established following the notorious gang rape and murder of a local woman in 2012. There have been several instances of sexual attacks on tourists over the last few years, though it's worth bearing in mind that the vast majority of visits are trouble free.

Unwanted Attention

Unwanted attention from men is a common problem.

➡ Be prepared to be stared at; it's something you'll simply have to live with, so don't allow it to get the better of you.

➡ Refrain from returning male stares; this will be considered encouragement.

➡ Dark glasses, phones, books or electronic tablets are useful props for averting unwanted conversations.

➡ Wearing a wedding ring and saying you're married, and due to meet your husband shortly, is another way to ward off unwanted interest.

Clothing

Although in upper/middle-class Delhi, Mumbai and Chennai, you'll see local women dressing as they might in New York or London, elsewhere women are dressed traditionally. For travellers, culturally appropri-ate clothing will help reduce undesirable attention.

➡ Steer clear of sleeveless tops, shorts, short skirts (ankle-length skirts are recommended) and anything else that's skimpy, see-through, tight-fitting, or reveals too much skin.

➡ Wearing Indian-style clothes is viewed favourably.

➡ Draping a dupatta (long scarf) over T-shirts is another good way to avoid stares – it's also handy if you visit a shrine that requires your head to be covered.

➡ Wearing a salwar kameez (traditional dresslike tunic and trousers) will help you blend in; a smart alternative is a kurta (long shirt) worn over jeans or trousers.

➡ Avoid going out in public wearing a choli (sari blouse) or a sari petticoat (which some foreign women mistake for a skirt); it's like being half-dressed.

➡ Aside from at pools, many Indian women wear long shorts and a T-shirt when swimming in public view; it's wise to wear a sarong from the beach to your hotel.

Sexual Harassment

Many female travellers have reported sexual harassment while in India, most commonly lewd comments and groping.

➡ Women travellers have experienced provocative gestures, jeering, getting 'accidentally' bumped into on the street and being followed.

➡ Incidents are particularly common at exuberant (and crowded) public events such as the Holi festival. If a crowd is gathering, make yourself scarce or find a safer place overlooking the event so that you're away from wandering hands.

➡ Women travelling with a male partner will receive less hassle.

Staying Safe

The following tips will help you avoid uncomfortable or dangerous situations during your journey:

➡ Always be aware of your surroundings. If it feels wrong, trust your instincts. Tread with care. Don't be scared, but don't be reckless either.

➡ Keep conversations with unknown men short – getting involved in an inane conversation with someone you barely know can be misinterpreted.

➡ If you feel that a guy is encroaching on your space, he probably is. A firm request to keep away may well do the trick, especially if your tone is loud and curt enough to draw the attention of passers-by. The silent treatment can also be effective.

➡ Follow local women's cues and instead of shaking hands say namaste – the traditional, respectful Hindu greeting.

➡ Avoid wearing expensive-looking jewellery and carrying flashy accessories.

➡ Female filmgoers will lessen the chances of harassment by going to the cinema with a companion.

➡ At hotels, keep your door locked, as staff (particularly at budget and midrange places) could knock and walk in without waiting for your permission.

➡ Don't let anyone you don't know or have just met into your hotel room, even if they work for the tourist company with whom you're travelling and claim it's to discuss an aspect of your trip.

➡ Avoid wandering alone in isolated areas, even during daylight. Steer clear of *gallis* (narrow lanes), deserted roads, beaches and ruins.

➡ Act confidently in public; to avoid looking lost (and thus more vulnerable) consult maps at your hotel (or at a restaurant) rather than on the street.

Taxis & Public Transport

Being female has some advantages; women can usually queue-jump for buses and trains without consequence and on trains there are special ladies-only carriages. There are also women-only waiting rooms at some stations.

➡ Prearrange an airport pick-up from your hotel. This is essential if your flight is scheduled to arrive after dark.

➡ Avoid taking taxis alone late at night and never agree to have more than one man (the driver) in the car – ignore claims that this is 'just my brother' etc.

➡ Delhi and some other cities have licensed prepaid radio cab services such as Easycabs – they're more expensive than the regular prepaid taxis, but promote themselves as being safe, with drivers who have been vetted as part of their recruitment.

➡ Uber and Ola Taxis are also useful, as the rates are fixed and you get the driver's license plate in advance so you can check it's definitely the right taxi and pass details on to someone else if you want to be on the safe side.

➡ When taking rickshaws alone, pretend to call/text someone to indicate someone knows where you are.

➡ Don't organise your travel in such a way that means you're hanging out at bus/train stations or arriving late at night, or even after dark.

➡ Solo women have reported less hassle by opting for the more expensive classes on trains.

➡ If you're travelling overnight by train, the best option is the upper outer berth in 2AC; you're out of the way of wandering hands, but surrounded by plenty of other people and not locked in a four-person 1AC room (which might only have one other person in it).

➡ On public transport, don't hesitate to return any errant limbs, put an item of luggage between you and others, be vocal (attracting public attention), or simply find a new spot.

Health & Hygiene

➡ Sanitary pads are widely available but tampons are usually restricted to pharmacies.

Websites

Peruse personal experiences proffered by fellow female travellers at www.journeywoman.com and www.wanderlustandlipstick.com. Blogs such as Breathe, Dream, Go (breathedreamgo.com) and Hippie in Heels (hippie-inheels.com) are also full of tips.

Solo Travellers

Travelling solo in India may be great, because local people are often so friendly,

helpful and interested. You're more likely to be 'adopted' by families, especially if you're commuting together on a long rail journey. It's a great opportunity to make friends and get a deeper understanding of local culture. If you're keen to hook up with fellow travellers, tourist hubs such as Delhi, Goa, Rajasthan, Kerala, Manali, McLeod Ganj, Leh, Agra and Varanasi are some popular places to do so. You may also be able to find travel companions on Lonely Planet's Thorn Tree Travel Forum (www.lonelyplanet.com/thorntree).

Cost

The most significant issue facing solo travellers is cost.

➡ Single-room accommodation rates are sometimes not much lower than double rates.

➡ Some midrange and top-end places don't even offer a single tariff.

➡ It's always worth trying to negotiate a lower rate for single occupancy.

Safety

Most solo travellers experience no major problems in India but, like anywhere else, it's wise to stay on your toes in unfamiliar surroundings.

➡ Some less honourable souls (locals and travellers alike) view lone tourists as an easy target for theft and sexual assault.

➡ Single men wandering around isolated areas have been mugged, even during the day.

Transport

➡ You'll save money if you find others to share taxis and autorickshaws, as well as when hiring a car for longer trips.

➡ Solo bus travellers may be able to get the 'co-pilot' (near the driver) seat on buses, which not only has a good view out front, but also handy if you've got a big bag.

Directory A–Z

Accommodation

Accommodation ranges from grungy backpacker hostels with concrete floors and cold 'bucket' showers to opulent palaces fit for a maharaja.

Categories

As a general rule, budget covers everything from basic hostels and railway retiring rooms to simple guest-houses in traditional village homes.

Midrange hotels tend to be modern-style concrete blocks that usually offer extras such as cable/satellite TV and air-conditioning.

Top-end places stretch from gorgeous heritage ho-tels to luxury five-star inter-national chains.

Reservations

➡ It's a good idea to book ahead, online or by phone, especially when travelling to more popular destinations. Some hotels require a credit-card deposit at the time of booking.

➡ Some budget options won't take reservations as

they don't know when people are going to check out. Call ahead to check.

➡ Other places may ask for a deposit at check-in – ask for a receipt and be wary of any request to sign a blank impression of your credit card. If the hotel insists, pay cash and get a receipt.

➡ Verify the check-out time when you check in – some hotels have a fixed check-out time, while others give you 24-hour check-out.

Seasons

➡ Rates are full price in high season, which coincides with the best weather (October to mid-February). In areas popular with tourists there are additional peak periods over Diwali, Christmas and New Year – make reservations well in advance. At other times, you may find significant discounts; if the hotel seems quiet, ask for a discount.

➡ Many temple towns (such as Pushkar) have additional peak seasons around major festivals and pilgrimages.

Taxes & Service Charges

➡ At midrange and top-end accommodation, you usually have to pay an 8% or 10% 'luxury' tax on rooms over ₹3000, plus 14.5% to 20% on food and beverages in hotels that attract the luxury tax on their rooms.

➡ Luxury tax does not apply in the off season (May to July).

➡ Many midrange and upmarket hotels also add a 'service charge' (usually 6% to 10%).

➡ Rates quoted include taxes unless noted.

➡ Note that India's new Goods & Service Tax (GST), due to come into force in 2017, may affect accommodation taxes and charges across the country.

Accommodation Types

BUDGET & MIDRANGE HOTELS

➡ Room quality can vary considerably within hotels, so try to inspect a few rooms first.

➡ Shared bathrooms (often with squat toilets) are usually only found at the cheapest lodgings.

➡ Most rooms have ceiling fans and better rooms have electric mosquito-killers and/or window nets, though cheaper rooms may lack windows altogether.

BOOK YOUR STAY ONLINE

For more accommodation reviews by Lonely Planet authors, check out http://lonelyplanet.com/hotels/. You'll find independent reviews, as well as recommen-dations on the best places to stay. Best of all, you can book online.

SLEEPING PRICE RANGES

Accommodation prices refer to a double room with bathroom and are inclusive of taxes, unless otherwise noted:

$ below ₹1500

$$ ₹1500 to ₹5000

$$$ above ₹5000

➡ If staying at the very cheapest of hotels, bring your own sheet or sleeping-bag liner along with a towel.

➡ Traffic noise can be irksome; pack good-quality earplugs and request a room that doesn't face a busy road.

➡ It's wise to keep your door locked, as some staff (particularly in budget accommodation) may knock and walk in without first seeking your permission.

➡ Note that some hotels lock their doors at night. Members of staff may sleep in the lobby but waking them up can be a challenge. Let the hotel know in advance if you'll be arriving or returning to your room late in the evening.

➡ Away from tourist areas, cheaper hotels may not take foreigners because they don't have the necessary foreigner-registration forms.

DORMITORY ACCOMMODATION

A number of hotels have cheap dormitories, though these may be mixed and, in less touristy places, full of drunken drivers – not ideal conditions for women. More traveller-friendly dorms are found at the handful of hostels run by the YMCA, YWCA, Salvation Army and HI-associated hostels. There are a few small private chains slowly developing well-thought-out backpacker dorms and rooms.

PAYING GUEST HOUSE SCHEME (HOMESTAYS)

Rajasthan pioneered the Paying Guest House Scheme, so it's well developed in the state. Prices range from budget to upper midrange – contact the local Rajasthan Tourism Development Corporation (RTDC) tourist reception centres for details.

RAILWAY RETIRING ROOMS

Most large train stations have basic rooms for travellers holding an ongoing train ticket or Indrail Pass. Some are grim, others are surprisingly pleasant, but all are noisy from the sound of trains and passengers. Nevertheless, they're useful for early-morning train departures and there's usually a choice of dormitories or private rooms (24-hour check-out).

PALACES, FORTS & HAVELIS

Rajasthan is famous for its wonderful heritage hotels created from palaces, forts and *havelis* (traditional, ornately decorated residences). There are hundreds and it often doesn't cost a fortune to stay in one: some are the height of luxury and priced accordingly, but many are simpler, packed with character and set in stunning locations.

TOP-END HOTELS

As a major tourist destination, Rajasthan has a bevy of top-end hotels. If you're staying at a top-end hotel, it's often cheaper to book it online. Nevertheless, unless the hotel is busy, you can nearly always score a discount from the rack rates.

Customs Regulations

➡ You are supposed to declare any amount of cash over US$5000 or total amount of currency over US$10,000 on arrival. Indian rupees shouldn't be taken out of India.

➡ Officials very occasionally ask tourists to enter expensive items such as video cameras and laptop computers on a 'Tourist Baggage Re-export' form to ensure they're taken out of India at the time of departure.

➡ Exporting antiques (defined as objects of historical interest not less than 100 years old) from

PRACTICALITIES

Newspapers & Magazines Major English-language dailies include the *Hindustan Times, Times of India, Indian Express, Hindu, Statesman, Telegraph, Daily News & Analysis (DNA)* and *Economic Times*. Current-affairs magazines include *Frontline, India Today,* the *Week, Tehelka* and *Outlook.*

Radio Government-controlled All India Radio (AIR) is India's national broadcaster with more than 220 stations broadcasting local and international news. There are also private FM channels broadcasting music, current affairs, talkback and more.

TV & Video The national (government) TV broadcaster is Doordarshan. Most people watch satellite and cable TV; English-language channels include BBC, CNN, Star World, HBO and Discovery.

Weights & Measures Officially India is metric. Terms you're likely to hear are: lakhs (one lakh = 100,000) and crores (one crore = 10 million).

India is explicitly prohibited. Reputable antique dealers know the laws and can make arrangements for an export-clearance certificate for old items that are OK to export, but it's best to look for quality reproductions instead.

Electricity

230V/50Hz. Plugs have two round pins.

Type C
230V/50Hz

Type D
230V/50Hz

Embassies & Consulates

Many foreign diplomatic missions have certain timings for visa applications (usually mornings), so phone for details.

The following consulates are all based in Delhi.

Australian (☏011-41399900; www.india.highcommission.gov.au; 1/50G Shantipath, Chanakyapuri; Ⓜ Racecourse)

Bangladeshi (☏011-24121394; www.bdhcdelhi.org; EP39 Dr Radakrishnan Marg, Chanakyapuri; Ⓜ Chanakyapuri)

Bhutanese (☏011-26889230; www.bhutan.gov.bt; Chandragupta Marg, Chanakyapuri; Ⓜ Chanakyapuri)

Canadian (☏011-41782000; www.canadainternational.gc.ca/india-inde; 7/8 Shantipath, Chanakyapuri; ☺ consular services 9am-noon Mon-Fri)

Chinese (☏011-26112345; http://in.china-embassy.org; 50-D Shantipath, Chanakyapuri; Ⓜ Chanakyapuri)

French (☏011-24196100; www.ambafrance-in.org; 2/50E Shantipath, Chanakyapuri; Ⓜ Chanakyapuri)

German (☏011-44199199; www.new-delhi.diplo.de; 6/50G Shantipath, Chanakyapuri; Ⓜ Chanakyapuri)

Irish (☏011-24940 3200; www.dfa.ie/irish-embassy/india; C17 Malcha Marg, Chanakyapuri; Ⓜ Chanakyapuri)

Israeli (☏011-30414500; www.embassies.gov.il/delhi; 3 Dr APJ Abdul Kalam Rd; ☺9.30am-1pm Mon-Fri)

Japanese (☏011-26876581; www.in.emb-japan.go.jp; 50G Shantipath, Chanakyapuri; ☺9am-1pm & 2-5.30pm Mon-Fri)

Malaysian (☏011-24159300; www.kln.gov.my/web/ind_new-delhi/home; 50M Satya Marg, Chanakyapuri; ☺8.30am-4.30pm Mon-Fri)

Maldivian (☏011-41435701; www.maldiveshigh com.in; B2 Anand Niketan)

Myanmar (☏011-24678822; www.myanmedelhi.com; 3/50F Nyaya Marg; ☺9.30am-4.30pm Mon-Fri)

Nepali (☏011-23476200; www.nepalembassy.in; Mandi House, Barakhamba Rd; ☺9am-1pm & 2-5pm)

Netherlands (☏011-2419 7600; www.netherlandsworldwide.nl/countries/india; 6/50F Shantipath, Chanakyapuri; ☺9am-5pm Mon-Fri)

New Zealand (☏011-46883170; www.nzembassy.com/india; Sir Edmund Hillary Marg, Chanakyapuri; ☺8.30am-5pm Mon-Fri)

Pakistan (☏011-26110601; pakhcnewdelhi.org.pk; 2/50G Shantipath, Chanakyapuri; ☺9-11am Mon-Fri)

Singaporean (☏011-46000915; www.mfa.gov.sg/newdelhi; E6 Chandragupta Marg, Chanakyapuri; ☺9am-1pm & 1.30-5pm Mon-Fri)

Sri Lankan (☏011-23010201; 27 Kautilya Marg, Chanakyapuri; ☺8.45am-5pm Mon-Fri)

Thai (☏011-49774100; http://newdelhi.thaiembassy.org; D-1/3 Vasant Vihar; ☺9am-5pm Mon-Fri)

UK (☏011-24192100; Shantipath; Ⓜ Racecourse)

US (☏011-24198000; http://newdelhi.usembassy.gov; Shantipath)

Food & Drink

See the Rajasthani Food chapter (p227) for details on this region's cuisine.

Taxes & Service Charges

Most upscale or midrange restaurants add a service charge (around 10%) on meals. They also add a service tax of around 13% on 40% of your bill (the 'service' part), plus VAT, which can be 5% to 20% depending on the state. Menu prices in Lonely Planet listings do not include

DIRECTORY A–Z GLBTI TRAVELLERS

**EATING
PRICE RANGES**

Prices reflect the cost of a standard main meal (unless otherwise indicated). Reviews are listed by writer preference within the following price categories:

$ below ₹150

$$ ₹150 to ₹300

$$$ above ₹300

taxes. Note that India's new Goods & Service Tax (GST), due to come into force in 2017, may affect restaurant taxes and charges across the country.

GLBTI Travellers

Homosexuality was made illegal in India in 2013, having only been decriminalised since 2009. Trans rights have fared better: in 2014, there was a ruling that gave legal recognition of a third gender in India, a step towards increased acceptance of the large yet marginalised transgender (*hijra*) population. LGBT visitors should be discreet in this conservative country. Public displays of affection are frowned upon for both homosexual and heterosexual couples.

Despite the ban, there are are low-key gay scenes in many larger cities, including Delhi and Mumbai.

Gay Delhi (www.gaydelhi.org) LGBT support group, organising social events in Delhi.

Gaysi Zine (http://gaysifamily.com) A thoughtful monthly magazine and website featuring gay writing and issues.

Indian Dost (www.indiandost.com/gay.php) News and information including contact groups in India.

Indja Pink (www.indjapink.co.in) India's first 'gay travel boutique', founded by a well-known Indian fashion designer.

Queer Ink (www.queer-ink.com) Online bookstore specialising in gay- and lesbian-interest books from the subcontinent.

Insurance

➺ Comprehensive travel insurance to cover theft, loss and medical problems (as well as air evacuation) is strongly recommended.

➺ Some policies specifically exclude potentially dangerous activities such as scuba diving, skiing, motorcycling, paragliding and trekking – read the fine print.

➺ If you plan to hire a motorcycle in India make sure the rental policy includes at least third-party insurance.

➺ Check in advance if your insurance policy will pay doctors and hospitals directly or reimburse you later for overseas health expenditures (keep all documentation for your claim).

➺ It's crucial to get a police report in India if you've had anything stolen; insurance companies may refuse to reimburse you without one.

➺ Worldwide travel insurance is available at www.lonelyplanet.com/travel-insurance. You can buy, extend and claim online anytime – even if you're already on the road.

Internet Access

Internet cafes are becoming less common as wi-fi and 3G and 4G phone services increase. Wi-fi access is widely available in hotels and it's usually free.

Laptops

➺ The simplest way to connect to the internet when away from a wi-fi connection is to use your smartphone as a personal wi-fi hotspot (use a local SIM to avoid roaming charges).

➺ Alternatively, companies that offer prepaid wireless 3G/4G modem sticks (dongles) include Reliance, Airtel, Tata Docomo, MTS and Vodafone. To connect, you have to submit your proof of identity and address in India (get a letter from your hotel) and often provide a passport photo. A local phone number is also essential to receive the modem activation code – the whole thing can take up to 24 hours. Costs are around ₹2000, which includes around 10GB of data (20GB recharges cost around ₹2000).

➺ Make sure the areas you're travelling to are covered by your service provider.

➺ Consider purchasing a fuse-protected universal AC adaptor to protect your device from power surges.

➺ Plug adaptors are widely available throughout India, but bring spare plug fuses from home.

Internet Cafes

➺ Internet charges vary regionally, falling anywhere between ₹15 and ₹80 per hour and often with a 15- to 30-minute minimum.

➺ Bandwidth load tends to be lowest in the early morning and early afternoon.

➺ Some internet cafes may ask to see your passport.

SECURITY

➺ Be wary of sending sensitive financial information from internet cafes; some places can use keystroke-capturing technology to access passwords and emails.

➺ Avoid sending credit-card details or other personal data over a wireless connection; using online banking on any nonsecure system is generally unwise.

Legal Matters

If you're in a sticky legal situation, contact your embassy as soon as possible. However, be aware that all your embassy may be able to do is monitor your treatment in custody and arrange a lawyer. In the Indian justice system, the burden of proof can often be on the accused and stints in prison before trial are not unheard of. Travellers should note that they can be prosecuted under the law of their home country regarding age of consent, even when abroad.

Antisocial Behaviour

Smoking in public places is illegal, but this is rarely enforced; if caught, you'll be fined ₹200, which could rise to ₹1000 if proposed changes go ahead. People can smoke inside their homes and in most open spaces such as streets (heed any signs stating otherwise). The status of e-cigarettes is in flux, but there are currently bans in several states and this could be expanded at any time.

A number of Indian cities have banned spitting and littering, but, as is obvious to everyone, this is hardly enforced.

Drugs

➡ Indian law doesn't distinguish between 'hard' and 'soft' drugs; possession of any illegal drug is regarded as a criminal offence, which will result in a custodial sentence.

➡ Sentences may be up to a year for possession of a small amount for personal use, to a minimum of 10 years if it's deemed the purpose was for sale or distribution.

➡ Cases can take months, even several years, to appear before a court while the accused may have to wait in prison. There's also usually a hefty monetary fine on top of any custodial sentence.

➡ Be aware that travellers have been targeted in sting operations in some backpacker enclaves.

➡ Marijuana grows wild in various parts of India, but consuming it is still an offence, except in towns where bhang is legally sold for religious rituals.

➡ Police are getting particularly tough on foreigners who use drugs, so you should take this risk very seriously.

Police

➡ You should always carry your passport; police are entitled to ask you for identification at any time.

➡ If you're arrested for an alleged offence and asked for a bribe, note: it is illegal to pay a bribe in India. Many people deal with an on-the-spot fine by just paying it to avoid trumped-up charges.

➡ Corruption is rife, so the less you have to do with local police the better; avoid potentially risky situations.

Maps

Maps available inside India are of variable quality. Throughout Rajasthan, most state government tourist offices stock basic local maps. The following maps are available at good bookshops:

Eicher (www.eicherworld.com) Road, state and city maps.

Nelles (www.nelles-verlag.de) Western India.

Survey of India (www.survey-ofindia.gov.in) City, state and country maps but some titles are restricted for security reasons.

Money

The Indian rupee (₹) is divided into 100 paise, but paise coins are rare. Coins come in denominations of ₹1, ₹2, ₹5 and ₹10; notes come in ₹5, ₹10, ₹20, ₹50, ₹100, ₹500 and ₹2000. The Indian rupee is linked to a basket of currencies and has been subject to fluctuations in recent years.

In 2016, the government demonetised ₹1000 and ₹500 notes; these have now been superseded by new ₹2000 and ₹500 notes.

ATMs & Eftpos

➡ ATMs are found in most urban centres. Visa, MasterCard, Cirrus, Maestro and Plus are the most commonly accepted cards.

➡ Some banks in India that accept foreign cards include Axis Bank, Citibank, HDFC, HSBC, ICICI, Standard Chartered, State Bank of India (SBI) and State Bank of Bikaner & Jaipur (SBBJ).

➡ Before your trip, check whether your card can reliably access banking networks in India and ask for details of charges.

➡ Most ATMs have withdrawal limits of ₹10,000 to ₹15,000.

➡ Notify your bank that you'll be using your card in India (provide dates) to avoid having your card blocked; take along your bank's phone number just in case.

➡ Always keep the emergency lost-and-stolen numbers for your credit cards in a safe place, separate from your cards, and report any loss or theft immediately.

➡ Away from major towns, always carry cash as backup.

Cash

➡ Major currencies such as US dollars, British pounds and euros are easy to change throughout India. Many banks in Rajasthan also accept other currencies such as Australian and Canadian dollars, and Swiss francs.

➡ Private moneychangers deal with a wider range of currencies.

➡ When travelling off the beaten track, always carry an adequate stock of rupees.

➡ Whenever changing money, check every note. Don't accept any filthy, ripped or disintegrating notes, as these may be difficult to use.

➡ It can be tough getting change in India: jealously hoard your ₹10, ₹20 and ₹50 notes.

➡ Officially, you cannot take rupees out of India, but this rule is laxly enforced. You can most easily change any leftover rupees back into foreign currency at the airport (some banks have a ₹1000 minimum). You may be required to present your encashment certificates or credit-card/ATM receipts and show your passport and airline ticket.

Credit Cards

➡ Credit cards are accepted at a growing number of shops, upmarket restaurants and midrange and top-end hotels; they can usually be used to pay for flights and train tickets.

➡ Cash advances on major credit cards are also possible at some banks.

➡ MasterCard and Visa are the most widely accepted cards.

Encashment Certificates

➡ Indian law states that all foreign currency must be changed at official moneychangers or banks.

➡ For every (official) foreign-exchange transaction, you'll receive an encashment certificate (receipt), which will allow you to exchange rupees back into foreign currency when departing India.

➡ Encashment certificates should be able to cover the amount of rupees you intend changing back to foreign currency.

➡ Printed receipts from ATMs are also accepted as evidence of an international transaction at most banks.

INTERNATIONAL TRANSFERS

If you run out of money, someone back home can wire you cash via money-changers affiliated with Moneygram (www.money-gram.com) or Western Union (www.westernunion.com). A fee is added to the trans-action. To collect cash, bring your passport and the name and reference number of the person who sent the funds.

Moneychangers

Private moneychangers are usually open for longer hours than banks and are found almost everywhere (many also double as travel agents). Upmarket hotels may also change money, but their rates are usually not as competitive.

Tipping

➡ A service fee is usually already added to your bill and tipping is optional. Elsewhere, a tip is appreciated.

➡ Hotel bellboys and train/airport porters appreciate anything from around ₹20 to ₹100.

➡ It's not mandatory to tip taxi or rickshaw drivers.

➡ If you hire a car with driver for more than a couple of days, a tip is recommended for good service.

Travellers Cheques

➡ No longer widely accepted.

➡ Where accepted, some banks may only accept cheques from American Express (Amex) and Thomas Cook.

➡ Pounds sterling and US dollars are the safest currencies, especially in smaller towns.

➡ Keep a record of the cheques' serial numbers separate from your cheques, along with the proof-of-purchase slips, encashment vouchers and photocopied passport details. If you lose your cheques, contact the Amex or Thomas Cook offices in Delhi.

➡ To replace lost travellers cheques, you need the proof-of-purchase slip and the numbers of the missing cheques (some places require a photocopy of the police report and a passport photo). If you don't have the numbers of your missing cheques, the company that issued them will contact the place where you bought them.

Opening Hours

Official business hours are 9.30am to 5.30pm Monday to Friday, with many offices closing for a lunch hour around 1pm. Many sights are open from dawn to dusk.

Banks 10am–2pm or 4pm Monday to Friday, to noon or 1pm Saturday

Post Offices 10am–4pm Monday to Friday, to noon Saturday

Restaurants 8am–10pm or lunch: noon–2.30pm or 3pm; dinner: 7–10pm or 11pm

Shops 9am–9pm, some closed Sunday

Photography

For useful tips and techniques on travel photography, read Lonely Planet's guide to *Travel Photography*.

➡ Memory cards for digital cameras are available from photographic shops in most large cities and towns.

➡ To be safe, regularly back up your memory cards, email and Cloud storage.

Restrictions

➡ Indian authorities are touchy about anyone taking photographs of military installations – this can include train stations, bridges, airports, military sites and sensitive border regions.

→ Photography from the air is officially prohibited, although airlines rarely enforce this.

→ Many places of worship, such as monasteries, temples and mosques, also prohibit photography. Taking photos inside a shrine, at a funeral, at a religious ceremony or of people publicly bathing (including rivers) can also be offensive – ask first.

→ Flash photography may be prohibited in certain areas of a shrine or may not be permitted at all.

→ Exercise sensitivity when taking photos of people, especially women, who may find it offensive – obtain permission in advance.

→ When photographing people use your instincts; some people may demand money afterwards.

Post

India has the biggest postal network on earth, with over 155,000 post offices. Mail and poste-restante services are generally good, although the speed of delivery will depend on the efficiency of any given office. Airmail is faster and more reliable than sea mail, although it's best

to use courier services (such as DHL) to send and receive items of value – expect to pay around ₹3500 per kilogram to Europe, Australia or the USA. Private couriers are often cheaper, but goods may be repacked into large packages to cut costs and things sometimes go missing.

Receiving Mail

→ Ask senders to address letters to you with your surname in capital letters and underlined, followed by poste restante, GPO (main post office) and the city or town in question. To claim mail you'll need to show your passport.

→ It's best to have any parcels sent to you by registered post.

Sending Mail
LETTERS

→ Posting letters/aerogrammes to anywhere overseas costs ₹25/15.

→ International postcards cost around ₹12.

→ For postcards, stick on the stamps *before* writing on them, as post offices can give you as many as four stamps per card.

→ Sending a letter overseas by registered post adds ₹50 to the cost.

PARCELS

→ Posting parcels can be relatively straightforward or involve multiple counters and a fair amount of queuing; get to the post office in the morning.

→ Prices vary depending on weight (including packing material).

→ An (unregistered) airmail package costs around ₹400 to ₹1000 (up to 250g) to any country and ₹50 to ₹150 per additional 250g (up to a maximum of 2kg; different charges apply for higher weights).

→ Parcel post has a maximum of 20kg to 30kg depending on the destination.

→ Choose either airmail (delivery in one to three weeks); sea mail (two to four months); or Surface Air-Lifted (SAL), a curious hybrid where parcels travel by both air and sea (around one month).

→ Another option is EMS (express mail service; delivery within three days) for around 30% more than the normal airmail price.

→ Parcels must be stitched up in white linen and the seams sealed with wax – agents at the post office offer this service for a fee. It's a joy to watch.

→ The post office can provide the necessary customs declaration forms and these must be stitched or pasted to the parcel. If the contents are a gift under the value of ₹1000, you won't be required to pay duty at the delivery end.

→ Carry a permanent marker to write on the parcel any information requested by the desk.

→ Books or printed matter can go by international book post for ₹350 (maximum

GOVERNMENT TRAVEL ADVICE

The following government websites offer travel advice and information on current hot spots.

Australian Department of Foreign Affairs (www.smartraveller.gov.au)

British Foreign Office (www.fco.gov.uk/en)

Canadian Department of Foreign Affairs (www.voyage.gc.ca)

German Foreign Office (www.auswaertiges-amt.de)

Japan Ministry of Foreign Affairs (www.mofa.go.jp)

Netherlands Ministry of Foreign Affairs (www.government.nl)

Swiss Department of Foreign Affairs (www.eda.admin.ch)

US State Department (http://travel.state.gov)

5kg), the parcel has to be packed with an opening so it can be checked by customs.

⇒ **India Post** (www.indiapost. gov.in) has an online calculator for domestic and international postal tariffs.

Public Holidays

There are officially three national public holidays – Republic and Independence Days and Gandhi's birthday (Gandhi Jayanti). Every state celebrates its own official holidays, which cover bank holidays for government workers as well as major religious festivals. Most businesses (offices, shops etc) and tourist sites close on public holidays, but transport is usually unaffected. It's wise to make transport and hotel reservations well in advance if you intend visiting during major festivals.

Republic Day 26 January

Holi February/March

Ramanavani March/April

Dr BL Ambedkar's Birthday 14 April

Mahavir Jayanti March/April

Good Friday March/April

Buddha Purnima April/May

Eid al-Fitr June

Independence Day 15 August

Janmastani August/September

Eid al-Adha August/September

Dussehra September/October

Gandhi Jayanti 2 October

Diwali October/November

Guru Nanak Jayanti November

Eid-Milad-un-Nabi November/ December

Christmas 25 December

Safe Travel

Travellers to India's major cities may fall prey to petty and opportunistic crime. Have a look at the India branch of Lonely Planet's Thorn Tree travel forum (www. lonelyplanet.com/thorntree),

SECURE IT OR LOSE IT

⇒ The safest place for your money and your passport is next to your skin, in a concealed moneybelt or pouch. Never, ever carry these things in your luggage or a shoulder bag. Bum bags are not recommended either, as they advertise that you have a stash of goodies.

⇒ Never leave your valuable documents and travellers cheques in your hotel room. If the hotel is a reputable one, you should be able to use the hotel safe.

⇒ It's wise to peel off at least US$100 and keep it stashed away separately from your main horde, for emergencies.

⇒ Separate your big notes from your small ones so you don't display large wads of cash when you are paying for things.

where travellers often post timely warnings about problems they've encountered on the road. And speaking of the road, India's roads are lethal places and visitors should approach all road travel with care and definitely avoid any driving or riding at night.

India has a bit of a reputation for scams (see p242) and these are indeed common in the tourist hot spots in Rajasthan. Always check your government's travel advisory warnings.

Telephone

⇒ Private PCO/STD/ISD telephone offices offer inexpensive local, interstate and international calls at lower prices than calls made from hotel rooms.

⇒ A digital meter displays how much the call is costing and usually provides a printed receipt when the call is finished.

⇒ Costs vary depending on the operator and destination but can range from ₹1 per minute for local calls and between ₹5 and ₹10 for international calls.

⇒ Some booths also offer a 'call-back' service – you ring home, provide the phone number of the booth and wait for people at home to call

you back, for a fee of around ₹10 on top of the cost of the preliminary call.

⇒ Useful online resources include the Yellow Pages (www.indiayellowpages.com) and Justdial (www.justdial. com).

Mobile Phones

Roaming connections are excellent in urban areas, poor in the countryside. Local prepaid SIMs are widely available; the paperwork is fairly straightforward but you'll have to wait 24 hours for activation.

INDIAN MOBILE PHONE SERVICES

⇒ Indian mobile phone numbers usually have 10 digits typically beginning with 9 (sometimes also 7 or 8).

⇒ There's roaming coverage for international GSM phones in most cities and large towns.

⇒ To avoid expensive roaming costs (often highest for incoming calls), get hooked up to the local mobile-phone network. You'll need to have an unlocked phone to use an Indian SIM card or buy a local handset (from ₹2000).

⇒ The leading service providers include Airtel, Vodafone and Reliance.

Coverage varies from region to region.

GETTING CONNECTED

➡ Getting connected is inexpensive and fairly straightforward in many areas. It's easiest to obtain a local SIM card when you arrive if you're flying into a large city.

➡ Foreigners must supply between one and five passport photos, their passport and photocopies of their passport identity and visa pages. Often mobile shops can arrange all this for you, or you can ask your hotel to help you. It's best to try to do this in tourist centres and cities.

➡ You must also supply a residential address, which can be the address of your hotel. Usually, the phone company will call your hotel (warn the hotel a call will come through) any time up to 24 hours after your application to verify that you are staying there.

➡ It's a good idea to obtain the SIM card somewhere where you're staying for a day or two so that you can return to the vendor if there's any problem. Only obtain your SIM card from a reputable branded phone store to avoid scams.

➡ Another option is to ask a friendly local to register the phone using their local ID.

➡ Prepaid mobile-phone kits (SIM card and phone number, plus an allocation of calls) are available in most Indian towns from around ₹250 from a phone shop or grocery store.

➡ Credit must usually be used within a set time limit and costs vary with the amount of credit on the card.

➡ The amount you pay for a credit top-up is not the amount you get on your phone – state taxes and service charges come off first.

CHARGES

➡ Calls made within the state or city in which you bought the SIM card are cheap – ₹1 per minute – and you can call internationally for less than ₹10 per minute.

➡ SMS messaging is even cheaper. Usually, the more credit you have on your phone, the cheaper the call rate.

➡ Most SIM cards are state specific; they can be used in other states, but you pay for calls at roaming rates and you'll be charged for incoming calls as well as outgoing calls.

Phone Codes

Calling India from abroad Dial your country's international access code, then 📞91 (India's country code), then the area code (without the initial zero), then the local number.

Calling internationally from India Dial 📞00 (the international access code), then the country code of the country you're calling, then the area code (without the initial zero if there is one) and the local number.

Toll-free numbers These begin with 📞1800.1

Time

India uses the 12-hour clock and the local standard time is known as IST (Indian Standard Time). IST is 5½ hours ahead of GMT/UTC.

CITY	NOON IN DELHI
Beijing	2.30pm
Dhaka	12.30pm
Islamabad	11.30am
London	6.30am
Kathmandu	12.15pm
New York	1.30am
San Francisco	10.30pm
Sydney	5.30pm
Tokyo	3.30pm

Toilets

Public toilets are most easily found in major cities and tourist sites and the cleanest toilets (usually with sit-down and squat choices) are most reliably found at modern restaurants, shopping complexes and cinemas. Beyond urban centres, toilets are of the squat variety and locals will use the 'hand-and-water' technique, which involves performing ablutions with a small jug of water and the left hand. It's always a good idea to carry your own toilet paper/wipes and hand sanitiser.

Tourist Information

In addition to the Government of India tourist offices (also known as 'India Tourism'), each state maintains its own network of tourist offices. In Rajasthan, the **Rajasthan Tourism Development Corporation** (RTDC; http://rtdc.tourism.rajasthan.gov.in) operates Tourist Reception Centres in most places of interest. These vary in their efficiency and usefulness, but most have free brochures and often a free local map.

The tourism website of the Government of India is Incredible India (www.incredibleindia.org).

Travellers with Disabilities

India's crowded public transport, hectic urban life and variable infrastructure can test even the hardiest able-bodied traveller. If you have a physical disability or you are vision impaired, these factors can pose even more of a challenge. If your mobility is considerably restricted, you may like to ease the stress by travelling with an able-bodied companion.

Accommodation Wheelchair-friendly hotels are almost

exclusively top end. Make pre-trip enquiries and book ground-floor rooms at hotels that lack adequate facilities.

Accessibility Some restaurants and offices have ramps; most tend to have at least one step. Staircases are often steep and uneven.

Footpaths Where pavements exist, they can be riddled with holes, littered with debris and packed with pedestrians and parked motorcycles.

Transport Hiring a car with a driver will make moving around a lot easier; if you use a wheelchair, make sure the car-hire company can provide an appropriate vehicle to carry it.

Further advice Consult your doctor about your specific requirements before heading to India.

Resources

Download Lonely Planet's free Accessible Travel guide from http://lptravel.to/AccessibleTravel. Other resources include the following:

Access-Able Travel Source (www.access-able.com)

Accessible Journeys (www.disabilitytravel.com)

Enable Holidays (www.enableholidays.com)

Global Access News (www.globalaccessnews.com)

Mobility International USA (MIUSA; www.miusa.org)

Visas

Visa on Arrival

Citizens from over 100 countries, from Albania to Zimbabwe, can apply for a 30-day e-Tourist visa online at indianvisaonline.gov.in a minimum of four and a maximum of 30 days before they are due to travel.The fee is US$60 and it's necessary to upload a photograph as well as a copy of your passport, have at least six month's validity in your passport and at least two pages blank. The facility is available at 16 airports, including Delhi, Mumbai, Bengaluru (Bangalore), Chennai (Madras), Kochi (Cochin), Goa, Hyderabad, Kolkata and Thiruvanathapuram (Trivandrum) airports, though you can exit through any airport. You should also have a return or onward ticket, though proof of this is not usually requested. If your application is approved, you will receive an attachment to an email, which you'll need to print out and take with you to the airport. You'll then have the e-Tourist visa stamped into your passport at the airport, hence the term 'Visa on Arrival', though you need to apply for it beforehand. It is valid from the date of arrival.

Travellers have reported being asked for documentation showing their hotel confirmation at the airport, though this is not specified on the VOA website.

Other Visas

If you want to stay for longer than 30 days, or if you are not covered by the VOA scheme, you must get a visa before arriving in India (apart from Nepali or Bhutanese citizens, but with the exception of Nepali citizens who are entering via China). Visas are available at Indian missions worldwide, though in many countries, applications are processed by a separate private company. In some countries, including the UK, you must apply in person at the designated office as well as file an application online.

Note that your passport needs to be valid for at least six months beyond your intended stay in India, with at least two blank pages. Most people are issued a standard six-month tourist visa, which for most nationalities permits multiple entries.

➡ Student, business and journalist visas have strict conditions (consult the Indian embassy for details).

➡ Tourist visas are valid from the date of issue, not the date you arrive in India.

➡ Five- and 10-year tourist visas are available to US citizens only under a bilateral arrangement; however, you can still only stay in the country for up to 180 days continuously.

➡ Currently, you are required to submit two passport photographs with your visa application; these must be in colour and must be 5.08cm by 5.08cm (2in by 2in; larger than regular passport photos).

➡ An onward travel ticket is a requirement for some visas, but this isn't always enforced (check in advance).

➡ Additional restrictions apply to travellers from Bangladesh and Pakistan, as well as certain Eastern European, African and Central Asian countries. Check any special conditions for your nationality with the Indian embassy in your country.

➡ Visas are priced in the local currency and may have an added service fee.

➡ Extended visas are possible for people of Indian origin (excluding those in Pakistan and Bangladesh) who hold a non-Indian passport and live abroad.

➡ For visas lasting more than six months, you're supposed to register at the **Foreigners' Regional Registration Office** (FRRO; ☏011-26711443; frrodil@nic.in; Level 2, East Block 8, Sector 1, Rama Krishna Puram; ⊙9.30am-3pm Mon-Fri; Ⓜ Green Park) in Delhi within 14 days of arriving in India; enquire about these special conditions when you apply for your visa.

Visa Extensions

India is extremely stringent with visa extensions. At the time of writing, the only circumstances where this might conceivably happen are in *extreme* medical emergencies or if you were robbed of your passport just before you planned to leave the country (at the end of your visa).

In such cases, you should contact the FRRO in Delhi. This is also the place to come for a replacement visa if you need your lost/stolen passport replaced (required before you can leave the country). Note that regional FRROs are even less likely to grant an extension.

Assuming you meet the stringent criteria, the FRRO is permitted to issue an extension of 14 days (free for nationals of most countries; enquire on application). You must bring your confirmed air ticket, one passport photo (take two, just in case) and a photocopy of your passport identity and visa pages. Note that this system is designed to get you out of the country promptly with the correct official stamps, not to give you two extra weeks of travel.

Volunteering

Many charities and international aid agencies work in India and there are numerous opportunities for volunteers. It may be possible to find a placement after you arrive in India, but charities and NGOs normally prefer volunteers who have applied in advance and been approved for the kind of work involved.

Lonely Planet does not endorse any organisations that we do not work with directly, so it is essential that you do your own thorough research before agreeing to volunteer with any organisation.

The website www.ethical volunteering.org has useful tips on choosing an ethical volunteer organisation.

The **Concern India Foundation** (☏011-26224483,

011-26210998; www.concern indiafoundation.org; Lajpat Nagar 4, Room A52, 1st fl, Amar Colony) may be able to link volunteers with current projects around the country; contact it well in advance for information.

Overseas Volunteer Placement Agencies

For long-term posts and information on volunteering, check out the following organisations:

AidCamps International (www. aidcamps.org)

Coordinating Committee for International Voluntary Service (www.ccivs.org)

Global Volunteers (www. globalvolunteers.org)

Idealist (www.idealist.org)

Indicorps (www.indicorps.org)

Voluntary Service Overseas (www.vso.org.uk)

Volunteer Abroad (www.go abroad.com/volunteer-abroad)

Working Abroad (www.working abroad.com)

Worldwide Volunteering (www. worldwidevolunteering.org.uk)

Aid Programs in Rajasthan

The following programs may have opportunities for volunteers with specific skills.

Animal Aid Unlimited (☏9352511435, 9602055895; www.animalaidunlimited.com; Badi Village) Volunteers can help rescue, treat and care for injured, abandoned or stray animals (mostly dogs, cows and donkeys) at its spacious premises a few kilometres outside Udaipur. Make an appointment before going to see it. There's no minimum period, but volunteers are encouraged to stay long enough to learn the routines and develop relationships with individual animals.

Help in Suffering (☏0141-3245673; www.his-india.in; Maharani Farm, Durgapura, Jaipur) Jaipur-based animal welfare charity. Welcomes qualified voluntary vets (three-/six-/12-month commitments). Apply first in writing.

Marwar Medical & Relief Society (☏0291-2545210; www.mandore.com; Dadwari Lane, c/o Mandore Guesthouse) Runs educational, health, environmental and other projects in villages in the Jodhpur district. Guests at its guesthouse in Mandore and other short- or long-term volunteers are welcomed.

Sambhali Trust (☏0291-2512385; www.sambhali-trust. org; c/o Durag Niwas Guest House, 1st Old Public Park, Raika Bagh, Jodhpur) Organisation aiming to empower disadvantaged women and girls in Jodhpur city and Setrawa village, primarily through textile production, literacy and English-language learning. Volunteers can teach and help organise workshops on topics such as health, women's rights and nutrition.

Seva Mandir (☏0294-2451041; www.sevamandir.org; Old Fatehpura, Udaipur) A long-established NGO working with rural and tribal people in southern Rajasthan on a host of projects including afforestation, water resources, health, education and empowerment of women and village institutions. Volunteers and interns can get involved in a wide range of activities.

URMUL Trust (☏0151-2523093; www.urmul.org; Ganganagar Rd, Urmul Bhawan, Bikaner) Provides primary health care and education to desert dwellers in arid western Rajasthan, as well as promoting their handicrafts and women's rights. Volunteer placements (minimum one month) are available in teaching English, health care, documentation and other work.

Transport

GETTING THERE & AWAY

Plenty of international airlines service India and overland routes are open to and from Nepal, Bangladesh, Bhutan and Pakistan. Flights, cars and tours can be booked online at www.lonelyplanet.com/bookings.

Entering the Country

Entering India by air or land is relatively straightforward, with standard immigration and customs procedures. A frustrating law barring re-entry into India within two months of the previous date of departure has now been done away with (except for citizens of some Asian countries), thus allowing most travellers to combine their India tour with side trips to neighbouring countries.

Passport

To enter India you need a valid passport and an onward/return ticket. You'll also need a visa (p255). Your passport should be valid for at least six months beyond your intended stay in India, with at least two blank pages. If your passport is lost or stolen, immediately contact your country's representative. Keep photocopies of your airline ticket and the identity and visa pages of your passport in case of emergency. Better yet, scan and email copies to yourself. Check with the Indian embassy in your home country for any special conditions that may exist for your nationality.

Air

Airports & Airlines

India has six main gateways for international flights. Most

Rajasthan-bound travellers fly into Delhi's **Indira Gandhi International Airport** (p71) . A growing number of international flights from the Middle East, Thailand and Singapore serve **Jaipur** (p124) – for details, enquire at travel agencies and see www.aai.aero.

India's national carrier is **Air India** (☑1800-1801407; www.airindia.com), which also runs an extensive service of domestic flights. Air India has had a relatively decent air safety record in recent years.

Tickets

Departure tax and other charges are included in the prive of airline tickets. You are required to show a copy of your ticket (or e-ticket) and your passport in order to enter the airport, whether flying internationally or within India.

CLIMATE CHANGE & TRAVEL

Every form of transport that relies on carbon-based fuel generates CO_2, the main cause of human-induced climate change. Modern travel is dependent on aeroplanes, which might use less fuel per kilometre per person than most cars but travel much greater distances. The altitude at which aircraft emit gases (including CO_2) and particles also contributes to their climate change impact. Many websites offer 'carbon calculators' that allow people to estimate the carbon emissions generated by their journey and, for those who wish to do so, to offset the impact of the greenhouse gases emitted with contributions to portfolios of climate-friendly initiatives throughout the world. Lonely Planet offsets the carbon footprint of all staff and author travel.

Land

It is possible to travel from Rajasthan to Pakistan on the train that links Jodhpur and Karachi. To reach Nepal overland, you'll have to transit through Delhi and take a bus or train to the border.

Rajasthan to Pakistan

Given the rocky relationship between India and Pakistan, crossing by land depends on the current state of relations between the two countries – check locally. If the crossings are open, you can travel from Rajasthan to Pakistan by train from Jodhpur, on a weekly train to Karachi.

You must have a visa to enter Pakistan. It's easiest to obtain this from the Pakistan mission in your home country. At the time of research, the **Pakistan embassy** (☏011-26110601; pakhcnewdelhi.org.pk; 2/50G Shantipath, Chanakyapuri; ☺9-11am Mon-Fri) in Delhi was not issuing tourist visas for most nationalities, but this could change.

GETTING AROUND

Air

Within Rajasthan, there are airports in Jaipur (p124), Jaisalmer, Jodhpur and Udaipur. However, Jaisalmer may be closed as efforts to reopen it have stalled.

Security at airports is stringent. In smaller airports, all hold baggage must be x-rayed prior to check-in. Every item of cabin baggage needs a label, which must be stamped as part of the security check (don't forget to collect tags at the check-in counter). You may also have to allow for a spot-check of your cabin baggage on the tarmac before you board.

Keeping peak hour congestion in mind, the recommended check-in time for domestic flights is two hours before departure – the deadline is 45 minutes. The usual baggage allowance is 20kg (10kg for smaller aircraft) in economy class.

Airlines in India

With vast numbers of passengers travelling annually, India has a very competitive domestic airline industry. Major carriers include Air India, **Jet Airways** (☏9139893333; www.jetairways.com), **IndiGo** (☏9212783838; www.goindigo.in) and **SpiceJet** (☏0987-1803333; www.spicejet.com).

Airline seats can be booked cheaply over the internet or through travel agencies. Apart from airline sites, bookings can be made through reliable ticketing portals such as Cleartrip (www.cleartrip.com), Make My Trip (www.makemytrip.com) and Yatra (www.yatra.com). Keep in mind that fares fluctuate dramatically, affected by holidays, festivals and seasons.

Bicycle

Rajasthan offers an immense array of experiences for a long-distance cyclist. Nevertheless, long-distance cycling is not for the faint of heart or weak of knee. You'll need physical endurance to cope with the roads, traffic and climate.

There are no restrictions on bringing a bicycle into the country. However, bicycles sent by sea can take a few weeks to clear customs in India, so it's better to fly bikes in. It may actually be cheaper (and less hassle) to hire or buy a bicycle in India itself. Read up on bicycle touring before you travel – Rob Van Der Plas's *The Bicycle Touring Manual* and Stephen Lord's *Adventure Cycle-Touring Handbook* are good places to start. The **Cycling Federation of India** (☏011-23753529; www.cyclingfederationofindia.org; 12 Pandit Pant Marg; ☺10am-6pm Mon-Fri; ⊕Patel Chowk) in Delhi can provide local information.

Hire

➡ Tourist centres and traveller hang-outs are the easiest spots to find bicycles for hire.

➡ Prices vary between ₹40 and ₹200 per day for roadworthy, Indian-made bicycles. Mountain bikes are usually upwards of ₹600 per day.

➡ Hire places may require a cash security deposit (avoid leaving your airline ticket or passport).

Practicalities

➡ Roadside cycle mechanics abound but you should still bring spare tyres and brake cables, lubricating oil, a chain repair kit and plenty of puncture-repair patches.

➡ Bikes can often be carried for free, or for a small luggage fee, on the roof of public buses – handy for uphill stretches.

➡ Contact your airline for information about transporting your bike and customs formalities in your home country.

Buying a Bike

➡ Indian mountain bikes such as Hero and Atlas start at around ₹6000.

➡ Reselling is easy: ask at local cycle or hire shops or put up an advert on travel noticeboards. If you purchased a new bike and it's still in reasonable condition, you should be able to recoup around 50% of what you originally paid.

On the Road

➡ Vehicles drive on the left side in India but, otherwise, road rules are virtually nonexistent.

➡ Cities and national highways can be hazardous places to cycle, so, where possible, stick to the backroads.

➡ Be conservative about the distances you expect to cover – an experienced cyclist can manage around 60km to 100km a day on the plains and 40km or less on dirt roads.

Bus

➡ The Rajasthan state government bus service is Rajasthan State Road Transport Corporation (RSRTC; http://transport.rajasthan.gov.in/rsrtc/), sometimes still known as Rajasthan Roadways.

➡ Often there are privately owned local bus services as well as luxury private coaches running between major cities – these can be booked through travel agencies.

➡ Avoid night buses unless there's no alternative, as driving conditions are more hazardous and drivers may be suffering from lack of sleep.

➡ All buses make snack and toilet stops (some more frequently than others), providing a break but possibly adding hours to journey times.

➡ Females enjoy a 30% discount on RSRTC buses in Rajasthan (often extended to some private buses).

Bus Types & Classes
➡ On the main routes in Rajasthan you have a choice of ordinary, express and deluxe. Express and deluxe buses make fewer stops than ordinary buses – they're still usually crowded though. The fare is marginally higher than ordinary buses, but worth every rupee.

➡ On selected routes there are AG Sleeper buses – these have beds and make overnight trips more comfortable. Beds have a bunk-bed arrangement, with

rows of single beds, each with a curtain for privacy.

➡ Air-conditioned Volvo and Volvo-Mercedes Line buses are the best bus options and serve the Jaipur–Delhi and Agra–Udaipur routes.

➡ Private buses also operate on most Rajasthani routes; apart from often being quicker and usually more comfortable, the booking procedure is much simpler than for state-run buses. However, private companies can often change schedules at the last minute to get as many bums on seats as possible.

Luggage
➡ Luggage is either stored in compartments underneath the bus (sometimes for a small fee) or carried on the roof.

➡ Arrive at least an hour ahead of the scheduled departure time – some buses cover the roof-stored bags with a large canvas, making last-minute additions inconvenient/impossible.

➡ If your baggage is stored on the roof, make sure it is securely locked and tied to the metal baggage rack.

➡ Theft is a risk – keep an eye on your bags at snack and toilet stops and *never* leave your daypack or valuables unattended inside the bus.

Reservations
➡ Most deluxe buses can be booked in advance – usually up to a month in advance for government buses – at bus stations or local travel agencies.

➡ Online bookings for many routes can be made through the portals Cleartrip (www.cleartrip.com) and Redbus (www.redbus.in).

➡ Reservations are rarely possible on 'ordinary' buses and travellers often get left behind in the mad rush for a seat.

➡ To maximise your chances of securing a spot, send a travelling companion ahead to grab some space.

➡ Many buses only depart when full – you may find your bus suddenly empties to join another bus that's ready to leave before yours.

➡ At many bus stations there's a separate women's queue, although this isn't always obvious because signs are often in Hindi and men frequently join the melee. Women travellers should sharpen their elbows and make their way to the front, where they will get almost immediate service (and a 30% discount on the bus fare).

Car

Few people bother with organising self-drive car rental – not only because of the hair-raising driving conditions, but also because hiring a car with a driver is wonderfully affordable in India, particularly if several people share the cost. Hertz (www.hertz.com) is one of the few international rental companies with representatives in India.

Hiring a Car & Driver
➡ Most towns have taxi stands or car-hire companies where you can arrange short or long tours.

➡ Use your hotel to find a car and driver – this achieves a good level of security and reliability and often a better rate.

➡ Not all hire cars are licensed to travel beyond their home state. Even those vehicles that are licensed to enter different states have to pay extra (often hefty) state taxes, which will add to the rental charge.

➡ Ask for a driver who speaks some English and knows the region you intend visiting, and try to see the car and meet the driver before paying any money.

➡ Ambassador cars look great but are rather slow and uncomfortable if travelling long distances – consider them for touring cities.

➡ For multiday trips, the charge should cover the driver's meals and accommodation. Drivers should make their own sleeping and eating arrangements.

➡ It is *essential* to set the ground rules with the driver from day one, in order to avoid anguish later.

Costs

➡ The price depends on the distance and sometimes the terrain (driving on mountain roads uses more petrol, hence the 'hill charges').

➡ One-way trips usually cost the same as return ones (to cover the petrol and driver charges for getting back).

➡ To avoid potential misunderstandings, ensure you get *in writing* what you've been promised (quotes should include petrol, sightseeing stops, all your chosen destinations, and meals and accommodation for the driver).

➡ If a driver asks you for money to pay for petrol en route (reasonable on long trips), keep a record (he will do the same).

➡ Operators usually charge from ₹8 to ₹10 per kilometre per day (depending on the car and if it has AC), with a 250km minimum per day and an overnight charge of up to ₹300 (covering driver expenses).

➡ For sightseeing day trips around a single city, expect to pay anywhere upwards of ₹1400/1800 for a non-AC/AC car with an eight-hour, 80km limit per day (extra charges apply beyond this limit).

➡ A tip is customary at the end of your journey; ₹150 to ₹200 per day is fair.

Motorcycle

➡ Cruising solo around India by motorcycle offers the freedom to go when and where you desire. There are also some excellent motorcycle tours available, which take the hassle out of doing it alone.

➡ Helmets, leathers, gloves, goggles, boots, waterproofs and other types of protective gear are best brought from your home country, as they're either unavailable in India or are of variable quality.

Driving Licences

➡ To hire a motorcycle in India, technically you're required to have a valid international driver's permit in addition to your domestic licence.

➡ In tourist areas, some places may rent out a motorcycle without asking for a driving permit/licence, but you won't be covered by insurance in the event of an accident and may also face a fine.

Hire

➡ The classic way to motorcycle round India is on an Enfield Bullet, still built to many of the original 1940s specifications. As well as making a satisfying sound, these bikes are easy to repair (parts can be found almost everywhere in India). On the other hand, Enfields are less reliable than the newer, Japanese-designed bikes.

➡ Plenty of places rent out motorcycles for local trips and longer tours. Japanese- and Indian-made bikes in the 100cc to 150cc range are cheaper than the big 350cc and 500cc Enfields.

➡ As a deposit, you'll need to leave a large cash lump sum (ensure you get a receipt that also stipulates the refundable amount), your passport or your air ticket. It's strongly advisable to

avoid leaving your passport, which you'll need to check in at hotels and which the police can demand to see at any time.

➡ For three weeks' hire, a 500cc Enfield costs from ₹25,000; a 350cc costs ₹18,000. The price can include excellent advice and an invaluable crash course in Enfield mechanics and repairs.

Purchase

Secondhand bikes are widely available and the paperwork is a lot easier than buying a new machine.

Finding a secondhand motorcycle is a matter of asking around, checking travellers' noticeboards and approaching local motorcycle mechanics.

A looked-after, second-hand 350cc Enfield motorcycle will cost anywhere from ₹50,000 to ₹120,000. The 500cc model costs anywhere from ₹85,000 to ₹140,000. You will also have to pay for insurance. It's advisable to get any second-hand bike serviced before you set off.

When reselling your bike, expect to get between half and two-thirds of the price you paid if the bike is still in reasonable condition. Shipping an Indian bike overseas is complicated and expensive – and you may find it can't be registered owing to safety and pollution regulations in your home country.

Helmets are available for ₹800 to ₹2000 and extras like panniers, luggage racks, protection bars, rear-view mirrors, lockable fuel caps, petrol filters and tools are easy to come by. One useful extra is a customised fuel tank, which will increase the range you can cover between fuel stops. An Enfield 500cc gives about 25km/L; the 350cc model gives slightly more. A good site for Enfield models is www.royalenfield.com.

The following dealers come recommended:

→ **Delhi** Run by the knowledgable Lalli Singh, **Lalli Motorbike Exports** (☎011-28750869; www.lallisingh.com; 1740-A/55 Hari Singh Nalwa St, Abdul Aziz Rd, Delhi; ⏱10am-7pm Tue-Sun; Ⓜ Karol Bagh) sells and rents out Enfields and parts, and buyers get a crash course in running and maintaining these lovable but temperamental machines. He can also recommend other reputable dealers in the area.

→ **Jaipur** For hiring, fixing or purchasing a motorcycle, visit **Rajasthan Auto Centre** (☎0141-2568074, 9829188064; www.royalenfieldsalim.com; Sanganeri Gate, Sanjay Bazaar; ⏱10am-8pm Mon-Sat, to 2pm Sun). To hire a 350cc Bullet costs ₹600 per day (including helmet); if you take the bike outside Jaipur, it costs ₹700 per day. Ask for Saleem, the Bullet specialist.

Ownership Papers

There's plenty of paperwork associated with owning a motorcycle; the registration papers are signed by the local registration authority when the bike is first sold and you'll need these papers when you buy a secondhand bike.

Foreign nationals cannot simply change the name that is on the registration like the locals. Instead, you must fill out the forms for a change of ownership and transfer of insurance. If you buy a new bike, the company selling it must register the machine for you, adding to the cost.

For any bike, the registration must be renewed every 15 years (for around ₹5000) and you must make absolutely sure that it states the 'fitness' of the vehicle, and that there are no outstanding debts or criminal proceedings associated with the bike.

The process is complicated and it makes sense to seek advice from the company selling the bike – allow two weeks to tackle the paperwork and get on the road.

Fuel, Spare Parts & Extras

→ If you're going to remote regions it's also important to carry basic spares (valves, fuel lines, piston rings etc).

→ Spare parts for Indian and Japanese machines are widely available in cities and larger towns, and Delhi's Karol Bagh is a good place to find parts.

→ Make sure you regularly check and tighten all nuts and bolts, as Indian roads and engine vibration tend to work things loose quite quickly.

→ Check the engine and gearbox oil level regularly (at least every 500km) and clean the oil filter every few thousand kilometres.

→ Given the road conditions, the chances are you'll make at least a couple of visits to a puncture-wallah – start your trip with new tyres and carry spanners to remove your own wheels.

Insurance

→ Only hire a bike with third-party insurance – if you hit someone without insurance, the consequences can be very costly. Reputable companies will include third-party cover in their policies; those that don't probably aren't trustworthy.

→ You must also arrange insurance if you buy a motorcycle (usually you can organise this through the person selling the bike).

→ The minimum level of cover is third-party insurance – available for ₹500 to ₹600 per year. This will cover repair and medical costs for any other vehicles, people or property you might hit, but no cover for your own machine. Comprehensive insurance (recommended) costs upwards of ₹1000 per year.

Road Conditions

→ Given the varied road conditions, India can be challenging for novice riders.

→ Hazards range from cows and chickens crossing the carriageway to broken-down trucks, pedestrians on the road and perpetual potholes and unmarked speed humps. Rural roads sometimes have grain crops strewn across them to be threshed by passing vehicles – a serious sliding hazard for bikers.

→ Try not to cover too much territory in one day and avoid travelling after dark – many vehicles drive without lights and dynamo-powered motorcycle headlamps are useless at low revs while negotiating around potholes.

→ On busy national highways expect to average 45km/h without stops; on winding backroads and dirt tracks this can drop to 10km/h.

Organised Motorcycle Tours

Dozens of companies offer organised motorcycle tours around India with a support vehicle, mechanic and guide.

Blazing Trails (☎in UK +44 (0)5603-666788; www.blazingtrailstours.com)

Classic Bike Adventure (www.classic-bike-india.com)

H-C Travel (☎in UK +44 (0)1256-770775; www.hctravel.com)

Indian Motorcycle Adventures (☎in New Zealand +64 (0)9-420 6002; www.indianmotorcycleadventures.com)

Lalli Mobike Adventures (☎011-47652551; www.lallisingh.com; 1266/4 Naiwala St, Payarelal Rd; ⏱10am-7pm Tue-Sun; Ⓜ Karol Bagh)

Moto Discovery (📞in USA +1 830-438-7744; www.motodiscovery.com)

World on Wheels (📞in Australia +61 (0)2-9970 6370; www.worldonwheels.tours)

Local Transport

➡ Buses, cycle-rickshaws, autorickshaws, taxis and urban trains provide transport around cities.

➡ Apps such as Uber and Ola Cabs have transformed local transport. If you have a smartphone, you can call a taxi and the fare is electronically calculated – no arguments and often cheaper than an autorickshaw.

➡ On any form of transport without a fixed fare, agree on the price *before* you start your journey and make sure that it covers your luggage and every passenger.

➡ Fares usually increase at night (by up to 100%) and some drivers charge a few rupees extra for luggage.

➡ Carry plenty of small bills for taxi and rickshaw fares as drivers rarely have change.

➡ Carry a business card of the hotel in which you are staying, as your pronunciation of streets, hotel names etc may be incomprehensible to drivers. Some hotel cards even have a sketch map clearly indicating their location.

➡ Some taxi/autorickshaw drivers are involved in the commission racket.

Autorickshaw & Tempo

➡ The Indian autorickshaw is basically a smog-belching three-wheeled contraption with a low tin or canvas roof and sides, providing room for two passengers and limited luggage.

➡ They are also referred to as autos, tuk-tuks, Indian helicopters or Ferraris.

➡ Jaipur has increasing numbers of quiet, comfortable, electric autorickshaws.

➡ Autorickshaws are mostly cheaper than taxis (except Uber and Ola Cabs) and while most have meters, getting the driver to turn on the meter can be a challenge.

➡ Tempos and *vikrams* (large tempos) are outsized autorickshaws with room for more than two passengers, running on fixed routes for fixed fares.

Bus

Urban buses, particularly in the big cities, are fume-belching, human-stuffed mechanical monsters that travel at breakneck speed (except during morning and evening rush hours, when they can be endlessly stuck in traffic). It's usually far more convenient and comfortable to opt for an autorickshaw or taxi.

Cycle-Rickshaw

➡ A cycle-rickshaw is a pedal cycle with two rear wheels, supporting a bench seat for passengers. Most have a canopy that can be raised in wet weather, or lowered to provide extra space for luggage.

➡ Many of the big cities have phased out (or reduced) the number of cycle-rickshaws, but you can still find them in Jaipur and they remain a major means of local transport in many smaller towns.

➡ Fares must be agreed upon in advance – speak to locals to get an idea of what is a fair price. Remember, this is extremely strenuous work and the wallahs are among India's poorest, so a tip is appreciated and haggling over a few rupees unnecessary.

Metro

Metro systems have transformed urban transport in India's biggest cities and are expanding. Joining, Delhi,

Kolkata (Calcutta), Mumbai (Bombay) and Chennai (Madras) is Jaipur's new Metro (📞0141-2385790; www.jaipurmetrorail.info), which cuts right under the Pink City.

Share Jeep

➡ Share jeeps supplement the bus service in many parts of Rajasthan, especially in areas off the main road routes, such as many of the towns in Shekhawati.

➡ Jeeps leave when (very) full, from well-established 'passenger stations' on the outskirts of towns and villages; locals should be able to point you in the right direction. They are usually dirt cheap and jam-packed and tend to be more dangerous than buses.

Taxi

Most Indian airports and many train stations have prepaid taxi and radio cab booths, normally just outside the terminal building. Here, you can book a taxi for a fixed price (which will include baggage) and thus avoid commission scams. However, officials advise holding on to the payment coupon until you reach your chosen destination, in case the driver has any other ideas.

Radio cabs cost marginally more than prepaid taxis, but are air-conditioned and manned by the company's chauffeurs. Cabs have electronic, receipt-generating fare meters and are fitted with GPS units, so the company can monitor the vehicle's movement around town. These minimise chances of errant driving or unreasonable demands for extra cash by the driver afterward.

Smaller airports and stations may have prepaid autorickshaw booths instead.

Train

Travelling by train is a quintessential Indian experience. Trains offer a smoother ride than buses and are especially recommended for long journeys that include overnight travel. India's rail network is one of the largest and busiest in the world and Indian Railways is the largest utility employer on earth, with roughly 1.5 million workers. There are around 7000 train stations scattered across the country.

Although we list the most useful, there are hundreds of train services. The best way of sourcing updated railway information is to use relevant internet sites such as Indian Railways (rbs.indianrail.gov. in), India Rail Info (http:// indiarailinfo.com), IRCTC enquiry (erail.in) and the useful www.seat61.com/ India.htm. There's also *Trains at a Glance* (₹45), available at many train station bookstands and good bookshops/ news stands, but it's published annually so it's not as up to date as websites. Nevertheless, it offers comprehensive timetables covering all the main lines.

Booking Tickets in India

You can either book tickets online, through a travel agency or a hotel (for a commission) or in person at the train station. Larger stations often have some English-speaking staff who can help with reservations. At smaller stations, the stationmaster and his deputy usually speak English.

➡ **At the station** Get a reservation slip from the information window, fill in the name of the departure station, destination station, the class you want to travel and the name and number of the train. Join the long queue to the ticket window where your ticket will be printed. Women should use the separate women's queue – if there isn't one, go to the front of the regular queue. Larger stations often have a counter for foreigners.

➡ **Tourist Reservation Bureau** Larger cities and major tourist centres have an International Tourist Bureau, which allows you to book certain tickets in relative peace – check http://india railinfo.com for a list of these stations.

BOOKING ONLINE
You can book online through **IRCTC** (www.irctc.co.in), the e-ticketing division of the government's Indian Railways, or portals such as **Cleartrip** (www.cleartrip. com), **Make My Trip** (www. makemytrip.com) and **Yatra** (www.yatra.com). Remember, however, that online booking of train tickets has its share of glitches: travellers have reported problems with registering themselves on some portals and using certain overseas credit cards; you may also need an Indian phone number to register.

When booking online, it pays to know the details of your journey – particularly station names, train numbers, days of operation and available classes. Start by visiting http://erail.in – the search engine will bring up a list of all trains running between your chosen destinations, along with information on classes and fares.

Step two is to register online for an account with IRCTC. This is required even if you plan to use a private ticket agency. Registration is a complex process, involving passwords, emails, scans of your passport and texts to your mobile phone. The ever-helpful Man in Seat 61 (www.seat61.com/India. htm) has a detailed guide to all the steps.

Once registered, you can use a credit card to book travel on specific trains, either directly with IRCTC or with private agencies.

You'll be issued with an e-ticket, which you must print out ready to present alongside your passport and

TRAIN CLASSES

Air-Conditioned 1st Class (1AC) The most expensive class of train travel; two- or four-berth compartments with locking doors and meals included.

Air-Conditioned 2-Tier (2AC) Two-tier berths arranged in groups of four and two in an open-plan carriage. The bunks convert to seats by day and there are curtains for some semblance of privacy.

Air-Conditioned 3-Tier (3AC) Three-tier berths arranged in groups of six in an open-plan carriage; no curtains.

AC Executive Chair (ECC) Comfortable, reclining chairs and plenty of space; usually found on Shatabdi express trains.

AC Chair (CC) Similar to the Executive Chair carriage but with less-fancy seating.

Sleeper Class (sl) Open-plan carriages with three-tier bunks and no AC; the open windows afford great views.

Unreserved/reserved 2nd Class (II/SS) Wooden or plastic seats and *a lot* of people – but cheap!

PALACES ON WHEELS

To travel maharaja style, try the Palace on Wheels, Royal Rajasthan on Wheels and Maharajas Express train services.

➡ The Palace on Wheels (www.palaceonwheels.net) operates one-week luxury tours of Rajasthan, departing from Delhi. The itinerary includes Jaipur, Jaisalmer, Jodhpur, Ranthambhore National Park, Chittorgarh, Udaipur, Keoladeo National Park and Agra. Fit-for-a-maharaja carriages are sumptuously decked out and there are dining cars, a bar, a lounge and a library. Trains run on fixed dates from September to April; the fare per person for seven nights starts at US$6500/4890/4325 (in a single/double/triple cabin). Try to book 10 months in advance.

➡ The Royal Rajasthan on Wheels (www.royalrajasthanonwheels.co.in) is the most luxurious and runs one-week trips from October to March, starting and finishing in Delhi. The route takes in Jodhpur, Udaipur, Chittorgarh, Ranthambhore National Park, Jaipur, Khajuraho, Varanasi and Agra. The fare (seven nights) per person per night is US$875/625 for single/twin occupancy of deluxe suites.

➡ The Maharajas Express (www.palacetours.com) operates three- to seven-night packages starting from US$4125 per person. All itineraries include parts of Rajasthan.

booking reference once you board the train.

Reservations

Bookings open 120 days before departure and you must make a reservation for all chair-car, sleeper, and 1AC, 2AC and 3AC carriages. No reservations are required for general (2nd class) compartments. Trains are always busy in India so it's wise to book as far in advance as possible; advanced booking for overnight trains is *strongly recommended*. Train services to certain destinations are often increased during major festivals but it's still worth booking well in advance.

Reserved tickets show your seat/berth number and the carriage number. When the train pulls in, keep an eye out for your carriage number written on the side of the train (station staff and porters can also point you in the right direction). A list of names and berths is also posted on the side of each reserved carriage.

Be aware that train trips can be delayed at any time of the journey, so, to avoid stress, factor some leeway into your travel plans.

If the train you want to travel on is sold out, be

sure to enquire about the following:

Reservation Against Cancellation (RAC) Even when a train is fully booked, Indian Railways sells a handful of RAC seats in each class. This means that if you have an RAC ticket and someone cancels before the departure date, you will get that seat (or berth). You'll have to check the reservation list at the station on the day of travel to see where you've been allocated to sit. Even if no one cancels, as an RAC ticket holder you can still board the train and, even if you don't get a seat, you can still travel.

Taktal Tickets Indian Railways holds back a limited number of tickets on key trains and releases them at 8am two days before the train is due to depart. A charge of ₹10 to ₹500 is added to each ticket price. 1AC and Executive Chair tickets are excluded from the scheme.

Tourist Quota A special (albeit small) tourist quota is set aside for foreign tourists travelling between popular stations. These seats can only be booked at dedicated reservation offices in major cities, and you need to show your passport and visa as ID. Tickets can be paid for in rupees (some offices may ask to see foreign exchange certificates – ATM receipts will suffice).

Waitlist (WL) Trains are frequently overbooked, but many passengers cancel and there are regular no-shows. So if you buy a ticket on the waiting list you're still quite likely to get a seat, even if there are a number of people ahead of you on the list. Check your booking status at rbs.indianrail.gov.in/pnr_Enq.html by entering your tickets' PNR number. A refund is available if you fail to get a seat – ask the ticket office about your chances.

Refunds

Tickets are refundable but fees apply. If you present more than one day in advance, a fee of ₹20 to ₹70 applies. Steeper charges apply if you seek a refund less than four hours prior to departure, but you can get some sort of refund as late as 12 hours afterwards.

Classes & Costs

Shatabdi express trains are same-day services between major and regional cities. These are the fastest and most expensive trains, with only two classes; AC Executive Chair and AC Chair. Shatabdis are comfortable, but the glass windows cut the views considerably compared to non-AC classes on slower trains, which have barred windows and fresh air.

Rajdhani express trains are long-distance express services running between Delhi and the state capitals, and offer 1AC, 2AC, 3AC and 2nd class. Two-tier means there are two levels of bunks in each compartment, which are a little wider and longer than their counterparts in 3-tier. Costing, respectively, a half and a third as much as 1AC, the classes 2AC and 3AC are perfectly adequate for an overnight trip.

Fares are calculated by distance and class of travel; Rajdhani and Shatabdi trains are slightly more expensive, but the price includes meals. Most air-conditioned carriages have a catering service (meals are brought to your seat). In unreserved classes, it's a good idea to carry portable snacks. Male/female seniors (those over 60/58) get 40/50% off all fares in all classes on all types of trains. Children below the age of six travel for free; those aged between six and 12 are charged half price, up to 300km.

Health

There is huge geographical variation in India, so in different areas, heat, cold and altitude can cause health problems. Hygiene is poor in most regions so food and water-borne illnesses are common. A number of insect-borne diseases are present, particularly in tropical areas. Medical care is basic in various areas (especially beyond the larger cities) so it's essential to be well prepared.

Pre-existing medical conditions and accidental injury (especially traffic accidents) account for most life-threatening problems. Becoming ill in some way, however, is common. Fortunately, most travellers' illnesses can be prevented with some common-sense behaviour or treated with a well-stocked travellers' medical kit – however, never hesitate to consult a doctor while on the road, as self-diagnosis can be hazardous.

BEFORE YOU GO

You can buy many medications over the counter in India without a doctor's prescription, but it can be difficult to find some of the newer drugs, particularly the latest antidepressant drugs, blood-pressure medications and contraceptive pills. Be circumspect about self-medicating, as travellers mixing the wrong drugs or overdosing has on occasion ended in tragedy.

Bring the following:

➡ medications in their original, labelled containers

➡ a signed, dated letter from your physician describing your medical conditions and medications, including generic names

➡ a doctor's letter documenting the medical necessity of any syringes you bring

➡ if you have a heart condition, a copy of your ECG taken just prior to travelling

➡ any regular medication (double your ordinary needs).

Insurance

Don't travel without health insurance. Emergency evacuation is expensive. There are various factors to consider when choosing insurance. Read the small print.

➡ You may require extra cover for adventure activities such as rock climbing and scuba diving.

➡ In India, doctors usually require immediate payment in cash. Your insurance plan may make payments directly to providers or it will reimburse you later for overseas health expenditures. If you do have to claim later, make sure you keep all relevant documentation.

➡ Some policies ask that you telephone back (reverse charges) to a centre in your home country where an immediate assessment of your problem will be made.

Vaccinations

Specialised travel-medicine clinics are your best source of up-to-date information; they stock all available vaccines and can give specific recommendations for your trip. Most vaccines don't give immunity until at least two weeks after they're given, so visit a doctor well before departure. Ask your doctor for an International Certificate of Vaccination (sometimes known as the 'yellow booklet'), which will list all the vaccinations you've received.

Medical Checklist

Recommended items for a personal medical kit:

➡ Antifungal cream, eg clotrimazole

➡ Antibacterial cream, eg mupirocin

➡ Antibiotic for skin infections, eg amoxicillin/clavulanate or cephalexin

➡ Antihistamine – there are many options, eg cetrizine for daytime and promethazine for night

➡ Antiseptic, eg Betadine

➡ Antispasmodic for stomach cramps, eg Buscopam

➡ Contraceptive

→ Decongestant, eg pseudoephedrine

→ DEET-based insect repellent

→ Diarrhoea medication – consider an oral rehydration solution (eg Gastrolyte), diarrhoea 'stopper' (eg loperamide) and antinausea medication (eg prochlorperazine). Antibiotics for diarrhoea include ciprofloxacin; for bacterial diarrhoea

azithromycin; for giardia or amoebic dysentery tinidazole

→ First-aid items such as scissors, elastoplasts, bandages, gauze, thermometer (but not mercury), sterile needles and syringes, safety pins and tweezers

→ Ibuprofen or another anti-inflammatory

→ Iodine tablets (unless you are pregnant or have a thyroid problem) to purify water

→ Migraine medication if you suffer from migraines

→ Paracetamol

→ Pyrethrin to impregnate clothing and mosquito nets

→ Steroid cream for allergic or itchy rashes, eg 1% to 2% hydrocortisone

→ High-factor sunscreen

→ Throat lozenges

→ Thrush (vaginal yeast infection) treatment,

REQUIRED & RECOMMENDED VACCINATIONS

The only vaccine required by international regulations is **yellow fever**. Proof of vaccination will only be required if you have visited a country in the yellow-fever zone within the six days prior to entering India. If you are travelling to India from Africa or South America, you should check to see if you require proof of vaccination.

The World Health Organization (WHO) recommends the following vaccinations for travellers going to India (as well as being up to date with measles, mumps and rubella vaccinations):

Adult diphtheria & tetanus Single booster recommended if none in the previous 10 years. Side effects include sore arm and fever.

Hepatitis A Provides almost 100% protection for up to a year; a booster after 12 months provides at least another 20 years' protection. Mild side effects such as headache and sore arm occur in 5% to 10% of people.

Hepatitis B Now considered routine for most travellers. Given as three shots over six months. A rapid schedule is also available, as is a combined vaccination with hepatitis A. Side effects are mild and uncommon, usually headache and a sore arm. In 95% of people lifetime protection results.

Polio Only one booster is required as an adult for lifetime protection. Inactivated polio vaccine is safe during pregnancy.

Typhoid Recommended for all travellers to India, even those only visiting urban areas. The vaccine offers around 70% protection, lasts for two to three years and comes as a single shot. Tablets are also available, but the injection is usually recommended as it has fewer side effects. Sore arm and fever may occur.

Varicella If you haven't had chickenpox, discuss this vaccination with your doctor.

These immunisations are recommended for long-term travellers (more than one month) or those at special risk (seek further advice from your doctor):

Japanese B encephalitis Three injections in all. Booster recommended after two years. Sore arm and headache are the most common side effects. In rare cases, an allergic reaction comprising hives and swelling can occur up to 10 days after any of the three doses.

Meningitis Single injection. There are two types of vaccination: the quadravalent vaccine gives two to three years' protection; meningitis group C vaccine gives around 10 years' protection. Recommended for long-term backpackers aged under 25.

Rabies Three injections in all. A booster after one year will then provide 10 years' protection. Side effects are rare – occasionally headache and sore arm.

Tuberculosis (TB) A complex issue. Adult long-term travellers are usually recommended to have a TB skin test before and after travel, rather than vaccination. Only one vaccine given in a lifetime.

eg clotrimazole pessaries or Diflucan tablet

➡ Ural or equivalent if prone to urine infections

Websites

There is a wealth of travel-health advice on the internet; www.lonelyplanet.com is a good place to start. Some other suggestions:

Centers for Disease Control and Prevention (CDC; www.cdc. gov) Good general information.

MD Travel Health (www.mdtrav elhealth.com) Provides complete travel-health recommendations for every country; updated daily.

World Health Organization (WHO; www.who.int/ith) Its superb book *International Travel & Health* is revised annually and is available online

Further Reading

Recommended references include *Travellers' Health* by Dr Richard Dawood and *Travelling Well* by Dr Deborah Mills, which is now also available as an app; check out the website (www.travellingwell. com.au) too.

IN INDIA

Availability & Cost of Health Care

Medical care is hugely variable in India. Some cities now have clinics catering specifically to travellers and expatriates; these clinics are usually more expensive than local medical facilities, and offer a higher standard of care. Additionally, they know the local system, including reputable local hospitals and specialists. They may also liaise with insurance companies should you require evacuation. It is usually difficult to find reliable medical care in rural areas.

Self-treatment may be appropriate if your problem is minor (eg traveller's diarrhoea), you are carrying the relevant medication, and you cannot attend a recommended clinic. If you suspect a serious disease, especially malaria, travel to the nearest quality facility.

Before buying medication over the counter, check the use-by date, and ensure the packet is sealed and properly stored (eg not exposed to the sunshine).

Infectious Diseases

Malaria

This is a serious and potentially deadly disease. Before you travel, seek expert advice according to your itinerary (rural areas are especially risky) and on medication and side effects.

Malaria is caused by a parasite transmitted by the bite of an infected mosquito. The most important symptom of malaria is fever, but general symptoms, such as headache, diarrhoea, cough or chills, may also occur. Diagnosis can only be properly made by taking a blood sample.

Two strategies should be combined to prevent malaria: mosquito avoidance and antimalarial medications. Most people who catch malaria are taking inadequate or no antimalarial medication.

Travellers are advised to prevent mosquito bites by taking these steps:

➡ Use a DEET-based insect repellent on exposed skin. Wash this off at night – as long as you are sleeping under a mosquito net. Natural repellents such as citronella can be effective, but must be applied more frequently than products containing DEET.

➡ Sleep under a mosquito net impregnated with pyrethrin.

➡ Choose accommodation with proper screens and fans (if not air-conditioned).

➡ Impregnate clothing with pyrethrin in high-risk areas.

➡ Wear long sleeves and trousers in light colours.

➡ Use mosquito coils.

➡ Spray your room with insect repellent before going out for your evening meal.

There are a variety of medications available:

Chloroquine & Paludrine combination Limited effectiveness in many parts of South Asia. Common side effects include nausea (40% of people) and mouth ulcers.

Doxycycline (daily tablet) A broad-spectrum antibiotic that helps prevent a variety of tropical diseases, including leptospirosis, tick-borne disease and typhus. Potential side effects include photosensitivity (a tendency to sunburn), thrush (in women), indigestion, heartburn, nausea and interference with the contraceptive pill. More serious side effects include ulceration of the oesophagus – take your tablet with a meal and a large glass of water, and never lie down within half an hour of taking it.

HEALTH ADVISORIES

It's a good idea to consult your government's travel-health website before departure, if one is available:

Australia (www.smartraveller.gov.au)

Canada (www.travelhealth.gc.ca)

New Zealand (safetravel.govt.nz/health-and-travel)

UK (www.fco.gov.uk/en/travelling-and-living-overseas)

US (www.cdc.gov/travel)

It must be taken for four weeks after leaving the risk area.

Lariam (mefloquine) This weekly tablet suits many people. Serious side effects are rare but include depression, anxiety, psychosis and seizures. Anyone with a history of depression, anxiety, other psychological disorders or epilepsy should not take Lariam. It is considered safe in the second and third trimesters of pregnancy. Tablets must be taken for four weeks after leaving the risk area.

Malarone A combination of atovaquone and proguanil. Side effects are uncommon and mild, most commonly nausea and headache. It is the best tablet for scuba divers and for those on short trips to high-risk areas. It must be taken for one week after leaving the risk area.

Other Diseases

Avian flu 'Bird flu' or Influenza A (H5N1) is a subtype of the type A influenza virus. Contact with dead or sick birds is the principal source of infection and bird-to-human transmission does not easily occur. Symptoms include high fever and flu-like symptoms with rapid deterioration, leading to respiratory failure and death in many cases. Immediate medical care should be sought if bird flu is suspected. Check www.who.int/en/or www.avian influenza.com.au.

Cholera There are occasional outbreaks of cholera in India. This acute gastrointestinal infection is transmitted through contaminated water and food, including raw or undercooked fish and shellfish. Cases are rare among travellers, but those who are travelling to an area of active transmission should consult with their healthcare practitioner regarding vaccination.

Dengue fever This mosquito-borne disease is becomingly increasingly problematic, especially in the cities. As there is no vaccine available it can only be prevented by avoiding mosquito bites at all times. Symptoms include high fever, severe headache and body ache and sometimes a rash and

diarrhoea. Treatment is rest and paracetamol – do not take aspirin or ibuprofen as it increases the likelihood of haemorrhaging. Make sure you see a doctor to be diagnosed and monitored.

Hepatitis A This food- and water-borne virus infects the liver, causing jaundice (yellow skin and eyes), nausea and lethargy. There is no specific treatment for hepatitis A, you just need to allow time for the liver to heal. All travellers to India should be vaccinated against hepatitis A.

Hepatitis B This sexually transmitted disease is spread by body fluids and can be prevented by vaccination. The long-term consequences can include liver cancer and cirrhosis.

Hepatitis E Transmitted through contaminated food and water, hepatitis E has similar symptoms to hepatitis A, but is far less common. It is a severe problem in pregnant women and can result in the death of both mother and baby. There is no commercially available vaccine, and prevention is by following safe eating and drinking guidelines.

HIV Spread via contaminated body fluids. Avoid unsafe sex, unsterile needles (including in medical facilities) and procedures such as tattoos. The growth rate of HIV in India is one of the highest in the world.

Influenza Present year-round in the tropics, influenza (flu) symptoms include fever, muscle aches, a runny nose, cough and sore throat. It can be severe in people over the age of 65 or in those with medical conditions such as heart disease or diabetes – vaccination is recommended for these individuals. There is no specific treatment, just rest and paracetamol.

Japanese B encephalitis This viral disease is transmitted by mosquitoes and is rare in travellers. Most cases occur in rural areas and vaccination is recommended for travellers spending more than one month outside of cities. There is no treatment, and it may result in permanent brain damage or death. Ask your doctor for further details.

Rabies This fatal disease is spread by the bite or possibly even the lick of an infected animal – most commonly a dog or monkey. You should seek medical advice immediately after any animal bite and commence postexposure treatment. Having pretravel vaccination means the posttbite treatment is greatly simplified. If an animal bites you, gently wash the wound with soap and water, and apply iodine-based antiseptic. If you are not prevaccinated you will need to receive rabies immunoglobulin as soon as possible, and this is very difficult to obtain in much of India.

Tuberculosis While TB is rare in travellers, those who have significant contact with the local population (such as medical and aid workers and long-term travellers) should take precautions. Vaccination is usually only given to children under the age of five, but adults at risk are recommended to have pre- and post-travel TB testing. The main symptoms are fever, cough, weight loss, night sweats and fatigue.

Typhoid This serious bacterial infection is also spread via food and water. It gives a high and slowly progressive fever and headache, and may be accompanied by a dry cough and stomach pain. It is diagnosed by blood tests and treated with antibiotics. Vaccination is recommended for all travellers who are spending more than a week in India. Be aware that vaccination is not 100% effective, so you must still be careful with what you eat and drink.

Traveller's Diarrhoea

This is by far the most common problem affecting travellers in India – between 30% and 70% of people will suffer from it within two weeks of starting their trip. It's usually caused by a bacteria, and thus responds promptly to treatment with antibiotics.

Traveller's diarrhoea is defined as the passage of more than three watery bowel actions within 24 hours, plus at least one other symptom,

CARBON-MONOXIDE POISONING

Some mountain areas rely on charcoal burners for warmth, but these should be avoided due to the risk of fatal carbon-monoxide poisoning. The thick, mattress-like blankets used in many mountain areas are amazingly warm once you get beneath the covers. If you're still cold, improvise a hot-water bottle by filling your drinking-water bottle with boiled water and covering it with a sock.

such as fever, cramps, nausea, vomiting or feeling generally unwell.

Treatment consists of staying well hydrated; rehydration solutions like Gastrolyte are the best for this. Antibiotics such as ciprofloxacin or azithromycin should kill the bacteria quickly. Seek medical attention quickly if you do not respond to an appropriate antibiotic.

Loperamide is just a 'stopper' and doesn't get to the cause of the problem. It can be helpful, though (eg if you have to go on a long bus ride). Don't take loperamide if you have a fever or blood in your stools.

Amoebic dysentery Amoebic dysentery is very rare in travellers but is quite often misdiagnosed by poor-quality labs. Symptoms are similar to bacterial diarrhoea: fever, bloody diarrhoea and generally feeling unwell. You should always seek reliable medical care if you have blood in your diarrhoea. Treatment involves two drugs: tinidazole or metronidazole to kill the parasite in your gut and then a second drug to kill the cysts. If left untreated complications such as liver or gut abscesses can occur.

Giardiasis Giardia is a parasite that is relatively common in travellers. Symptoms include nausea, bloating, excess gas, fatigue and intermittent diarrhoea. The parasite will eventually go away if left untreated but this can take months; the best advice is to seek medical treatment. The treatment of choice is tinidazole, with metronidazole being a second-line option.

Environmental Hazards

Air Pollution

Air pollution, particularly vehicle pollution, is an increasing problem in most of India's urban hubs. If you have severe respiratory problems, speak with your doctor before travelling to India. All travellers are advised to listen to advisories on pollution levels from the press or government officials (if the Air Quality Index measures 100 or above in any of its eight pollutant categories, this is poor). It's worth taking a disposable face mask if you are affected by air quality.

Diving & Surfing

Divers and surfers should seek specialised advice before they travel to ensure their medical kit contains treatment for coral cuts and tropical ear infections. Divers should ensure their insurance covers them for decompression illness – get specialised dive insurance through an organisation such as Divers Alert Network (www.danasiapacific.org). Certain medical conditions are incompatible with diving; check with your doctor.

Food

Dining out brings with it the possibility of contracting diarrhoea. Ways to help avoid food-related illness:

➧ eat only freshly cooked food

➧ avoid shellfish and buffets

➧ peel fruit

➧ cook vegetables

➧ soak salads in iodine water for at least 20 minutes

➧ eat in busy restaurants with a high turnover of customers.

Heat

Many parts of India, especially down south, are hot and humid throughout the year. For most visitors it takes around two weeks to comfortably adapt to the hot climate. Swelling of the feet and ankles is common, as are muscle cramps caused by excessive sweating. Prevent these by avoiding dehydration and excessive activity in the heat. Don't eat salt tablets (they aggravate the gut); drinking rehydration solution or eating salty food helps. Treat cramps by resting, rehydrating with double-strength rehydration solution and gently stretching.

Dehydration is the main contributor to heat exhaustion. Recovery is usually rapid and it is common to feel weak for some days afterwards. Symptoms include:

➧ feeling weak

➧ headache

➧ irritability

➧ nausea or vomiting

➧ sweaty skin

➧ a fast, weak pulse

➧ normal or slightly elevated body temperature.

Treatment:

➧ get out of the heat

➧ fan the sufferer

➧ apply cool, wet cloths to the skin

➧ lay the sufferer flat with their legs raised

➧ rehydrate with water containing one-quarter teaspoon of salt per litre.

Heatstroke is a serious medical emergency. Symptoms include:

➧ weakness

➧ nausea

→ a hot, dry body

→ temperature of over 41°C

→ dizziness

→ confusion

→ loss of coordination

→ seizures

→ eventual collapse.

Treatment:

→ get out of the heat

→ fan the sufferer

→ apply cool, wet cloths to the skin or ice to the body, especially to the groin and armpits.

Prickly heat is a common skin rash in the tropics, caused by sweat trapped under the skin. Treat it by moving out of the heat for a few hours and by having cool showers. Creams and ointments clog the skin so they should be avoided. Locally bought prickly-heat powder can be helpful.

Altitude Sickness

If you are going to altitudes above 3000m, acute mountain sickness (AMS) is an issue. The biggest risk factor is going too high too quickly – follow a conservative acclimatisation schedule found in good trekking guides, and *never* go to a higher altitude when you have any symptoms that could be altitude related. There is no way to predict who will get altitude sickness and it is quite often the younger, fitter members of a group who succumb.

Symptoms usually develop during the first 24 hours at altitude but may be delayed up to three weeks. Mild symptoms include:

→ headache

→ lethargy

→ dizziness

→ difficulty sleeping

→ loss of appetite.

AMS may become more severe without warning and can

be fatal. Severe symptoms include:

→ breathlessness

→ a dry, irritative cough (which may progress to the production of pink, frothy sputum)

→ severe headache

→ lack of coordination and balance

→ confusion

→ irrational behaviour

→ vomiting

→ drowsiness

→ unconsciousness.

Treat mild symptoms by resting at the same altitude until recovery, which usually takes a day or two. Paracetamol or aspirin can be taken for headaches. If symptoms persist or become worse, immediate descent is necessary; even 500m can help. Drug treatments should never be used to avoid descent or to enable further ascent.

The drugs acetazolamide and dexamethasone are recommended by some doctors for the prevention of AMS; however, their use is controversial. They can reduce the symptoms, but

they may also mask warning signs; severe and fatal AMS has occurred in people taking these drugs.

To prevent AMS:

→ ascend slowly – have frequent rest days, spending two to three nights at each rise of 1000m

→ sleep at a lower altitude than the greatest height reached during the day, if possible. Above 3000m, don't increase sleeping altitude by more than 300m daily

→ drink extra fluids

→ eat light, high-carbohydrate meals

→ avoid alcohol and sedatives.

Insect Bites & Stings

Bedbugs Don't carry disease but their bites can be itchy. You can treat the itch with an antihistamine.

Lice Most commonly appear on the head and pubic areas. You may need numerous applications of an antilice shampoo such as pyrethrin.

Ticks Contracted walking in rural areas. Ticks are commonly found behind the ears, on the belly and in armpits. If you have had a tick bite and have a rash at the site

DRINKING WATER

→ Never drink tap water.

→ Bottled water is generally safe – check the seal is intact at purchase.

→ Avoid ice unless you know it has been made hygienically.

→ Be careful of fresh juices served at street stalls in particular – they may have been watered down or may be served in unhygienic jugs/glasses.

→ Boiling water is usually the most efficient method of purifying it.

→ The best chemical purifier is iodine. It should not be used by pregnant women or those with thyroid problems.

→ Water filters should also filter out most viruses. Ensure your filter has a chemical barrier such as iodine and a small pore size (less than four microns).

of the bite or elsewhere, fever or muscle aches, see a doctor. Doxycycline prevents tick-borne diseases.

Leeches Found in humid rainforest areas. They do not transmit any disease but their bites are often itchy for weeks and can easily become infected. Apply an iodine-based antiseptic to any leech bite to help prevent infection.

Bee and wasp stings Anyone with a serious bee or wasp allergy should carry an injection of adrenalin (eg an Epipen).

Skin Problems

Fungal rashes There are two common fungal rashes that affect travellers. The first occurs in moist areas, such as the groin, armpits and between the toes. It starts as a red patch that slowly spreads and is usually itchy. Treatment involves keeping the skin dry, avoiding chafing and using an antifungal cream such as clotrimazole or Lamisil. The second, *Tinea versicolor,* causes light-coloured patches, most commonly on the back, chest and shoulders. Consult a doctor.

Cuts and scratches These become easily infected in humid climates. Immediately wash all wounds in clean water and apply antiseptic. If you develop signs of infection (increasing pain and redness), see a doctor.

Sunburn

Even on a cloudy day sunburn can occur rapidly.

➡ Use a strong sunscreen (factor 50+) and reapply after a swim.

➡ Wear a wide-brimmed hat and sunglasses.

➡ Avoid lying in the sun during the hottest part of the day (10am to 2pm).

➡ Be vigilant above 3000m – you can get burnt very easily at altitude.

If you become sunburnt, stay out of the sun until you have recovered, apply cool com-

presses and, if necessary, take painkillers for the discomfort. One per cent hydrocortisone cream applied twice daily is also helpful.

Women's Health

For gynaecological health issues, seek out a female doctor.

Birth control Bring adequate supplies of your own form of contraception.

Sanitary products Pads, but rarely tampons, are readily available.

Thrush Heat, humidity and antibiotics can all contribute to thrush. Treatment is with antifungal creams and pessaries such as clotrimazole. A practical alternative is a single tablet of fluconazole (Diflucan).

Urinary-tract infections These can be precipitated by dehydration or long bus journeys without toilet stops; bring suitable antibiotics.

Language

India's linguistic landscape is varied – 23 languages (including English) are recognised in the constitution, and more than 1600 minor languages are spoken. This large number of languages certainly helps explain why English is still widely spoken in India and why it's still in official use. Despite major efforts to promote Hindi as the national language of India, phasing out English, many educated Indians speak English as virtually their first language. For the large number of Indians who speak more than one language, it's often their second tongue. Although you'll find it very easy to get around India with English, it's always good to know a little of the local language.

While the locals in Rajasthan, Agra and Delhi may speak Punjabi, Urdu, Marwari, Jaipuri, Malvi or Mewati to each other, for you, Hindi will be the local language of choice. Hindi has about 600 million speakers worldwide, of which 180 million are in India. It developed from Classical Sanskrit, and is written in Devanagari script. In 1947 it was granted official status along with English.

Pronunciation

Most Hindi sounds are similar to their English counterparts. The main difference is that Hindi has both 'aspirated' consonants (pronounced with a puff of air, like saying 'h' after the sound) and unaspirated ones, as well as 'retroflex' (pronounced with the tongue bent backwards) and nonretroflex consonants.

WANT MORE?

For in-depth language information and handy phrases, check out Lonely Planet's *India Phrasebook*. You'll find them at **shop.lonelyplanet.com**, or you can buy Lonely Planet's iPhone phrasebooks at the Apple App Store.

Our simplified pronunciation guides don't include these distinctions – read them as if they were English and you'll be understood.

Pronouncing the vowels correctly is important, especially their length (eg a and aa). The consonant combination ng after a vowel indicates nasalisation (ie the vowel is pronounced 'through the nose'). Note also that au is pronounced as the 'ow' in 'how'. Word stress is very light – we've indicated the stressed syllables with italics.

Basics

Hindi verbs change form depending on the gender of the speaker (or the subject of the sentence in general), so it's the verbs, not the pronouns 'he' or 'she' (as is the case in English) which show whether the subject of the sentence is masculine or feminine. In these phrases we include the options for male and female speakers, marked 'm' and 'f' respectively.

Hello./Goodbye.	नमस्ते ।	na·ma·*ste*
Yes.	जी हाँ ।	jee haang
No.	जी नहीं ।	jee na·*heeng*
Excuse me.	सुनिये ।	su·ni·ye
Sorry.	माफ़ कीजिये ।	maaf *kee*·ji·ye
Please ...	कृपया ...	kri·pa·*yaa* ...
Thank you.	थैंक्यू ।	*thayn*·kyoo
You're welcome.	कोई बात नहीं ।	*ko*·ee baat na·*heeng*

How are you?
आप कैसे/कैसी हैं?   aap *kay*·se/*kay*·see hayng **(m/f)**

Fine. And you?
मैं ठीक हूँ ।
आप सुनाइये ।   mayng teek hoong
aap su·*naa*·i·ye

What's your name?

आप का नाम क्या है?	aap kaa naam kyaa hay	

My name is ...

मेरा नाम ... है।	me·raa naam ... hay

Do you speak English?

क्या आपको अंग्रेज़ी	kyaa aap ko an·gre·zee
आती है?	aa·tee hay

I don't understand.

मैं नहीं समझा/	mayng na·heeng sam·jaa/
समझी।	sam·jee (m/f)

Accommodation

Where's a ...?

... कहाँ है?	... ka·haang hay
guesthouse	गेस्ट हाउस	gest haa·us
hotel	होटल	ho·tal
youth hostel	यूथ हास्टल	yoot haas·tal

Do you have a ... room?

क्या ... कमरा	kyaa ... kam·raa
है?	hay
single	सिंगल	sin·gal
double	डबल	da·bal

How much is it per ...?

... के लिये	... ke li·ye
कितने पैसे	kit·ne pay·se
लगते हैं?	lag·te hayng
night	एक रात	ek raat
person	हर व्यक्ति	har vyak·ti

air-con	ए० सी०	e see
bathroom	बाथरूम	baat·room
hot water	गर्म पानी	garm paa·nee
mosquito net	मसहरी	mas·ha·ree
washerman	धोबी	do·bee
window	खिड़की	kir·kee

Directions

Where's ...?

... कहाँ है?	... ka·haang hay

How far is it?

वह कितनी दूर है?	voh kit·nee door hay

What's the address?

पता क्या है?	pa·taa kyaa hay

Can you show me (on the map)?

(नक्शे में) दिखा	(nak·she meng) di·kaa
सकते है?	sak·te hayng

Turn left/right.

लेफ्ट/राइट मुड़िये।	left/raa·it mu·ri·ye

NUMBERS

1	१	एक	ek
2	२	दो	do
3	३	तीन	teen
4	४	चार	chaar
5	५	पाँच	paanch
6	६	छह	chay
7	७	सात	saat
8	८	आठ	aat
9	९	नौ	nau
10	१०	दस	das
20	२०	बीस	bees
30	३०	तीस	tees
40	४०	चालीस	chaa·lees
50	५०	पचास	pa·chaas
60	६०	साठ	saat
70	७०	सत्तर	sat·tar
80	८०	अस्सी	as·see
90	९०	नब्बे	nab·be
100	१००	सौ	sau
1000	१०००	एक हज़ार	ek ha·zaar

at the corner	कोने पर	ko·ne par
at the traffic lights	सिगनल पर	sig·nal par
behind ...	... के पीछे	... ke pee·che
in front of ...	... के सामने	... ke saam·ne
near ...	... के पास	... ke paas
opposite ...	... के सामने	... ke saam·ne
straight ahead	सीधे	see·de

Eating & Drinking

What would you recommend?

आपके ख़्याल में	aap ke kyaal meng
क्या अच्छा होगा?	kyaa ach·chaa ho·gaa

Do you have vegetarian food?

क्या आप का खाना	kyaa aap kaa kaa·naa
शाकाहारी है?	shaa·kaa·haa·ree hay

I don't eat (meat).

मैं (गोश्त) नहीं	mayng (gosht) na·heeng
खाता/खाती।	kaa·taa/kaa·tee (m/f)

I'll have ...

मुझे ... दीजिये।	mu·je ... dee·ji·ye

That was delicious.

बहुत मज़ेदार हुआ।	ba·hut ma·ze·daar hu·aa

Please bring the menu/bill.

मेन्यू/बिल लाइये।	men·yoo/bil laa·i·ye

Key Words

bottle	बोतल	*bo·tal*
bowl	कटोरी	ka·to·ree
breakfast	नाश्ता	*naash·taa*
dessert	मीठा	*mee·taa*
dinner	रात का खाना	*raat kaa kaa·naa*
drinks	पीने की चीज़ें	*pee·ne kee chee·zeng*
food	खाना	*kaa·naa*
fork	काँटा	*kaan·taa*
glass	गिलास	glaas
knife	चाकू	*chaa·koo*
local eatery	ढाबा	*daa·baa*
lunch	दिन का खाना	din kaa kaa·naa
market	बाज़ार	*baa·zaar*
plate	प्लेट	plet
restaurant	रेस्टोरेंट	*res·to·rent*
set meal	थाली	*taa·lee*
snack	नाश्ता	*naash·taa*
spoon	चम्मच	*cham·mach*

Meat & Fish

beef	गाय का गोश्त	gaai kaa gosht
chicken	मुर्ग़ी	*mur·gee*
duck	बतख़	ba·tak
fish	मछली	*mach·lee*
goat	बकरा	bak·raa
lobster	बड़ी झींगा	ba·ree jeeng·gaa
meat	गोश्त	gosht
meatballs	कोफ़्ता	kof·taa
pork	सुअर का गोश्त	*su·ar kaa gosht*
prawn	झींगी मछली	jeeng·gee mach·lee
seafood	मछली	*mach·lee*

Fruit & Vegetables

apple	सेब	seb
apricot	ख़ुबानी	ku·baa·nee
banana	केला	ke·laa
capsicum	मिर्च	mirch

carrot	गाजर	*gaa·*jar
cauliflower	फूल गोभी	pool go·bee
corn	मक्का	*mak·kaa*
cucumber	ककड़ी	kak·ree
date	खजूर	ka·joor
eggplant	बैंगन	*bayng·gan*
fruit	फल	pal
garlic	लहसुन	leh·sun
grape	अंगूर	an·goor
grapefruit	चकोतरा	cha·kot·raa
lemon	निम्बू	*nim·boo*
lentils	दाल	daal
mandarin	संतरा	san·ta·raa
mango	आम	aam
mushroom	खुम्बी	kum·bee
nuts	मेवे	me·ve
orange	नारंगी	naa·ran·gee
papaya	पपीता	pa·pee·taa
peach	आड़ू	aa·roo
peas	मटर	ma·tar
pineapple	अनन्नास	a·nan·naas
potato	आलू	aa·loo
pumpkin	कद्दू	kad·doo
spinach	पालक	paa·lak
vegetables	सब्ज़ी	sab·zee
watermelon	तरबूज़	tar·booz

Other

bread	चपाती/ नान/रोटी	cha·paa·tee/ naan/ro·tee
butter	मक्खन	mak·kan
chilli	मिर्च	mirch
chutney	चटनी	chat·nee
egg	अंडे	an·de
honey	मधु	ma·dhu
ice	बर्फ़	barf
ice cream	कुल्फ़ी	kul·fee
pappadams	पपड़	pa·par
pepper	काली मिर्च	kaa·lee mirch
relish	अचार	a·chaar
rice	चावल	chaa·val
salt	नमक	na·mak
spices	मिर्च मसाला	mirch ma·saa·laa
sugar	चीनी	chee·nee
tofu	टोफू	to·foo

Drinks

beer	बियर	bi·yar
coffee	काॅफ़ी	kaa·fee

QUESTION WORDS

How?	कैस?	kay·se
What?	क्या?	kyaa
Which?	कौनसा?	kaun·saa
When?	कब?	kab
Where?	कहाँ?	ka·haang
Who?	कौन?	kaun
Why?	क्यों?	kyong

milk	दूध	dood
red wine	लाल शराब	laal sha·*raab*
sweet fruit drink	शरबत	*shar*·bat
tea	चाय	chaai
water	पानी	*paa*·nee
white wine	सफ़ेद शराब	sa·*fed* sha·*raab*
yoghurt	लस्सी	*las*·see

Emergencies

Help!
मदद कीजिये! · ma·*dad kee*·ji·ye

Go away!
जाओ! · *jaa*·o

I'm lost.
मैं रास्ता भूल गया/गयी हूँ। · mayng *raas*·taa bool ga·*yaa*/ga·*yee* hoong (m/f)

Call a doctor!
डॉक्टर को बुलाओ! · *daak*·tar ko bu·*laa*·o

Call the police!
पुलिस को बुलाओ! · pu·*lis* ko bu·*laa*·o

I'm ill.
मैं बीमार हूँ। · mayng *bee*·maar hoong

Where is the toilet?
टॉइलेट कहाँ है? · *taa*·i·let ka·*haang* hay

Shopping & Services

I'd like to buy ...
मुझे ... चाहिये। · mu·*je* ... *chaa*·hi·ye

I'm just looking.
सिर्फ़ देखने आया/आयी हूँ। · sirf *dek*·ne aa·*yaa*/aa·*yee* hoong (m/f)

Can I look at it?
दिखाइये। · di·*kaa*·i·ye

How much is it?
कितने का है? · *kit*·ne kaa hay

It's too expensive.
यह बहुत महंगा/महंगी है। · yeh ba·*hut* ma·*han*·gaa/ma·*han*·gee hay (m/f)

There's a mistake in the bill.
बिल में गलती है। · bil meng *gal*·tee hay

bank	बैंक	baynk
post office	डाक ख़ाना	daak *kaa*·naa
public phone	सार्वजनिक फ़ोन	*saar*·va·ja·nik fon
tourist office	पर्यटन ऑफिस	*par*·ya·tan *aa*·fis

Time & Dates

What time is it?
टाइम क्या है? · *taa*·im kyaa hay

It's (10) o'clock.
(दस) बजे हैं। · (das) ba·*je* hayng

Half past (10).
साढ़े (दस)। · *saa*·re (das)

morning	सुबह	su·*bah*
afternoon	दोपहर	*do*·pa·har
evening	शाम	shaam
Monday	सोमवार	*som*·vaar
Tuesday	मंगलवार	man·*gal*·vaar
Wednesday	बुधवार	*bud*·vaar
Thursday	गुरुवार	gu·ru·*vaar*
Friday	शुक्रवार	*shuk*·ra·vaar
Saturday	शनिवार	sha·ni·*vaar*
Sunday	रविवार	ra·vi·*vaar*

TRANSPORT

Public Transport

When's the ... (bus)?	... (बस) कब जाती है?	... (bas) kab *jaa*·tee hay
first	पहली	*peh*·lee
last	आख़िरी	*aa*·ki·ree
bicycle rickshaw	साइकिल रिक्शा	*saa*·i·kil *rik*·shaa
boat	जहाज़	ja·*haaz*
bus	बस	bas
plane	हवाई जहाज़	ha·*vaa*·ee ja·*haaz*
train	ट्रेन	tren

At what time does it leave?
कितने बजे जाता/जाती है? · *kit*·ne ba·*je jaa*·taa/*jaa*·tee hay (m/f)

How long does the trip take?
जाने में कितनी देर लगती है? · *jaa*·ne meng *kit*·nee der *lag*·tee hay

How long will it be delayed?
उसे कितनी देर हुई है? · u·*se kit*·nee der hu·*ee* hay

Does it stop at ...?
क्या ... में रुकती है? · kyaa ... meng *ruk*·tee hay

Please tell me when we get to ...

जब ... आता है,   *jab ... aa*·taa hay
मुझे बताइये।   *mu*·je ba·*taa*·i·ye

Please go straight to this address.

इसी जगह को   *is*·ee *ja*·gah ko
फ़ौरन जाइए।   *fau*·ran *jaa*·i·ye

Please stop here.

यहाँ रुकिये।   ya·*haang* ru·ki·ye

A ... ticket (to ...).	(...) के लिये ... टिकट दीजिये।	(...) ke li·ye ... ti·*kat* *dee*·ji·ye
1st-class	फ़र्स्ट क्लास	*farst* klaas
2nd-class	सेकन्ड क्लास	se·*kand* klaas
one-way	एक तरफ़ा	ek ta·ra·*faa*
return	आने जाने का	*aa*·ne *jaa*·ne kaa

I'd like a/an ... seat.	मुझे ... सीट चाहिये।	*mu*·je ... seet *chaa*·hi·ye
aisle	किनारे	ki·*naa*·re
window	खिड़की के पास	*kir*·kee ke paas

bus stop	बस स्टॉप	bas *is*·taap
ticket office	टिकटघर	ti·*kat*·gar
timetable	समय सारणी	sa·*mai* *saa*·ra·nee
train station	स्टेशन	*ste*·shan

Driving & Cycling

I'd like to hire a ...	मुझे ... किराये पर लेना है।	*mu*·je ... ki·*raa*·ye par *le*·naa hay
4WD	फ़ोर व्हील ड्राइव	for vheel *draa*·iv
bicycle	साइकिल	*saa*·i·kil
car	कार	kaar
motorbike	मोटर साइकिल	*mo*·tar *saa*·i·kil

Is this the road to ...?

क्या यह ... का   kyaa ych ... kaa
रास्ता है?   *raas*·taa hay

Can I park here?

यहाँ पार्क कर सकता/   ya·*haang* paark kar *sak*·taa/
सकती हूँ?   *sak*·tee hoong (m/f)

Where's a service station?

पेट्रोल पम्प कहाँ है?   *pet*·rol pamp ka·*haang* hay

I need a mechanic.

मुझे मरम्मत करने   *mu*·je ma·*ram*·mat
वाला चाहिये।   *kar*·ne vaa·laa *chaa*·hi·ye

The car/motorbike has broken down at ...

कार/मोटर साइकिल   kaar/*mo*·tar *saa*·i·kil
...मेश ख़राब   ... meng ka·*raab*
हो गयी है।   ho ga·*yee* hay

I have a flat tyre.

टायर पंक्चर हो   *taa*·yar *pank*·char ho
गया है।   ga·*yaa* hay

I've run out of petrol.

पेट्रोल ख़त्म हो   *pet*·rol katm ho
गया है।   ga·*yaa* hay

GLOSSARY

ahimsa – nonviolence and reverence for all life

apsara – celestial maiden

Aryan – Sanskrit word for 'noble'; people who migrated from Persia and settled in northern India

ashram – spiritual community or retreat

autorickshaw – a noisy three-wheeled device that has a motorbike engine and seats for two passengers behind the driver

Ayurveda – the ancient and complex science of Indian herbal medicine and healing

bagh – garden

baithak – salon in a *haveli* where merchants received guests

baksheesh – tip, donation (alms) or bribe

bandhani – tie-dye

baori – well, particularly a step-well with landings and galleries

betel – nut of the betel tree; chewed as a stimulant and digestive in a concoction know as *paan*

bhang – dried leaves and flowering shoots of the marijuana plant

Bhil – tribal people of southern Rajasthan

bindi – forehead mark

Bishnoi – tribe known for their reverence for the environment

Bodhi Tree – *Ficus religiosa*, under which Buddha attained enlightenment

Brahmin – member of the priest caste, the highest Hindu caste

Buddha – Awakened One; the originator of Buddhism, who is also regarded by Hindus as the ninth incarnation of Vishnu

bund – embankment, dyke

chajera – mason employed by Marwari businessmen of Shekhawati to build *havelis*

charpoy – simple bed made of ropes knotted together on a wooden frame

chaupar – town square formed by the intersection of major roads

chhatri – cenotaph (literally 'umbrella')

choli – sari blouse

chowk – town square, intersection or marketplace

chowkidar – caretaker; night watchman

crore – 10 million

cycle-rickshaw – three-wheeled bicycle with seats for two passengers behind the rider

dacoit – bandit

Dalit – preferred term for India's *Untouchable* caste

dalwar – sword

dargah – shrine or place of burial of a Muslim saint

dharamsala – pilgrims guest house

dhobi – laundry

dhurrie – cotton rug

Digambara – Sky Clad; a Jain sect whose monks show disdain for worldly goods by going naked

Diwan-i-Am – hall of public audience

Diwan-i-Khas – hall of private audience

dupatta – long scarf for women often worn with the *salwar kameez*

durbar – royal court; also a government

garh – fort

ghat – steps or landing on a river; range of hills or road up hills

ghazal – Urdu song derived from poetry; sad love theme

ghoomer – dance performed by women during festivals and weddings

gopis – milkmaids; Krishna was very fond of them

guru – teacher or holy person

Harijan – name (no longer considered acceptable) given by Gandhi to India's *Untouchables*, meaning 'children of god'

hathi – elephant

haveli – traditional, ornately decorated rseidence

hijra – eunuch

hookah – water pipe

howdah – seat for carrying people on an elephant's back

jali – carved marble lattice screen; also refers to the holes or spaces produced through carving timber

Jats – traditionally people who were engaged in agriculture; today the Jats play a strong role in administration and politics

jauhar – ritual mass suicide by immolation, traditionally performed by *Rajput* women after military defeat to avoid dishonour

jootis – traditional leather shoes of Rajasthan; men's *jootis* often have curled-up toes; also known as *mojaris*

kabas – the holy rats believed to be the incarnations of local families at Karni Mata Temple at Deshnok

Kalbelias – nomadic tribal group associated with snake charming

karma – Hindu, Buddhist and Sikh principle of retributive justice for past deeds

kashida – embroidery on *jootis*

kathputli – puppeteer

khadi – homespun cloth; Mahatma Gandhi encouraged people to spin *khadi* rather than buy English cloth

khadim – Muslim holy servant or mosque attendant

kotwali – police station

Kshatriya – warrior or administrator caste, second in the caste hierarchy; Rajputs claim lineage from the Kshatriyas

kundan – type of jewellery featuring *meenakari* on one side and precious stones on the other

kurta – long cotton shirt with either a short collar or no collar

lakh – 100,000
lingam – phallic symbol; symbol of Shiva

madrasa – Islamic college
Mahabharata – Vedic epic poem of the Bharata dynasty; describes the battle between the Pandavas and the Kauravas
mahal – house, palace
maharaja – literally 'great king'; princely ruler; also known as ma-harana, maharao and maharawal
maharani – wife of a princely ruler or a ruler in her own right
Mahavir – the 24th and last *tirthankar*
mahout – elephant driver/keeper
mandapa – chamber before the inner sanctum of a temple
mandir – temple
mantra – sacred word or syllable used by Buddhists and Hindus to aid concentration; metric psalms of praise found in the *Vedas*
Marathas – warlike central Indians who controlled much of India at times and fought against the *Mughals* and *Rajputs*
marg – major road
masjid – mosque
Marwar – kingdom of the Rathore dynasty that ruled from Mandore, and later from Jodhpur
meenakari – type of enamel-work used on ornaments and jewellery
mehfilkhana – Islamic building in which religious songs are sung
mehndi – henna; intricate henna designs applied by women to their hands and feet
mela – fair, festival
Mewar – kingdom of the Sisodia dynasty; ruled Udaipur and Chittorgarh
moksha – release from the cycle of birth and death
monsoon – rainy season; June to October
mosar – death feast
Mughal – Muslim dynasty of Indian emperors from Babur to Aurangzeb (16th to 18th centuries)

nawab – Muslim ruling prince or powerful landowner
nilgai – antelope

niwas – house, building
NRI – nonresident Indian

odhni – headscarf
Om – sacred invocation that represents the essence of the divine principle

paan – chewable preparation made from betel leaves, nuts and lime
PCO – public call office
pol – gate
prasad – sacred food offered to the gods
puja – literally 'respect'; offering or prayer
purdah – custom among some conservative Muslims (also adopted by some Hindus, es-pecially the Rajputs) of keeping women in seclusion; veiled

raga – any conventional pattern of melody and rhythm that forms the basis for free composition
raj – rule or sovereignty; British Raj (sometimes just Raj) refers to British rule before 1947
raja – king; also *rana*
Rajputs – Sons of Princes; Hindu warrior caste, former rulers of western India
rana – see *raja*
rani – female ruler; wife of a king
rawal – nobleman
Road – railway town that serves as a communication point to a larger town off the line, eg Mt Abu and Abu Road
RSRTC – Rajasthan State Road Transport Corporation
RTDC – Rajasthan Tourism Development Corporation

sadar – main
sadhu – ascetic, holy person, one who is trying to achieve en-lightenment; usually addressed as 'swamiji' or 'babaji'
sagar – lake, reservoir
sahib – respectful title applied to a gentleman
sal – gallery in a palace
salwar kameez – traditional dresslike tunic and trouser combination for women
sambar – deer

sati – suicide by immolation; banned more than a century ago, it is still occasionally performed
Scheduled Tribes – government classification for tribal groups of Rajasthan; the tribes are grouped with the lowest caste-less class, the Dalits
shikar – hunting expedition
Sikh – member of the mono-theistic religion Sikhism, which separated from Hinduism in the 16th century and has a military tradition; Sikh men can be recog-nised by their beards and turbans
sikhara – temple-spire or temple
silavat – stone carvers
Singh – literally 'lion'; a surname adopted by Rajputs and Sikhs
Sufi – Muslim mystic

tabla – pair of drums
tempo – noisy three-wheeled public transport; bigger than an autorickshaw
thakur – Hindu caste; nobleman
tikka – a mark devout Hindus put on their foreheads with *tikka* powder; also known as a *bor* or *rakhadi*
tirthankars – the 24 great Jain teachers
tonga – two-wheeled passenger vehicle drawn by horse or pony
toran – shield-shaped device above a lintel, which a bride-groom pierces with his sword before claiming his bride
torana – elaborately sculpted gateway before temples
tripolia – triple gateway

Vaishya – merchant caste; the third caste in the hierarchy
Vedas – Hindu sacred books; collection of hymns composed during the 2nd millennium BC and divided into four books: Rig-Veda, Yajur-Veda, Sama-Veda and Atharva-Veda

wallah – man; added onto al-most anything, eg *dhobi-wallah*, *chai-wallah*, *taxi-wallah*

yagna – self-mortification

zenana – women's quarters

Behind the Scenes

SEND US YOUR FEEDBACK

We love to hear from travellers – your comments keep us on our toes and help make our books better. Our well-travelled team reads every word on what you loved or loathed about this book. Although we cannot reply individually to your submissions, we always guarantee that your feedback goes straight to the appropriate authors, in time for the next edition. Each person who sends us information is thanked in the next edition – the most useful submissions are rewarded with a selection of digital PDF chapters.

Visit **lonelyplanet.com/contact** to submit your updates and suggestions or to ask for help. Our award-winning website also features inspirational travel stories, news and discussions.

Note: We may edit, reproduce and incorporate your comments in Lonely Planet products such as guidebooks, websites and digital products, so let us know if you don't want your comments reproduced or your name acknowledged. For a copy of our privacy policy visit lonelyplanet.com/privacy.

OUR READERS

Many thanks to the travellers who used the last edition and wrote to us with helpful hints, useful advice and interesting anecdotes:

Barbara Illingworth, Bhuvnesh Gupta, Chuck Burton, Dom Rudd, Frank Clarke, George Barrow, Helen Scurfield, Kerry Nicholls, Lucy Graubart, Magda Bedkowska, Michael Beer, Renée Keulers, Sutej Sharma, Suzanne Hopwood, Terri Drage, Vincenzo Coppola

WRITER THANKS
Lindsay Brown

I am very grateful for the help and encouragement provided by Satinder, Karan & Ritu and Dicky & Kavita in Jaipur, Anoop in Pushkhar, Usha in Ranthambhore, Harsh in Bikaner, Siddharth in Jaisalmer, Ramesh Jangid in Nawalgarh, Laxmi Kant Jangid in Jhunjhunu and many many others who helped out along the road. Last but not least, thanks to Jenny.

Abigail Blasi

Thanks to all the people who helped me in Delhi, including my Delhi family Jyoti and Niranjan Desai, to Danish Abbas, Nicholas Thompson, Sarah Fotheringham, Toby Sinclair and the Delhi Walla himself, Mayank Austen Soofi. Special gratitude to Joe Bindloss and to all the other India authors for their help and knowledge. Huge thanks to my Mum, Ant & Luca for looking after everyone at home.

ACKNOWLEDGEMENTS

Climate map data adapted from Peel MC, Finlayson BL & McMahon TA (2007) 'Updated World Map of the Köppen-Geiger Climate Classification', Hydrology and Earth System Sciences, 11, 1633–44.

Cover photograph: Rajasthani woman passing street mural in Bundi, Ian Trower/AWL ©

Illustrations pp36–7 and pp82–3 by Javier Zarracina; pp98–9 by Michael Weldon.

THIS BOOK

This 5th edition of Lonely Planet's *Rajasthan, Delhi & Agra* guidebook was researched and written by Lindsay Brown and Abigail Blasi. The previous edition was written by Paul Clammer, Abigail Blasi and Kevin Raub. This guidebook was produced by the following:

Destination Editor Joe Bindloss

Product Editors Alison Ridgway, Kathryn Rowan

Cartographers Lonely Planet Cartography

Book Designer Michael Buick

Assisting Editors Imogen Bannister, Anne Mulvaney, Gabrielle Stefanos

Cover Researcher Naomi Parker

Thanks to Joel Cotterell, Daniel Fahey, Gemma Graham, Claire Naylor, Karyn Noble, Tom Stainer

Index

A

Abhaneri 127
accessible travel 254-5
accommodation 246-7, *see also individual locations*
　children, travel with 26
　language 274
　palaces 16
activities 19-21, *see also individual activities*
Agra 9, 28, 78-97, **79**, **86**, **88**, 2-3, 8-9, 17
　accommodation 78, 88-91
　activities 87
　climate 78
　drinking & nightlife 93
　emergencies 94
　festivals & events 91
　food 78, 91-3
　highlights 79
　medical services 94
　scams 94
　shopping 93-4
　sights 79-87
　tourist information 95
　tours 87-8
　travel seasons 78
　travel to/from 95-6
　travel within 96
Agra Fort 84-6, 17
air pollution 270
air travel
　to/from India 257
　within India 258
Ajmer 135-8, **136**
altitude sickness 271
Alwar 131-3
Amber 127-8
Amber Fort 9, 127-8, 9
amoebic dysentery 270
animals 237-40, *see also individual species*

Map Pages **000**
Photo Pages **000**

—

antelopes 237
archaeological sites
　Mehrauli Archaeological Park 75
　Qutb Minar Complex 75
architecture 234-5
area codes 15, 254
art galleries, *see* museums & galleries
arts 102-3, 232-3, *see also individual arts*
ATMs 250
autorickshaws 262
avian flu 269
ayurveda
　Delhi 53
　Jaipur 115
　Pushkar 139-40
　Udaipur 158

B

baoris 235
bathrooms 254
bazaars, *see* markets & bazaars
bears 97, 239
beer 231
begging 219
Bhagavad Gita 225
Bharatpur 128-31, **129**
Bhil people 222
bicycle travel, *see* cycling
Bikaner 196-202, **198-9**
bird flu 269
birdwatching 16, 21, 239-40, 17
　Desert National Park 196
　Guda Bishnoi 185
　Keoladeo National Park 129-30, 17
　Kota 150
　Kumbhalgarh Wildlife Sanctuary 165
　Mt Abu 169
　Ranthambhore National Park 11, 143-5, 11

—

Rao Jodha Desert Rock Park 178-9
Sultanpur National Park 76
Bishnoi people 222
block printing 103, 105, 105
boat trips
　Kota 150
　Udaipur 156
books 204
border crossings to Pakistan 185, 258
Brahma 224
Brahman 224
British East India Company 213
British empire 213-15
budgeting 15
Bundi 13, 145-50, **146**, 13
bus travel
　local transport 262
　within Rajasthan 259
business hours 15, 251

C

camel safaris 13, 17-18, 13
　Bikaner 197
　Jaisalmer 192-3
　Osian 186
　Sam Sand Dunes 195
camels 11, 13, 17-18, 11, 13
car travel 259-60
carbon-monoxide poisoning 270
carpets 103, 234, 102, 103
caste system 223
cell phones 14, 253-4
cenotaphs 235
chai 230-1
Chand Baori 127
chhatris 235
children, travel with 25-6
chinkaras 237
Chittorgarh (Chittor) 12, 151-4, **152**, 5, 12
cholera 269

—

City Palace (Alwar) 131-2
City Palace (Jaipur) 107, 110-11, 105
City Palace (Kota) 150
City Palace (Udaipur) 155, 12
climate 14, 19-21, *see also individual regions*
climate change 257
coffee 230
consulates 248
cooking courses
　Delhi 54
　Jaipur 115
　Pushkar 140
　Udaipur 158
costs 15
courses, *see also individual locations*
　cooking 54, 115, 140, 158
　language 54
　meditation 54, 115
　yoga 54, 115, 140, 158
crafts 103, 233-4, 102, 103, 104, 105
credit cards 242, 251
cricket 222
culture 204-5, 219-22
currency 250
customs regulations 247-8
cycle-rickshaws 262
cycling 258-9
　Delhi 53
　Jaipur 115
　Udaipur 158-9

D

dance 232
dangers, *see* safety
Deeg 132
dehydration 270
Delhi 10, 27, 30-77, **32-3**, 10
　accommodation 30, 54-9
　activities 53
　climate 30
　Connaught Place 42-3, 57, 61-2, 69, **42-3**

Delhi *continued*
  courses 54
  drinking & nightlife 65-6
  entertainment 67
  food 30, 59-65
  highlights 32-3
  internet access 71
  medical services 71
  New Delhi 43-9, 58, 62-4, 69-70, **46-7**
  Old Delhi 34-42, 54-5, 59-60, 68-9, **38-9**
  Paharganj 55-7, 60-1, **56**
  safety 70-1
  shopping 67-70
  sights 31-53
  South Delhi 50-2, 58-9, 64-5, 70, **50-1**
  tourist information 71
  tours 53-4
  travel seasons 30
  travel to/from 71-2
  travel within 72-5
  West Delhi 57-8, 60-1
dengue fever 269
Desert National Park 196
deserts 17-18, 204, 237
diarrhoea 269-70
disabilities, travellers with 254-5
divorce 220
Diwali 21
drinking water 271
drinks 230-1
driving 259-60
droughts 204
drugs 242, 250
dysentery, amoebic 270

E
economy 204-5
electricity 248
embassies 248
embroidery 234
emergencies 15, 276
enamelwork 233
encephalitis, Japanese B 269
endangered species 239
environmental issues 204
events, *see* festivals & events
exchange rates 15

Map Pages **000**
Photo Pages **000**

F
Fatehpur 174
Fatehpur Sikri 97-101, **98-9**, **373-4**
festivals & events 17, 19-21, 28
  Delhi 31
  Dussehra Mela 114
  Gangaur 114
  Jodhpur Flamenco & Gypsy Festival 180
  Kailash Fair 91
  Marwar Festival 180
  Mewar Festival 159
  Pushkar Camel Fair 140
  Rajasthan 114
  Rajasthan International Folk Festival 180
  Ram Barat 91
  Taj Mahotsav 91
  Teej 114
film 204, 233
food 27, 227-31, 248-9, *see also individual locations*
  children, travel with 25-6
  cooking courses 54, 115, 140, 158
  language 274-6
  safety 242, 270
  vegetarian travellers 228
forts 16, 28, 235, *see also* palaces
  accommodation 247
  Agra Fort 84-6, **17**
  Amber Fort 9, 127-8, **9**
  Bala Quila 132-3
  Chittorgarh Fort 12, 151-3, **5**, **12**
  Jaigarh 128
  Jaisalmer Fort 11, 186, **11**
  Junagarh 196-7
  Kankwari Fort 134
  Kumbhalgarh 165
  Lohagarh 129
  Mehrangarh 10, 177, **10**
  Nahargarh 113-14
  Purana Qila 47-8
  Red Fort 34-5, 36-7, **36-7**
  Taragarh 147
  Tughlaqabad 75
frescoes 233, **102-3**

G
galleries, *see* museums & galleries
Gandhi, Indira 45, 216
Gandhi, Mahatma 21, 41, 45, 215, 216

Ganesh 224
gardens, *see* parks & gardens
gay travellers 249
gazelles 237
gems 233, 242-3
geography 236-7
giardiasis 270
golf 53
Guda Bishnoi 185
Gurgaon (Gurugram) 76-7
Guru Shikhar 169

H
Hanuman 224
havelis 235, 247, **12**
  Bhagton ki Choti Haveli 171
  Binsidhar Newatia Haveli 175
  Le Prince Haveli 174
  Modi Havelis 173
  Mohanlal Ishwardas Modi Haveli 173
  Murmuria Haveli 175
  Nathmal-ki-Haveli 189
  Patwa-ki-Haveli 188-9
  Shekhawati 175
Hawa Mahal 113
health 266-72
  books 268
  checklist 266-7
  children, travel with 26
  environmental hazards 270-2
  insurance 266
  services 268
  vaccinations 266, 267
  websites 268
heatstroke 271
hepatitis 269
hijras 221
hiking 169
Hindu temples
  Akshardham Temple 52
  Brahma Temple 138-9
  Chhatarpur Mandir 51-2
  Galta 114-15
  Jagdish Temple 157
  Jhandewalan Hanuman Temple 42
  Karni Mata Temple 200
  Lakshmi Narayan Temple 41-2
  Laxminarayan Temple 188
  Old Rangji Temple 138
  Pap Mochani (Gayatri) Temple 139
  Savitri Mata Temple 138

Hinduism 223-5
history 206-18
HIV 269
Holi 19, **2**, **18**
holidays 253
horse riding 158

I
immigration 257
independence 214-16
indigenous peoples 222
influenza 269
insect bites & stings 271-2
insurance
  health 266
  motorcycle 261
  travel 249
internet access 249
internet resources 15
Islam 225
Iswari Minar Swarga Sal 113
itineraries 22-4, **22**, **23**, **24**

J
jackals 238
Jagmandir Island 156-7
Jain temples
  Bhandasar Temple 197
  Delwara Temples 167
  Digambara Jain Temple 35
  Jaisalmer 187
  Mahavira Temple 185
  Nasiyan (Red) Temple 136-7
  Ranakpur 166
Jainism 226
Jaipur 9, 107-27, **110-11**, **9**
  accommodation 117-19
  activities 115
  courses 115
  drinking & nightlife 122
  entertainment 122-3
  food 120-1
  internet access 124
  medical services 124
  shopping 123-7
  sights 107-15
  tourist information 124
  tours 115-17
  travel to/from 124-6
  travel within 126-7
  walking tours 116, **116**
Jaipur Elephant Festival 19
Jaipur Literature Festival 19

Jaisalmer 11, 186-95, **188-9**, 11
  accommodation 190-1
  drinking 191-4
  food 191-4
  history 186
  shopping 194
  sights 186-90
  tourist information 194
  tours 190
  travel to/from 194-5
  travel within 195
Jaisalmer Desert Festival 19
Jaisalmer Fort 11, 186, 11
Jama Masjid (Agra) 87
Jama Masjid (Delhi) 40-1, 10
Jama Masjid (Fatehpur Sikri) 97
Japanese B encephalitis 269
jeep travel 262
jewellery 233
Jhunjhunu 173-4
Jodhpur 10, 176-85, **178-9**, 10, 102, 103
  accommodation 180-3
  activities 177-80
  drinking & nightlife 183
  festivals & events 180
  history 177
  shopping 18
  sights 177-80
  tourist information 184
  travel to/from 184-5
  travel within 185
jodhpurs 183

K
Kali 224
Keoladeo National Park 128-31, 17
Khejadali 185
Khuri 195-6
Kota 150-1
Krishna 224
Kumbhalgarh 165-6
Kumbhalgarh Wildlife Sanctuary 165
kushti 67

L
lakes
  Jait Sagar 147
  Lake Pichola 156
  Nakki Lake 168
language 14, 273-9

language courses 54
legal matters 250
leopards 168, 238
lesbian travellers 249
literature 204

M
magazines 247
Mahabharata 225
Majnu-ka-Tilla 59
malaria 268-9
Mandawa 174-6
maps 250
markets & bazaars 18, 27
  Delhi 67, 68, 68-9, 69, 70
  Jaipur 123
  Pushkar 143
marriage 219-20
mausoleums, see tombs, shrines & mausoleums
measures 247
medical services 268
meditation courses
  Delhi 54
  Jaipur 115
Mehrangarh 10, 177, 10
metro travel 262
Mina people 222
mobile phones 14, 253-4
money 14, 15, 250-1
monkeys 238-9
monuments & statues
  Agrasen ki Baoli 43
  Clock Tower 180
  Coronation Durbar Site 41
  Raj Ghat 41
  Royal Gaitor 114
mosques
  Fatehpuri Masjid 35-40
  Jama Masjid (Agra) 87
  Jama Masjid (Delhi) 40-1, 10
  Jama Masjid (Fatehpur Sikri) 97
  Sunehri Masjid 35
motorcycle travel 260-2
Mt Abu 167-71, **168**
Mughal dynasty 27, 28, 210-13
museums & galleries
  Anokhi Museum of Hand Printing 128
  Archaeological Museum (Fatehpur Sikri) 100-1
  Bagore-ki-Haveli 157
  Central Museum (Jaipur) 113

City Palace (Kota) 150
City Palace Museum (Udaipur) 155
Crafts Museum 48
Desert Cultural Centre & Museum 190
Dr Ramnath A Podar Haveli Museum 171
Gandhi Smriti 45
Government Museum 155-6
Indira Gandhi Memorial Museum 45
Mehrangarh Museum 177-8
Morarka Haveli Museum 171
Museo Camera 76
National Bal Bhavan 41
National Gallery of Modern Art 45
National Gandhi Museum 41
National Museum 45
National Rail Museum 48
National Research Centre on Camels 202
Nehru Memorial Museum 45-6
Prachina Cultural Centre & Museum 197
Rashtrapati Bhavan Museum 45
Sanskriti Museums 52-3
Shankar's International Dolls Museum 41
SRC Museum of Indology 113
Sulabh International Museum of Toilets 52
Taj Museum 84
Thar Heritage Museum 190
Vintage & Classic Car Collection 158

N
National Gallery of Modern Art 45
National Museum 45
national parks & reserves 238, see also wildlife sanctuaries
  Desert National Park 196
  Keoladeo National Park 128-31, 17
  Ranthambhore National Park 11, 143-5, 11
  Sariska Tiger Reserve & National Park 133-5
  Sultanpur National Park 76

Nawalgarh 171-3
newspapers 247

O
observatories
  Jantar Mantar (Delhi) 43
  Jantar Mantar (Jaipur) 111-13
opening hours 15, 251
Osian 185-6

P
paan 230
painting 232-3, 102-3
Pakistan, border crossings 185, 258
palaces 16, 235, see also forts
  accommodation 247
  Bundi Palace 13, 147, 13
  Chitrasala 147
  City Palace (Alwar) 131-2
  City Palace (Jaipur) 107, 110-11, 105
  City Palace (Kota) 150
  City Palace (Udaipur) 155, 12
  Fatehpur Sikri 97-100, 373-4
  Fort Palace 186-7
  Hawa Mahal 113
  Jal Mahal 114
  Sajjan Garh 157-8
  Suraj Mahl's Palace 132
  Umaid Bhawan Palace 180
parks & gardens
  Lodi Gardens 44
  Mehtab Bagh 84
  Mughal Gardens 45
  Rao Jodha Desert Rock Park 178-9
Partition 215-16
Parvati 224
passports 257
phad 232-3
photography 251-2
planning, see also individual regions
  budgeting 15
  calendar of events 19-21
  children, travel with 25-6
  India basics 14
  internet resources 15
  itineraries 22-4, **22**, **23**, **24**
  regional overviews 27-8
  travel seasons 14, 19-21

police 250
politics 204-5
pollution 270
polo 123
population 205
postal services 252-3
pottery 234
prickly heat 271
public holidays 253
puppetry 234
Puranas 224-5
Pushkar 11, 138-43, **139**, **2**, **11**
Pushkar Camel Fair 11, 21, 140, **11**

R
rabies 269
radio 247
Rajasthan 28, 106-202, **108-9**
  accommodation 106
  climate 106
  highlights 108-9
Rajputs 28
Ramayana 225
Ranakpur 166-7
Ranthambhore National Park 11, 143-5, **11**
Red Fort 34-5, 36-7, **36-7**
religion 205, 223-6
rickshaws 262
rugs 103, 234, **103**
ruins
  Adhai-din-ka-Jhonpra 137
  Bhangarh 134
  Feroz Shah Kotla 41
  Mehrauli Archaeological Park 75
  Qutb Minar Complex 75

S
sacred texts 223-5
safaris 13, 17-18, **13**
  Bikaner 197
  Jaisalmer 192-3
  Osian 186
  Sam Sand Dunes 195
safety 242-3, 252, 253
  Delhi 70-1
  drinking water 242, 271
  drugs 242
  food 242, 270

Map Pages **000**
Photo Pages **000**

scams 242-3
  solo travellers 245
  women travellers 244-5
Salawas 185
Sam Sand Dunes 195
saris 244, **104**
Sariska Tiger Reserve & National Park 133-5
scams 94, 242-3
Shekhawati 12, 171-6, **172**, **12**
Shiva 224
shopping 18, 27
shrines, see tombs, shrines & mausoleums
Sikh temples
  Gurdwara Bangla Sahib 49-50
  Sisganj Gurdwara 35
Sikhism 225-6
Sisodia dynasty 208
sloth bears 97, 239
smoking 250
solo travellers 245
spa treatments 53
sports
  cricket 222
  kushti 67
  polo 123
statues, see monuments & statues
step-wells 235
Sufism 225
Sultanpur National Park 76
sunburn 272

T
Taj Mahal 9, 80-4, **88**, **2-3**, **8-9**, **82-3**
taxes
  accommodation 246
  air travel 257
  car travel 259
  food 248-9
taxis 262
tea 230-1
telephone services 14, 15, 253-4
temples 235, see also Hindu temples, Jain temples, Sikh temples
tempos 262
textiles 103, 233-4, **103**, **104**, **105**
thalis 229
Thar Desert 13, 192-3, 204, 236, 240, **13**
theft 243, 245, 249, 259

tigers 11, 237-8
  Ranthambhore National Park 144, **11**
  Sariska Tiger Reserve 134
time 14
toilets 254
tombs, shrines & mausoleums 28
  Akbar's Mausoleum 86
  Chini-ka-Rauza 87
  Dargah of Khwaja Muin-ud-din Chishti 135-6
  Hazrat Nizam-ud-din Dargah 43-4
  Humayun's Tomb 43
  Itimad-ud-Daulah 86-7
  Khan-i-Khanan's Tomb 49
  Safdarjang's Tomb 49
  Taj Mahal 9, 80-4, **88**, **2-3**, **8-9**, **82-3**
tour scams 243
tourism 204-5
tourist information 254
tours, see individual locations
touts 243
train travel 262-5
travel to/from India 257-8
travel within India 15, 258-65
trekking 169
tribal peoples 221-2
tuberculosis 269
TV 247
typhoid 269

U
Udaipur 12, 154-65, **156**, **12**
  accommodation 159-61
  activities 158
  courses 158
  drinking & nightlife 162
  emergencies 163
  entertainment 162-3
  festivals & events 159
  food 161-2
  internet access 163
  medical services 163
  shopping 163
  sights 155-8
  tourist information 164
  tours 158-9
  travel to/from 164
  travel within 164-5

V
vacations 253
vaccinations 266, 267
Vedas 223-4
vegetarian travellers 228
wvisas 14, 255-6
Vishnu 224
volunteering 256

W
walking tours
  Delhi 53-4
  Jaipur 116, **116**
  Udaipur 159
water, drinking 271
weather 14, 19-21, see also individual regions
weaving 234
websites 15
weights 247
wildlife sanctuaries 16, 28, 237-40, see also national parks & reserves
  Kumbhalgarh Wildlife Sanctuary 165
  Mt Abu Wildlife Sanctuary 168
  Sajjan Garh Wildlife Sanctuary 158
  Sariska Tiger Reserve & National Park 133-5
  Tal Chhapar Wildlife Sanctuary 238
wine 231
women in Rajasthan 220-1
women travellers 244-5
women's health 272
World Heritage Sites
  Fatehpur Sikri 97-101, **98-9**, **373-4**
  Jantar Mantar (Jaipur) 111-13
  Keoladeo National Park 128-31, **17**
  Taj Mahal 9, 80-4, **88**, **2-3**, **8-9**, **82-3**
work 205, 256
wrestling 67

Y
yoga courses
  Delhi 54
  Jaipur 115
  Pushkar 140
  Udaipur 158

Z
zoos 48-9

LONELY PLANET IN THE WILD

Map Legend

Sights
- Beach
- Bird Sanctuary
- Buddhist
- Castle/Palace
- Christian
- Confucian
- Hindu
- Islamic
- Jain
- Jewish
- Monument
- Museum/Gallery/Historic Building
- Ruin
- Shinto
- Sikh
- Taoist
- Winery/Vineyard
- Zoo/Wildlife Sanctuary
- Other Sight

Activities, Courses & Tours
- Bodysurfing
- Diving
- Canoeing/Kayaking
- Course/Tour
- Sento Hot Baths/Onsen
- Skiing
- Snorkelling
- Surfing
- Swimming/Pool
- Walking
- Windsurfing
- Other Activity

Sleeping
- Sleeping
- Camping

Eating
- Eating

Drinking & Nightlife
- Drinking & Nightlife
- Cafe

Entertainment
- Entertainment

Shopping
- Shopping

Information
- Bank
- Embassy/Consulate
- Hospital/Medical
- Internet
- Police
- Post Office
- Telephone
- Toilet
- Tourist Information
- Other Information

Geographic
- Beach
- Hut/Shelter
- Lighthouse
- Lookout
- Mountain/Volcano
- Oasis
- Park
- Pass
- Picnic Area
- Waterfall

Population
- Capital (National)
- Capital (State/Province)
- City/Large Town
- Town/Village

Transport
- Airport
- Border crossing
- Bus
- Cable car/Funicular
- Cycling
- Ferry
- Metro station
- Monorail
- Parking
- Petrol station
- Subway station
- Taxi
- Train station/Railway
- Tram
- Underground station
- Other Transport

Note: Not all symbols displayed above appear on the maps in this book

Routes
- Tollway
- Freeway
- Primary
- Secondary
- Tertiary
- Lane
- Unsealed road
- Road under construction
- Plaza/Mall
- Steps
- Tunnel
- Pedestrian overpass
- Walking Tour
- Walking Tour detour
- Path/Walking Trail

Boundaries
- International
- State/Province
- Disputed
- Regional/Suburb
- Marine Park
- Cliff
- Wall

Hydrography
- River, Creek
- Intermittent River
- Canal
- Water
- Dry/Salt/Intermittent Lake
- Reef

Areas
- Airport/Runway
- Beach/Desert
- Cemetery (Christian)
- Cemetery (Other)
- Glacier
- Mudflat
- Park/Forest
- Sight (Building)
- Sportsground
- Swamp/Mangrove

OUR STORY

A beat-up old car, a few dollars in the pocket and a sense of adventure. In 1972 that's all Tony and Maureen Wheeler needed for the trip of a lifetime – across Europe and Asia overland to Australia. It took several months, and at the end – broke but inspired – they sat at their kitchen table writing and stapling together their first travel guide, *Across Asia on the Cheap*. Within a week they'd sold 1500 copies. Lonely Planet was born.

Today, Lonely Planet has offices in Franklin, London, Melbourne, Oakland, Dublin, Beijing and Delhi, with more than 600 staff and writers. We share Tony's belief that 'a great guidebook should do three things: inform, educate and amuse'.

OUR WRITERS

Lindsay Brown

Lindsay started travelling as a young bushwalker exploring the Blue Mountains west of Sydney. Then as a marine biologist he dived the coastal and island waters of southeastern Australia. He continued travelling whenever he could while employed at Lonely Planet as an editor and publishing manager. On becoming a freelance writer and photographer he has co-authored more than 30 Lonely Planet guides to Australia, Bhutan, India, Nepal, Pakistan and Papua New Guinea.

Abigail Blasi

A freelance travel writer, Abigail has lived and worked in London, Rome, Hong Kong, and Copenhagen. Lonely Planet have sent her to India, Egypt, Tunisia, Mauritania, Mali, Italy, Portugal, Malta and around Britain. She writes regularly for newspapers and magazines, such as the *Independent*, the *Telegraph*, and *Lonely Planet Traveller*. She has three children and they often come along for the ride. Twitter/Instagram: @abiwhere

Published by Lonely Planet Global Limited
CRN 554153
5th edition – October 2017
ISBN 978 1 78657 143 4
© Lonely Planet 2017   Photographs © as indicated 2017
10 9 8 7 6 5 4 3 2 1
Printed in China